MICROECONOMICS
Principles and Policy
Eleventh Edition 2010 Update

MICROECONOMICS
Principles and Policy
Eleventh Edition 2010 Update

William J. Baumol

New York University and Princeton University

Alan S. Blinder

Princeton University

SOUTH-WESTERN
CENGAGE Learning

Australia • Brazil • Japan • Korea • Mexico • Singapore • Spain • United Kingdom • United States

Microeconomics: Principles and Policy,
Eleventh Edition 2010 Update
William J. Baumol, Alan S. Blinder

VP Editorial Director: Jack W. Calhoun

Publisher: Joe Sabatino

Executive Editor: Michael Worls

Supervising Developmental Editor: Katie Yanos

Editorial Assistant: Lena Mortis

Senior Marketing Manager: John Carey

Senior Marketing Communications Manager:
Sarah Greber

Marketing Coordinator: Suellen Ruttkay

Media Editor: Deepak Kumar

Director, Content and Media Production:
Barbara Fuller Jacobsen

Content Project Manager: Emily Nesheim

Senior Frontlist Buyer, Manufacturing:
Sandee Milewski

Production Service: Pre-PressPMG

Senior Art Director: Michelle Kunkler

Cover and Internal Designer: Lisa Albonetti

Cover Images: © Getty Images; © First Light
Associated Photographers, Inc.

Senior Rights Acquisitions Account Manager,
Text: Mardell Glinski Schultz

Text Permissions Researcher: Sue Howard

Senior Rights Acquisitions Account Manager,
Images: Deanna Ettinger

Images Permissions Researcher: Scott Rosen,
Bill Smith Group

For product information and technology assistance, contact us at
Cengage Learning Customer & Sales Support, 1-800-354-9706

For permission to use material from this text or product,
submit all requests online at **www.cengage.com/permissions**
Further permissions questions can be emailed to
permissionrequest@cengage.com

Exam*View*® is a registered trademark of eInstruction Corp. Windows is a registered trademark of the Microsoft Corporation used herein under license. Macintosh and Power Macintosh are registered trademarks of Apple Computer, Inc. used herein under license.

© 2008 Cengage Learning. All Rights Reserved.

Library of Congress Control Number: 2010924201
ISBN-13: 978-1-4390-3899-4
ISBN-10: 1-4390-3899-6

South-Western Cengage Learning
5191 Natorp Boulevard
Mason, OH 45040
USA

Cengage Learning products are represented in Canada by Nelson Education, Ltd.

For your course and learning solutions, visit **www.cengage.com**

Purchase any of our products at your local college store or at our preferred online store **www.cengagebrain.com**

Printed in the United States of America
1 2 3 4 5 6 7 14 13 12 11 10

To Sue Anne Batey Blackman: wise, beloved, and irreplaceable.

BRIEF CONTENTS

TABLE OF CONTENTS

PREFACE

As usual, when updating an edition, we have made many small changes to improve clarity of exposition and to update the text both for recent economics events—the global downturn—and for relevant advances in the literature. But this time we have focused on one particular addition that will, so far as we have been able to find out, differentiate this book from all other introductory texts.

We have included in the eleventh edition a substantial discussion of the role of the entrepreneurs and of the microtheory of their activities, their pricing and their earnings, and the implications for economic growth. Several studies of the place of the entrepreneur in economics textbooks (including earlier editions of this one) have all reached the same conclusion: that entrepreneurs are either completely invisible or are virtually so. Indeed, in a substantial set of the textbooks the word *entrepreneur* does not even appear in the index.

Now, this omission should appear strange because entrepreneurs are often classified as one of the four factors of production—but the only one to which no chapter is devoted. More than that, it seems universally recognized by economists that economic growth is the prime contributor to the general welfare and that more than 80 percent of the current income of the average American was contributed by growth in the past century alone. Moreover, it is clear that, even though entrepreneurs did not produce this growth by themselves, much, if not most, of this historically unprecedented achievement would not have occurred without them. Yet, in the textbooks, they have been the invisible men and women.

More than that, the description and analysis of the activities of entrepreneurs is evidently a topic in microeconomics: the incentives and the responses of *the individual actors* in the economy. This means that analysis of economic growth and policies for its stimulation need to be examined from two sides: the macroeconomic, where issues such as the requisite savings and investment are studied, and the microeconomic, where the twin activities of invention and entrepreneurship are analyzed. Yet the discussion of growth in most textbooks is entirely confined to the macro sections of the volume, with the subject completely absent from the micro analysis. In our new edition, as the reader will see, this is no longer so. There is a complete chapter on the *microeconomics* of growth and half a chapter on the entrepreneur as one of the two human factors of production.

This eleventh edition is the product of nearly 30 years of the existence and modification of this book. In the responses to a survey of faculty users, it became clear that a number of chapters were generally not covered by instructors for lack of time, although the material is of considerable interest to students and is not—or need not be—technically demanding. So we simplified several such chapters further—notably Chapter 9 on the stock and bond markets, Chapter 13 on regulation and antitrust, Chapter 17 on environmental economics, and Chapter 21 on poverty and inequality—to make it practical for an instructor to assign any or all of them to the students for reading entirely by themselves.

We have added a number of new materials in response to requests by correspondents. For example, in the material on the static-optimality properties of perfect competition, we added a discussion of the Coase theorem and more on behavioral economics. But as already indicated, the primary change was in the new material on the microeconomics of growth and entrepreneurship.

We ended this section of the preface to the tenth edition by singling out the critical contributions of one colleague and friend of amazingly long duration. We now repeat some of our words about the late Sue Anne Batey Blackman, who worked closely with us through 10 editions of this book; for all practical purposes, she had become a co-author. Indeed, the chapter on environmental matters is now largely her product. Her creative mind guided our efforts; her eagle eyes caught our errors; and her stimulating and pleasant company kept us going. Perhaps most important, we loved and valued her most profoundly. Unfortunately, she has been taken from us much too young. Our children and grandchildren will understand and surely support our decision not to dedicate this edition of the book to them, but rather to our precious lost friend, Sue Anne.

NOTE TO THE STUDENT

May we offer a suggestion for success in your economics course? Unlike some of the other subjects you may be studying, economics is cumulative: Each week's lesson builds on what you have learned before. You will save yourself a lot of frustration—and a lot of work—by keeping up on a week-to-week basis.

To assist you in doing so, we provide a chapter summary, a list of important terms and concepts, a selection of questions to help you review the contents of each chapter, as well as the answers to odd-numbered Test Yourself questions. Making use of these learning aids will help you to master the material in your economics course. For additional assistance, we have prepared student supplements to help in the reinforcement of the concepts in this book and provide opportunities for practice and feedback.

The following list indicates the ancillary materials and learning tools that have been designed specifically to be helpful to you. If you believe any of these resources could benefit you in your course of study, you may want to discuss them with your instructor. Further information on these resources is available at www.cengage.com/economics/baumol.

We hope our book is helpful to you in your study of economics and welcome your comments or suggestions for improving student experience with economics. Please write to us in care of Baumol and Blinder, Editor for Economics, South-Western/Cengage Learning 5191 Natorp Boulevard, Mason, Ohio, 45040, or through the book's web site at www.cengage.com/economics/baumol.

CourseMate

Multiple resources for learning and reinforcing principles concepts are now available in one place! CourseMate is your one-stop shop for the learning tools and activities to help you succeed.

Access online resources like ABC News Videos, Ask the Instructor Videos, Flash Cards, Interactive Quizzing, the Graphing Workshop, News Articles, Economic debates, Links to Economic Data, and more. Visit www.cengagebrain.com to see the study options available with this text.

Study Guide

The study guide assists you in understanding the text's main concepts. It includes learning objectives, lists of important concepts and terms for each chapter, quizzes, multiple-choice tests, lists of supplementary readings, and study questions for each chapter—all of which help you test your understanding and comprehension of the key concepts.

IN GRATITUDE

Finally, we are pleased to acknowledge our mounting indebtedness to the many who have generously helped us in our efforts through the nearly 30-year history of this book. We often have needed help in dealing with some of the many subjects that an introductory textbook must cover. Our friends and colleagues Charles Berry, *Princeton University*; Rebecca

Blank, *University of Michigan;* William Branson, *Princeton University;* Gregory Chow, *Princeton University;* Avinash Dixit, *Princeton University;* Susan Feiner, *University of Southern Maine;* Claudia Goldin, *Harvard University;* Ronald Grieson, *University of California, Santa Cruz;* Daniel Hamermesh, *University of Texas;* Yuzo Honda, *Osaka University;* Peter Kenen, *Princeton University;* Melvin Krauss, *Stanford University;* Herbert Levine, *University of Pennsylvania;* Burton Malkiel, *Princeton University;* Edwin Mills, *Northwestern University;* Janusz Ordover, *New York University;* David H. Reiley Jr., *University of Arizona;* Uwe Reinhardt, *Princeton University;* Harvey Rosen, *Princeton University;* Laura Tyson, *University of California, Berkeley;* and Martin Weitzman, *Harvard University* have all given generously of their knowledge in particular areas over the course of 10 editions. We have learned much from them and have shamelessly relied on their help.

Economists and students at colleges and universities other than ours offered numerous useful suggestions for improvements, many of which we have incorporated into this eleventh edition. We wish to thank Larry Allen, *Lamar University;* Nestor M. Arguea, *University of West Florida;* Gerald Bialka, *University of North Florida;* Kyongwook Choi, *Ohio University;* Basil G. Coley, *North Carolina A &T State University;* Carol A. Conrad, *Cerro Coso Community College;* Brendan Cushing-Daniels, *Gettysburg College;* Edward J. Deak, *Fairfield University;* Kruti Dholakia, *The University of Texas at Dallas;* Aimee Dimmerman, *George Washington University;* Mark Gius, *Quinnipiac University;* Ahmed Ispahani, *University of La Verne;* Jin Kim, *Georgetown University;* Christine B. Lloyd, *Western Illinois University;* Laura Maghoney, *Solano Community College;* Kosmas Marinakis, *North Carolina State University;* Carl B. Montano, *Lamar University;* Steve Pecsok, *Middlebury College;* J. M. Pogodzinski, *San Jose State University;* Adina Schwartz, *Lakeland College;* David Tufte, *Southern Utah University;* and Thierry Warin, *Middlebury College;* for their insightful reviews.

Obviously, the book you hold in your hands was not produced by us alone. An essential role was played by Susan Walsh, who stepped into the space vacated by Sue Anne and handled the tasks superbly, with insight and reliability, and did so in a most pleasant manner. In updating the eleventh edition, Anne Noyes Saini helped to refresh data and information throughout the book, and our colleague William Silber, New York University, generously helped us draft new content on derivatives and securitization—we thank both for their contributions. We also appreciate the contribution of the staff at South-Western Cengage Learning, including Joe Sabatino, Editor-in-Chief; Michael Worls, Executive Editor; John Carey, Senior Marketing Manager; Katie Yanos, Supervising Developmental Editor; Emily Nesheim, Content Project Manager; Deepak Kumar, Media Editor; Michelle Kunkler, Senior Art Director; Deanna Ettinger, Photo Manager; and Sandee Milewski, Senior Manufacturing Coordinator. It was a pleasure to deal with them, and we appreciate their understanding of our approaches, our goals, and our idiosyncrasies. We also thank our intelligent and delightful assistants at Princeton University and New York University, Kathleen Hurley and Janeece Roderick Lewis, who struggled successfully with the myriad tasks involved in completing the manuscript.

And, finally, we must not omit our continuing debt to our wives, Hilda Baumol and Madeline Blinder. They have now suffered through 11 editions and the inescapable neglect and distraction the preparation of each new edition imposes. Their tolerance and understanding has been no minor contribution to the project.

William J. Baumol
Alan S. Blinder

ABOUT THE AUTHORS

WILLIAM J. BAUMOL

William J. Baumol was born in New York City and received his BSS at the College of the City of New York and his Ph.D. at the University of London.

He is the Harold Price Professor of Entrepreneurship and Academic Director of the Berkley Center for Entrepreneurial Studies at New York University, where he teaches a course in introductory microeconomics, and the Joseph Douglas Green, 1895, Professor of Economics Emeritus and Senior Economist at Princeton University. He is a frequent consultant to the management of major firms in a wide variety of industries in the United States and other countries as well as to a number of governmental agencies. In several fields, including the telecommunications and electric utility industries, current regulatory policy is based on his explicit recommendations. Among his many contributions to economics are research on the theory of the firm, the contestability of markets, the economics of the arts and other services—the "cost disease of the services" is often referred to as "Baumol's disease"—and economic growth, entrepreneurship, and innovation. In addition to economics, he taught a course in wood sculpture at Princeton for about 20 years and is an accomplished painter (you may view some of his paintings at http://pages.stern.nyu.edu/~wbaumol/).

Alan Blinder and Will Baumol

Professor Baumol has been president of the American Economic Association and three other professional societies. He is an elected member of the National Academy of Sciences, created by the U.S. Congress, and of the American Philosophical Society, founded by Benjamin Franklin. He is also on the board of trustees of the National Council on Economic Education and of the Theater Development Fund. He is the recipient of 11 honorary degrees.

Baumol is the author of hundreds of journal and newspaper articles and more than 35 books, including *Global Trade and Conflicting National Interests* (2000); *The Free-Market Innovation Machine* (2002); *Good Capitalism, Bad Capitalism* (2007); and *The Microtheory of Innovative Entrepreneurship* (2010). His writings have been translated into more than a dozen languages.

ALAN S. BLINDER

Alan S. Blinder was born in New York City and attended Princeton University, where one of his teachers was William Baumol. After earning a master's degree at the London School of Economics and a Ph.D. at MIT, Blinder returned to Princeton, where he has taught since 1971, including teaching introductory macroeconomics since 1977. He is currently the Gordon S. Rentschler Memorial Professor of Economics and Public Affairs and co-director of Princeton's Center for Economic Policy Studies, which he founded.

In January 1993, Blinder went to Washington as part of President Clinton's first Council of Economic Advisers. Then, from June 1994 through January 1996, he served as vice chairman of the Federal Reserve Board. He thus played a role in formulating both the fiscal and monetary policies of the 1990s, topics discussed extensively in this book. He has also advised several presidential campaigns.

Blinder has consulted for a number of the world's largest financial institutions, testified dozens of times before congressional committees, and been involved in several entrepreneurial start-ups. For many years, he has written newspaper and magazine articles on economic policy, and he currently has a regular column in the *Wall Street Journal*. In addition, Blinder's op-ed pieces still appear periodically in other newspapers. He also appears frequently on PBS, CNN, CNBC, and Bloomberg TV.

Blinder has served as president of the Eastern Economic Association and vice president of the American Economic Association and is a member of the American Philosophical Society, the American Academy of Arts and Sciences, and the Council on Foreign Relations. He has two grown sons, two grandsons, and lives in Princeton with his wife, where he plays tennis as often as he can.

MICROECONOMICS
Principles and Policy
Eleventh Edition 2010 Update

Part 1

Getting Acquainted with Economics

Welcome to economics! Some of your fellow students may have warned you that "econ is boring." Don't believe them—or at least, don't believe them too much. It is true that studying economics is hardly pure fun. But a first course in economics can be an eye-opening experience. There is a vast and important world out there—the economic world—and this book is designed to help you understand it.

Have you ever wondered whether jobs will be plentiful or scarce when you graduate, or why a college education becomes more and more expensive? Should the government be suspicious of big firms? Why can't pollution be eliminated? How did the U.S. economy manage to grow so rapidly in the 1990s while Japan's economy stagnated? If any of these questions have piqued your curiosity, read on. You may find economics is more interesting than you had thought!

It is only in later chapters that we will begin to give you the tools you need to begin carrying out your own economic analyses. However, the four chapters of Part 1 that we list next will introduce you to both the subject matter of economics and some of the methods that economists use to study their subject.

CHAPTERS

WHAT IS ECONOMICS?

Why does public discussion of economic policy so often show the abysmal ignorance of the participants? Why do I so often want to cry at what public figures, the press, and television commentators say about economic affairs?

**ROBERT M. SOLOW, WINNER OF THE
1987 NOBEL PRIZE IN ECONOMICS**

conomics is a broad-ranging discipline, both in the questions it asks and the methods it uses to seek answers. Many of the world's most pressing problems are economic in nature. The first part of this chapter is intended to give you some idea of the sorts of issues that economic analysis helps to clarify and the kinds of solutions that economic principles suggest. The second part briefly introduces the tools that economists use—tools you are likely to find useful in your career, personal life, and role as an informed citizen, long after this course is over.

CONTENTS

IDEAS FOR BEYOND THE FINAL EXAM

Elephants may never forget, but people do. We realize that most students inevitably forget much of what they learn in a course—perhaps with a sense of relief—soon after the final exam. Nevertheless, we hope that you will remember some of the most significant economic ideas and, even more important, the ways of thinking about economic issues that will help you evaluate the economic issues that arise in our economy.

To help you identify some of the most crucial concepts, we have selected seven from the many in this book. Some offer key insights into the workings of the economy, and several bear on important policy issues that appear in newspapers; others point out common misunderstandings that occur among even the most thoughtful lay observers. Most of them indicate that it takes more than just good common sense to analyze economic issues effectively. As the opening quote of this chapter suggests, many learned judges, politicians, and university administrators who failed to understand basic economic principles could have made wiser decisions.

Try this one on for size. Imagine you own a widget manufacturing company that rents a warehouse. Your landlord raises your rent by $10,000 per year. Should you raise the price of your widgets to try to recoup some of your higher costs or should you do the opposite—lower your price to try to sell more and spread the so-called overhead costs over more products? In fact, as we shall see in Chapter 8, both answers are probably wrong!

IDEAS FOR BEYOND THE FINAL EXAM

Each of the seven *Ideas for Beyond the Final Exam*, many of which are counterintuitive, will be sketched briefly here. More important, each will be discussed in depth when it occurs in the course of the book, where it will be called to your attention by a special icon in the margin. Don't expect to master these ideas fully now, but do notice how some of the ideas arise again and again as we deal with different topics. By the end of the course you will have a better grasp of when common sense works and when it fails, and you will be able to recognize common fallacies that are all too often offered by public figures, the press, and television commentators.

Idea 1: How Much Does It Really Cost?

Because no one has infinite riches, people are constantly forced to make choices. If you purchase a new computer, you may have to give up that trip you had planned. If a business decides to retool its factories, it may have to postpone its plans for new executive offices. If a government expands its defense program, it may be forced to reduce its outlays on school buildings.

Economists say that the true costs of such decisions are not the number of dollars spent on the computer, the new equipment, or the military, but rather *the value of what must be given up in order to acquire the item*—the vacation trip, the new executive offices, and the new schools. These are called **opportunity costs** because they represent the *opportunities* the individual, firm, or government must forgo to make the desired expenditure. Economists maintain that rational decision making must be based on opportunity costs, not just dollar costs (see Chapters 3, 8, 10, and 15).

The **opportunity cost** of a decision is the value of the next best alternative that must be given up because of that decision (for example, working instead of going to school).

The cost of a college education provides a vivid example. How much do you think it *costs* to go to college? Most people are likely to answer by adding together their expenditures on tuition, room and board, books, and the like, and then deducting any scholarship funds they may receive. Suppose that amount comes to $15,000.

Economists keep score differently. They first want to know how much you would be earning if you were not attending college. Suppose that salary is $20,000 per year. This may seem irrelevant, but because you *give up* these earnings by attending college, they must be added to your tuition bill. You have that much less income because of your education. On the other side of the ledger, economists would not count *all* of the university's bill for room and board as part of the costs of your education. They would want to know how much *more* it costs you to live at school rather than at home. Economists would count only these *extra* costs as an educational expense because you would have incurred these costs whether or not you attend college. On balance, college is probably costing you much more than you think. And, as we will see later, taking opportunity cost into account in any personal planning will help you to make more rational decisions.

Idea 2: Attempts to Repeal the Laws of Supply and Demand—The Market Strikes Back

When a commodity is in short supply, its price naturally tends to rise. Sometimes disgruntled consumers badger politicians into "solving" this problem by making the high prices illegal—by imposing a ceiling on the price. Similarly, when supplies are plentiful—say, when fine weather produces extraordinarily abundant crops—prices tend to fall. Falling prices naturally dismay producers, who often succeed in getting legislators to impose price floors.

Such attempts to repeal the laws of supply and demand usually backfire and sometimes produce results virtually the opposite of those intended. Where rent controls are adopted to protect tenants, housing grows scarce because the law makes it unprofitable to build and maintain apartments. When price floors are placed under agricultural products, surpluses pile up because people buy less.

As we will see in Chapter 4 and elsewhere in this book, such consequences of interference with the price mechanism are not accidental. They follow inevitably from the way in which free markets work.

Idea 3: The Surprising Principle of Comparative Advantage

China today produces many products that Americans buy in huge quantities, including toys, textiles, and electronic equipment. American manufacturers often complain about Chinese competition and demand protection from the flood of imports that, in their view, threatens American standards of living. Is this view justified?

Economists think that it is often false. They maintain that both sides normally gain from international trade, but what if the Chinese were able to produce *everything* more cheaply than we can? Wouldn't Americans be thrown out of work and our nation be impoverished?

A remarkable result, called the law of *comparative advantage*, shows that, even in this extreme case, the two nations could still benefit by trading and that each could gain as a result! We will explain this principle first in Chapter 3 and then use it frequently. For now, a simple parable will make the reason clear.

Suppose Sally grows up on a farm and is a whiz at plowing, but she is also a successful country singer who earns $4,000 per performance. Should Sally turn down singing engagements to leave time to work the fields? Of course not. Instead, she should hire Alfie, a much less efficient farmer, to do the plowing for her. Sally may be better at plowing, but she earns so much more by singing that it makes sense for her to specialize in that and leave the farming to Alfie. Although Alfie is a less skilled farmer than Sally, he is an even worse singer.

So Alfie earns his living in the job at which he at least has a *comparative* advantage (his farming is not as inferior as his singing), and both Alfie and Sally gain. The same is true of two countries. Even if one of them is more efficient at everything, both countries can gain by producing the things they do best *comparatively*.

Idea 4: Trade Is a Win-Win Situation

One of the most fundamental ideas of economics is that both parties must expect to gain something in a voluntary exchange. Otherwise, why would they both agree to trade? This principle seems self-evident, yet it is amazing how often it is ignored in practice.

For example, it was widely believed for centuries that in international trade one country's gain from an exchange must be the other country's loss (Chapter 22). Analogously, some people feel instinctively that if Ms. A profits handsomely from a deal with

Mr. B, then Mr. B must have been exploited. Laws sometimes prohibit mutually beneficial exchanges between buyers and sellers—as when a loan transaction is banned because the interest rate is "too high" (Chapter 19), or when a willing worker is condemned to remain unemployed because the wage she is offered is "too low" (Chapter 20), or when the resale of tickets to sporting events ("ticket scalping") is outlawed even though the buyer is happy to get the ticket that he could not obtain at a lower price (Chapter 4).

In every one of these cases, well-intentioned but misguided reasoning blocks the possible mutual gains that arise from voluntary exchange and thereby interferes with one of the most basic functions of an economic system (see Chapter 3).

Idea 5: The Importance of Thinking at the Margin

We will devote many pages of this book to explaining and extolling a type of decision-making process called *marginal analysis* (see especially Chapters 5, 7, 8, and 14), which we can best illustrate through an example.

Suppose an airline is told by its accountants that the full average cost of transporting one passenger from Los Angeles to New York is $300. Can the airline profit by offering a reduced fare of $200 to students who fly on a standby basis? The surprising answer is probably yes. The reason is that most of the costs of the flight must be paid whether the plane carries 20 passengers or 120 passengers.

Costs such as maintenance, landing rights, and ground crews are irrelevant to the decision of whether to carry *additional* standby passengers at reduced rates. The only costs that are relevant are the extra costs of writing and processing additional tickets, the food and beverages consumed by these passengers, the additional fuel required, and so on. These so-called *marginal costs* are probably quite small in this example. A passenger who pays the airline any amount more than it costs the airline to give her a seat that would otherwise be unused (its marginal cost of flying her) adds something to the company's profit. So it probably is more profitable to let students ride at low fares than to leave the seats empty.

In many real cases, a failure to understand marginal analysis leads decision makers to reject advantageous possibilities, like the reduced fare in our example. These people are misled by using *average* rather than *marginal* cost figures in their calculations—an error that can be very costly.

Idea 6: Externalities—A Shortcoming of the Market Cured by Market Methods

Markets are adept at producing the goods that consumers want and in just the quantities they desire. They do so by rewarding those who respond to what consumers want and who produce these commodities economically. This all works out well as long as each exchange involves only the buyer and the seller—and no one else. However, some transactions affect third parties who were not involved in the decision. Examples abound: Electric utilities that generate power for midwestern states also produce pollution that kills freshwater fish in upstate New York. A farmer sprays crops with toxic pesticides, but the poison seeps into the groundwater and affects the health of neighboring communities.

Such social costs are called *externalities* because they affect parties *external* to the economic transactions that cause them. Externalities escape the control of the market mechanism because no financial incentive motivates polluters to minimize the damage they do—as we will learn in Chapters 15 and 17. So business firms make their products as cheaply as possible, disregarding any environmental harm they may cause.

Yet Chapters 15 and 17 will point out a way for the government to use the market mechanism to control undesirable externalities. If the electric utility and the farmer are charged for the clean air and water they use, just as they are charged for any coal and fertilizer they consume, then they will have a financial incentive to reduce the amount of pollution they generate. Thus, in this case, economists believe that market methods are often the best way to cure one of the market's most important shortcomings.

Idea 7: The Trade-Off between Efficiency and Equality

Wages and income have grown more unequal in the United States since the late 1970s. Highly skilled workers have pulled away from low-skilled workers. The rich have grown richer while the poor have become (relatively) poorer, yet U.S. unemployment has been much lower than that in Europe for many years. In many European countries inequality has not grown more extreme.

Many economists see these phenomena as two sides of the same coin. Europe and the United States have made different choices regarding how best to balance the conflicting claims of greater economic efficiency (more output and jobs) versus greater equality.

Roughly speaking, the American solution is to let markets work to promote efficiency—something they are very good at doing—with only minimal government interferences to reduce economic inequalities. (Some of these interferences are studied in Chapter 21.) However, much of continental Europe takes a different view. They find it scandalous that many Americans work for less than $6 per hour, with virtually no fringe benefits and no job security. European laws mandate not only relatively high minimum wages but also substantial fringe benefits and employment protections; of course, European taxes must be much higher to pay for these programs.

As economists see it, each system's virtue is also its vice. There is an agonizing *trade-off* between the *size* of a nation's output and the degree of *equality* with which that output is distributed. European-style policies designed to divide the proverbial economic pie more equally inadvertently can cause the size of the pie to shrink. American-style arrangements that promote maximal efficiency and output may permit or even breed huge inequalities and poverty. Which system is better? There is no clear answer, but we will examine the issue in detail in Chapter 21.

Epilogue

These ideas are some of the more fundamental concepts you will find in this book—ideas that we hope you will retain beyond the final exam. There is no need to master them right now, for you will hear much more about each as you progress through the book. By the end of the course, you may be amazed to see how natural, or even obvious, they will seem.

INSIDE THE ECONOMIST'S TOOL KIT

We turn now from the kinds of issues economists deal with to some of the tools they use to grapple with them.

Economics as a Discipline

Although economics is clearly the most rigorous of the social sciences, it nevertheless looks decidedly more "social" than "scientific" when compared with, say, physics. An economist must be a jack of several trades, borrowing modes of analysis from numerous fields. Mathematical reasoning is often used in economics, but so is historical study. And neither looks quite the same as when practiced by a mathematician or a historian. Statistics play a major role in modern economic inquiry, although economists had to modify standard statistical procedures to fit their kinds of data.

The Need for Abstraction

Some students find economics unduly abstract and "unrealistic." The stylized world envisioned by economic theory seems only a distant cousin to the world they know. There is an old joke about three people—a chemist, a physicist, and an economist—stranded on an desert island with an ample supply of canned food but no tools to open the cans. The

"Yes, John, we'd all like to make economics less dismal . . . "

NOTE: The nineteenth-century British writer Thomas Carlyle described economics as the "dismal science," a label that stuck.

SOURCE: From *The Wall Street Journal*. Permission, Cartoon Features Syndicate.

chemist thinks that lighting a fire under the cans would burst the cans. The physicist advocates building a catapult with which to smash the cans against some boulders. The economist's suggestion? "Assume a can opener."

Economic theory *does* make some unrealistic assumptions—you will encounter some of them in this book—but some abstraction from reality is necessary because of the incredible complexity of the economic world, not because economists like to sound absurd.

Compare the chemist's simple task of explaining the interactions of compounds in a chemical reaction with the economist's complex task of explaining the interactions of people in an economy. Are molecules motivated by greed or altruism, by envy or ambition? Do they ever imitate other molecules? Do forecasts about them influence their behavior? People, of course, do all these things and many, many more. It is therefore vastly more difficult to predict human behavior than to predict chemical reactions. If economists tried to keep track of every feature of human behavior, they would never get anywhere. Thus:

Abstraction from unimportant details is necessary to understand the functioning of anything as complex as the economy.

Abstraction means ignoring many details so as to focus on the most important elements of a problem.

An analogy will make it clear why economists **abstract** from details. Suppose you have just arrived for the first time in Los Angeles. You are now at the Los Angeles Civic Center—the point marked *A* in Maps 1 and 2, which are alternative maps of part of Los Angeles. You want to drive to the Los Angeles County Museum of Art, point *B* on each map. Which map would be more useful?

Map 1 has complete details of the Los Angeles road system, but this makes it hard to read and hard to use as a way to find the art museum. For this purpose, Map 1 is far too

MAP 1

Detailed Road Map of Los Angeles

Map © by Rand McNally, RL. 08-S-32. Reprinted by permission.

NOTE: Point *A* marks the Los Angeles Civic Center, and Point *B* marks the Los Angeles County Museum of Art.

detailed, although for other purposes (for example, locating a small street in Hollywood) it may be far better than Map 2.

In contrast, Map 2 omits many minor roads—you might say they are *assumed away*—so that the freeways and major arteries stand out more clearly. As a result of this simplification, several routes from the Civic Center to the Los Angeles County Museum of Art emerge. For example, we can take the Hollywood Freeway west to Alvarado Boulevard, go south to Wilshire Boulevard, and then head west again. Although we *might* find a shorter route by poring over the details in Map 1, most strangers to the city would be better off with Map 2. Similarly, economists try to *abstract* from a lot of confusing details while retaining the essentials.

Map 3, however, illustrates that simplification can go too far. It shows little more than the major interstate routes that pass through the greater Los Angeles area and therefore will not help a visitor find the art museum. Of course, this map was never intended to be used as a detailed tourist guide, which brings us to an important point:

> **There is no such thing as one "right" degree of abstraction and simplification for all analytic purposes. The proper degree of abstraction depends on the objective of the analysis. A model that is a gross oversimplification for one purpose may be needlessly complicated for another.**

Economists are constantly seeking analogies to Map 2 rather than Map 3, walking the thin line between useful generalizations about complex issues and gross distortions of the pertinent facts. For example, suppose you want to learn why some people are fabulously rich whereas others are abjectly poor. People differ in many ways, too many to enumerate, much less to study. The economist must ignore most of these details to focus on the important ones. The color of a person's hair or eyes is probably not important for the problem but, unfortunately, the color of his or her skin probably is because racial discrimination can depress a person's income. Height and weight may not matter, but education probably does. Proceeding in this way, we can pare Map 1 down to the

MAP 2

Major Los Angeles Arteries and Freeways

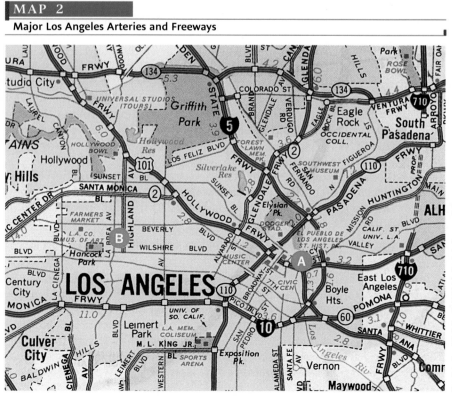

MAP 3
Greater Los Angeles Freeways

SOURCE: California Department of Transportation

manageable dimensions of Map 2. But there is a danger of going too far, stripping away some of the crucial factors, so that we wind up with Map 3.

The Role of Economic Theory

A **theory** is a deliberate simplification of relationships used to explain how those relationships work.

Some students find economics "too theoretical." To see why we can't avoid it, let's consider what we mean by a **theory**.

To an economist or natural scientist, the word *theory* means something different from what it means in common speech. In science, a theory is *not* an untested assertion of alleged fact. The statement that aspirin provides protection against heart attacks is not a theory; it is a *hypothesis*, that is, a reasoned guess, which will prove to be true or false once the right sorts of experiments have been completed. But a theory is different. It is a deliberate simplification (abstraction) of reality that attempts to explain how some relationships work. It is an *explanation* of the mechanism behind observed phenomena. Thus, gravity forms the basis of theories that describe and explain the paths of the planets. Similarly, price theory (discussed in Parts 2 and 3) seeks to describe and explain how buyers and sellers interact in markets to determine prices.

People who have never studied economics often draw a false distinction between *theory* and *practical policy*. Politicians and businesspeople, in particular, often reject abstract economic theory as something that is best ignored by "practical" people. The irony of these statements is that

It is precisely the concern for policy that makes economic theory so necessary and important.

To analyze policy options, economists are forced to deal with *possibilities that have not actually occurred.* For example, to learn how to shorten periods of high unemployment, they must investigate whether a proposed new policy that has never been tried can help. Or to determine which environmental programs will be most effective, they must understand how and why a market economy produces pollution and what might happen if the government taxed industrial waste discharges and automobile emissions. Such questions require some *theorizing*, not just examination of the facts, because we need to consider possibilities that have never occurred.

The facts, moreover, can sometimes be highly misleading. Data often indicate that two variables move up and down together. But this statistical **correlation** does not prove that either variable *causes* the other. For example, when it rains, people drive slower and there are also more traffic accidents, but no one thinks slower driving causes more accidents when it's raining. Rather, we understand that both phenomena are caused by a common underlying factor—more rain. How do we know this? Not just by looking at the correlation between data on accidents and driving speeds. Data alone tell us little about cause and effect. We must use some simple *theory* as part of our analysis. In this case, the theory might explain that drivers are more apt to have accidents on wet roads.

> Two variables are said to be **correlated** if they tend to go up or down together. Correlation need not imply causation.

Similarly, we must use theoretical analysis, and not just data alone, to understand *how,* if at all, different government policies will lead to lower unemployment or *how* a tax on emissions will reduce pollution.

Statistical correlation need not imply causation. Some theory is usually needed to interpret data.

What Is an Economic Model?

An **economic model** is a representation of a theory or a part of a theory, often used to gain insight into cause and effect. The notion of a "model" is familiar enough to children; and economists—like other researchers—use the term the same way children do.

> An **economic model** is a simplified, small-scale version of an aspect of the economy. Economic models are often expressed in equations, by graphs, or in words.

A child's model airplane looks and operates much like the real thing, but it is smaller and simpler, so it is easier to manipulate and understand. Engineers for Boeing also build models of planes. Although their models are far larger and much more elaborate than a child's toy, they use them for the same purposes: to observe the workings of these aircraft "up close" and to experiment to see how the models behave under different circumstances. ("What happens if I do this?") From these experiments, they make educated guesses as to how the real-life version will perform.

Economists use models for similar purposes. The late A. W. Phillips, famous engineer-turned-economist who discovered the "Phillips curve", was talented enough to construct a working model of the determination of national income in a simple economy by using colored water flowing through pipes. For years this contraption has graced the basement of the London School of Economics. Although we will explain the models with words and diagrams, Phillips's engineering background enabled him to depict the theory with tubes, valves, and pumps.

Because many of the models used in this book are depicted in diagrams, for those of you who need review, we explain the construction and use of various types of graphs in the appendix to this chapter. Don't be put off by seemingly abstract models. Think of them as useful road maps and remember how hard it would be to find your way around Los Angeles without one.

Reasons for Disagreements: Imperfect Information and Value Judgments

"If all the earth's economists were laid end to end, they could not reach an agreement," the saying goes. Politicians and reporters are fond of pointing out that economists can be found on both sides of many public policy issues. If economics is a science, why do economists so often disagree? After all, astronomers do not debate whether the earth revolves around the sun or vice versa.

This question reflects a misunderstanding of the nature of science. Disputes are normal at the frontier of any science.

SOURCE: Science Museum/Science & Society Picture Library

A. W. Phillips built this model in the early 1950s to illustrate Keynesian theory.

For example, astronomers once argued vociferously over whether the earth revolves around the sun. Nowadays, they argue about gamma-ray bursts, dark matter, and other esoterica. These arguments go mostly unnoticed by the public because few of us understand what they are talking about. But economics is a *social* science, so its disputes are aired in public and all sorts of people feel competent to join economic debates.

Furthermore, economists actually agree on much more than is commonly supposed. Virtually all economists, regardless of their politics, agree that taxing polluters is one of the best ways to protect the environment (see Chapters 15 and 17), that rent controls can ruin a city (Chapter 4), and that free trade among nations is usually preferable to the erection of barriers through tariffs and quotas (see Chapter 22). The list could go on and on. It is probably true that the issues about which economists agree *far* exceed the subjects on which they disagree.

Finally, many disputes among economists are not scientific disputes at all. Sometimes the pertinent facts are simply unknown. For example, you will learn in Chapter 17 that the appropriate financial penalty to levy on a polluter depends on quantitative estimates of the harm done by the pollutant; however, good estimates of this damage may not be available. Similarly, although there is wide scientific agreement that the earth is slowly warming, there are disagreements over the costs of global warming. Such disputes make it difficult to agree on a concrete policy proposal.

Another important source of disagreements is that economists, like other people, come in all political stripes: conservative, middle-of-the-road, liberal, radical. Each may have different values, and so each may hold a different view of the "right" solution to a public policy problem—even if they agree on the underlying analysis. Here are two examples:

1. In Idea 6 of our *Ideas for Beyond the Final Exam*, we noted that prices can be used to control pollution. Charge polluters a high price for each gallon of gunk they dump into a beautiful river and they will think twice before doing it. While economists generally agree that this approach will work and many advocate it, some object to such a "license to pollute," which gives anyone the right to destroy society's natural resources if they are just willing to pay the price.
2. In designing an income tax, society must decide how much of the burden to put on upper-income taxpayers. Some people believe the rich should pay a disproportionate share of the taxes. Others disagree, believing it is fairer to levy the same income tax rate on everyone.

Economists cannot answer questions like these any more than nuclear physicists could have determined whether dropping the atomic bomb on Hiroshima was a good idea. The decisions rest on moral judgments that can be made only by the citizenry through its elected officials.

Although economic science can contribute theoretical and factual knowledge on a particular issue, the final decision on policy questions often rests either on information that is not currently available or on social values and ethical opinions about which people differ, or on both.

| SUMMARY |

1. To help you get the most out of your first course in economics, we have devised a list of seven important ideas that you will want to retain beyond the final exam. Briefly, they are the following:

   a. *Opportunity cost* is the correct measure of cost.

   b. Attempts to fight market forces often backfire.

   c. Nations can gain from trade by exploiting their *comparative advantages.*

   d. Both parties can gain in a voluntary exchange.

   e. Good decisions typically require *marginal analysis,* which weighs added costs against added benefits.

   f. Externalities may cause the market mechanism to malfunction, but this defect can often be repaired by market methods.

   g. There is a trade-off between efficiency and equality. Many policies that promote one damage the other.

2. Common sense is not always a reliable guide in explaining economic issues or in making economic decisions.

3. Because of the great complexity of human behavior, economists are forced to *abstract* from many details, to make generalizations that they know are not quite true,

and to organize what knowledge they have in terms of some theoretical structure called a "model."

4. Correlation need not imply causation.

5. Economists use simplified models to understand the real world and predict its behavior, much as a child uses a model railroad to learn how trains work.

6. Although these models, if skillfully constructed, can illuminate important economic problems, they rarely can answer the questions that confront policy makers. Value judgments involving such matters as ethics are needed for this purpose, and the economist is no better equipped than anyone else to make them.

| KEY TERMS |

abstraction   8

correlation   11

economic model   11

opportunity cost   4

theory   10

| DISCUSSION QUESTIONS |

1. Think about a way you would construct a model of how your college is governed. Which officers and administrators would you include and exclude from your model if the objective were one of the following:

   a. To explain how decisions on financial aid are made

   b. To explain the quality of the faculty

   Relate this to the map example in the chapter.

2. Relate the process of abstraction to the way you take notes in a lecture. Why do you not try to transcribe every word uttered by the lecturer? Why don't you write down just the title of the lecture and stop there? How do you decide, roughly speaking, on the correct amount of detail?

3. Explain why a government policy maker cannot afford to ignore economic theory.

| APPENDIX | *Using Graphs: A Review*[1]

As noted in the chapter, economists often explain and analyze models with the help of graphs. Indeed, this book is full of them. But that is not the only reason for studying how graphs work. Most college students will deal with graphs in the future, perhaps frequently. You will see them in newspapers. If you become a doctor, you will use graphs to keep track of your patients' progress. If you join a business firm, you will use them to check profit or performance at a glance. This appendix introduces some of the techniques of graphic analysis—tools you will use throughout the book and, more important, very likely throughout your working career.

GRAPHS USED IN ECONOMIC ANALYSIS

Economic graphs are invaluable because they can display a large quantity of data quickly and because they facilitate data interpretation and analysis. They enable the eye to take in at a glance important statistical relationships that would be far less apparent from written descriptions or long lists of numbers.

TWO-VARIABLE DIAGRAMS

Much of the economic analysis found in this and other books requires that we keep track of two **variables** simultaneously.

A **variable** is something measured by a number; it is used to analyze what happens to other things when the size of that number changes (varies).

For example, in studying how markets operate, we will want to keep one eye on the *price* of a commodity and the other on the *quantity* of that commodity that is bought and sold.

For this reason, economists frequently find it useful to display real or imaginary figures in a two-variable diagram, which simultaneously represents the behavior of two economic variables. The numerical value of one variable is measured along the horizontal line at the bottom of the graph (called the *horizontal axis*), starting from the **origin** (the point labeled "0"), and the numerical value of the other variable is measured up the vertical line on the left side of the graph (called the *vertical axis*), also starting from the origin.

The "0" point in the lower-left corner of a graph where the axes meet is called the **origin**. Both variables are equal to zero at the origin.

Figures 1(a) and 1(b) are typical graphs of economic analysis. They depict an imaginary *demand curve*, represented by the brick-colored dots in Figure 1(a) and the heavy brick-colored line in Figure 1(b). The graphs show the price of natural gas on their vertical axes and the quantity of gas people want to buy at each price on the horizontal axes. The dots in Figure 1(a) are connected by the continuous brick-colored curve labeled *DD* in Figure 1(b).

Economic diagrams are generally read just as one would read latitudes and longitudes on a map. On the

---

[1] Students who have some acquaintance with geometry and feel quite comfortable with graphs can safely skip this appendix.

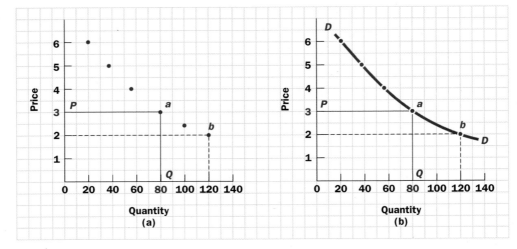

FIGURE 1

A Hypothetical
Demand Curve for
Natural Gas in St. Louis

NOTE: Price is in dollars per thousand cubic feet; quantity is in billions of cubic feet per year.

TABLE 1

Quantities of Natural Gas Demanded at Various Prices

Price (per thousand cubic feet)	$2	$3	$4	$5	$6
Quantity demanded (billions of cubic feet per year)	120	80	56	38	20

demand curve in Figure 1, the point marked *a* represents a hypothetical combination of price and quantity of natural gas demanded by customers in St. Louis. By drawing a horizontal line leftward from that point to the vertical axis, we learn that at this point the average price for gas in St. Louis is $3 per thousand cubic feet. By dropping a line straight down to the horizontal axis, we find that consumers want 80 billion cubic feet per year at this price, just as the statistics in Table 1 show. The other points on the graph give similar information. For example, point *b* indicates that if natural gas in St. Louis were to cost only $2 per thousand cubic feet, quantity demanded would be higher—it would reach 120 billion cubic feet per year.

Notice that information about price and quantity is *all* we can learn from the diagram. The demand curve will not tell us what kinds of people live in St. Louis, the size of their homes, or the condition of their furnaces. It tells us about the quantity demanded at each possible price—no more, no less.

A diagram abstracts from many details, some of which may be quite interesting, so as to focus on the two variables of primary interest—in this case, the price of natural gas and the amount of gas that is demanded at each price. All of the diagrams used in this book share this basic feature. They cannot tell the reader the "whole story," any more than a map's latitude and longitude figures for a particular city can make someone an authority on that city.

THE DEFINITION AND MEASUREMENT OF SLOPE

One of the most important features of economic diagrams is the rate at which the line or curve being sketched runs uphill or downhill as we move to the right. The demand curve in Figure 1 clearly slopes downhill (the price falls) as we follow it to the right (that is, as consumers demand more gas). In such instances, we say that *the curve has a negative slope, or is negatively sloped, because one variable falls as the other one rises.*

The **slope of a straight line** is the ratio of the vertical change to the corresponding horizontal change as we move to the right along the line between two points on that line, or, as it is often said, the ratio of the "rise" over the "run."

The four panels of Figure 2 show all possible types of slope for a straight-line relationship between two unnamed variables called Y (measured along the vertical axis) and X (measured along the horizontal axis). Figure 2(a) shows a *negative slope*, much like our demand curve in the previous graph. Figure 2(b) shows a *positive slope*, because variable Y rises (we go uphill) as variable X rises (as we move to the right). Figure 2(c) shows a *zero slope*, where the value of Y is the same irrespective of the value of X. Figure 2(d) shows an *infinite slope*, meaning that the value of X is the same irrespective of the value of Y.

Slope is a numerical concept, not just a qualitative one. The two panels of Figure 3 show two positively sloped straight lines with different slopes. The line in Figure 3(b) is clearly steeper. But by how much? The labels should help you compute the answer. In Figure 3(a) a horizontal movement, AB, of 10 units $(13 - 3)$ corresponds to a vertical movement, BC, of 1 unit

FIGURE 2

Different Types of Slope of a Straight-Line Graph

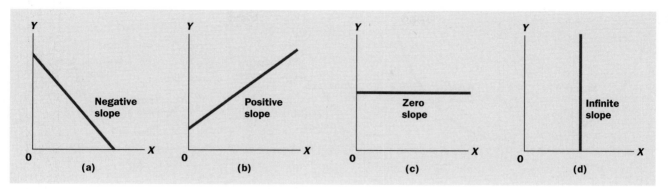

(a) Negative slope   (b) Positive slope   (c) Zero slope   (d) Infinite slope

FIGURE 3

How to Measure Slope

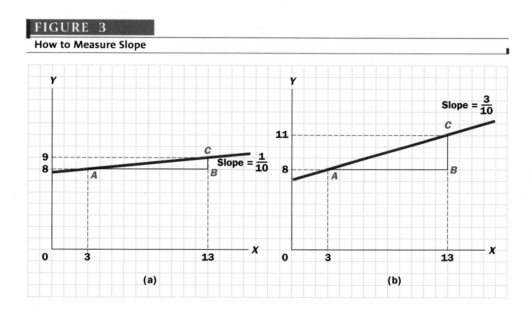

(a)   Slope $= \frac{1}{10}$ (b)   Slope $= \frac{3}{10}$

$(9 - 8)$. So the slope is $BC/AB = 1/10$. In Figure 3(b), the same horizontal movement of 10 units corresponds to a vertical movement of 3 units $(11 - 8)$. So the slope is $3/10$, which is larger—the rise divided by the run is greater in Figure 3(b).

By definition, the slope of any particular straight line remains the same, no matter where on that line we choose to measure it. That is why we can pick any horizontal distance, *AB,* and the corresponding slope triangle, *ABC,* to measure slope. But this is not true for curved lines.

> Curved lines also have slopes, but the numerical value of the slope differs at every point along the curve as we move from left to right.

The four panels of Figure 4 provide some examples of *slopes of curved lines.* The curve in Figure 4(a) has a negative slope everywhere, and the curve in Figure 4(b) has a positive slope everywhere. But these are not the only possibilities. In Figure 4(c) we encounter a curve that has a positive slope at first but a negative slope later on. Figure 4(d) shows the opposite case: a negative slope followed by a positive slope.

We can measure the slope of a smooth curved line numerically *at any particular point* by drawing a *straight* line that *touches,* but does not *cut,* the curve at the point in question. Such a line is called a **tangent** to the curve.

> The **slope of a curved line** at a particular point is defined as the slope of the straight line that is tangent to the curve at that point.

Figure 5 shows tangents to the brick-colored curve at two points. Line *tt* is tangent at point *T,* and line *rr* is tangent at point *R.* We can measure the slope of the

FIGURE 4

Behavior of Slopes in Curved Graphs

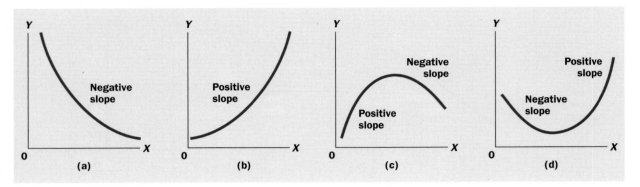

(a)   (b)   (c)   (d)

FIGURE 5

How to Measure Slope at a Point on a Curved Graph

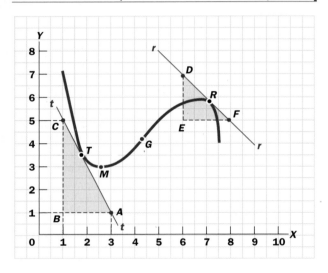

curve at these two points by applying the definition. The calculation for point *T*, then, is the following:

Slope at point *T* = Slope of line *tt*

$$= \frac{\text{Distance } BC}{\text{Distance } BA}$$

$$= \frac{(1 - 5)}{(3 - 1)} = \frac{-4}{2} = -2$$

A similar calculation yields the slope of the curve at point *R*, which, as we can see from Figure 5, must be smaller numerically. That is, the tangent line *rr* is less steep than line *tt*:

Slope at point *R* = Slope of line *rr*

$$= \frac{(5 - 7)}{(8 - 6)} = \frac{-2}{2} = -1$$

Exercise Show that the slope of the curve at point *G* is about 1.

What would happen if we tried to apply this graphical technique to the high point in Figure 4(c) or to the low point in Figure 4(d)? Take a ruler and try it. The tangents that you construct should be horizontal, meaning that they should have a slope exactly equal to zero. It is always true that where the slope of a *smooth* curve changes from positive to negative, or vice versa, there will be at least one point whose slope is zero.

Curves shaped like smooth hills, as in Figure 4(c), have a zero slope at their *highest* point. Curves shaped like valleys, as in Figure 4(d), have a zero slope at their *lowest* point.

RAYS THROUGH THE ORIGIN AND 45° LINES

The point at which a straight line cuts the vertical (*Y*) axis is called the **Y-intercept**.

> The **Y-intercept** of a line or a curve is the point at which it touches the vertical axis (the *Y*-axis). The *X*-intercept is defined similarly.

For example, the *Y*-intercept of the line in Figure 3(a) is a bit less than 8.

> Lines whose *Y*-intercept is zero have so many special uses in economics and other disciplines that they have been given a special name: a **ray through the origin**, or a **ray**.

Figure 6 shows three rays through the origin, and the slope of each is indicated in the diagram. The ray in the center (whose slope is 1) is particularly useful in many economic applications because it marks points where *X* and *Y* are equal (as long as *X* and *Y* are measured in the same units). For example, at point *A* we have *X* = 3 and *Y* = 3; at point *B*, *X* = 4 and *Y* = 4. A similar relation holds at any other point on that ray.

FIGURE 6

Rays through the Origin

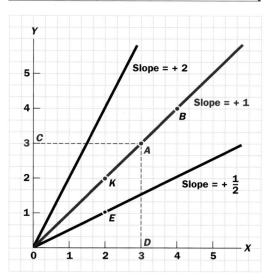

This implies that the vertical change and the horizontal change are always equal, so the two variables must always remain equal. Any point along that ray (for example, point *A*) is exactly equal in distance from the horizontal and vertical axes (length *DA* = length *CA*)—the number on the *X*-axis (the abscissa) will be the same as the number on the *Y*-axis (the ordinate).

Rays through the origin with a slope of 1 are called 45° lines because they form an angle of 45° with the horizontal axis. A 45° line marks off points where the variables measured on each axis have equal values.[2]

If a point representing some data is above the 45° line, we know that the value of *Y* exceeds the value of *X*. Similarly, whenever we find a point below the 45° line, we know that *X* is larger than *Y*.

SQUEEZING THREE DIMENSIONS INTO TWO: CONTOUR MAPS

Sometimes problems involve more than two variables, so two dimensions just are not enough to depict them on a graph. This is unfortunate, because the surface of a sheet of paper is only two-dimensional. When we study a business firm's decision-making process, for example, we may want to keep track simultaneously of three variables: how much labor it employs, how much raw material it imports from foreign countries, and how much output it creates.

How do we know that this is always true for a ray whose slope is 1? If we start from the origin (where both *X* and *Y* are zero) and the slope of the ray is 1, we know from the definition of slope that

$$\text{Slope} = \frac{\text{Vertical change}}{\text{Horizontal change}} = 1$$

Luckily, economists can use a well-known device for collapsing three dimensions into two—a *contour map*. Figure 7 is a contour map of the summit of the highest mountain in the world, Mt. Everest, on the border of Nepal and Tibet. On some of the irregularly shaped "rings" on this map, we find numbers (like 8500) indicating the height (in meters) above sea level at that particular spot on the mountain. Thus, unlike other maps, which give only latitudes and longitudes, this contour map (also called a topographical map) exhibits *three* pieces

FIGURE 7

A Geographic Contour Map

SOURCE: Mount Everest. Alpenvereinskarte. Vienna: Kartographische Anstalt Freytag-Berndt und Artaria, 1957, 1988.

---

[2] The definition assumes that both variables are measured in the same units.

of information about each point: latitude, longitude, and altitude.

Figure 8 looks more like the contour maps encountered in economics. It shows how a third variable, called Z (think of it as a firm's output, for example), varies as we change either variable X (think of it as a firm's employment of labor) or variable Y (think of it as the use of imported raw material). Just like the map of Mt. Everest, any point on the diagram conveys three pieces of data. At point *A*, we can read off the values of X and Y in the conventional way (X is 30 and Y is 40), and we can also note the value of Z by finding out on which contour line point *A* falls. (It is on the Z = 20 contour.) So point *A* is able to tell us that 30 hours of labor and 40 yards of cloth produce 20 units of output per day. The contour line that indicates 20 units of output shows the various combinations of labor and cloth a manufacturer can use to produce 20 units of output. Economists call such maps **production indifference maps.**

A **production indifference map** is a graph whose axes show the quantities of two inputs that are used to produce some output. A curve in the graph corresponds to some given quantity of that output, and the different points on that curve show the different quantities of the two inputs that are just enough to produce the given output.

FIGURE 8

An Economic Contour Map

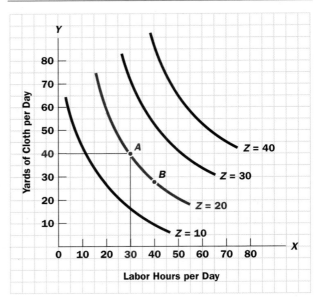

Labor Hours per Day

Although most of the analyses presented in this book rely on the simpler two-variable diagrams, contour maps will find their applications, especially in the appendixes to Chapters 5 and 7.

| SUMMARY |

1. Because graphs are used so often to portray economic models, it is important for students to acquire some understanding of their construction and use. Fortunately, the graphics used in economics are usually not very complex.

2. Most economic models are depicted in two-variable diagrams. We read data from these diagrams just as we read the latitude and longitude on a map: each point represents the values of two variables at the same time.

3. In some instances, three variables must be shown at once. In these cases, economists use contour maps, which, as the name suggests, show "latitude," "longitude," and "altitude" all at the same time.

4. Often, the most important property of a line or curve drawn on a diagram will be its slope, which is defined as the ratio of the "rise" over the "run," or the vertical change divided by the horizontal change when one moves along the curve. Curves that go uphill as we move to the right have positive slopes; curves that go downhill have negative slopes.

5. By definition, a straight line has the same slope wherever we choose to measure it. The slope of a curved line changes, but the slope at any point on the curve can be calculated by measuring the slope of a straight line tangent to the curve at that point.

| KEY TERMS |

45° line   17

origin (of a graph)   13

production indifference map   18

ray through the origin, or ray   16

slope of a straight
(or curved) line   14, 15

tangent to a curve   15

variable   13

Y-intercept   16

THE ECONOMY: MYTH AND REALITY

E pluribus unum (Out of many, one)

MOTTO ON U.S. CURRENCY

This chapter introduces you to the U.S. economy and its role in the world. It may seem that no such introduction is necessary, for you have probably lived your entire life in the United States. Every time you work at a summer or part-time job, pay your college bills, or buy a slice of pizza, you not only participate in the American economy—you also observe something about it.

But the casual impressions we acquire in our everyday lives, though sometimes correct, are often misleading. Experience shows that most Americans—not just students—either are unaware of or harbor grave misconceptions about some of the most basic economic facts. One popular myth holds that most of the goods that Americans buy are made in China. Another is that business profits account for a third of the price we pay for a typical good or service. Also, "everyone knows" that federal government jobs have grown rapidly over the past few decades. In fact, none of these things is remotely close to true.

So, before we begin to develop theories of how the economy works, it is useful to get an accurate picture of what our economy is really like.

CONTENTS

THE AMERICAN ECONOMY: A THUMBNAIL SKETCH

"And may we continue to be worthy of consuming a disproportionate share of this planet's resources."

The U.S. economy is the biggest national economy on earth, for two very different reasons. First, there are a lot of us. The population of the United States is just over 300 million—making it the third most populous nation on earth after China and India. That vast total includes children, retirees, full-time students, institutionalized people, and the unemployed, none of whom produce much output. But the *working population* of the United States numbers about 140 million. As long as they are reasonably productive, that many people are bound to produce vast amounts of goods and services. And they do.

But population is not the main reason why the U.S. economy is by far the world's biggest. After all, India has nearly four times the population of the United States, but its economy is smaller than that of Texas. The second reason why the U.S. economy is so large is that we are a very rich country. Because American workers are among the most productive in the world, our economy produces more than $47,000 worth of goods and services for every living American—nearly $100,000 for every *working* American. If each of the 50 states was a separate country, California would be the eighth-largest national economy on earth!

Why are some countries (like the United States) so rich and others (like India) so poor? That is one of the central questions facing economists. It is useful to think of an economic system as a machine that takes **inputs**, such as labor and other things we call **factors of production**, and transforms them into **outputs**, or the things people want to consume. The American economic machine performs this task with extraordinary efficiency, whereas the

Inputs or **factors of production** are the labor, machinery, buildings, and natural resources used to make outputs.

Outputs are the goods and services that consumers and others want to acquire.

U.S. Share of World GDP—It's Nice to Be Rich

The approximately 6.8 billion people of the world produced approximately $70 trillion worth of goods and services in 2008. The United States, with only about 4.6 percent of that population, turned out approximately 21 percent of total output. As the accompanying graph shows, the United States is still the leader in goods and services, with over $47,000 worth of GDP produced per person (or per capita). Just seven major industrial economies (the United States, Japan, Germany, France, Italy, the United Kingdom, and Canada—which account for just 11 percent of global population) generated 42 percent of world output. But their share has been falling as giant nations like China and India grow rapidly.

SOURCE: International Monetary Fund, *World Economic Outlook Database*, October 2009, http://www.imf.org, accessed December 2009; and Central Intelligence Agency, *The World Factbook*, 2009. Note: Foreign GDPs are converted to U.S. dollars using exchange rates.

2008 Gross Domestic Product (GDP) per Capita in 7 Industrial Countries

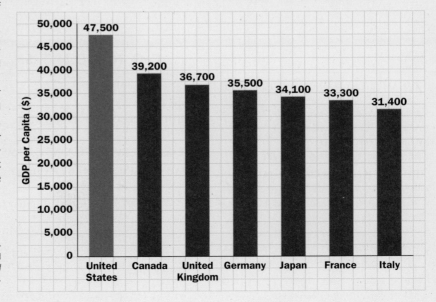

Country	GDP per Capita ($)
United States	47,500
Canada	39,200
United Kingdom	36,700
Germany	35,500
Japan	34,100
France	33,300
Italy	31,400

Indian machine runs quite inefficiently (though it is improving rapidly). Learning why this is so is one of the chief reasons to study economics.

Thus, what makes the American economy the center of world attention is our unique combination of prosperity and population. There are other rich countries in the world, like Switzerland, and there are other countries with huge populations, like India. But no nation combines a huge population with high per capita income the way the United States does. Japan, with an economy well under half the size of ours, is the only nation that comes close—although China, with its immense population, is moving up rapidly.

Although the United States is a rich and populous country, the 50 states certainly were not created equal. Population density varies enormously—from a high of about 1,200 people per square mile in crowded New Jersey to a low of just one person per square mile in the wide-open spaces of Alaska. Income variations are much less pronounced, but still, the average income in West Virginia is only about half that in Connecticut.

A Private-Enterprise Economy

Part of the secret of America's economic success is that free markets and private enterprise have flourished here. These days, private enterprise and capitalism are the rule, not the exception, around the globe. But the United States has taken the idea of free markets—where individuals and businesses voluntarily buy and sell things—further than almost any other country. It remains the "land of opportunity."

Every country has a mixture of public and private ownership of property. Even in the darkest days of communism, Russians owned their own personal possessions. In our country, the post office and the electricity-producing Tennessee Valley Authority are enterprises of the federal government, and many cities and states own and operate mass transit facilities and sports stadiums. But the United States stands out among the world's nations as one of the most "privatized." Few industrial assets are publicly owned in the United States. Even many city bus companies and almost all utilities (such as electricity, gas, and telephones) are run as private companies in the United States. In Europe, they are often government enterprises, though there is substantial movement toward transfer of government firms to private ownership.

The United States also has one of the most "marketized" economies on earth. The standard measure of the total output of an economy is called **gross domestic product (GDP)**, a term that appears frequently in the news. The share of GDP that passes through markets in the United States is enormous. Although government purchases of goods and services amount to about 20 percent of GDP, much of that is purchased from private businesses. Direct government production of goods is extremely rare in our society.

Gross domestic product (GDP) is a measure of the size of the economy—the total amount it produces in a year. *Real GDP* adjusts this measure for changes in the purchasing power of money; that is, it corrects for inflation.

A Relatively "Closed" Economy

All nations trade with one another, and the United States is no exception. Our annual exports exceed $1.6 trillion and our annual imports exceed $2 trillion. That's a lot of money, and so is the gap between them. But America's international trade often gets more attention than it deserves. The fact is that we still produce most of what we consume and consume most of what we produce, although the shares of imports and exports have been growing, as Figure 1 shows. In 1959, the average of exports and imports was only about 4 percent of GDP, a tiny fraction of the total. It has since gone up to over 15 percent. Although this is no longer negligible, it still means that almost 85 percent of what Americans buy every year is made in the United States.

Among the most severe misconceptions about the U.S. economy is the myth that this country no longer manufactures anything, but imports everything from, say, China. In fact, only about 18 percent of U.S. GDP is imported, with imports from China making up less than one-seventh of this—or a little over 2 percent of GDP. It may surprise you to learn that we actually import more merchandise from Canada than we do from China.

Economists use the terms *open* and *closed* to indicate how important international trade is to a nation. A common measure of "openness" is the average of exports and imports,

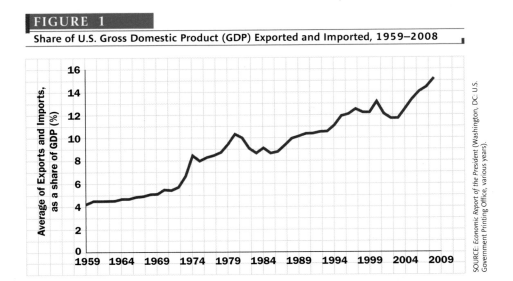

SOURCE: *Economic Report of the President* (Washington, DC: U.S. Government Printing Office, various years).

An economy is called relatively **open** if its exports and imports constitute a large share of its GDP.

An economy is considered relatively **closed** if they constitute a small share.

expressed as a share of GDP. Thus, the Netherlands is considered an extremely **open economy** because it imports and exports about three-quarters of its GDP. (See Table 1.) By this criterion, the United States stands out as among the most **closed economies** among the advanced, industrial nations. We export and import a smaller share of GDP than all of the countries listed in the table.

A Growing Economy . . .

The next salient fact about the U.S. economy is its growth; it gets bigger almost every year (see Figure 2). Gross domestic product in 2008 was over $14 trillion; as noted earlier, that's over $47,000 per American. Measured in dollars of constant purchasing power,[1] the U.S. GDP was almost five times as large in 2008 as it was in 1959. Of course, there were many more people in America in 2008 than there were 49 years earlier. But even correcting for population growth, America's real GDP *per capita* was about 2.8 times higher in 2008 than in 1959. That's still not a bad performance: Living standards nearly tripled in 49 years.

Looking back further, the purchasing power of the average American increased nearly 600 percent over the entire twentieth century! That's a remarkable number. To get an idea of what it means, just think how much poorer your family would become if it started out with an average U.S. income and then, suddenly, six dollars out of seven were taken away.

A **recession** is a period of time during which the total output of the economy falls.

Most Americans at the end of the nineteenth century could not afford vacations, the men had one good suit of clothing which they listed in their wills, and they wrote with ink that was kept in inkwells (and that froze every winter).

But with Bumps along the Growth Path

Although the cumulative growth performance depicted in Figure 2 is impressive, America's economic growth has been quite irregular. We have experienced alternating periods of good and bad times, which are called *economic fluctuations* or sometimes just *business cycles*. In some years—five since 1959, to be exact—GDP actually declined. Such periods of *declining* economic activity are called **recessions.**

TABLE 1

Openness of Various National Economies, 2008

	Openness
Netherlands	75%
Germany	47
Canada	34
United Kingdom	25
Mexico	19
Japan	17
Russia	17
China	16
United States	**15**

NOTE: Openness calculated as the average of imports and exports as a percentage of GDP.

SOURCE: For United States, Bureau of Economic Analysis; for all other countries, Central Intelligence Agency, *The World Factbook,* https://www.cia.gov/library/publications/the-world-factbook/index.html accessed December 2009.

---

[1] This concept is called *real* GDP.

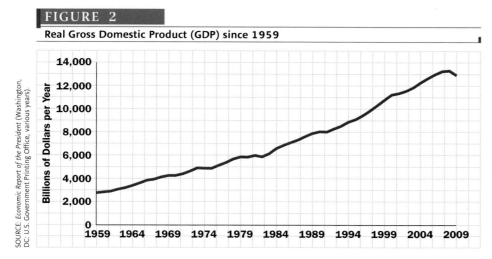

FIGURE 2

Real Gross Domestic Product (GDP) since 1959

SOURCE: *Economic Report of the President* (Washington, DC: U.S. Government Printing Office, various years).

NOTE: Real (inflation-adjusted) GDP figures are in 2005 dollars.

The bumps along the American economy's historic growth path are barely visible in Figure 2, but they stand out more clearly in Figure 3, which displays the same data in a different way. Here we plot not the *level* of real GDP each year but, rather, its *growth rate*—the percentage change from one year to the next. Now the booms and busts that delight and distress people—and swing elections—stand out clearly. From 1983 to 1984, for example, real GDP grew by over 7 percent, which helped ensure Ronald Reagan's landslide reelection. But from 2008 to 2009, real GDP actually dropped sharply, causing all sorts of social distress.

One important consequence of these ups and downs in economic growth is that *unemployment* varies considerably from one year to the next (see Figure 4). During the Great Depression of the 1930s, unemployment ran as high as 25 percent of the workforce, but it fell to barely over 1 percent during World War II. Just within the past few years, the national unemployment rate has been as high as 10.1 percent (in October 2009) and as low as 3.8 percent (in April 2000). In human terms, that 6.3 percentage point difference represents approximately 10 million jobless workers. Understanding why joblessness varies so dramatically, and what we can do about it, is another major reason for studying economics.

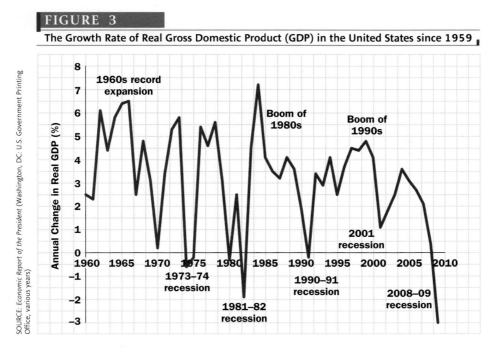

FIGURE 3

The Growth Rate of Real Gross Domestic Product (GDP) in the United States since 1959

SOURCE: *Economic Report of the President* (Washington, DC: U.S. Government Printing Office, various years).

NOTE: Growth rates are for 1959–1960, 1960–1961, and so on.

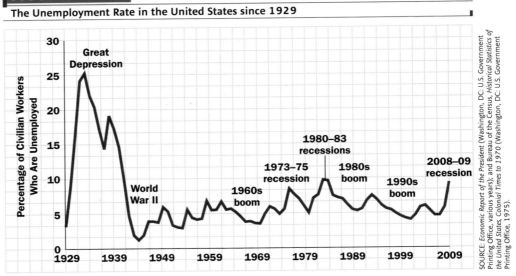

FIGURE 4

The Unemployment Rate in the United States since 1929

SOURCE: *Economic Report of the President* (Washington, DC: U.S. Government Printing Office, various years); and Bureau of the Census, *Historical Statistics of the United States, Colonial Times to 1970* (Washington, DC: U.S. Government Printing Office, 1975).

THE INPUTS: LABOR AND CAPITAL

Let's now return to the analogy of an economy as a machine turning inputs into outputs. The most important input is human labor: the men and women who run the machines, work behind the desks, and serve you in stores.

Unemployment Rates in Europe

For roughly the first quarter-century after World War II, unemployment rates in the industrialized countries of Europe were significantly lower than those in the United States. Then, in the mid-1970s, rates of joblessness in Europe leaped, with double digits becoming common. And they have been higher than U.S. unemployment rates in almost every year since. Where employment is concerned, the U.S. economy has become the envy of Europe—with the exception of the United Kingdom. Put on a comparable basis by the U.S. Bureau of Labor Statistics, unemployment rates in the various countries in the fall of 2008 were:

U.S.	5.8%
Canada	5.3
Australia	4.2
Japan	4.0
France	7.5
Germany	7.5
Italy	6.8
Sweden	6.2
United Kingdom	5.7

SOURCE: U.S. Bureau of Labor Statistics.

SOURCE: © Joel Stettenheim/CORBIS

The American Workforce: Who Is in It?

We have already mentioned that about 140 million Americans hold jobs. Almost 53 percent of these workers are men; over 47 percent are women. This ratio represents a drastic change from two generations ago, when most women worked only at home (see Figure 5). Indeed, the massive entrance of women into the paid labor force was one of the major social transformations of American life during the second half of the twentieth century. In 1950, just 29 percent of women worked in the marketplace; now almost 60 percent do. As Figure 6 shows, the share of women in the labor forces of other industrial countries has also been growing. The expanding role of women in the labor market has raised many controversial questions—whether they are discriminated against (the evidence suggests that they are), whether the government should compel employers to provide maternity leave, and so on.

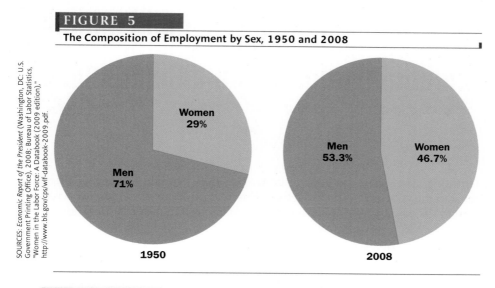

FIGURE 5

The Composition of Employment by Sex, 1950 and 2008

SOURCES: *Economic Report of the President* (Washington, DC: U.S. Government Printing Office), 2008; Bureau of Labor Statistics, "Women in the Labor Force: A Databook (2009 edition)," http://www.bls.gov/cps/wlf-databook-2009.pdf.

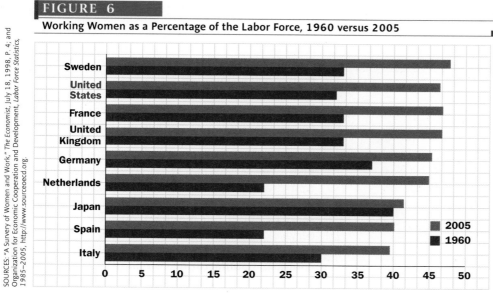

FIGURE 6

Working Women as a Percentage of the Labor Force, 1960 versus 2005

SOURCES: "A Survey of Women and Work," *The Economist*, July 18, 1998, P. 4; and Organization for Economic Cooperation and Development, *Labor Force Statistics, 1985–2005*, http://www.sourceoecd.org.

In contrast to women, the percentage of teenagers in the workforce has dropped significantly since its peak in the mid-1970s (see Figure 7). Young men and women aged 16 to 19 accounted for 8.6 percent of employment in 1974 but only 3.8 percent in 2008. As the baby boom gave way to the baby bust, people under 20 became scarce resources! Still,

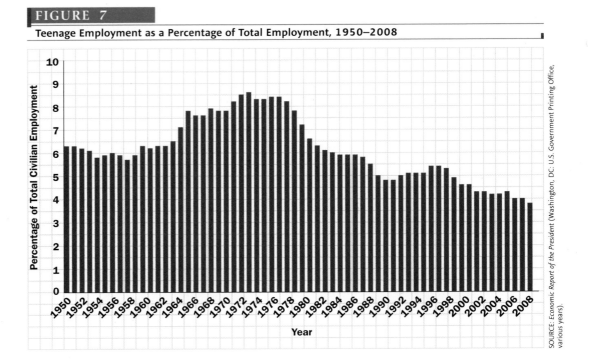

SOURCE: *Economic Report of the President* (Washington, DC: U.S. Government Printing Office, various years).

nearly 6 million teenagers hold jobs in the U.S. economy today—a number that has been pretty stable in the past few years. Most teenagers fill low-wage jobs at fast-food restaurants, amusement parks, and the like. Relatively few can be found in the nation's factories.

The American Workforce: What Does It Do?

What do these 140 million working Americans do? The only real answer is: almost anything you can imagine. In May 2008, America had 110,990 architects, 394,230 computer programmers, more than 899,920 carpenters, more than 2.6 million truck drivers, 553,690 lawyers, roughly 1.5 million secretaries, 174,530 kindergarten teachers, 29,170 pediatricians, 63,030 tax preparers, 6,900 geological engineers, 298,900 fire fighters, and 12,600 economists.[2]

Figure 8 shows the breakdown by sector. It holds some surprises for most people. The majority of American workers—like workers in all developed countries—produce services, not goods. In 2009, about 68 percent of all non-farm workers in the United States were employed by private service industries, whereas only about 14 percent produced goods. These legions of service workers included about 16.5 million in educational and health services, about 17.7 million in business and professional services, and over 15 million in retail trade. (The biggest single private employer in the country is Wal-Mart.) By contrast, manufacturing companies in the United States employed only 12 million people, and almost a third of those worked in offices rather than in the factory. The Homer Simpson image of the typical American worker as a blue-collar worker is really quite misleading.

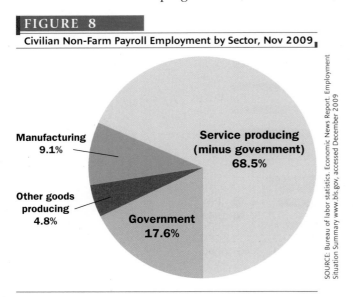

SOURCE: Bureau of labor statistics. Economic News Report. Employment Situation Summary www.bls.gov, accessed December 2009

NOTE: Numbers may not add to 100% due to rounding.

[2] SOURCE: U.S. Bureau of Labor Statistics, *Occupational Employment and Wages, May 2008,* http://www.bls.gov.

Federal, state, and local governments employed about 22 million people but, contrary to another popular misconception, few of these civil servants work for the *federal* government. Federal *civilian* employment is about 2.7 million—about 10 percent lower than it was in the 1980s. (The armed forces employ about another 1.5 million men and women in uniform.) State and local governments provide about 19.5 million jobs—or about seven times the number of federal government jobs. In addition to the jobs categorized in Figure 8, approximately 2 million Americans work on farms and over 10 million are self-employed.

As Figure 9 shows, *all* industrialized countries have become "service economies" in recent decades. To a considerable degree, this shift to services reflects the arrival of the "Information Age." Activities related to computers, to research, to the transmission of information by teaching and publication, and other information-related activities are providing many of the new jobs. This means that, in the rich economies, workers who moved out of manufacturing jobs into the service sectors have not gone predominantly into low-skill jobs such as dishwashing or housecleaning. Many found employment in service jobs in which education and experience provide a great advantage. At the same time, technological change has made it possible to produce more and more manufactured products using fewer and fewer workers. Such labor-saving innovation in manufacturing has allowed a considerable share of the labor force to move out of goods-producing jobs and into services.

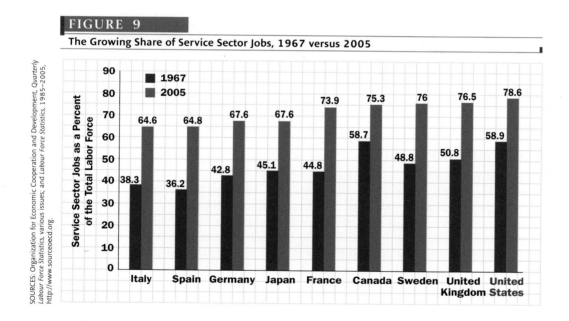

FIGURE 9

The Growing Share of Service Sector Jobs, 1967 versus 2005

SOURCES: Organization for Economic Cooperation and Development, *Quarterly Labour Force Statistics*, various issues; and *Labour Force Statistics, 1985–2005*, http://www.sourceoecd.org.

The American Workforce: What It Earns

Altogether, these workers' wages account for over 70 percent of the income that the production process generates. That figures up to an average hourly wage of over $18—plus fringe benefits like health insurance and pensions, which can contribute an additional 30 to 40 percent for some workers. Because the average workweek is about 34 hours long, a typical weekly paycheck in the United States is about $630 before taxes (but excluding the value of benefits). That is hardly a princely sum, and most college graduates can expect to earn substantially more.[3] But it is typical of average wage rates in a rich country like the United States.

---

[3] These days, college graduates typically earn over 80 percent more than workers with only high school diplomas. SOURCE: Bureau of Labor Statistics, "Labor Force Statistics from the Current Population Survey." Earnings by education, http://www.bls.gov.

Wages throughout northern Europe are similar. Indeed, workers in a number of other industrial countries now receive higher compensation than American workers do—a big change from the situation a few decades ago. According to the U.S. Bureau of Labor Statistics, in 2007 workers in U.S. manufacturing industries made less than those in many European countries (see Figure 10). However, U.S. compensation levels still remain above those in Japan and many other countries.

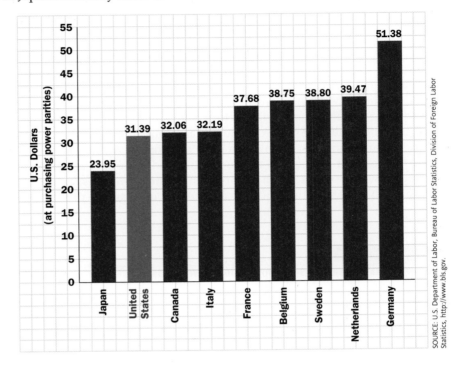

FIGURE 10

Average Hourly Compensation Rates in Manufacturing, 2007

SOURCE: U.S. Department of Labor, Bureau of Labor Statistics, Division of Foreign Labor Statistics, http://www.bls.gov.

Capital and Its Earnings

The rest of national income (after deducting the small sliver of income that goes to the owners of land and natural resources) mainly accrues to the owners of *capital*—the machines and buildings that make up the nation's industrial plant.

The total market value of these business assets—a tough number to estimate—is believed to be in the neighborhood of $30 trillion. Because that capital earns an average rate of return of about 10 percent before taxes, total earnings of capital—including corporate profits, interest, and all the rest—come to about $3 trillion.

Public opinion polls routinely show that Americans have a distorted view of the level of business profits in our society. The man and woman on the street believe that corporate profits after tax account for about 30 percent of the price of a typical product (see the box "Public Opinion on Profits" on the next page). The right number is closer to 8 percent.

THE OUTPUTS: WHAT DOES AMERICA PRODUCE?

What does all this labor and capital produce? Consumer spending accounts for about 70 percent of GDP. And what an amazing variety of goods and services it buys. American households spend roughly 66 percent of their budgets on services, with housing commanding the largest share. They also spend about $168 billion annually on their telephone bills, over $35 billion on airline tickets, and $90 billion on dentists. The other 34 percent of American budgets goes for goods—ranging from about $342 billion per year on motor vehicles to almost $60 billion on shoes.

Public Opinion on Profits

Most Americans think corporate profits are much higher than they actually are. One public opinion poll years ago found that the average citizen thought that corporate profits *after taxes* amounted to 32 percent of sales for the typical manufacturing company. The actual profit rate at the time was closer to 4 percent!* Interestingly, when a previous poll asked how much profit was "reasonable," the response was 26 cents on every dollar of sales—more than six times as large as profits actually were.

* This poll was conducted in 1986. Corporate profit rates increased considerably in the 1990s and 2000s.

SOURCE: "Public Attitudes toward Corporate Profits," *Public Opinion Index* (Princeton, NJ: Opinion Research Corporation, June 1986).

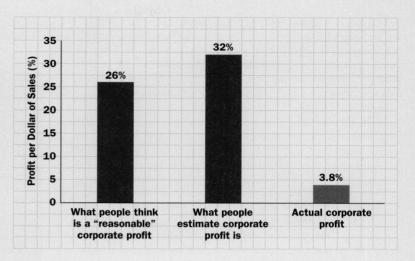

This leaves about 30 percent of GDP for all *nonconsumption* uses. That includes government services (buying such things as airplanes, guns, and the services of soldiers, teachers, and bureaucrats), business purchases of machinery and industrial structures, and consumer purchases of new houses.

THE CENTRAL ROLE OF BUSINESS FIRMS

Calvin Coolidge once said that "the business of America is business." Although this statement often has been ridiculed, he was largely right. When we peer inside the economic machine that turns inputs into outputs, we see mainly private companies. Astonishingly, the United States has more than 25 million business firms—about one for every 12 people!

The owners and managers of these businesses hire people, acquire or rent capital goods, and arrange to produce things consumers want to buy. Sound simple? It isn't. Over 80,000 businesses fail every year. A few succeed spectacularly. Some do both. Fortunately for the U.S. economy, however, the lure of riches induces hundreds of thousands of people to start new businesses every year—against the odds.

A number of the biggest firms do business all over the world, just as foreign-based *multinational corporations* do business here. Indeed, some people claim that it is now impossible to determine the true "nationality" of a multinational corporation—which may have factories in ten or more countries, sell its wares all over the world, and have stockholders in dozens of nations. (See the box "Is That an American Company?" on the next page). Ford, for example, generates more profits abroad than at home, and the Toyota you drive was probably assembled in the United States.

Firms compete with other companies in their *industry*. Most economists believe that this *competition* is the key to industrial efficiency. A sole supplier of a commodity will find it easy to make money, and may therefore fail to innovate or control costs. Its management is liable to become relaxed and sloppy. But a company besieged by dozens of competitors eager to take its business away must constantly seek ways to innovate, to cut costs, and to

Is That an American Company?

Robert Reich, who was Secretary of Labor in the Clinton administration, argued some years ago that it was already nearly impossible to define the nationality of a multinational company. Although many scholars think Reich exaggerated the point, no one doubts that he had one—nor that the nationalities of corporations have become increasingly blurred since then. He wrote in 1991:

What's the difference between an "American" corporation that makes or buys abroad much of what it sells around the world and a "foreign" corporation that makes or buys in the United States much of what it sells? . . . The mind struggles to keep the players straight. In 1990, Canada's Northern Telecom was selling to its American customers telecommunications equipment made by Japan's NTT at NTT's factory in North Carolina.

If you found that one too easy, try this: Beginning in 1991, Japan's Mazda would be producing Ford Probes at Mazda's plant in Flat Rock, Michigan. Some of these cars would be exported to Japan and sold there under Ford's trademark.

A Mazda-designed compact utility vehicle would be built at a Ford plant in Louisville, Kentucky, and then sold at Mazda dealerships in the United States. Nissan, meanwhile, was designing a new light truck at its San Diego, California, design center. The trucks would be assembled at Ford's Ohio truck plant, using panel parts fabricated by Nissan at its Tennessee factory, and then marketed by both Ford and Nissan in the United States and in Japan. Who is Ford? Nissan? Mazda?

SOURCE: © AP IMAGES/Greg Campbell

SOURCE: Robert B. Reich, *The Work of Nations* (New York: Knopf, 1991), pp. 124, 131.

build a better mousetrap. The rewards for business success can be magnificent. But the punishment for failure is severe.

WHAT'S MISSING FROM THE PICTURE? GOVERNMENT

Thus far, we have the following capsule summary of how the U.S. economy works: More than 25 million private businesses, energized by the profit motive, employ about 140 million workers and about $30 trillion of capital. These firms bring their enormously diverse wares to a bewildering variety of different markets, where they try to sell them to over 300 million consumers.

It is in *markets*—places where goods and services are bought and sold—that these millions of households and businesses meet to conduct transactions, as depicted in Figure 11. Only a few of these markets are concrete physical locations, such as fish markets or stock exchanges. Most are more abstract "places," where business may be conducted by telephone or the Internet—even if the commodity being traded is a physical object. For example, there are no centralized *physical* marketplaces for buying cars or computers, but there are highly competitive markets for these goods nonetheless.

As Figure 11 suggests, firms use their receipts from selling goods and services in the markets for *outputs* to pay wages to employees and interest and profits to the people who provide capital in the markets for *inputs*. These income flows, in turn, enable consumers to purchase the goods and services that companies produce. This circular flow of money, goods, and factors of production lies at the center of the analysis of how the national economy works. All these activities are linked by a series of interconnected markets, some of which are highly competitive and others of which are less so.

FIGURE 11

The Circular Flow of Goods and Money

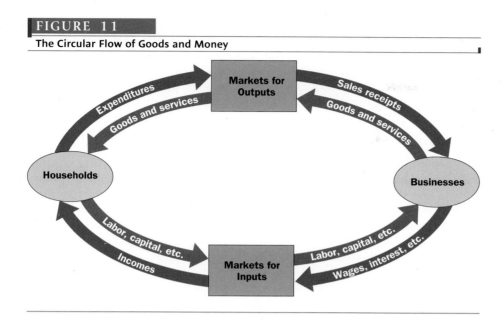

All very well and good. But the story leaves out something important: the role of *government*, which is pervasive even in our decidedly free-market economy. Just what does government do in the U.S. economy—and why?

Although an increasing number of tasks seem to get assigned to the state each year, the traditional role of government in a market economy revolves around five jobs:

- Making and enforcing the laws
- Regulating business
- Providing certain goods and services such as national defense
- Levying taxes to pay for these goods and services
- Redistributing income

Every one of these tasks is steeped in controversy and surrounded by intense political debate. We conclude this chapter with a brief look at each.

The Government as Referee

For the most part, power is diffused in our economy, and people "play by the rules." But, in the scramble for competitive advantage, disputes are bound to arise. Did Company A live up to its contract? Who owns that disputed piece of property? In addition, some unscrupulous businesses are liable to step over the line now and then—as we saw in many cases of fraud that helped bring on the debacle in sub-prime mortgages in 2007–2009.

Enter the government as rule maker, referee, and arbitrator. Congress and state and local legislatures pass the laws that define the rules of the economic game. The executive branches of all three governmental levels share the responsibility for enforcing them. And the courts interpret the laws and adjudicate disputes.

The Government as Business Regulator

Nothing is pure in this world of ours. Even in "free-market" economies, governments interfere with the workings of free markets in many ways and for myriad reasons. Some government activities seek to make markets work better. For example, America's *antitrust laws* are used to protect competition against possible encroachment by monopoly. Some regulations seek to promote social objectives that unfettered markets do not foster—environmental regulations are a particularly clear case. But, as critics like to point out, some economic regulations have no clear rationale at all.

We mentioned earlier that the American belief in free enterprise runs deep. For this reason, the regulatory role of government is more contentious here than in most other countries. After all, Thomas Jefferson said that government is best that governs least. Two hundred years later, Presidents Reagan, Bush (both of them), and Clinton all pledged to dismantle inappropriate regulations—and sometimes did. But the financial crisis of 2007–2009 has led to many calls for new and tighter regulations, especially in finance.

Government Expenditures

The most contentious political issues often involve taxing and spending because those are the government's most prominent roles. Democrats and Republicans, both in the White House and in Congress, have frequently battled fiercely over the federal budget. In 1995 and 1996, such disputes even led to some temporary shutdowns of the federal government. Under President Bill Clinton, the government managed to achieve a sizable surplus in its budget—meaning that tax receipts exceeded expenditures. But it didn't last long. Today the federal budget is deeply in the red, and prospects for getting it balanced are poor.

During fiscal year 2008, the federal government spent over $3.1 *trillion*—a sum that is literally beyond comprehension. Figure 12 shows where the money went. Over 31 percent went for *pensions and income security programs,* which include both social insurance programs (such as Social Security and unemployment compensation) and programs designed to assist the poor. About 21 percent went for *national defense.* Another 25 percent was absorbed by *health-care* expenditures, mainly on Medicare and Medicaid. Adding in *interest on the national debt,* these four functions alone accounted for over 86 percent of all federal spending. The rest went for a miscellany of other purposes including education, transportation, agriculture, housing, and foreign aid.

Government spending at the state and local levels was about $2.0 trillion. Education claimed the largest share of state and local government budgets (35 percent), with health and public welfare programs a distant second (26 percent). Despite this vast outpouring of public funds, many observers believe that serious social needs remain unmet. Critics claim that our public infrastructure (such as bridges and roads) is adequate, that our educational system is lacking, that we are not spending enough on homeland defense, and so on.

Although the scale and scope of government activity in the United States is substantial, it is quite moderate when we compare it to other leading economies, as we will see next.

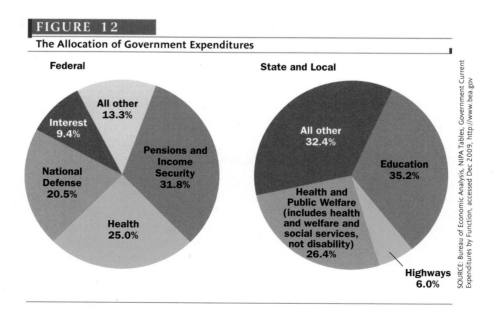

FIGURE 12

The Allocation of Government Expenditures

Federal

- All other 13.3%
- Interest 9.4%
- National Defense 20.5%
- Pensions and Income Security 31.8%
- Health 25.0%

State and Local

- All other 32.4%
- Education 35.2%
- Health and Public Welfare (includes health and welfare and social services, not disability) 26.4%
- Highways 6.0%

SOURCE: Bureau of Economic Analysis, NIPA Tables, Government Current Expenditures by Function, accessed Dec 2009, http://www.bea.gov

Taxes in America

Taxes finance this array of goods and services, and sometimes it seems that the tax collector is everywhere. We have income and payroll taxes withheld from our paychecks, sales taxes added to our purchases, property taxes levied on our homes; we pay gasoline taxes, liquor taxes, and telephone taxes.

Americans have always felt that taxes are both too many and too high. In the 1980s and 1990s, antitax sentiment became a dominant feature of the U.S. political scene. The old slogan "no taxation without representation" gave way to the new slogan "no new taxes." Yet, by international standards, Americans are among the most lightly taxed people in the world. Figure 13 compares the fraction of income paid in taxes in the United States with those paid by residents of other wealthy nations. The tax share in the United States fell notably during the early years of George W. Bush's presidency, but has since crept up a bit and threatens to go higher.

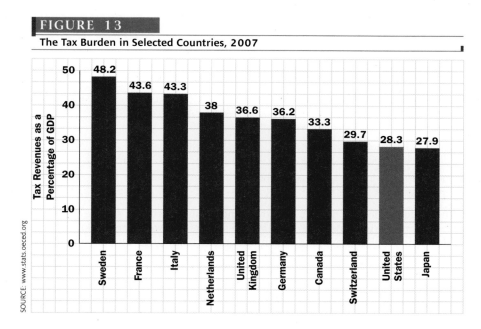

FIGURE 13

The Tax Burden in Selected Countries, 2007

SOURCE: www.stats.oeced.org

The Government as Redistributor

In a market economy, people earn incomes according to what they have to sell. Unfortunately, many people have nothing to sell but unskilled labor, which commands a paltry price. Others lack even that. Such people fare poorly in unfettered markets. In extreme cases, they are homeless, hungry, and ill. Robin Hood transferred money from the rich to the poor. Some think the government should do the same; others disagree.

If poverty amid riches offends your moral sensibilities—a personal judgment that each of us must make for ourselves—two basic remedial approaches are possible. The socialist idea is to force the distribution of income to be more equal by overriding the decisions of the market. "From each according to his ability, to each according to his needs" was Marx's ideal. In practice, things were not quite so noble under socialism, but there was little doubt that incomes in the old Soviet Union were more equally distributed than those in the United States.

The liberal idea is to let free markets determine the distribution of *before-tax* incomes, but then to use the tax system and **transfer payments** to reduce inequality—just as Robin Hood did. This is the rationale for, among other things, **progressive taxation** and antipoverty programs. Americans who support redistribution line up solidly behind the liberal approach. But which ways are the best, and how much is enough? No simple answers have emerged from many decades of debate on these highly contentious questions. Lately, as wage disparities have widened, the inequality issue has gained prominence on the national political agenda. It figured prominently in the 2008 presidential campaign, for example.

Transfer payments are sums of money that certain individuals receive as outright grants from the government rather than as payments for services rendered.

A tax is **progressive** if the ratio of taxes to income rises as income rises.

CONCLUSION: IT'S A MIXED ECONOMY

A **mixed economy** is one with some public influence over the workings of free markets. There may also be some public ownership mixed in with private property.

Ideology notwithstanding, all nations at all times blend public and private ownership of property in some proportions. All rely on markets for some purposes, but all also assign some role to government. Hence, people speak of the ubiquity of **mixed economies**. But mixing is not homogenization; different countries can and do blend the state and market sectors in different ways. Even today, the Russian economy is a far cry from the Italian economy, which is vastly different from that of Hong Kong.

Shortly after most of you were born, a stunning historical event occurred: Communism collapsed all over Europe. For years, the formerly socialist economies suffered through a painful transition from a system in which private property, free enterprise, and markets played subsidiary roles to one in which they are central. These nations have changed the mix, if you will—and dramatically so. To understand why this transformation is at once so difficult and so important, we need to explore the main theme of this book: *What does the market do well, and what does it do poorly?* This task begins in the next chapter.

| SUMMARY |

1. The U.S. economy is the biggest national economy on earth, both because Americans are rich by world standards and because we are a populous nation. Relative to most other advanced countries, our economy is also exceptionally "privatized" and **closed**.

2. The U.S. economy has grown dramatically over the years. But this growth has been interrupted by periodic **recessions**, during which unemployment rises.

3. The United States has a big, diverse workforce whose composition by age and sex has been changing substantially. Relatively few workers these days work in factories or on farms; most work in service industries.

4. Employees take home most of the nation's income. Most of the rest goes, in the forms of interest and profits, to those who provide the capital.

5. Governments at the federal, state, and local levels employ one-sixth of the American workforce (including the armed forces). These governments finance their expenditures by taxes, which account for about 28 percent of GDP. This percentage is one of the lowest in the industrialized world.

6. In addition to raising taxes and making expenditures, the government in a market economy serves as referee and enforcer of the rules, regulates business in a variety of ways, and redistributes income through taxes and **transfer payments**. For all these reasons, we say that we have a **mixed economy**, which blends private and public elements.

| KEY TERMS |

closed economy 24	mixed economy 36	progressive tax 35
factors of production, or inputs 22	open economy 24	recession 24
gross domestic product (GDP) 23	outputs 22	transfer payments 35

| DISCUSSION QUESTIONS |

1. Which are the two biggest national economies on earth? Why are they so much bigger than the others?

2. What is meant by a "factor of production"? Have you ever sold any on a market?

3. Why do you think per capita income in Connecticut is nearly double that in West Virginia?

4. Roughly speaking, what fraction of U.S. labor works in factories? In service businesses? In government?

5. Most American businesses are small, but most of the output is produced by large businesses. That sounds paradoxical. How can it be true?

6. What is the role of government in a mixed economy?

THE FUNDAMENTAL ECONOMIC PROBLEM: SCARCITY AND CHOICE

Our necessities are few but our wants are endless.

INSCRIPTION ON A FORTUNE COOKIE

Understanding what the market system does well and what it does badly is this book's central task. To address this complex issue, we must first answer a simpler one: What do economists expect the market to accomplish?

The most common answer is that the market resolves what is often called *the* fundamental economic problem: how best to manage the resources of society, doing as well as possible with them, despite their scarcity. All decisions are constrained by the scarcity of available resources. A dreamer may envision a world free of want, in which everyone, even in Africa and Central America, drives a BMW and eats caviar, but the earth lacks the resources needed to make that dream come true. Because resources are scarce, all economic decisions involve *trade-offs*. Should you use that $5 bill to buy pizza or a new writing pad for econ class? Should General Motors invest more money in improving assembly lines or in research? A well-functioning market system facilitates and guides such decisions, assigning each hour of labor and each kilowatt-hour of electricity to the task where, it is hoped, the input will best serve the public.

This chapter shows how economists analyze choices like these. The same basic principles, founded on the concept of *opportunity cost,* apply to the decisions made by business firms, governments, and society as a whole. Many of the most basic ideas of economics, such as *efficiency, division of labor, comparative advantage, exchange,* and *the role of markets* appear here for the first time.

CONTENTS

ISSUE: WHAT TO DO ABOUT THE BUDGET DEFICIT?

For roughly 15 years, from the early 1980s until the late 1990s, the top economic issue of the day was how to reduce the federal budget deficit. Presidents Ronald Reagan, George H. W. Bush, and Bill Clinton all battled with Congress over tax and spending *priorities*. Which programs should be cut? What taxes should be raised?

Then, thanks to a combination of strong economic growth and deficit-reducing policies, the budget deficit melted away like springtime snow and actually turned into a budget *surplus* for a few fiscal years (1998 through 2001). For a while, the need to make agonizing *choices* seemed to disappear—or so it seemed. But it was an illusion. Even during that brief era of budget surpluses, hard choices still had to be made. The U.S. government could not afford *everything*. Then, as the stock market collapsed, the economy slowed, and President George W. Bush pushed a series of tax cuts through Congress, the budget surpluses quickly turned back into deficits again—the largest deficits in our history.

The fiscal questions in the 2008 presidential campaign were the familiar ones of the 1980s and 1990s. Which spending programs should be cut and which ones should be increased? Which, if any, of the Bush tax cuts should be repealed? Even a government with an annual budget of over $2 *trillion* was forced to set priorities and make hard choices.

Even when resources are quite generous, they are never unlimited; thus, everyone must still make tough choices. An *optimal* decision is one that chooses the most desirable alternative *among the possibilities permitted by the available resources*, which are always scarce in this sense.

SCARCITY, CHOICE, AND OPPORTUNITY COST

Resources are the instruments provided by nature or by people that are used to create goods and services. Natural resources include minerals, soil, water, and air. Labor is a scarce resource, partly because of time limitations (the day has only 24 hours) and partly because the number of skilled workers is limited. Factories and machines are resources made by people. These three types of resources are often referred to as *land, labor,* and *capital.* They are also called *inputs* or *factors of production.*

One of the basic themes of economics is scarcity—the fact that **resources** are always limited. Even Philip II, of Spanish Armada fame and ruler of one of the greatest empires in history, had to cope with frequent rebellions in his armies when he could not meet their payrolls or even get them basic provisions. He is reported to have undergone bankruptcy an astonishing eight times during his reign. In more recent years, the U.S. government has been agonizing over difficult budget decisions even though it spends more than $2 *trillion* annually.

But the scarcity of *physical resources* is more fundamental than the scarcity of funds. Fuel supplies, for example, are not limitless, and some environmentalists claim that we should now be making some hard choices—such as keeping our homes cooler in winter and warmer in summer and saving gas by living closer to our jobs. Although energy may be the most widely discussed scarcity, the general principle applies to all of the earth's resources—iron, copper, uranium, and so on. Even goods produced by human effort are in limited supply because they require fuel, labor, and other scarce resources as inputs. We can manufacture more cars, but the increased use of labor, steel, and fuel in auto production will mean that we must cut back on something else, perhaps the production of refrigerators.

This all adds up to the following fundamental principle of economics, which we will encounter again and again in this text:

> Virtually all resources are *scarce*, meaning that people have less of them than they would like. Therefore, choices must be made among a *limited* set of possibilities, in full recognition of the inescapable fact that a decision to have more of one thing means that people will have less of something else.

In fact, one popular definition of economics is the study of how best to use *limited* means to pursue *unlimited* ends. Although this definition, like any short statement, cannot possibly cover the sweep of the entire discipline, it does convey the flavor of the economist's stock in trade.

To illustrate the true cost of an item, consider the decision to produce additional cars and therefore to produce fewer refrigerators. Although the production of a car may cost $15,000 per vehicle, for example, *its real cost to society is the refrigerators that society must forgo to get an additional car.* If the labor, steel, and energy needed to manufacture a car would be sufficient to make 30 refrigerators instead of the car, the **opportunity cost** of a car is 30 refrigerators. The principle of opportunity cost is so important that we will spend most of this chapter elaborating on it in various ways.

The **opportunity cost** of any decision is the value of the next best alternative that the decision forces the decision maker to forgo.

HOW MUCH DOES IT REALLY COST? The Principle of Opportunity Cost Economics examines the options available to households, businesses, governments, and entire societies, given the limited resources at their command. It studies the logic of how people can make optimal decisions from among competing alternatives. One overriding principle governs this logic—a principle we introduced in Chapter 1 as one of the *Ideas for Beyond the Final Exam:* With limited resources, a decision to have *more* of one thing is simultaneously a decision to have *less* of something else. Hence, the relevant *cost* of any decision is its *opportunity cost*—the value of the next best alternative that is given up. Optimal decision making must be based on opportunity-cost calculations.

IDEAS FOR BEYOND THE FINAL EXAM

Opportunity Cost and Money Cost

Because we live in a market economy where (almost) everything has its price, students often wonder about the connection or difference between an item's *opportunity cost* and its *market price*. This statement seems to divorce the two concepts: The true opportunity cost of a car is not its market price but the value to their potential purchasers of the other things (like refrigerators) that could have been made or purchased instead.

But isn't the opportunity cost of a car related to its money cost? The normal answer is yes. The two costs are usually closely tied to one another because of the way in which a market economy

"O.K. who *can* put a price on love? Jim?"

sets prices. Steel, for example, is used to manufacture both automobiles and refrigerators. If consumers value items that can be made with steel (such as refrigerators) highly, then economists would say that the *opportunity cost* of making a car is high. But, under these circumstances, strong demand for this highly valued resource will bid up its market price. In this way, a well-functioning price system will assign a high price to steel, which will make the *money cost* of manufacturing a car high as well. In summary:

> If the market functions well, goods that have high opportunity costs will also have high money costs. In turn, goods that have low opportunity costs will also have low money costs.

Nevertheless, it would be a mistake to treat opportunity costs and explicit monetary costs as identical. For one thing, sometimes the market does not function well and hence assigns prices that do not accurately reflect opportunity costs. Moreover, some valuable items may not bear explicit price tags at all. We encountered one such example in Chapter 1, where we noted that the opportunity cost of a college education may differ sharply from its explicit money cost. Why? Because one important item is typically omitted from the money-cost calculation: the *market value of your time*; that is, the wages you could earn by working instead of attending college. Because you give up these potential wages, which can amount to $15,000 per year or more in order to acquire an education, they must be counted as a major part of the opportunity cost of going to college.

Other common examples where money costs and opportunity costs diverge are goods and services that are given away "free." For example, some early settlers of the American West destroyed natural amenities such as forests and buffalo herds, which had no market price, leaving later generations to pay the opportunity costs in terms of lost resources. Similarly, you incur no explicit monetary cost to acquire an item that is given away for free. However, if you must wait in line to get the "free" commodity, you incur an opportunity cost equal to the value of the next best use of your time.

Optimal Choice: Not Just *Any* Choice

How do people and firms make decisions? There are many ways, some of them based on hunches with little forethought; some are even based on superstition or the advice of a fortune teller. Often, when the required information is scarce and the necessary research and calculations are costly and difficult, the decision maker will settle on the first possibility that he can "live with"—a choice that promises to yield results that are not too bad and that seem fairly safe. The decision maker may be willing to choose this course even though he recognizes that there might be other options that are better but are unknown to him. This way of deciding is called *satisficing*.

In this book, we will assume that decision makers seek to do better than mere satisficing. Rather, we will assume that they seek to reach decisions that are optimal—decisions that do better in achieving the decision makers' goals than any other possible choice. We will assume that the required information is available to the decision makers and we will study the procedures that enable them to determine the optimal choices.

An **optimal decision** is one that best serves the objectives of the decision maker, whatever those objectives may be. It is selected by explicit or implicit comparison with the possible alternative choices. The term *optimal* does not mean that we, the observers or analysts, approve or disapprove of the objective itself.

> An **optimal decision** for individual X is one that is selected *after implicit or explicit comparison of the consequences of each of the possible choices* and that is shown by analysis to be the one that most effectively promotes the goals of person X.

We will study optimal decision making by various parties—consumers, producers, and sellers—in a variety of situations. The methods of analysis for determining what choice is optimal in each case will be remarkably similar. So, if you understand one of them, you will already be well on your way to understanding them all. A technique called *marginal analysis* will be used for this purpose. But one fundamental idea underlies any method used for optimal decision making: *To determine whether a possible decision is or is not optimal, its consequences must be compared with those of each of the other possible choices.*

SCARCITY AND CHOICE FOR A SINGLE FIRM

The **outputs** of a firm or an economy are the goods and services it produces.

The **inputs** used by a firm or an economy are the labor, raw materials, electricity, and other resources it uses to produce its outputs.

The nature of opportunity cost is perhaps clearest in the case of a single business firm that produces two **outputs** from a fixed supply of **inputs**. Given current technology and the limited resources at its disposal, the more of one good the firm produces, the less of the other it will be able to make. Unless managers explicitly weigh the desirability of each product against the other, they are unlikely to make rational production decisions.

Consider the example of Jones, a farmer whose available supplies of land, machinery, labor, and fertilizer are capable of producing the various combinations of soybeans and wheat listed in Table 1. Obviously, devoting more resources to soybean production means that Jones will produce less wheat. Table 1 indicates, for example, that if Jones grows only soybeans, the harvest will be 40,000 bushels. But if he reduces his soybean production to 30,000 bushels, he can also grow 38,000 bushels of wheat. Thus, *the opportunity cost of obtaining 38,000 bushels of wheat is 10,000 fewer bushels of soybeans.* Put another way, the opportunity cost of 10,000 more bushels of soybeans is 38,000 bushels of wheat. The other numbers in Table 1 have similar interpretations.

TABLE 1

Production Possibilities Open to a Farmer

Bushels of Soybeans	Bushels of Wheat	Label in Figure 1
40,000	0	A
30,000	38,000	B
20,000	52,000	C
10,000	60,000	D
0	65,000	E

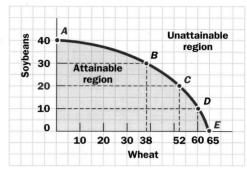

NOTE: Quantities are in thousands of bushels per year.

FIGURE 1

Production Possibilities Frontier for Production by a Single Farmer

The situation becomes a little more complicated when the objective of the farmer is to earn as large a *money profit* as possible, rather than maximizing quantity of wheat or soybeans. Suppose producing 38,000 bushels of wheat requires Jones to give up 10,000, bushels of soybeans and $4,000 is the profit he would earn if he chose the wheat output, whereas $1,200 is the profit offered by the soybean option (that would have to be given up if wheat specialization were decided upon). Then the opportunity cost that our farmer would incur is not the 10,000 bushels of soybeans, but the $12,000 in profits that substitution of soybean production would offer.

The Production Possibilities Frontier

Figure 1 presents this same information graphically. Point *A* indicates that one of the options available to the farmer is to produce 40,000 bushels of soybeans and 0 wheat. Thus, point *A* corresponds to the first line of Table 1, point *B* to the second line, and so on. Curves similar to *AE* appear frequently in this book; they are called **production possibilities frontiers.** Any point *on or inside* the production possibilities frontier is attainable because it does not entail larger outputs than currently available resources permit. Points *outside* the frontier, representing very large quantities of output, are figments of the imagination given current circumstances because they cannot be achieved with the available resources and technology.

A **production possibilities frontier** shows the different combinations of various goods, any one of which a producer can turn out, given the available resources and existing technology.

Because resources are limited, the production possibilities frontier always slopes downward to the right. The farmer can *increase* wheat production (move to the right in Figure 1) only by devoting more land and labor to growing wheat, but this choice simultaneously *reduces* soybean production (the curve must move downward) because less land and labor remain available for growing soybeans.

Notice that, in addition to having a negative slope, our production possibilities frontier *AE* has another characteristic: It is "bowed outward." What does this curvature mean? In short, as larger and larger quantities of resources are transferred from the production of one output to the production of another, the additions to the second product decline.

Suppose farmer Jones initially produces only soybeans, using even land that is comparatively most productive in wheat cultivation (point *A*). Now he decides to switch some land from soybean production into wheat production. Which part of the land will he switch? If Jones is sensible, he will use the part that, because of its chemical content, direction in relation to sunlight, and so on, is relatively most productive in growing wheat. As he shifts to point *B*, soybean production falls from 40,000 bushels to 30,000 bushels as wheat production rises from 0 to 38,000 bushels. A sacrifice of only 10,000 bushels of soybeans "buys" 38,000 bushels of wheat.

Imagine now that our farmer wants to produce still more wheat. Figure 1 tells us that the sacrifice of an additional 10,000 bushels of soybeans (from 30,000 bushels to 20,000 bushels) will yield only 14,000 more bushels of wheat (see point *C*). Why? The main reason is that *inputs tend to be specialized.* As we noted at point *A*, the farmer was using resources for soybean production that were relatively more productive in growing wheat.

Consequently, their relative productivity in soybean production was low. When these resources are switched to wheat production, the yield is high.

This trend cannot continue forever, of course. As more wheat is produced, the farmer must utilize land and machinery with a greater productivity advantage in growing soybeans and a smaller productivity advantage in growing wheat. This is why the first 10,000 bushels of soybeans forgone "buys" the farmer 38,000 bushels of wheat, whereas the second 10,000 bushels of soybeans "buys" only 14,000 bushels of wheat. Figure 1 and Table 1 show that these returns continue to decline as wheat production expands: The next 10,000-bushel reduction in soybean production yields only 8,000 bushels of additional wheat, and so on.

If the farmer's objective is to maximize the amount of wheat or soybean product he gets out of his land and labor then, as we can see, the *slope* of the production possibilities frontier graphically represents the concept of *opportunity cost*. Between points *C* and *B*, for example, the opportunity cost of acquiring 10,000 additional bushels of soybeans is shown on the graph to be 14,000 bushels of forgone wheat; between points *B* and *A*, the opportunity cost of 10,000 bushels of soybeans is 38,000 bushels of forgone wheat. In general, as we move upward to the left along the production possibilities frontier (toward more soybeans and less wheat), the opportunity cost of soybeans in terms of wheat increases. Looking at the same thing the other way, as we move downward to the right, the opportunity cost of acquiring wheat by giving up soybeans increases—more and more soybeans must be forgone per added bushel of wheat and successive addition to wheat output occur.

The Principle of Increasing Costs

The **principle of increasing costs** states that as the production of a good expands, the opportunity cost of producing another unit generally increases.

We have just described a very general phenomenon with applications well beyond farming. The **principle of increasing costs** states that as the production of one good expands, the opportunity cost of producing another unit of this good generally increases. This principle is not a universal fact—exceptions do arise—but it does seem to be a technological regularity that applies to a wide range of economic activities. As our farming example suggests, the principle of increasing costs is based on the fact that resources tend to be at least somewhat specialized. So we lose some of their productivity when those resources are transferred from doing what they are relatively *good* at to what they are relatively *bad* at. In terms of diagrams such as Figure 1, the principle simply asserts that the production possibilities frontier is bowed outward.

Perhaps the best way to understand this idea is to contrast it with a case in which no resources are specialized so costs do not increase as output proportion changes. Figure 2 depicts a production possibilities frontier for producing black shoes and brown shoes. Because the labor and machinery used to produce black shoes are just as good at producing brown shoes, the frontier is a straight line. If the firm cuts back its production of black shoes by 10,000 pairs, it can produce 10,000 additional pairs of brown shoes, no matter how big the shift between these two outputs. It loses no productivity in the switch because resources are not specialized.

More typically, however, as a firm concentrates more of its productive capacity on one commodity, it is forced to employ inputs that are better suited to making another commodity. The firm is forced to vary the proportions in which it uses inputs because of the limited quantities of some of those inputs. This fact also explains the typical curvature of the firm's production possibilities frontier.

FIGURE 2

Production Possibilities Frontier without Specialized Resources

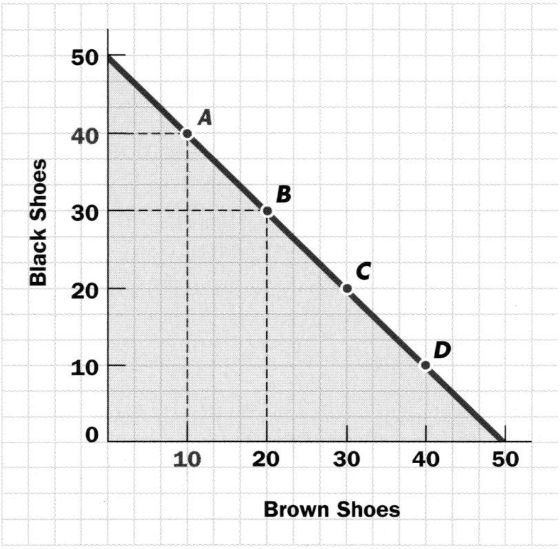

NOTE: Quantities are in thousands of pairs per week.

SCARCITY AND CHOICE FOR THE ENTIRE SOCIETY

Like an individual firm, the entire economy is also constrained by its limited resources and technology. If the public wants more aircraft and tanks, it will have to give up some boats and automobiles. If it wants to build more factories and stores, it will have to build fewer homes and sports arenas. In general:

> **The position and shape of the production possibilities frontier that constrains society's choices are determined by the economy's physical resources, its skills and technology, its willingness to work, and how much it has devoted in the past to the construction of factories, research, and innovation.**

Because so many nations have long debated whether to reduce or augment military spending, let us exemplify the nature of society's choices by deciding between military might (represented by missiles) and civilian consumption (represented by automobiles). Just like a single firm, the economy as a whole faces a production possibilities frontier for missiles and autos, determined by its technology and the available resources of land, labor, capital, and raw materials. This production possibilities frontier may look like curve *BC* in Figure 3. If most workers are employed in auto plants, car production will be large, but the output of missiles will be small. If the economy transfers resources out of auto manufacturing when consumer demand declines, it can, by congressional action, alter the output mix toward more missiles (the move from *D* to *E*). However, something is likely to be lost in the process because physical resources are specialized. The fabric used to make car seats will not help much in missile production. The principle of increasing costs strongly suggests that the production possibilities frontier curves downward toward the axes.

We may even reach a point where the only resources left are not very useful outside of auto manufacturing. In that case, even a large sacrifice of automobiles will get the economy few additional missiles. That is the meaning of the steep segment, *FC*, on the frontier. At point *C*, there is little additional output of missiles as compared to point *F*, even though at *C* automobile production has been given up entirely.

FIGURE 3

Production Possibilities Frontier for the Entire Economy

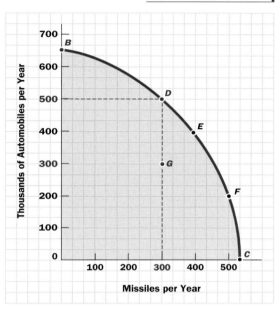

> **The downward slope of society's production possibilities frontier implies that hard choices must be made. Civilian consumption (automobiles) can be increased only by decreasing military expenditure, not by rhetoric or wishing. The curvature of the production possibilities frontier implies that as defense spending increases, it becomes progressively more expensive to "buy" additional military strength ("missiles") in terms of the resulting sacrifice of civilian consumption.**

Scarcity and Choice Elsewhere in the Economy

We have emphasized that limited resources force hard choices on business managers and society as a whole, but the same type of choices arises elsewhere—in households, universities, and other nonprofit organizations, as well as the government.

The nature of opportunity cost is perhaps most obvious for a household that must decide how to divide its income among the goods and services that compete for the family's attention. If the Simpson family buys an expensive new car, they may be forced to cut back sharply on some other purchases. This fact does not make it unwise to buy the car, but it does make it unwise to buy the car until the family considers the full implications for its overall budget. If the Simpsons are to utilize their limited resources most effectively, they must recognize the opportunity costs of the car—the things they will forgo as a result— perhaps a vacation and an expensive new TV set. The decision to buy the car will be rational if the benefit to the family from the automobile (however measured) is greater than the opportunity cost—their benefit if they buy an equally expensive vacation or TV set instead.

Hard Choices in the Real World

This excerpt from a recent newspaper story brings home the realities of scarcity and choice:

"President Barack Obama delivered a $3.6 trillion budget blueprint to Congress Thursday. . . .

The budget blueprint for fiscal year 2010 is one of the most ambitious policy prescriptions in decades, a reordering of the federal government to provide national health care, shift the energy economy away from oil and gas, and boost the federal commitment to education. . . .

Mr. Obama proposes large increases in education funding, including indexing Pell Grants for higher education to inflation and converting the popular scholarship to an automatic 'entitlement' program. High-speed rail would gain a $1 billion-a-year grant program, part of a larger effort to boost infrastructure spending. . . .

To finance his proposals, the president has clearly chosen winners and losers—with the affluent heading the list of losers. . . .

As expected, taxes will rise for singles earning $200,000 and couples earning $250,000, beginning in 2011—for a total windfall of $656 billion over 10 years. Income tax hikes would raise $339 billion alone. Limits on personal exemptions and itemized deductions would bring in another $180 billion. Higher capital gains rates would bring in $118 billion. The estate tax, scheduled to be repealed next year, would instead be preserved. . . ."

SOURCE: Excerpted from Jonathan Weisman, "Obama Budget Pushes Sweeping Change", '*The Wall Street Journal*', February 27, 2009. Reprinted by permission of *The Wall Street Journal*. Copyright © 2009 Dow Jones & Company, Inc. All Rights Reserved Worldwide.

SOURCE: © AP Photo/J. David Ake

ISSUE REVISITED   COPING WITH THE BUDGET DEFICIT

As already noted, even a rich and powerful nation like the United States must cope with the limitations implied by scarce resources. The necessity for choice imposed on governments by the limited amount they feel they can afford to spend is similar in character to the problems faced by business firms and households. For the goods and services that it buys from others, a government must prepare a budget similar to that of a very large household. For the items it produces itself—education, police protection, libraries, and so on—it faces a production possibilities frontier much like a business firm does. Even though the U.S. government spent over $2.6 trillion in 2006, some of the most acrimonious debates between then President Bush and his critics arose from disagreements about how the government's limited resources should be allocated among competing uses. Even if unstated, the concept of opportunity cost is central to these debates.

THE CONCEPT OF EFFICIENCY

So far, our discussion of scarcity and choice has assumed that either the firm or the economy always operates on its production possibilities frontier rather than *below* it. In other words, we have tacitly assumed that whatever the firm or economy decides to do, it does so **efficiently**.

Economists define efficiency as the absence of waste. An efficient economy wastes none of its available resources and produces the maximum amount of output that its technology permits.

To see why any point on the economy's production possibilities frontier in Figure 3 (in a choice between missiles or automobiles or some combination of the two) represents an efficient decision, suppose for a moment that society has decided to produce 300 missiles. The production possibilities frontier tells us that if 300 missiles are to be produced, then the maximum number of automobiles that can be made is 500,000 (point *D* in Figure 3). The economy is therefore operating efficiently only if it produces 500,000 automobiles (when it manufactures 300 missiles) rather than some smaller number of cars, such as 300,000 (as at point *G*).

Point *D* is efficient, but point *G* is not, because the economy is capable of moving from *G* to *D*, thereby producing 200,000 more automobiles without giving up any missiles (or anything else). Clearly, failure to take advantage of the option of choosing point *D* rather than point *G* constitutes a wasted opportunity—an inefficiency.

Note that the concept of efficiency does not tell us which point on the production possibilities frontier is *best*. Rather, it tells us only that any point *below* the frontier cannot be best, because any such point represents wasted resources. For example, should society ever find itself at a point such as *G*, the necessity of making hard choices would (temporarily) disappear. It would be possible to increase production of *both* missiles *and* automobiles by moving to a point such as *E*.

Why, then, would a society ever find itself at a point below its production possibilities frontier? Why are resources wasted in real life? The most important reason in today's economy is *unemployment*. When many workers are unemployed, the economy must be at a point such as *G*, below the frontier, because by putting the unemployed to work in each industry, the economy could produce both more missiles *and* more automobiles. The economy would then move from point *G* to the right (more missiles) and upward (more automobiles) toward a point such as *E* on the production possibilities frontier. Only when no resources are wasted is the economy operating on the frontier.

Inefficiency occurs in other ways, too. A prime example is assigning inputs to the wrong task—as when wheat is grown on land best suited to soybean cultivation. Another important type of inefficiency occurs when large firms produce goods that smaller enterprises could make better because they can pay closer attention to detail, or when small firms produce outputs best suited to large-scale production. Some other examples are the outright waste that occurs because of favoritism (for example, promotion of an incompetent brother-in-law to a job he cannot do very well) or restrictive labor practices (for example, requiring a railroad to keep a fireman on a diesel-electric locomotive where there is no longer a fire to tend).

A particularly deplorable form of waste is caused by discrimination against minority or female workers. When a job is given, for example, to a white male in preference to an African-American woman who is more qualified, society sacrifices potential output and the entire community is apt to be affected adversely. Every one of these inefficiencies means that the community obtains less output than it could have, given the available inputs.

THE THREE COORDINATION TASKS OF ANY ECONOMY

In deciding how to **allocate its scarce resources,** every society must somehow make three sorts of decisions:

- First, as we have emphasized, it must figure out *how to utilize its resources efficiently;* that is, it must find a way to reach its production possibilities frontier.
- Second, it must decide *which of the possible combinations of goods to produce*—how many missiles, automobiles, and so on; that is, it must select one specific point on

A set of outputs is said to be produced **efficiently** if, given current technological knowledge, there is no way one can produce larger amounts of any output without using larger input amounts or giving up some quantity of another output.

Allocation of resources refers to society's decisions on how to divide up its scarce input resources among the different outputs produced in the economy and among the different firms or other organizations that produce those outputs.

the production possibilities frontier among all of the points (that is, all of the output combinations) on the frontier.

- Third, it must decide *how much of the total output of each good to distribute to each person,* doing so in a sensible way that does not assign meat to vegetarians and wine to teetotalers.

There are many ways in which societies can and do make each of these decisions—to which economists often refer as *how, what,* and *to whom?* For example, a central planner may tell people how to produce, what to produce, and what to consume, as the authorities used to do, at least to some extent, in the former Soviet Union. But in a market economy, no one group or individual makes all such resource allocation decisions explicitly. Rather, consumer demands and production costs allocate resources *automatically* and *anonymously* through a system of prices and markets. As the formerly socialist countries learned, markets do an impressively effective job in carrying out these tasks. For our introduction to the ways in which markets do all this, let's consider each task in turn.

TASK 1. HOW THE MARKET FOSTERS EFFICIENT RESOURCE ALLOCATION

Production efficiency is one of the economy's three basic tasks, and societies pursue it in many ways. However, one source of efficiency is so fundamental that we must single it out for special attention: the tremendous productivity gains that stem from *specialization.*

The Wonders of the Division of Labor

Division of labor means breaking up a task into a number of smaller, more *specialized* tasks so that each worker can become more adept at a particular job.

Adam Smith, the founder of modern economics, first marveled at how **division of labor** raises efficiency and productivity when he visited a pin factory. In a famous passage near the beginning of his monumental book *The Wealth of Nations* (1776), he described what he saw:

> One man draws out the wire, another straightens it, a third cuts it, a fourth points it, a fifth grinds it at the top for receiving the head. To make the head requires two or three distinct operations; to put it on is a peculiar business, to whiten the pins is another; it is even a trade by itself to put them into the paper.[1]

Smith observed that by dividing the work to be done in this way, each worker became quite skilled in a particular specialty, and the productivity of the group of workers as a whole was greatly enhanced. As Smith related it:

> I have seen a small manufactory of this kind where ten men only were employed. . . . Those ten persons . . . could make among them upwards of forty-eight thousand pins in a day. . . . But if they had all wrought separately and independently . . . they certainly could not each of them have made twenty, *perhaps not one pin in a day.*[2]

In other words, through the miracle of division of labor and specialization, 10 workers accomplished what might otherwise have required thousands. This was one of the secrets of the Industrial Revolution, which helped lift humanity out of the abject poverty that had been its lot for centuries.

Adam Smith, L.L.D.

SOURCE: © Courtesy of the Library of Congress

---

[1] Adam Smith, *The Wealth of Nations* (New York: Random House, 1937), p. 4.
[2] Ibid., p. 5.

The Amazing Principle of Comparative Advantage

Specialization in production fosters efficiency in an even more profound sense. Adam Smith noticed that *how* goods are produced can make a huge difference to productivity, but so can *which* goods are produced. The reason is that people (and businesses and nations) have different abilities. Some can repair automobiles, whereas others are wizards with numbers. Some are handy with computers, and others can cook. An economy will be most efficient if people specialize in doing what they do best and then trade with one another, so that the accountant gets her car repaired and the computer programmer gets to eat tasty and nutritious meals.

This much is obvious. What is less obvious—and is one of the great ideas of economics—is that two people (or two businesses or two countries) can generally gain from trade *even if one of them is more efficient than the other in producing everything.* A simple example will help explain why.

Some lawyers can type better than their administrative assistants. Should such a lawyer fire her assistant and do her own typing? Not likely. Even though the lawyer may type better than the assistant, good judgment tells her to concentrate on practicing law and leave the typing to a lower-paid assistant. Why? Because the *opportunity cost* of an hour devoted to typing is the amount that she could earn from an hour less spent with clients, which is a far more lucrative activity.

This example illustrates the principle of **comparative advantage** at work. The lawyer specializes in arguing cases despite her advantage as a typist because she has a *still greater* advantage as an attorney. She suffers some direct loss by leaving the typing to a less efficient employee, but she more than makes up for that loss by the income she earns selling her legal services to clients.

Precisely the same principle applies to nations. As we shall learn in greater detail in Chapter 34, comparative advantage underlies the economic analysis of international trade patterns. A country that is particularly adept at producing certain items—such as aircraft in the United States, coffee in Brazil, and oil in Saudi Arabia—should specialize in those activities, producing more than it wants for its own use. The country can then take the money it earns from its exports and purchase from other nations items that it does not make for itself. And this is still true if one of the trading nations is the most efficient producer of almost everything. The underlying logic is precisely the same as in our lawyer-typist example. The United States might, for example, be better than South Korea at manufacturing both computers and television sets. But if the United States is vastly more efficient at producing computers, but only slightly more efficient at making TV sets, it pays for the United States to specialize in computer manufacturing, for South Korea to specialize in TV production, and for the two countries to trade.

This principle, called the *law of comparative advantage,* was discovered by David Ricardo, another giant in the history of economic analysis, almost 200 years ago. It is one of the *Ideas for Beyond the Final Exam* introduced in Chapter 1.

> One country is said to have a **comparative advantage** over another in the production of a particular good *relative to other goods* if it produces that good less inefficiently than it **produces** other goods, as compared with the other country.

THE SURPRISING PRINCIPLE OF COMPARATIVE ADVANTAGE Even if one country (or one worker) is worse than another country (or another worker) in the production of *every* good, it is said to have a *comparative advantage* in making the good at which it is *least inefficient*—compared to the other country. Ricardo discovered that two countries can gain by trading even if one country is more efficient than another in the production of *every* commodity. Precisely the same logic applies to individual workers or to businesses.

In determining the most efficient patterns of production and trade, it is *comparative advantage* that matters. Thus, a country can gain by importing a good from abroad even if that good can be produced more efficiently at home. Such imports make sense if they enable the country to specialize in producing those goods at which it is *even more efficient.* And the other, less efficient country should specialize in exporting the goods in whose production it is *least inefficient.*

IDEAS FOR
BEYOND THE
FINAL EXAM

TASK 2. MARKET EXCHANGE AND DECIDING HOW MUCH OF EACH GOOD TO PRODUCE

The gains from specialization are welcome, but they create a problem: With specialization, people no longer produce only what they want to consume themselves. The workers in Adam Smith's pin factory had no use for the thousands of pins they produced each day; they wanted to trade them for things like food, clothing, and shelter. Similarly, the administrative assistant in our law office example has no personal use for the legal briefs he types. Thus, specialization requires some mechanism by which workers producing pins can *exchange* their wares with workers producing such things as cloth and potatoes and office workers can turn their typing skills into things they want to consume.

> **Without a system of exchange, the productivity miracle achieved by comparative advantage and the division of labor would do society little good, because each producer in an efficient arrangement would be left with only the commodities in whose production its comparative efficiency was greatest and would have no other goods to consume. With it, standards of living have risen enormously.**

Although people can and do trade goods for other goods, a system of exchange works better when everyone agrees to use some common item (such as pieces of paper with unique markings printed on them) for buying and selling things. Enter *money*. Then workers in pin factories, for example, can be paid in money rather than in pins, and they can use this money to purchase cloth and potatoes. Textile workers and farmers can do the same.

In a market in which trading is carried out by means of exchange between money and goods or services, the market mechanism also makes the second of our three crucial decisions: how much of each good should be produced with the resources that are available to the economy. For what happens is that if more widgets are produced than consumers want to buy at current prices, those who make widgets will be left with unsold widgets on their hands. Widget price will be driven down, and manufacturers will be forced to cut production, with some being driven out of business altogether. The opposite will happen if producers supply fewer widgets than consumers want at the prevailing prices. Then prices will be driven up by scarcity and manufacturers will be led to increase their output. In this way, the output and price of each and every commodity will be driven toward levels at which supply matches demand or comes very close to it. That is how the market automatically deals with the second critical decision: how much of each commodity will be produced by the economy given the economy's productive capacity (as shown by the production possibility frontier).

TASK 3. HOW TO DISTRIBUTE THE ECONOMY'S OUTPUTS AMONG CONSUMERS

These two phenomena—specialization and exchange (assisted by money)—working in tandem led to vast increases in the abundance that the more prosperous economies of the world were able to supply. But that leaves us with the third basic issue: What forces allow those outputs to be distributed among the population in reasonable ways? What forces establish a smoothly functioning system of exchange so that people can first exploit their comparative advantages and then acquire what they want to consume? One alternative is to have a central authority telling people what to do. Adam Smith explained and extolled yet another way of organizing and coordinating economic activity—markets and prices can coordinate those activities. Smith noted that people are adept at pursuing their own self-interests and that a **market system** harnesses this self-interest remarkably well. As he put it—with clear religious overtones—in doing what is best for themselves, people are "led by an invisible hand" to promote the economic well-being of society as a whole.

Those of us who live in a well-functioning market economy like that found in the United States tend to take the achievements of the market for granted, much like the daily rising and setting of the sun. Few bother to think about, say, the reason why Hawaiian pineapples show up daily in Vermont supermarkets in quantities desired by Vermont consumers. The

A **market system** is a form of economic organization in which resource allocation decisions are left to individual producers and consumers acting in their own best interests without central direction.

market deals with this issue through the profit motive, which guides firms' output decisions, matching quantities produced to consumer preferences. A rise in the price of wheat because of increased demand for bread, for example, will persuade farmers to produce more wheat and devote less of their land to soybeans. Such a price system also distributes goods among consumers in accord with their tastes and preferences, using voluntary exchange to determine who gets what. Consumers spend their income on the things they like best (among those they can afford). Vegetarians do not waste their income on beef, and teetotalers do

SOURCE: © Plush Studios/Blend Images/Jupiterimages

not spend money on gin. So consumers, by controlling their spending patterns, can ensure that the goods they buy at the supermarket are compatible with their preferences. That is how the market mechanism ensures that the products of the economy are divided among consumers in a rational manner, meaning that this distribution tends to fit in with the preferences of the different purchasers. But there is at least one problem here; the ability to buy goods is hardly divided equally. Workers with valuable skills and owners of scarce resources can sell what they have at attractive prices. With the incomes they earn, they can purchase generous amounts of goods and services. Those who are less successful in selling what they own receive lower incomes and so can afford to buy less. In extreme cases, they may suffer severe deprivation.

The past few pages explain, in broad terms, how a market economy solves the three basic problems facing any society: how to produce any given combination of goods efficiently, how to select an appropriate combination of goods to produce, and how to distribute these goods sensibly among people. As we proceed through the following chapters, you will learn much more about these issues. You will see that they constitute the central theme that permeates not only this text but the work of economists in general. As you progress through this book, keep in mind two questions:

- What does the market do well?
- What does it do poorly?

There are numerous answers to both questions, as you will learn in subsequent chapters.

Society has many important goals. Some of them, such as producing goods and services with maximum efficiency (minimum waste), can be achieved extraordinarily well by letting markets operate more or less freely.

Free markets will not, however, achieve all of society's goals. For example, they often have trouble keeping unemployment low. In fact, the unfettered operations of markets may even run counter to some goals, such as protection of the environment. Many observers also believe that markets do not necessarily distribute income in accord with ethical or moral norms. Even in cases in which markets do not perform well, there may be ways of harnessing the power of the market mechanism to remedy its own deficiencies, as you will learn in later chapters.

Economic debates often have political and ideological overtones. So we will close this chapter by emphasizing that the central theme we have just outlined is neither a *defense of* nor an *attack on* the capitalist system. Nor is it a "conservative" position. One does not have to be a conservative to recognize that the market mechanism can be an extraordinarily helpful instrument for the pursuit of economic goals. Most of the formerly socialist countries of Europe have been working hard to "marketize" their economies, and even the communist People's Republic of China has made huge strides in that direction.

The point is not to confuse ends with means in deciding how much to rely on market forces. Liberals and conservatives surely have different goals, but the means chosen to pursue these goals should, for the most part, be chosen on the basis of how effective the selected means are, not on some ideological prejudgments. Even Karl Marx emphasized that the market is remarkably efficient at producing an abundance of goods and services that had never been seen in precapitalist history. Such wealth can be used to promote conservative goals, such as reducing tax rates, or to facilitate goals favored by liberals, such as providing more generous public aid for the poor.

Certainly the market cannot deal with every economic problem. Indeed, we have just noted that the market is the *source* of a number of significant problems. Even so, the evidence accumulated over centuries leads economists to believe that most economic problems are best handled by market techniques. The analysis in this book is intended to help you identify both the objectives that the market mechanism can reliably achieve and those that it will fail to promote, or at least not promote very effectively. We urge you to forget the slogans you have heard—whether from the left or from the right—and make up your own mind after learning the material in this book.

| SUMMARY |

1. Supplies of all **resources** are limited. Because resources are **scarce,** an **optimal decision** is one that chooses the best alternative among the options that are possible with the available resources.

2. With limited resources, a decision to obtain more of one item is also a decision to give up some of another. The value of what we give up is called the **opportunity cost** of what we get. The opportunity cost is the true cost of any decision. This is one of the *Ideas for Beyond the Final Exam.*

3. When markets function effectively, firms are led to use resources efficiently and to produce the things that consumers want most. In such cases, opportunity costs and money costs (prices) correspond closely. When the market performs poorly, or when important, socially costly items are provided without charging an appropriate price, or are given away free, opportunity costs and money costs can diverge.

4. A firm's **production possibilities frontier** shows the combinations of goods it can produce, given the current technology and the resources at its disposal. The frontier is usually bowed outward because resources tend to be specialized.

5. The **principle of increasing costs** states that as the production of one good expands, the opportunity cost of producing another unit of that good generally increases.

6. Like a firm, the economy as a whole has a production possibilities frontier whose position is determined by its technology and by the available resources of land, labor, capital, and raw materials.

7. A firm or an economy that ends up at a point below its production possibilities frontier is using its resources inefficiently or wastefully. This is what happens, for example, when there is unemployment.

8. Economists define **efficiency** as the absence of waste. It is achieved primarily by the gains in productivity brought about through **specialization** that exploits **division of labor** and **comparative advantage** and by a system of exchange.

9. Two countries (or two people) can gain by specializing in the activity in which each has a *comparative* advantage and then trading with one another. These gains from trade remain available even if one country is inferior at producing everything but specializes in producing those items at which it is least inefficient. This so-called principle of comparative advantage is one of our *Ideas for Beyond the Final Exam.*

10. If an exchange between two individuals is voluntary, both parties must benefit, even if no additional goods are produced. This is another of the *Ideas for Beyond the Final Exam.*

11. Every economic system must find a way to answer three basic questions: How can goods be produced most efficiently? How much of each good should be produced? How should goods be distributed among users?

12. The **market system** works very well in solving some of society's basic problems, but it fails to remedy others and may, indeed, create some of its own. Where and how it succeeds and fails constitute the central theme of this book and characterize the work of economists in general.

| KEY TERMS |

allocation of scarce resources   47

comparative advantage   49

division of labor   48

efficiency   47

inputs   42

market system   50

opportunity cost   41

optimal decision   42

outputs   42

principle of increasing costs   44

production possibilities frontier   43

resources   40

| TEST YOURSELF |

1. A person rents a house for $24,000 per year. The house can be purchased for $200,000, and the tenant has this much money in a bank account that pays 4 percent interest per year. Is buying the house a good deal for the tenant? Where does opportunity cost enter the picture?

2. Graphically show the production possibilities frontier for the nation of Stromboli, using the data given in the following table. Does the principle of increasing cost hold in Stromboli?

Stromboli's 2004 Production Possibilities	
Pizzas per Year	Pizza Ovens per Year
75,000,000	0
60,000,000	6,000
45,000,000	11,000
30,000,000	15,000
15,000,000	18,000
0	18,000

3. Consider two alternatives for Stromboli in 2009. In case (a), its inhabitants eat 60 million pizzas and build 6,000 pizza ovens. In case (b), the population eats 15 million pizzas but builds 18,000 ovens. Which case will lead to a more generous production possibilities frontier for Stromboli in 2009?

4. Jasmine's Snack Shop sells two brands of potato chips. She produces them by buying them from a wholesale supplier. Brand X costs Jasmine $1 per bag, and Brand Y costs her $1.40. Draw Jasmine's production possibilities frontier if she has $280 budgeted to spend on the purchase of potato chips from the wholesaler. Why is it not "bowed out"?

| DISCUSSION QUESTIONS |

1. Discuss the resource limitations that affect
   a. the poorest person on earth
   b. Bill Gates, the richest person on earth
   c. a farmer in Kansas
   d. the government of Indonesia

2. If you were president of your college, what would you change if your budget were cut by 10 percent? By 25 percent? By 50 percent?

3. If you were to leave college, what things would change in your life? What, then, is the opportunity cost of your education?

4. Raising chickens requires several types of feed, such as corn and soy meal. Consider a farm in the former Soviet Union. Try to describe how decisions on the number of chickens to be raised, and the amount of each feed to use in raising them, were made under the old communist regime. If the farm is now privately owned, how does the market guide the decisions that used to be made by the central planning agency?

5. The United States is one of the world's wealthiest countries. Think of a recent case in which the decisions of the U.S. government were severely constrained by scarcity. Describe the trade-offs that were involved. What were the opportunity costs of the decisions that were actually made?

SUPPLY AND DEMAND: AN INITIAL LOOK

The free enterprise system is absolutely too important to be left to the voluntary action of the marketplace.

FLORIDA CONGRESSMAN RICHARD KELLY, 1979

In this chapter, we study the economist's most basic investigative tool: the mechanism of supply and demand. Whether your econ course concentrates on macroeconomics or microeconomics, you will find that the so-called law of supply and demand is a fundamental tool of economic analysis. Economists use supply and demand analysis to study issues as diverse as inflation and unemployment, the effects of taxes on prices, government regulation of business, and environmental protection. Supply and demand curves—graphs that relate price to quantity supplied and quantity demanded, respectively—show how prices and quantities are determined in a free market.[1]

A major theme of the chapter is that governments around the world and throughout recorded history have tampered with the price mechanism. As we will see, these bouts with Adam Smith's "invisible hand" have produced undesirable side effects that often surprised and dismayed the authorities. The invisible hand fights back!

CONTENTS

---

[1] This chapter, like much of the rest of this book, uses many graphs like those described in the appendix to Chapter 1. If you have difficulties with these graphs, we suggest that you review that material before proceeding.

| PUZZLE: | WHAT HAPPENED TO OIL PRICES? |

Since 1949, the dollars of purchasing power that a buyer had to pay to buy a barrel of oil had remained remarkably steady, and gasoline had generally remained a bargain. But during two exceptional time periods—one from about 1975 through 1985 and one beginning in 2003—oil prices exploded, and filling up the automobile gas tank became painful to consumers. Clearly, supply and demand changes must have been behind these developments, but what led them to change so much and so suddenly? Later in the chapter, we will provide excerpts from a newspaper story about how dramatic and unexpected events can suddenly shift supply and will help to bring the analysis of this chapter to life.

SOURCE: © AP Images/Paul Sakuma

THE INVISIBLE HAND

Invisible hand is a phrase used by Adam Smith to describe how, by pursuing their own self-interests, people in a market system are "led by an invisible hand" to promote the well-being of the community.

Adam Smith, the father of modern economic analysis, greatly admired the price system. He marveled at its accomplishments—both as an efficient producer of goods and as a guarantor that consumers' preferences are obeyed. Although many people since Smith's time have shared his enthusiasm for the concept of the **invisible hand,** many have not. Smith's contemporaries in the American colonies, for example, were often unhappy with the prices produced by free markets and thought they could do better by legislative decree. Such attempts failed, as explained in the accompanying box "Price Controls at Valley Forge." In countless other instances, the public was outraged by the prices charged on the open market, particularly in the case of housing rents, interest rates, and insurance rates.

Attempts to control interest rates (which are the price of borrowing money) go back hundreds of years before the birth of Christ, at least to the code of laws compiled under the Babylonian king Hammurabi in about 1800 B.C. Our historical legacy also includes a rather long list of price ceilings on foods and other products imposed in the reign of Diocletian, emperor of the declining Roman Empire. More recently, Americans have been offered the "protection" of a variety of price controls. Laws have placed ceilings on some prices (such as rents) to protect buyers, whereas legislation has placed floors under other prices (such as farm products) to protect sellers. Yet, somehow, everything such regulation touches seems to end up in even greater disarray than it was before. Despite rent controls, rents in New York City have soared. Despite laws against "scalping," tickets for popular shows and sports events sell at tremendous premiums—tickets to the Super Bowl, for example, often fetch thousands of dollars on the "gray" market. To understand what goes wrong when we tamper with markets, we must first learn how they operate unfettered. This chapter takes a first step in that direction by studying the machinery of supply and demand. Then, at the end of the chapter, we return to the issue of price controls.

Every market has both buyers and sellers. We begin our analysis on the consumers' side of the market.

Price Controls at Valley Forge

George Washington, the history books tell us, was beset by many enemies during the winter of 1777–1778, including the British, their Hessian mercenaries, and the merciless winter weather. However, he had another enemy that the history books ignore—an enemy that meant well but almost destroyed his army at Valley Forge. As the following excerpt explains, that enemy was the Pennsylvania legislature:

> In Pennsylvania, where the main force of Washington's army was quartered . . . the legislature . . . decided to try a period of price control limited to those commodities needed for use by the army. . . . The result might have been anticipated by those with some knowledge of the trials and tribulations of other states. The prices of uncontrolled goods, mostly imported, rose to record heights. Most farmers kept back their produce, refusing to sell at what they regarded as an unfair price. Some who had large families to take care of even secretly sold their food to the British, who paid in gold.

After the disastrous winter at Valley Forge when Washington's army nearly starved to death (thanks largely to these well-intentioned but misdirected laws), the ill-fated experiment in price controls was finally ended. The Continental Congress on June 4, 1778, adopted the following resolution:

> "Whereas . . . it hath been found by experience that limitations upon the prices of commodities are not only ineffectual for

Valley Forge.

the purposes proposed, but likewise productive of very evil consequences . . . resolved, that it be recommended to the several states to repeal or suspend all laws or resolutions within the said states respectively limiting, regulating or restraining the Price of any Article, Manufacture or Commodity."

DEMAND AND QUANTITY DEMANDED

People commonly think of consumer demands as fixed amounts. For example, when product designers propose a new computer model, management asks: "What is its market potential?"; that is, just how many are likely to be sold? Similarly, government bureaus conduct studies to determine how many engineers or doctors the United States will require (demand) in subsequent years.

Economists respond that such questions are not well posed—that there is no single answer to such a question. Rather, they say, the "market potential" for computers or the number of engineers that will be "required" depends on a great number of influences, including the price charged for each.

The quantity demanded of any product normally depends on its price. Quantity demanded also depends on a number of other determinants, including population size, consumer incomes, tastes, and the prices of other products.

Because prices play a central role in a market economy, we begin our study of demand by focusing on how quantity demanded depends on price. A little later, we will bring the other determinants of quantity demanded back into the picture. For now, we will consider all influences other than price to be fixed. This assumption, often expressed as "other things being equal," is used in much of economic analysis. As an example of the relationship between price and demand, let's think about the quantity of beef demanded. If the price of beef is very high, its "market potential" may be very small. People will find ways to get along with less beef, perhaps by switching to pork or fish. If the price of beef declines, people will tend to eat more beef. They may serve it more frequently or eat larger portions or switch away from fish. Thus:

There is no one demand figure for beef, or for computers, or for engineers. Rather, there is a different quantity demanded at each possible price, all other influences being held constant.

The **quantity demanded** is the number of units of a good that consumers are willing and can afford to buy over a specified period of time.

The Demand Schedule

A **demand schedule** is a table showing how the quantity demanded of some product during a specified period of time changes as the price of that product changes, holding all other determinants of quantity demanded constant.

A **demand curve** is a graphical depiction of a demand schedule. It shows how the quantity demanded of some product will change as the price of that product changes during a specified period of time, holding all other determinants of quantity demanded constant.

Table 1 shows how such information for beef can be recorded in a **demand schedule.** It indicates how much beef consumers in a particular area are willing and able to buy at different possible prices during a specified period of time, other things held equal. Specifically, the table shows the quantity of beef that will be demanded in a year at each possible price ranging from $6.90 to $7.50 per pound. At a relatively low price, such as $7.00 per pound, customers wish to purchase 70 (million) pounds per year. But if the price were to rise to, say, $7.40 per pound, quantity demanded would fall to 50 million pounds.

Common sense tells us why this happens.[2] First, as prices rise, some customers will reduce the quantity of beef they consume. Second, higher prices will induce some customers to drop out of the market entirely—for example, by switching to pork or fish. On both counts, quantity demanded will decline as the price rises.

TABLE 1		
Demand Schedule for Beef		
Price per Pound	Quantity Demanded	Label in Figure 1
$7.50	45	A
7.40	50	B
7.30	55	C
7.20	60	E
7.10	65	F
7.00	70	G
6.90	75	H

NOTE: Quantity is in pounds per year.

As the price of an item rises, the quantity demanded normally falls. As the price falls, the quantity demanded normally rises, all other things held constant.

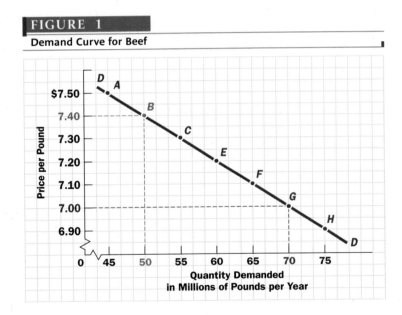

FIGURE 1

Demand Curve for Beef

Price per Pound — Quantity Demanded in Millions of Pounds per Year

The Demand Curve

The information contained in Table 1 can be summarized in a graph like Figure 1, which is called a **demand curve.** Each point in the graph corresponds to a line in the table. This curve shows the relationship between price and quantity demanded. For example, it tells us that to sell 65 million pounds per year, the price must be $7.10 per pound. This relationship is shown at point *G* in Figure 1. If the price were $7.40, however, consumers would demand only 50 million pounds (point *B*). Because the quantity demanded declines as the price increases, the demand curve has a negative slope.[3]

Notice the last phrase in the definitions of the demand schedule and the demand curve: "holding all other determinants of quantity demanded constant." What are some of these "other things," and how do they affect the demand curve?

Shifts of the Demand Curve

The quantity of beef demanded is subject to a variety of influences other than the price of beef. Changes in population size and characteristics, consumer incomes and tastes, and the prices of alternative products such as pork and fish presumably change the quantity of beef demanded, even if the price of beef does not change.

Because the demand curve for beef depicts only the relationship between the quantity of beef demanded and the price of beef, holding all other factors constant, a change in beef

---

[2] This commonsense answer is examined more fully in later chapters.

[3] If you need to review the concept of slope, refer back to Chapter 1's appendix.

price moves the market for beef from one point on the demand curve to another point on the same curve. However, a change in any of these other influences on demand causes a **shift of the entire demand curve.** More generally:

> A change in the price of a good produces a movement *along* a fixed demand curve. By contrast, a change in any other variable that influences quantity demanded produces a shift of the *entire* demand curve.

If consumers want to buy more beef at every given price than they wanted previously, the demand curve shifts to the right (or outward). If they desire less at every given price, the demand curve shifts to the left (or inward toward the origin).

Figure 2 shows this distinction graphically. If the price of beef falls from $7.30 to $7.10 per pound, and quantity demanded rises accordingly, we move along demand curve D_0D_0 from point C to point F, as shown by the blue arrow. If, on the other hand, consumers suddenly decide that they like beef better than before, or if they embrace a study that reports the health benefits of beef, the entire demand curve shifts outward from D_0D_0 to D_1D_1, as indicated by the brown arrows, meaning that at *any* given price consumers are now willing to buy more beef than before. To make this general idea more concrete, and to show some of its many applications, let us consider some specific examples of those "other things" that can shift demand curves.

Consumer Incomes If average incomes rise, consumers will purchase more of most goods, including beef, even if the prices of those goods remain the same. That is, increases in income normally shift demand curves outward to the right, as depicted in Figure 3(a), where the demand curve shifts outward from D_0D_0 to D_1D_1, establishing a new price and output quantity.

A **shift in a demand curve** occurs when any relevant variable other than price changes. If consumers want to buy *more* at any and all given prices than they wanted previously, the demand curve shifts to the right (or outward). If they desire *less* at any given price, the demand curve shifts to the left (or inward).

FIGURE 2

Movements along versus Shifts of a Demand Curve

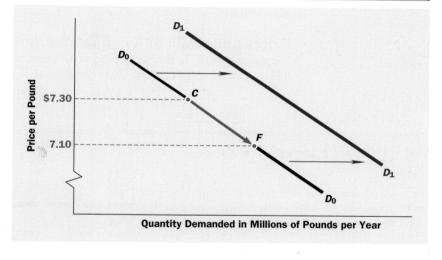

Population Population growth affects quantity demanded in more or less the same way as increases in average incomes. For instance, a larger population will presumably want to consume more beef, even if the price of beef and average incomes do not change, thus shifting the entire demand curve to the right, as in Figure 3(a). The equilibrium price and quantity both rise. Increases in particular population segments can also elicit shifts in demand—for example, the United States experienced a miniature population boom between the late 1970s and mid-1990s. This group (which is dubbed Generation Y and includes most users of this book) has sparked higher demand for such items as cell phones and video games.

In Figure 3(b), we see that a decrease in population should shift the demand curve for beef to the left, from D_0D_0 to D_2D_2.

Consumer Preferences If the beef industry mounts a successful advertising campaign extolling the benefits of eating beef, families may decide to buy more at any given price. If so, the entire demand curve for beef would shift to the right, as in Figure 3(a). Alternatively, a medical report on the dangers of high cholesterol may persuade consumers to eat less beef, thereby shifting the demand curve to the left, as in Figure 3(b). Again, these are general phenomena:

> If consumer preferences shift in favor of a particular item, its demand curve will shift outward to the right, as in Figure 3(a).

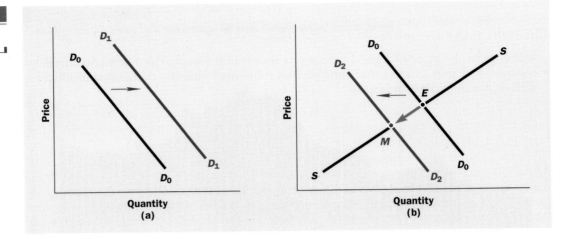

FIGURE 3
Shifts of the Demand Curve

An example is the ever-shifting "rage" in children's toys—be it Yu-Gi-Oh! cards, electronic Elmo dolls, or the latest video games. These items become the object of desperate hunts as parents snap them up for their offspring, and stores are unable to keep up with the demand.

Prices and Availability of Related Goods Because pork, fish, and chicken are popular products that compete with beef, a change in the price of any of these other items can be expected to shift the demand curve for beef. If any of these alternative

Volatility in Electricity Prices

The following newspaper story excerpts highlight the volatility of the electricity industry and its susceptibility to manipulation of the supply-demand mechanism and soaring prices. Although the industry was deregulated more than a decade ago, electricity prices have generally not fallen and, in many cases, have risen sharply. The Federal Energy Regulatory Commission contends that allowing competition among producers should guarantee the lowest possible price. Why have electricity prices not fallen, unlike other previously regulated industries?

> Rising fuel costs are one major reason. . . . Another factor is the very nature of electricity, which must be produced, transmitted and consumed in an instant . . . electricity cannot be held in inventory.

Critics point to opportunities for suppliers to interfere in the market system, including the withholding of power or limiting of production during periods of high demand, leading to skyrocketing prices.

> "Shutting down a power plant in July is like the mall closing on the weekend before Christmas, but in July last year, 20 percent of generating capacity was shut down in California," said Robert McCullough, an economist whose Oregon consulting business is advising some of those contending in lawsuits that prices are being manipulated.

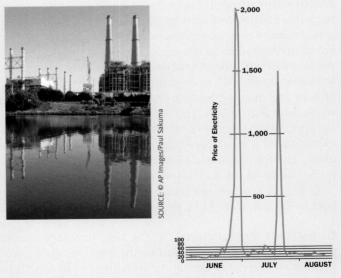

SOURCE: © AP Images/Paul Sakuma

NOTE: Quantity is in billions of quarts per year.

SOURCE: "Flaws Seen In Market for Utilities; Power Play: The Bidding Game" by David Cay Johnston, *The New York Times*, Late Edition (East Coast), November 21, 2006, p.C1.

items becomes cheaper, some consumers will switch away from beef. Thus, the demand curve for beef will shift to the left, as in Figure 3(b). Other price changes may shift the demand curve for beef in the opposite direction. For example, suppose that hamburger buns and ketchup become less expensive. This may induce some consumers to eat more beef and thus shift the demand curve for beef to the right, as in Figure 3(a). In general:

> **Increases in the prices of goods that are substitutes for the good in question (as pork, fish, and chicken are for beef) move the demand curve to the right. Increases in the prices of goods that are normally used together with the good in question (such as hamburger buns and beef) shift the demand curve to the left.**

This is just what happened when a frost wiped out almost half of Brazil's coffee bean harvest in 1995. The three largest U.S. coffee producers raised their prices by 45 percent, and, as a result, the demand curve for alternative beverages such as tea shifted to the right. Then in 1998, coffee prices dropped about 34 percent, which in turn caused the demand curve for tea to shift toward the left (or toward the origin).

Although the preceding list does not exhaust the possible influences on quantity demanded, we have said enough to suggest the principles followed by demand and shifts of demand. Let's turn now to the supply side of the market.

SUPPLY AND QUANTITY SUPPLIED

Like quantity demanded, the quantity of beef that is supplied by business firms such as farms is not a fixed number; it also depends on many things. Obviously, we expect more beef to be supplied if there are more farms or more cows per farm. Cows may provide less meat if bad weather deprives them of their feed. As before, however, let's turn our attention first to the relationship between the price and quantity of beef supplied.

Economists generally suppose that a higher price calls forth a greater **quantity supplied.** Why? Remember our analysis of the principle of increasing costs in Chapter 3 (page 44). According to that principle, as more of any farmer's (or the nation's) resources are devoted to beef production, the opportunity cost of obtaining another pound of beef increases. Farmers will therefore find it profitable to increase beef production only if they can sell the beef at a higher price—high enough to cover the additional costs incurred to expand production. In other words, it normally will take higher prices to persuade farmers to raise beef production. This idea is quite general and applies to the supply of most goods and services.[4] As long as suppliers want to make profits and the principle of increasing costs holds:

The **quantity supplied** is the number of units that sellers want to sell over a specified period of time.

> **As the price of any commodity rises, the quantity supplied normally rises. As the price falls, the quantity supplied normally falls.**

The Supply Schedule and the Supply Curve

Table 2 shows the relationship between the price of beef and its quantity supplied. Tables such as this one are called **supply schedules;** they show how much sellers are willing to provide during a specified period at alternative possible prices. This particular supply schedule tells us that a low price like $7.00 per pound will induce suppliers to provide only 50 million pounds, whereas a higher price like $7.30 will induce them to provide much more—55 million pounds.

A **supply schedule** is a table showing how the quantity supplied of some product changes as the price of that product changes during a specified period of time, holding all other determinants of quantity supplied constant.

---

[4] This analysis is carried out in much greater detail in later chapters.

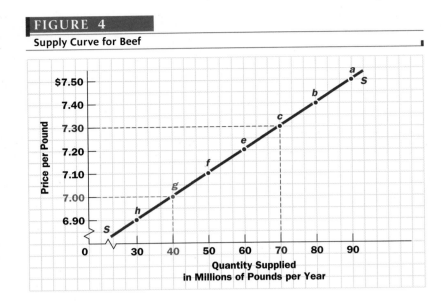

FIGURE 4

Supply Curve for Beef

TABLE 2

Supply Schedule for Beef

Price per Pound	Quantity Supplied	Label in Figure 4
$7.50	90	a
7.40	80	b
7.30	70	c
7.20	60	e
7.10	50	f
7.00	40	g
6.90	30	h

NOTE: Quantity is in pounds per year.

A **supply curve** is a graphical depiction of a supply schedule. It shows how the quantity supplied of a product will change as the price of that product changes during a specified period of time, holding all other determinants of quantity supplied constant.

As you might have guessed, when such information is plotted on a graph, it is called a **supply curve.** Figure 4 is the supply curve corresponding to the supply schedule in Table 2, showing the relationship between the price of beef and the quantity supplied. It slopes upward—it has a positive slope—because quantity supplied is higher when price is higher. Notice again the same phrase in the definition: "holding all other determinants of quantity supplied constant." What are these "other determinants"?

Shifts of the Supply Curve

Like quantity demanded, the quantity supplied in a market typically responds to many influences other than price. The weather, the cost of feed, the number and size of farms, and a variety of other factors all influence how much beef will be brought to market. Because the supply curve depicts only the relationship between the price of beef and the quantity of beef supplied, holding all other influences constant, a change in any of these other determinants of quantity supplied will cause the entire supply curve to shift. That is:

> A change in the price of the good causes a movement *along* a fixed supply curve. Price is not the only influence on quantity supplied, however. If any of these other influences change, the *entire* supply curve shifts.

Figure 5 depicts this distinction graphically. A rise in price from $7.10 to $7.30 will raise quantity supplied by moving along supply curve S_0S_0 from point *f* to point *c*. Any rise in quantity supplied attributable to an influence other than price, however, will shift the *entire* supply curve outward to the right, from S_0S_0 to S_1S_1, as shown by the brown arrows. Let us consider what some of these other influences are and how they shift the supply curve.

Size of the Industry   We begin with the most obvious influence. If more farmers enter the beef industry, the quantity supplied at any given price will increase. For example, if each farm provides 60,000 pounds of beef per year at a price of $7.10 per pound, then 100,000 farmers would provide 600 million pounds, but 130,000 farmers would provide 780,000 million. Thus, when more farms are in the industry, the quantity of beef supplied will be greater at any given price—and hence the supply curve will move farther to the right.

Figure 6(a) illustrates the effect of an expansion of the industry from 100,000 farms to 130,000 farms—a rightward shift of the supply curve from $S_0 S_0$ to $S_1 S_1$. Figure 6(b) illustrates the opposite case: a contraction of the industry from 100,000 farms to 62,500 farms. The supply curve shifts inward to the left, from $S_0 S_0$ to $S_2 S_2$. Even if no farmers enter or leave the industry, results like those depicted in Figure 6 can be produced by expansion or contraction of the *existing* farms.

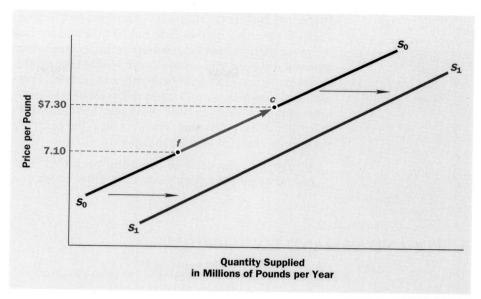

Technological Progress

Another influence that shifts supply curves is technological change. Suppose an enterprising farmer invents a new growth hormone that increases the body mass of cattle. Thereafter, at any given price, farms will be able to produce more beef; that is, the supply curve will shift outward to the right, as in Figure 6(a). This example, again, illustrates a general influence that applies to most industries:

> **Technological progress that reduces costs will shift the supply curve outward to the right.**

Automakers, for example, have been able to reduce production costs since industrial technology invented robots that can be programmed to work on several different car models. This technological advance has shifted the supply curve outward.

Prices of Inputs

Changes in input prices also shift supply curves. Suppose a drought raises the price of animal feed. Farmers will have to pay more to keep their cows alive and healthy and consequently will no longer be able to provide the same quantity of beef at each possible price. This example illustrates that

> **Increases in the prices of inputs that suppliers must buy will shift the supply curve inward to the left.**

FIGURE 5

Movements along versus Shifts of a Supply Curve

FIGURE 6

Shifts of the Supply Curve

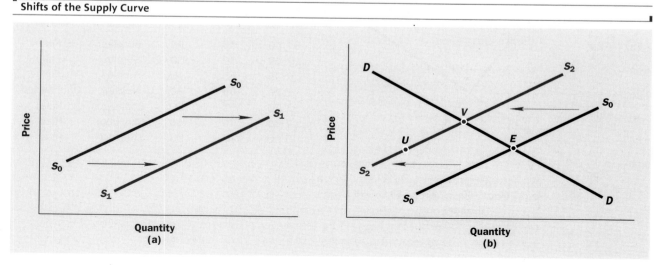

Prices of Related Outputs   Ranchers sell hides as well as meat. If leather prices rise sharply, ranchers may decide not to fatten their cattle as much as they used to, before bringing them to market, thereby reducing the quantity of beef supplied. On a supply-demand diagram, the supply curve would then shift inward, as in Figure 6(b).

Similar phenomena occur in other industries, and sometimes the effect goes the other way. For example, suppose that the price of beef goes up, which increases the quantity of meat supplied. That, in turn, will raise the number of cowhides supplied even if the price of leather does not change. Thus, a rise in the price of beef will lead to a rightward shift in the supply curve of leather. In general:

> **A change in the price of one good produced by a multiproduct industry may be expected to shift the supply curves of other goods produced by that industry.**

SUPPLY AND DEMAND EQUILIBRIUM

A **supply-demand diagram** graphs the supply and demand curves together. It also determines the equilibrium price and quantity.

To analyze how the free market determines price, we must compare the desires of consumers (demand) with the desires of producers (supply) to see whether the two plans are consistent. Table 3 and Figure 7 help us do this.

Table 3 brings together the demand schedule from Table 1 and the supply schedule from Table 2. Similarly, Figure 7 puts the demand curve from Figure 1 and the supply curve from Figure 4 on a single graph. Such graphs are called **supply-demand diagrams,** and you will encounter many of them in this book. Notice that, for reasons already discussed, the demand curve has a negative slope and the supply curve has a positive slope. That is generally true of supply-demand diagrams.

In a free market, price and quantity are determined by the intersection of the supply and demand curves. At only one point in Figure 7, point *E*, do the supply curve and the demand curve intersect. At the price corresponding to point *E*, which is $7.20 per pound, the quantity supplied and the quantity demanded are both 60 million pounds per year. This means that at a price of $7.20 per pound, consumers are willing to buy exactly what producers are willing to sell.

At a lower price, such as $7.00 per pound, only 40 million pounds of beef will be supplied (point *g*), whereas 70 million pounds will be demanded (point *G*).

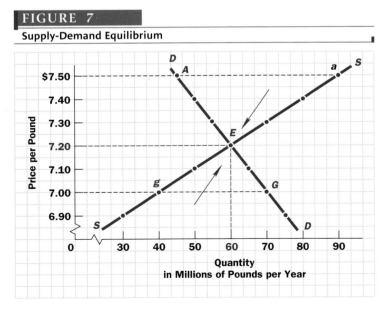

FIGURE 7

Supply-Demand Equilibrium

TABLE 3

Determination of the Equilibrium Price and Quantity of Beef

Price per Pound	Quantity Demanded	Quantity Supplied	Surplus or Shortage	Price Direction
$7.50	45	90	**Surplus**	**Fall**
7.40	50	80	Surplus	Fall
7.30	55	70	Surplus	Fall
7.20	60	60	**Neither**	**Unchanged**
7.10	65	50	Shortage	Rise
7.00	70	40	**Shortage**	**Rise**
6.90	75	30	Shortage	Rise

Thus, quantity demanded will exceed quantity supplied. There will be a **shortage** equal to 70 minus 40, or 30 million pounds. Price will thus be driven up by unsatisfied demand. Alternatively, at a higher price, such as $7.50 per pound, quantity supplied will be 90 million pounds (point *a*) and quantity demanded will be only 45 million (point *A*). Quantity supplied will exceed quantity demanded—creating a **surplus** equal to 90 minus 45, or 45 million pounds. The unsold output can then be expected to push the price down.

Because $7.20 is the only price in this graph at which quantity supplied and quantity demanded are equal, we say that $7.20 per pound is the equilibrium price (or the "market clearing" price) in this market. Similarly, 60 million pounds per year is the equilibrium quantity of beef. The term **equilibrium** merits a little explanation, because it arises so frequently in economic analysis.

An equilibrium is a situation in which there are no inherent forces that produce change. Think, for example, of a pendulum resting at its center point. If no outside force (such as a person's hand) comes to push it, the pendulum will remain exactly where it is; it is therefore in equilibrium.

If you give the pendulum a shove, however, its equilibrium will be disturbed and it will start to move. When it reaches the top of its arc, the pendulum will, for an instant, be at rest again. This point is not an equilibrium position, for the force of gravity will pull the pendulum downward. Thereafter, gravity and friction will govern its motion from side to side. Eventually, the pendulum will return to its original position. The fact that the pendulum tends to return to its original position is described by saying that this position is a *stable* equilibrium. That position is also the only equilibrium position of the pendulum. At any other point, inherent forces will cause the pendulum to move.

The concept of equilibrium in economics is similar and can be illustrated by our supply-and-demand example. Why is no price other than $7.20 an equilibrium price in Table 3 or Figure 7? What forces will change any other price?

Consider first a low price such as $7.00, at which quantity demanded (70 million pounds) exceeds quantity supplied (40 million pounds). If the price were this low, many frustrated customers would be unable to purchase the quantities they desired. In their scramble for the available supply of beef, some would offer to pay more. As customers sought to outbid one another, the market price would be forced up. Thus, a price below the equilibrium price cannot persist in a free market because a shortage sets in motion powerful economic forces that push the price upward.

Similar forces operate in the opposite direction if the market price exceeds the equilibrium price. If, for example, the price should somehow reach $7.50, Table 3 tells us that quantity supplied (90 million pounds) would far exceed the quantity demanded (45 million pounds). Producers would be unable to sell their desired quantities of beef at the prevailing price, and some would undercut their competitors by reducing price. Such competitive price cutting would continue as long as the surplus remained—that is, as long as quantity supplied exceeded quantity demanded. Thus, a price above the equilibrium price cannot persist indefinitely.

We are left with a clear conclusion. The price of $7.20 per pound and the quantity of 60 million pounds per year constitute the only price-quantity combination that does not sow the seeds of its own destruction. It is thus the only equilibrium for this market. Any lower price must rise, and any higher price must fall. It is as if natural economic forces place a magnet at point *E* that attracts the market, just as gravity attracts a pendulum.

The pendulum analogy is worth pursuing further. Most pendulums are more frequently in motion than at rest. However, unless they are repeatedly buffeted by outside forces (which, of course, is exactly what happens to economic equilibria in reality), pendulums gradually return to their resting points. The same is true of price and quantity in a free market. They are moved about by shifts in the supply and demand curves that we have already described. As a consequence, markets are not always in equilibrium. But, if nothing interferes with them, experience shows that they normally move toward equilibrium.

A **shortage** is an excess of quantity demanded over quantity supplied. When there is a shortage, buyers cannot purchase the quantities they desire at the current price.

A **surplus** is an excess of quantity supplied over quantity demanded. When there is a surplus, sellers cannot sell the quantities they desire to supply at the current price.

An **equilibrium** is a situation in which there are no inherent forces that produce change. Changes away from an equilibrium position will occur only as a result of "outside events" that disturb the status quo.

The **law of supply and demand** states that in a free market the forces of supply and demand generally push the price toward the level at which quantity supplied and quantity demanded are equal.

The Law of Supply and Demand

In a free market, the forces of supply and demand generally push the price toward its equilibrium level, the price at which quantity supplied and quantity demanded are equal. Like most economic "laws," some markets will occasionally disobey the **law of supply and demand.** Markets sometimes display shortages or surpluses for long periods of time. Prices sometimes fail to move toward equilibrium. But the "law" is a fair generalization that is right far more often than it is wrong.

EFFECTS OF DEMAND SHIFTS ON SUPPLY-DEMAND EQUILIBRIUM

Figure 3 showed how developments other than changes in price—such as increases in consumer income—can shift the demand curve. We saw that a rise in income, for example, will shift the demand curve to the right, meaning that at any given price, consumers—with their increased purchasing power—will buy more of the good than before. This, in turn, will move the equilibrium point, changing both market price and quantity sold.

This market adjustment is shown in Figure 8(a). It adds a supply curve to Figure 3(a) so that we can see what happens to the supply-demand equilibrium. In the example in the graph, the quantity demanded at the old equilibrium price of $7.20 increases from 60 million pounds per year (point E on the demand curve D_0D_0) to 75 million pounds per year (point R on the demand curve D_1D_1). We know that $7.20 is no longer the equilibrium price, because at this price quantity demanded (75 million pounds) exceeds quantity supplied (60 million pounds). To restore equilibrium, the price must rise. The new equilibrium occurs at point T, the intersection point of the supply curve and the shifted demand curve, where the price is $7.30 per pound and both quantities demanded and supplied are 70 million pounds per year. This example illustrates a general result, which is true when the supply curve slopes upward:

Any influence that makes the demand curve shift outward to the right, and does not affect an upward-sloped supply curve, will raise the equilibrium price and the equilibrium quantity.[5]

FIGURE 8

The Effects of Shifts of the Demand Curve

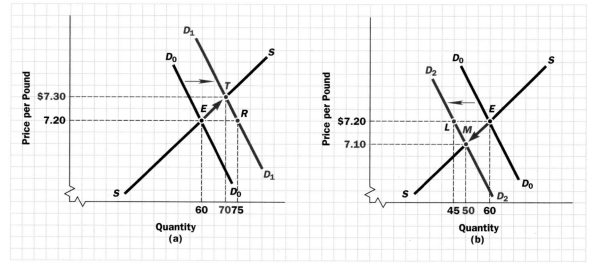

NOTE: Quantity is in millions of pounds per year.

---

[5] For example, when incomes rise rapidly, in many developing countries the demand curves for a variety of consumer goods shift rapidly outward to the right. In Japan, for example, the demand for used Levi's jeans and Nike running shoes from the United States skyrocketed in the early 1990s as status-conscious Japanese consumers searched for outlets for their then-rising incomes.

The Ups and Downs of Milk Consumption

The following excerpt from a U.S. Department of Agriculture publication discusses some of the things that have affected the consumption of milk in the last century.

In 1909, Americans consumed a total of 34 gallons of fluid milk per person—27 gallons of whole milk and 7 gallons of milks lower in fat than whole milk, mostly buttermilk. . . . Fluid milk consumption shot up from 34 gallons per person in 1941 to a peak of 45 gallons per person in 1945. War production lifted Americans' incomes but curbed civilian production and the goods consumers could buy. Many food items were rationed, including meats, butter and sugar. Milk was not rationed, and consumption soared. Since 1945, however, milk consumption has fallen steadily, reaching a record low of just under 23 gallons per person in 2001 (the latest year for which data are available). Steep declines in consumption of whole milk and buttermilk far outpaced an increase in other lower fat milks. By 2001, Americans were consuming less than 8 gallons per person of whole milk, compared with nearly 41 gallons in 1945 and 25 gallons in 1970. In contrast, per capita consumption of total lower fat milks was 15 gallons in 2001, up from 4 gallons in 1945 and 6 gallons

in 1970. These changes are consistent with increased public concern about cholesterol, saturated fat, and calories. However, decline in per capita consumption of fluid milk also may be attributed to competition from other beverages, especially carbonated soft drinks and bottled water, a smaller percentage of children and adolescents in the U.S., and a more ethnically diverse population whose diet does not normally include milk.

SOURCE: Judy Putnam and Jane Allshouse, "Trends in U.S. Per Capita Consumption of Dairy Products, 1909 to 2001," *Amber Waves: The Economics of Food, Farming, Natural Resources and Rural America,* June 2003, U.S. Department of Agriculture, available at http://www.usda.gov.

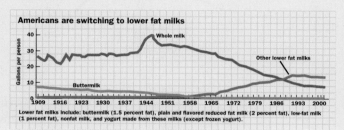

Lower fat milks include: buttermilk (1.5 percent fat), plain and flavored reduced fat milk (2 percent fat), low-fat milk (1 percent fat), nonfat milk, and yogurt made from these milks (except frozen yogurt).

Everything works in reverse if consumer incomes fall. Figure 8(b) depicts a leftward (inward) shift of the demand curve that results from a decline in consumer incomes. For example, the quantity demanded at the previous equilibrium price ($7.20) falls from 60 million pounds (point *E*) to 45 million pounds (point *L* on the demand curve D_2D_2). The initial price is now too high and must fall. The new equilibrium will eventually be established at point *M,* where the price is $7.10 and both quantity demanded and quantity supplied are 50 million pounds. In general:

Any influence that shifts the demand curve inward to the left, and that does not affect the supply curve, will lower both the equilibrium price and the equilibrium quantity.

SUPPLY SHIFTS AND SUPPLY-DEMAND EQUILIBRIUM

A story precisely analogous to that of the effects of a demand shift on equilibrium price and quantity applies to supply shifts. Figure 6 described the effects on the supply curve of beef if the number of farms increases. Figure 9(a) now adds a demand curve to the supply curves of Figure 6 so that we can see the supply-demand equilibrium. Notice that at the initial price of $7.20, the quantity supplied after the shift is 780 million pounds (point *I* on the supply curve S_1S_1), which is 30 percent more than the original quantity demanded of 600 million pounds (point *E* on the supply curve S_0S_0). We can see from the graph that the price of $7.20 is too high to be the equilibrium price; the price must fall. The new equilibrium point is *J,* where the price is $7.10 per pound and the quantity is 650 million pounds per year. In general:

Any change that shifts the supply curve outward to the right, and does not affect the demand curve, will lower the equilibrium price and raise the equilibrium quantity.

This must always be true if the industry's demand curve has a negative slope, because the greater quantity supplied can be sold only if the price is decreased so as to induce customers to buy more.[6] The cellular phone industry is a case in point. As more providers

---

[6] Graphically, whenever a positively sloped curve shifts to the right, its intersection point with a negatively sloping curve must always move lower. Just try drawing it yourself.

FIGURE 9

Effects of Shifts of the Supply Curve

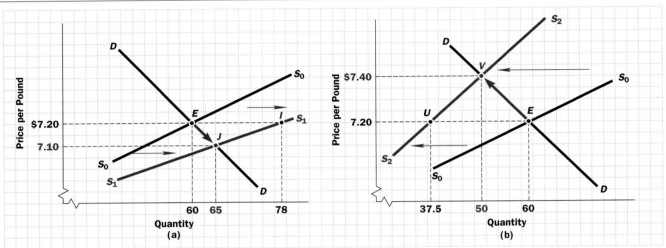

Quantity
(a)

Quantity
(b)

have entered the industry, the cost of cellular service has plummeted. Some cellular carriers have even given away telephones as sign-up bonuses.

Figure 9(b) illustrates the opposite case: a contraction of the industry. The supply curve shifts inward to the left and equilibrium moves from point *E* to point *V*, where the price is $7.40 and quantity is 500 million pounds per year. In general:

> **Any influence that shifts the supply curve to the left, and does not affect the demand curve, will raise the equilibrium price and reduce the equilibrium quantity.**

Many outside forces can disturb equilibrium in a market by shifting the demand curve or the supply curve, either temporarily or permanently. In 1998, for example, gasoline prices dropped because a recession in Asia shifted the demand curve downward, as did a reduction in use of petroleum that resulted from a mild winter. In the summer of 1998, severely hot weather and lack of rain damaged the cotton crop in the United States, shifting the supply curve downward. Such outside influences change the equilibrium price and quantity. If you look again at Figures 8 and 9, you can see clearly that any event that causes either the demand curve or the supply curve to shift will also change the equilibrium price and quantity.

PUZZLE RESOLVED: THOSE LEAPING OIL PRICES

The disturbing increases in the price of gasoline, and of the oil from which it is made, is attributable to large shifts in both demand and supply conditions. Americans are, for example, driving more and are buying gas-guzzling vehicles, and the resulting upward shift in the demand curve raises price. Instability in the Middle East and Russia has undermined supply, and that also raised prices. We have seen the results at the gas pumps. The following newspaper story describes a sensational sort of change in supply conditions:

Aug. 10 (Bloomberg)—BP Plc and its partners in the Prudhoe Bay oil field in Alaska will spend about $170 million inspecting and repairing corroded pipelines that shut most of the production from the largest U.S. oil field.

Including costs to clean up and repair a line that leaked in March, the "rough estimate" rises to about $200 million, said Kemp Copeland, field manager for BP's Prudhoe Bay operations. The figures include the cost of replacing 16 miles of feeder pipeline in the field.

The worst cost to BP will probably be the hit to its reputation, said Mark Gilman, an analyst at The Benchmark Company LLC in New York, who rates the shares "sell."

"At some point this is going to prove very costly, as you're going to be competing with folks whose reputation has not been subject to the same degree of punishment," Gilman, who owns a "small" number of BP shares, said today in a phone interview.

The Prudhoe Bay shutdown is the latest blow for Chief Executive Officer John Browne, who faces a grand jury probe for an earlier Alaska spill, charges of market manipulation in the U.S. propane industry and fines from a Texas refinery blast that killed 15 workers. BP, which gets 40 percent of its sales from the U.S., last month said it will boost spending there to improve safety and maintenance.

London-based BP Plc said today it will know by the start of next week whether it can keep operating the western half of the field, which is currently producing as much as 137,000 barrels of oil a day. The entire field pumps 400,000 barrels a day, or 8 percent of U.S. output, when fully operational.

LOOKING FOR STEEL SUPPLIES

BP is asking suppliers U.S. Steel Corp. and Nippon Steel Corp. for faster delivery to a total of 51,000 feet of pipe it has already ordered for the repairs, BP Alaska President Steve Marshall said in conference call on Aug. 8. The pipe is scheduled to be delivered in October the earliest.

A supplier for another 30,000 feet of 24-inch pipe and 52,000 feet of 18-inch pipe is still needed, said Marshall.

BP, Houston-based ConocoPhillips and Exxon Mobil Corp. of Irving, Texas, are joint owners in the Prudhoe Bay field. ConocoPhillips, the third-largest U.S. oil company, earlier today declared force majeure on oil deliveries from Prudhoe Bay.

Force majeure allows companies to avoid penalties for failing to fulfill contracts because of unforeseen events. ConocoPhillips sells its Alaskan crude oil to refineries and brokers, according to spokesman Bill Tanner.

SOURCE: Ian McKinnon and Sonja Franklin, "BP Says Prudhoe Bay Repair Costs May Be $200 Million," with reporting by Jim Kennett in Houston. Editor: Jordan (rsd).

Application: Who Really Pays That Tax?

Supply-and-demand analysis offers insights that may not be readily apparent. Here is an example. Suppose your state legislature raises the gasoline tax by 10 cents per gallon. Service station operators will then have to collect 10 additional cents in taxes on every gallon they pump. They will consider this higher tax as an addition to their costs and will pass it on to you and other consumers by raising the price of gas by 10 cents per gallon. Right? No, wrong—or rather, partly wrong.

The gas station owners would certainly *like* to pass on the entire tax to buyers, but the market mechanism will allow them to shift only *part* of it—perhaps 6 cents per gallon. They will then be stuck with the remainder—4 cents in our example. Figure 10, which is just another supply-demand graph, shows why.

The demand curve is the blue curve *DD*. The supply curve before the tax is the black curve S_0S_0. Before the new tax, the equilibrium point is E_0 and the price is $2.54. We can interpret the supply curve as telling us at what price sellers are willing to provide any given quantity. For example, they are willing to supply quantity $Q_1 = 50$ million gallons per year if the price is $2.54 per gallon.

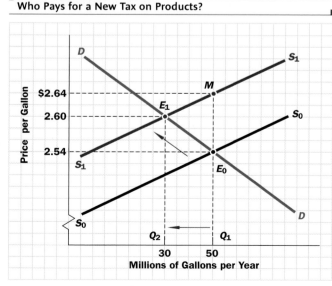

FIGURE 10

Who Pays for a New Tax on Products?

So what happens as a result of the new tax? Because they must now turn 10 cents per gallon over to the government, gas station owners will be willing to supply any given quantity only if they get 10 cents more per gallon than before. Therefore, to get them to supply quantity $Q_1 = 50$ million gallons, a price of $2.54 per gallon will no longer suffice. Only a price of $2.64 per gallon will now induce them to supply 50 million gallons. Thus, at quantity $Q_1 = 50$, the point on the supply curve will move up by 10 cents, from point E_0 to point M. Because firms will insist on the same 10-cent price increase for any other quantity they supply, the *entire* supply curve will shift up by the 10-cent tax—from the black curve S_0S_0 to the new brick-colored supply curve S_1S_1. And, as a result, the supply-demand equilibrium point will move from E_0 to E_1 and the price will increase from $2.54 to $2.60.

The supply curve shift may give the impression that gas station owners have succeeded in passing the entire 10-cent increase on to consumers—the distance from E_0 to M—but look again. The *equilibrium* price has only gone up from $2.54 to $2.60. That is, the price has risen by only 6 cents, not by the full 10-cent amount of the tax. The gas station will have to absorb the remaining 4 cents of the tax.

Now this really *looks* as though we have pulled a fast one on you—a magician's sleight of hand. After all, the supply curve has shifted upward by the full amount of the tax, and yet the resulting price increase has covered only part of the tax rise. However, a second look reveals that, like most apparent acts of magic, this one has a simple explanation. The explanation arises from the *demand* side of the supply-demand mechanism. The negative slope of the demand curve means that when prices rise, at least some consumers will reduce the quantity of gasoline they demand. That will force sellers to give up part of the price increase. In other words, firms must absorb the part of the tax—4 cents—that consumers are unwilling to pay. But note that the equilibrium quantity Q_1 has fallen from 50 million gallons to $Q_2 = 30$ million gallons—so both consumers and suppliers lose out in some sense.

This example is not an oddball case. Indeed, the result is almost always true. The cost of any increase in a tax on any commodity will usually be paid partly by the consumer and partly by the seller. This is so no matter whether the legislature says that it is imposing the tax on the sellers or on the buyers. Whichever way it is phrased, the economics are the same: The supply-demand mechanism ensures that the tax will be shared by both of the parties.

BATTLING THE INVISIBLE HAND: THE MARKET FIGHTS BACK

IDEAS FOR BEYOND THE FINAL EXAM

As we noted in our *Ideas for Beyond the Final Exam* in Chapter 1, lawmakers and rulers have often been dissatisfied with the outcomes of free markets. From Rome to Reno, and from biblical times to the space age, they have battled the invisible hand. Sometimes, rather than trying to adjust the workings of the market, governments have tried to raise or lower the prices of specific commodities by decree. In many such cases, the authorities felt that market prices were, in some sense, immorally low or immorally high. Penalties were therefore imposed on anyone offering the commodities in question at prices above or below those established by the authorities. Such legally imposed constraints on prices are called "price ceilings" and "price floors." To see their result, we will focus on the use of price ceilings.

Restraining the Market Mechanism: Price Ceilings

The market has proven itself a formidable foe that strongly resists attempts to get around its decisions. In case after case where legal **price ceilings** are imposed, virtually the same series of consequences ensues:

A **price ceiling** is a maximum that the price charged for a commodity cannot legally exceed.

1. *A persistent shortage develops because quantity demanded exceeds quantity supplied.* Queuing (people waiting in lines), direct rationing (with everyone getting a fixed allotment), or any of a variety of other devices, usually inefficient and unpleasant, must substitute for the distribution process provided by the price mechanism. Example: Rampant shortages in Eastern Europe and the former Soviet Union helped precipitate the revolts that ended communism.

POLICY DEBATE

ECONOMIC ASPECTS OF THE WAR ON DRUGS

For years now, the U.S. government has engaged in a highly publicized "war on drugs." Billions of dollars have been spent on trying to stop illegal drugs at the country's borders. In some sense, interdiction has succeeded: Federal agents have seized literally tons of cocaine and other drugs. Yet these efforts have made barely a dent in the flow of drugs to America's city streets. Simple economic reasoning explains why.

When drug interdiction works, it shifts the supply curve of drugs to the left, thereby driving up street prices. But that, in turn, raises the rewards for potential smugglers and attracts more criminals into the "industry," which shifts the supply curve back to the right. The net result is that increased shipments of drugs to U.S. shores replace much of what the authorities confiscate. This is why many economists believe that any successful antidrug program must concentrate on reducing demand, which would lower the street price of drugs, not on reducing supply, which can only raise it.

Some people suggest that the government should go even further and legalize many drugs. Although this idea remains a highly controversial position that few are ready to endorse, the reasoning behind it is straightforward. A stunningly high fraction of all the violent crimes committed in America—especially robberies and murders—are drug-related. One

SOURCE: © AP Images/Angela Gaul

major reason is that street prices of drugs are so high that addicts must steal to get the money, and drug traffickers are all too willing to kill to protect their highly profitable "businesses."

How would things differ if drugs were legal? Because South American farmers earn pennies for drugs that sell for hundreds of dollars on the streets of Los Angeles and New York, we may safely assume that legalized drugs would be vastly cheaper. In fact, according to one estimate, a dose of cocaine would cost less than 50 cents. That, proponents point out, would reduce drug-related crimes dramatically. When, for example, was the last time you heard of a gang killing connected with the distribution of cigarettes or alcoholic beverages?

The argument against legalization of drugs is largely moral: Should the state sanction potentially lethal substances? But there is an economic aspect to this position as well: The vastly lower street prices of drugs that would surely follow legalization would increase drug use. Thus, although legalization would almost certainly reduce crime, it may also produce more addicts. The key question here is, How many more addicts? (No one has a good answer.) If you think the increase in quantity demanded would be large, you are unlikely to find legalization an attractive option.

2. *An illegal, or "black" market often arises to supply the commodity.* Usually some individuals are willing to take the risks involved in meeting unsatisfied demands illegally. Example: Although most states ban the practice, ticket "scalping" (the sale of tickets at higher than regular prices) occurs at most popular sporting events and rock concerts.

3. *The prices charged on illegal markets are almost certainly higher than those that would prevail in free markets.* After all, lawbreakers expect some compensation for the risk of being caught and punished. Example: Illegal drugs are normally quite expensive. (See the accompanying Policy Debate box "Economic Aspects of the War on Drugs.")

4. A substantial portion of the price falls into the hands of the illicit supplier instead of going to those who produce the good or perform the service. Example: A constant complaint during the public hearings that marked the history of theater-ticket price controls in New York City was that the "ice" (the illegal excess charge) fell into the hands of ticket scalpers rather than going to those who invested in, produced, or acted in the play.

5. *Investment in the industry generally dries up.* Because price ceilings reduce the monetary returns that investors can legally earn, less money will be invested in industries that are subject to price controls. Even fear of impending price controls can have this effect. Example: Price controls on farm products in Zambia have prompted peasant farmers and large agricultural conglomerates alike to cut back production rather than grow crops at a loss. The result has been thousands of lost jobs and widespread food shortages.

Case Study: Rent Controls in New York City

These points and others are best illustrated by considering a concrete example involving price ceilings. New York is the only major city in the United States that has continuously legislated rent controls in much of its rental housing, since World War II. Rent controls, of course, are intended to protect the consumer from high rents. But most economists believe that rent control does not help the cities or their residents and that, in the long run, it leaves almost everyone worse off. Elementary supply-demand analysis shows us why.

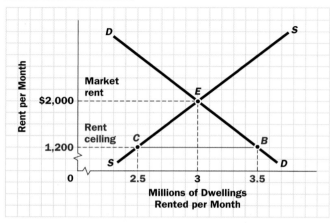

FIGURE 11

Supply-Demand Diagram for Rental Housing

Figure 11 is a supply-demand diagram for rental units in New York. Curve *DD* is the demand curve and curve *SS* is the supply curve. Without controls, equilibrium would be at point *E*, where rents average $2,000 per month and 3 million housing units are occupied. If rent controls are effective, the ceiling price must be below the equilibrium price of $2,000. But with a low rent ceiling, such as $1,200, the quantity of housing demanded will be 3.5 million units (point *B*), whereas the quantity supplied will be only 2.5 million units (point *C*).

The diagram shows a shortage of 1 million apartments. This theoretical concept of a "shortage" manifests itself in New York City as an abnormally low vacancy rate, that is, a low share of unoccupied apartments available for rental—typically about half the national urban average. Naturally, rent controls have spawned a lively black market in New York. The black market raises the effective price of rent-controlled apartments in many ways, including bribes, so-called key money paid to move up on a waiting list, or the requirement that prospective tenants purchase worthless furniture at inflated prices.

According to Figure 11, rent controls reduce the quantity supplied from 3 million to 2.5 million apartments. How does this reduction show up in New York? First, some property owners, discouraged by the low rents, have converted apartment buildings into office space or other uses. Second, some apartments have been inadequately maintained. After all, rent controls create a shortage, which makes even dilapidated apartments easy to rent. Third, some landlords have actually abandoned their buildings rather than pay rising tax and fuel bills. These abandoned buildings rapidly become eyesores and eventually pose threats to public health and safety.

"If you leave me, you know, you'll never see this kind of rent again."

An important implication of these last observations is that rent controls—and price controls more generally—harm consumers in ways that offset part or all of the benefits to those who are fortunate enough to find and acquire at lower prices the product that the reduced prices has made scarce. Tenants must undergo long waits and undertake time-consuming searches to find an apartment. The apartment they obtain is likely to be poorly maintained or even decrepit, and normal landlord services are apt to disappear. Thus, even for the lucky beneficiaries, rent control is always far less of a bargain than the reduced monthly payments make them appear to be. The same problems generally apply with other forms of price control as well.

With all of these problems, why does rent control persist in New York City? And why do other cities sometimes move in the same direction?

Part of the explanation is that most people simply do not understand the problems that rent controls create. Another part is that landlords are unpopular politically. But a third, and very important, part of the explanation is that not everyone is hurt by rent controls—and those who benefit from controls fight hard to preserve them. In New York, for example, many tenants pay rents that are only a fraction of what their apartments would fetch on the open market. They are, naturally enough, quite happy with this situation. This last point illustrates another very general phenomenon:

Virtually every price ceiling or floor creates a class of people that benefits from the regulations. These people use their political influence to protect their gains by preserving the status quo, which is one reason why it is so difficult to eliminate price ceilings or floors.

Restraining the Market Mechanism: Price Floors

Interferences with the market mechanism are not always designed to keep prices low. Agricultural price supports and minimum wage laws are two notable examples in which the law keeps prices *above* free-market levels. Such **price floors** are typically accompanied by a standard series of symptoms:

A **price floor** is a legal minimum below which the price charged for a commodity is not permitted to fall.

1. *A surplus develops as sellers cannot find enough buyers.* Example: Surpluses of various agricultural products have been a persistent—and costly—problem for the U.S. government. The problem is even worse in the European Union (EU), where the common agricultural policy holds prices even higher. One source estimates that this policy accounts for half of all EU spending.[7]

2. *Where goods, rather than services, are involved, the surplus creates a problem of disposal.* Something must be done about the excess of quantity supplied over quantity demanded. Example: The U.S. government has often been forced to purchase, store, and then dispose of large amounts of surplus agricultural commodities.

3. *To get around the regulations, sellers may offer discounts in disguised—and often unwanted—forms.* Example: Back when airline fares were regulated by the government, airlines offered more and better food and more stylishly uniformed flight attendants instead of lowering fares. Today, the food is worse, but tickets cost much less.

4. *Regulations that keep prices artificially high encourage overinvestment in the industry.* Even inefficient businesses whose high operating costs would doom them in an unrestricted market can survive beneath the shelter of a generous price floor. Example: This is why the airline and trucking industries both went through painful "shakeouts" of the weaker companies in the 1980s, after they were deregulated and allowed to charge market-determined prices.

Once again, a specific example is useful for understanding how price floors work.

Case Study: Farm Price Supports and the Case of Sugar Prices

America's extensive program of farm price supports began in 1933 as a "temporary method of dealing with an emergency"—in the years of the Great Depression, farmers were going broke in droves. These price supports are still with us today, even though farmers account for less than 2 percent of the U.S. workforce.[8]

One of the consequences of these price supports has been the creation of unsellable surpluses—more output of crops such as grains than consumers were willing to buy at the inflated prices yielded by the supports. Warehouses were filled to overflowing. New storage facilities had to be built, and the government was forced to set up programs in

---

[7] *The Economist*, February 20, 1999.

[8] Under major legislation passed in 1996, many agricultural price supports were supposed to be phased out over a seven-year period. In reality, many support programs, especially that for sugar, have changed little.

which grain from the unmanageable surpluses was shipped to poor foreign countries to combat malnutrition and starvation in those nations. Realistically, if price supports are to be effective in keeping prices above the equilibrium level, then *someone* must be prepared to purchase the surpluses that invariably result. Otherwise, those surpluses will somehow find their way into the market and drive down prices, undermining the price support program. In the United States (and elsewhere), the buyer of the surpluses has usually turned out to be the government, which makes its purchases at the expense of taxpayers who are forced to pay twice—once through taxes to finance the government purchases and a second time in the form of higher prices for the farm products bought by the American public.

One of the more controversial farm price supports involves the U.S. sugar industry. Sugar producers receive low-interest loans from the federal government and a guarantee that the price of sugar will not fall below a certain level.

In a market economy such as that found in the United States, Congress cannot simply set prices by decree; rather, it must take some action to enforce the price floor. In the case of sugar, that "something" is limiting both domestic production and foreign imports, thereby shifting the supply curve inward to the left. Figure 12 shows the mechanics involved in this price floor. Government policies shift the supply curve inward from S_0S_0 to S_1S_1 and drive the U.S. price up from 25¢ to 50¢ per pound. The more the supply curve shifts inward, the higher the price.

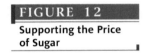

FIGURE 12

Supporting the Price of Sugar

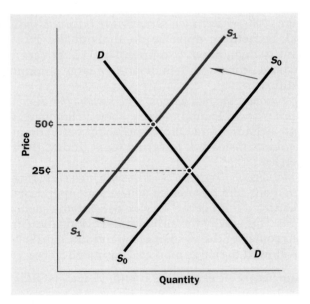

The sugar industry obviously benefits from the price-control program, but consumers pay for it in the form of higher prices for sugar and sugar-filled products such as soft drinks, candy bars, and cookies. Although estimates vary, the federal sugar price support program appears to cost consumers approximately $1.5 billion per year.

If all of this sounds a bit abstract to you, take a look at the ingredients in a U.S.-made soft drink. Instead of sugar, you will likely find "high-fructose corn syrup" listed as a sweetener. Foreign producers generally use sugar, but sugar is simply too expensive to be used for this purpose in the United States.

A Can of Worms

Our two case studies—rent controls and sugar price supports—illustrate some of the major side effects of price floors and ceilings but barely hint at others. Difficulties arise that we have not even mentioned, for the market mechanism is a tough bird that imposes suitable retribution on those who seek to evade it by government decree. Here is a partial list of other problems that may arise when prices are controlled.

Favoritism and Corruption   When price ceilings or floors create shortages or surpluses, someone must decide who gets to buy or sell the limited quantity that is available. This decision-making process can lead to discrimination along racial or religious lines, political favoritism, or corruption in government. For example, many prices were held at artificially low levels in the former Soviet Union, making queuing for certain goods quite common. Even so, Communist Party officials and other favored groups were somehow able to purchase the scarce commodities that others could not get.

Unenforceability   Attempts to limit prices are almost certain to fail in industries with numerous suppliers, simply because the regulating agency must monitor the behavior of so many sellers. People will usually find ways to evade or violate the law, and something like the free-market price will generally reappear. However, there is an important difference: Because the evasion process, whatever its form, will have some operating costs, those costs must be borne by someone. Normally, that someone is the consumer, who must pay higher prices to the suppliers for taking the risk of breaking the law.

Auxiliary Restrictions   Fears that a system of price controls will break down invariably lead to regulations designed to shore up the shaky edifice. Consumers may be told when and from whom they are permitted to buy. The powers of the police and the courts may be used to prevent the entry of new suppliers. Occasionally, an intricate system of market subdivision is imposed, giving each class of firms a protected sphere in which others are not permitted to operate. For example, in New York City, there are laws banning conversion of rent-controlled apartments to condominiums.

Limitation of Volume of Transactions   To the extent that controls succeed in affecting prices, they can be expected to reduce the volume of transactions. Curiously, this is true regardless of whether the regulated price is above or below the free-market equilibrium price. If it is set above the equilibrium price, the quantity demanded will be below the equilibrium quantity. On the other hand, if the imposed price is set below the free-market level, the quantity supplied will be reduced. Because sales volume cannot exceed either the quantity supplied or the quantity demanded, a reduction in the volume of transactions is the result.[9]

Misallocation of Resources   Departures from free-market prices are likely to result in misuse of the economy's resources because the connection between production costs and prices is broken. For example, Russian farmers used to feed their farm animals bread instead of unprocessed grains because price ceilings kept the price of bread ludicrously low. In addition, just as more complex locks lead to more sophisticated burglary tools, more complex regulations lead to the use of yet more resources for their avoidance.

Economists put it this way: Free markets are capable of dealing efficiently with the three basic coordination tasks outlined in Chapter 3: deciding what to produce, how to produce it, and to whom the goods should be distributed. Price controls throw a monkey wrench into the market mechanism. Although the market is surely not flawless, and government interferences often have praiseworthy goals, good intentions are not enough. Any government that sets out to repair what it sees as a defect in the market mechanism runs the risk of causing even more serious damage elsewhere. As a prominent economist

---

[9] See Discussion Question 4 at the end of this chapter.

once quipped, societies that are too willing to interfere with the operation of free markets soon find that the invisible hand is nowhere to be seen.

A SIMPLE BUT POWERFUL LESSON

Astonishing as it may seem, many people in authority do not understand the law of supply and demand, or they act as if it does not exist. For example, a few years ago *The New York Times* carried a dramatic front-page picture of the president of Kenya setting fire to a large pile of elephant tusks that had been confiscated from poachers. The accompanying story explained that the burning was intended as a symbolic act to persuade the world to halt the ivory trade.[10] One may certainly doubt whether the burning really touched the hearts of criminal poachers, but one economic effect was clear: By reducing the supply of ivory on the world market, the burning of tusks forced up the price of ivory, which raised the illicit rewards reaped by those who slaughter elephants. That could only encourage more poaching—precisely the opposite of what the Kenyan government sought to accomplish.

| SUMMARY |

1. An attempt to use government regulations to force prices above or below their equilibrium levels is likely to lead to **shortages** or **surpluses,** to black markets in which goods are sold at illegal prices, and to a variety of other problems. The market always strikes back at attempts to repeal the law of supply and demand.

2. The quantity of a product that is demanded is not a fixed number. Rather, **quantity demanded** depends on such influences as the price of the product, consumer incomes, and the prices of other products.

3. The relationship between quantity demanded and price, holding all other things constant, can be displayed graphically on a **demand curve.**

4. For most products, the higher the price, the lower the quantity demanded. As a result, the demand curve usually has a negative slope.

5. The quantity of a product that is supplied depends on its price and many other influences. A **supply curve** is a graphical representation of the relationship between **quantity supplied** and price, holding all other influences constant.

6. For most products, supply curves have positive slopes, meaning that higher prices lead to supply of greater quantities.

7. A change in quantity demanded that is caused by a change in the price of the good is represented by a movement *along* a fixed demand curve. A change in quantity demanded that is caused by a change in any other determinant of quantity demanded is represented by a **shift of the demand curve.**

8. This same distinction applies to the supply curve: Changes in price lead to movements along a fixed supply curve; changes in other determinants of quantity supplied lead to shifts of the entire supply curve.

9. A market is said to be in **equilibrium** when quantity supplied is equal to quantity demanded. The equilibrium price and quantity are shown by the point on the supply-demand graph where the supply and demand curves intersect. The **law of supply and demand** states that price and quantity tend to gravitate to this point in a free market.

10. Changes in consumer incomes, tastes, technology, prices of competing products, and many other influences lead to shifts in either the demand curve or the supply curve and produce changes in price and quantity that can be determined from **supply-demand diagrams.**

11. A tax on a good generally leads to a rise in the price at which the taxed product is sold. The rise in price is generally less than the tax, so consumers usually pay less than the entire tax.

12. Consumers generally pay only part of a tax because the resulting rise in price leads them to buy less and the cut in the quantity they demand helps to force price down.

---

[10] *The New York Times,* July 19, 1989.

| KEY TERMS |

demand curve 58

demand schedule 58

equilibrium 65

invisible hand 56

law of supply and demand 66

price ceiling 70

price floor 73

quantity demanded 57

quantity supplied 61

shift in a demand curve 59

shortage 65

supply curve 62

supply schedule 61

supply-demand diagram 64

surplus 65

| TEST YOURSELF |

1. What shapes would you expect for demand curves for the following:

    a. A medicine that means life or death for a patient

    b. French fries in a food court with kiosks offering many types of food

2. The following are the assumed supply and demand schedules for hamburgers in Collegetown:

Demand Schedule		Supply Schedule	
Price	Quantity Demanded per Year (thousands)	Price	Quantity Supplied per Year (thousands)
$2.75	14	$2.75	32
2.50	18	2.50	30
2.25	22	2.25	28
2.00	26	2.00	26
1.75	30	1.75	24
1.50	34	1.50	22

    a. Plot the supply and demand curves and indicate the equilibrium price and quantity.

    b. What effect would a decrease in the price of beef (a hamburger input) have on the equilibrium price and quantity of hamburgers, assuming all other things remained constant? Explain your answer with the help of a diagram.

    c. What effect would an increase in the price of pizza (a substitute commodity) have on the equilibrium price and quantity of hamburgers, assuming again that all other things remain constant? Use a diagram in your answer.

3. Suppose the supply and demand schedules for bicycles are as they appear in the following table.

    a. Graph these curves and show the equilibrium price and quantity.

Price	Quantity Demanded per Year (millions)	Quantity Supplied per Year (millions)
$170	43	27
210	39	31
250	35	35
300	31	39
330	27	43
370	23	47

    b. Now suppose that it becomes unfashionable to ride a bicycle, so that the quantity demanded at each price falls by 9 million bikes per year. What is the new equilibrium price and quantity? Show this solution graphically. Explain why the quantity falls by less than 9 million bikes per year.

    c. Suppose instead that several major bicycle producers go out of business, thereby reducing the quantity supplied by 9 million bikes at every price. Find the new equilibrium price and quantity, and show it graphically. Explain again why quantity falls by less than 9 million.

    d. What are the equilibrium price and quantity if the shifts described in Test Yourself Questions 3(b) and 3(c) happen at the same time?

4. The following table summarizes information about the market for principles of economics textbooks:

Price	Quantity Demanded per Year	Quantity Supplied per Year
$45	4,300	300
55	2,300	700
65	1,300	1,300
75	800	2,100
85	650	3,100

    a. What is the market equilibrium price and quantity of textbooks?

b. To quell outrage over tuition increases, the college places a $55 limit on the price of textbooks. How many textbooks will be sold now?

c. While the price limit is still in effect, automated publishing increases the efficiency of textbook production. Show graphically the likely effect of this innovation on the market price and quantity.

5. How are the following demand curves likely to shift in response to the indicated changes?

a. The effect of a drought on the demand curve for umbrellas

b. The effect of higher popcorn prices on the demand curve for movie tickets

c. The effect on the demand curve for coffee of a decline in the price of Coca-Cola

6. The two accompanying diagrams show supply and demand curves for two substitute commodities: tapes and compact discs (CDs).

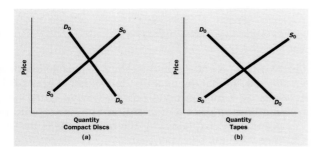

a. On the right-hand diagram, show what happens when rising raw material prices make it costlier to produce tapes.

b. On the left-hand diagram, show what happens to the market for CDs.

7. Consider the market for beef discussed in this chapter (Tables 1 through 4 and Figures 1 and 8). Suppose that the government decides to fight cholesterol by levying a tax of 50 cents per pound on sales of beef. Follow these steps to analyze the effects of the tax:

a. Construct the new supply schedule (to replace Table 2) that relates quantity supplied to the price that consumers pay.

b. Graph the new supply curve constructed in Test Yourself Question 7(a) on the supply-demand diagram depicted in Figure 7.

c. Does the tax succeed in its goal of reducing the consumption of beef?

d. Is the price rise greater than, equal to, or less than the 50 cent tax?

e. Who actually pays the tax, consumers or producers? (This may be a good question to discuss in class.)

8. **(More difficult)** The demand and supply curves for T-shirts in Touristtown, U.S.A., are given by the following equations:

$$Q = 24{,}000 - 500P \qquad Q = 6{,}000 + 1{,}000P$$

where P is measured in dollars and Q is the number of T-shirts sold per year.

a. Find the equilibrium price and quantity algebraically.

b. If tourists decide they do not really like T-shirts that much, which of the following might be the new demand curve?

$$Q = 21{,}000 - 500P \qquad Q = 27{,}000 - 500P$$

Find the equilibrium price and quantity after the shift of the demand curve.

c. If, instead, two new stores that sell T-shirts open up in town, which of the following might be the new supply curve?

$$Q = 4{,}000 + 1{,}000P \qquad Q = 9{,}000 + 1{,}000P$$

Find the equilibrium price and quantity after the shift of the supply curve.

| DISCUSSION QUESTIONS |

1. How often do you rent videos? Would you do so more often if a rental cost half as much? Distinguish between your demand curve for home videos and your "quantity demanded" at the current price.

2. Discuss the likely effects of the following:

a. Rent ceilings on the market for apartments

b. Floors under wheat prices on the market for wheat

Use supply-demand diagrams to show what may happen in each case.

3. U.S. government price supports for milk led to an unceasing surplus of milk. In an effort to reduce the surplus about a decade ago, Congress offered to pay dairy farmers to slaughter cows. Use two diagrams, one for the milk market and one for the meat market, to illustrate how this policy should have affected the price of meat. (Assume that meat is sold in an unregulated market.)

4. It is claimed in this chapter that either price floors or price ceilings reduce the actual quantity exchanged in a market. Use a diagram or diagrams to test this conclusion, and explain the common sense behind it.

5. The same rightward shift of the demand curve may produce a very small or a very large increase in quantity, depending on the slope of the supply curve. Explain this conclusion with diagrams.

6. In 1981, when regulations were holding the price of natural gas below its free-market level, then-Congressman Jack Kemp of New York said the following in an interview with *The New York Times*: "We need to decontrol natural gas, and get production of natural gas up to a higher level so we can bring down the price."[11] Evaluate the congressman's statement.

7. From 1990 to 1997 in the United States, the number of working men grew by 6.7 percent; the number of working women grew by 11 percent. During this time, average wages for men grew by 20 percent, whereas average wages for women grew by 25 percent. Which of the following two explanations seems more consistent with the data?

a. Women decided to work more, raising their relative supply (relative to men).

b. Discrimination against women declined, raising the relative (to men) demand for female workers.

---

[11] *The New York Times*, December 24, 1981.

Part 2

THE BUILDING BLOCKS
OF DEMAND AND SUPPLY

The next four chapters describe and analyze the basic building blocks with which economists analyze markets and their two essential elements: buyers (consumers) and sellers (producers). As in a piece of machinery, all the parts of a market operate simultaneously together, so there is no logical place to begin the story. Furthermore, the heart of the story is not found in the individual components, but in the way they fit together. The four central microeconomics chapters start off with the separate components but then assemble them into a working model of how firms determine price and output simultaneously. Then Chapter 9 deals with stocks and bonds as tools that help business firms obtain the finances they need to operate and as earnings opportunities for potential investors in firms.

CHAPTERS

CONSUMER CHOICE:
INDIVIDUAL AND MARKET DEMAND

Everything is worth what its purchaser will pay for it.

PUBLILIUS SYRUS (1ST CENTURY B.C.)

Y ou are about to start a new year in college, and your favorite clothing store is having a sale. So you decide to stock up on jeans. How do you decide how many pairs
to buy? How is your decision affected by the price of the jeans and the amount of
money you earned in your summer job? How can you get the most for your money?
Economic analysis provides some rational ways to make these decisions. Do you think
about your decision as an economist would, either consciously or unconsciously?
Should you? By the end of the chapter, you will be able to analyze such purchase decisions using concepts called *utility* and *marginal analysis.*

Chapter 4 introduced you to the idea of supply and demand and the use of supply
and demand curves to analyze how markets determine prices and quantities of products sold. This chapter will investigate the underpinnings of the demand curve, which,
as we have already seen, shows us half of the market picture.

CONTENTS

PUZZLE: WHY SHOULDN'T WATER BE WORTH MORE THAN DIAMONDS?

When Adam Smith lectured at the University of Glasgow in the 1760s, he introduced the study of demand by posing a puzzle. Common sense, he said, suggests that the price of a commodity must somehow depend on what that good is worth to consumers—on the amount of *utility* that the commodity offers. Yet, Smith pointed out, some cases suggest that a good's utility may have little influence on its price.

Smith cited diamonds and water as examples. He noted that water has enormous value to most consumers; indeed, its availability can be a matter of life and death. Yet water often sells at a very low price or is even free of charge, whereas diamonds sell for very high prices even though few people would consider them necessities. We will soon be in a position to see how marginal analysis, the powerful method of analysis introduced in this chapter, helps to resolve this paradox.

SOURCE: © Comstock Images/Jupiterimages

SOURCE: Larry Larminer/Brand X Pictures/Jupiterimages

SCARCITY AND DEMAND

When economists use the term *demand*, they do not mean mere wishes, needs, requirements, or preferences. Rather, demand refers to actions of consumers who, so to speak, put their money where their mouths are. Demand assumes that consumers *can* pay for the goods in question and that they are also *willing* to pay out the necessary money. Some of us may, for example, dream of owning a racehorse or a Lear jet, but only a few wealthy individuals can turn such fantasies into effective demands.

Any individual consumer's choices are subject to one overriding constraint that is at least partly beyond that consumer's control: The individual has only a limited income available to spend. This scarcity of income is the obvious reason why less affluent consumers demand fewer computers, trips to foreign countries, and expensive restaurant meals than wealthy consumers do. The scarcity of income affects even the richest of all spenders—the government. The U.S. government spends billions of dollars on the armed services, education, and a variety of other services, but governments rarely, if ever, have the funds to buy everything they want.

Because income is limited (and thus is a scarce resource), any consumer's purchase decisions for different commodities must be *interdependent*. The number of movies that Jane can afford to see depends on the amount she spends on new clothing. If John's parents have just sunk a lot of money into an expensive addition to their home, they may have to give up a vacation trip. Thus, no one can truly understand the demand curves for movies and clothing, or for homes and vacation trips, without considering demand curves for alternative goods.

The quantity of movies demanded, for example, probably depends not only on ticket prices but also on the prices of clothing. Thus, a big sale on shirts might induce Jane to splurge on several, leaving her with little or no cash to spend on movies. So, an analysis of consumer demand that focuses on only one commodity at a time leaves out an essential part of the story. Nevertheless, to make the analysis easier to follow, we begin by considering products in isolation. That is, we employ what is called "partial analysis," using a standard simplifying assumption. This assumption requires that all other variables remain unchanged. Later in the chapter and in the appendix, we will tell a fuller story.

UTILITY: A TOOL TO ANALYZE PURCHASE DECISIONS

In the American economy, millions of consumers make millions of decisions every day. You decide to buy a movie ticket instead of a paperback novel. Your roommate decides to buy two tubes of toothpaste rather than one tube or three tubes. How do people make these decisions?

Economists have constructed a simple theory of consumer choice based on the hypothesis that each consumer spends income in the way that yields the greatest amount of satisfaction, or *utility*. This seems to be a reasonable starting point, because it says only that people do what they prefer. To make the theory operational, we need a way to measure utility.

A century ago, economists envisioned utility as an indicator of the pleasure a person derives from consuming some set of goods, and they thought that utility could be measured directly in some kind of psychological units (sometimes called *utils*) after somehow reading the consumer's mind. Gradually, they came to realize that this was an unnecessary and, perhaps, impossible task. How many utils did you get from the last movie you saw? You probably cannot answer that question because you have no idea what a util is. Neither does anyone else.

But you may be able to answer a different question like, "How many hamburgers would you give up to get that movie ticket?" If you answer "three," no one can say how many utils you get from seeing a film, but they can say that you get more from the movie than from a single hamburger. When economists approach the issue in this manner, hamburgers, rather than the more vague "utility," become the unit of measurement. They can say that the utility of a movie (to you) is three hamburgers.

Early in the twentieth century, economists concluded that this indirect way of measuring consumer benefit gave them all they needed to build a theory of consumer choice. One can measure the benefit of a movie ticket by asking how much of some other commodity (like hamburgers) you are willing to give up for it. Any commodity will do for this purpose, but the simplest, most commonly used choice, and the one that we will use in this book, is money.[1] So we will use phrases like "the money utility of a pair of shoes" to mean how large an amount of money the individual in question is willing to give up for those shoes.

YOUR PIZZA DOLLAR

RENT
WAGES
GAS
ELECTRICITY
TAXES
INSURANCE
MUSHROOMS
PEPPERONI
EXTRA CHEESE

The Purpose of Utility Analysis: Analyzing How People *Behave*, Not What They *Think*

Here, a very important warning is required: Money (or hamburgers, for that matter) is an imperfect measure of utility. The reason is that measuring utility by means of money is like measuring the length of a table with a rubber yardstick. The value of a dollar changes—sometimes a great deal—depending on circumstances. For example, if you win $10 million in the lottery, an additional dollar can confidently be expected to add much less to your well-being than it would have one week earlier. After you hit the jackpot, you may not hesitate to spend $9 on a hamburger, whereas before you would not have spent more than $3. This difference does not mean that you now love hamburgers three times as much as before. Consequently, although we use money as an indicator of utility in this book, it should not be taken as an accurate indicator of consumers' psychological attitude toward the goods they buy.

So why do we use the concept of money utility? There are two good reasons. First, we do know how to approach *measuring* it (see next section), although we do not know how to measure what is going on inside the consumer's mind. Second, and much more important, it

---

[1] Note to Instructors: You will recognize that, although not using the terms, we are distinguishing here between neoclassical *cardinal utility* and *ordinal utility*. Moreover, throughout the book, *marginal utility in money terms* (or *money marginal utility*) is used as a synonym for the *marginal rate of substitution* between money and the commodity.

is extremely useful for analyzing demand behavior—what consumers will spend to buy some good, even though it is *not* a good indicator of what is going on deep inside their brains.

Total versus Marginal Utility

The **total monetary utility** of a quantity of a good to a consumer (measured in money terms) is the maximum amount of money that he or she is willing to give up in exchange for it.

Thus, we define the **total monetary utility** of a particular bundle of goods to a particular consumer as *the largest sum of money that person will voluntarily give up in exchange for those goods.* For example, imagine that you love pizza and are planning to buy four pizzas for a party you are hosting. You are, as usual, a bit low on cash. Taking this into account, you decide that you are willing to buy the four pies if they cost up to $52 in total, but you're not willing to pay more than $52. As economists, we then say that the *total utility* of four pizzas to you is $52, the maximum amount you are willing to spend to have them.

Total monetary utility (from which we will drop the word *monetary* from here on) measures your dollar evaluation of the benefit that you derive from your total purchases of some commodity during some selected period of time. *Total* utility is what really matters to you. But to understand which decisions most effectively promote total utility, we must make use of a related concept, **marginal (monetary) utility.** This concept is not a measure of the amount of benefit you get from your purchase decision but, rather, provides *a tool* with which you can analyze how much of a commodity that you must buy to make your total utility as large as possible. Your marginal utility of some good, X, is defined as *the addition to total utility that you derive by consuming one more unit of X.*[2] If you consumed two pizzas last month, marginal utility indicates how much additional pleasure you would have received by increasing your consumption to three pizzas. Before showing how marginal utility helps to find what quantity of purchases makes total utility as large as possible, we must first discuss how these two figures are calculated and just what they mean.

The **marginal utility** of a commodity to a consumer (measured in money terms) is the maximum amount of money that she or he is willing to pay for *one more unit* of that commodity.

Table 1 helps to clarify the distinction between marginal and total utility and shows how the two are related. The first two columns show how much *total* utility (measured in money terms) you derive from various quantities of pizza, ranging from zero to eight per month. For example, a single pizza pie is worth (no more than) $15 to you, two are worth $28 in total, and so on. The *marginal* utility is the *difference* between any two successive total utility figures. For example, assuming you have consumed three pizzas (worth $40.50 to you), suppose an additional pie brings your total utility to $52. Your marginal utility is thus the difference between the two, or $11.50.

Remember: Whenever we use the terms *total utility* and *marginal utility,* we define them in terms of the consumer's willingness to part with *money* for the commodity, not in some unobservable (and imaginary) psychological units.

TABLE 1
Your Total and Marginal Utility for Pizza This Month

(1) Quantity (Q) Pizzas per Month	(2) Total Utility (TU)	(3) Point in Marginal Utility (MU) = (ΔTU/ΔQ)	(4) Figure 1
0	$0.00		
		$15.00	A
1	15.00		
		13.00	B
2	28.00		
		12.50	C
3	40.50		
		11.50	D
4	52.00		
		8.00	E
5	60.00		
		5.00	F
6	65.00		
		3.00	G
7	68.00		
		0.00	H
8	68.00		

NOTE: Each entry in Column (3) is the difference between successive entries in Column (2). This is what is indicated by the zigzag lines.

The "Law" of Diminishing Marginal Utility

With these definitions, we can now propose a simple hypothesis about consumer tastes:

The more of a good a consumer has, the less *marginal* utility an additional unit contributes to overall satisfaction, if all other things remain unchanged.

Economists use this plausible proposition widely. The idea is based on the assumption that every person has a *hierarchy* of uses for a particular commodity. All of these uses are valuable, but some are more valuable than others. Take pizza, for example. Perhaps you consider your *own* appetite for pizza first—you buy enough pizza to satiate your own personal taste for it. But pizza may also provide you with an opportunity to satisfy your

---

[2] For those of you who have taken a course in differential calculus it may help to recognize that "marginal utility" is just another name for the first derivative of total utility with respect to (an increase in) the quantity of the commodity consumed.

social needs. So instead of eating all the pizza you buy, you decide to have a pizza party. First on your guest list may be your boyfriend or girlfriend. Next priority is your room-mate, and, if you feel really flush, you may even invite your economics instructor! So, if you buy only one pizza, you eat it yourself. If you buy a second pizza, you share it with your friend. A third is shared with your roommate, and so on.

The point is: Each pizza contributes something to your satisfaction, but each *additional* pizza contributes less (measured in terms of money) than its predecessor because it satisfies a lower-priority use. This idea, in essence, is the logic behind the **"law" of diminishing marginal utility,** which asserts that the more of a commodity you already possess, the smaller the amount of (marginal) utility you derive from acquisition of yet another unit of the commodity.

The third column of Table 1 illustrates this concept. The marginal utility (abbreviated MU) of the first pizza is $15; that is, you are willing to pay *up to* $15 for the first pie. The second is worth no more than $13 to you, the third pizza only $12.50, and so on, until you are willing to pay only $5 for the sixth pizza (the MU of that pizza is $5).

Figure 1, a marginal utility curve, shows a graph of the numbers in the first and third columns of Table 1. For example, point *D* indicates that the MU of a fourth pizza is $11.50. So, at any higher price, you will not buy a fourth pizza.

Note that the curve for marginal utility has a nega-tive slope; this is yet another way of representing the assertion that marginal utility diminishes as the pos-sessed quantity of the good rises. Like most laws, however, the "law" of diminishing marginal utility has exceptions. Some people feel that the value to them of getting one more unit of some good *rises rather than falls* as they acquire more of that item. This can be so when the person is consumed by or ad-dicted to that product. Stamp collectors and alco-holics provide good examples. The stamp collector who has a few stamps may consider the acquisition of one more to be mildly amusing. The person who has a large and valuable collection may be prepared to go to the ends of the earth for another stamp. Similarly, an alcoholic who finds the first beer quite pleasant may find the fourth or fifth to be absolutely irresistible. Economists generally treat such cases of increasing marginal utility as anomalies. For most goods and most people, marginal utility declines as consumption increases.

Table 1 illustrates another noteworthy relationship. Observe that as someone buys more and more units of the commodity—that is, as that person moves further down the table—the *total* utility numbers get larger and larger, whereas the *marginal* utility numbers get smaller and smaller. The reasons should now be fairly clear. The marginal utility numbers keep declining, as the "law" of diminishing marginal utility tells us they will, but *total* utility keeps rising so long as marginal utility remains positive. A person who owns ten compact disks, other things being equal, is better off (has higher total utility) than a person who possesses only nine, as long as the MU of the tenth CD is positive. In summary:

As a rule, as a person acquires more of a commodity, total utility increases and marginal utility from that good decreases, all other things being equal. In particular, when a commodity is very scarce, economists expect it to have a high marginal utility, even though it may provide little total utility because people have so little of the item.

Using Marginal Utility: The Optimal Purchase Rule

Now let us use the concept of marginal utility to analyze consumer choices. Consumers must always choose among the many commodities that

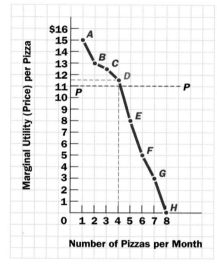

The **"law" of diminishing marginal utility** asserts that additional units of a commodity are worth less and less to a consumer in money terms. As the individual's consumption increases, the marginal utility of each additional unit declines.

FIGURE 1

A Marginal Utility (or Demand) Curve: Your Demand for Pizza This Month

"It's been fun, Dave, but I think we're entering the diminished marginal utility phase of our relationship."

compete for their limited supply of dollars. How can you use the idea of utility to help you understand the purchase choices permitted by those dollars that best serve your preferences?

You can obviously choose among many different quantities of pizza, any of which will add to your total utility. But which of these quantities will yield the greatest net benefits? If pizza were all that you were considering buying, in theory the choice would involve a simple calculation. We would need a statistical table that listed all of the alternative numbers of pizzas that you may conceivably buy. The table should indicate the *net* utility that each possible choice yields. That is, it should include the total utility that you would get from a particular number of pizzas, minus the utility of the other purchases you would forgo by having to pay for them—their opportunity cost. We could then simply read your optimal choice from this imaginary table—the number of pizzas that would give you the highest net utility number.

Even in theory, calculating optimal decisions is, unfortunately, more difficult than that. No real table of net utilities exists; an increase in expenditure on pizzas would mean less money available for clothing or movies, and you must balance the benefits of spending on each of these items against spending on the others. All of this means that we must find a more effective technique to determine optimal pizza purchases (as well as purchases of clothing, entertainment, and other things). That technique is **marginal analysis.**

Marginal analysis is a method for calculating optimal choices—the choices that best promote the decision maker's objective. It works by testing whether, and by how much, a small change in a decision will move things toward or away from the goal.

To see how marginal analysis helps to explain how consumers determine their optimal purchase decisions, first recall our assumption that you are trying to maximize the total *net* utility you obtain from your pizza purchases. That is, you are trying to select the number of pies that maximizes the total utility the pizzas provide you *minus the total utility you give up with the money you must pay for them.*

We can compare the analysis of the optimal decision-making process to the process of climbing a hill. First, imagine that you consider the possibility of buying only one pizza. Then suppose you consider buying two pizzas, and so on. If two pizzas give you a higher total net utility than one pizza, you may think of yourself as moving higher up the *total* net utility hill. Buying more pizzas enables you to ascend that hill higher and higher, until at some quantity you reach the top—*the optimal purchase quantity.* Then, if you buy any more, you will have overshot the peak and begun to descend the hill.

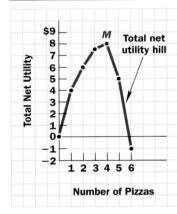

FIGURE 2

Finding Your Optimal Pizza Purchase Quantity: Maximizing Total Net Utility

Figure 2 shows such a hill and describes how your total net utility changes when you change the number of pizzas you buy. It shows the upward-sloping part of the hill, where the number of purchases has not yet brought you to the top. Then it shows the point (M) at which you have bought enough pizzas to make your net utility as large as possible (the peak occurs at four pizzas). At any point to the right of M, you have overshot the optimal purchase. You are on the downward side of the hill because you have bought more than enough pizzas to best serve your interests; you have bought too many to maximize your net utility.

How does marginal analysis help you to find that optimal purchase quantity, and how does it warn you if you are planning to purchase too little (so that you are still on the ascending portion of the hill) or too much (so that you are descending)? The numerical example in Table 1 will help reveal the answers. The marginal utility of, for example, a third pizza is $12.50. This means that the total utility you obtain from three pizzas ($40.50) is exactly $12.50 higher than the total utility you get from two pizzas ($28). As long as marginal utility is a positive number, the more you purchase, the more total utility you will get.

Total Net Utility equals Total Utility minus Total Expenditure (Price × Quantity)

That shows the benefit side of the purchase, but such a transaction also has a debit side—the amount you must pay for the purchase. Suppose that the price is $11 per pizza. Then the marginal *net* utility of the third pizza is marginal utility minus price, $12.50 minus $11, or $1.50. This is the amount that the third pizza adds to your total net utility. (See the third and fourth lines of Table 1.) So you really *are* better off with three pizzas than with two.

We can generalize the logic of the previous paragraph to show how marginal analysis solves the problem of finding the optimal purchase quantity, given the price of the commodity being purchased:

IDEAS FOR BEYOND THE FINAL EXAM

RULE 1: If marginal net utility is positive, the consumer must be buying too small a quantity to maximize total net utility. Because marginal utility exceeds price, the

consumer can increase total net utility further by buying (at least) one more unit of the product. In other words, since marginal net utility (which is marginal utility minus price) tells us how much the purchase of an additional unit raises or lowers total net utility, a positive marginal net utility means that total net utility is still going uphill. The consumer has not yet bought enough to get to the top of the hill.

RULE 2: No purchase quantity for which marginal net utility is a negative number can ever be optimal. In such a case, a buyer can get a higher total net utility by cutting back the purchase quantity. The purchaser would have climbed too far on the net utility hill, passing the topmost point and beginning to descend.

This leaves only one option. The consumer cannot be at the top of the hill if marginal net utility $(MU - P)$ is greater than zero—that is, if MU is greater than P. Similarly, the purchase quantity cannot be optimal if marginal net utility at that quantity $(MU - P)$ is less than zero—that is, if MU is less than P. The purchase quantity can be optimal, giving the consumer the highest possible total net utility, only if

$$\text{Marginal net utility} = MU - P = 0; \text{ that is, if } MU = P$$

Consequently, the hypothesis that the consumer chooses purchases to make the largest net contribution to total utility leads to the following *optimal purchase rule:*

It always pays the consumer to buy more of any commodity whose marginal utility (measured in money) exceeds its price and less of any commodity whose marginal utility is less than its price. When possible, the consumer should buy a quantity of each good at which price (P) and marginal utility (MU) are exactly equal—that is, at which

$$MU = P$$

because only these quantities will maximize the *net total utility* that the consumer gains from purchases, given the fact that these decisions must divide available money among all purchases.[3]

Notice that, although the consumer really cares about maximizing total *net* utility (and marginal utility is not the goal), we have used marginal analysis as a *guide* to the optimal purchase quantity. Marginal analysis serves only as an analytic method—as a means to an end. This goal is maximization of total net utility, not marginal utility or marginal net utility. In Chapter 8, after several other applications of marginal analysis, we will generalize the discussion to show how thinking "at the margin" allows us to make optimal decisions in a wide variety of fields besides consumer purchases.

Let's briefly review graphically how the underlying logic of the marginal way of thinking leads to the optimal purchase rule, $MU = P$. Refer back to the graph of marginal utilities of pizzas (Figure 1). Suppose that Paul's Pizza Parlor currently sells pizzas at a price of $11 (the dashed line *PP* in the graph). At this price, five pizzas (point *E*) is *not* an optimal purchase because the $8 marginal utility of the fifth pizza is less than its $11 price. You would be better off buying only four pizzas because that choice would save $11 with only an $8 loss in utility—a net gain of $3—from the decision to buy one less pizza.

You should note that, in practice, there may not exist a number of pizzas at which MU is *exactly* equal to *P*. In our example, the fourth pizza is worth $11.50, whereas the fifth pizza is worth $8—neither of them is *exactly* equal to their $11 price. If you could purchase an appropriate, in-between quantity (say, 4.38 pizzas), then MU would, indeed, exactly equal *P*. But Paul's Pizza Parlor will not sell you 4.38 pizzas, so you must do the best you can. You buy four pizzas, for which MU comes as close as possible to equality with *P*.

The rule for optimal purchases states that you should not buy a quantity at which MU is higher than price (points like *A, B,* and *C* in Figure 1) because a larger purchase would

---

[3] Economists can equate a dollar price with marginal utility only because they measure marginal utility in money terms (or, as they more commonly state, because they deal with the marginal rate of substitution of money for the commodity). If marginal utility were measured in some psychological units not directly translatable into money terms, a comparison of *P* and MU would have no meaning. However, MU could also be measured in terms of any commodity other than money. (Example: How many pizzas are you willing to trade for an additional ticket to a basketball game?)

make you even better off. Similarly, you should not end up at points *E, F, G,* and *H,* at which MU is below price, because you would be better off buying less. Rather, you should buy four pizzas (point *D*), where *P* = MU (approximately). Thus, marginal analysis leads naturally to the rule for optimal purchase quantities:

> **The decision to purchase a quantity of a good that leaves marginal utility greater than price cannot maximize total net utility, because buying an additional unit would add more to total utility than it would increase cost. Similarly, it cannot be optimal for the consumer to buy a quantity of a good that leaves marginal utility less than price, because then a reduction in the quantity purchased would save more money than it would sacrifice in utility. Consequently, the consumer can maximize total net utility only if the purchase quantity brings marginal utility as close as possible to equality with price.**

Note that price is an objective, observable figure determined by the market, whereas marginal utility is subjective and reflects consumer tastes. Because individual consumers lack the power to influence the price, they must adjust purchase quantities to make their subjective marginal utility of each good equal to the price given by the market.

From Diminishing Marginal Utility to Downward-Sloping Demand Curves

We will see next that the marginal utility curve and the demand curve of a consumer who maximizes total net utility are one and the same. The two curves are identical. This observation enables us to use the optimal purchase rule to show that the "law" of diminishing marginal utility implies that demand curves typically slope downward to the right; that is, they have negative slopes.[4] To do this, we use the list of marginal utilities in Table 1 to determine how many pizzas you would buy at any particular price. For example, we see that at a price of $8, it pays for you to buy five pizzas, because the MU of the fifth pizza ordered is $8.

Table 2 gives several alternative prices and the optimal purchase quantity corresponding to each price derived in just this way. (To make sure you understand the logic behind the optimal purchase rule, verify that the entries in the right column of Table 2 are, in fact, correct.) This table, which was initially interpreted as a marginal utility schedule, can also to be interpreted as a demand schedule, because it tells us what quantity of the good the consumer in question will demand at each price, the exact function of a consumer's demand schedule. This *demand schedule* appears graphically as the *demand curve* shown in Figure 1. This demand curve is also simply the brick-colored marginal utility curve.

This is so because at any given price, the curve tells us what quantity of the good the consumer will want to buy (the quantity at which marginal utility is equal to the given price), and that is just how a demand curve is defined. So the curve in the graph must be a demand curve. But the curve also tells us the marginal utility at any such quantity, so it is also a marginal utility curve. You can also see its negative slope in the graph, which is a characteristic of demand curves.

Let's examine the logic underlying the negatively sloped demand curve a bit more carefully. Suppose you are purchasing the optimal number of pizzas, at which price equals marginal utility. But then, if the price falls, you will find that your marginal utility for that product is now *above* the newly reduced price. For example, Table 1 indicates that at a price of $12.50 per pizza, you would optimally buy three pizzas, because the MU of the fourth pizza is only $11.50. If price falls below $11.50, it then pays to purchase more—it pays to buy the fourth pizza because its MU now exceeds its price. The marginal utility of the next (fifth) pizza is only $8. Thus, if the price falls below $8, it would pay you to buy that fifth pizza. So, the lower the price, the more the consumer will find it advantageous to buy, which is what is meant by saying that the demand curve has a negative slope.

Note the critical role that the "law" of diminishing marginal utility plays here. If *P* falls, a consumer who wishes to maximize total utility must buy more, to the point that

TABLE 2

List of Optimal Quantities of Pizza for You to Purchase at Alternative Prices

Price	Quantity of Pizzas Purchased per Month
$ 3.00	7
5.00	6
8.00	5
11.50	4
12.50	3
13.00	2
15.00	1

NOTE: For simplicity of explanation, the prices shown have been chosen to equal the marginal utilities in Table 1. In-between prices would make the optimal choices involve fractions of pizzas (say, 2.6 pizzas).

---

[4] If you need to review the concept of slope, refer to the discussion of graphic analysis in Chapter 1's appendix.

MU falls enough to equal the new lower price. According to the "law" of diminishing marginal utility, the only way to do this is to increase the quantity purchased.

Although this explanation is a bit abstract, we can easily rephrase it in practical terms. We have noted that individuals put commodities to various uses, each of which has a different priority. For you, buying a pizza for your date has a higher priority than using the pizza to feed your roommate. If the price of pizzas is high, it makes sense for you to buy only enough for the high-priority uses—those that offer high marginal utilities. When price declines, however, it pays to purchase more of the good—enough for some lower-priority uses. The same general assumption about consumer psychology underlies both the "law" of diminishing marginal utility and the negative slope of the demand curve. They are really two different ways of describing the same assumed attitudes of the consumer.

Indeed, it may well have struck you that this chapter's discussion of the consumer's decision process—equating price and marginal utility—does not resemble the thought processes of any consumer you have ever met. Buyers may seem to make decisions much more instinctively and without any calculation of marginal utilities or anything like them. That is true—yet it need not undermine the pertinence of the discussion.

When you give a command to your computer, you actually activate some electronic switches and start some operations in what is referred to as *binary code.* Most computer users do not know they are having this effect and do not care, yet they are activating binary code nevertheless, and the analysis of the computation process does not misrepresent the facts by describing this sequence. In the same way, if a shopper divides her purchasing power among various purchase options in a way that yields the largest possible utility for her money, she *must* be following the rules of marginal analysis, even though she is totally unaware of this choice.

A growing body of experimental evidence, however, has pointed out some persistent deviations between reality and the picture of consumer behavior provided by marginal analysis. Experimental studies by groups of economists and psychologists have turned up many examples of behavior that seem to violate the optimal purchase rule. For instance, one study offered two groups of respondents what were really identical options, presumably yielding similar marginal utilities. Despite this equality, depending on differences in some *irrelevant* information that was also provided to the respondents, the two groups made very different choices.

> One group of subjects received the information in parentheses, and the other received the information in brackets. . . .
>
> [*Problem 1*]. Imagine that you are about to purchase. . . . a calculator for ($15)[$125]. The calculator salesman informs you that the calculator you wish to buy is on sale for ($10)[$120] at the other branch of the store, located a 20-minute drive away. Would you make the trip to the other store?
>
> The responses to the two versions of this problem were quite different. When the calculator cost $125 only 29 percent of the subjects said they would make the trip, whereas 68 percent said they would go when the calculator cost only $15.

Thus, in this problem *both* groups were really being told they could save $5 on the price of a product if they took a 20-minute trip to another store. Yet, depending on an irrelevant fact, whether the product was a cheap or an expensive model, the number of persons willing to make the same trip to save the same amount of money was very different. The point is that human purchase decisions are affected by the environment in which the decision is made, and not only by the price and marginal utility of the purchase.[5]

There are many examples—here are two. Two groups of people were asked what they would do if, desperately thirsty after coming off a long walk in the desert, they saw a place selling a cold beer for $10. The first group was told it was a luxury hotel, and the members of the group enthusiastically elected to purchase it, but the other group was told that the beer was sold by a shabby grocery store at the same high price, and they indignantly refused

[5]Richard H. Thaler, *Quasi Rational Economics* (New York: Russell Sage Foundation, 1992), pp. 148–150.

the offer. Here are individuals who, having purchased a bottle of wine for $15 some 20 years earlier and learning that such bottles now sell for $800, will not try to sell their bottle (suggesting it is worth more than $800 to them) but will also refuse to buy another at the current price (suggesting it is worth less than $800 to them).

One can go on and on with examples of consumers not behaving as economic theory describes. But do such actions make a substantial difference to the performance of the economy? For example, would the price of the old wine fall substantially if most of the people who still own bottles offered them for sale? The answer is sometimes. But sometimes the market mechanism offsets the effects of such "irrationality." A striking illustration arose when President Dwight Eisenhower had a heart attack. The next morning, the bottom dropped out of the stock market. Brokers were besieged by terrified investors who demanded immediate sale of their stockholdings at whatever price they could fetch. But there were many other potential stock buyers who recognized that, even if the president did not survive, there would be no radical change in the U.S. economy. The collapse of the market was an opportunity to acquire valuable securities at bargain prices, and they bought. By the next day, the market had fully recovered, and the effect of the irrational terror of the sellers of the previous day had evaporated. The bottom line is that human behavior is often far from the "rational decision making" assumed by the theory, but that does not always make a big difference in the behavior of the market.

BEHAVIORAL ECONOMICS: ARE ECONOMIC DECISIONS REALLY MADE "RATIONALLY"?

Economic theory has traditionally focused on optimality in decision making. What bundle of supermarket purchases maximizes the consumer's utility? What business decisions maximize company profits? In recent years, a number of economists and psychologists have questioned the implied assumption that economic decisions are made rationally, after careful calculation and comparison of the payoffs in terms of the decision makers' goals. As you might expect, they have found much evidence of behavior that is inconsistent with economists' typical rationality assumptions. This research has led to a school of thought called *behavioral economics* that investigates how consumers and other economic decision makers really behave.

CONSUMER CHOICE AS A TRADE-OFF: OPPORTUNITY COST

We have expressed the optimal purchase rule as the principle guiding a decision about how much of one commodity to buy. However, we have already observed that the scarcity of income lurking in the background turns every decision into a trade-off. Given each consumer's limited income, a decision to buy a new car usually means giving up some travel or postponing furniture purchases. The money that the consumer gives up when making a purchase—the expenditure on that purchase—is only one measure of the true underlying cost—what must be given up in exchange, and that is what we have defined as the opportunity cost of the purchase.

IDEAS FOR BEYOND THE FINAL EXAM

HOW MUCH DOES IT REALLY COST? The real cost is the *opportunity cost* of the purchase—the commodities that we must give up as a result of the purchase decision. This opportunity-cost calculation has already been noted in one of our *Ideas for Beyond the Final Exam*—we must always consider the real cost of our purchase decisions, which take into account how much of *other* things they force us to forgo. Any decision to buy implies some such trade-off because scarcity constrains all economic decisions. Although their dilemmas may not inspire much pity, even billionaires face very real trade-offs: Invest $200 million in an office building, or go for the $300 million baseball team?

This last example has another important implication. The trade-off from a consumer's purchase decision does not always involve giving up another *consumer good*. This is true, for example, of the choice between consumption and saving. Consider a high school student who is deciding whether to buy a new car or to save the money to pay for college. If she saves the money, it can grow by earning interest, so that the original amount plus interest earned will be available to pay for tuition and board three years later. A decision to cut down on consumption now and put the money into the bank means that the student will be wealthier in the future because of the interest she will earn. This, in turn, will enable the student to afford more of her college expenses at the future date when those expenses arise. So the opportunity cost of a new car today is the forgone opportunity to save funds for the future. We conclude:

> **From the viewpoint of economic analysis, the true cost of any purchase is the opportunity cost of that purchase, rather than the amount of money that is spent on it.**

The opportunity cost of a purchase can be either higher or lower than its price. For example, if your computer cost you $1,800, but the purchase required you to take off two hours from your job that pays $20 per hour, the true cost of the computer—that is, the opportunity cost—is the amount of goods you could have bought with $1,840 (the $1,800 price plus the $40 in earnings that the purchase of the computer required you to give up). In this case, the opportunity cost ($1,840, measured in money terms) is higher than the price of the purchase ($1,800). (For an example in which price is higher than opportunity cost, see Test Yourself Question 4 at the end of the chapter.)

Consumer's Surplus: The Net Gain from a Purchase

The optimal purchase rule, MU (approximately) = *P*, assumes that the consumer always tries to maximize the money value of the total utility from the purchase *minus* the amount spent to make that purchase.[6] Thus, any difference between the price consumers *actually* pay for a commodity and the price they would be *willing* to pay for that item represents a net utility gain in some sense. Economists give the name **consumer's surplus** to that difference—that is, to the net gain in total utility that a purchase brings to a buyer. The consumer is trying to make the purchase decisions that maximize

> **Consumer's surplus = Total utility (in money terms) − Total expenditures**

Thus, just as economists assume that business firms maximize total profit (equal to total revenue minus total cost), they assume that consumers maximize consumer's surplus; that is, the difference between the total utility of the purchased commodity and the amount that consumers spend on it.

The concept of *consumer's surplus* seems to suggest that the consumer gains some sort of free bonus, or *surplus,* for every purchase. In many cases, this idea seems absurd. How can it be true, particularly for goods whose prices seem to be outrageous?

We hinted at the answer in Chapter 1, where we observed that, if there is no cheating, both parties must gain from a voluntary exchange or else one of them will refuse to participate. The same must be true when a consumer makes a *voluntary* purchase from a supermarket or an appliance store. If the consumer did not expect a net gain from the transaction, he or she would simply not bother to buy the good. Even if the seller were to "overcharge" by some standard, that would merely reduce the size of the consumer's net gain, not eliminate it entirely. If the seller is so greedy as to charge a price that wipes out the net gain altogether, the punishment will fit the crime: The consumer will refuse to buy, and the greedy seller's would-be gains will never materialize. The basic principle states that every purchase that is not on the borderline—that is, every purchase except those about which the consumer is indifferent—must yield *some* consumer's surplus.

But how large is that surplus? At least in theory, it can be measured with the aid of a table or graph of marginal utilities (Table 1 and Figure 1). Suppose that, as in our earlier example, the price of a large pizza is $11 and you purchase four pizzas. Table 3 reproduces the marginal utility numbers from Table 1. It shows that the first pizza is worth $15 to you,

Consumer's surplus is the difference between the value to the consumer of the quantity of Commodity X purchased and the amount that the market requires the consumer to pay for that quantity of X.

---

[6] Again, in practice, the consumer can often only approximately equate MU and *P*.

so at the $11 price, you reap a net gain (surplus) of $15 minus $11, or $4, by buying that pizza. The second pizza also brings you some surplus, but less than the first one does, because the marginal utility diminishes. Specifically, the second pizza provides a surplus of $13 minus $11, or $2. Reasoning in the same way, the third pizza gives you a surplus of $12.50 minus $11, or $1.50. It is only the fourth serving—the last one that you purchase—that offers little or no surplus because, by the optimal purchase rule, the marginal utility of the last unit is approximately equal to its price. We can now easily determine the total consumer's surplus that you obtain by buying four pizzas. It is simply the sum of the surpluses received from each pizza. Table 3 shows that this consumer's total surplus is

$$\$4 + \$2 + \$1.50 + \$0.50 = \$8$$

This way of looking at the optimal purchase rule shows why a buyer must always gain some consumer's surplus if buying more than one unit of a good. Note that the price of each unit remains the same, but the marginal utility diminishes as more units are purchased. The last unit bought yields only a tiny consumer's surplus because MU (approximately) = *P*, but all prior units must have had marginal utilities greater than the MU of the last unit because of diminishing marginal utility.

We can be more precise about the calculation of the consumer's surplus with the help of a graph showing marginal utility as a set of bars. The bars labeled *A*, *B*, *C*, and *D* in Figure 3 come from the corresponding points on the marginal utility curve (demand curve) in Figure 1. The consumer's surplus from each pizza equals the marginal utility of that pizza minus the price paid for it. By representing consumer's surplus graphically, we can determine just how much surplus was obtained from the entire purchase by measuring the area between the marginal utility curve and the horizontal line representing the price of pizzas—in this case, the horizontal line *PP* represents the (fixed) $11 price.

In Figure 3, the bar whose upper-right corner is labeled *A* represents the $15 marginal utility derived from the first pizza; the same interpretation applies to bars *B*, *C*, and *D*. Clearly, the first serving purchased yields a consumer's surplus of $4, indicated by the shaded part of bar *A*. The height of that part of the bar is equal to the $15 marginal utility minus the $11 price. In the same way, the next two shaded areas represent the surpluses offered by the second and third pizzas. The fourth pizza has the smallest shaded area because the height representing marginal utility is (as close as you can get to being) equal to the height representing price. Sum up the shaded areas in the graph to obtain, once

TABLE 3

Calculating Marginal Net Utility (Marginal Consumer's Surplus) from Your Pizza Purchases

Quantity	Marginal Utility	Price	Marginal Net Utility (Surplus)
0	$15.00	$11.00	$4.00
1	13.00	11.00	2.00
2	12.50	11.00	1.50
3	11.50	11.00	0.50
4			
Total			$8.00

FIGURE 3

Graphic Calculation of Consumer's Surplus

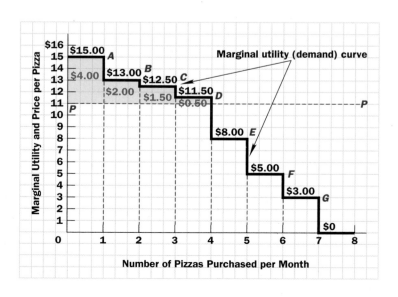

again, the total consumer's surplus ($4 + $2 + $1.50 + $0.50 = $8) from a four-pizza purchase.

> The consumer's surplus derived from buying a certain number of units of a good is obtained graphically by drawing the person's demand curve as a set of bars whose heights represent the marginal utilities of the corresponding quantities of the good and then drawing a horizontal line whose height is the price of the good. The sum of the heights of the bars above the horizontal line—that is, the area of the demand (marginal utility) bars above that horizontal line—measures the *total* consumer's surplus that the purchase yields.

PUZZLE: RESOLVING THE DIAMOND–WATER PUZZLE

We can now use marginal utility analysis to analyze Adam Smith's paradox (which he was never able to explain) that diamonds are very expensive, whereas water is generally very cheap, even though water seems to offer far more utility. The resolution of the diamond–water puzzle is based on the distinction between marginal and total utility.

The *total* utility of water—its role as a necessity of life—is indeed much higher than that of diamonds, but price, as we have seen, is not related directly to *total* utility. Rather, the optimal purchase rule tells us that price tends to equal *marginal* utility. We have every reason to expect the marginal utility of water to be very low, whereas the marginal utility of a diamond is very high.

Given normal conditions, water is comparatively cheap to provide, so its price is generally quite low. Consumers thus use correspondingly large quantities of water. The principle of diminishing marginal utility, therefore, pushes down the marginal utility of water for a typical household to a low level. As the consumer's surplus diagram (Figure 3) suggests, this also means that its *total* utility is likely to be high.

In contrast, high-quality diamonds are scarce (partly because a monopoly keeps them so). As a result, the quantity of diamonds consumed is not large enough to drive down the MU of diamonds very far, so buyers of such luxuries must pay high prices for them. As a commodity becomes more scarce, its *marginal* utility and its market price rise, regardless of the size of its *total* utility. Also, as we have seen, because so little of the commodity is consumed, its *total* utility is likely to be comparatively low, despite its large *marginal* utility.

Thus, like many paradoxes, the diamond–water puzzle has a straightforward explanation. In this case, all one has to remember is that

> Scarcity raises price and *marginal* utility, but it generally reduces *total* utility. And although total utility measures the benefits consumers get from their consumption, it is marginal utility that is equal (approximately) to price.

Income and Quantity Demanded

Our application of marginal analysis has enabled us to examine the relationship between the *price* of a commodity and the quantity that will be purchased. But things other than price also influence the amount of a good that a consumer will purchase. As an example, we'll look at how quantity demanded responds to changes in *income*.

To be concrete, consider what happens to the number of ballpoint pens consumers will buy when their real income rises. It may seem almost certain that they will buy more ballpoint pens than before, but that is not necessarily so. A rise in real income can either increase or decrease the quantity of any particular good purchased.

Why might an increase in income lead a consumer to buy fewer ballpoint pens? People buy some goods and services only because they cannot afford anything better. They may purchase used cars instead of new ones. They may use inexpensive ballpoint pens instead of finely crafted fountain pens or buy clothing secondhand instead of new. If their real incomes rise, they may then drop out of the used car market and buy brand-new automobiles or buy more fountain pens and fewer ballpoint pens. Thus, a rise in real income will *reduce* the quantities of cheap pens and used cars demanded. Economists have given the rather descriptive name **inferior goods** to the class of commodities for which quantity demanded falls when income rises.

An **inferior good** is a commodity whose quantity demanded falls when the purchaser's real income rises, all other things remaining equal.

The upshot of this discussion is that economists cannot draw definite conclusions about the effects of a rise in consumer incomes on quantity demanded. But for most commodities, if incomes rise and prices do not change, quantity demanded will increase. Such an item is often called a *normal good.*

FROM INDIVIDUAL DEMAND CURVES TO MARKET DEMAND CURVES

So far in this chapter, we have studied how *individual demand curves* are obtained from the logic of consumer choice. To understand how the market system works, we must derive the relationship between price and quantity demanded *in the market as a whole*—the **market demand curve.** For example, the demand for laptops in Cleveland, Ohio, is described by such a demand curve. It is this market demand curve that plays a key role in the supply-demand analysis of price and output determination that we studied in Chapter 4.

A **market demand curve** shows how the total quantity of some product demanded by *all* consumers in the market during a specified period of time changes as the price of that product changes, holding all other things constant.

Market Demand Curves as a Horizontal Sum of the Demand Curves of Individual Buyers

If each individual pays no attention to other people's purchase decisions when making his or her own, then we can easily derive the market demand curve from consumers' individual demand curves: As we will see next, we simply *add* the individual consumers' demand curves, as shown in Figure 4. The figure gives the individual demand curves *DD* and *ZZ* for two people, Alex and Naomi, and the total (market) demand curve, *MM*. Alex and Naomi are both consumers of the product.

We can derive this market demand curve in the following straightforward way:

Step 1: Pick any relevant price, say, $10.

Step 2: At that price, determine Alex's quantity demanded (9 units) from his demand curve in Panel (a) of Figure 4 and Naomi's quantity demanded (6 units) from her demand curve in Panel (b) of Figure 4. Note that these quantities are indicated by the line segment labeled *AA* for Alex and that labeled *NN* for Naomi.

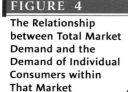

FIGURE 4

The Relationship between Total Market Demand and the Demand of Individual Consumers within That Market

Step 3: Add Naomi's and Alex's quantities demanded at the $10 price (segment *AA* + segment *NN* = 9 + 6 = 15) to yield the total quantity demanded by the market at that price. This gives segment *CC*, with total quantity demanded

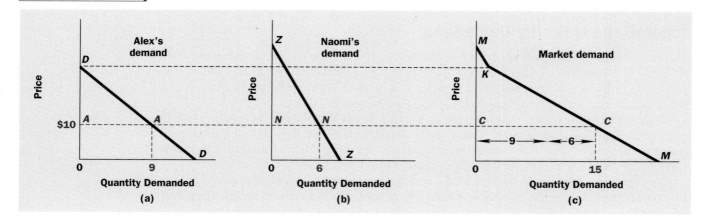

equal to 15 units, in Panel (c) of Figure 4. Notice that the addition constitutes a *horizontal* movement in the graph because we are adding quantities purchased, and those quantities are measured by horizontal distances from the zero points of each of the graphs.

Now repeat the process for each alternative price to obtain other points on the market demand curve until the shape of the entire curve *MM* appears. (The sharp angle at point *K* on the market curve occurs because that point corresponds to the price at which Alex, whose demand pattern is different from Naomi's, first enters the market. At any higher price, only Naomi is willing to buy anything.) That is all there is to the adding-up process. (Question: What would happen to the market demand curve if, say, another consumer entered the market?)

The "Law" of Demand

Just as in the case of an individual's demand curve, we expect the total quantity demanded by the market to move in the opposite direction from price, so the slope of the market demand curve will also be negative. Economists call this relationship the **"law" of demand.** Notice that we have put the word *law* in quotation marks. By now you will have observed that economic laws are not always obeyed, and we shall see in a moment that the "law" of demand is not without exceptions. But first let us see why the "law" usually holds.

> The **"law" of demand** states that a lower price generally increases the amount of a commodity that people in a market are willing to buy and also tends to increase the number of buyers. Therefore, for most goods, market demand curves have negative slopes.

Earlier in this chapter, we explained that individual demand curves usually slope downward because of the "law" of diminishing marginal utility. If individual demand curves slope downward, then the preceding discussion of the adding-up process implies that market demand curves must also slope downward. This is just common sense; if every consumer in the market buys fewer pizzas when the price of pizza rises, then the total quantity demanded in the market must surely fall.

But market demand curves may slope downward even if individual demand curves do not, because not all consumers are alike. Consider two examples where the individual's demand curve does not slope downward. If a bookstore reduces the price of a popular novel, it may draw many new customers, but few of the customers who already own a copy will buy a second one, despite the reduced price. Similarly, true devotees of pizza may maintain their pizza purchases unchanged even if prices rise to exorbitant levels, whereas others would not eat pizza even if you gave it to them free of charge. But the market demand curves for books and pizzas can still have a negative slope. As the price of pizza rises, less enthusiastic pizza eaters may drop out of the market entirely, leaving the expensive pie to the more devoted consumers. Thus, the quantity demanded declines as price rises, simply because higher prices induce more people to give up pizza completely. And for many commodities, lower prices encourage new customers to come into the *market* (for example, new book buyers), and it is these "fair-weather" customers (rather than the negative slope of *individual* demand curves) who can be most important for the "law" of demand.

This is also illustrated in Figure 4, in which only Naomi will buy the product at a price higher than *D*. At a price lower than *D*, Alex will also purchase the product. Hence, below point *K*, the market demand curve lies farther to the right than it would have if Alex had not entered the market. Put another way, a rise in price from a level below *D* to a level above *D* would cut quantity demanded for two reasons: (1) because Naomi's demand curve has a negative slope and (2) because it would drive Alex out of the market.

We conclude, therefore, that the "law" of demand stands on fairly solid ground. If individual demand curves slope downward, then the market demand curve surely will, too. Furthermore, the market demand curve may slope downward even when individual demand curves do not.

Exceptions to the "Law" of Demand

Some exceptions to the "law" of demand have been noted. One common exception occurs when people judge quality on the basis of price—they perceive a more expensive commodity as offering better quality. For example, many people buy name-brand aspirin, even if right next to it on the drugstore shelf they see an unbranded, generic aspirin with an identical chemical formula selling at half the price. The consumers who do buy the name-brand aspirin may well use comparative price to judge the relative qualities of different brands. They may prefer Brand X to Brand Y *because* X is slightly more expensive. If Brand X were to reduce its price below that of Brand Y, consumers might assume that it was no longer superior and actually reduce their purchases of X.

Another possible cause of an upward-sloping demand curve is snob appeal. If part of the reason for purchasing a $300,000 Rolls-Royce is to advertise one's wealth, a decrease in the car's price may actually reduce sales, even if the quality of the car remains unchanged. Other types of exceptions have also been noted by economists, but for most commodities, it seems quite reasonable to assume that demand curves have negative slopes, an assumption that is supported by the data.

This chapter has begun to take us behind the demand curve, to discuss how it is determined by the preferences of individual consumers. Chapter 6 will explore the demand curve further by examining other things that determine its shape and the implications of that shape for consumer behavior.

| SUMMARY |

1. Economists distinguish between **total and marginal utility**. Total utility, or the benefit consumers derive from a purchase, is measured by the maximum amount of money they would give up to obtain the good. Rational consumers seek to maximize (net) total utility, or **consumer's surplus**: the total utility derived from a commodity minus the value of the money spent in buying it.

2. Marginal utility is the maximum amount of money that a consumer is willing to pay for an *additional* unit of a particular commodity. *Marginal* utility is useful in calculating the set of purchases that maximizes net *total* utility. This illustrates one of our *Ideas for Beyond the Final Exam.*

3. The **"law" of diminishing marginal utility** is a psychological hypothesis stating that as a consumer acquires more of a commodity, the marginal utility of additional units of the commodity decreases.

4. To maximize the total utility obtained by spending money on Commodity X, given the fact that other goods can be purchased only with the money that remains after buying X, the consumer must purchase a quantity of X such that the price equals (or approximately equals) the commodity's marginal utility (in monetary terms).

5. If the consumer acts to maximize utility, and if the marginal utility of some good declines when purchased in larger quantities, then the consumer's demand curve for the good will have a negative slope. A reduction in price will induce the consumer to purchase more units, leading to a lower marginal utility.

6. Abundant goods tend to have low prices and low marginal utilities regardless of whether their total utilities are high or low. That is why water can have a lower price than diamonds despite its higher total utility.

7. An **inferior good**, such as secondhand clothing, is a commodity of which consumers buy less when they get richer, all other things held equal.

8. Consumers usually earn a surplus when they purchase a commodity voluntarily. This means that the quantity of the good that they buy is worth more to them than the money they give up in exchange for it. Otherwise, they would not buy it. That is why consumer's surplus is normally positive.

9. As another of our *Ideas for Beyond the Final Exam*, "How Much Does It Really Cost?," tells us, the true economic cost of the purchase of Commodity X is its opportunity cost—that is, the value of the alternative purchases that the acquisition of X requires the consumer to forgo. The money value of the opportunity cost of a unit of good X can be higher or lower than the price of X.

10. A rise in a consumer's income can push quantity demanded either up or down. For normal goods, a rise in income raises the quantity demanded; for inferior goods, which are generally purchased in an effort to save money, a higher income reduces the quantity demanded.

11. The demand curve for an entire market is obtained by taking a horizontal sum of the demand curves of all individuals who buy or consider buying in that market. This sum is obtained by adding up, for each price, the quantity of the commodity in question that every such consumer is willing to purchase at that price.

| KEY TERMS |

consumer's surplus   93

inferior good   96

"law" of demand   97

"law" of diminishing marginal utility   87

marginal analysis   88

marginal utility   86

market demand curve   96

total monetary utility   86

| TEST YOURSELF |

1. Which gives you greater *total* utility: 14 gallons of water per day or 22 gallons per day? Why?

2. At which level do you get greater *marginal* utility: 14 gallons per day or 22 gallons per day? Why?

3. Which of the following items are likely to be normal goods for a typical consumer? Which are likely to be inferior goods?

   a. Expensive perfume

   b. Paper plates

   c. Secondhand clothing

   d. Overseas trips

4. Emily buys an air conditioner that costs $700. Because the air in her home is cleaner, its use saves her $250 in curtain cleaning costs over the lifetime of the air conditioner. In money terms, what is the opportunity cost of the air conditioner?

5. Suppose that strawberries sell for $3 per basket. Jim is considering whether to buy zero, one, two, three, or four baskets. On your own, create a plausible set of total and marginal utility numbers for the different quantities of strawberries (as we did for pizza in Table 1), and arrange them in a table. From your table, calculate how many baskets Jim would buy.

6. Draw a graph showing the consumer's surplus Jim would get from his strawberry purchase in Test Yourself Question 5, and check your answer with the help of your marginal utility table.

7. Consider a market with two consumers, Jasmine and Jim. Draw a demand curve for each of the two consumers, and use those curves to construct the demand curve for the entire market.

| DISCUSSION QUESTIONS |

1. Describe some of the different ways you use water. Which would you give up if the price of water were to rise a little? If it were to rise by a fairly large amount? If it were to rise by a very large amount?

2. Suppose that you wanted to measure the marginal utility of a commodity to a consumer by directly determining the consumer's psychological attitude or strength of feeling toward the commodity rather than by seeing how much money the consumer would give up for the commodity. Why would you find it difficult to make such a psychological measurement?

3. Some people who do not understand the optimal purchase rule argue that if a consumer buys so much of a good that its price equals its marginal utility, the consumer could not possibly be behaving optimally. Rather, they say, the consumer would be better off quitting while ahead or buying a quantity such that marginal utility is much greater than price. What is wrong with this argument? (*Hint:* What opportunity would the consumer then miss? Is it maximization of marginal or total utility that serves the consumer's interests?)

4. What inferior goods do you purchase? Why do you buy them? Do you think you will continue to buy them when your income is higher?

| APPENDIX | *Analyzing Consumer Choice Graphically: Indifference Curve Analysis*

The consumer demand analysis presented in this chapter, although correct as far as it goes, has (at least) one shortcoming: By treating the consumer's decision about the purchase of each commodity as an isolated event, it conceals the fact that consumers must *choose* among commodities because of their limited budgets. The analysis so far does not explicitly indicate the hard choice behind every purchase decision—the sacrifice of some goods to obtain others.

The idea is included implicitly, of course, because the purchase of any commodity involves a trade-off between that good and money. If you spend more money on rent, you have less to spend on entertainment. If you buy more clothing, you have less money for food. But to represent the consumer's *choice* problem explicitly, economists have invented two geometric devices, the *budget line* and the *indifference curve*, which are described in this appendix.

GEOMETRY OF AVAILABLE CHOICES: THE BUDGET LINE

Suppose, for simplicity, that only two commodities are produced in the world: cheese and rubber bands. The decision problem of any household is then to allocate its income between these two goods. Clearly, the more it spends on one, the less it can have of the other. But just what is the trade-off? A numerical example will answer this question and introduce the graphical device that economists use to portray the trade-off.

Suppose that cheese costs $2 per pound, boxes of rubber bands sell at $3 each, and a consumer has $12 at his disposal. He obviously has a variety of choices, as displayed in Table 4. For example, if he buys no rubber bands, the consumer can go home with six pounds of cheese, and so on. Each of the combinations of cheese and rubber bands that the consumer can afford can be shown in a diagram in which the axes measure the quantities purchased of each commodity. In Figure 5, pounds of cheese are measured along the vertical axis, the number of boxes of rubber bands is measured along the horizontal axis, and a labeled point represents each of the combinations enumerated in Table 4. This budget line *AE* shows the possible combinations of cheese and rubber bands that the consumer can buy with $12 if cheese costs $2 per pound and a box of rubber bands costs $3. For example, point *A* corresponds to spending everything on cheese; point *E* corresponds to spending everything on rubber bands. At intermediate points on the budget line (such as *C*), the consumer buys some of both goods (at *C*, two boxes of rubber bands and three pounds of cheese), which together use up the $12 available.

TABLE 4

Alternative Purchase Combinations for a $12 Budget

Boxes of Rubber Bands (at $3 each)	Expenditure on Rubber Bands	Remaining Funds	Pounds of Cheese (at $2 each)	Label in Figure 5
0	$0	$12	6	A
1	3	9	4.5	B
2	6	6	3	C
3	9	3	1.5	D
4	12	0	0	E

If a straight line connects points *A* through *E*, the brown line in the diagram, it traces all possible ways to divide the $12 between the two goods. For example, at point *D*, if the consumer buys three boxes of rubber bands, he will have enough money left to purchase only 1½ pounds of cheese. This is readily seen to be correct from Table 4. Line *AE* is therefore called the **budget line.**

FIGURE 5

A Budget Line

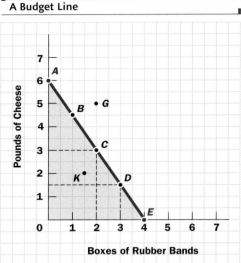

Boxes of Rubber Bands

The **budget line** for a household graphically represents all possible combinations of two commodities that it can purchase, given the prices of the commodities and some fixed amount of money at its disposal.

Properties of the Budget Line

Let us now use *r* to represent the number of boxes of rubber bands purchased by the consumer and *c* to indicate the amount of cheese that he acquires. Thus, at $2 per pound, he spends on cheese a total of $2 times the number of pounds of cheese bought, or $2*c*. Similarly, the consumer spends $3*r* on rubber bands, making a total of $2*c* plus $3*r*, which must equal $12 if he spends the entire $12 on the two commodities. Thus, $2c + 3r = 12$ is the equation of the budget line. It is also the equation of the straight line drawn in the diagram.[7]

Note also that the budget line represents the *maximum* amounts of the commodities that the consumer can afford. Thus, for any given purchase of rubber bands, it indicates the greatest amount of cheese that his money can buy. If the consumer wants to be thrifty, he can choose to end up at a point *below* the budget line, such as *K*. Clearly, then, the choices he has available include not only those points on the budget line, *AE*, but also any point in the shaded triangle formed by that line and the two axes, because at any such point the consumer buys smaller quantities of cheese and/or rubber bands than at points on *AE* and so spends less than the available $12. By contrast, points above the budget line, such as *G*, are not available to the

---

[7] You may have noticed one problem that arises in this formulation. If every point on the budget line *AE* is a possible way for the consumer to spend his money, he must be able to buy *fractional* boxes of rubber bands. Perhaps the purchase of 1Ω boxes can be interpreted to include a down payment of $1.50 on a box of rubber bands to be purchased on the next shopping trip!

consumer, given his limited budget. A bundle of five pounds of cheese and two boxes of rubber bands would cost $16, which is more than he has to spend.

Changes in the Budget Line

The position of the budget line is determined by two types of data: the prices of the commodities purchased and the income at the buyer's disposal. We can complete our discussion of the graphics of the budget line by examining briefly how a change in either prices or income affects the location of that line.

Obviously, any increase in the income of the household increases the range of options available to it. Specifically, *increases in income produce parallel shifts in the budget line,* as shown in Figure 6. The reason is simple: An increase in available income of, say, 50 percent, if spent entirely on these two goods, would permit the consumer's family to purchase exactly 50 percent more of *either* commodity. Point *A* in Figure 5 would shift upward by 50 percent of its distance from the origin, whereas point *E* would move to the right by 50 percent.[8] Figure 6 shows three such budget lines corresponding to incomes of $9, $12, and $18, respectively.

Finally, we can ask what happens to the budget line when the price of some commodity changes. In Figure 7, when the price of the rubber bands

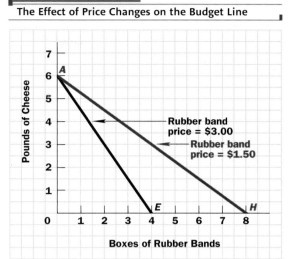

FIGURE 7

The Effect of Price Changes on the Budget Line

decreases, the budget line moves outward, but the move is no longer parallel because the point on the cheese axis remains fixed. Once again, the reason is fairly straightforward. A 50 percent reduction in the price of rubber bands (from $3.00 to $1.50) permits the consumer to buy twice as many boxes of rubber bands with his $12 as before: Point *E* moves rightward to point *H*, where the buyer can obtain eight boxes of rubber bands. However, since the price of cheese has not changed, the amount of cheese that can be bought for $12 is unaffected, meaning that the end of the budget line at point *A* does not move. This gives the general result about the determination of the budget line: *A reduction in the price of one of the two commodities swings the budget line outward along the axis representing the quantity of that item while leaving the location of the other end of the line unchanged.* Thus a fall in the price of rubber bands from $3.00 to $1.50 swings the price line from *AE* to blue line *AH*. This happens because at the higher price, $12 buys only four boxes of rubber bands, but at the lower price, it can buy eight boxes.

WHAT THE CONSUMER PREFERS: PROPERTIES OF THE INDIFFERENCE CURVE

The budget line indicates what choices are *available* to the consumer, given the size of his income and the commodity prices fixed by the market. Next, we must examine the consumer's *preferences* to determine which of these available possibilities he will choose with the given income and prices.

After much investigation, economists have determined what they believe to be the minimum amount of information they need about a purchaser in order to analyze his choices. Economists only need to know how a

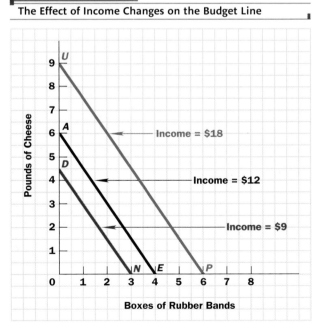

FIGURE 6

The Effect of Income Changes on the Budget Line

---

[8] An algebraic proof is simple. Let *M* (which is initially $12) be the amount of money available to the consumer's household. The equation of the budget line can be solved for *c*, obtaining $c = -(3/2)r + M/2$. This equation corresponds to a straight line with a slope of $-3/2$ and a vertical intercept of $M/2$. A change in *M*, the quantity of money available, will not change the *slope* of the budget line; rather, it will lead to parallel shifts in that line.

consumer *ranks* alternative bundles of available commodities, deciding which of every relevant pair of bundles he likes better but making no effort to find out *how much* more he likes the preferred bundle. Suppose, for instance, that the consumer can choose between two bundles of goods, Bundle W, which contains three boxes of rubber bands and one pound of cheese, and Bundle T, which contains two boxes of rubber bands and three pounds of cheese. The economist wants to know for this purpose only whether the consumer prefers W to T or T to W, or whether he is *indifferent* about which one he gets. Note that the analysis requires no information about the *degree* of preference—whether the consumer is wildly more enthusiastic about one of the bundles or just prefers it slightly.

Graphically, the preference information is provided by a group of curves called **indifference curves** (Figure 8).

> An **indifference curve** connects all combinations of the commodities that are equally desirable to the consumer.

Any point on the diagram represents a combination of cheese and rubber bands. (For example, point T on indifference curve I_b represents two boxes of rubber bands and three pounds of cheese.) Any two points on the same indifference curve (for example, S and W, on indifference curve I_a) represent two combinations of the goods that the consumer likes equally well. If two points, such as T and W, lie on different indifference curves, the consumer prefers the one on the higher indifference curve.

Before we examine these curves, let us see how to interpret one. A single point on an indifference curve says nothing about preferences. For example, point R on curve I_a simply represents the bundle of goods composed of four boxes of rubber bands and

½ pound of cheese. It does *not* suggest that the consumer is indifferent between ½ pound of cheese and four boxes of rubber bands. For the curve to indicate anything, one must consider at least two of its points—for example, points S and W. An indifference curve, by definition, represents all such combinations that provide equal total utility to the consumer.

We do not know yet which bundle, among all of the bundles he can afford, the consumer will choose to buy; this analysis indicates only that a change in which of two such bundles the consumer selects will make him neither better off nor worse off, in terms of the items received. Before using indifference curves to analyze the consumer's choices, one must examine a few of its properties. Most important is the fact that

> As long as the consumer desires *more* of each of the goods in question, *every* point on a higher indifference curve (that is, a curve farther from the origin in the graph) will be preferred to *any* point on a lower indifference curve.

In other words, among indifference curves, *higher is better.* The reason is obvious. Given two indifference curves, say, I_b and I_c in Figure 8, the higher curve will contain points lying above and to the right of some points on the lower curve. Thus, point U on curve I_c lies above and to the right of point T on curve I_b. This means that the consumer gets more rubber bands *and* more cheese at U than at T. Assuming that he desires both commodities, the consumer must prefer U to T.

Because every point on curve I_c is, by definition, equal in desirability to point U, and the same relation holds for point T and all other points along curve I_b, the consumer will prefer *every* point on curve I_c to *any* point on curve I_b.

This implies a second property of indifference curves: *They never intersect.* This is so because if an indifference curve, say, I_b, is anywhere above another indifference curve, say, I_a, then I_b must be above I_a everywhere, because every point on I_b is preferred to every point on I_a.

Another property that characterizes the indifference curve is its *negative slope.* Again, this holds only if the consumer wants more of both commodities. Consider two points, such as S and R, on the same indifference curve. If the consumer is indifferent between them, one point cannot represent more of *both* commodities than the other point. Given that point S represents more cheese than point R, R must offer more rubber bands than S, or the consumer would not be indifferent about which he gets. As a result, any movement toward the point with the larger number of rubber bands implies a decrease in the quantity of cheese. The curve will always slope downhill toward the right, giving a negative slope.

FIGURE 8

Three Indifference Curves for Cheese and Rubber Bands

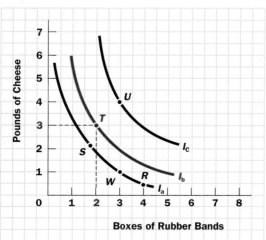

Boxes of Rubber Bands

A final property of indifference curves is the nature of their curvature—the way *they round toward the axes.* They are drawn "bowed in"—they flatten out (they become less and less steep) as they extend from left to right. To understand why this is so, we must first examine the economic interpretation of the slope of an indifference curve.

THE SLOPES OF INDIFFERENCE CURVES AND BUDGET LINES

In Figure 9, the average slope of the indifference curve between points M and N is represented by RM/RN.

> The **slope of an indifference curve**, referred to as the **marginal rate of substitution (MRS)** between the commodities, represents the maximum amount of one commodity that the consumer is willing to give up in exchange for one more unit of another commodity.

RM is the quantity of cheese that the consumer gives up in moving from M to N. Similarly, RN is the increased number of boxes of rubber bands acquired in this move. Because the consumer is indifferent between bundles M and N, the gain of RN rubber bands must just suffice to compensate him for the loss of RM pounds of cheese. Thus, the ratio RM/RN represents the terms on which the consumer is willing—*according to his own preference*—to trade one good for the other. If RM/RN equals 2, the consumer is willing to give up (no more than) two pounds of cheese for one additional box of rubber bands.

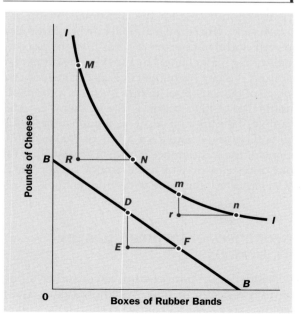

FIGURE 9

Slopes of a Budget Line and an Indifference Curve

The **slope of the budget line,** *BB,* in Figure 9 is also a rate of exchange between cheese and rubber bands, but it no longer reflects the consumer's subjective willingness to trade. Rather, the slope represents the rate of exchange that *the market* offers to the consumer when he gives up money in exchange for cheese and rubber bands. Recall that the budget line represents all commodity combinations that a consumer can get by spending a fixed amount of money. The budget line is, therefore, a curve of constant expenditure. At current prices, if the consumer reduces his purchase of cheese by amount DE in Figure 9, he will save just enough money to buy an additional amount, EF, of rubber bands, because at points D and F he is spending the same total number of dollars.

> The **slope of a budget line** is the amount of one commodity that the market requires an individual to give up to obtain one additional unit of another commodity without any change in the amount of money spent.

The slopes of the two types of curves, then, are perfectly analogous in their meaning. The slope of the indifference curve indicates the terms on which the *consumer* is willing to trade one commodity for another, whereas the slope of the budget line reports the terms on which the market allows the consumer to trade one good for another.

It is useful to carry our interpretation of the slope of the budget line one step further. Common sense suggests that the market's rate of exchange between cheese and rubber bands should be related to their prices, pc and pr, and it is easy to show that this is so. Specifically, the slope of the budget line is equal to the ratio of the prices of the two commodities. To see why, note that if the consumer gives up one box of rubber bands, he has pr more dollars to spend on cheese. But the quantity of cheese this money will enable him to buy is *inversely* related to its price; that is, the lower the price of cheese, the more cheese that money can buy—each dollar permits him to buy $1/pc$ pounds of cheese. So the additional pr dollars the consumer has available when he forgoes the purchase of one box of rubber bands permit him to buy pr times $1/pc = pr/pc$ more pounds of cheese. Thus, the slope of the budget line, which indicates how much additional cheese the consumer can buy when he gives up one box of rubber bands, is pr/pc.

Before returning to our main subject, the study of consumer choice, we pause briefly and use our interpretation of the slope of the indifference curve to discuss the third of the properties of the indifference curve—its characteristic curvature—which we left unexplained earlier. The shape of indifference curves means that the slope decreases with movement from left to right. In Figure 9, at point m, toward the right of the diagram, the consumer is willing to give up far less cheese for one more box of rubber bands (quantity *rm*) than he is willing to trade at point *M*, toward the left. This situation occurs because at *M* the consumer initially has a large quantity of cheese and few rubber bands, whereas at *m* his initial stock of cheese is low and he has many rubber bands. In general terms, the curvature premise on which indifference curves are usually drawn asserts that consumers are relatively eager to trade away some part of what they own of a commodity of which they have a large amount but are more reluctant to trade away part of the goods of which they hold small quantities. This psychological premise underlies the curvature of the indifference curve.

We can now use our indifference curve apparatus to analyze how the consumer chooses among the combinations that he can afford to buy—that is, the combinations of rubber bands and cheese shown by the budget line. Figure 10 brings together in the same diagram the budget line from Figure 5 and the indifference curves from Figure 8.

Tangency Conditions

Because, according to the first of the properties of indifference curves, the consumer prefers higher curves to lower ones, he will go to the point on the budget line that lies on the highest indifference curve attainable. This will be point *T* on indifference curve *I*_b. He can afford no other point that he likes as well. For example, neither point *K* below the budget line nor point *W* on the budget line puts the consumer on such a high indifference curve. Further, any point on an indifference curve above *I*_b, such as point *U*, is out of the question because it lies beyond his financial means. We end up with a simple rule of consumer choice:

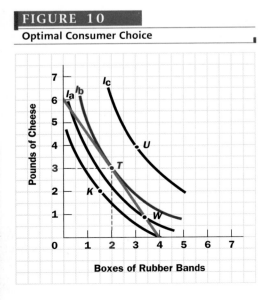

FIGURE 10

Optimal Consumer Choice

Boxes of Rubber Bands

Consumers will select the most desired combination of goods obtainable for their money. The choice will be that point on the budget line at which the budget line is tangent to an indifference curve.

We can see why only the point of tangency, *T* (two boxes of rubber bands and three pounds of cheese), will give the consumer the largest utility that his money can buy. Suppose that the consumer were instead to consider buying 3½ boxes of rubber bands and one pound of cheese. This would put him at point *W* on the budget line and on the indifference curve *I*_a. By buying fewer rubber bands and more cheese (a move upward and to the left on the budget line), he could get to another indifference curve, *I*_b, that would be higher and therefore more desirable without spending any more money. It clearly does not pay to end up at *W*. Only the point of tangency, *T*, leaves no room for further improvement.

At a point of tangency, where the consumer's benefits from purchasing cheese and rubber bands are maximized, the slope of the budget line equals the slope of the indifference curve. This is true by the definition of a point of tangency. We have just seen that the slope of the indifference curve is the marginal rate of substitution between cheese and rubber bands and that the slope of the budget line is the ratio of the prices of rubber bands and cheese. We can therefore restate the requirement for the optimal division of the consumer's money between the two commodities in slightly more technical language:

Consumers will get the most benefit from their money when they choose combinations of commodities whose marginal rates of substitution equal the ratios of their prices.

It is worth reviewing the logic behind this conclusion. Why is it not advisable for the consumer to stop at a point such as *W*, where the marginal rate of substitution (slope of the indifference curve) is less than the price ratio (slope of the budget line)? By moving upward and to the left from *W* along his budget line, he can instead take advantage of market opportunities to obtain a commodity bundle that he likes better. This will always be true, for example, if the amount of cheese the consumer is *personally* willing to exchange for a box of rubber bands (the slope of the indifference curve) is greater than the amount of cheese for which the box of rubber bands trades *on the market* (the slope of the budget line).

Consequences of Income Changes: Inferior Goods

Now consider what happens to the consumer's purchases after a rise in income. We know that a rise in income produces a parallel outward shift in the budget line, such as the shift from *BB* to *CC* in Figure 11. The

FIGURE 11

Effects of a Rise in Income When Neither Good Is Inferior

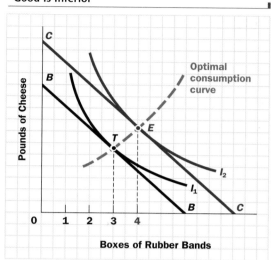

Boxes of Rubber Bands

quantity of rubber bands demanded rises from three to four boxes, and the quantity demanded of cheese increases as well. This change moves the consumer's equilibrium from tangency point *T* to tangency point *E* on a higher indifference curve.

A rise in income may or may not increase the demand for a commodity. In Figure 11, the rise in income does lead the consumer to buy more cheese *and* more rubber bands, but indifference curves need not always be positioned in a way that yields this sort of result. In Figure 12, as the consumer's budget line rises from *BB* to *CC*, the tangency point moves leftward from *H* to *G*. As a result, when his income rises, the consumer actually buys *fewer* rubber bands. This implies that for this consumer rubber bands are an *inferior good.*

FIGURE 12

Effects of a Rise in Income When Rubber Bands Are an Inferior Good

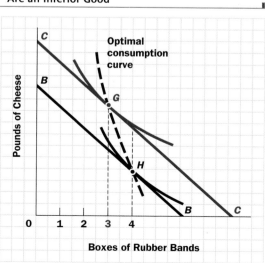

Boxes of Rubber Bands

Consequences of Price Changes: Deriving the Demand Curve

Finally, we come to the main question underlying demand curves: How does a consumer's choice change if the price of one good changes? We explained earlier that a reduction in the price of a box of rubber bands causes the budget line to swing outward along the horizontal axis while leaving its vertical intercept unchanged. In Figure 13, we depict the effect of a decline in the price of rubber bands on the quantity of rubber bands demanded. As the price of rubber bands falls, the budget line swings from *BC* to *BD*. The tangency points, *T* and *E*, also move in a corresponding direction, causing the quantity demanded to rise from two to three boxes. The price of rubber bands has fallen and the quantity demanded has risen, so the demand curve for rubber bands has a negative slope. The desired purchase of rubber bands increases from two to three boxes, and the desired purchase of cheese also increases, from 3 pounds to 3¾ pounds.

The demand curve for rubber bands can be constructed directly from Figure 13. Point *T* shows that the consumer will buy two boxes of rubber bands when the price of a box is $3.00. Point *E* indicates that when the price falls to $1.50, quantity demanded rises to three boxes of rubber bands.[9] These two pieces of information are shown in Figure 14 as points *t* and *e* on the demand curve for rubber bands. By examining the effects of other possible prices for rubber bands (other budget lines emanating from point *B* in Figure 13), we can find all the other points on the demand curve in

FIGURE 13

Consequences of Price Changes

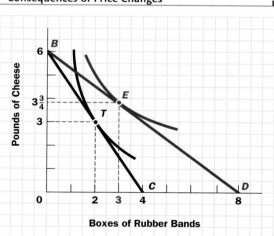

Boxes of Rubber Bands

---

[9] How do we know that the price of rubber bands corresponding to the budget line *BD* is $1.50? Because the $12.00 total budget will purchase at most eight boxes (point *D*), the price per box must be $12.00/8 = $1.50.

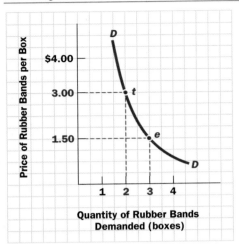

FIGURE 14

Deriving the Demand Curve for Rubber Bands

exactly the same way. The demand curve is derived from the indifference curve by varying the price of the commodity to see the effects of all other possible prices.

The indifference curve diagram also brings out an important idea that the demand curve does not show. A change in the *price of rubber bands* also has consequences for the *quantity of cheese demanded* because it affects the amount of money left over for cheese purchases. In the example illustrated in Figure 13, the decrease in the price of rubber bands increases the demand for cheese from 3 to 3¾ pounds.

| SUMMARY |

1. Indifference curve analysis permits economists to study the interrelationships of the demands for two (or more) commodities.

2. The basic tools of indifference curve analysis are the consumer's **budget line** and **indifference curves.**

3. A budget line shows all combinations of two commodities that the consumer can afford, given the prices of the commodities and the amount of money the consumer has available to spend.

4. The budget line is a straight line whose slope equals the ratio of the prices of the commodities. A change in price changes the **slope of the budget line.** A change in the consumer's income causes a parallel shift in the budget line.

5. Two points on an indifference curve represent two combinations of commodities such that the consumer does not prefer one combination over the other.

6. Indifference curves normally have negative slopes and are bowed in toward the origin. The **slope of an indifference curve** indicates how much of one commodity the consumer is willing to give up to get an additional unit of the other commodity.

7. The consumer will choose the point on the budget line that gets him to the highest attainable indifference curve. Normally this will occur at the point of tangency between the two curves. This point indicates the combination of commodities that gives the consumer the greatest benefits for the amount of money he has available to spend.

8. The consumer's demand curve can be derived from his indifference curve.

| KEY TERMS |

budget line   100

indifference curve   102

slope of a budget line   103

slope of an indifference curve
(marginal rate of
substitution)   103

| TEST YOURSELF |

1. John Q. Public spends all of his income on gasoline and hot dogs. Draw his budget line under several conditions:

   a. His income is $100, and one gallon of gasoline and one hot dog each cost $2.

   b. His income is $150, and the two prices remain the same.

   c. His income is $100, hot dogs cost $2 each, and gasoline costs $2.50 per gallon.

2. Draw some hypothetical indifference curves for John Q. Public on a diagram identical to the one you constructed for Test Yourself Question 1.

   a. Approximately how much gasoline and how many hot dogs will Mr. Public buy?

   b. How will these choices change if his income increases to $140? Is either good an inferior good?

   c. How will these choices change if gasoline price rises to $3.00 per gallon?

3. Explain the information that the *slope* of an indifference curve conveys about a consumer's preferences. Use this relationship to explain the typical U-shaped curvature of indifference curves.

DEMAND AND ELASTICITY

*A high cross elasticity of demand [between two goods indicates that they] compete in the same market.
[This can prevent a supplier of one of the products] from possessing monopoly power over price.*

U.S. SUPREME COURT, DUPONT CELLOPHANE DECISION, 1956

I n this chapter, we continue our study of demand and demand curves, which we began in the previous chapter. Here we explain the way economists *measure* how much quantity demanded responds to price changes and what such responsiveness implies about the revenue that producers will receive if they change prices. In particular, we introduce and explain an important concept called *elasticity* that economists use to examine the relationship between quantity demanded and price.

CONTENTS

ISSUE: **WILL TAXING CIGARETTES MAKE TEENAGERS STOP SMOKING?**

Public health experts believe that increasing taxes on cigarettes can be a major weapon in the battle to cut teenage smoking. Imagine yourself on a panel of consultants helping a congressional committee draft new legislation to deal with this issue. As the youngest member of the group, you are asked for your opinion about how effective a big tax increase on cigarettes would be in persuading young people to stop smoking. How would you respond? What sorts of statistical data, if any, would you use to help form your opinion? How might you go about analyzing the relevant numbers?

This chapter will help you answer such questions. As often happens in economics, we will see that careful investigation brings some surprises. This is true in the case of taxes to discourage teenage smoking. A tax on cigarettes may actually benefit teenagers'—and other citizens'—health. And it will, of course, benefit government finances by bringing in more tax money. Nothing surprising so far. Instead, the surprise is this: The more effective the tax is in curbing teenage smoking, the less beneficial it will be to the government's finances, and vice versa; the more the tax benefits the government, the less it will contribute to health. The concept of elasticity of demand will make this point clearer.

ELASTICITY: THE MEASURE OF RESPONSIVENESS

Governments, business firms, supermarkets, and law courts all need a way to measure how responsive demand is to price changes—for example, will a 10 percent cut in the price of commodity X increase quantity of X demanded a little or a lot? Economists measure the responsiveness of quantity demanded to price changes via a concept called *elasticity*. Marketers sometimes use estimates of elasticity to decide how to price their products or whether to add new product models. A relatively flat demand curve like Figure 1(a)

FIGURE 1

Hypothetical Demand Curves for Film

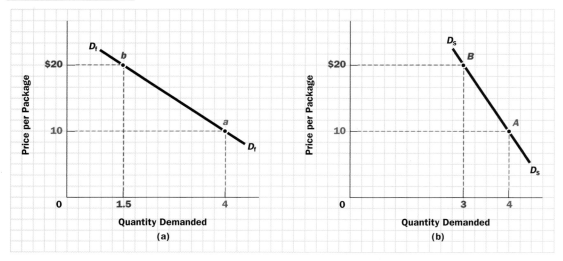

NOTE: Quantities are in millions of packages of film per year.

indicates that consumers respond sharply to a change in price—the quantity they demand falls by 2.5 units (from 4 units to 1.5 units) when price rises $10. That is, they demand or buy much less of the product when price rises even a little bit. Such a "touchy" curve is called *elastic* or *highly elastic*. A relatively steep demand curve like Figure 1(b), which indicates that consumers respond hardly at all to a price change, is called *inelastic*. In this graph, a $10 price rise cuts quantity demanded by only 1 unit.

The precise measure used for this purpose is called the **price elasticity of demand,** or simply the **elasticity of demand.** We define elasticity of demand as the ratio of the *percentage* change in quantity demanded to the associated *percentage* change in price.

Demand is called *elastic* if, say, a 10 percent rise in price reduces quantity demanded by *more* than 10 percent. Demand is called *inelastic* if such a rise in price reduces quantity demanded by *less* than 10 percent.

> The **(price) elasticity of demand** is the ratio of the *percentage* change in quantity demanded to the *percentage* change in price that brings about the change in quantity demanded.

Why do we need these definitions to analyze the responsiveness to price shown by a particular demand curve? At first, it may seem that the *slope* of the demand curve conveys the needed information: Curve D_sD_s is much steeper than curve D_fD_f in Figure 1, so any given change in price appears to correspond to a much smaller change in quantity demanded in Figure 1(b) than in Figure 1(a). For this reason, it is tempting to call demand in Panel (a) "more elastic." Slope will not do the job because the slope of any curve depends on the particular units of measurement, and economists use no standardized units of measurement. For example, cloth output may be measured in yards or in meters, milk in quarts or liters, and coal in tons or hundred-weights. Figure 2(a) brings out this point explicitly. In this graph, we return to a pizza example like that in Chapter 5, measuring quantity demanded in terms of pizzas and price in dollars per pizza. A fall in price from $14 to $10 per large pizza (points *A* and *B*) raises quantity demanded at Paul's Pizza Parlor from 280 pizzas to 360 per week—that is, by 80 pizzas.

Now look at Figure 2(b), which provides *exactly* the same information but measures quantity demanded in *slices* of pizza rather than whole pizzas (with one pizza yielding eight slices). Here, the same price change as before increases quantity demanded, from $8 \times 280 = 2{,}240$ slices to $8 \times 360 = 2{,}880$ slices—that is, by 640 slices, rather than by 80 pizzas.

Visually, the increase in quantity demanded looks eight times as great in Panel (b) as in Panel (a), but all that has changed is the unit of measurement. The 640-unit increase in

FIGURE 2

The Sensitivity of Slope to Units of Measurement at Paul's Pizza Parlor

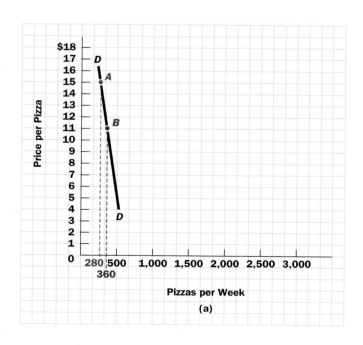

(a)

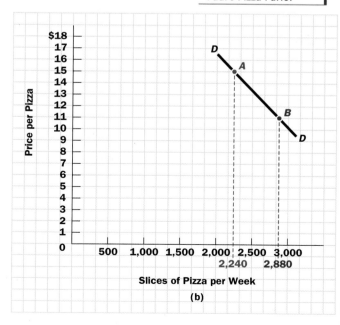

(b)

Figure 2(b) represents the same increase in quantity demanded as the 80-unit increase in Figure 2(a). Just as you get different numbers for a given rise in temperature, depending on whether you measure it in Celsius or Fahrenheit, so the slopes of demand curves differ, depending on whether you measure quantity in pizzas or in pizza slices. Clearly, then, slope does not really measure responsiveness of quantity demanded to price, because the measure changes whenever the units of measurement change.

Economists created the elasticity concept precisely in response to this problem. Elasticity measures responsiveness on the basis of *percentage* changes in price and quantity rather than on *absolute* changes. The elasticity formula solves the units problem because percentages are unaffected by units of measurement. If the government defense budget doubles, it goes up by 100 percent, whether measured in millions or billions of dollars. If demand for pizza triples, it rises by 200 percent, whether we measure the quantity demanded in number of pies or slices. The elasticity formula given earlier therefore expresses both the change in quantity demanded and the change in price as *percentages*.[1]

Furthermore, elasticity calculates the change in quantity demanded *as a percentage of the average of the two quantities:* the quantity demanded *before* the change in price has occurred (Q_0) and the quantity demanded *after* the price change (Q_1). In our example, the "before" pizza purchase is 280 (Q_0), the quantity sold after the price fall is 360 (Q_1), and the average of these two numbers is 320. The increase in number of pizzas bought is 80 pizzas, which is 25 percent of the 320 average of the sales before and after the price change. So 25 percent is the number we use as the purchase increase measure in our elasticity calculation. This procedure is a useful compromise between viewing the change in quantity demanded (80 pizzas) as a percentage of the initial quantity (280) or as a percentage of the final quantity (360).

Similarly, the change in price is expressed as a percentage of the average of the "before" and "after" prices, so that, in effect, it represents elasticity at the price halfway between those two prices; that is, the price falls by $4 (from $14 to $10). Because $4 is 33 percent of the average of $14 ($P_0$) and $10 ($P_1$) (that is, $12), we say that in this case a 33 percent fall in price led to a 25 percent rise in quantity of pizza demanded.

To summarize, the elasticity formula has two basic attributes:

- **Each of the changes with which it deals is measured as a *percentage* change.**
- **Each of the percentage changes is calculated in terms of the average values of the before and after quantities and prices.**

In addition, economists often adjust the price elasticity of demand formula in a third way. Note that when the price *increases*, the quantity demanded usually *declines*. Thus, when the price change is a positive number, the quantity change will normally be a negative number; when the price change is a negative number, the quantity change will normally be a positive number. As a consequence, the ratio of the two percentage changes will be a negative number. We customarily express elasticity as a positive number, however. Hence:

- **Each percentage change is taken as an "absolute value," meaning that the calculation drops all minus signs.[2]**

---

[1] The remainder of this section involves fairly technical computational issues. On a first reading, you may prefer to go directly to the new section that begins on the next page.

[2] This third attribute of the elasticity formula—the removal of all minus signs—applies only when the formula is used to measure the responsiveness of *quantity demanded* of product X to a change in the *price* of product X. Later in the chapter, we will show that similar formulas are used to measure the responsiveness between other pairs of variables. For example, the elasticity of supply uses a similar formula to measure the responsiveness of quantity supplied to price. In such cases, it is not customary to drop minus signs when calculating elasticity. The reasons will become clearer later in the chapter.

We can now state the formula for price elasticity of demand, keeping all three features of the formula in mind:

Price elasticity of demand = Change in quantity demanded, expressed as a percentage of the average of the before and after quantities *divided by* the corresponding percentage change in price.

In our example:

Elasticity of demand for pizzas =

$$\frac{(Q_1-Q_0)/\text{average of } Q_0 \text{ and } Q_1}{(P_1-P_0)/\text{average of } P_0 \text{ and } P_1} = \frac{80/320}{4/12} = \frac{25\%}{33\%} = 0.76 \text{ (approximately)}$$

Price Elasticity of Demand and the Shapes of Demand Curves

We noted earlier that looks can be deceiving in some demand curves because their units of measurement are arbitrary. Economists have provided the elasticity formula to overcome that problem. Nonetheless, the shape of a demand curve does convey some information about its elasticity. Let's see what information some demand curve shapes give with the aid of Figure 3.

1. Perfectly Elastic Demand Curves   Panel (a) of Figure 3 depicts a horizontal demand curve. Such a curve is called *perfectly elastic* (or *infinitely elastic*). At any price higher than $0.75, quantity demanded will drop to zero; that is, the comparative change in quantity demanded will be infinitely large. Perfect elasticity typically occurs when many producers sell a product and consumers can switch easily from one seller to another if any particular producer raises the price. For example, suppose you and the other students in your economics class are required to buy a newspaper every day to keep up with economic events. If news dealer X, from whom you have been buying the newspaper, raises the price from 75 cents to 80 cents, but the competitor, Y, across the street keeps the old price, then X may lose all her newspaper customers to Y. This situation is likely to prevail whenever an acceptable rival product is available at the going price (75 cents in the diagram). In cases in which no one will pay more than the going price, the seller will lose all of her customers if she raises her price by even a penny.

FIGURE 3

Demand Curves with Different Elasticities

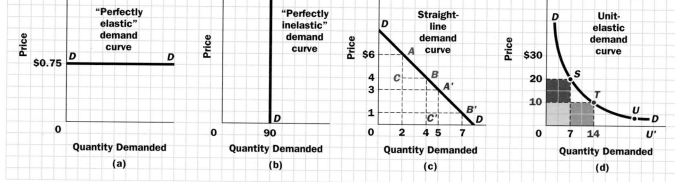

2. Perfectly Inelastic Demand Curves

Figure 3(b) shows the opposite extreme: a completely vertical demand curve. Such a curve is called *perfectly inelastic* throughout because its elasticity is zero at every point on the curve. Because quantity demanded remains at 90 units no matter what the price, the percentage change in quantity is always zero, and hence the elasticity (which equals percentage change in quantity divided by percentage change in price) is always zero. In this case, consumer purchases do not respond at all to any change in price.

Vertical demand curves, such as the one shown in Figure 3(b), occur when a commodity is very inexpensive. For example, you probably will not buy more rubber bands if their prices fall. The demand curve may also be vertical when consumers consider the item in question to be an absolute necessity. For example, if your roommate's grandfather has a heart attack, the family will buy whatever medicine the doctor prescribes, regardless of the price, and will not purchase any more even if the price falls.

3. (Seemingly Simple) Straight-Line Demand Curves

Figure 3(c) depicts a case between these two extremes: a *straight-line* demand curve that runs neither vertically nor horizontally. Note that, although the *slope* of a straight-line demand curve remains constant throughout its length, its *elasticity* does not. For example, the elasticity of demand between points *A* and *B* in Figure 3(c) is

$$\frac{\text{Change in } Q \text{ as a percentage of average } Q}{\text{Change in } P \text{ as a percentage of average } P} = \frac{2/3}{2/5} = \frac{66.67\%}{40\%} = 1.67$$

The elasticity of demand between points *A'* and *B'* is

$$\frac{2 \text{ as a percentage of } 6}{2 \text{ as a percentage of } 2} = \frac{33.33 \text{ percent}}{100 \text{ percent}} = 0.33$$

The general point is that

> Along a straight-line demand curve, the price elasticity of demand grows steadily smaller as you move from left to right. That is so because the quantity keeps getting larger, so that a given *numerical* change in quantity becomes an ever-smaller *percentage* change. But, simultaneously, the price keeps going lower, so that a given numerical change in price becomes an ever-larger percentage change. So, as one moves from left to right along the demand curve, the numerator of the elasticity fraction keeps falling and the denominator keeps growing larger; thus the fraction that is the elasticity formula keeps declining.

A **demand curve** is **elastic** when a given percentage price change leads to a larger percentage change in quantity demanded.

A **demand curve** is **inelastic** when a given percentage price change leads to a smaller percentage change in quantity demanded.

A demand curve is **unit-elastic** when a given percentage price change leads to the same percentage change in quantity demanded.

4. Unit-Elastic Demand Curves

If the elasticity of a straight-line demand curve varies from one part of the curve to another, what does a demand curve with the same elasticity throughout its length look like? For reasons explained in the next section, it has the general shape indicated in Figure 3(d). That panel shows a curve with elasticity equal to 1 throughout (a *unit-elastic* demand curve). A unit-elastic demand curve bends in the middle toward the origin of the graph—at either end, it moves closer and closer to the axes but never touches or crosses them.

As we have noted, a curve with an elasticity greater than 1 is called an **elastic demand curve** (one for which the percentage change in quantity demanded will be greater than the percentage change in price); a curve whose elasticity is less than 1 is known as an **inelastic curve.** When elasticity is exactly 1, economists say that the curve is **unit-elastic.**

Real-world price elasticities of demand seem to vary considerably from product to product. Because people can get along without them, moderately luxurious goods, such as expensive vacations, are generally more price elastic—people give them up more readily when their prices rise—than goods such as milk and shirts, which are considered necessities. Products with close substitutes, such as Coke and Pepsi, tend to have relatively high elasticities because if one soft drink becomes expensive, many of its consumers will switch to the other. Also, the elasticities of demand for goods that business firms buy, such as raw materials and machinery, tend to be higher on the whole than those for consumers' goods. This is because competition forces firms to buy their supplies wherever they can get them most cheaply. The exception occurs when a firm requires a particular input for which no reasonable substitutes exist or the available substitutes are substantially inferior. Table 1 gives actual statistical estimates of elasticities for some industries in the economy.

TABLE 1

Estimates of Price Elasticities

Product	Price Elasticity
Industrial chemicals	0.4
Shoe repairs and cleaning	0.4
Food, tobacco, and beverages	0.5
Newspapers and magazines	0.5
Data processing, precision and optical instruments	0.7
Medical care and hospitalization insurance	0.8
Metal products	1.1
Purchased meals (excluding alcoholic beverages)	1.6
Electricity (household utility)	1.9
Boats, pleasure aircraft	2.4
Public transportation	3.5
China, tableware	8.8

SOURCES: H. S. Houthakker and Lester D. Taylor, *Consumer Demand in the United States*, 2d ed. (Cambridge, MA: Harvard University Press, 1970), pp. 153–158; and Joachim Möller, "Income and Price Elasticities in Different Sectors of the Economy: An Analysis of Structural Change for Germany, the UK and the USA," in Thjis ten Raa and Ronald Schettkat (eds.), *The Growth of Service Industries: The Paradox of Exploding Costs and Persistent Demand*, 2001, pp.167–208.

PRICE ELASTICITY OF DEMAND: ITS EFFECT ON TOTAL REVENUE AND TOTAL EXPENDITURE

Aside from its role as a measure of the responsiveness of demand to a change in price, elasticity serves a second, very important purpose. As a real illustration at the end of this chapter will show, a firm often wants to know whether an increase in price will increase or decrease its total revenue—the money it obtains from sales to its customers. The price elasticity of demand provides a simple guide to the answer:

If demand for the seller's product is elastic, a price *increase* will *actually decrease* total revenue. If demand is exactly unit-elastic, a rise in price will leave total revenue unaffected. If demand is inelastic, a rise in price will raise total revenue. The opposite changes will occur when price falls.

A corresponding story must be true about the expenditures made by the *buyers* of the product. After all, the expenditures of the buyers are exactly the same thing as the revenues of the seller.

These relationships between elasticity and total revenue hold because total revenue (or expenditure) equals price times quantity demanded, $P \times Q$, and because a drop in price has two opposing effects on the two components of that formula. It decreases P, and, if the demand curve is negatively sloped, it increases Q. The first effect *decreases* revenues by cutting the amount of money that consumers spend on each unit of the good. The second effect *increases* revenues by raising the number of units of the good that the firm sells.

The net effect on total revenue (or total expenditure) depends on the elasticity. If price goes down by 10 percent and quantity demanded increases by 10 percent (a case of *unit elasticity*), the two effects cancel out: $P \times Q$ remains constant. In contrast, if price goes down by 10 percent and quantity demanded rises by 15 percent (a case of *elastic* demand), $P \times Q$ increases. Finally, if a 10 percent price fall leads to only a 5 percent rise in quantity demanded (*inelastic* demand), $P \times Q$ falls.

We can easily see the relationship between elasticity and total revenue in a graph. First, note that

The total revenue (or expenditure) represented by any point on a demand curve (any price-quantity combination), such as point *S* in Figure 4, equals the area of the rectangle under that point (the area of rectangle *ORST* in the figure). This is true because the

FIGURE 4

An Elastic Demand
Curve

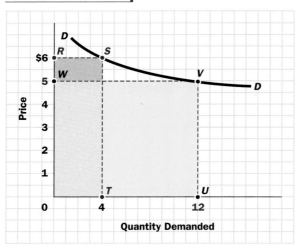

FIGURE 4

An Elastic Demand
Curve

area of a rectangle equals its height times the width, or *OR* × *RS* in Figure 4. Clearly, that is price times quantity, which is exactly total revenue.

To illustrate the connection between elasticity and consumer expenditure, Figure 4 shows an elastic portion of a demand curve, *DD*. In this figure, when price falls, quantity demanded rises by a greater percentage, increasing total expenditure. At a price of $6 per unit, the quantity sold is 4 units, so total expenditure is 4 × $6 = $24, represented by the vertical rectangle whose upper-right corner is point *S*. When price falls to $5 per unit, 12 units are sold. Consequently, the new expenditure ($60 = $5 × 12), measured by the rectangle 0*WVU*, exceeds the old expenditure.

In contrast, Figure 3(d), the unit-elastic demand curve, shows constant expenditures even though price changes. Total spending is $140 whether the price is $20 and 7 units are sold (point *S*) or the price is $10 and 14 units are sold (point *T*).

This discussion also indicates why a unit-elastic demand curve must have the shape depicted in Figure 3(d), hugging the axes closer and closer but never touching or crossing them. When demand is unit-elastic, total expenditure must be the same at every point on the curve; that is, it must equal $140 at point *S* and point *T* and point *U* in Figure 3(d). Suppose that at point *U* (or some other point on the curve), the demand curve were to touch the horizontal axis, meaning that the price would equal zero. Then total expenditure would be zero, not $140. Therefore, if the demand curve remains unit-elastic along its entire length, it can never cross the horizontal axis (where *P* = 0). By the same reasoning, it cannot cross the vertical axis (where *Q* = 0). Because the slope of the demand curve is negative, any unit-elastic curve simply must get closer and closer to the axes as it moves away from its middle points, as illustrated in Figure 3(d), though it will never touch either axis.

We can now see why demand elasticity is so important for business decisions. A firm should not jump to the conclusion that a price increase will automatically add to its profits, or it may find that consumers take their revenge by cutting back a great deal on their purchases. In fact, if its demand curve is elastic, a firm that raises price will end up selling so many fewer units that its total revenue will actually fall, even though it makes more money than before on each unit it sells.

Price *cuts* can also be hazardous—if the elasticity of demand is low. For example, among adult smokers cigarettes have an estimated price elasticity of between 0.25 and 0.50 meaning that we can expect a 10 percent drop in price to induce only a 2.5–5 percent rise in demand.[3] This relationship may explain why, when Philip Morris cut the price of Marlboros by about 18 percent, the company's profits dropped by 25 percent within months. Thus, the strategic value to a business firm of a price rise or a price cut depends very much on the elasticity of demand for its product. But elasticity tells us only how a price change affects a firm's *revenues*; we must also consider the effect of costs on the firm's output decisions, as we will do in Chapter 8.

ISSUE REVISITED: WILL A CIGARETTE TAX DECREASE

TEENAGE SMOKING SIGNIFICANTLY?

We're back to the issue with which we began this chapter: Will a tax on cigarettes, which increases their price, effectively reduce teenage smoking? We can express the answer to this question in terms of the price elasticity of demand for cigarettes by teenagers. If that demand elasticity is high, the

---

[3] Source: Frank J. Chaloupka, K. Michael Cummings, Christopher P. Morley, and Judith K. Horan, "Tax, Price and Cigarette Smoking: Evidence from the Tobacco Documents and Implications for Tobacco Company Marketing Strategies," *Tobacco Control*, 11 (Supplement 1), (2002), pp. i62–i72.

tax will be effective, because a small increase in cigarette taxes will lead to a sharp cut in purchases by teenagers. The opposite will clearly be true if this demand elasticity is small.

It turns out that young people *are* more sensitive to price increases than adult smokers. The estimates of teenagers' price elasticity of demand for cigarettes range from about 0.5 all the way up to 1.7.[4] This means that if, for example, a tax on cigarettes raises their price by 10 percent, the number of teenage smokers will fall by somewhere between 5 and 17 percent. As we just noted, adults have been found to have a price elasticity of demand for cigarettes of between 0.25 and 0.50—their response to the 10 percent increase in the price of cigarettes will be a decrease of only 2.5–5 percent in the number of adult smokers. So we can expect that a substantial tax on cigarettes that resulted in a significant price increase would cause a higher percentage of teenagers than adults to stop smoking.

We said earlier in the chapter that if a cigarette tax program failed to curb teen smoking, it would benefit the government's tax collectors a great deal. On the other hand, if the program successfully curbed teenage smoking, then government finances would benefit only a little. The logic of this argument should now be clear. If teen cigarette demand were inelastic, the tax program would fail to make a dent in teen smoking. That would mean that many teenagers would continue to buy cigarettes and government tax revenue would grow substantially as a result of the rise in tax rate. But when elasticity is high, a price rise *decreases* total revenue (in this case, the amount of tax revenues collected) because quantity demanded falls by a greater percentage than the price rises. That is, with an elastic demand, relatively few teen smokers will remain after the tax increase, so there will be few of them to pay the new taxes. The government will "lose out." Of course, in this case the tax seeks to change behavior, so the government would no doubt rejoice at its small revenues!

WHAT DETERMINES DEMAND ELASTICITY?

What kinds of goods have elastic demand curves, meaning that quantity demanded responds strongly to price? What kinds of goods have inelastic demand curves? Several influences affect consumers' sensitivity to price changes.

1. Nature of the Good   *Necessities,* such as basic foodstuffs, normally have relatively inelastic demand curves, meaning that the quantities consumers demand of these products respond very little to price changes. For example, people buy roughly the same quantity of potatoes even when the price of potatoes rises. One study estimated that the price elasticity of demand for potatoes is just 0.3, meaning that when the price rises 10 percent, the quantity of potatoes purchased falls only 3 percent. In contrast, many *luxury goods,* such as restaurant meals, have rather elastic demand curves. One estimate found that the price elasticity of demand for restaurant meals is 1.6, so that we can expect a 10 percent price rise to cut purchases by 16 percent.

2. Availability of Close Substitutes   If consumers can easily obtain an acceptable substitute for a product whose price increases, they will switch readily. Thus, when the

[4] Source: Lisa M. Powell, John A. Tauras, and Hana Ross, "The Importance of Peer Effects, Cigarette Prices and Tobacco Control Policies for Youth Smoking Behavior," *Journal of Health Economics*, 24, no. 5 (September 2005), pp. 950–968.

market offers close substitutes for a given product, its demand will be more elastic. Substitutability is often a critical determinant of elasticity. The demand for gasoline is inelastic because we cannot easily run a car without it, but the demand for *any particular brand* of gasoline is extremely elastic, because other brands will work just as well. This example suggests a general principle: The demand for narrowly defined commodities (such as romaine lettuce) is more elastic than the demand for more broadly defined commodities (such as vegetables).

Selling Short

"Why does it have to be us who prove that price elasticity really works?"

3. Share of Consumer's Budget   The share of the consumer's budget represented by the purchase of a particular item also affects its elasticity. Very inexpensive items that absorb little of a consumer's budget tend to have inelastic demand curves. Who is going to buy fewer paper clips if their price rises 10 percent? Hardly anyone. However, many families will be forced to postpone buying a new car, or will buy a used car instead, if auto prices go up by 10 percent.

4. Passage of Time   The time period is relevant because the demand for many products is more elastic in the long run than in the short run. For example, when the price of home heating oil rose in the 1970s, some homeowners switched from oil heat to gas heat. Very few of them switched immediately, however, because they needed to retrofit their furnaces to accommodate the other fuel. So, the short-term demand for oil for home heating was quite inelastic. As time passed and more homeowners had the opportunity to purchase and install new furnaces, the demand curve gradually became more elastic.

ELASTICITY AS A GENERAL CONCEPT

So far we have looked only at how quantity demanded responds to price changes—that is, the *price* elasticity of demand. But elasticity has a more general use in measuring how any one economic variable responds to changes in another. From our earlier discussion, we know that a firm will be keenly interested in the price elasticity of its demand curve, but its interest in demand does not end there. As we have noted, quantity demanded depends on other things besides price. Business firms will be interested in consumer responsiveness to changes in these variables as well.

1. Income Elasticity

Income elasticity of demand is the ratio of the percentage change in quantity demanded to the percentage change in income.

For example, quantity demanded depends on consumer incomes. A business firm's managers will, therefore, want to know how much a change in consumer income will affect the quantity of its product demanded. Fortunately, an elasticity measure can be helpful here, too. An increase in consumer incomes clearly raises the amounts of most goods that consumers will demand. To measure the response, economists use the **income elasticity of demand,** which is the ratio of the percentage change in quantity demanded to the percentage change in income. For example, foreign travel is quite income-elastic, with middle-income and higher-income people traveling abroad much more extensively than poor people. In contrast, blue jeans, worn by rich and poor alike, show little demand increase as income increases.

2. Price Elasticity of Supply

Economists also use elasticity to measure other responses. For example, to measure the response of quantity *supplied* to a change in price, we use the *price elasticity of supply*—defined as the ratio of the percentage change in quantity supplied to the percentage change in price, for example, by what percent the supply of wheat increases when the price (at the time of planting) goes up by, say, 7 percent. The logic and analysis of all such elasticity concepts are, of course, perfectly analogous to those for price elasticity of demand.

3. Cross Elasticity of Demand

Consumers' demands for many products are substantially affected by the quantities and prices of *other* available products. This brings us to the important concept called *cross elasticity of demand,* which measures how much the demand for product X is affected by a change in the price of another good, Y.

This elasticity number is significantly affected by the fact that some products make other products *more* desirable, but some products *decrease* consumer demand for other products. There are some products that just naturally go together; for example, for many consumers cream and sugar increase the desirability of coffee, and vice versa. The same is true of mustard or ketchup and hamburgers. In some extreme cases, neither product ordinarily has any use without the other—automobiles and tires, shoes and shoelaces, and so on. Such goods, each of which makes the other more valuable, are called **complements.**

> Two goods are called **complements** if an increase in the quantity consumed of one increases the quantity demanded of the other, all other things remaining constant.

The demand curves of complements are interrelated; that is, a rise in the price of coffee is likely to reduce the quantity of sugar demanded. Why? When coffee prices rise, people drink less coffee and therefore demand less sugar to sweeten it. The opposite will be true of a fall in coffee prices. A similar relationship holds for other complementary goods.

At the other extreme, some goods make other goods *less* valuable. These products are called **substitutes.** Ownership of a motorcycle, for example, may decrease one's desire for a bicycle. If your pantry is stocked with cans of tuna fish, you are less likely to rush out and buy cans of salmon. As you may expect, demand curves for substitutes are also related, but in the opposite direction. When the price of motorcycles falls, people may desire fewer bicycles, so the quantity of bicycles demanded falls while that for motorcycles rises. When the price of salmon goes up, people may eat more tuna.

> Two goods are called **substitutes** if an increase in the quantity consumed of one cuts the quantity demanded of the other, all other things remaining constant.

Economists use **cross elasticity of demand** to determine whether two products are substitutes or complements. This measure is defined much like the ordinary price elasticity of demand, except that instead of measuring the responsiveness of the quantity demanded of, say, coffee, to a change in its own price, cross elasticity of demand measures how quantity demanded of one good (coffee) responds to a change in the price of another, say, sugar. For example, if a 20 percent rise in the price of sugar reduces the quantity of coffee demanded by 5 percent (a change of *minus* 5 percent in quantity demanded), then the cross elasticity of demand will be

> The **cross elasticity of demand** for product X to a change in the price of another product, Y, is the ratio of the percentage change in quantity demanded of X to the percentage change in the price of Y that brings about the change in quantity demanded.

$$\frac{\text{Percentage change in quantity of coffee demanded}}{\text{Percentage change in sugar price}} = \frac{-5\%}{20\%} = -0.25$$

Obviously, cross elasticity is important for business firms, especially when rival firms' prices are concerned. American Airlines, for example, knows all too well that it will lose customers if it does not match price cuts by Continental or United. Coke and Pepsi provide another clear case in which cross elasticity of demand is crucial, but firms other than direct competitors may well take a substantial interest in cross elasticity. For example, the prices of DVD players and DVD rentals may profoundly affect the quantity of theater tickets that consumers demand.

The cross elasticity of demand measure underlies the following rule about complements and substitutes:

If two goods are substitutes, a rise in the price of one of them tends to increase the quantity demanded of the other, so their cross elasticities of demand will normally be positive. If two goods are complements, a rise in the price of one of them tends to decrease the quantity demanded of the other item, so their cross elasticities will normally be negative. Notice that, because cross elasticities can be positive or negative, we do *not* customarily drop minus signs as we do in a calculation of the ordinary price elasticity of demand.

This result is really a matter of common sense. If the price of a good rises and buyers can find a substitute, they will tend to switch to the substitute. If the price of Japanese-made cameras goes up and the price of American-made cameras does not, at least some people will switch to the American product. Thus, a *rise* in the price of Japanese cameras causes a *rise* in the quantity of American cameras demanded. Both percentage changes are positive numbers and so their ratio—the cross elasticity of demand—is also positive.

However, if two goods are complements, a rise in the price of one will discourage both its own use and use of the complementary good. Automobiles and car radios are obviously complements. A large increase in automobile prices will depress car sales, and this in turn will reduce sales of car radios. Thus, a positive percentage change in the price of cars leads to a negative percentage change in the quantity of car radios demanded. The ratio of these numbers—the cross elasticity of demand for cars and radios—is therefore negative.

In practice, courts of law often evaluate cross elasticity of demand to determine whether particular business firms face strong competition that can prevent them from overcharging consumers—hence, the quotation from the U.S. Supreme Court at the beginning of this chapter. The quotation is one of the earliest examples of the courts using the concept of cross elasticities. It tells us that if two substitute (that is, rival) products have a high cross elasticity of demand (for example, between McDonald's and Burger King), then neither firm can raise its price much without losing customers to the other. In such a case, no one can legitimately claim that either firm has a monopoly. If a rise in Firm X's price causes its consumers to switch in droves to a Firm Y's product, then the cross elasticity of demand for Firm Y's product with respect to the price of Firm X's product will be high. That, in turn, means that competition is really powerful enough to prevent Firm X from raising its price arbitrarily. This relationship explains why cross elasticity is used so often in litigation before courts or government regulatory agencies when the degree of competition is an important issue, because the higher the cross elasticity of demand between two products, the stronger must be the competition between them. So cross elasticity is an effective measure of the strength of such competition.

The cross elasticity issue keeps coming up in the antitrust context whenever courts need to determine whether or not a firm has monopoly power. For example, in a 2007 dispute between Sun Microsystems and Versata Enterprises, Versata's claim charging monopolistic behavior by Sun Microsystems was dismissed because Versata failed to adequately address cross elasticities. The issue also appeared when the United States Federal Trade Commission challenged a merger between Whole Foods Market and Wild Oats Markets, claiming that the combination would create a monopoly. (See "How Large Is A Firm's Market Share? Cross Elasticity as a Test," on page 119, for more on cross elasticity.)

THE TIME PERIOD OF THE DEMAND CURVE AND ECONOMIC DECISION MAKING

One more important feature of a demand curve does not appear on a graph. A demand curve indicates, at each possible price, the quantity of the good that is demanded *during a particular time period*; that is, all of the alternative prices considered in a demand curve must refer to the same time period. Economists do not compare a price of $10 for Commodity X in January with a price of $8 in September.

How Large Is a Firm's Market Share? Cross Elasticity as a Test

A firm's "market share" is often a crucial element in antitrust lawsuits (see Chapter 13) for a simple reason. If the firm supplies no more than, say, 20 percent of the industry's output, courts and regulators presume that the firm is not a monopoly, as its customers can switch their business to competitors if the firm tries to charge too high a price. On the other hand, if the defendant firm in the lawsuit accounts for 90 percent of the industry's output, courts may have good reason to worry about monopoly power (which we cover in Chapter 11).

Such court cases often provide lively debates in which the defendant firms try to prove that they have very small market shares and the plaintiffs seek to establish the opposite. Each side knows how much the defendant firm actually produces and sells, so what do they find to argue about? The dispute is about *the size of the total relevant market,* which clearly affects the magnitude of the firm's market *share.* Ambiguity arises here because different firms do not produce identical products. For instance, are Rice Krispies in the same market as Cheerios? And how about Quaker Oatmeal, which users eat hot? What about frozen waffles? Are all of these products part of the same market? If they are, then the overall market is large, and each seller therefore has a smaller share. If these products are in different markets, the opposite will be true.

Many observers argue, as the Supreme Court did in the famous DuPont cellophane case, that one proper criterion for determining the borders of the relevant market is *cross elasticity of demand.* More recently, in 2008, this issue reappeared in the government's suit challenging Whole Foods Market's acquisition of Wild Oats Markets, a case which hinged largely on whether the relevant market consisted of only "premium, natural and organic supermarkets" or whether it included conventional supermarkets, as well. If two products have a high and positive cross elasticity, they must be close enough substitutes to compete closely; that is, they must be in the same market. But how large must the cross elasticity be before the court decides that two products are in the same market? Although the law has not established a clear elasticity benchmark to determine whether a particular firm is in a relevant market, several courts have determined that a very high cross elasticity number clearly indicates effective competition between two products, meaning that the two items must be in the same market.

SOURCE: FTC v. Whole Foods Market, Inc., 548 F.3d 1028 (D.C. Cir. 2008).

SOURCE: © Jon Fisher/Workbook Stock/Jupiterimages

This feature imparts a peculiar character to the demand curve and complicates statistical calculations. For obvious reasons, actual observed data show different prices and quantities only for different dates. Statistical data may show, for example, the one price that prevailed in January and another that occurred at a later date, when that price had changed. Why, then, do economists adopt the apparently peculiar approach of dealing in a demand curve only with the hypothetical prices that may conceivably occur (as alternative possibilities) in one and the same time period? The answer is that the demand curve's strictly defined time dimension arises inescapably from the logic of decision making and the use of demand curves as a tool in attempts to reach an **optimal decision**—the decision that moves the decision maker as close to the goal as is possible under the circumstances.

When a business seeks to price one of its products for, say, the following six months, it must consider the range of *alternative* prices available for that six-month period and the consequences of each of these possible prices. For example, if management is reasonably certain that the best price for the six-month period lies somewhere between $3.50 and $5.00, it should perhaps consider each of four possibilities—$3.50, $4.00, $4.50, and $5.00—and estimate how much it can expect to sell at each of these potential prices during that given six-month period. The result of these estimates may appear in a format similar to that of the following table:

This table supplies managers with the information that they need to make optimal pricing decisions. Because the price selected will be the one at which goods are sold *during the period in question,* all the prices considered in that decision must be alternative possible prices for that same period. The table therefore also contains precisely the information an economist uses to draw a demand curve.

An **optimal decision** is the one that best serves the objectives of the decision maker, whatever those objectives may be. It is selected by explicit or implicit comparison with the possible alternative choices. The term *optimal* connotes neither approval nor disapproval of the objective itself.

Potential Six-Month Price	Expected Quantity Demanded
$3.50	75,000
4.00	73,000
4.50	70,000
5.00	60,000

The demand curve describes a set of hypothetical quantity responses to a set of potential prices, but the firm can actually charge only one of these prices. All of the points on the demand curve refer to alternative possibilities for the *same time period*—the period for which the decision is to be made.

Thus, a demand curve of the sort just described is not just an abstract notion that is useful primarily in academic discussions. Rather, it offers precisely the information that businesses or government agencies need to make rational decisions. However, the fact that all points on the demand curve are hypothetical possibilities for the same period of time causes problems for statistical estimation of demand curves. These problems are discussed in the appendix to this chapter.

REAL-WORLD APPLICATION: POLAROID VERSUS KODAK[5]

Let's look at an example from the real world to show how the elasticity concept helps to resolve a concrete problem rather different from those we have been discussing. In 1989, a lengthy trial in a U.S. district court resulted in a judgment against the photographic products manufacturing company Eastman-Kodak for patent infringement of technology that rival firm Polaroid had designed. The court then set out to determine the amount of money Kodak owed Polaroid for its patent infringement during the 10-year period 1976 to 1986, when Kodak had sold very similar instant cameras and film. The key issue was how much profit Polaroid had lost as a result of Kodak's entry into the field of instant photography, because that would determine how much Kodak would be required to pay Polaroid. Both price elasticity of demand and cross elasticity of demand played crucial roles in the court's decisions.

The court needed accurate estimates of the price elasticity of demand to determine whether the explosive growth in instant camera sales between 1976 and 1979 was mainly attributable to the fall in price that resulted from Kodak's competition or was attributable to Kodak's good reputation and the resulting rise in consumer confidence in the quality of instant cameras. If the latter were true, then Polaroid might actually have *benefited* from Kodak's entry into the instant camera market rather than *losing* profits, because Kodak's presence in the market would have increased the total number of potential customers aware of and eager to try instant cameras.

After 1980, instant camera and film sales began to drop sharply. On this issue, the *cross elasticity of demand* between instant and conventional (35-millimeter) cameras and film was crucial to the explanation. Why? Because the decline in the instant camera market occurred just as the prices of 35-millimeter cameras, film, developing, and printing all began to fall significantly. So, if the decline in Polaroid's overall sales was attributable to the decreasing cost of 35-millimeter photography, then Kodak's instant photography activity was *not* to blame. In that case, the amount that Kodak would be required to pay to Polaroid would decrease significantly. But if the cross elasticity of demand between 35-millimeter photography prices and the demand for instant cameras and film was low, then the cause of the decline in Polaroid's sales might well have been Kodak's patent-infringing activity—thus *adding* to the damage compensation payments to which Polaroid was entitled.

On the basis of its elasticity calculations, Polaroid at one point claimed that Kodak was obligated to pay it $9 *billion* or more. Kodak, however, claimed that it owed Polaroid something in the neighborhood of $450 million. A lot of money was at stake. The judge's verdict came out with a number very close to Kodak's figure.

---

[5] Here it should be pointed out that William Baumol was a witness in this court case, testifying on behalf of Kodak.

IN CONCLUSION

In this chapter, we have continued our study of the demand side of the market. Rather than focusing on what underlies demand formation, as we did in Chapter 5, we applied demand analysis to business decisions. Most notably, we described and analyzed the economist's measure of the responsiveness of consumer demand to changes in price, and we showed how this assessment determines the effect of a firm's price change on the revenues of that enterprise. We illustrated how these concepts throw light not only on business sales and revenues but also on a number of rather different issues, such as smoking and health, the effectiveness of competition among business firms as studied by courts of law, and the determination of penalties for patent infringement. In the next chapter, we turn to the supply side of the market and move a step closer to completing the framework we need to understand how markets work.

| SUMMARY |

1. To measure the responsiveness of the quantity demanded to price, economists calculate the **elasticity of demand,** which is defined as the percentage change in quantity demanded divided by the percentage change in price, after elimination of the minus sign.

2. If demand is **elastic** (elasticity is greater than 1), then a rise in price will reduce total expenditures on the product (= sellers' total revenue). If demand is **unit-elastic** (elasticity is equal to 1), then a rise in price will not change total expenditures. If demand is **inelastic** (elasticity is less than 1), then a rise in price will increase total expenditure.

3. Goods that make each other more desirable (hot dogs and mustard, wristwatches and watch straps) are called **complements.** When two goods are such that when consumers get more of one of them, they want less of the other (steaks and hamburgers, Coke and Pepsi), economists call those goods **substitutes.**

4. **Cross elasticity of demand** is defined as the percentage change in the quantity demanded of one good divided by the percentage change in the price of another good. Two substitute products normally have a positive cross elasticity of demand. Two complementary products normally have a negative cross elasticity of demand.

5. A rise in the price of one of two substitute products can be expected to *shift the demand curve* of the other product to the right. A rise in the price of one of two complementary goods tends to shift the other good's demand curve to the left.

6. All points on a demand curve refer to the *same time period*—the time during which the price that is being decided upon or otherwise considered will be in effect.

| KEY TERMS |

complements   117

cross elasticity of demand   117

(price) elasticity of demand   109

elastic, inelastic, and unit-elastic demand curves   112

income elasticity of demand   116

optimal decision   119

substitutes   117

| TEST YOURSELF |

1. What variables other than price and advertising are likely to affect the quantity demanded of a product?

2. Describe the probable shifts in the demand curves for
   a. Airplane trips when airlines' on-time performance improves
   b. Automobiles when airplane fares increase
   c. Automobiles when gasoline prices increase
   d. Electricity when the average temperature in the United States rises during a particular year (*Note:* The demand curve for electricity in Maine and the demand curve for electricity in Florida should respond in different ways. Why?)

3. Taxes on particular goods discourage their consumption. Economists say that such taxes "distort consumer demands." In terms of the elasticity of demand or elasticity of supply for the commodities in question, what sort of goods would you choose to tax to achieve the following objectives?
   a. Collect a large amount of tax revenue
   b. Distort demand as little as possible

c. Discourage consumption of harmful commodities

d. Discourage production of polluting commodities

4. Give examples of commodities whose demand you would expect to be elastic and commodities whose demand you would expect to be inelastic.

5. A rise in the price of a certain commodity from $20 to $25 reduces quantity demanded from 25,000 to 10,000 units. Calculate the price elasticity of demand.

6. If the price elasticity of demand for gasoline is 0.3 and the current price is $3.20 per gallon, what rise in the price of gasoline will reduce its consumption by 10 percent?

7. Which of the following product pairs would you expect to be substitutes, and which would you expect to be complements?

a. Shoes and sneakers

b. Gasoline and sport-utility vehicles

c. Bread and butter

d. Instant camera film and regular camera film

8. For each of the product pairs given in Test Yourself Question 7, what would you guess about the products' cross elasticity of demand?

a. Do you expect it to be positive or negative?

b. Do you expect it to be a large or small number? Why?

| DISCUSSION QUESTIONS |

1. Explain why elasticity of demand is measured in *percentages*.

2. Explain why the elasticity of demand formula normally eliminates minus signs.

3. Explain why the elasticity of a straight-line demand curve varies from one part of the curve to another.

4. A rise in the price of a product whose demand is elastic will reduce the total revenue of the firm. Explain.

5. Name some events that will cause a demand curve to shift.

6. Explain why the following statement is true: "A firm with a demand curve that is inelastic at its current output level can always increase its profits by raising its price and selling less." (*Hint:* Refer back to the discussion of elasticity and total expenditure/total revenue on pages 113–114.)

| APPENDIX | *How Can We Find a Legitimate Demand Curve from Historical Statistics?*

The peculiar time dimension of the demand curve, in conjunction with the fact that many variables other than price influence quantity demanded, makes it surprisingly difficult to derive a product's demand curve from historical statistical data. Specialists can and often do derive such estimates, but the task is full of booby traps and usually requires advanced statistical methods and interpretation. This appendix seeks to warn you about the booby traps. It implies, for example, that if you become the marketing manager of a business firm after you graduate from college and you need demand analysis, you will need experts to do the job. This appendix will also show you some mistakes to look for as you interpret the results, if you have reason to doubt the qualifications of the statisticians you hire to calculate or forecast your demand curve. It also gives an intuitive explanation of the legitimate ways in which demand curves may be determined from the statistics.

The most obvious way to go about estimating a demand curve statistically is to collect a set of figures on prices and quantities sold in different periods, like those given in Table 2. These points can be plotted on a diagram with price and quantity on the axes, as shown in Figure 5. We can then draw a line (the dashed line *TT*) that comes as close as possible to connecting these points (labeled Jan., Feb., and so on), and in this graph the line follows them reasonably well. This line may therefore appear to approximate the demand curve that we are seeking, but unfortunately line *TT*, which summarizes the data for different points of time, may bear no relationship to the true demand curve. Let us see why, and get some idea as to what can be done about it.

You may notice that the prices and quantities represented by the historical points in Figure 5 refer to different periods of time, and that each point on the graph represents an *actual* (not hypothetical) price and quantity sold at a particular period of time (for example, one point gives the data for January, another for February, and so on). The distinction is significant. Over the entire period covered by the historical data (January through May), the true demand curve, which is what an economist really needs to analyze decision

TABLE 2

Historical Data on Price and Quantity

	January	February	March	April	May
Quantity Sold	95,000	91,500	95,000	90,000	91,000
Price	$7.20	$8.00	$7.70	$8.00	$8.20

FIGURE 5

Plot of Historical Data on Price and Quantity

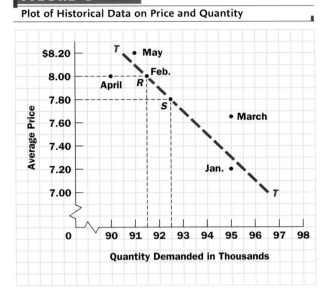

Quantity Demanded in Thousands

FIGURE 6

Plot of Historical Data and True Demand Curves for January, February, and March

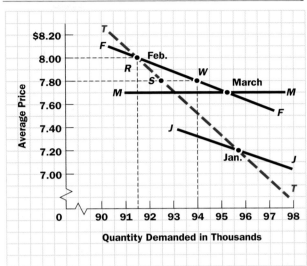

Quantity Demanded in Thousands

problems, may well have shifted because of changes in some of the other variables affecting quantity demanded.

The actual events may appear as shown in Figure 6. In January, the demand curve was given by *JJ*, but by February the curve had shifted to *FF*, by March to *MM*, and so on. This figure shows a separate and distinct demand curve for each of the relevant months, and none of them needs to resemble the line we drew as a plot of historical data, *TT*.

In fact, the slope of the historical plot curve, *TT*, can be very different from the slopes of the true underlying demand curves, as is the case in Figure 6. As a consequence, the decision maker can be seriously misled if she selects her price on the basis of the historical data. She may, for example, think that quantity demanded is quite insensitive to changes in price (as the steepness of line *TT* seems to indicate), and so may conclude that a price reduction is not advisable. In fact, the true demand curves show that a price reduction would increase quantity demanded substantially, because they are much more elastic than the shape of the estimated line *TT* in Figure 5 would suggest.

For example, if the decision maker were to charge a price of $7.80 rather than $8.00 in February, the historical plot would lead her to expect a rise in quantity demanded of only 1,000 units. (Compare point *R*, with sales of 91,500 units, and point *S*, with sales of 92,500 units, in Figure 5.) The true demand curve for February (line *FF* in Figure 6), however, indicates an increase in sales of 2,500 units (from point *R*, with sales of 91,500 units, to point *W*, with sales of 94,000 units). A manager who based her decision on the historical plot,

rather than on the true February demand curve, might be led into serious error. Nevertheless, it is astonishing how often people make this mistake in practice, even when using apparently sophisticated techniques.

AN ILLUSTRATION: DID THE ADVERTISING PROGRAM WORK?

Some years ago, one of the largest producers of packaged foods in the United States conducted a statistical study to judge the effectiveness of its advertising expenditures, which amounted to nearly $100 million per year. A company statistician collected year-by-year figures on company sales and advertising outlays and discovered, to his delight, that they showed a remarkably close relationship to one another: Quantity demanded always rose as advertising rose. The trouble was that the relationship seemed just too perfect. In economics, data about demand and any one of the elements that influence it almost never show such a neat pattern. Human tastes and other pertinent influences are too variable to permit such regularity.

Suspicious company executives asked one of the authors of this book to examine the analysis. A little thought showed that the suspiciously close statistical relationship between sales and advertising expenditures resulted from a disregard for the principles just presented. The investigator had, in fact, constructed a graph of *historical* data on sales and advertising expenditure, analogous to *TT* in Figures 5 and 6 and therefore not necessarily similar to the truly relevant relationship.

It became apparent, after study of the situation, that the stability of the relationship actually arose from the fact that, in the past, the company had based its advertising spending on its sales, automatically allocating a fixed percentage of its sales revenues to advertising. The *historical* relationship between advertising and demand therefore described only the company's budgeting practices, not the effectiveness of its advertising program. It showed the effect of sales on advertising, not the effect of advertising on sales, which was the desired information. If the firm's management had used this curve in planning future advertising campaigns, it might have made some regrettable decisions. *The moral of the story:* Avoid the use of purely historical curves like *TT* in making economic decisions.

HOW CAN WE FIND A LEGITIMATE DEMAND CURVE FROM THE STATISTICS?

The trouble with the discussion so far is that it tells you only what you *cannot* legitimately do, but business executives and economists often need information about demand curves—for example, to analyze a pricing decision for next April. How can the true demand curves be found? In practice, statisticians use complex methods that go well beyond what we can cover in an introductory course. Nevertheless, we can (and will) give you a feeling for the advanced methods used by statisticians via a simple illustration in which a straightforward approach helps to locate the demand curve statistically.

The problem described in this appendix occurs because demand curves and supply curves (like other curves in economics) shift from time to time. They always shift for some reason, however. As we saw in the chapter, they shift because quantity demanded or supplied is influenced by variables other than price, such as advertising, consumer incomes, and so forth. Recognizing this relationship can help us track down the demand curve—if we can determine the "other things" that affect the demand for, say, widgets, and observe when those other things changed and when they did not, we can infer when the demand curve may have been moving and when it probably wasn't.

Consider the demand for umbrellas. Umbrellas are rarely advertised and are relatively inexpensive, so neither advertising nor consumer incomes should

have much effect on their sales. In fact, it is reasonable to assume that the quantity of umbrellas demanded in a year depends largely on two influences: their price and the amount of rainfall. As we know, a change in price will lead to a movement *along the demand curve* without shifting it. Heavy rains will *shift the demand curve* outward, because people will need to buy more umbrellas, whereas the curve will shift inward in a drought year. Ideally, we would like to find some dates *when the demand curve stayed in the same position but the supply curve shifted* so that we can obtain a number of different equilibrium points, all of which lie on or near *the same* demand curve.

Suppose that rainfall in St. Louis was as given in Table 3 for the period 2001–2009 and that prices and quantities of umbrellas sold in those years were as indicated by the dots in Figure 7. Notice, first, that in years in which rainfall was highest, such as 2005 and 2009, the dots in the graph lie farthest to the right, whereas the dots for low-rain years lie toward the left, meaning that in rainier years more umbrellas were sold, as our hypothesis about the effect of rain on sales suggests. More important for our purposes, for the four years 2001, 2003, 2004, and 2008, rainfall was about the same—nearly 27 inches. Thus, the demand curve did *not* shift from one of these years to the next. It is reasonable to conclude that the dots for these four years fell close to the same true demand curve.

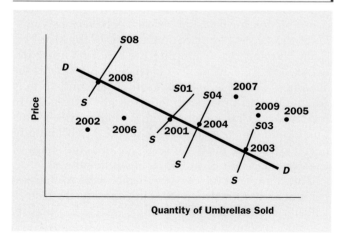

FIGURE 7

Legitimate Demand Curve Estimation from Statistical Data

Year	2001	2002	2003	2004	2005	2006	2007	2008	2009
Inches of rain	**26**	18	**28**	**29**	35	20	32	**27**	34

TABLE 3

But the dots for those four years are quite far apart from one another. This separation means that in those years, with the demand curve in the same position, the supply curve must have been shifting. So, if we wish, we can check this supposition statistically, by observing that the supply curve can be expected to shift when there is a change in the cost of the raw materials that go into the production of umbrellas—cloth, steel for the ribs, and plastic for the handles. Changes in this cost variable can be expected to shift the supply curve but not the demand curve, because consumers do not even know these cost numbers. So, just as the rainfall data indicated in what years the demand curve probably moved and when it did not, the input price data can give us such information about the supply curve.

To see this, imagine that we have a year-by-year table for those input costs similar to the table for rainfall (the cost table is not shown here); and suppose it tells us that in the four years of interest (2001, 2003, 2004, and 2008), those costs were very different from one another. We can infer that the supply curves in those years were quite different even though, as we have just seen, the demand curve was unchanging in the same years. Accordingly, the graph shows line DD drawn close to these four dots, with their four supply curves—$SS01$, $SS03$, $SS04$, and $SS08$—also going through the corresponding points, which are the equilibrium points for those four years. We can therefore infer that all four points are close to the *same* demand curve and can therefore legitimately interpret DD as a valid statistical estimate of the true demand curve for those years. We derived it by recognizing as irrelevant the dots for the years with much higher or much lower rainfall amounts, in which the demand curve can be expected to have shifted, and by drawing the statistical demand curve through the relevant dots—those that, according to the data on the variables that shift the curves, were probably generated by different supply curves but a common demand curve.

The actual methods used to derive statistical demand curves are far more complex. The underlying logic, however, is analogous to that of the process used in this example.

PRODUCTION, INPUTS, AND COST: BUILDING BLOCKS FOR SUPPLY ANALYSIS

Of course, that's only an estimate. The actual cost will be higher.

AUTO MECHANIC TO CUSTOMER

Suppose you take a summer job working for Al's Building Contractors, a producer of standardized, inexpensive garages. On your first day of work, you find that Al has bought or signed contracts to buy enough lumber, electric wiring, tools, and other materials to meet his estimated needs for the next two years. The only input choice that has not been made is the number of carpenters that he will hire. So Al is left with only one decision about input purchases: How many carpenters should he sign up for his company? In this chapter, we explore this kind of decision and answer the following question: What input choice constitutes the most profitable way for a business firm to produce its output?

When firms make their supply (output) decisions, they examine the likely demand for the products they create. We have already studied demand in the last two chapters, but to understand the firm's decisions about the supply side of its markets, we must also study its production costs. A firm's costs depend on the quantities of labor, raw materials, machinery, and other inputs that it buys and on the price it pays for each input. This chapter examines how businesses can select optimal input combinations—that is, the combinations that enable firms to produce whatever output they decide on at the minimum cost for that output. We will discuss the firm's profit-seeking decisions about output and price in Chapter 8.

To make the analysis of optimal input quantities easier to follow, we approach this task in two stages. We begin the chapter with the simpler case, in which the firm can vary the quantity of only one input while all other input quantities are already determined. This assumption vastly simplifies the analysis and enables us to answer two key questions:

- How does the quantity of input affect the quantity of output?
- How can the firm select the optimal quantity of an input?

After that, we deal with the more realistic case where the firm simultaneously selects the quantities of several inputs. We will use the results of that analysis to deduce the firm's cost curves that will ultimately lead us to analysis of the supply curves that play so important a role in the supply-demand mechanism that we have already discussed.[1]

CONTENTS

[1] Some instructors may prefer to postpone discussion of this topic until later in the course.

PUZZLE: HOW CAN WE TELL IF LARGE FIRMS ARE MORE EFFICIENT?

Modern industrial societies enjoy cost advantages as a result of automation, assembly lines, and sophisticated machinery, all of which often reduce production costs dramatically. But in industries in which equipment with such enormous capacity requires a very large investment, small companies will be unable to reap many of these benefits of modern technology. Only large firms will be able to take advantage of the associated cost savings. When firms can take advantage of such *economies of scale,* as economists call them, production costs per unit will decline as output expands.

The relationship between large size and low costs does not always fit every industry. Sometimes the courts must decide whether a giant firm should be broken up into smaller units. The most celebrated case of this kind involved American Telephone and Telegraph Company (AT&T), which had a monopoly over most of the phone service in the United States for nearly 50 years.[2] Government agencies and analysts who urged a breakup of AT&T argued that such a giant firm has great economic power and deprives consumers of the benefits of competition. Opponents of the breakup, including AT&T itself, pointed out that if AT&T's large size brought significant economies of scale, then smaller firms would be much less efficient producers than the larger one and costs to consumers would have to be correspondingly higher. Who was right? To settle the issue, the courts needed to know whether AT&T had significant economies of scale.

Sometimes data like those shown in Figure 1 are offered to the courts when they consider such cases. The data in the figure, which were provided by AT&T, indicate that as the volume of telephone messages rose after 1942, the capital cost of long-distance communication by telephone dropped enormously and eventually fell below 8 percent of its 1942 level. Economists maintain that this graph does *not* constitute legitimate evidence, one way or another, about the presence of economies of scale. Why do they say this? At the end of this chapter, we will study precisely what is wrong with the evidence presented in Figure 1 and consider what sort of evidence really would legitimately have determined whether AT&T had economies of scale.

FIGURE 1
Historical Costs for Long-Distance Telephone Transmissions

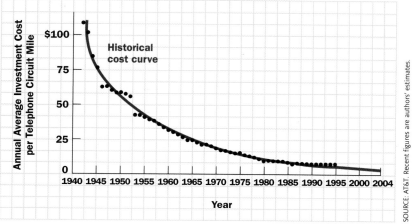

Note: Figures are in dollars per year.

SOURCE: AT&T. Recent figures are authors' estimates.

SHORT-RUN VERSUS LONG-RUN COSTS: WHAT MAKES AN INPUT VARIABLE?

As firms make input and output decisions, their actions are limited by previous commitments to equipment, plant, and other production matters. At any point in time, many input choices are *precommitted* by past decisions. If, for example, a firm purchased machinery a year ago, it has committed itself to that production decision for the remainder of the

---

[2] AT&T is a descendant of the original Bell Telephone Company, affectionately known as "Ma Bell." The company relinquished the use of the name "Bell" when it was forced by the courts to divest itself of its 22 regional companies in 1982. The companies were reorganized into the "Baby Bells"—seven regional phone companies called Nynex, Bell Atlantic, Ameritech, Bell-South, Southwestern Bell, USWest, and Pacific Telesis Group. In the 1990s, several of these "Baby Bells" merged once again (Bell Atlantic, for example, bough Nynex in 1996). Since then, the consolidation has continued. In 2000, Bell Atlantic bought GTE and changed its name to Verizon. Then, in 2005, Verizon acquired MCI. In the same year, Southwestern Bell (SBC Communications) bought the parent company of the "Baby Bells," AT&T (along with Cingular), and is now known as AT&T Inc.

machine's economic life, unless the company is willing to take the loss involved in replacing that equipment sooner. An economist would say that these temporarily unalterable capital commitments are not variable for the time period in question. Firms that employ unionized labor forces may also incur costs that are temporarily not variable if labor contracts commit the firms to employing a certain number of employees or to using employees for a required number of weeks per year. Costs are not variable for some period if they are set by a longer-term financial commitment, such as a contract to buy a raw material, lease a warehouse, or invest in equipment that cannot be resold or transferred without substantial loss of the investment. Even if the firm has not paid for these commitments ahead of time, legally it must still pay for the contracted goods or services.

The Economic Short Run versus the Economic Long Run

A two-year-old machine with a nine-year economic life can be an inescapable commitment and therefore represent a cost that is not variable for the next seven years. But that investment is not an unchangeable commitment in plans that extend *beyond* those seven years, because by then it may benefit the firm to replace the machine in any case. Economists summarize this notion by speaking of two different "runs" (or periods of time) for decision making: the **short run** and the **long run.**

The **short run** is a period of time during which some of the firm's cost commitments will *not* have ended.

The **long run** is a period of time long enough for all of the firm's current commitments to come to an end.

These terms recur time and again throughout this book. In the short run, firms have relatively little opportunity to change production processes so as to adopt the most efficient way of producing their current outputs, because plant sizes and other input quantities have largely been predetermined by past decisions. Managers may be able to hire more workers to work overtime and buy more supplies, but they can't easily increase factory size, even if sales turn out to be much greater than expected. Over the long run, however, all such inputs, including plant size, become adjustable.

As an example, let's examine Al's Building Contractors and consider the number of carpenters that it hires, the amount of lumber that it purchases, and the amounts of the other inputs that it buys. Suppose the company has signed a five-year rental contract for the warehouse space in which it stores its lumber. Ultimately—that is, in the long run—the firm may be able to reduce the amount of warehouse space to which it is committed, and if warehouse space in the area is scarce in the long run, more can be built. Once he has signed the warehouse contract, Al has relatively little immediate discretion over its capacity. Over a longer planning horizon, however, Al will need to replace the original contract, and he will be free to decide all over again how large a warehouse to rent or construct.

Much the same is true of large industrial firms. Companies have little control over their plant and equipment capacities in the short run. But with some advance planning, they can acquire different types of machines, redesign factories, and make other choices. For instance, General Motors continued producing the Chevrolet Caprice and other big, rear-wheel-drive cars at its plant in Arlington, Texas, for the 1995 and 1996 model years even though the vehicles were not selling well. That was partly because the company knew that it would need time to convert the plant to manufacture its popular full-size pickup trucks, which were in short supply. By the 1997 model year, however, GM engineers were able to convert the plant to truck production.

Note that the short run and the long run do not refer to the same time periods for all firms; rather, those periods vary in length, depending on the nature of each firm's commitments. If, for example, the firm can change its workforce every week, its machines every two years, and its factory every twenty years, then twenty years will be the long run, and any period less than twenty years will constitute the short run.

A **fixed cost** is the cost of an input whose quantity does not rise when output goes up, one that the firm requires to produce any output at all. The total cost of such indivisible inputs does not change when the output changes. Any other cost of the firm's operation is called a **variable cost**.

Fixed Costs and Variable Costs

This distinction between the short run and the long run also determines which of the firm's costs rise or fall when there is a change in the amount of output produced by the firm. Some costs cannot be varied *no matter how long the period in question.* These are called **fixed costs,** and they arise when some types of inputs can be bought only in big batches or when inputs have a large productive capacity. For example, there is no such thing as a "mini" automobile assembly line capable of producing two cars per week, and, except for extreme luxury models, it is impractical to turn out automobiles without an assembly line. For these reasons, the fixed cost of automobile manufacturing includes the cost of the smallest (least expensive) assembly line that the firm can acquire. These costs are called *fixed* because the total amount of money spent in buying the assembly line does not vary, whether it is used to produce 10 cars or 100 cars each day, so long as the output quantity does not exceed the assembly line's capacity.

In the short run, some other costs behave very much as fixed costs do; in other words, they are predetermined by previous decisions and are *temporarily* fixed. But in the long run, firms can change both their capital and labor commitments, which causes more costs to become **variable.** We will have more to say about fixed and variable costs as we examine other key input and cost relationships.

PRODUCTION, INPUT CHOICE, AND COST WITH ONE VARIABLE INPUT

In reality, all businesses use many different inputs whose quantities must be decided. Nevertheless, we will begin our discussion with the short-run case in which there is *only a single input that is variable*—that is, in which the quantities of all other inputs will not be changed. In doing so, we are trying to replicate in our theoretical analysis what physicists or biologists do in the laboratory when they conduct a *controlled* experiment: changing just one variable at a time to enable us to see the influence of that one variable in isolation. Thus, we will study the effects of variation in the quantity of one input under the assumption that all other things remain unchanged—that is, other things being equal.

TABLE 1

Total Physical Product Schedule for Al's Building Company

(1)	(2)
Number of Carpenters	Total Product (Garages per Year)
0	0
1	4
2	12
3	24
4	32
5	35
6	30

Total, Average, and Marginal Physical Products

We begin the analysis with the first of the firm's three main questions: What is the relationship between the quantity of inputs utilized and the quantity of production? Al has studied how many of its inexpensive standardized garages his firm can turn out in a year, depending on the number of carpenters it uses. The relevant data are displayed in Table 1.

The table begins by confirming the commonsense observation that garages cannot be built without labor. Thus, output is zero when Al hires zero labor input (see the first line of the table). After that, the table shows the rising total garage outputs that additional amounts of labor yield, assuming that the firm's employees work on one garage at a time and, after it is finished, move on to the next garage. For instance, with a one-carpenter input, total output is 4 garages per year; with two carpenters helping one another and specializing in different tasks, annual output can be increased to 12 garages. After five carpenters are employed in building a garage, they begin to get in one another's way. As a result, employment of a sixth carpenter actually reduces output from 35 to 30 garages.

Total Physical Product   The data in Table 1 appear graphically in Figure 2, which is called a **total physical product (TPP)** curve. This curve reports how many garages Al can produce with different quantities of carpenters, holding the quantities of all other inputs constant.

Average Physical Product   To understand more about how the number of carpenters contributes to output, Al can use two other physical product relationships given in Table 2. The **average physical product (APP)** measures output per unit of input; it is simply the total physical product divided by the quantity of variable input used—the number of garages produced in a year per carpenter employed. For Al's firm, it is the total number of garages produced in a year divided by the number of carpenters hired. APP is shown in column (5) of Table 2. For example, because four carpenters can turn out 32 garages annually, the APP of four carpenters is 32/4, or 8 garages per carpenter.

The firm's **total physical product (TPP)** is the amount of output it obtains in total from a given quantity of input.

The **average physical product (APP)** is the total physical product (TPP) divided by the quantity of input. Thus, APP = TPP/X, where X = the quantity of input.

Total Physical Product with Different Quantities of Carpenters Used by Al's Firm

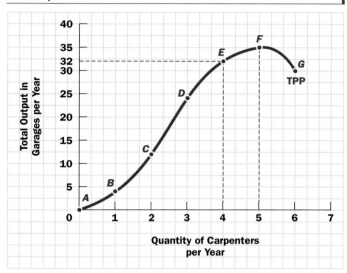

Al's Product Schedules: Total, Average, and Marginal Physical Product and Marginal Revenue Product

(1)	(2)	(3)	(4)	(5)
Number of Carpenters	Total Physical Product (Garages per year)	Marginal Physical Product (Garages per added carpenter)	Marginal Revenue Product (Thousands of $ per year per added carpenter)	Average Physical Product (Garages per carpenter)
0	0			0
1	4	4	$ 60	4
2	12	8	120	6
3	24	12	180	8
4	32	8	120	8
5	35	3	45	7
6	30	−5	−75	5

Note: Each entry in column (3) is the difference between successive entries in column (2). This is what is indicated by the zigzag lines.

Marginal Physical Product

To decide how many carpenters to hire, Al should know how many *additional* garages to expect from each *additional* carpenter.[3] This concept is known as **marginal physical product (MPP),** and Al can calculate it from the total physical product data using the same method we introduced to derive marginal utility from total utility in Chapter 5. For example, the marginal physical product of the fourth carpenter is the total output when Al uses four carpenters *minus* the total output when he hires only three carpenters. That is, the MPP of the fourth carpenter = 32 − 24 = 8 garages. We calculate the other MPP entries in the third column of Table 2 in exactly the same way. Figure 3 displays these numbers in a graph called a *marginal physical product curve.*

The **marginal physical product (MPP)** of an input is the increase in total output that results from a one-unit increase in the input quantity, holding the amounts of all other inputs constant.

Marginal Physical Product and the "Law" of Diminishing Marginal Returns

The shape of the marginal physical product curve in Figure 3 has important implications for Al's garage building. Compare the TPP curve in Figure 2 with the MPP curve in Figure 3. The MPP curve can be described as the curve that reports the *rate* at which the TPP curve is changing. MPP is equal to the *slope* of the TPP curve[4] because it tells us how much of an increase in garage output results from each additional carpenter Al hires. Thus, until input reaches three carpenters, the marginal physical product of carpenters *increases* when Al hires more of them. That is, TPP increases at

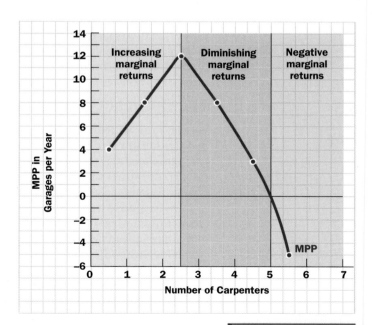

Al's Marginal Physical Product (MPP) Curve

---

[3] If you have studied any calculus, you will recognize "marginal physical product," which is in essence the first derivative of number of garages produced with respect to number of carpenters hired.

[4] The same is true of any total and marginal curves: at any output level the marginal is the slope of the total curve. For example, the slope of an individual's total utility curve when he has five apples is the change in his total utility when he acquires a sixth apple. But that, by definition, is the marginal utility of the sixth apple.

an increasing rate (its slope becomes steeper) between points *A* and *D* in Figure 2. Between three carpenters and five carpenters, the MPP (the slope of TPP) *decreases* but still has *positive* values throughout (that is, it lies above the horizontal axis). Consequently, in this range, TPP is still increasing (its slope, MPP, is greater than zero), but its rate of increase is slower (its slope, MPP, is still positive, but is a declining positive number). That is, in this region, between points *D* and *F* in Figure 2, each additional carpenter contributes garage output but adds less than the previous carpenter added. Beyond five carpenters, to the right of point *F* in Figure 2, the MPP of carpenters actually becomes *negative*: The total physical product curve starts to decrease as additional carpenters get in one another's way.

Figure 3 is divided into three zones to illustrate these three cases. Note that the marginal returns to additional carpenters increase at first and then diminish. This is the typical pattern, and it parallels what we said about the utility of consumption in Chapter 5. Each additional unit adds some production, but at a decreasing rate. In the leftmost zone of Figure 3 (the region of increasing marginal returns), each additional carpenter adds more to TPP than the previous one did.

**IDEAS FOR
BEYOND THE
FINAL EXAM**

The "law" of diminishing marginal returns, which has played a key role in economics for two centuries, states that an increase in the amount of any one input, *holding the amounts of all others constant,* ultimately leads to lower marginal returns to the expanding input.

This so-called law rests simply on observed facts; economists did not deduce the relationship analytically. Returns to a single input usually diminish because of the "law" of variable input proportions. When the quantity of one input increases while all others remain constant, the variable input whose quantity increases gradually becomes more abundant relative to the others and gradually becomes overabundant. (For example, the proportion of labor increases and the proportions of other inputs, such as lumber, decrease.) As Al uses more carpenters with fixed quantities of other inputs, the proportion of labor time to other inputs becomes unbalanced. Adding more carpenter time does little good and eventually begins to harm production. At this last point, the marginal physical product of carpenters becomes *negative*.

Many real-world cases seem to follow the law of variable input proportions. In China, for instance, farmers have been using increasingly more fertilizer as they try to produce larger grain harvests to feed the country's burgeoning population. Although its consumption of fertilizer is four times higher than it was 15 years ago, China's grain output has increased by only 50 percent. This relationship certainly suggests that fertilizer use has reached the zone of diminishing returns.

The Optimal Quantity of an Input and Diminishing Returns

We can now address the second question that all firms must ask as they make production decisions: How can the firm select the optimal quantity of an input? To answer this question, look again at the first and third columns of Table 2, which show the firm's marginal physical product schedule. We will assume for now that a carpenter is paid $50,000 per year and that Al can sell his inexpensive garages for $15,000 each.

Now suppose that Al is considering using just one carpenter. Is this choice optimal? Does it maximize his profits? To answer this question we have to consider not only how many garages an additional carpenter provides but also the money value of each garage; that is, we must first translate the marginal *physical* product into its money equivalent. In this case, the monetary evaluation of TPP shows that the answer is no, one carpenter is not enough to maximize profit, because the marginal physical product of a second carpenter is 8 garages per year, the second entry in marginal physical product column (3) of Table 2. At a price of $15,000 per garage, this extra output would add $120,000 to total revenue. Because the added revenue exceeds the $50,000 cost of the second carpenter, the firm comes out ahead by $120,000 − $50,000, or $70,000 per year.

Marginal Revenue Product and Input Prices   The additional *money revenue* that a firm receives when it increases the quantity of some input by one unit is called the input's

marginal revenue product (MRP). If Al's garages sell at a fixed price, say $15,000, the marginal revenue product of the input equals its marginal physical product multiplied by the output price:

$$MRP = MPP \times Price\ of\ output$$

For example, we have just shown that the marginal revenue product of the second carpenter is $120,000, which we obtained by multiplying the MPP of 8 garages by the price of $15,000 per garage. The other MRP entries in column (4) of Table 2 are calculated in the same way. The MRP concept enables us to formulate a simple rule for the optimal use of any input. Specifically:

> When the marginal revenue product of an input exceeds its price, it pays the firm to use more of that input. Similarly, when the marginal revenue product of the input is less than its price, it pays the firm to use less of that input.

Let's test this rule in the case of Al's garages. We have observed that two carpenters cannot be the optimal input because the MRP of a second carpenter ($120,000) exceeds his wages ($50,000). What about a third carpenter? Table 2 shows that the MRP of the third carpenter ($12 \times \$15,000 = \$180,000$) also exceeds his wages; thus, stopping at three carpenters also is not optimal. The same is true for a fourth carpenter, because his MRP of $120,000 still exceeds his $50,000 price. The situation is different with a fifth carpenter, however. Hiring a fifth carpenter is not a good idea because his MRP, which is $3 \times \$15,000 = \$45,000$, is less than his $50,000 cost. Thus, the optimal number of carpenters for Al to hire is four, yielding a total output of 32 garages.

Notice the crucial role of diminishing returns in this analysis. When the marginal *physical* product of carpenter begins to decline, the money value of that product falls as well—that is, the marginal *revenue* product also declines. The producer always profits by expanding input use until diminishing returns set in and reduce the MRP to the price of the input. So Al should stop *increasing* his carpenter purchases when MRP *falls* to the price of a carpenter.

> A common expression suggests that it does not pay to continue doing something "beyond the point of diminishing returns." As we see from this analysis, quite to the contrary, it normally *does* pay to do so! The firm has employed the proper amount of input only when diminishing returns reduce the marginal revenue product of the input to the level of its price, because then the firm will be wasting no opportunity to *add* to its total profit. Thus, the optimal quantity of an input is that at which MRP equals its price (*P*). In symbols:

$$MRP = P\ of\ input$$

The logic of this analysis is exactly the same as that used in our discussion of marginal utility and price in Chapter 5. Al is trying to maximize *profits*—the difference between the *total* revenue yielded by his carpenter input and the *total* cost of buying that input. To do so, he must increase his carpenter usage to the point where price equals marginal revenue product, just as an optimizing consumer keeps buying until price equals marginal utility.

The **marginal revenue product (MRP)** of an input is the additional revenue that the producer earns from the increased sales when it uses an additional unit of the input.

MULTIPLE INPUT DECISIONS: THE CHOICE OF OPTIMAL INPUT COMBINATIONS[5]

Up to this point we have simplified our analysis by assuming that the firm can change the quantity of only one of its inputs and that the price the product can command does not change, no matter how large a quantity the producer offers for sale (the fixed price is $15,000 for Al's garages). Of course, neither of these assumptions is true in reality. In Chapter 8, we will explore the effect of product quantity decisions on prices by bringing

---

[5] Instructors may want to teach this part of the chapter (up to page 133) now, or they may prefer to wait until they come to Chapters 19 and 20 on the determination of wages, interest rates, profit, and rent.

Closer to Home: The Diminishing Marginal Returns to Studying

The "law" of diminishing marginal returns crops up a lot in ordinary life, not just in the world of business. Consider Jason and his study habits: He has a tendency to procrastinate and then cram for exams the night before he takes them, pulling "all-nighters" regularly. How might an economist describe Jason's payoff from an additional hour of study in the wee hours of the morning, relative to that of Colin, who studies for two hours every night?

SOURCE: © PNC/Brand X Pictures/Jupiterimages

in the demand curve. First we must deal with the obvious fact that a firm must decide on the quantities of each of the many inputs it uses, not just one input at a time. That is, Al must decide not only how many carpenters to hire but how much lumber and how many tools to buy. Both of the latter decisions clearly depend on the number of carpenters in his team. So, once again, we must examine the two basic and closely interrelated issues: production levels and optimal input quantities. But this time, we will allow the firm to select the quantities of *many* inputs. By expanding our analysis in this way, we can study a key issue: how a firm, by its choice of production method (also called its production technology), can make up for decreased availability of one input by using more of another input.

Substitutability: The Choice of Input Proportions

Just as we found it useful to start the analysis with physical output or product in the one-variable-input case, we will start with physical production in the multiple-variable-input case. Firms can choose among alternative types of technology to produce any given product. Many people mistakenly believe that management really has very little choice when selecting its input proportions. Technological considerations alone, they believe, dictate such choices. For example, a particular type of furniture-cutting machine may require two operators working for an hour on a certain amount of wood to make five desks—no more and no less. But this way of looking at the possibilities is an overly narrow view of the matter.

In reality, the furniture manufacturer can choose among several alternative production processes for making desks. For example, simpler and cheaper machines might be able to change the same pile of wood into five desks, but only by using more than two hours of labor. Or, the firm might choose to create the desks with simple hand tools, which would require many more workers and no machinery at all. The firm will seek the method of production that is *least costly*.

In advanced industrial societies, where labor is expensive and machinery is cheap, it may pay to use the most automated process. For example, Caterpillar, a U.S. heavy-vehicle and machinery producer, curbed its high labor costs by investing in computers that enabled it to manufacture twice as many truck engines with the same number of people. However, in less developed countries, where machinery is scarce and labor is abundant, making things by hand may be the most economical solution. An interesting example can be found in rural India, where company records are often still handwritten, not computerized, as is widely true in the United States.

We conclude that firms can generally substitute one input for another. A firm can produce the same number of desks with less labor, *if* it is prepared to sink more money into machinery. Whether or not it *pays* to make such a substitution depends on the relative costs of labor and machinery. Several general conclusions follow from this discussion:

- Normally, a firm can choose among different technological options to produce a particular volume of output. Technological considerations rarely fix input proportions immutably.
- Given a target production level, a firm that cuts down on the use of one input (say, labor) will normally have to increase its use of another input (say, machinery). This trade-off is what we mean when we speak of *substituting* one input for another.
- The combination of inputs that represents the *least costly* way to produce the desired level of output depends on the relative prices of the various inputs.

The Marginal Rule for Optimal Input Proportions

Choosing the input proportions that minimize the cost of producing a given output is really a matter of common sense. To understand why, let us turn, once again, to marginal analysis of the decision. As before, Al is considering whether to buy more expensive tools that will enable him to produce his garages using fewer carpenters or to do the reverse. The two inputs, tools and carpenters, are substitutes; if the firm spends more on tools, it needs fewer carpenters. *But the tools are not perfect substitutes for labor.* Tools need carpenters to operate them, and tools are not endowed with the judgment and common sense that are needed if something goes wrong. Of course, a carpenter without tools is also not very productive, so Al gains a considerable benefit by acquiring balanced relative quantities of the two inputs. If he uses too much of one and too little of the other, the output of the firm will suffer. In other words, it is reasonable to assume that *diminishing returns* will accompany excessive substitution of either input for the other. As he substitutes more and more labor for expensive machinery, the marginal physical product of the added labor will begin to decline.

How should Al decide whether to spend more on tools and less on labor, or vice versa? The obvious—and correct—answer is that he should compare what he gets for his money by spending, say, $100 more on labor or on tools. If he gets more (a greater marginal revenue product) by spending this amount on labor than by spending it on tools, clearly it pays Al to spend that money on labor rather than on tools. In that case, it pays him to spend somewhat less on tools than he had been planning to do and to transfer the money he thereby saves to purchasing more carpenter labor. So we have the following three conclusions:

1. If the marginal revenue product of the additional labor that Al gets by spending, say, a dollar more on carpenters is greater than the marginal revenue product he receives from spending the same amount on tools, he should change his plans and devote more of his spending to labor than he had planned and less to tools.
2. If the marginal revenue product of an additional dollar spent on labor is less than the marginal revenue product of an additional dollar spent on tools, Al should increase his spending on tools and cut his planned spending on labor.
3. If the marginal revenue products of an additional dollar spent on either labor or tools are the same, Al should stick to his current purchase plans. There is nothing to be gained by switching the proportions of his spending on the two inputs.[6]

There is only one more step. Suppose, for example, that the MRP per dollar is greater for labor than that for tools. Then, as we have just seen, Al should spend more money on labor than originally planned and less on tools. But where should this switch in spending stop? Should the transfer of funds continue until Al stops spending on tools altogether, because the MRP per dollar is greater for labor than for tools? Such an answer makes no

---

[6] Calculation of the marginal revenue product per dollar spent on an input is easy if we know the marginal revenue product of the input and the price of the input. For example, we know from Table 2 that the MRP of a third carpenter is $180,000 and his wage is $50,000. Thus, his MRP per dollar spent on his wages is $180,000/$50,000 = $3.60. More generally, the MRP per dollar spent on any input, X, is the MRP of X divided by the price of X.

Beyond Farms and Firms: The General Rule for Optimal Input Proportions

We have just discussed how a firm can determine the most economical input combination for any given level of output. This analysis does not apply only to business enterprises. Nonprofit organizations such as your own college are interested in finding the least costly ways to accomplish a variety of tasks (for example, maintaining the grounds and buildings); government agencies (sometimes) seek to meet their objectives at minimum costs; even in the home, we can find many ways to save money. Thus, our present analysis of *cost minimization* is widely applicable.

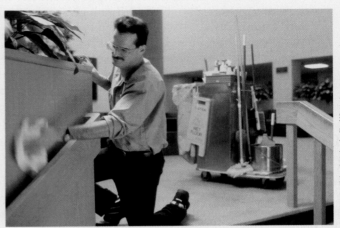

sense—a worker without tools is not very productive. The correct answer is that, by the "law" of diminishing returns, when Al buys more and more carpenter time, the initially higher MRP of carpenters will decline. As he spends less and less on tools, tools will become scarcer and more valuable and their initially lower MRP will rise. So, as Al transfers more money from tools to carpenters, the MRPs per dollar for the inputs will get closer and closer to one another, and they will eventually meet, which is when the proportions of Al's spending allocated to the two inputs will have reached the optimal level. At that point, there is no way he can get more for his money by changing the proportions of those inputs that he hires or buys.

Changes in Input Prices and Optimal Input Proportions

The commonsense reasoning behind the rule for optimal input proportions leads to an important conclusion. Let's say that Al is producing seven garages at minimum cost. Suppose that the wage of a carpenter falls, but the price of tools remains the same. This means that a dollar will now buy a larger quantity of labor than before, thus increasing the marginal revenue product *per dollar* spent on carpenters—a dollar will now buy more carpenter labor and more of its product than it did before. But because tool prices have not changed, the marginal revenue product obtainable by spending an additional dollar on tools will also be unchanged. So, if Al had previously devoted the right proportions to spending on carpenters and spending on tools, that will no longer be true. If, previously, the marginal revenue product per dollar spent on carpenters equaled the marginal revenue product per dollar spent on tools, this relationship will have changed so that

Marginal revenue product per dollar spent on carpenters > Marginal revenue product per dollar spent on tools

That is, the proportion between the two inputs will no longer be optimal. Clearly, Al will be better off if he increases his spending on carpenters and reduces his spending on tools.

Looked at another way, to restore optimality, the MRP per dollar spent on carpenters must fall to match the MRP per dollar spent on tools. But, by the "law" of diminishing returns, the MRP of carpenters will *fall* when the use of carpenters is increased. Thus, a fall in the price of carpenters prompts Al to use *more* carpenter time, and if the increase is sufficiently large, it will restore equality in the marginal revenue products per dollar spent on the two inputs. In general, we have the commonsense result that

As any one input becomes more costly relative to competing inputs, the firm is likely to substitute one input for another—that is, to use less of the input that has become more expensive and to use more of competing inputs.

COST AND ITS DEPENDENCE ON OUTPUT

Having analyzed how the firm decides on its input quantities, we now take the next step toward our analysis of the implications for pricing and output quantity of the product it sells to consumers. For this purpose, the firm needs to know, among other things, how much it will cost to produce different output quantities. Clearly, this cost—the amount of money that the firm spends on production—will depend on how much it produces and what quantities of input it will need to do the job. How do we measure the cost relationships?

Input Quantities and Total, Average, and Marginal Cost Curves

We must turn now to the third of the three main questions that a firm must ask: How do we derive the firm's cost relationships from the input decisions that we have just explained? We will use these cost relationships when we analyze the firm's output and pricing decisions in Chapter 8, in which we will study the last of the main components of our analysis of the market mechanism: How much of its product or service should the profit-maximizing firm produce?

The most desirable output quantity for the firm clearly depends on how costs change as output varies. Economists typically display and analyze such information in the form of *cost curves*. Indeed, because we will use marginal analysis again in our discussion, we will need three different cost curves: the *total cost curve*, the *average cost curve*, and the *marginal cost curve*.

These curves follow directly from the nature of production. The technological production relationships for garage-building dictate the amount of carpenter time, the type and quantity of tools, the amount of lumber, and the quantities of the other inputs that Al uses to produce any given number of garages. This technological relationship for carpenters appeared earlier in Figure 2. From these data on carpenter usage and the price of a carpenter, plus similar information on tools, lumber, and other inputs, and the decision on the optimal proportions among those inputs, Al can determine how much it will cost to produce any given number of garages. Therefore, the relevant cost relationships depend directly on the production relationships we have just discussed. The calculation of the firm's total costs from its physical product schedule that we use here assumes that the firm cannot influence the market price of carpenters or the prices of other inputs, because these are fixed by union contracts and other such influences. Using this assumption, let us begin with the portion of the cost calculation that applies to carpenters.

The method is simple: For each quantity of output, record from Table 1 or Figure 2 the number of carpenters required to produce it. Then multiply that quantity of carpenters by the assumed annual average wage of $50,000.

Total Costs   In addition to the cost of carpenters, Al must spend money on his other inputs, such as tools and lumber. Furthermore, his costs must include the *opportunity costs* of any inputs that Al himself contributes—such as his own labor, which he could have used to earn wages by taking a job in another firm, and his own capital that he has invested in the firm, which he could have invested, say, in interest-paying government bonds. The costs of the other inputs are calculated, essentially, in the same manner as the cost of carpenters—by determining the quantity of each input that will optimally be used in producing any given number of garages and then multiplying that input quantity by its price. To calculate the total cost Al must cover to build, say, four garages per year, we have the following simple formula:

The total cost of four garages = (The number of carpenters used × The wage per carpenter) + (The amount of lumber that will be used × The price of lumber) + (The number of pounds of nails that will be used × The price of nails) + . . .

Using this calculation and data such as those in Table 1, we obtain directly the total costs for different output quantities shown in Table 3. For example, row (4), column (2), of Table 3 indicates that if he wants to produce three garages per year, Al needs to purchase quantities of labor time, lumber, and other inputs whose total cost is $54,000. The other numbers in the second column of Table 3 are interpreted similarly. To summarize the story:

TABLE 3

Al's (Variable) Cost Schedules

(1)	(2)	(3)	(4)
Total Product (Garages per year)	Total Variable Cost (Thousands of $ per year)	Marginal Variable Cost (Thousands of $ per added garage)	Average Variable Cost (Thousands of $ per garage)
0	$ 0		$ 0
		$28	
1	28		28
		16	
2	44		22
		10	
3	54		18
		8	
4	62		15.5
		6	
5	68		13.6
		7	
6	75		12.5
		9	
7	84		12
		16	
8	100		12.5
		32	
9	132		14.7 (approx.)
		46	
10	178		17.8

The marginal product relationships enable the firm to determine the input proportions and quantities needed to produce any given output at lowest total cost. From those input quantities and the prices of the inputs, we can determine the *total cost* (TC) of producing any level of output. Thus, the relationship of total cost to output is determined by the technological production relationships between inputs and outputs and by input prices.

Total, Average, and Marginal Cost Curves

Two other cost curves—the average cost (AC) and marginal cost (MC) curves—provide information crucial for our analysis. We can calculate these curves directly from the total cost curve, just as Table 2 calculated average and marginal physical product from total physical product.

For any given output, *average cost* is defined as total cost divided by quantity produced. For example, Table 3 shows that the total cost of producing seven garages is $84,000, so the average cost is $84,000/7, or $12,000 per garage.

Similarly, we define the *marginal cost* as the increase in total cost that arises from the production of an additional garage. For example, the marginal cost of the fifth garage is the difference between the total cost of producing five garages, $68,000, and the total cost of producing four garages, $62,000; that is, the marginal cost of the fifth garage is $6,000. Figure 4 shows all three curves—the total, average, and marginal cost curves. The TC curve is generally assumed to rise fairly steadily as the firm's output increases. After all, Al cannot expect to produce eight garages at a lower total cost than he can produce five, six, or seven garages. The AC curve and the MC curve both look roughly like the letter U—first going downhill, then gradually turning uphill again. We will explore the reason for and implications of this U-shape later in the chapter.

So far, we have taken into account only the *variable* costs, or the costs that depend on the number of garages Al's firm builds. That's why these costs are labeled as "variable" in the table and the graph. But there are other costs, such as the rent Al pays for the company office, that are fixed; that is, they stay the same in total, no matter how many garages he produces, at least within some limits. Of course, Al cannot obtain these fixed-cost inputs for free. Their costs, however, are constants—they are positive numbers and not zero.

Total Fixed Cost and Average Fixed Cost Curves   Although variable costs are only part of combined total costs (which include both fixed and variable costs), the total and average cost curves that include both types of costs have the same general shape as those shown in Figure 4. In contrast, the curves that record *total fixed costs* (TFC) and *average fixed costs* (AFC) have very special shapes, illustrated in Figure 5. By definition, TFC remains the same whether the firm produces a little or a lot—so long as it produces something. As a result, any TFC curve is a horizontal straight line like the one shown in Figure 5(a). It has the same height at every output.

FIGURE   4

Al's Total Variable Cost, Average Variable Cost, and Marginal Variable Cost

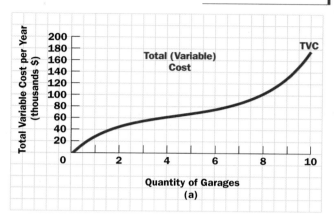

Average fixed cost, however, gets smaller and smaller as output increases, because AFC (which equals TFC/Q) (where Q represents quantity of output) falls as output (the denominator) rises for constant TFC. Businesspeople typically put the point another way: Any increase in output spreads the fixed cost (which they often call "overhead") among more units, meaning that less of it is carried by any one unit. For example, suppose that Al's firm's total fixed cost is $12,000 per year. When he produces only two garages, the entire $12,000 of fixed cost must be borne by those two garages; that is, the average fixed cost is $6,000 per garage. But if Al produces three garages, the fixed cost per garage falls to $4,000 = $12,000/3 (Table 4).

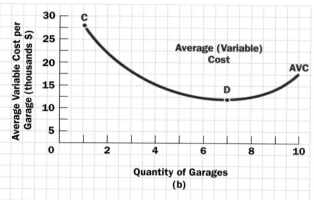

AFC can never reach zero. Even if Al were to produce one million garages per year, each garage would have to bear, on average, one-millionth of the TFC—which is still a positive number (although minuscule). It follows that the AFC curve gets lower and lower as output increases, moving closer and closer to the horizontal axis but never crossing it. This pattern appears in Figure 5(b).

Finally, we may note that marginal fixed costs exhibit a very simple behavior: *Marginal fixed costs are always zero.* Building an additional garage does not add a penny to Al's annual office rent, which is fixed at $12,000, according to the lease. Looked at another way, because the total fixed cost stays unchanged at $12,000, no matter how many garages are produced, the marginal fixed cost of, say, a fifth garage is the total fixed cost of five garages minus the total fixed cost of four garages = $12,000 − $12,000 = 0.

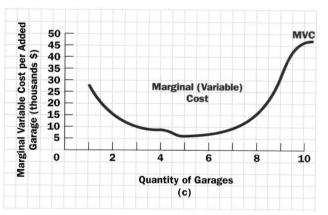

Note: Quantity is in garages per year.

Having divided costs into fixed costs (FC) and variable costs (VC), we can express corresponding rules for total average and marginal costs:

$$TC = TFC + TVC$$
$$AC = AFC + AVC$$
$$MC = MFC + MVC$$
$$= 0 + MVC$$
$$= MVC$$

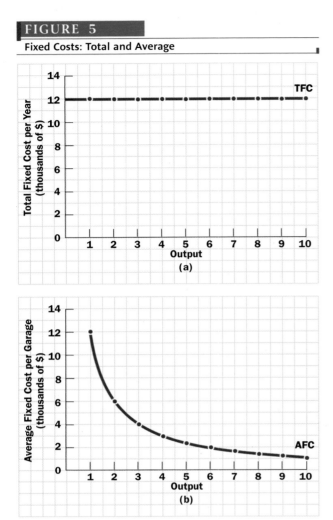

FIGURE 5

Fixed Costs: Total and Average

(a)

(b)

NOTE: Output is in garages per year.

TABLE 4

Al's Fixed Costs

(1) Number of Garages	(2) Total Fixed Cost (Thousands of $ per year)	(3) Marginal Fixed Cost	(4) Average Fixed Cost (Thousands of $ per garage)
0	$ 12		—
1	12	$0	$ 12
2	12	0	6
3	12	0	4
4	12	0	3
5	12	0	2.4
6	12	0	2
7	12	0	1.7
8	12	0	1.5
9	12	0	1.33
10	12	0	1.2

The Law of Diminishing Marginal Productivity and the U-Shaped Average Cost Curve

The preceding discussion of fixed and variable costs enables us to consider the configuration of the average cost curve and the production implications of its typical U-shape. The typical curve looks like Figure 4(b) and is roughly U-shaped: The left-hand portion of the curve is downward-sloping and the right-hand portion is upward-sloping. AC declines when output increases in the left-hand portion of the curve for two reasons.

The first reason makes intuitive sense and pertains to the fixed-cost portion of AC and the fact that these fixed costs are divided over more units of product as output increases. As Figure 5(b) shows, the average *fixed*-cost curve always falls as output increases, and it falls very sharply at the left-hand end of the AFC curve. Because AC equals AFC plus average variable costs (AVC), the AC curve for virtually any product contains a fixed-cost portion, AFC, which falls steeply at first when output increases. So, as these fixed costs are spread over more units as output increases, the AC curve for any product should have a downward-sloping portion such as *CD* in Figure 4(b), which is characterized by decreasing average cost.

The second reason why AC curves have a downward-sloping section relates to changing input proportions. As the firm increases the quantity of one input while holding other inputs constant, the marginal physical product relationship tells us that MPP will first rise. As a result, average costs will decrease. For example, if Al is using very few carpenters relative to the amounts of other inputs, a rise in the quantity of carpenters will, at first, yield increasing additions to output (in the range of increasing marginal physical product of carpenters illustrated in the left-hand part of Figure 3). As the quantity produced increases, the average cost of output falls.

Now look at any point to the right of point *D* in Figure 4(b). Average cost rises as output increases along this section of the curve. Why does the portion of the curve with decreasing AC end? Although it may not seem very important in our example, increasing administrative costs are a major source of increasing average cost in practice.

Sheer size makes firms more complicated to run. Large firms tend to be relatively bureau-cratic, impersonal, and costly to manage. As a firm becomes very large and loses top management's personal touch, bureaucratic costs ultimately rise disproportionately. Typi-cally, this change ultimately drives average cost upward.

The output at which average costs stop decreasing and begin to rise varies from indus-try to industry. Other things being equal, the greater the relative size of fixed costs, the higher the output at which the switch-over occurs.[7] For example, it occurs at a much larger volume of output in automobile production than in farming, which is why no farms are as big as even the smallest auto producer. Automobile producers must be larger than farms because the fixed costs of automobile production are far greater than those in farm-ing, so spreading the fixed cost over an increasing number of units of output keeps AC falling far longer in auto production than in farming. Thus, although firms in both indus-tries may have U-shaped AC curves, the bottom of the U occurs at a far larger output in auto production than in farming.

The AC curve for a typical firm is U-shaped. We can attribute its downward-sloping seg-ment to increasing marginal physical products and to the fact that the firm spreads its fixed costs over ever-larger quantities of outputs. Similarly, we can attribute the upward-sloping segment primarily to the disproportionate rise in administrative costs that occurs as firms grow large.

The Average Cost Curve in the Short and Long Run

At the beginning of this chapter, we observed that some inputs are variable and some are precommitted, depending on the pertinent time horizon. It follows that

The average (and marginal and total) cost curve depends on the firm's planning horizon—how far into the future it tries to look when making its plans. The average (and total) cost curve for the long run differs from that for the short run because, in the long run, input quantities generally become variable.

We can, in fact, be much more specific about the relationships between the short-run and long-run average cost curves. Consider, as an example, the capacity of Naomi's poul-try farm. In the short run, she can choose to raise, at most, only the number of chickens that she can crowd into her coops' current capacity. Of course, she can always build more chicken coops; however, if it turns out that the coops are much larger than she needs, Naomi cannot simply undo the excessive space and get back the money that she has spent on it. But, in the long run, when they need to be replaced, she can choose among new coops of different sizes.

If she constructs a smaller coop, Naomi's AC curve looks like curve *SL* in Figure 6. That means that if she is pleasantly surprised as sales grow to 100 pounds of chicken per week, av-erage cost will be $0.40 per pound of chicken (point *V*). She may then wish she had built bigger coops with an AC curve of *BG*, which would have enabled her to cut the cost per pound of chicken to $0.35 (point *W*). In the short run, though, Naomi can do nothing about this decision; the AC curve remains *SL*. Similarly, had she built the larger coops, the short-run AC curve would be *BG*, and the farm would be committed to this cost curve even if her sales were to decline sharply.

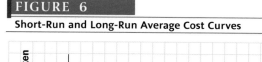

FIGURE 6

Short-Run and Long-Run Average Cost Curves

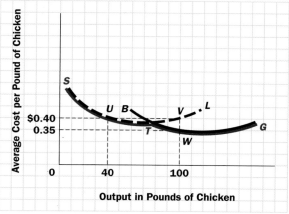

Average Cost per Pound of Chicken

Output in Pounds of Chicken

---

[7] Empirical evidence confirms this view, although it suggests that the bottom of the U is often long and flat. That is to say, a considerable range of outputs often fall between the regions of decreasing and increasing average cost. In this intermediate region, the AC curve is approximately horizontal, meaning that, in this range, AC does not change when output increases.

In the long run, however, Naomi must replace the coops, and she is free to decide their size all over again. If Naomi expects sales of 100 pounds of chicken per week, she will construct larger coops and have an average cost of $0.35 per pound of chicken (point *W*). If she expects sales of only 40 pounds of chicken per week, she will arrange for smaller buildings with an average cost of $0.40 per pound of chicken (point *U*).

In sum, in the long run, a firm will select the plant size (that is, the short-run AC curve) that is most economical for the output level that it expects to produce. The long-run average cost curve therefore consists of all of the *lower* segments of the short-run AC curves. In Figure 6, this composite curve is the brick-colored curve, *STG*. The long-run average cost curve shows the lowest possible short-run average cost corresponding to each output level.

ECONOMIES OF SCALE

We have now put together the basic tools we need to address the question posed at the beginning of this chapter: Does a large firm benefit from substantial economies of scale that allow it to operate more efficiently than smaller firms? To answer this question, we need a precise definition of this concept.

An enterprise's scale of operation arises from the quantities of the various inputs that it uses. Consider what happens when the firm doubles its scale of operations. For example, suppose Al's garage-building firm were to double the number of carpenters, the amount of lumber, the number of tools, and the quantity of every other input that it uses. Suppose as a result that the number of garages built per year increased from 12 to 26; that is, output more than doubled. Because output goes up by a greater percentage than the increase in each of the inputs, Al's production is said to be characterized by **increasing returns to scale** (or **economies of scale**), at least in this range of input and output quantities.

Economies of scale affect operations in many modern industries. Where they exist, they give larger firms cost advantages over smaller ones and thereby foster large firm sizes. Automobile production and telecommunications are two common examples of industries that enjoy significant economies of scale. Predictably, firms in these industries are, indeed, huge.

Technology generally determines whether a specific economic activity is characterized by economies of scale. One particularly clear example of a way in which this can happen is provided by warehouse space. Imagine two warehouses, each shaped like a perfect cube, where the length, width, and height of Warehouse 2 are twice as large as the corresponding measurements for Warehouse 1. Now remember your high school geometry. The surface area of any side of a cube is equal to the square of its length. Therefore, the amount of material needed to build Warehouse 2 will be 2^2, or four times as great as that needed for Warehouse 1. However, because the volume of a cube is equal to the cube of its length, Warehouse 2 will have 2^3, or eight times, as much storage space as Warehouse 1. Thus, in a cubic building, multiplying the input quantities by 4 leads to eight times the storage space—an example of strongly increasing returns to scale.

This example is, of course, oversimplified. It omits such complications as the need for stronger supports in taller buildings, the increased difficulty of moving goods in and out of taller buildings, and the like. Still, the basic idea is correct, and the example shows why, up to a point, the very nature of warehousing creates technological relationships that lead to economies of scale.

Our definition of economies of scale, although based on the type of production, relates closely to the shape of the *long-run* average cost curve. Notice that the definition requires that a doubling of *every* input must bring about more than a doubling of output. If all input quantities are doubled, total cost must double, but if output *more* than doubles when

Production is said to involve **economies of scale**, also referred to as **increasing returns to scale**, if, when all input quantities are increased by *X* percent, the quantity of output rises by *more* than *X* percent.

input quantities are doubled, then cost per unit (average cost) must decline when output increases. In other words:

Production relationships with economies of scale lead to long-run average cost curves that decline as output expands.

Figure 7(a) depicts a decreasing average cost curve but shows only one of three possible shapes that the long-run average cost curve can take. Figure 7(b) shows the curve for *constant* returns to scale. Here, if all input quantities double, both total cost (TC) and the quantity of output (Q) double, so average cost (AC = TC/Q) remains *constant*. There is also a third possibility. Output may also increase, but less than double, when all inputs double. This case of *decreasing* returns to scale leads to a *rising* long-run average cost curve like the one depicted in Figure 7(c). The figure reveals a close association between the slope of the AC curve and the nature of the firm's returns to scale.

Note that the same production function can display increasing returns to scale in some ranges, constant returns to scale in other ranges, and decreasing returns to scale in yet others. This is true of all the U-shaped average cost curves we have discussed, as shown in Figure 4(b).

The "Law" of Diminishing Returns and Returns to Scale

Earlier in this chapter, we discussed the "law" of diminishing marginal returns. Is there any relationship between economies of scale and the phenomenon of diminishing returns? At first, the two ideas may seem contradictory. After all, if a producer gets diminishing returns from her inputs as she uses more of each of them, doesn't it follow that by using more of *every* input, she must encounter decreasing returns to scale? In fact, the two principles do not contradict one another, for they deal with fundamentally different issues.

- *Returns to a single input.* This asks the question, How much does output expand if a firm increases the quantity of just *one* input, *holding all other input quantities unchanged?*
- *Returns to scale.* Here the question is, How much does output expand if all inputs are increased simultaneously by the same percentage?

The "law" of diminishing returns pertains to the first question, because it examines the effects of increasing only one input at a time. It is plausible that the firm will encounter diminishing returns as this one input becomes relatively overabundant as compared to the quantities of the firm's other inputs. Thus, for example, the addition of too much carpenter time relative to a given quantity of lumber will contribute relatively little to total garage production, yielding diminishing returns. To get the most benefit out of the hiring of an additional carpenter, the firm needs to acquire more tools and raw materials.

FIGURE 7

Three Possible Shapes for the Long-Run Average Cost Curve

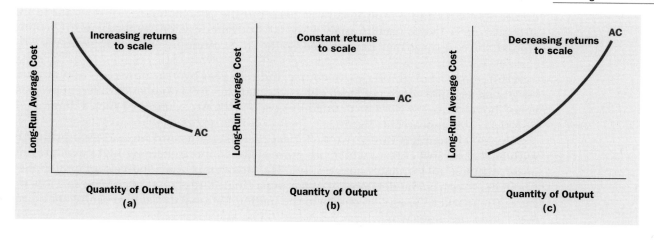

(a) Increasing returns to scale — AC — Long-Run Average Cost / Quantity of Output

(b) Constant returns to scale — AC — Long-Run Average Cost / Quantity of Output

(c) Decreasing returns to scale — AC — Long-Run Average Cost / Quantity of Output

Returns to scale pertain to proportionate increases in *all* inputs and therefore answer the second question. If Al doubles carpenter time and all other inputs as well, the carpenters need not become redundant. However, increasing the amount of one input without expanding any other inputs clearly threatens redundancy of the expanded item, even in a factory where simultaneous expansion of *all* inputs will lead to a very big jump in output. Thus, the "law" of diminishing returns (to a single input) is compatible with *any* sort of returns to scale. In summary:

> **Returns to scale and returns to a single input (holding all other inputs constant) refer to two distinct aspects of a firm's technology. A production function that displays diminishing returns to *a single input* may show diminishing, constant, or increasing returns when *all input quantities are increased proportionately*.**

Historical Costs versus Analytical Cost Curves

In Chapter 5, we noted that all points on a demand curve pertain to the *same* period of time. Decision makers must use this common time period for the analysis of an optimal decision for a given period, because the demand curve describes the alternative choices available *for the period of time to which the decision will apply*. The same is true of a cost curve. All points on a cost curve pertain to exactly the same time period, because the graph examines the cost of each alternative output level that the firm can choose for that period, thus providing the information needed to compare the alternatives and their consequences and thereby to make an optimal decision for that period.

It follows that a graph of historical data on prices and quantities at *different points in time* is normally *not* the cost curve that the decision maker needs. This observation will help us resolve the problem posed at the beginning of the chapter, which raised the question whether declining historical costs were evidence of economies of scale as information needed to decide on the optimal size of the firm in question.

> **All points on any of the cost curves used in economic analysis refer to the same period of time.**

One point on an auto manufacturer's cost curve may show, for example, how much it would cost the firm to produce 2.5 million cars during 2011. Another point on the same curve may show what would happen to the firm's costs if, *instead*, it were to produce 3 million cars in that same year. Such a curve is called an *analytical cost curve* or, when there is no possibility of confusion, simply a cost curve. This curve must be distinguished from a diagram of *historical costs*, which shows how costs have changed from year to year.

The different points on an analytical cost curve represent *alternative possibilities*, all for the same time period. In 2011, the car manufacturer will produce either 2.5 million or 3 million cars (or some other amount), but certainly not both. Thus, at most, only one point on this cost curve will ever be observed. The company may, indeed, produce 2.5 million cars in 2011 and 3 million cars in 2012, but the 2012 data are not relevant to the 2011 cost curve that is used to analyze the 2011 output decision. By the time 2012 comes around, the cost curve may have shifted, so the 2012 cost figure will not apply to the 2011 cost curve.

A different sort of graph can, of course, indicate year by year how costs and outputs vary. Such a graph, which gathers together the statistics for a number of different periods, is not, however, a *cost curve* as defined by economists. An example of such a diagram of historical costs appeared in Figure 1.

Why do economists rarely use historical cost diagrams and instead deal primarily with analytical cost curves, which are more abstract, more challenging to explain, and more difficult to estimate statistically? The answer is that analysis of real policy problems—such as the desirability of having a single supplier of telephone services for the entire market—leaves no choice in the matter. Rational decisions require analytical cost curves. Let's see why.

PUZZLE: RESOLVING THE ECONOMIES OF SCALE PUZZLE

Recall the problem that we introduced early in the chapter. We examined the divestiture of AT&T's components and concluded that, to determine whether it made sense to break up such a large company, economists would have to know whether the industry provided economies of scale. Among the data offered as evidence was a graph that showed a precipitous drop in the capital cost of long-distance communications as the volume of calls rose after 1942. But we did not answer a more pertinent question: Why didn't this information constitute legitimate evidence about the presence or absence of economies of scale?

It all boils down to the following: To determine whether a single large firm can provide telephone service more cheaply in, say, 2007 than a number of smaller firms can, we must compare the costs of *both large-scale and small-scale production in 2007*. It does no good to compare the cost of a large supplier in 2007 with its own costs as a smaller firm back in 1942, because that cannot possibly provide the needed information. The cost situation in 1942 is irrelevant for today's decision between large and small suppliers, because no small firm today would use the obsolete techniques employed in 1942.

Since the 1940s, great technical progress has taken the telephone industry from ordinary open-wire circuits to microwave systems, telecommunications satellites, coaxial cables of enormous capacity, and fiber optics. As a result, the *entire* analytical cost curve of telecommunications must have shifted downward quite dramatically from year to year. Innovation must have reduced not only the cost of large-scale operations *but also the cost of smaller-scale operations*. Until decision makers compare the costs of large and small suppliers *today*, they cannot make a rational choice between single-firm and multifirm production. It is the analytical cost curve, all of whose points refer to the same period, that, by definition, supplies this information.

Figures 8 and 9 show two extreme hypothetical cases: one that entails true economies of scale and one that does not. Both are based on the same historical cost data (in black) with their very sharply declining costs. (This curve is reproduced from Figure 1.) They also show (in brick and blue) two possible average cost (AC) curves, one for 1942 and one for 2007.

In Figure 8, the analytical AC curve has shifted downward very sharply from 1942 to 2007, as technological change reduced all costs. Moreover, both of the AC curves slope downward to the right, meaning that, in either year, a larger firm has lower average costs. Thus, the situation shown in Figure 8 really does entail scale economies, so that one large firm can serve the market at lower cost than many small ones.

Now look at Figure 9, which shows exactly the same historical costs as Figure 8. Here, however, both analytical AC curves are U-shaped. In particular, the 2007 AC curve has its minimum point at an output level, *A*, that is less than one-half of the current output, *B*, of the large supplier. Thus, the shape of the analytical cost curves does *not* show economies of scale. This means that, for the situation shown in Figure 9, a smaller company can produce more cheaply than a large one can. In this case, one cannot justify

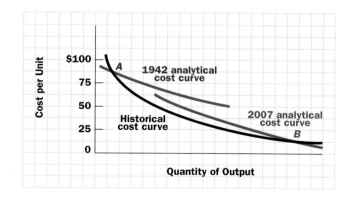

FIGURE 8

Declining Historical Cost Curve with the Analytical Average Cost Curve Also Declining in Each Year

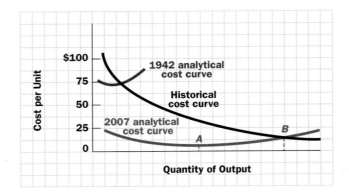

FIGURE 9

Declining Historical Cost
Curve with U-Shaped
Analytical Cost Curves in
Each Year

domination of the market by a single large firm on the grounds that its costs are lower—despite the sharp downward trend of historical costs.

In sum, the behavior of historical costs reveals nothing about the cost advantages or disadvantages of a single large firm. More generally:

> **Because a diagram of historical costs does not compare the costs of large and small firms *at the same point in time*, it cannot be used to determine whether an industry provides economies of large-scale production. Only the analytical cost curve can supply this information.**

In the case of telephone service, some estimates indicate that economies of large-scale production do indeed exist. Presumably because of this influence, 20 years after the Bell telephone system's breakup, the typical firm providing traditional long-distance telephone service is still very large, with AT&T and Verizon dominating the industry. Yet half a dozen or so other smaller firms still compete in this arena. It is perhaps ironic that a substantial proportion of the "Baby Bell" local telephone companies that were pulled away from AT&T by the courts in 1982 have recombined in order to obtain cost and other advantages of larger size. Cellular and Internet-based long-distance service has also gained ground at a rapid pace.

Cost Minimization in Theory and Practice

Lest you be tempted to run out and open a business, confident that you now understand how to minimize costs, we should point out that business decisions are a good deal more complicated than we have indicated here. Rare is the business executive who knows for sure the exact shapes of marginal physical product schedules, or the precise nature of cost curves. No one can provide an instruction book for instant success in business. What we have presented here is, instead, a set of principles that constitutes a guide to the logic of good decision making.

Business management has been described as the art of making critical decisions on the basis of inadequate information, and our complex and ever-changing world often leaves people no alternative but to make educated guesses. Actual business decisions will at best approximate the cost-minimizing ideal outlined in this chapter. Certainly, practicing managers will make mistakes, but when they do their jobs well and the market system functions smoothly, the approximation may prove amazingly good. Although no system is perfect, inducing firms to produce the output they select at the lowest possible cost is undoubtedly one of the jobs the market system does best.

POLICY DEBATE

Should Water Be Provided to Western Farmers at Subsidized Prices?

Farmers in the western United States use a great deal of water. Because most of the area's climate is high desert, agriculture there requires artificial irrigation—indeed, water is critical. In California, for example, farmers use 30 million acre-feet of water a year (almost 10 trillion gallons) to irrigate their crops—about 80 percent of that state's developed water supply. Yet western farmers and ranchers have traditionally paid very low prices for the water they use. Government controls have kept the price of water used for agriculture artificially low, so California farmers pay only a small fraction of the price that urban residents pay for water. Even during droughts, farmers in that state continued to use vast quantities of water, while residents in the cities were forced to ration.

This situation has given rise to an intense debate between farmers and environmentalists. There is no question that water is scarce in the western states, exacerbated by an increase in population, leading to predictions of a looming shortage of disastrous proportions. It is also clear that farmers pay a price that is much lower than the true marginal cost of water, particularly because that cost includes a very high *opportunity cost*—that is, the value of the other uses of water that must be forgone as a result of its extensive employment in agriculture.

As analysis in this chapter shows, a low price for an input increases the amount that producers use, and there is little doubt that the low price of water substantially increases its consumption by western farmers. Environmentalists and economists have joined forces in arguing that western water users should pay prices that cover its true marginal cost. Indeed, it has been suggested that at such a price any shortage would simply disappear.

But the farmers argue that long practice entitles them to continued low water prices and that low prices in the past induced them to invest extensively in their agricultural properties, so that a price

increase now would be tantamount to confiscating their investments. Recent small price increases for water have, in fact, encouraged farmers to utilize water-saving methods such as drip irrigation, with some farmers now eager to sell their resulting surplus water to California cities. State water authorities are working toward creating a market for farmers, cities, and private businesses to buy and sell water. This shows how higher prices can sometimes benefit society, but it also illustrates how it can raise issues of fairness to some of the persons affected.

SOURCE: © Bob Rowan; Progressive Image/CORBIS

SOURCES: Dean E. Murphy, "Water Contract Renewals Stir Debate Between Environmentalists and Farmers in California," *The New York Times*, December 15, 2004, p. A.22; James Flanigan, "Creating a Free-Flowing Market to Buy, Sell Water," *Los Angeles Times*, October 24, 2001, http://www.latimes.com; "California's Economy: The Real Trouble," *The Economist*, July 28, 2001, p. 31; and California Department of Water Resources, http://www.owue.water.ca.gov.

| SUMMARY |

1. A firm's total cost curve shows its lowest possible cost of producing any given quantity of output. This curve is derived from the input combination that the firm uses to produce any given output and the prices of the inputs.

2. The **marginal physical product** (MPP) of an input is the increase in total output resulting from a one-unit increase in that input, holding the quantities of all other inputs constant.

3. The "law" of diminishing marginal returns states that if a firm increases the amount of one input (holding all other input quantities constant), the marginal physical product of the expanding input will eventually begin to decline.

4. To maximize profits, a firm must purchase an input up to the point at which diminishing returns reduce the input's **marginal revenue product** (MRP) to equal its price ($P = MRP = MPP \times price$).

5. Average and marginal variable cost curves tend to be U-shaped, meaning that these costs decline up to a certain level of output and then begin to rise again at larger output quantities.

6. The **long run** is a period sufficiently long for the firm's plant to require replacement and for all of its current contractual commitments to expire. The **short run** is any period briefer than the long run.

7. **Fixed costs** are costs whose total amounts do not vary when output increases. All other costs are called **variable costs.** Some costs are variable in the long run but not in the short run.

8. At all levels of output, the total fixed cost (TFC) curve is horizontal and the average fixed cost (AFC) curve declines toward the horizontal axis but never crosses it.

9. TC = TFC + TVC; AC = AFC + AVC; MFC = 0.

10. It is usually possible to produce the same quantity of output in a variety of ways by substituting more of one input for less of another input. Firms normally seek the combination of inputs that offers the least costly way to produce any given output.

11. A firm that wants to minimize costs will select input quantities at which the ratios of the marginal revenue product of each input to the input's price—its MRP per dollar—are equal for all inputs.

12. If a doubling of all the firm's inputs just doubles its output, the firm is said to have constant returns to scale. If a doubling of all inputs leads to more than twice as much output, it has **increasing returns to scale** (or **economies of scale**). If a doubling of inputs produces less than a doubling of output, the firm has decreasing returns to scale.

13. With increasing returns to scale, the firm's long-run average costs are decreasing; constant returns to scale are associated with constant long-run average costs; decreasing returns to scale are associated with increasing long-run average costs.

14. Economists cannot tell if an industry offers economies of scale (increasing returns to scale) simply by inspecting a diagram of historical cost data. Only the underlying analytical cost curve can supply this information.

| KEY TERMS |

average physical product (APP)   130

economies of scale (increasing returns to scale)   142

fixed cost   129

long run   129

marginal physical product (MPP)   131

marginal revenue product (MRP)   133

short run   129

total physical product (TPP)   130

variable cost   129

| TEST YOURSELF |

1. A firm's total fixed cost is $360,000. Construct a table of its total and average fixed costs for output levels varying from zero to 6 units. Draw the corresponding TFC and AFC curves.

2. With the following data, calculate the firm's AVC and MVC and draw the graphs for TVC, AVC, and MVC. Why is MVC the same as MC?

Quantity	Total Variable Costs
1	$40,000
2	80,000
3	120,000
4	176,000
5	240,000
6	360,000

3. From the data in Test Yourself Questions 1 and 2, calculate TC and AC for each of the output levels from 1 to 6 units and draw the two graphs.

4. If a firm's commitments in 2008 include machinery that will need replacement in 5 years, a factory building rented for 12 years, and a 3-year union contract specifying how many workers it must employ, when, from its point of view in 2008, does the firm's long run begin?

5. If the marginal revenue product of a gallon of oil used as input by a firm is $2.20 and the price of oil is $2.07 per gallon, what can the firm do to increase its profits?

6. A firm hires two workers and rents 15 acres of land for a season. It produces 150,000 bushels of crop. If it had doubled its land and labor, production would have been 325,000 bushels. Does it have constant, decreasing, or increasing returns to scale?

7. Suppose that wages are $20,000 per season per person and land rent per acre is $3,000. Calculate the average cost of 150,000 bushels and the average cost of 325,000 bushels, using the figures in Test Yourself Question 6. (Note that average costs increase when output increases.) What connection do these figures have with the firm's returns to scale?

8. Naomi has stockpiled a great deal of chicken feed. Suppose now that she buys more chicks, but not more chicken feed, and divides the feed she has evenly among the larger number of chickens. What is likely to happen to the marginal physical product of feed? What, therefore, is the role of input proportions in the determination of marginal physical product?

9. Labor costs $12 per hour. Nine workers produce 180 bushels of product per hour, whereas 10 workers produce 196 bushels. Land rents for $1,200 per acre per year. With 10 acres worked by nine workers, the marginal physical product of an acre of land is 1,400 bushels per year. Does the farmer minimize costs by hiring nine workers and renting 10 acres of land? If not, which input should he use in larger relative quantity?

10. Suppose that Al's total costs increase by $5,000 per year at every output level. Show in Table 2 how this change affects his total and average costs.

| DISCUSSION QUESTION |

1. A firm experiences a sudden increase in the demand for its product. In the short run, it must operate longer hours and pay higher overtime wage rates to satisfy this new demand. In the long run, the firm can install more machines instead of operating fewer machines for longer hours. Which do you think will be lower, the short-run or the long-run average cost of the increased output? How is your answer affected by the fact that the long-run average cost includes the new machines the firm buys, whereas the short-run average cost includes no machine purchases?

| APPENDIX | *Production Indifference Curves*

To describe a production function—that is, the relationship between input combinations and the size of a firm's total output—economists use a graphic device called the **production indifference curve.** Each indifference curve indicates *all* combinations of input quantities just capable of producing a *given* quantity of output; thus, a separate indifference curve corresponds to each possible quantity of output. These production indifference curves are perfectly analogous to the consumer indifference curves discussed in the appendix to Chapter 5.

> A production indifference curve (sometimes called an *isoquant*) is a curve showing all the different quantities of two inputs that are just sufficient to produce a given quantity of output.

Figure 10 represents different quantities of labor and capital capable of producing given amounts of wheat. The figure shows three indifference curves: one for the production of 220,000 bushels of wheat, one for 240,000 bushels, and one for 260,000 bushels. The indifference curve labeled 220,000 bushels indicates that a farm can generate an output of 220,000 bushels of wheat using *any one* of the combinations of inputs represented by points on that curve. For example, it can employ 10 years of labor and 200 acres of land (point *A*) or the labor–land combination shown by point *B* on the same curve. Because it lies considerably below and to the right of point *B,* point *A* represents a productive process that uses more labor and less land.

Points *A* and *B* can be considered *technologically* indifferent because each represents a bundle of inputs just capable of yielding the same quantity of finished goods. However, "indifference" in this sense does not mean that the producer will be unable to decide between input combinations *A* and *B.* Input prices will permit the producer to arrive at a decision.

The production indifference curves in a diagram such as Figure 10 show for each combination of inputs how much output can be produced. Because production indifference curves are drawn in two dimensions, they represent only two inputs at a time. In more realistic situations, firms are likely to need more than two inputs,

FIGURE 10

A Production Indifference Map

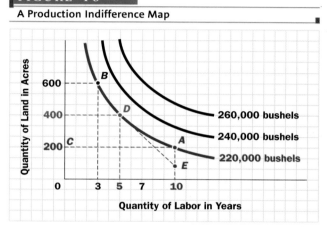

so, to study the subject, economists must conduct an algebraic analysis. Even so, all the principles we need to analyze such a situation can be derived from the two-variable case.

CHARACTERISTICS OF THE PRODUCTION INDIFFERENCE CURVES, OR ISOQUANTS

Before discussing input pricing and quantity decisions, we first examine what is known about the shapes of production indifference curves.

Characteristic 1: *Higher curves correspond to larger outputs.* Points on a higher indifference curve represent larger quantities of *both* inputs than the corresponding points on a lower curve. Thus, a higher curve represents a larger output.

Characteristic 2: *An indifference curve will generally have a negative slope.* It goes downhill as we move toward the right. Thus, if a firm reduces the quantity of one input, and if it does not want to cut production, it must use more of another input.

Characteristic 3: *An indifference curve is typically assumed to curve inward toward the origin near its middle.* This shape reflects the "law" of diminishing returns to a single input. For example, in Figure 10, points B, D, and A represent three different input combinations capable of producing the same quantity of output. At point B, the firm uses a large amount of land and relatively little labor, whereas the opposite is true at point A. Point D is intermediate between the two.

Now consider the choice among these input combinations. When the farmer considers moving from point B to point D, he gives up 200 acres of land and instead hires 2 additional years of labor. Similarly, the move from D to A involves giving up another 200 acres of land. This time, however, hiring an additional 2 years of labor does not make up for the reduced use of land. Diminishing returns to labor as the farmer hires more and more workers to replace more and more land means that the farm now needs a much larger quantity of additional labor—5 person-years rather than 2—to make up for the reduction in the use of land. Without such diminishing returns, the indifference curve would have been a straight line, DE. The curvature of the indifference curve through points D and A reflects diminishing returns to substitution of inputs.

THE CHOICE OF INPUT COMBINATIONS

A production indifference curve describes only the input combinations that *can* produce a given output; it indicates just what is technologically possible. To decide which of the available options suits its purposes best, a business needs the corresponding cost information: the relative prices of the inputs.

The **budget line** in Figure 11 represents all equally costly input combinations for a firm. For example, if farmhands are paid $9,000 per year and land rents for $1,000 per acre per year, then a farmer who spends $360,000 can hire 40 farmhands but rent no land (point K), or he can rent 360 acres but have no money left for farmhands (point J). It is undoubtedly more sensible to pick some intermediate point on his budget line at which he divides the $360,000 between the two inputs. The slope of the budget line represents the amount of land the farmer must give up if he wants to hire one more worker without increasing his budget.

A budget line is the locus of all points representing every input combination of inputs that the producer can afford to buy with a given amount of money and given input prices.

If the prices of the inputs do not change, then the slope of the budget line will not change anywhere in the graph. It will be the same at every point on a given

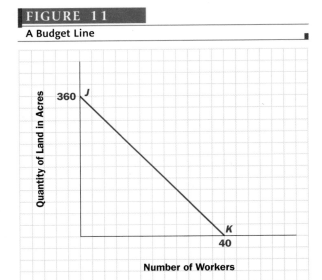

FIGURE 11

A Budget Line

budget line, and it will be the same on the $360,000 budget line as on the $400,000 budget line or on the budget line for any other level of spending. For if the price of hiring a worker is nine times as high as the cost of renting an acre, then the farmer must rent nine fewer acres to hire an additional farmhand without changing the total amount of money he spends on these inputs. Thus, the slope will be acres given up per added farmhand = $-9/1 = -9$.

With the input prices given, the slope of any budget line does not change and the slopes of the different budget lines for different amounts of expenditures are all the same. Two results follow: (1) The budget lines are straight lines because their slopes remain the same throughout their length, and (2) because they all have the same slope, the budget lines in the graph will all be parallel, as in Figure 12.

A firm that is seeking to minimize costs does not necessarily have a fixed budget. Instead, it wants to produce a given quantity of output (say, 240,000 bushels) with *the smallest possible budget*.

Figure 12 combines the indifference curve for 240,000 bushels from Figure 10 with a variety of budget lines similar to JK in Figure 11. The firm's task is to find the lowest budget line that will allow it to reach the 240,000-bushel indifference curve. Clearly, an expenditure of $270,000 is too little; no point on the budget line, AB, permits production of 240,000 bushels. Similarly, an expenditure of $450,000 is too much, because the firm can produce its target level of output more cheaply. The solution is at point T where the farmer uses 15 workers and 225 acres of land to produce the 240,000 bushels of wheat. That budget line, the one that is tangent to the relevant indifference curve, is evidently the lowest budget line that meets

FIGURE 12

Cost Minimization

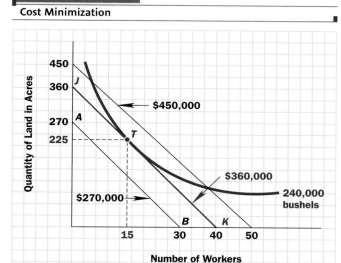

FIGURE 13

The Firm's Expansion Path

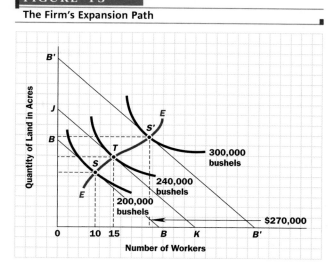

the indifference curve anywhere, so it represents the lowest-cost input combination capable of producing the desired output. In general:

> The least costly way to produce any given level of output is indicated by the point of tangency between a budget line and the production indifference curve corresponding to that level of output.

COST MINIMIZATION, EXPANSION PATH, AND COST CURVES

Figure 12 shows how to determine the input combination that minimizes the cost of producing 240,000 bushels of output. The farmer can repeat this procedure exactly for any other output quantity, such as 200,000 bushels or 300,000 bushels. In each case, we draw the corresponding production indifference curve and find the lowest budget line that permits the farm to produce that much. For example, in Figure 13, budget line *BB* is tangent to the indifference curve for 200,000 units of output; similarly, budget line *JK* is tangent to the indifference curve for 240,000 bushels; and budget line *B'B'* is tangent to the indifference curve for 300,000 units of output. This gives us three tangency points: *S*, which gives the input combination that produces a 200,000-bushel output at lowest cost; *T*, which gives the same information for a 240,000-bushel output; and *S'*, which indicates the cost-minimizing input combination for the production of 300,000 bushels.

This process can be repeated for as many other levels of output as we like. For each such output we draw the corresponding production indifference curve and find its point of tangency with a budget line. The brick-colored

curve *EE* in Figure 13 connects all of the cost-minimizing points; that is, it is the locus of *S, T, S',* and all other points of tangency between a production indifference curve and a budget line. Curve *EE* is called the firm's **expansion path.**

> The expansion path is the locus of the firm's cost-minimizing input combinations for all relevant output levels.

Point *T* in Figure 12 shows the quantity of output (given by the production indifference curve through that point) and the total cost (shown by the tangent budget line). Similarly, we can determine the output and total cost for every other point on the expansion path, *EE,* in Figure 13. For example, at point *S,* output is 200,000 bushels and total cost is $270,000. These data are precisely the sort of information we need to find the firm's total cost curve; that is, they are the sort of information contained in Table 3, which is the source of the total cost curve and the average and marginal cost curves in Figure 4. Thus:

> The points of tangency between a firm's production indifference curves and its budget lines yield its expansion path, which shows the firm's cost-minimizing input combination for each pertinent output level. This information also yields the output and total cost for each point on the expansion path, which is what we need to draw the firm's cost curves.

Suppose that the cost of renting land increases and the wage rate of labor decreases. These changes mean that the budget lines will differ from those depicted in Figure 12. Specifically, with land becoming more expensive, any given sum of money will rent fewer acres, so the intercept of each budget line on the vertical (land) axis will shift *downward*. Conversely, with cheaper labor, any given sum of money will buy more labor, so the intercept of the budget line on the horizontal (labor) axis will shift to the *right*. Figure 14 depicts a series of budget lines corresponding to a $1,500 per acre rental rate for land and a $6,000 annual wage for labor. If input prices change, the combination of inputs that minimizes costs will normally change. In this diagram, the land rent at $1,500 per acre is more than it was in Figure 12, whereas labor costs $6,000 per year (less than in Figure 12). As a result, these budget lines are less steep than those shown in Figure 12, and point E now represents the least costly way to produce 240,000 bushels of wheat.

To assist you in seeing how things change, Figure 15 combines, in a single graph, budget line *JK* and tangency point *T* from Figure 12 with budget line *WV* and tangency point *E* from Figure 14. When land becomes more expensive and labor becomes cheaper, the budget lines (such as *JK*) become less steep than they were previously (see *WV*). As a result, the least costly way to produce 240,000 bushels shifts from point *T* to point *E*, at which the firm uses more labor and less land. As common sense suggests, when the price of one input rises in comparison with that of another, it will pay the firm to use less of the more expensive input and more of the other input.

In addition to substituting one input for another, a change in the price of an input may induce the firm to alter its level of output. We will cover this subject in the next chapter.

FIGURE 14

Optimal Input Choice at a Different Set of Input Prices

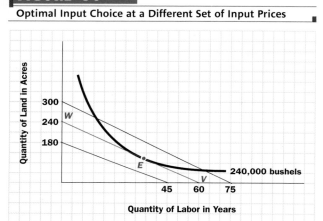

FIGURE 15

How Changes in Input Prices Affect Input Proportions

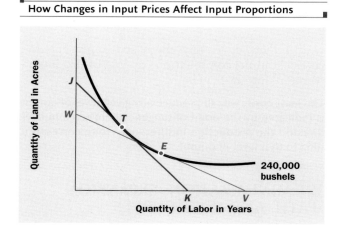

| SUMMARY |

1. A production relationship can be described by a series of **production indifference curves,** each of which shows all input combinations capable of producing a specified amount of output.

2. As long as each input has a positive marginal physical product, production indifference curves will have negative slopes and the higher curves will represent larger amounts of output than the lower curves. Because of diminishing returns, these curves characteristically bend toward the origin near the middle.

3. The optimal input combination for any given level of output is indicated by the point of tangency between a **budget line** and the corresponding production indifference curve.

4. The firm's **expansion path** shows, for each of its possible output levels, the combination of input quantities that minimizes the cost of producing that output.

5. Total cost for each output level can be derived from the production indifference curves and the budget lines tangent to them along the expansion path. These figures can be used to determine the firm's total cost, average cost, and marginal cost curves.

6. When input prices change, firms will normally use more of the input that becomes relatively less expensive and less of the input that becomes relatively more expensive.

| KEY TERMS |

| TEST YOURSELF |

1. Compound Consolidated Corporation (CCC) produces containers using two inputs: labor and glue. If labor costs $10 per hour and glue costs $5 per gallon, draw CCC's budget line for a total expenditure of $100,000. In this same diagram, sketch a production indifference curve indicating that CCC can produce no more than 1,000 containers with this expenditure.

2. With respect to Test Yourself Question 1, suppose that wages rise to $20 per hour and glue prices rise to $6 per gallon. How are CCC's optimal input proportions likely to change? (Use a diagram to explain your answer.)

3. What happens to the location of the expansion path of the firm in Test Yourself Question 2?

OUTPUT, PRICE, AND PROFIT:
THE IMPORTANCE OF MARGINAL ANALYSIS

Business is a good game. . . . You keep score with money.

**NOLAN BUSNELL, FOUNDER OF ATARI
(AN EARLY VIDEO GAME MAKER)**

Suppose you become president of a firm that makes video games. One of your most critical decisions will be how many video games to produce and at what price to offer them for sale. The owners of the company presumably want to make as much profit as possible. This chapter explores the logic underlying the decisions that lead to achievement of this goal.

With this chapter, we cap off our discussion of the fundamental building blocks of microeconomics. Chapters 5 and 6 dealt with the behavior of consumers. Chapter 7 introduced the other main participant in microeconomics, the firm. The firm's two main roles are, first, to produce its product efficiently and, second, to sell that product at a profit. Chapter 7 described production decisions and demonstrated that this process yields cost data. We will soon see in the current chapter that this is cost information the firm's management needs to determine the price and output of its product that will yield a profit as high as market conditions permit. In Chapter 9, we will discuss stocks and bonds as instruments that enable business firms to obtain the money needed to finance their production and sales activities and as an earnings opportunity for individuals who consider investing in firms.

Throughout Part 2, we have described how firms and consumers can make *optimal decisions,* meaning that their decisions go as far as possible, given the circumstances, to promote the consumer's and producer's goals. In this chapter, we will continue to assume that business firms seek primarily to maximize total profit, just as we assumed that consumers maximize utility. (See the box "Do Firms Really Maximize Profits?" on the following page, for a discussion of other objectives of business firms.)

CONTENTS

Do Firms Really Maximize Profits?

Naturally, many people question whether firms really try to maximize profits to the exclusion of all other goals. But businesspeople are like other human beings: Their motives are varied and complex. Given the choice, many executives may prefer to control the *largest* firm rather than the most profitable one. Some may be fascinated by technology and therefore spend so much on research and development that it cuts down on profit. Some may want to "do good" and therefore give away some of the stockholders' money to hospitals and colleges. Different managers within the same firm may not always agree with one another on goals, so that it may not even make sense to speak about "the" goal of the firm. Thus, any attempt to summarize the objectives of management in terms of a single number (profit) is bound to be an oversimplification.

In addition, the exacting requirements for maximizing profits are tough to satisfy. In deciding how much to invest, what price to set for a product, or how much to allocate to the advertising budget, the range of available alternatives is enormous. Also, information about each alternative is often expensive and difficult to acquire. As a result, when a firm's management decides on, say, an $18 million construction budget, it rarely compares the consequences of that decision in any detail with the consequences of all possible alternatives—such as budgets of $17 million or $19 million. Unless all the available possibilities are compared, management cannot be sure that it has chosen the one that brings in the highest possible profit.

Often, management's concern is whether the decision's results are likely to be acceptable—whether its risks will be acceptably low, whether its profits will be acceptably high—so that the company can live satisfactorily with the outcome. Such analysis cannot be expected to bring in the maximum possible profit. The decision may be good, but some unexplored alternative may be even better.

Decision making that seeks only solutions that are acceptable has been called *satisficing,* to contrast it with optimizing (profit maximization). Some analysts, such as the late Nobel Prize winner

Herbert Simon of Carnegie-Mellon University, have concluded that decision making in industry and government is often of the satisficing variety.

Even if this assertion is true, it does not necessarily make profit maximization a bad assumption. Recall our discussion of abstraction and model building in Chapter 1. A map of Los Angeles that omits hundreds of roads is no doubt "wrong" if interpreted as a literal description of the city. Nonetheless, by capturing the most important elements of reality, it may help us understand the city better than a map that is cluttered with too much detail. Similarly, we can learn much about the behavior of business firms by assuming that they try to maximize profits, even though we know that not all of them act this way all of the time.

"It's true that more is not necessarily better, Edward, but it frequently is."

An optimal decision is one which, among all the decisions that are actually possible, best achieves the decision maker's goals. For example, if profit is the sole objective of some firm, the price that makes the firm's profit as large as possible is optimal for that company.

As in the previous three chapters, marginal analysis helps us to determine what constitutes an **optimal decision.** Because that method of analysis is so useful, this chapter summarizes and generalizes what we have learned about the methods of marginal analysis, showing also how this analysis applies in many other situations in which optimality is an issue.

Marginal analysis leads to some surprising conclusions that show how misleading unaided "common sense" can sometimes be. Here's an example. Suppose a firm suffers a sharp increase in its rent or some other fixed cost. How should the firm react? Some would argue that the firm should raise the price of its product to cover the higher rent; others would argue that it should cut its price so as to increase its sales enough to pay the increased rent. We will see in this chapter that *both* of these answers are incorrect! A profit-maximizing firm faced with a rent increase should neither raise nor lower its price if it wants to prevent its net earnings from falling.

| **PUZZLE:** | CAN A COMPANY MAKE A PROFIT BY SELLING BELOW ITS COSTS? |

Price and output decisions can sometimes perplex even the most experienced businesspeople. The following real-life illustration seems to show that it is possible for a firm to make a profit by selling at a price that is apparently below its cost.[1]

In a recent legal battle between two manufacturers of pocket calculators, Company B accused Company A of selling 10 million sophisticated calculators at a price of $12, which Company A allegedly knew was too low to cover costs. Company B claimed that Company A was cutting its price simply to drive Company B out of business. At first, Company A's records, as revealed to the court, appeared to confirm Company B's accusations. The cost of materials, labor, advertising, and other direct costs of the calculators came to $10.30 per calculator. Company A's accountants also assigned to this product its share of the company's annual expenditure on overhead—such items as general administration, research, and the like—which amounted to $4.25 per calculator. The $12 price clearly did not cover the $14.55 cost attributed to each calculator. Yet economists representing Company A were able to convince the court that, at the $12 price, manufacturing the calculator was a profitable activity for Company A, so there was no basis on which to conclude that its only purpose was to destroy B. At the end of the chapter, we'll see how ordinary good sense is not necessarily the best guide in business decisions and how marginal analysis helped solve this problem.

PRICE AND QUANTITY: ONE DECISION, NOT TWO

When your company introduces a new line of video games, the marketing department has to decide what price to charge and how many games to produce. These crucial decisions strongly influence the firm's labor requirements, the consumer response to the product, and, indeed, the company's future success. This chapter's main focus is on how to determine these two quantities so as to maximize the firm's profits.

When the firm selects a *price* and a *quantity* of output that maximize profits, it seems that it must choose two numbers. In fact, however, the firm can pick only one. Once it has selected the *price*, the *quantity* it can sell is up to consumers. Alternatively, the firm may decide how many units it would like to sell, but then the market will determine the *price* at which this quantity can be sold. The firm's dilemma explicitly illustrates the powerful role that consumers play in the market. Management gets two numbers by making only one decision because the firm's demand curve tells it, for any quantity it may decide to market, the highest possible price its product can bring.

To illustrate, we return to Chapter 7's garage-building example. Al's Building Contractors sells garages to individual homeowners, and Al is trying to figure out how best to make money on his building operation. To do this, he must estimate his *firm's demand curve*. The firm's demand curve is different from the demand curves we encountered in earlier chapters—the demand curve of an individual consumer and the market demand curve (which is the combined demand of all consumers in the market). Now we are dealing with a single firm (Al's Building Contractors) that is only one among possibly many firms that serve the market. The demand curve of any one supplier depends on the number and activities of the other firms in the market, as each competes for its share of total market demand. The demand curve of a single firm is actually a complicated matter that we will deal with several times in subsequent chapters.[2] For now, suffice it to say that Al's

---

[1] The following case is disguised to protect the confidentiality of the firms involved.

[2] In one case, the relation between market demand and firm demand is very easy. That is the case where the firm has no competitors—it is a *monopoly*. Since it has the entire market to itself, its demand curve and the market demand curve are one and the same. We deal with monopoly in Chapter 11. Another fairly straightforward case, called perfect competition, will be studied in Chapter 10.

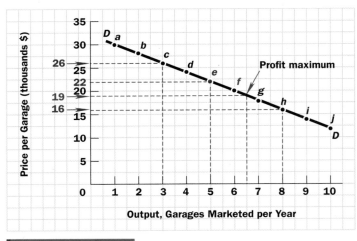

FIGURE 1

Demand Curve for
Al's Garages

demand curve will lie closer to the market demand curve (meaning that Al has a greater share of the market), the better his service, the more effective his advertising, the stronger his reputation for quality, and so on.

Suppose Al faces the demand curve for his garages shown as *DD* in Figure 1. The curve depicts the quantity demanded at each price. For example, the curve shows that at a price of $22,000 per garage (point *e*), Al's customers will demand five garages. If Al gets greedy and tries to charge the higher price of $26,000 per garage (point *c* on the curve), he can sell only three garages. If he wants to sell eight garages, he can find the required number of customers only by offering the garages at the lower price of $16,000 each (point *h*). In summary:

Each point on the demand curve represents a price–quantity pair. The firm can pick any such pair. It can never pick the price corresponding to one point on the demand curve and the quantity corresponding to another point, however, because such an output cannot be sold at the selected price.

For this reason, we will not discuss price and output decisions separately throughout this chapter, for they are actually two different aspects of the same decision. To analyze this decision, we will make an imperfectly realistic assumption about the behavior of business firms—the assumption that firms strive for the largest possible total profit to the exclusion of any other goal. We will therefore assume throughout this chapter (and for most of the book) that the firm has only one objective: It wants to make its total profit as large as possible. Our analytic strategy will seek to determine what output level (or price) achieves this goal, but you should keep in mind that many of our results depend on this simplifying assumption, so the conclusions will not apply to every case. Our decision to base the analysis on the profit-maximizing assumption gives us sharper insights, but we pay for it with some loss of realism.

The **total profit** of a firm is its net earnings during some period of time. It is equal to the total amount of money the firm gets from sales of its products (the firm's total revenue) minus the total amount that it spends to make and market those products (total cost).

TOTAL PROFIT: KEEP YOUR EYE ON THE GOAL

Total profit, then, is the firm's assumed goal. By definition, total profit is the difference between what the company earns in the form of sales revenue and what it pays out in the form of costs:

Total profit = Total revenue − Total cost (including opportunity cost)

IDEAS FOR
BEYOND THE
FINAL EXAM

OPPORTUNITY COST AND PROFIT Total profit defined in this way is called *economic profit* to distinguish it from an accountant's definition of profit. The two concepts of profit differ because an economist's total cost counts the *opportunity cost* of any capital, labor, or other inputs supplied by the firm's owner. For example, let's say that Naomi, who owns a small business, earns just enough to pay herself the money that her labor and capital could have earned if they had been sold to others (say, $60,000 per year). Then, as we saw in Chapter 3, economists would say that she is earning zero economic profit. (Naomi is just covering all her costs, including her opportunity costs.) In contrast, most accountants would say her profit is $60,000, referring to the difference between her gross receipts and gross costs.

ECONOMIC PROFIT AND OPTIMAL DECISION MAKING

Why do economists use this apparently strange definition of profits, in which they subtract not only the costs that would ordinarily be deducted from total revenue but also the opportunity costs? The answer is that doing so tells us directly whether the firm has made an *optimal* decision, in other words, whether the firm has chosen the price and quantity that maximizes profits. Specifically:

1. If economic profit is positive, then the firm's decisions are optimal; that is, its price and output yield a profit larger than any alternative prices and outputs.
2. If economic profit is zero, then the firm's choices are still satisfactory, because its price and output yield as much profit as the best available alternative.
3. If economic profit is negative, then the choice is not optimal; there exists at least one alternative price–output combination that is more profitable.

This reasoning explains why we pay so much attention to opportunity cost: because it helps us to determine whether or not a decision is optimal. It works for all decisions, not only those about prices and quantities. But how does it do so? An example will make it clear. Suppose a firm has $100,000 to spend on either packaging or advertising. Suppose further that if the $100,000 is spent on packaging, it will bring in an accounting profit (that is, a profit as ordinarily defined: total revenue minus total ordinary cost, leaving out opportunity cost) of $20,000. If, instead, the (accounting) profit it could obtain from a $100,000 investment in advertising is $X, then by definition, $X is the opportunity cost of the decision to invest in packaging. In other words, $X is the earnings that could have been obtained from the alternative opportunity that the firm gives up by investing in packaging. So, for the possible decision to invest in packaging:

Economic **profit = Accounting profit − Opportunity cost = $20,000 − $X = The difference between the earnings offered by the two alternative investments**

This immediately illustrates our three conclusions above, because:

1. If $X < $20,000, then economic profit > 0, because packaging, which yields $20,000, is the more profitable investment choice.
2. If $X = $20,000, then economic profit = 0, and the two investment options are equally profitable.
3. And if $X > $20,000, then the economic profit of packaging ($20,000 − $X) is negative, so advertising must be a more profitable investment than packaging.

The reason economic profit performs this test is simple:

Economic profit of the decision in question = its accounting profit − its opportunity cost = accounting profit of the decision in question − accounting profit of the best available alternative. So, the economic profit of the decision in question will be positive only if it is more profitable (in the accountant's measurement) than the alternative, and so on.

Economic profit equals net earnings, in the accountant's sense, minus the *opportunity costs* of capital and of any other inputs supplied by the firm's owners.

Total, Average, and Marginal Revenue

To see how total profit depends on output, we must study how the two components of total profit, total revenue (TR) and total cost (TC), behave when output changes. It should be obvious that both total revenue and total cost depend on the output–price combination the firm selects; we will study these relationships presently.

We can calculate **total revenue** directly from the firm's demand curve because, by definition, it is the product of price times the quantity that consumers will buy at that price:

$$TR = P \times Q$$

Table 1 shows how we derive the total revenue schedule from the demand schedule for Al's garages. The first two columns simply give the relevant quantities and the price of the corresponding quantity, so that they express Figure 1's demand curve in tabular form. The third column gives, for each quantity, the product of price times quantity. For example, if Al sells seven garages at a price of $18,000 per garage, his annual sales revenue will be 7 garages × $18,000 per garage = $126,000.

The **total revenue** of a supplier firm is the total amount of money it receives from the purchasers of its products, without any deduction of costs.

TABLE 1

Demand for Al's Garages: His Total Revenue Schedule and His Marginal Revenue Schedule

(1)	(2)	(3)	(4)
	Price = Average Revenue	Total Revenue	Marginal Revenue per Added
Garages per Year	per Garage (in thousands)	per Year (in thousands)	Garage (in thousands)
0	—	$ 0	
1	$30	30	$30
2	28	56	26
3	26	78	22
4	24	96	18
5	22	110	14
6	20	120	10
7	18	126	6
8	16	128	2
9	14	126	-2
10	12	120	-6

The **average revenue (AR)** is **total revenue (TR)** divided by quantity.

Marginal revenue (MR) is the addition to total revenue resulting from the addition of one unit to total output. Geometrically, marginal revenue is the slope of the total revenue curve at the pertinent output quantity. Its formula is $MR_1 = TR_1 - TR_0$, and so on.

Figure 2 displays Al's total revenue schedule in graphic form as the black TR curve. This graph shows precisely the same information as the demand curve in Figure 1, but in a somewhat different form. For example, point f on the demand curve in Figure 1, which shows a price–quantity combination of $P = \$20,000$ per garage and $Q = 6$ garages per year, appears as point F in Figure 2 as a total revenue of $120,000 per year ($20,000 per garage $\times$ 6 garages). Similarly, each other point on the TR curve in Figure 2 corresponds to the similarly labeled point in Figure 1.

We can speak of the relationship between the demand curve and the TR curve in a slightly different and more useful way than that shown in Figure 1. Because the product price is the revenue per unit that the firm receives, we can view the demand curve as an **average revenue (AR)** curve. To see why this is so, observe that average revenue and total revenue are, by definition, related to one another by the formula $AR = TR/Q$ and, as we have seen, $TR = P \times Q$. Therefore,[3]

$$AR = TR/Q = P \times Q/Q = P$$

As you can see, average revenue and price are just different names for the same thing. The reason should be clear. If a supermarket sells a brand of candy bars *at the same price*—say, $1—to each and every customer who wants one, then the average revenue that the store derives from each sale of these candy bars must also be $1.

Finally, the last column of Table 1 shows the **marginal revenue (MR)** for each level of output. Marginal revenue provides us with an analytic tool whose use we will explain presently. This concept (analogous to marginal utility and marginal cost) refers to the *addition* to total revenue that results from raising output by one unit. Thus, in Table 1, we see that when output rises from two to three garages, total revenue goes up from $56,000 to $78,000, so marginal revenue is $78,000 minus $56,000, or $22,000.

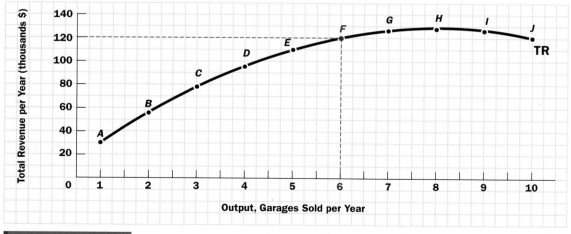

FIGURE 2

Total Revenue Curve for Al's Garages

[3] See the appendix to this chapter for a general discussion of the relationship between totals and averages.

Total, Average, and Marginal Cost

The revenue side is, of course, only half of the firm's profit picture. We must turn to the cost side for the other half. As we saw in Chapter 7, average cost (AC) and marginal cost (MC) are obtained directly from total cost (TC) in exactly the same way that average and marginal revenue are calculated from total revenue.

Figure 3 plots the numbers in Table 2 and thus shows the total, average, and marginal cost curves for Al's garage-building operation. As we learned in Chapter 7, the U-shapes of the average cost and marginal cost curves depicted here are considered typical. The shapes mean that, in any given industry, there is one size of firm that is most efficient in producing the output. Smaller enterprises lose any advantages that derive from a large volume of production, and so their average cost (the cost per unit of output) will be greater than that of a firm operating at the most efficient size of output. Similarly, firms that are too large will suffer from difficulties of supervision and coordination, and perhaps from bureaucratic controls, so that their costs per unit of output will also be higher than those of a firm of the most efficient size.

Maximization of Total Profit

We now have all the tools to answer our central question: What combination of output and price will yield the largest possible total profit? To study how total profit depends on output, Table 3 brings together the total revenue and total cost schedules from Tables 1 and 2. The fourth column in Table 3—called, appropriately enough, total profit—is just the difference between total revenue and total cost at each level of output.

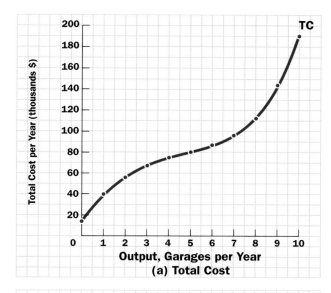

(a) Total Cost

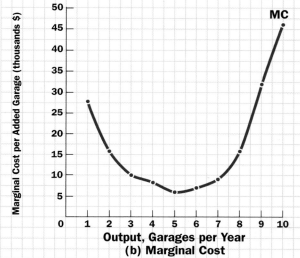

(b) Marginal Cost

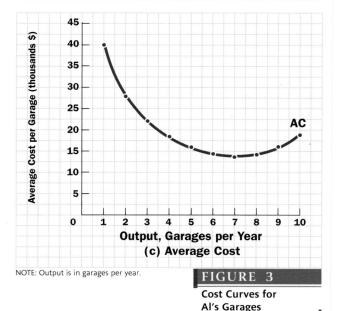

(c) Average Cost

NOTE: Output is in garages per year.

FIGURE 3

Cost Curves for Al's Garages

TABLE 2

Al's Total, Average, and Marginal Costs

(1) Garages per Year	(2) Total Cost per Year (in thousands)	(3) Marginal Cost per Added Garage (in thousands)	(4) Average Cost per Garage (in thousands)
0	$ 12		—
1	40	$28	$40
2	56	16	28
3	66	10	22
4	74	8	18.5
5	80	6	16
6	87	7	14.5
7	96	9	13.7 (approx.)
8	112	16	14
9	144	32	16
10	190	46	19

TABLE 3
Total Revenues, Costs, and Profit for Al's Garages

(1) Garages per Year	(2) Total Revenue (TR) (in thousands)	(3) Total Cost (TC) (in thousands)	(4) Total Profit (TR – TC) (in thousands)	(5) Marginal Profit (in thousands)
0	$ 0	$ 12	$–12	
1	30	40	–10	$ 2
2	56	56	0	10
3	78	66	12	12
4	96	74	22	10
5	110	80	30	8
6	120	87	33	3
7	126	96	30	–3
8	128	112	16	–14
9	126	144	–18	–34
10	120	190	–70	–52

Because we assume that Al's objective is to maximize profits, it is simple enough to determine the level of production he will choose. The table indicates that by producing and selling six garages per year, Al's garage-building operation obtains the highest level of profit it is capable of earning—$33,000 per year (actually, we will see in a moment that it pays Al to produce a little more than this amount). Any higher or lower rate of production would lead to lower profits. For example, profits would drop to $30,000 if output increased to seven garages. If Al were to make the mistake of producing ten garages per season, he would actually suffer a net loss.

Profit Maximization: A Graphical Interpretation

We can present the same information on a graph. In Figure 4(a), we bring together into a single diagram the relevant portion of the total revenue curve from Figure 2 and the total cost curve from

FIGURE 4
Profit Maximization:
A Graphical
Interpretation

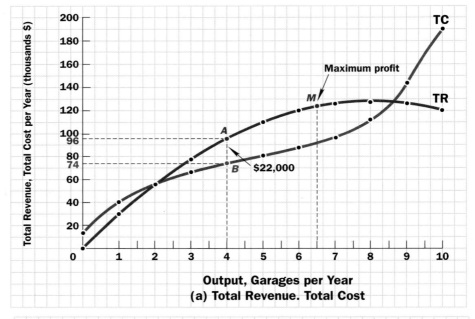

(a) Total Revenue. Total Cost

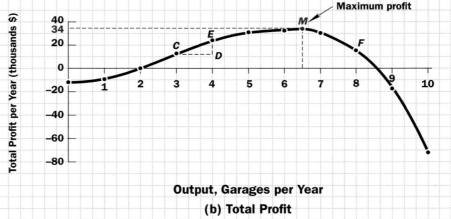

(b) Total Profit

NOTE: Output is in garages per year.

Figure 3. Total profit, which is the difference between total revenue and total cost, appears in the diagram as the vertical distance between the TR and TC curves. For example, when output is four garages, total revenue is $96,000 (point *A*), total cost is $74,000 (point *B*), and total profit is the distance between points *A* and *B*, or $22,000.

In this graphical view of the problem, Al wants to maximize total profit, which is the vertical distance between the TR and TC curves. Figure 4(b) plots these vertical differences derived from Figure 4(a) and so it shows the curve of total profit—that is, TR − TC. We see that it reaches its maximum value of about $34,000 (point *M*) at an output level of 6.5 garages per year—that is, 13 garages every two years. This graph shows that the conclusion we reached by looking at Table 3 was approximately right, but not perfectly accurate. Why? Because the table did not consider the possibility that the labor and material it pays Al to acquire may make it profitable to start on the construction of yet another garage after the first six are completed, with this garage being finished in the next year. We will consider this possibility in more detail in a few paragraphs.

The total profit curve in Figure 4(b) is shaped like a hill. Although such a shape is not inevitable, we expect a hill shape to be typical for the following reason: If a firm produces nothing, it certainly earns no profit. At the other extreme, a firm can produce so much output that it swamps the market, forcing price down so low that it loses money. Only at intermediate levels of output—something between zero and the amount that floods the market—can the company earn a positive profit. Consequently, the total profit curve will rise from zero (or negative) levels at a very small output to positive levels at intermediate outputs; finally, it will fall to negative levels when output gets too large.

MARGINAL ANALYSIS AND MAXIMIZATION OF TOTAL PROFIT

We see from Figure 4 and Table 3 that many levels of output may yield a positive profit, but the firm is not aiming for just any level of profit. Instead, it wants the largest possible profit. If management knew the exact shape of its profit hill, choosing the optimal level of output would be a simple task indeed. It would merely have to locate the point, such as M in Figure 4(b), that defined the top of its profit hill. However, management rarely, if ever, has so much information, so a different technique for finding the optimum is required. That technique is marginal analysis, which is the same set of tools we used to analyze the firm's input purchase decisions in Chapter 7 and the consumer's buying decisions in Chapters 5 and 6.

This time we will use a concept known as **marginal profit** to solve Al's problem. Referring back to Table 3, we see that an increase in Al's output from three to four garages would raise total profit from $12,000 to $22,000; that is, it would generate $10,000 in additional profit, as shown in the last column of Table 3. We call this amount the marginal profit resulting from the addition of the fourth garage. Similarly, marginal profit from the seventh garage would be

> **Marginal profit** is the addition to total profit resulting from one more unit of output.

$$\text{Total profit from 7 garages} - \text{Total profit from 6 garages} =$$
$$\$30{,}000 - \$33{,}000 = -\$3{,}000$$

The marginal rule for finding the optimal level of output is easy to understand:

If the marginal profit from increasing output by one unit is positive, then output should be increased. If the marginal profit from increasing output by one unit is negative, then output should be decreased. Thus, an output level can maximize total profit only if marginal profit is neither positive nor negative—that is, if it equals zero at that output.

For Al's Building Contractors, the marginal profit from the sixth unit of output (a sixth garage) is $3,000. This means that building six garages is not enough. Because marginal profit is still positive at six garages per year, it pays to produce more than six garages per year. However, marginal profit from the seventh garage is $30,000 − $33,000, or −$3,000, so

the firm should produce less than seven garages because production of the seventh garage would reduce total profit by $3,000. Only at something between six and seven garages, where marginal profit is neither positive nor negative (as is approximately true for 6.5 garages), can total profit be as big as possible, because neither increasing nor reducing output can add to total profit.

The marginal profit numbers in Table 3 indicate one way in which marginal analysis helps to improve decisions. If we had looked only at the total profit figures in the fourth column of the table, we might have concluded that six garages is the profit-maximizing output for Al. The marginal profit column (column 5) tells us that this is not so. We see that the marginal profit of a seventh garage is −$3,000, so Al should, indeed, produce fewer than seven garages per year. But *the marginal profit of the sixth garage is +$3,000, so it pays Al to produce **more** than six garages.* Thus, a production level somewhere between six and seven garages per year, that is, approximately 13 garages every two years, really maximizes profits, as the total profit graph confirms.

The profit hill in Figure 4(b) is a graphical representation of the condition stating that to maximize profit, marginal profit should be zero (or as close to zero as possible). Marginal profit is defined as the additional profit that accrues to the firm when output rises by one unit. For example, when output is increased, say, from three units to four units, or the distance *CD* in Figure 4(b), total profit rises by $10,000 (the distance *DE*) and marginal profit is therefore *DE/CD* (see the triangle *CDE* in the graph). This is precisely the definition of the slope of the total profit curve between points *C* and *E*. In general:

Marginal profit at any output is the slope of the total profit curve at that level of output.

With this geometric interpretation in hand, we can easily understand the logic of the marginal profit rule. At a point such as *C* in Figure 4(b), where the total profit curve is rising, marginal profit (which equals slope) is positive. Profit cannot be maximal at such a point, because we can increase profits by moving farther to the right. A firm that decided to stick to point *C* would be wasting the opportunity to increase profits by increasing output, thereby going further up the profit hill. Similarly, the firm cannot be maximizing profits at a point such as *F*, where the slope of the curve is negative, because there marginal profit (which, again, equals slope) is negative. If it finds itself at a point such as *F*, the firm can raise its profit by decreasing its output.

Only at a point such as *M* in Figure 4(b), where the total profit curve is neither rising nor falling, can the firm possibly be at the top of the profit hill rather than on one of the sides of the hill. Point *M* is precisely where the slope of the curve—and hence the marginal profit—is zero. Thus:

An output decision cannot be optimal unless the corresponding marginal profit is zero.

It is important to recognize once again that the firm is *not* interested in marginal profit for its own sake, but rather for what it implies about total profit. Marginal profit is like the needle on the temperature gauge of a car: The needle itself is of no concern to anyone, but failure to watch it can have dire consequences.

One common misunderstanding about marginal analysis is the idea that it seems foolish to go to a point where marginal profit is zero. "Isn't it better to earn a positive marginal profit?" This notion springs from confusion between the quantity one is seeking to maximize (total profit) and the gauge that indicates whether such a maximum has actually been attained (marginal profit). Of course, it is better to have a positive *total* profit than a zero total profit. In contrast, a zero value on the marginal profit gauge merely indicates that all is well—that total profit is at its maximum, that we are at the top of the profit hill, where the *slope* is zero.

THE IMPORTANCE OF THINKING AT THE MARGIN *Marginal Analysis*: You are likely to have noticed a recurrent theme in this chapter, which is a cornerstone of any economic analysis and thus one of our *Ideas for Beyond the Final Exam*. In any decision about whether to expand an activity, it is always the marginal cost and marginal benefit that are the relevant factors. A calculation based on average data is likely to lead the decision maker to miss all sorts of opportunities, some of them critical.

More generally, if one wants to make optimal decisions, marginal analysis should be used in the planning calculations. This is true whether the decision applies to a business firm seeking to maximize total profit or minimize the cost of the output it has selected, to a consumer trying to maximize utility, or to a less developed country striving to maximize per-capita output. It applies as much to decisions on input proportions and advertising as to decisions about output levels and prices.

Marginal Revenue and Marginal Cost: Guides to Optimization

An alternative version of the marginal analysis of profit maximization can be derived from the cost and revenue components of profit. For this purpose, refer back to Figure 4, where we used total revenue (TR) and total cost (TC) curves to construct the profit hill. There is another way of finding the profit-maximizing solution.

We want to maximize the firm's profit, which is measured by the vertical distance between the TR and TC curves. This distance is not maximal at an output level such as three units, because there the two curves are growing farther apart. If we move farther to the right, the vertical distance between them (which is total profit) will increase. Similarly, we have not maximized the vertical distance between TR and TC at an output level such as eight units, because there the two curves are coming closer together. We can add to profit by moving farther to the left (reducing output). The conclusion from the graph, then, is that total profit—the vertical distance between TR and TC—is maximized only when the two curves are neither growing farther apart nor coming closer together—that is, when their slopes are equal (in the case of Al's Building Contractors in Figure 4, at 6.5 garages).

Marginal revenue and marginal cost curves, which we learned about earlier in the chapter, will help us understand this concept better. For precisely the same reason that marginal profit is the slope of the total profit curve, marginal revenue is the slope of the total revenue curve—because it represents the increase in total revenue resulting from the sale of one additional unit. Similarly, marginal cost is equal to the slope of the total cost curve. This interpretation of marginal revenue and marginal cost, respectively, as the slopes of the total revenue and total cost curves permits us to restate the geometric conclusion we have just reached in an economically significant way:

Profit can be maximized only at an output level at which marginal revenue is (approximately) equal to marginal cost. In symbols:

$$MR = MC$$

The logic of the MR = MC rule for profit maximization is straightforward.[4] When MR is not equal to MC, profits cannot possibly be maximized because the firm can increase its profits by either raising or reducing its output. For example, if MR = $22,000 and MC = $10,000 (Table 4), an additional unit of output

TABLE 4		
Al's Marginal Revenue and Marginal Cost		
(1)	(2)	(3)
Garages per Year	Marginal Revenue (in thousands)	Marginal Cost (in thousands)
0	—	—
1	$30	$28
2	26	16
3	22	10
4	18	8
5	14	6
6	10	7
7	6	9
8	2	16
9	−2	32
10	−6	46

---

[4] You may have surmised by now that just as total profit = total revenue − total cost, it must be true that marginal profit = marginal revenue − marginal cost. This is, in fact, correct. It also shows that when marginal profit = 0, we must have MR = MC.

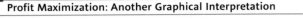

FIGURE 5

Profit Maximization: Another Graphical Interpretation

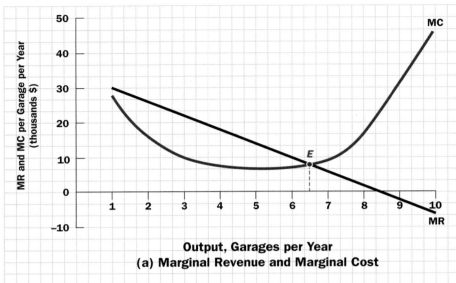

Output, Garages per Year
(a) Marginal Revenue and Marginal Cost

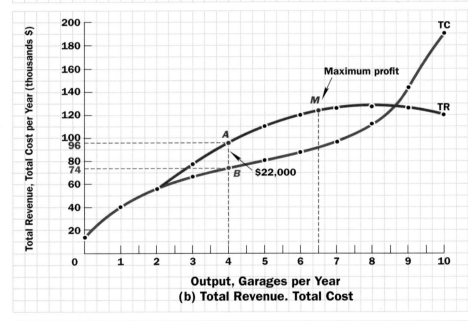

Output, Garages per Year
(b) Total Revenue. Total Cost

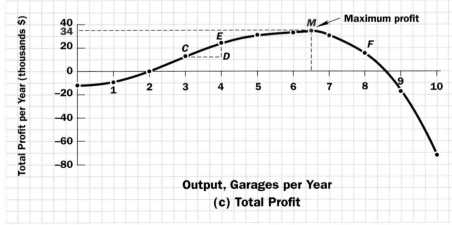

Output, Garages per Year
(c) Total Profit

NOTE: Output is in garages per year.

adds $22,000 to revenues but only $10,000 to costs. Hence, the firm can increase its net profit by $12,000 by producing and selling one more unit. Similarly, if MC exceeds MR, say, MR = $6,000 and MC = $9,000, then the firm loses $3,000 on its marginal unit, so it can add $3,000 to its profit by reducing output by one unit. Only when MR = MC (or comes as close as possible to equaling MC) is it impossible for the firm to add to its profit by changing its output level.

Table 4 reproduces marginal revenue and marginal cost data for Al's Building Contractors from Tables 1 and 2. The table shows, as must be true, that the MR = MC rule leads us to the same conclusion as Figure 4 and Table 3. If he wants to maximize his profits, Al should produce more than six but fewer than seven garages per year. The marginal revenue of the sixth garage is $10,000 ($120,000 from the sale of six garages less $110,000 from the sale of five garages), whereas the marginal cost is only $7,000 ($87,000 − $80,000). Therefore, MR > MC and the firm should produce more than the sixth unit. The seventh garage, however, brings in only $6,000 in marginal revenue and its marginal cost is $9,000—clearly a losing proposition. Only at about 6.5 units of output does MR equal MC *exactly*.

Because the graphs of marginal analysis will prove so useful in later chapters, Figure 5(a) shows the MR = MC condition for profit maximization graphically. The black curve labeled MR in the figure is the marginal revenue schedule from Table 4. The brick-colored curve labeled MC is the marginal cost schedule. The two curves intersect at point *E*, where marginal revenue and marginal cost are equal. The optimal output for

Al is 6.5 units.[5] Figures 5(b) and 5(c), respectively, reproduce the TR and TC curves from Figure 4(a) and the total profit curve from Figure 4(b). Note how MC and MR intersect at the same output at which the distance of TR above TC is greatest, which is also the output at which the profit hill reaches its peak.

Finding the Optimal Price from Optimal Output

At the beginning of this chapter, we set two goals—to determine the profit-maximizing output and to find the profit-maximizing price—and emphasized that once we know either of these, it can automatically tell us the other. So far, we have identified the profit-maximizing output, the output level at which MR = MC (6.5 garages per year in our garage-building example). That leaves us with the task of determining the profit-maximizing price.

Fortunately, this task requires only one more easy step. As we said earlier, once the firm has selected the output it wants to produce and sell, the demand curve determines the price it must charge to induce consumers to buy that amount of product. Consequently, if we know that the profit-maximizing output is 6.5 garages, the demand curve in Figure 1 tells us what price Al must charge to sell that profit-maximizing output. To sell an average of 6.5 garages per year (that is, 13 garages every two years), he must price each garage at $19,000 (between points *f* and *g*). The demand curve tells us that this amount is the only price at which this quantity will be demanded by customers.

> Once the profit-maximizing output quantity has been determined with the help of the MR = MC rule, it is easy to find the profit-maximizing price with the help of the demand curve. Just use that curve to find out at what price the optimal quantity will be demanded.

POLICY DEBATE

Profit and the New Market Economies

The failure of communism to produce economic abundance has led the nations of Eastern Europe, and even China, to turn to the market mechanism. These countries hope that the market will soon bring them the sort of prosperity achieved by the industrialized countries.

The market, as we know, is driven by the profit motive. In a free market, profits are not determined by a government agency, but rather by demand and cost conditions, as described by the demand and cost curves. Many citizens of these new market economies are appalled by the sizes of the profits that the free market affords to successful businesspeople, and they are upset by the greed that these entrepreneurs display. There are pressures to put limits on these profits.

The same thing happened in the United Kingdom and elsewhere as firms formerly owned by the government were sold to private individuals and returned to the market. In the United Kingdom, a number of the privatized firms were initially monopolies, and the government chose to protect consumers by putting ceilings on prices but not on profits to provide the firms with appropriate incentives. Yet when some of these firms proved to be quite profitable, the British government agencies reduced the price ceilings so as to cut those profits, a move that was attacked sharply not

only by the firms themselves but also by some British economists. The debate in the United Kingdom and elsewhere amounts to this: Should severe limits be placed on profits as a matter of fairness and to improve the ethical climate of society, or should such measures be avoided because ceilings on profits undermine the incentives for business success and therefore prevent the market mechanism from delivering the economic abundance of which it is capable?

"Please stand by, we are switching to a free-market economy"

---

[5] We must note one important qualification. Sometimes marginal revenue and marginal cost curves do not have the nice shapes depicted in Figure 5(a), and they may intersect more than once. In such cases, although it remains true that MR = MC at the output level that maximizes profits, there may be other output levels at which MR = MC but at which profits are not maximized.

GENERALIZATION: THE LOGIC OF MARGINAL ANALYSIS AND MAXIMIZATION

The logic of marginal analysis of profit maximization that we have just studied can be generalized, because essentially the same argument was already used in Chapters 5 and 7 and will recur in a number of chapters later in this book. To avoid having to master the argument each time all over again, it is useful to see how this concept can be applied in problems other than the determination of the firm's profit-maximizing output.

The general issue is this: Decision makers often are faced with the problem of selecting the magnitude of some variable, such as how much to spend on advertising, or how many bananas to buy, or how many school buildings to construct. Each of these acts brings benefits, so the larger the number selected by the decision maker, the larger the total benefits that will be derived. Unfortunately, as larger numbers are selected, the associated costs also grow. The problem is to take the trade-off properly into account and to calculate at what point the net gain—the difference between the total benefit and the total cost—will be greatest. Thus, we have the following general principle:

> **If a decision is to be made about the quantity of some variable, then to maximize**
> **Net benefit = Total benefit − Total cost,**
> **the decision maker must select a value of the variable at which**
> **Marginal benefit = (approximately) Marginal cost**

For example, if a community were to determine that the marginal benefit from building an additional school was greater than the cost of an additional school, it would clearly be better off if it built another school. But if the community were planning to build so many schools that the marginal benefit was less than the marginal cost, it would be better off if it switched to a more limited construction program. Only if the marginal benefit and cost are as close as possible to being equal will the community have the optimal number of schools.

We will apply this same concept in later chapters. Again and again, when we analyze a quantitative decision that brings together both benefits and costs, we conclude that the optimal decision occurs at the point where the marginal benefit equals the marginal cost. The logic is the same whether we are considering the net gains to a firm, to a consumer, or to society as a whole.

Application: Fixed Cost and the Profit-Maximizing Price

We can now use our analytic framework to offer an insight that is often unexpected. Suppose there is a rise in the firm's fixed cost; for example, imagine that the property taxes on Al's Building Contractors double. What will happen to the profit-maximizing price and output? Should Al raise his price to cover the increased cost, or should he produce a larger output even if it requires a drop in price? The answer is surprising: Neither!

> **When a firm's fixed cost increases, its profit-maximizing price and output remain completely unchanged, so long as it pays the firm to stay in business.**

In other words, there is nothing that the firm's management can do to offset the effect of the rise in fixed cost. This is surely a case where common sense is not a reliable guide to the right decision.

Why is this so? Recall that, by definition, a fixed cost does not change when output changes. The increase in Al's fixed costs is the same whether business is slow or booming, whether production is 2 garages or 20. This idea is illustrated in Table 5, which also reproduces Al's total profits from Table 3. The third column of the table shows that total fixed cost has risen (from zero) to $10,000 per year. As a result, total profit is $10,000 less than it would have been otherwise—no matter what the firm's output. For example, when output is four units, we see that total profit falls from $22,000 (second column) to $12,000 (last column).

Because profit is reduced by the same amount at every output level, whatever output was most profitable before the increase in fixed costs must still be most profitable. In Table 5, we see that $23,000 is the largest entry in the last column, which shows profits after the rise in fixed cost. This approximately highest possible profit is attained, as it was before, when

TABLE 5

Rise in Fixed Cost:
Total Profit Before and After

(1)	(2)	(3)	(4)
Garages per Year	Total Profit Before (in thousands)	Rise in Fixed Cost (in thousands)	Total Profit After (in thousands)
0	$−12	$10	$−22
1	−10	10	−20
2	0	10	−10
3	12	10	2
4	22	10	12
5	30	10	20
6	33	10	23
7	30	10	20
8	16	10	6
9	−18	10	−28
10	−70	10	−80

FIGURE 6

Fixed Cost Does Not Affect Profit-Maximizing Output

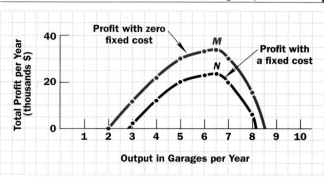

output is at six units. The actual profit-maximizing output will remain at 6.5 garages, exactly as before. In other words, the firm's profit-maximizing price and quantity remain unchanged.

This is shown graphically in Figure 6, which displays the firm's total profit hill before and after the rise in fixed cost (reproducing Al's initial profit hill from Figure 4). We see that the cost increase simply moves the profit hill straight downward by $10,000, so the highest point on the hill is just lowered from point *M* to point *N*. But the top of the hill is shifted neither left nor right. It remains at the 6.5-garage output level.[6]

PUZZLE RESOLVED: USING MARGINAL ANALYSIS TO UNRAVEL THE CASE OF THE "UNPROFITABLE" CALCULATOR

We can now put the marginal analysis of profit determination to work to solve the puzzle with which we began this chapter. The example was drawn from reality, and reality never works as neatly as a textbook illustration with a mechanical application of the MR = MC rule. However, we will see that the underlying reasoning does shed useful light on real problems.

Our "unprofitable" calculator puzzle concerned a firm that produced a number of electronic items, including calculators. The company was apparently losing money on calculator sales because the $12 price was less than the $14.55 average cost that the company's bookkeepers assigned to the product. This $14.55 figure included $10.30 of (marginal) costs caused directly by the manufacturing and marketing of each additional calculator, plus a $4.25 per-calculator share of the company's overall general expenses ("overhead"), such as compensation of the company president. When it was accused in a court of law of trying to drive a competitor out of business by deliberately selling below cost, the company turned to marginal analysis to show that the charge was untrue and that the calculators were indeed a profitable line of business.

To demonstrate this fact, a witness for the company explained that if selling the calculators really were unprofitable, then the company could increase its earnings by *ceasing* their production altogether. But, in fact, had the company done so, it would have lowered its profits.

To see why, let's look at the numbers again. If the company gave up the sale of 10 million calculators, its revenues would be reduced by $12 (the price of each calculator) × 10 million units sold—a (marginal) revenue reduction of $120 million. But how much cost would it save by giving up those sales? The answer is that the cost outlay

---

[6] EXERCISE: Does the added fixed cost change the marginal cost? Explain. What does this imply for optimal output?

actually caused by the production of each calculator was only the $10.30 in direct cost. Even if it stopped selling the calculators (which were just one part of its product line), the company would still have to continue to pay for costs like the salary of the company president and general advertising expenditures. In other words, none of the company's fixed overhead costs would be saved by ending calculator production. Rather, the (marginal) cost saving would be the direct cost of $10.30 per calculator × the 10 million calculator output—a total cost saving of just $103 million.

The bottom line was that eliminating calculators from the product line would have reduced total profit by $17 million per year—the $120 million in forgone revenue minus the $103 million cost. So, continued production of the calculators was not causing losses; on the contrary, it was contributing $17 million in profits every year, because each unit of output was bringing in $12 in revenue − $10.30 in marginal cost = $1.70. The court concluded that this reasoning was correct and used this conclusion in its decision.

This case illustrates a point that is encountered frequently. The calculator manufacturer was selling its product at a price that appeared not to cover the costs but really did. The appearance stems from the fact that the cost attributable to any one of a company's products is essentially its *marginal* cost—the cost the firm must pay to add the item to its product line. But bookkeepers usually don't think in terms of marginal costs, and in their calculations they often include other types of costs that are not affected by reducing the output of the product or by eliminating its production.

The same sort of issue faces airlines that offer discounted fares to students (or to senior citizens, or some other group), when those fares are lower than the average cost (including fuel cost, salaries of personnel, and so on) per passenger. If the discounted fares have the effect of filling up seats that would otherwise have flown empty, and if the fares cover more than their *marginal cost* (which consists only of the additional cost of selling the tickets and providing the students with a snack), then those fares clearly are *adding* to the airline's profits, even though they are below average cost per passenger. Nevertheless, such fare discounts sometimes lead to lawsuits by competitors of the airlines that offer such discounted fares.

CONCLUSION: THE FUNDAMENTAL ROLE OF MARGINAL ANALYSIS

**IDEAS FOR
BEYOND THE
FINAL EXAM**

THE IMPORTANCE OF THINKING AT THE MARGIN We saw in Chapter 7 how marginal analysis helps us to understand the firm's input choices. Similarly, in Chapters 5 and 6, it cast indispensable light on the consumer's purchase decisions. In this chapter, it enabled us to analyze output and pricing decisions. The logic of marginal analysis applies not only to economic decisions by consumers and firms but also to decisions made by governments, universities, hospitals, and other organizations. In short, this type of analysis applies to any individual or group that must make optimal choices about the use of scarce resources. Thus, one of the most important conclusions that can be drawn from this chapter, and a conclusion brought out vividly by the examples we have just discussed, is the importance of thinking "at the margin"—one of *our Ideas for Beyond the Final Exam.*

Another real-life example far removed from profit maximization will illustrate how marginal criteria are useful in decision making. For years before women were first admitted to Princeton University (and to several other colleges), administrators cited the cost of the proposed admission of women as a major obstacle. They had decided in advance that any women coming to the university would constitute a net addition to the student body because, for a variety of reasons involving relations with alumni and other groups, it was not feasible to reduce the number of male students. Presumably on the basis of a calculation of average cost, some critics spoke of cost figures as high as $80 million.

To economists, it was clear that the relevant figure was actually the *marginal cost*, or the addition to total cost that would result from the admission of the additional students. The women students would, of course, bring additional tuition fees (marginal revenues) to Princeton. If these fees were just sufficient to cover the amount that they would add to costs, the admission of the women would leave the university's financial picture unaffected.

A careful calculation showed that the admission of women would add far less to the university's financial problems than the average cost figures indicated. One reason was that women's course preferences at that time were characteristically different from men's, and hence women frequently selected courses that were undersubscribed in exclusively male institutions. Therefore, the admission of 1,000 women to a formerly all-male institution could be expected to require fewer additional classes than if 1,000 more men had been admitted.[7] More important, it was found that a number of classroom buildings were underutilized. The cost of operating these buildings was nearly fixed; their total utilization cost would be changed only slightly by the influx of women. The marginal cost for classroom space was therefore almost zero and certainly well below the average cost (the cost per student).

For all of these reasons, it turned out that the relevant marginal cost was much smaller than the figures that had been considered earlier. Indeed, this cost was something like one-third of the earlier estimates. There is little doubt that this careful marginal calculation played a critical role in the admission of women to Princeton at that time and to some other universities that subsequently made use of the calculations in the Princeton analysis. More recent data, incidentally, confirmed that the marginal calculations were amply justified.

THE THEORY AND REALITY: A WORD OF CAUTION

We have now completed two chapters describing how business managers can make optimal decisions. Can you go to Wall Street or Main Street and find executives calculating marginal cost and marginal revenue to decide how much to produce? Not very often—although in some important applications they do. Nor can you find consumers in stores using marginal analysis to decide what to buy. Like consumers, successful businesspeople often rely heavily on intuition and "hunches" that cannot be described by any set of rules. In fact, in a 1993 survey of CEOs conducted by Inc. magazine, nearly 20 percent of the respondents admitted to using guesswork to price their products or services.

Note that we have not sought to provide a literal description of business behavior but rather a model to help us analyze and predict this behavior. The four chapters that we have just completed constitute the core of microeconomics. We will find ourselves returning again and again to the principles learned in these chapters.

| SUMMARY |

1. A firm can choose the quantity of its product that it wants to sell or the price that it wants to charge, but it cannot choose both because price affects the quantity demanded.

2. In economic theory, we usually assume that firms seek to maximize **profits.** This assumption should not be taken literally, but rather interpreted as a useful simplification of reality.

3. The demand curve of a firm is determined from the market demand curve by the strength of the competitive efforts of the rival firms in the market.

4. **Marginal revenue** is the additional revenue earned by increasing quantity sold by one unit. Marginal cost is the additional cost incurred by increasing production by one unit.

[7] See Gardner Patterson, "The Education of Women at Princeton," *Princeton Alumni Weekly,* 69 (September 24, 1968).

5. Maximum profit requires the firm to choose the level of output at which marginal revenue is equal to (or most closely approximates) marginal cost.

6. Geometrically, the profit-maximizing output level occurs at the highest point on the total profit curve. There the slope of the total profit curve is zero (or as close to zero as possible), meaning that **marginal profit** is zero.

7. A change in fixed cost will not change the profit-maximizing level of output.

8. It will generally pay a firm to expand its output if it is selling at a price greater than marginal cost, even if that price happens to be below average cost.

9. **Optimal decisions** must be made on the basis of marginal cost and marginal revenue figures, not average cost and average revenue figures. This concept is one of the *Ideas for Beyond the Final Exam.*

| KEY TERMS |

average revenue (AR)   160

economic profit   159

marginal profit   163

marginal revenue (MR)   160

optimal decision   156

total profit   158

total revenue (TR)   159

| TEST YOURSELF |

1. Suppose that the firm's demand curve indicates that at a price of $10 per unit, customers will demand 2 million units of its product. Suppose that management decides to pick both price and output; the firm produces 3 million units of its product and prices them at $18 each. What will happen?

2. Suppose that a firm's management would be pleased to increase its share of the market but if it expands its production, the price of its product will fall. Will its profits necessarily fall? Why or why not?

3. Why does it make sense for a firm to seek to maximize *total* profit rather than to maximize *marginal* profit?

4. A firm's marginal revenue is $133 and its marginal cost is $90. What amount of profit does the firm fail to pick up by refusing to increase output by one unit?

5. Calculate average revenue (AR) and average cost (AC) in Table 3. How much profit does the firm earn at the output at which AC = AR? Why?

6. A firm's total cost is $1,000 if it produces one unit, $1,600 if it produces two units, and $2,000 if it produces three units of output. Draw up a table of total, average, and marginal costs for this firm.

7. Draw an average and marginal cost curve for the firm in Test Yourself Question 6 above. Describe the relationship between the two curves.

8. A firm has the demand and total cost schedules given in the following table. If it wants to maximize profits, how much output should it produce?

Quantity	Price	Total Cost
1	$6	$ 1.00
2	5	2.50
3	4	6.00
4	3	7.00
5	2	11.00

| DISCUSSION QUESTION |

1. "It may be rational for the management of a firm not to try to maximize profits." Discuss the circumstances under which this statement may be true.

| APPENDIX | *The Relationships Among Total, Average, and Marginal Data*

You may have surmised that there is a close connection between the average revenue curve and the marginal revenue curve and that there must be a similar relationship between the average cost curve and the marginal cost curve. After all, we derived our average revenue figures from the total revenues and also calculated our marginal revenue figures from the total revenues at the various possible output levels; a similar relationship applied to costs. In fact:

Marginal, average, and total figures are inextricably bound together. From any one of the three sets of figures, the other two can be calculated. The relationships among total, average, and marginal data are exactly the same for any variable—such as revenue, cost, or profit—to which the concepts apply.

To illustrate and emphasize the wide applicability of marginal analysis, we switch our example from profits, revenues, and costs to a noneconomic variable. As we are about to see, the same concepts can be applied to human body weights. We use this example because calculation of weights is more familiar to most people than calculation of profits, revenues, or costs, and it can illustrate several fundamental relationships between average and marginal figures.

In Table 6, we begin with an empty room. (The total weight of occupants is equal to zero.) A person weighing 100 pounds enters; total, marginal, and average weights are all, then, 100 pounds. If this person is followed by a person weighing 140 pounds (marginal weight equals 140 pounds), the total weight increases to 240 pounds, average weight rises to 120 pounds (240/2), and so on.[8]

TABLE 6

Weights of Persons in a Room (in pounds)

Number of Persons in a Room	Marginal Weight	Total Weight	Average Weight
0		0	—
1	100	100	100
2	140	240	120
3	135	375	125
4	**125**	**500**	**125**
5	100	600	120
6	60	660	110

---

[8] In this illustration, "persons in room" is analogous to units of output, "total weight" is analogous to total revenue or cost, and "marginal weight" is analogous to marginal revenue or cost in the discussions of marginal analysis in the body of the chapter.

The rule for converting totals to averages, and vice versa, is

Rule 1a. Average weight equals total weight divided by number of persons.

Rule 1b. Total weight equals average weight times number of persons.

This rule naturally applies equally well to cost, revenue, profit, or any other variable.

We calculate marginal weight from total weight by working with the same subtraction process already used to calculate marginal cost and marginal revenue. Specifically:

Rule 2a. The marginal weight of, say, the third person equals the total weight of three people minus the total weight of two people.

For example, when the fourth person enters the room, total weight rises from 375 to 500 pounds, and hence the corresponding marginal weight is $500 - 375 = 125$ pounds, as is shown in the second column of Table 6. We can also do the reverse—calculate total from marginal weight—through an addition process.

Rule 2b. The total weight of, say, three people equals the (marginal) weight of the first person who enters the room plus the (marginal) weight of the second person, plus the (marginal) weight of the third person.

You can verify Rule 2b by referring to Table 6, which shows that the total weight of three persons, 375 pounds, is indeed equal to $100 + 140 + 135$ pounds, the sum of the preceding marginal weights. A similar relation holds for any other total weight figure in the table, a fact that you should verify.

In addition to these familiar arithmetic relationships, there are two other useful relationships.

Rule 3. With an exception (fixed cost) that was discussed in Chapter 7, the marginal, average, and total figures for the first person must all be equal.

That is, when there is only one person in the room whose weight is X pounds, the average weight will obviously be X, the total weight must be X, and the marginal weight must also be X (because the total must have risen from zero to X pounds). Put another way, when the marginal person is alone, he or she is obviously the average person and also represents the totality of all relevant persons.

Our final and very important relationship is

Rule 4. If marginal weight is lower than average weight, then average weight must decrease when the number of persons increases. If marginal weight exceeds average weight, average weight must increase when the number of persons increases. If marginal and average weight are

equal, the average weight must remain constant when the number of persons increases.

These three possibilities are all illustrated in Table 6. Notice, for example, that when the third person enters the room, the average weight increases from 120 to 125 pounds. That increase occurs because this person's (marginal) weight is 135 pounds, which is above the average and therefore *pulls up the average*, as Rule 4 requires. Similarly, when the sixth person—who is a 60-pound child—enters the room, the average decreases from 120 to 110 pounds because marginal weight, 60 pounds, is below average weight and so pulls the average down.

It is essential to avoid a common misunderstanding of this rule. It does *not* state, for example, that if the average figure is rising, the *marginal* figure must be *rising*. When the average rises, the marginal figure may rise, fall, or remain unchanged. The arrival of two persons, both well above the average weight, will push the average up in two successive steps even if the second new arrival is lighter than the first. We see such a case in Table 6, where average weight rises successively from 100 to 120 to 125 pounds, whereas the marginal weight falls from 140 to 135 to 125 pounds.

GRAPHICAL REPRESENTATION OF MARGINAL AND AVERAGE CURVES

We have shown how, from a curve of total profit (or total cost or total anything else), we can determine the corresponding marginal figure. In the chapter, we noted repeatedly that the marginal value at any particular point is equal to the slope of the corresponding total curve at that point. But for some purposes, it is convenient to use a graph that records marginal and average values directly rather than deriving them from the curve of totals.

We can obtain such a graph by plotting the data in a table of average and marginal figures, such as Table 6. The result looks like the graph shown in Figure 7. In that graph, the number of persons in the room appears on the horizontal axis and the corresponding average and marginal figures appear on the vertical axis. The solid dots represent average weights; the small circles represent

FIGURE 7

The Relationship between Marginal and Average Curves

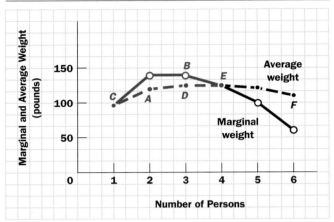

marginal weights. For example, point *A* shows that when two people are in the room, their average weight is 120 pounds, as recorded on the third line of Table 6. Similarly, point *B* on the graph represents information provided in the next column of the table—that is, that the marginal weight of the third person who enters the room is 135 pounds. We have connected these points into a marginal curve and an average curve, represented, respectively, by the solid and the broken curves in the diagram. This is the representation of marginal and average values economists most frequently use.

Figure 7 illustrates two of our rules. Rule 3 says that for the first unit, the marginal and average values will be the same; that is precisely why the two curves start out together at point *C*. The graph also depicts Rule 4 between points *C* and *E*: Where the average curve is rising, the marginal curve lies above the average. (Notice that over part of this range, the marginal curve falls even though the average curve is rising; Rule 4 says nothing about the rise or fall of the *marginal* curve.) We see also that over range *EF*, where the average curve is falling, the marginal curve is below the average curve, again in accord with Rule 4. Finally, at point *E*, where the average curve is neither rising nor falling, the marginal curve meets the average curve; the average and marginal weights are equal at that point, so the marginal weights do not pull the average weight either upward or downward.

| TEST YOURSELF |

1. Suppose that the following table is your record of exam grades in your Principles of Eonomics course:

   Use these data to make up a table of total, average, and marginal grades for the five exams.

Exam Date	Grade	Comment
September 30	65	A slow start
October 28	75	A big improvement
November 26	90	Happy Thanksgiving!
December 13	85	Slipped a little
January 24	95	A fast finish!

2. From the data in your exam-grade table in Test Yourself Question 1, illustrate each of the rules mentioned in this appendix. Be sure to point out an instance where the marginal grade falls but the average grade rises.

INVESTING IN BUSINESS: STOCKS AND BONDS

A bargain that is going to become a greater bargain is no bargain.

MARTIN SHUBIK, YALE UNIVERSITY

A firm does more than select inputs, outputs, and prices—which were the topics of previous chapters. In this chapter, we discuss how real firms finance their activities—notably with stocks and bonds. These days, a very large proportion of the nation's college graduates invests money in the stock and bond markets. You probably will as well, if you don't already. For this reason, it is important to understand something about how these markets work, but please do not think that this chapter will turn you into a super speculator who can beat the market consistently. Too many investors have thought that way and ended up losing their life's savings. Indeed, the main lesson of this chapter is that, for good reason, the future behavior of the stock market is virtually unpredictable. As you look toward the future, the stock market will undoubtedly go up and undoubtedly go down, but the unanswerable question is: When? History repeatedly teaches us that lesson, and as philosopher George Santayana once wrote, "Those who cannot remember the past are condemned to repeat it"—as many stock market investors have done.[1]

CONTENTS

---

[1] George Santayana, *The Life of Reason: Or, The Phases of Human Progress*, Vol. I (New York: C. Scribner's Sons, 1905–1906).

PUZZLE 1:   WHAT IN THE WORLD HAPPENED TO THE STOCK MARKET?

Sometimes a picture really is worth a thousand words. Figure 1 shows the remarkable behavior of share prices on the NASDAQ stock market (which we will describe later in the chapter) between 1990 and 2007. It looks a bit like the Rocky Mountains, rising spectacularly from the autumn of 1998 to early 2000, and then falling dramatically back down to earth. The numbers on the scale tell you that the index soared from about 1,600 in October 1998 to about 4,800 in March 2000—an astonishing gain of 200 percent in less than a year and a half! But by the fall of 2001, the index was back to about where it had been in October 1998. All in all, it was one of the most spectacular booms and busts in stock market history.

What in the world happened? In all honesty, most of the world's best economists and leading financial experts were left puzzled by this episode. As we will learn in this chapter, the value of a share of stock is supposed to reflect the current and future profits of the company that issues the stock. But that theory of stock prices will not explain why shares of Amazon.com, the online retailer, once sold for about $105 per share and then plunged to around $6 (it was about $131 as this book went to press), or why shares of Priceline.com (which sells airline tickets and books hotel reservations online) once sold for about $165 per share and dropped to around $4 (as against $241 at press time).

Alan Greenspan, former chairman of the Federal Reserve, once called the phenomenon that gripped America in the boom years "irrational exuberance"—and it was certainly that. One of the authors of this book called the upside of Figure 1 the "Wile E. Coyote stock market," after that old nemesis in Road Runner cartoons, who would run off cliffs and yet somehow manage to remain in the air—until he looked down.

FIGURE 1

NASDAQ Stock Market Composite Index, 1990–2007

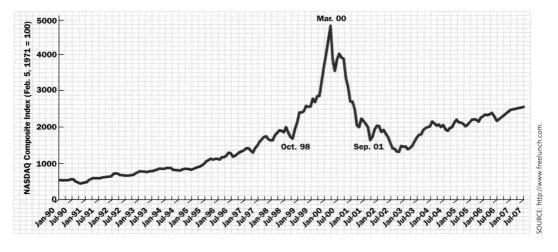

SOURCE: http://www.freelunch.com.

Apparently, investors in U.S. technology stocks "looked down" around March 2000. But why then? Why not before? And what made stock prices rise so high in the first place? As we said, the answers to such questions remain shrouded in mystery. Even so, we will be able to throw a little light on the subject by the end of the chapter.

PUZZLE 2:   THE STOCK MARKET'S UNPREDICTABILITY

The stock market is obviously something of an enigma. No other economic activity is reported in such detail in so many newspapers and other media and followed with such concern by so many people. Yet few activities have so successfully eluded prediction of their future. There is no shortage of well-paid "experts" prepared to forecast the future of the market or the price of a particular stock or the earnings of the company to which the stock price is related. But there are real questions about what these experts deliver.

For example, a famous study of leading stock market analysts' predictions of company earnings (on which they based their stock price forecasts) reports:

[W]e wrote to 19 major Wall Street firms . . . among the most respected names in the investment business.

We requested—and received—past earnings predictions on how these firms felt earnings for specific companies would behave over both a one-year and a five-year period. These estimates . . . were . . . compared with actual results to see how well the analysts forecast short-run and long-run earnings changes. . . .

Bluntly stated, the careful estimates of security analysts (based on industry studies, plant visits, etc.) do very little better than those that would be obtained by simple extrapolation of past trends. . . .

For example . . . the analysts' estimates were compared [with] the assumption that every company in the economy would enjoy a growth in earnings approximating the long-run rate of growth of the national income. It often turned out that . . . this naïve forecasting model . . . would make smaller errors in forecasting long-run earnings growth than . . . [did] the professional forecasts of the analysts. . . .

When confronted with the poor record of their five-year growth estimates, the security analysts honestly, if sheepishly, admitted that five years ahead is really too far in advance to make reliable projections. They protested that, although long-term projections are admittedly important, they really ought to be judged on their ability to project earnings changes one year ahead.

Believe it or not, it turned out that their one-year forecasts were even worse than their five-year projections.[2]

It has been said that an investor may as well pick stocks by throwing darts at the stock market page—it is far cheaper to buy a set of darts than to obtain the apparently useless advice of a professional analyst. Indeed, there have been at least two experiments, one by a U.S. senator and one by *Forbes* magazine, in which stocks picked by dart-throwing actually outperformed the mutual funds, the stocks of which are selected by experts.

Later in this chapter we will suggest an explanation for this poor performance.

CORPORATIONS AND THEIR UNIQUE CHARACTERISTICS

Stocks and bonds are created by corporations and are among the primary tools that these companies use to acquire the funds they need to operate. Corporations play a crucial role in the U.S. economy. Revenues of the top 50 American corporations totaled $4.9 trillion in 2008, or nearly 35 percent of the country's estimated $14.4 trillion gross domestic product (GDP). Some of these are true industrial giants. Wal-Mart Stores alone generated $378 billion in revenue in 2008, and Exxon Mobil and Chevron took in more than $372 billion and $210 billion, respectively. The combined revenues of just these three firms amounted to considerably more than the GDP of Belgium (and Denmark, Ireland, Norway, Switzerland, and many other countries).

But only 20 percent of American firms are incorporated, because most firms are small. Even many corporations are quite small—40 percent have business receipts of less than $100,000 per year.[3] That said, almost all large American firms are corporations. It's a word you've heard used many times. But what, exactly, is a "corporation"?

A **corporation** is a type of firm that is defined by law and to which the law assigns special privileges and special obligations. Three noteworthy features that their legal status entails are the following:

- Special limits are placed on the losses that may be suffered by those who invest in these firms.
- These firms are subjected to types of taxation from which other firms are exempt.

A **corporation** is a firm that has the legal status of a fictional individual. This fictional individual is owned by a number of people, called its stockholders, and is run by a set of elected officers and a board of directors, whose chairperson is often also in a powerful position.

---

[2] Burton G. Malkiel, *A Random Walk Down Wall Street* (New York: W. W. Norton; 1990), pp. 140–141.

[3] "Fortune 500: The 500 Largest U.S. Corporations," *Fortune magazine*, April 5, 2004, p. 289; and Organization for Economic Cooperation and Development, OECD in Figures, 2004, http://new.sourceoecd.org.

- The corporation is considered to be an entity that is distinct from any of its owners or its management, so that the corporation can outlast the association of any and all of the individuals who are currently connected with the firm.

Let us consider the logic behind these three features. To begin with, although it may seem strange, a corporation is considered an individual in the eyes of the law. Therefore, its earnings, like those of other individuals, are taxed. Thus the legal status leads to what is called "double taxation" of the stockholders. Unlike the earnings of other firms, corporate earnings are taxed twice—once when they are earned by the company and a second time when they go to investors in the form of dividends (and are subject to the personal income tax).

This disadvantage is counterbalanced by an important legal advantage, however: Any corporate debt is regarded as that fictitious individual's obligation, not any one stockholder's liability. In this way, stockholders benefit from the protection of **limited liability**—they can lose no more money than they have invested in the firm. In contrast, if you are part or sole owner of a firm that is not a corporation, and it loses money and cannot repay its debts, you can be sued by the people to whom the money is owed, who may be able to force you to pay them out of your own bank account or by selling your vacation home.

> **Limited liability** is a legal obligation of a firm's owners to pay back company debts only with the money they have already invested in the firm.

Limited liability is the main secret of the success of the corporate organizational form, and the reason that some corporations grow so big. Thanks to that provision, individuals throughout the world are willing to invest money in firms whose operations they do not understand and whose management personnel they do not know. Each shareholder receives in return a claim on the firm's profits and, at least in principle, a portion of the company's ownership.

The corporate form is a boon to investors because their liability for loss is limited to their investments. There is also a major disadvantage to this form of business organization: Corporate income is taxed twice.

Financing Corporate Activity: Stocks and Bonds

When a corporation needs money to add to its plant or equipment, or to finance other types of investment, it may reinvest its own earnings (rather than paying them out as dividends to stockholders), or print and sell new stock certificates or new bonds, or take out a loan. Stocks and bonds, in the last analysis, are pieces of paper printed by the firm under a variety of legal safeguards. If it can find buyers, the firm can sell these pieces of paper to the investing public when it wants to obtain more money to invest in its operations.

How can a firm obtain money in exchange for such printed paper as a stock or bond certificate? Doesn't the process seem a bit like counterfeiting? If done improperly, there are indeed grounds for the suspicion. But, carried out appropriately, it is a perfectly reasonable economic process. First, let's define our terms.

> A **common stock** (also called a share) of a corporation is a piece of paper that gives the holder of the stock a share of the ownership of the company.

Common stock represents partial ownership of a corporation. For example, if a company issues 100,000 shares, then a person who owns 1,000 shares owns 1 percent of the company and is entitled to 1 percent of the company's dividends, the corporation's annual payments to stockholders. This shareholder's vote also normally counts for 1 percent of the total votes in an election of corporate officers or in a referendum on corporate policy.

> A **bond** is simply an IOU sold by a corporation that promises to pay the holder of the bond a fixed sum of money at the specified maturity date and some other fixed amount of money (the coupon or interest payment) every year up to the date of maturity.

Bonds differ from stocks in several ways. First, the purchaser of a corporation's stock buys a share of its ownership and some control over its affairs, whereas a bond purchaser simply lends money to the firm and obtains no part of its ownership. Second, whereas stockholders have no idea how much they will receive when they sell their stocks or how much they will receive in dividends each year, bondholders know with a high degree of certainty how much money they will be paid if they hold their bonds to maturity (the date the firm has promised to repay the loan). For instance, a bond with a face value of $1,000 and an $80 coupon (the firm's annual interest payment to the bondholder) that matures in 2010 will provide $80 per year every year until 2010, and the firm will repay the bondholder's $1,000 in 2010. Unless the company goes bankrupt, this repayment schedule is guaranteed. Third, bondholders legally have a prior claim on company earnings, which means the stockholders receive no money until the firm has paid its bondholders. For all these reasons, bonds are considered less risky investments than stocks.[4]

To return to the question we asked earlier, a new issue of stocks and bonds is generally not like counterfeiting. As long as the funds obtained from the sale of the new **securities**[5] are used effectively to increase a firm's profit-earning capacity, these funds will automatically yield any required repayment and appropriate interest and dividends to purchasers. Occasionally, this payout does not happen. One of the favorite practices of the more notorious nineteenth-century market manipulators was "watering" company stocks—issuing stocks with little or nothing to back them up. The term is originally derived from the practice of some cattle dealers who would force their animals to drink large quantities of water just before bringing them to be weighed for sale.

> Stocks and bonds are also called **securities**.

Similarities Between Stocks and Bonds

In reality, the differences between stocks and bonds are not as clear-cut as just described. Two relevant misconceptions are worth noting. First, the ownership represented by a few shares of a company's stock may be more symbolic than real. A person who holds 0.02 percent of IBM Corporation stock—which, by the way, is a very large investment—exercises no real control over IBM's operations.

In fact, many economists believe that the ownership of large corporations is so diffuse that stockholders or stockholder groups rarely have any effective control over management. In this view, a corporation's management is a largely independent decision-making body; as long as it keeps enough cash flowing to stockholders to prevent discontent and organized rebellion, management can do anything it wants within the law. Looked at in this way, stockholders, like bondholders, merely provide loans to the company. The only real difference between the two groups, according to this interpretation, is that stockholders' loans are riskier and therefore entitled to higher payments.

Second, bonds actually can be a very risky investment. People who try to sell their bonds before maturity may find that the market price happens to be low; so if they need to raise cash in a hurry, they may incur substantial losses. Also, bondholders may be exposed to losses from **inflation**. Whether the $1,000 promised to the bondholder at the 2010 maturity date represents substantial (or very little) purchasing power depends on what happens to the general price level in the meantime (that is, how much price inflation occurs). No one can predict the price level this far in advance with any accuracy. Finally, a firm can issue bonds with little backing; that is, the firm may own little valuable property that it can use as a guarantee of repayment to the lender—the bondholder. This is often true of "junk bonds," and it helps to explain their high risk.

> **Inflation** occurs when prices in an economy rise rapidly. The rate of inflation is calculated by averaging the percentage growth rate of the prices of a selected sample of commodities.

Bond Prices and Interest Rates

What makes bond prices go up and down? A straightforward relationship exists between bond prices and current interest rates: Whenever one goes up, the other must go down. The term **interest rate** refers to the amount that borrowers currently pay to lenders per dollar of the money borrowed—it is the current market price of a loan.

For example, suppose that J.C. Penney issued 15-year bonds when interest rates were comparatively low, so the company had to pay only 6 percent to sell the bonds. People who invested $1,000 in those bonds received a contract that promised them $60 per year for 15 years plus the return of their $1,000 at the end of that period. Suppose, however, that interest rates rise, so that new 15-year bonds of similar companies now pay 12 percent. An investor with $1,000 can now buy a bond that offers $120 per year. Obviously, no one will now pay $1,000 for a bond that promises only $60 per year. Consequently, the market price of the old J.C. Penney bonds must fall.

> The **interest rate** is the amount that borrowers currently pay to lenders per dollar of the money borrowed—it is the current market price of a loan.

---

[4] An important exception involves so-called junk bonds—very risky bonds that became popular in the 1980s. They were used heavily by people trying to purchase enough of a corporation's stock to acquire control of that firm.

[5] Stocks and bonds are also called *securities*.

This example is not entirely hypothetical. Until a few years ago, bonds issued much earlier—at interest rates of 6 percent or lower—were still in circulation. In the 1980s' markets, when interest rates were well above 6 percent, such bonds sold for prices far below their original values.

When interest rates rise, the prices of previously issued bonds with lower interest earnings must fall. For the same reason, when interest rates fall, the prices of previously issued bonds must rise.

It follows that as interest rates change because of changes in government policy or other reasons, bond prices fluctuate. That is one reason why bonds can be a risky investment.

Corporate Choice Between Stocks and Bonds

If a corporation chooses to finance the construction of new factories and equipment through the issue of new stocks or bonds, how does it determine whether bonds or stocks best suit its purposes?

Two considerations are of prime importance. Although issuing bonds generally exposes a firm to more risk than issuing stocks, the corporation usually expects to pay more money to stockholders over the long run. In other words, to the firm that issues them, bonds are cheaper but riskier. The decision about which is better for the firm therefore involves a trade-off between the two considerations of expense and risk.

Why are bonds risky to a corporation? When it issues $20 million in new bonds at 10 percent, a company commits itself to pay out $2 million every year of the bond's life, whether business is booming or the firm is losing money. If the firm is unable to meet its obligation to bondholders in some year, bankruptcy may result.

Stocks do not burden the company with any such risk, because the firm does not promise to pay stockholders any fixed amount. Stockholders simply receive whatever is left of the company's net earnings after the firm makes its payments to bondholders. If nothing is left to pay the new stockholders in some years, legally speaking, that is just their bad luck. The higher risk faced by stockholders is the reason they normally obtain higher average payments than bondholders.

To the firm that issues them, bonds are riskier than stocks because they commit the firm to make a fixed annual payment, even in years when it is losing money. For the same reason, stocks are riskier than bonds to the buyers of securities. Therefore, stockholders expect to be paid more money than bondholders.

Plowback, or Retained Earnings

Plowback (or retained earnings) is the portion of a corporation's profits that management decides to keep and reinvest in the firm's operations rather than paying out as dividends to stockholders.

The final major source of funds for corporations, in addition to loans and the issue of stocks and bonds, is **plowback**, or **retained earnings**. For example, if a company earns $30 million after taxes and decides to pay only $10 million in dividends to its stockholders and reinvest the remaining $20 million in the firm, that $20 million is called "plowback."

When business is profitable, corporate managers will often prefer plowback to other sources of funding. For one thing, plowback usually involves lower risk. Also, plowback, unlike other sources of funding, does not come under the scrutiny of the Securities and Exchange Commission (SEC), the government agency that regulates stocks.[6] And, of course, plowback does not depend on the availability of eager customers for new company stocks and bonds. An issue of new securities can be a disappointment if there is little public demand when they are offered, but plowback runs no such risk.

Above all, a plowback decision generally does not call attention to the degree of success of management's operations, as a new stock issue does. When stock is issued, the SEC, potential buyers, and their professional advisers may all scrutinize the company carefully. No management has a perfect record, and the process may reveal things management would prefer to be overlooked.

---

[6] The Securities and Exchange Commission, established in 1934, protects the interests of people who buy securities. It requires firms that issue stock and other securities to provide information about their financial condition, and it regulates the issue and trading of securities.

Another reason for plowback's attractiveness is that issuing new stocks and bonds is usually an expensive and lengthy process. The SEC requires companies to gather masses of data in a prospectus—a document that describes a company's financial condition—before any new issue is approved.

Figure 2 shows the relative importance of each of the different funding sources to U.S. nonfinancial corporations. It indicates that plowback accounted for more than 100 percent of total corporate financing in 2007, while new bond issues and other forms of debt accounted for another 76 percent. How can this be? As the figure shows, new stock sales amounted to a stunning minus 81 percent of corporate financing, because corporations reduced the number of their stocks in the public's hands by buying some back.

What Determines Stock Prices? The Role of Expected Company Earnings

People invest in stocks because they believe (and hope) that the prices of the stocks they have purchased will rise. But will they? To answer that question, one should understand just what determines the price of a stock—but we do not really know the answer. We do know that, as with other things sold in markets, prices are determined by supply and demand. That merely raises the next question: What explains the behavior of supply and demand? That answer depends on the actions and expectations of the people who have stocks to sell or who wish to buy.

There is one apparently logical answer, although later we will see that there are reasons to question that explanation. This answer is that a stock is simply a share of the ownership of the firm that has issued it. The stock will therefore be valuable if the firm earns a good deal of money in the future, and it will rise in price if the firm earns more than investors had expected. The stock will fall in price if the earnings of the firm are poor or disappointing. That is why professional stock analysts who sell their advice to investors devote most of their efforts to studying individual firms and their markets, hoping to gain some insights into each company's future earnings prospects.

Though the stock market has generally been a good investment in the long run, it can be very risky over shorter periods, as we have seen. During the Great Depression that began in 1929, stock prices dropped precipitously and remained low for years. They did not re-attain their 1929 peaks until 1954. More recently, we have just lived through a decade in which stock market gains were zero.

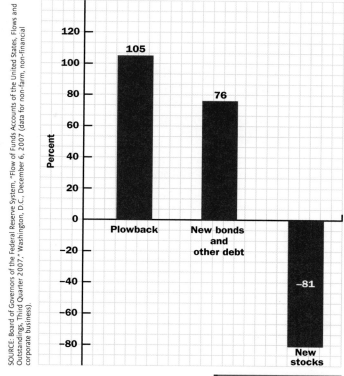

SOURCE: Board of Governors of the Federal Reserve System, "Flow of Funds Accounts of the United States, Flows and Outstanding, Third Quarter 2007," Washington, D.C., December 6, 2007 (data for non-farm, non-financial corporate business).

FIGURE 2

Sources of New Funds for U.S. Corporations, 2007

BUYING STOCKS AND BONDS

Although investors can purchase stocks and bonds through any brokerage firm, not all brokers charge the same fees. Bargain brokerage houses advertise in the newspapers' financial pages, offering investors very little service—no advice, no research, no other frills—other than merely buying or selling what the customer wants them to, at lower fees than those charged by higher-service brokerage firms. And during the late 1990s, it became possible to buy and sell shares over the Internet at very low cost—and millions of Americans did so.

Many investors are not aware of the various ways in which they can purchase (or sell) stocks. Two noteworthy arrangements are (1) a market order purchase, which simply tells the broker to buy a specified quantity of stock at the best price the market currently offers, and (2) a limit order, which is an agreement to buy a given amount of stock when its price falls to

"To hell with a balanced portfolio. I want to sell my Fenwick Chemical and sell it now."

Equities includes individual stocks, stock mutual funds, hybrid mutual funds, exchange-traded funds, and variable annuities.

Portfolio diversification means inclusion of a number and variety of stocks, bonds, and other such items in an individual's portfolio. If the individual owns airline stocks, for example, diversification requires the purchase of a stock or bond in a very different industry, such as breakfast cereal production.

A **mutual fund**, in which individual investors can buy shares, is a private investment firm that holds a portfolio of securities. Investors can choose among a large variety of mutual funds, such as stock funds, bond funds, and so forth.

An **index fund** is a mutual fund that chooses a particular stock price index and then buys the stocks (or most of the stocks) that are included in the index. The value of an investment in an index fund depends on what happens to the prices of all stocks in that index.

A **stock price index**, such as the S&P 500, is an average of the prices of a large set of stocks. These stocks are selected to represent the price movements of the entire stock market, or some specified segment of the market, and the chosen set is rarely changed.

a specified level. If the investor offers to buy at $18, then the broker will purchase shares if and when the market price falls to $18 per share or less.

One recent survey estimated that, in 2008, 47 percent of U.S. households (54.5 million) owned **equities**[7] and/or bonds—up from 39 percent of U.S. households in 1989, but down from a peak of about 57 percent of households in 2001. Of these, 60 percent of U.S. households owned both equities and bonds, 36 percent owned only equities, and 4 percent owned only bonds.[8]

Selecting a Portfolio: Diversification

Perhaps the first rule of safe investing is: Always diversify—never put all your eggs in one basket.[9] A person or an organization's holdings of securities from several different corporations is called a *portfolio of investments*. A portfolio tends to be far less risky than any of the individual securities it contains because of the benefits of **portfolio diversification**. Let's see why.

If, for example, Alex divides his holdings among Companies A, B, and C, then his portfolio may perform satisfactorily overall even if Company A goes broke. Moreover, suppose that Company A specializes in producing luxury items, which do well in prosperous periods but very badly during recessions, whereas Company B sells cheap clothing, whose cyclical demand pattern differs greatly from that of Company A. If Alex holds stock in both companies, his overall risk is obviously less than if he owned stock in only one. All other things being equal, a portfolio containing many different types of securities tends to be less risky than a portfolio with fewer types of securities.

Increasingly, institutional investors, such as mutual funds, have adopted portfolios composed of broad ranges of stocks typifying those offered by the entire stock market. **Mutual funds** are now among the largest U.S. investors in securities. They offer their customers portfolios of various groups of domestic stocks, foreign stocks, and bonds. Small investors can easily put their money into these funds, thereby reducing the risks of owning individual stocks and ensuring that the overall market does not significantly outperform their portfolios. Mutual fund transactions can be carried out by telephone or over the Internet, and investors can also easily check on the past performance of the different funds and obtain other pertinent information. Investors purchasing mutual fund shares should check on the fees charged by different funds, because fees vary surprisingly widely from one fund to another—and the difference can have a large effect on the relative earnings of an investment in a fund.

One kind of mutual fund, called an **index fund**, buys the securities used in one of the standard **stock price indexes** (such as Standard & Poor's 500—known as the S&P 500—or the broader Wilshire 5000 Index). A stock price index is an average of the prices of a group of stocks—weighted by the size of each company—that are believed to be representative of the overall stock market (or some specialized segment, such as Far Eastern stocks). When you invest in an index fund, the return on your money will therefore reflect the performance of the entire market, rather than any one or a few securities that you or your broker might have selected instead.

"A cheap alternative to traditional fund management arose more than 30 years ago, in the form of [index funds that simply buy and hold on to a large representative sample of securities] such as the S&P 500, [rarely incurring the cost of buying or selling]. . . . small investors ought to worry about cost. Figures from John Bogle, founder of the fund giant Vanguard, show that an S&P 500 index-fund returned 12.3% a year between 1980 and 2005,

---

[7] The term *equities* includes individual stocks, stock mutual funds, hybrid mutual funds, exchange-traded funds, and variable annuities.

[8] Investment Company Institute and the Securities Industry and Financial Markets Association, *Equity and Bond Ownership in America: 2008*, 2008, pp. 5–8, accessed online at http://www.ici.org/pdf/rpt_08_equity_owners.pdf.

[9] This was a bitter lesson for employees of Enron, the giant firm that went bankrupt so spectacularly in 2001. Many of its workers invested much of their savings in high-priced Enron stocks and lost virtually everything when the price of Enron stock later plunged.

"What Is a Share of Google Worth?"

It almost goes without saying that Google is one of the world's leading brands. Its Internet search engine is so ubiquitous that its very name is a verb for looking up information about someone or something.

So when its founders decided to "go public" and offer shares of the company for the public to buy, the announcement set off tremendous speculation about what the company would be worth. Google itself predicted a jaw-dropping price range of $108 to $135 for its shares, which would have translated into a company value of $36 billion dollars. That would put Google right up there with the bluest of the "blue chip" stocks—of the thousands of publicly listed companies in the United States, only about 70 companies have a market value that high.*

On August 19, 2004, Google made its debut on the NASDAQ stock market. Trading under the ticker symbol GOOG (you can "google it," if you like), the stock opened at $100, which was almost 18 percent higher than its initial offering price of $85. More than 22 million shares changed hands on that first day of trading, with Google selling a total of 19.6 million shares, thus raising about $1.2 billion for the company. That price implied a market value of $27.2 billion. Not bad for an idea conceived by two Stanford University grad students!

(As this book went to press, Google was selling for about $565 a share.)

SOURCE: © AP IMAGES / Ben Margot

SOURCES: Paul R. La Monica, "Google Jumps 18% in Debut," *CNN Money*, August 19, 2004, http://money.cnn.com; Ben Berkowitz, "Is Google Worth $135 a Share?," *MSN Money*, July 26, 2004, http://www.msn.com; Ben Elgin, "Commentary: Google This: Investor Beware," *Business Week Online*, August 9, 2004, http://www.businessweek.com; "Financial Release: Google Inc. Prices Initial Public Offering of Class A Common Stock," August 18, 2004, http://www.investor.google.com; and * "2004 Leaders: The Business Week Global 1000," *Business Week*, July 26, 2004, http://www.businessweekonline.com.

whereas the average mutual fund investor, because of costs and poor timing, earned just 7.3%. That makes an enormous difference to wealth: $10,000 invested in the index fund grew to $170,800; a typical mutual-fund investor saw his money grow to just to $48,200." (Source: *The Economist*, March 1, 2008, pp. 15–18.)

Institutional money managers increasingly use computer programs to decide on their portfolios and to buy or sell huge portfolios of stocks simultaneously and rapidly. Since 1982, some traders have also allowed their computers to decide when to jump in and make massive sales or purchases. This practice is called *program trading*. In 2003, program trading accounted for about 40 percent of the total New York Stock Exchange volume and a considerable amount of the volume in other stock exchanges. Program trading was heavily criticized for aggravating price fluctuations and contributing to the stock market crash of October 1987. Restrictions are now in place that curb program trading when stock markets decline sharply.

STOCK EXCHANGES AND THEIR FUNCTIONS

The New York Stock Exchange (NYSE)—"The Big Board"—is perhaps the world's most prestigious stock market. Located on Wall Street in New York City, it is "the establishment" of the securities industry. The NYSE deals with only the best-known and most heavily traded securities—2,447 companies in all, as of the end of 2008. Leading brokerage firms hold 1,366 "seats" on the stock exchange, which enable them to trade directly on the exchange floor. (In the NYSE's early years, members sat in assigned seats during roll call; the term lost its literal meaning with the advent of continuous trading in 1871.) Seats are traded on the open market. As of 2005, a seat on the exchange went for $3.5 million.

In 2008, the NYSE handled almost 36 percent of all stock market transactions, on average, in the United States (measured in volume of shares). A number of regional exchanges—such as the Chicago, Pacific, Philadelphia, Boston, and Cincinnati Stock Exchanges—deal in many of the stocks handled on the NYSE but mainly serve large institutional customers such as

banks, insurance companies, and mutual funds. In addition to these regional exchanges, the American Stock Exchange, acquired in 2008 by the NYSE's parent company, NYSE Euronext, handles about 10 percent of the total stock traded in the United States.

The remainder of all stock transactions are carried by NASDAQ (also known as the Nasdaq Stock Market), which draws its name from the National Association of Securities Dealers.[10] It is the home of most of the "tech" stocks that soared in the late 1990s, plummeted in 2000–2002, and have now returned to their pre-boom levels. Unlike the NYSE, NASDAQ has no physical trading floor, although it does have an outdoor display at its headquarters in New York City's Times Square, where a spectacular eight-story LED screen runs a continuous stock ticker, delivers market news, and shows advertisements and logos of NASDAQ member companies. All of its transactions are carried out on a computer network, with NASDAQ handling the stocks of approximately 3,300 companies, including such giants as Intel and Microsoft.

In recent years, the established stock markets have faced competition from another source. With the rapid growth of the Internet, people are now buying and selling stocks directly through their home computers. It is estimated that the number of online trading accounts at major U.S. brokerages increased from 1.5 million in 1997 to 19.7 million at the end of 2001, and topped 50 million in 2004.[11] According to one estimate, 12 million American households will be trading online by 2011—an increase of 48 percent from 8.1 million households in 2006.[12]

Regulation of the Stock Market

Both the government and the industry itself regulate the U.S. securities markets. At the base of the regulatory pyramid, stock brokerage firms maintain compliance departments to oversee their own operations. At the next level, the NYSE, the American Stock Exchange, NASDAQ, and the regional exchanges are responsible for monitoring their member firms' business practices, funding adequacy, compliance, and integrity. They also use sophisticated computer surveillance systems to scrutinize trading activity. The Securities and Exchange Commission (SEC) is the federal government agency that oversees the market's self-regulation.

You Are There: An Event on the Trading Floor of the New York Stock Exchange

You are standing on the trading floor of the New York Exchange, a crowded and noisy set of rooms cluttered with people, hundreds of computer monitors, and other electronic paraphernalia. It is a high-tech space in a 93-year-old architectural relic of bygone days. Around the floor are 17 stations, or "trading posts," presided over by specialists, each assigned responsibility for trading a particular set of stocks.

Suddenly the floor's frenetic activity focuses on one specialist's post. News has just come in that one of the companies whose stock she handles has earned more in the previous quarter than was expected. Brokers crowd around her, calling out orders to buy and sell the company's stock, as its price rises rapidly in the wake of the good news. Deals are completed verbally, as clerks record the trades and enter them into the computerized tape, making the information instantly available all over the globe.

SOURCE: Murray Teitelbaum, Communications Division, New York Stock Exchange.

[10] The NASD and Nasdaq have been separated legally.

[11] *The New York Times 2004 Almanac*, ed. John W. Wright (New York: Penguin Group, 2003), p. 342, which cites Gómez, Inc., an Internet research firm in Lincoln, Massachusetts; and the *Wall Street Journal*, "Trading Stocks Online," http://investing.wsj.com, which cites Forrester Research in Cambridge, Massachusetts.

[12] Bill Doyle, *US Online Trading Forecast: 2006 to 2011* (Cambridge, Mass.: Forrester Research), February 1, 2007.

One example of these self-imposed rules involves the steps that markets adopted after the October 1987 stock market crash to cushion future price falls. Starting in 1988, with amendments since then, the NYSE and other stock markets adopted a series of rules called *circuit breakers*, which now halt all trading for one hour, two hours, or the remainder of the trading day when the Dow Jones Industrial Average (a widely followed average price of a sample of stocks) declines below its previous day's closing value by defined percentage amounts (which are adjusted every quarter). These restrictions on trading vary with the severity of the drop in the Dow and with the time of day when the drop occurs. Circuit breakers were designed to head off panics among market participants and forestall crashes like the ones in October 1929 and October 1987.

Stock Exchanges and Corporate Capital Needs

Although corporations often raise needed funds by selling stock, they do not normally do so through the stock exchanges. New stock issues are typically handled by a special type of bank, called an *investment bank*. In contrast, the stock markets trade almost exclusively in "secondhand securities"—stocks in the hands of individuals and others who bought them earlier and now wish to sell them. Thus, the stock market does not provide funds to corporations needing financing to expand their productive activities. The markets provide money only to persons who already hold previously issued stocks.

Nevertheless, stock exchanges perform two critically important functions for corporate financing. First, by providing a secondhand market for stocks, they make individual investment in a company much less risky. Investors know that if they need money, they can always sell their stocks to other investors or to stock market specialists at the current

Corporate Scandals

Excerpted from the *The Economist* magazine, the following account provides details of some of the scandals that erupted in the corporate world in the early 2000s.

. . . After a tumultuous few years in which a series of corporate America's best-known names admitted to wrongdoing of one sort or another—the roll-call includes Enron, WorldCom, Qwest, Adelphia, Rite Aid, Tyco and Xerox—the focus shifted to Wall Street's banks and fund managers, giving industrial companies some breathing space. They are also relieved that the latest scandals—the billions missing from Italy's biggest dairy company, Parmalat, and questionable accounting at Adecco, a Swiss-based company that is the world's biggest temping agency—are unfolding thousands of miles away. . . .

Right now, the pack following the demise of one-time corporate titans is enraptured by the trial of Dennis Kozlowksi, former chief executive, and Mark Swartz, former chief financial officer, of Tyco. . . . [S]hareholders were appalled by revelations of excess, including $6,000 spent on a shower curtain and more than $100,000 on a mirror at a posh company apartment where Mr. Kozlowski lived. Prosecutors have alleged that Mr. Kozlowski and Mr. Swartz stole $170 million from the company, illegally gained $430 million from selling stock, and used dubious accounting to hide their actions—allegations the men have denied. . . .

So far, of the senior Enron executives, only [Andrew Fastow, former finance chief], has been indicted. The man who set up a series of offshore partnerships that disguised huge liabilities

had pleaded not guilty to charges of fraud, money laundering and conspiracy to inflate Enron's profits. . . . His wife, also a former Enron employee, was last week offered a deal under which she would plead guilty to a charge of filing a false tax return. . . .

February is scheduled to bring two trials, that of Scott Sullivan, former chief financial officer of WorldCom, and that of John Rigas, founder of Adelphia Communications, a cable television company. WorldCom is the holder of the record for the most deceptive accounts, to the tune of an estimated $11 billion over several years. Mr. Sullivan is charged with masterminding the fraud, though he denies this. . . .

While the rash of scandals did subside somewhat in 2003, another of the best-known corporate personalities of the late 1990s fell from grace. Dick Grasso resigned as chairman and chief executive of the New York Stock Exchange after a furore erupted over his $140 million pay packet (later revealed to have been $188m in total). . . .

"Our financial officer won't be at work today—he just called in guilty."

SOURCE: "A Trying Year," *The Economist,* January 13, 2004, http://www.economist.com.

A **derivative** is a complex financial instrument whose value depends in some way on the price movements of some specified set of investments, such as a group of stocks, bonds, or commodities. For example, a derivative contract may entitle its owner to buy 100 shares of Company X's stock at a price of $30 in four months, where $30 may be higher or lower than the market price of that stock at the specified date.

A **credit default swap (CDS)** is a financial instrument that functions like an insurance policy that protects a lender. The buyer of a CDS pays the seller for insuring against a third-party's default on a debt that is owed to the former. If the third party defaults on the debt, failing to make the required repayment, the seller of the CDS must pay a lump sum to the buyer of the CDS.

market price. This reduction in risk makes it far easier for corporations to issue new stocks. Second, the stock market determines the current price of the company's stocks. That, in turn, determines whether it will be difficult or easy for a corporation to raise money by selling new stocks.

Some people believe that a company's stock price is closely tied to its operational efficiency, its effectiveness in meeting consumer demands, and its diligence in going after profitable innovation. According to this view, firms that use funds effectively will usually have comparatively high stock prices, and that will enable the firms to raise more money when they issue new stocks through their investment banks and sell them at the high prices determined by the stock market. In this way, the stock market tends to channel the economy's funds to the firms that can make best use of the money.

Other people voice skepticism about the claim that the price of a company's stock is closely tied to efficiency. These observers believe that the demand for a stock is disproportionately influenced by short-term developments in the company's profitability and that the market pays little attention to management decisions affecting the firm's long-term earnings growth. These critics sometimes suggest that the stock market is similar to a gambling casino in which hunch, rumor, and superstition have a critical influence on prices. (We will learn more about this view later in the chapter.)

Whether or not stock prices are an accurate measure of a company's efficiency, if a company's stock price is very low in comparison with the value of its plant, equipment, and other assets, or when a company's earnings seem low compared to its potential level, that company becomes a tempting target for a **takeover**. Perhaps the firm's current management is believed not to be very competent, and those who seek to take control of the company believe that they can do better. Alternatively, if the demand for a company's stocks is believed to be inordinately influenced by short-term developments, such as temporarily low profits, others may believe that it is a bargain in terms of the low current price of

How to Lose Billions: Betting on Derivatives

Derivatives are complex financial instruments that "derive" their value from the price movements of an underlying investment, such as a group of stocks, bonds, or commodities. For example, a derivative may entitle its owner to buy 100 shares of Company X's stock at a price of $30 four months in the future.

Below, Professor William Silber of New York University's Stern School of Business, a widely recognized expert in securities markets, explains the role derivatives played in the most recent financial crisis:

"Businesses buy [derivatives] contracts in an effort to hedge or insure against sudden changes in interest rates or currency values. But they also can be used to speculate in the markets, and sometimes wind up creating bigger problems.

Derivatives exacerbated the financial crisis that began in August 2007 by adding to the potential liabilities of major financial institutions who had sold certain types of derivative contracts. **Credit Default Swaps (CDSs)** are derivatives that, under normal circumstances, allow investors to protect themselves in the event a bond they own goes into default. The seller of the CDS promises that the investor will receive the face value of the bond if the company defaults. The seller receives an up-front fee in exchange."

In the years leading up to the financial crisis of 2007–2008, U.S. investment banks bought CDSs as insurance to protect against potential losses related to the exotic financial products that they were buying and selling. When many American homeowners began defaulting on their mortgages, returns on these investments, which came from homeowners' mortgage payments, halted, and the value of these financial products declined rapidly. But when banks tried to redeem their CDS contracts, the insurers, who had not expected these new financial products to fail en masse, did not have enough cash on hand to cover the contracts.

Below, Professor Silber describes the dramatic events that followed:

"American International Group (AIG) was a major seller of CDSs to a wide variety of financial institutions. As a result of deteriorating credit conditions in September 2009, there was a high probability that AIG would not be able to make all of the payments that were due. It had miscalculated the default risks. Had AIG gone bankrupt, hundreds of other financial institutions that thought they had protection would have been left without any. The prospect of a cascade of bankruptcies forced the U.S. government to lend more than $100 billion to AIG to prevent a further collapse.

The lesson is that derivatives can be beneficial if they are used properly but can have unintended consequences unless they are monitored closely."

SOURCES: Professor William Silber, Director, Glucksman Institute for Research in Securities Markets, Stern School of Business, New York University; and Adam Davidson, "How AIG Fell Apart," September 18, 2008, accessed online at http:// www.thebigmoney.com.

the stock and its more promising future earnings prospects. A takeover occurs when a group of outside financiers buys a sufficient amount of company stock to gain control of the firm. Often, the new controlling group will simply fire the current management and substitute a new chairman, president, and other top officers.

> A **takeover** is the acquisition by an outside group (the raiders) of a controlling proportion of a company's stock. When the old management opposes the takeover attempt, it is called a *hostile takeover attempt*.

SPECULATION

Securities dealings are sometimes viewed with suspicion because they are thought to be an instrument of speculation. When something goes wrong in the stock market—when, say, prices suddenly fall—observers often blame **speculators**. Editorial writers, for example, often use the word *speculators* as a term of strong disapproval, implying that those who engage in the activity are parasites who produce no benefits for society and often cause considerable harm. (See "How to Lose Billions: Betting on Derivatives," on the previous page, for a description of a particularly risky speculative instrument, the derivative.)

> Individuals who engage in **speculation** deliberately invest in risky assets, hoping to obtain profits from future changes in the prices of these assets.

Economists disagree vehemently with this judgment. They argue that speculators perform two vital economic functions:

- Speculators sell protection from risk to other people, much as a fire insurance policy offers protection from risk to a homeowner.
- Speculators help to smooth out price fluctuations by purchasing items when they are abundant (and cheap) and holding them and reselling them when they are scarce (and expensive). In that way, speculators play a vital economic role in helping to alleviate and even prevent shortages.

Some examples from outside the securities markets will help clarify the role of speculators. Imagine that a Broadway ticket broker attends a preview of a new musical comedy and suspects it will be a hit. He decides to speculate by buying a large block of tickets for future performances. In that way, he takes over part of the producer's risk, while the play's producer reduces her inventory of risky tickets and receives some hard cash. If the show opens and is a flop, the broker will be stuck with the tickets. If the show is a hit, he can sell them at a premium, if the law allows (and he will be denounced as a speculator or a "scalper").

Similarly, speculators enable farmers (or producers of metals and other commodities whose future price is uncertain) to decrease their risk. Let's say Jasmine and Jim have planted a large crop of wheat but fear its price may fall before harvest time. They can protect themselves by signing a contract with a speculator for future delivery of the crop at an agreed-upon price. If the price then falls, the speculator—not Jasmine and Jim—will suffer the loss. Of course, if the price rises, the speculator will reap the rewards—but that is the nature of risk bearing. The speculator who has agreed to buy the crop at a preset price, regardless of market conditions at the time of the sale, has, in effect, sold an insurance policy to Jasmine and Jim. Surely this is a useful function.

The speculators' second role is perhaps even more important. In effect, they accumulate and store goods in periods of abundance and make goods available in periods of scarcity. Suppose that a speculator has reason to suspect that next year's crop of a storable commodity will not be nearly as abundant as this year's. She will buy some of the crop now, when it is cheap, for resale when it becomes scarce and expensive. In the process, she will smooth out the swing in prices by adding her purchases to the total market demand in the low-price period (which tends to bring the price up at that time) and bringing in her supplies during the high-price period (which tends to push this later-period price down).[13]

Thus, the successful speculator will help to relieve matters during periods of extreme shortage. Speculators have sometimes even helped to relieve famine by releasing supplies they had deliberately hoarded for such an occasion. Of course, speculators are cursed for their high prices when this happens. But those who curse them do not understand that prices would

---

[13] For a diagrammatic analysis of this role of speculation, see Discussion Question 3 at the end of this chapter.

have been even higher if the speculators' foresight and avid pursuit of profit had not provided for the emergency. On the securities market, famine and severe shortages are not an issue, but the fact remains that successful speculators tend to reduce price fluctuations by increasing demand for stocks when prices are low and contributing to supply when prices are high.

Far from aggravating instability and fluctuations, to earn a profit speculators *iron out* fluctuations by buying when prices are low and selling when prices are high.

PUZZLE 2 RESOLVED: UNPREDICTABLE STOCK PRICES AS "RANDOM WALKS"

In one of the puzzles at the beginning of this chapter, we cited evidence indicating that the best professional securities analysts have a forecasting record so miserable that investors may do as well predicting earnings by hunch, superstition, or any purely random process as they would by following professional advice. (See "Giving Up on Stock Gimmicks" on the next page to learn about some crazy ways of "predicting" the stock market's performance.)

Does this mean that analysts are incompetent people who do not know what they are doing? Not at all. Rather, there is fairly strong evidence that they have undertaken a task that is basically impossible.

How can this be so? The answer is that to make a good forecast of any variable—be it GDP, population, fuel usage, or stock market prices—there must be something in the past whose behavior is closely related to the future behavior of the variable whose path we wish to predict. If a 10 percent rise in this year's consumption always produces a 5 percent rise in next year's GDP, this fact can help us predict future GDP on the basis of current observations. But if we want to forecast the future of a variable whose behavior is completely unrelated to the behavior of any current or past variable, there is no objective evidence that can help us make that forecast. Throwing darts or gazing into a crystal ball are no less effective than analysts' calculations.

A mass of statistical evidence indicates that the behavior of stock prices is largely unpredictable. In other words, the behavior of stock prices is essentially random; the paths they follow approximate what statisticians call **random walks**. A random walk is like the path followed by a sleepwalker. All we know about his position after his next step is that it will be given by his current position plus whatever random direction his next haphazard step will take. The relevant feature of randomness, for our purposes, is that it is by nature unpredictable, which is just what the word *random* means.

If the evidence that stock prices approximate a random walk stands up to research in the future as it has so far, it is easy enough to understand why stock market predictions are so poor. Analysts are trying to forecast behavior that is basically random; in effect, they are trying to predict the unpredictable.

The time path of a variable such as the price of a stock is said to constitute a **random walk** if its magnitude in one period (say, May 2, 2005) is equal to its value in the preceding period (May 1, 2005) plus a completely random number. That is: Price on May 2, 2005 = Price on May 1, 2005 + Random number, where the random number (positive or negative) can be obtained by a roll of dice or some such procedure.

Two questions remain. First, does the evidence that stock prices follow a random walk mean that investment in stocks is a pure gamble and never worthwhile? Second, how does one explain the random behavior of stock prices?

To answer the first question, it is wrong to conclude that investment in stocks is generally not worthwhile. The statistical evidence is that, over the long run, stock prices as a whole have followed a fairly marked upward trend, perhaps reflecting the long-term growth of the economy. Thus, the random walk does not proceed in just any direction—rather, it represents a set of erratic movements around a basic upward trend in stock prices.

Moreover, it is not in the overall level of stock prices that the most pertinent random walk occurs, but in the performance of one company's stock as compared with another firm's stock. For this reason, professional advice may be able to predict that investment in the stock market is likely to be a good thing over the long haul. But, if

SOURCE: © 1990 Cartoonists & Writers Syndicate/cartoonweb.com

"Just a normal day at the nation's most important financial institution . . ."

Giving Up on Stock Gimmicks

"For a New Year's resolution. . ., I'm giving up stock market forecasting gimmicks.

The Super Bowl indicator. The January barometer. Others so numerous I can't think of them all right now. It won't be easy to do this cold turkey. The indicators are often ingenious, occasionally quite persuasive, and nearly always fun. They appeal to my yearning for a simple answer to a complicated problem.

The first indicator I bid goodbye to, the Super Bowl stock market predictor, is the easiest to forswear. It has suddenly and completely stopped functioning, breaking down like a rusty old car. That's too bad, because it added some zest to the National Football League championship extravaganza, which more than once has needed it.

The idea is this: If a team from the original National Football League before its 1970 merger with the American Football League won the Super Bowl, a good year for the stock market was in store. Conversely, if a team with AFL origins triumphed, tough times lay ahead.

An awareness of this pattern would have been especially helpful in the bear-market years 1969, 1970, 1973, 1974, and 1981, all of which began with wins by a team from the wrong side of the tracks. So what if everybody knew there was no possible causal link between football and the stock market?

As the years rolled by, though, the novelty of the Super Bowl indicator wore off, especially as analysts picked it apart looking for corollaries. Was the margin of victory important? What about which team scored first? Then along came John Elway to knock the whole thing down with a barrage of his famous bullet passes. The Denver Broncos quarterback led his team, a product of the AFL, to victories in '98 and '99, and yet the stock market boomed anyway.

SOURCE: © GABRIEL BOUYS/AFP/Getty Images

While Super Bowl indicator fans struggled to formulate the "Elway exception," the St. Louis Rams recaptured the Super Bowl in 2000 for the NFL originals. Contrarily, the stock market then dropped. . . .

A seasonal indicator with a stronger rationale, the January barometer long espoused by investment advisor Yale Hirsch, gave a better performance in 2000. In line with Hirsch's doctrine that "as January goes, so goes the year," it foreshadowed a down year for the market when the stock-price averages posted minus signs for the first month.

By Hirsch's reckoning, this rule has seen only three glaring exceptions since 1950. Most years, I readily confess, I find myself checking in January to see how it's shaping up.

But when the time comes to figure out how to put it into use, I'm at a loss. Trading on it seems impractical. Any long-term investor who sits out each January to await a signal misses a lot of gains: Measuring by the Standard & Poor's 500 Index, 3.3 percent in 1996, 6.1 percent in 1997, 1 percent in 1998 and 4.1 percent in 1999. . . .

Maybe you've got some favorite indicators of your own. If so, you're welcome to them. From now on, I never touch the stuff."

SOURCE: Chet Currier, "Investing: Giving Up on Stock Gimmicks," from *Newsday*, January 7, 2001, p. F13. Reprinted by permission of Tribune Media Services.

---

the random walk evidence is valid, there is no way professionals can tell us which of the available stocks is most likely to increase in price—that is, which combination of stocks is best for the investor to buy.

The only appropriate answer to the second question of how to account for the random behavior of stock prices is that no one is sure of the explanation. There are two widely offered hypotheses—each virtually the opposite of the other. The first asserts that stock prices are random because clever professional speculators are able to foresee almost perfectly every influence that is not random. For example, suppose that a change occurs that makes the probable earnings of some company higher than had previously been expected. Then, according to this view, the professionals will instantly become aware of this change and immediately buy enough shares to raise the price of the stock accordingly. Then the only thing for that stock price to do between this year and next is wander randomly, because the professionals cannot predict random movements, and hence they cannot force current stock prices to anticipate them.

The second explanation of the random behavior of stock prices is at the opposite extreme from the view that all nonrandom movements are wiped out by super-smart professionals. This is the view that people who buy and sell stocks have learned that they cannot predict future stock prices. As a result, they react to any signal, however irrational and irrelevant it appears. If the president catches cold, stock prices fall. If an astronaut's venture is successful, prices go up. According to this view, investors are, in the last analysis, trying to predict not the prospects of the economy or of the company whose shares they buy, but the supply and demand behavior of other investors, which will ultimately determine the course of stock prices. Because all investors are equally in the dark, their groping around can only result in the randomness that we observe.

The classic statement of this view of stock market behavior was provided in 1936 by the English economist John Maynard Keynes, a successful professional speculator himself:

> Professional investment may be likened to those newspaper competitions in which the competitors have to pick out the six prettiest faces from a hundred photographs, the prize being awarded to the competitor whose choice most nearly corresponds to the average preferences of the competitors as a whole; so that each competitor has to pick not those faces which he himself finds prettiest, but those which he thinks likeliest to catch the fancy of the other competitors, all of whom are looking at the problem from the same point of view. It is not a case of choosing those which, to the best of one's judgment, are really the prettiest, nor even those which average opinion genuinely thinks the prettiest. We have reached the third degree where we devote our intelligences to anticipating what average opinion expects the average opinion to be. And there are some, I believe, who practice the fourth, fifth and higher degrees.[14]

---

[14] John Maynard Keynes, *The General Theory of Employment, Interest, and Money* (New York: Harcourt Brace; 1936), p. 156.

PUZZLE 1 REDUX: THE BOOM AND BUST OF THE U.S. STOCK MARKET

This last quotation leads to some insights into the remarkable behavior of the U.S. stock market during the late 1990s and early 2000s—a phenomenon we mentioned at the start of this chapter. (Refer back to Figure 1.)

First, many people who buy stocks—both professionals and amateurs—do so for speculative purposes. They may not care (or even know!) what the company does; they care only that its stock price goes up. Second, in a speculative world, where people buy stocks in order to sell them later, a share of stock is basically worth what someone else will pay for it. So even if Smart Susan is convinced that Dotcon.com has poor business prospects, it may still be rational for her to buy the stock at $50 per share if she is convinced that she will be able to sell it to Foolish Frank next year for $100 per share. (This idea has been called the "greater fool" theory of investing: It makes sense to buy a stock at a foolishly high price if you can sell it at an even higher price—to an even greater fool!) Third, once something attains the status of a fad, waves of buying can drive prices up to ridiculous levels, as has happened many times in history. Fourth, America undoubtedly fell in love both with information technology (especially the Internet) and the stock market (especially Internet-related stocks) in the late 1990s.

All this set the stage for what is commonly called a financial "bubble." The metaphor is meant to conjure up images of things like balloons and soap bubbles that blow up and up and up . . . until they burst. Indeed, legions of economists were warning about a stock market bubble in 1998, in 1999, and into 2000. The problem is simply stated: No one ever knows when a bubble will burst. And for stock market speculators, timing is everything. Look back at Figure 1 again. Those who claimed in mid-1999 that technology stocks were overvalued looked pretty silly when stock prices doubled in less than one year. (Of course, they subsequently looked pretty smart when prices collapsed!) Technology enthusiasts ignored them as the stock market partied on. The only thing that is truly predictable about a bubble is that it will burst—eventually. But no one ever knows when. As was also the case more recently when the "housing bubble" burst, triggering the even larger economic crisis of 2007–2008, no one could say definitively that now was the time to sell technology stocks. As the saying goes, the rest is history.

| SUMMARY |

1. Most U.S. manufactured goods are produced by **corporations**.

2. Investors in corporations have greater risk protection than those who put their money into other types of firms because the corporate form gives them **limited liability**—they cannot be asked to pay more of the company's debts than they have invested in the firm.

3. Higher taxation of corporate earnings tends to limit the things in which corporations can invest and may lead to inefficiency in resource allocation.

4. A **common stock** is a share in a company's ownership. A **bond** is an IOU for money lent to a company by the bondholder. Many observers argue that a stock purchase really amounts to a loan to the company—a loan that is riskier than a bond purchase.

5. If **interest rates** rise, bond prices will fall. In other words, if some bond amounts to a contract to pay 8 percent and the market interest rate goes up to 10 percent, people will no longer be willing to pay the old price for that bond.

6. Corporations finance their activities mostly by **plowback** (that is, by retaining part of their earnings and reinvesting the funds in the company). They also obtain funds by selling stocks and bonds and by taking out more traditional loans.

7. If stock prices correctly reflect the future prospects of different companies, it is easier for promising firms to raise money because they are able to sell each stock issue at favorable prices.

8. Bonds are relatively risky for the firms that issue them, but they are fairly safe for their buyers, because they are a commitment by those firms to pay fixed annual amounts to the bondholders whether or not the companies make money that year. Stocks, which do not promise any fixed payment, are relatively safe for the companies but risky for their owners.

9. A **portfolio** is a collection of stocks, bonds, and other assets of a single owner. The greater the number and variety of securities and other assets a portfolio contains, the less risky it generally is.

10. A **takeover** of a corporation occurs when an outside group buys enough stock to get control of the firm's decisions. Takeovers are a useful way to get rid of incompetent management or to force management to be more efficient. However, the process is costly and leads to wasteful defensive and offensive activities.

11. **Speculation** affects stock market prices, but (contrary to widespread belief) it actually tends to reduce the frequency and size of price fluctuations. Speculators are also useful to the economy because they undertake risks that others wish to avoid, thereby, in effect, providing others with insurance against risk.

12. Statistical evidence indicates that individual stock prices behave **randomly** (in other words, unpredictably).

| KEY TERMS |

bond 180	index fund 184	portfolio diversification 184
common stock 180	inflation 181	random walk 190
corporation 179	interest rate 181	securities 181
credit default swap 188	limited liability 180	speculation 189
derivative 188	mutual fund 184	stock price index 184
equities 184	plowback (retained earnings) 182	takeover 188, 189

| TEST YOURSELF |

1. Suppose that interest rates are 6 percent in the economy and a safe bond promises to pay $3 per year in interest forever. What do you think the price of the bond will be? Why?

2. Suppose that in the economy described in Test Yourself 1, interest rates suddenly fall to 3 percent. What will happen to the price of the bond that pays $3 per year?

3. For whom are stocks riskier than bonds? For whom are bonds riskier than stocks?

4. If the price of a company's stock constitutes a random walk, next year its price will equal today's price plus what?

5. Company A sells heaters and Company B sells air conditioners. Which is the safer investment, Company A stock, Company B stock, or a portfolio containing half of each?

6. If you make a lucky prediction about the prices of the stocks of the two companies in Question 5, will you earn more or less if you invest in that company rather than the portfolio?

| DISCUSSION QUESTIONS |

1. If you hold shares in a corporation and management decides to plow back the company's earnings some year instead of paying dividends, what are the advantages and disadvantages to you?

2. If you want to buy a stock, when might it pay you to use a market order? When will it pay to use a limit order?

3. Show in diagrams that if a speculator were to buy when price is high and sell when price is low, he would increase price fluctuations. Why would it be in his best interest not to do so? (*Hint:* Draw two supply-demand diagrams, one for the high-price period and one for the low-price period. How would the speculator's activities affect these diagrams?)

4. If stock prices really do take a random walk, can you nevertheless think of good reasons for getting professional advice before investing?

5. Hostile takeovers often end up in court when management attempts to block such a maneuver and raiders accuse management of selfishly sacrificing the stockholders' interests. The courts often look askance at "coercive" offers by raiders—an offer to buy, say, 20 percent of the company's stock by a certain date from the first stockholders who offer to sell. By contrast, they take a more favorable attitude toward "noncoercive" offers to buy any and all stock supplied at announced prices. Do you think the courts are right to reject "coercive offers" and prevent management from blocking "noncoercive" offers? Why?

6. In program trading, computers decide when to buy or sell stocks on behalf of large, institutional investors. The computers then carry out those transactions with electronic speed. Critics claim that this practice is a major reason why stock prices rose and fell sharply in the 1980s. Is this idea plausible? Why or why not?

Part 3

Markets and the Price System

So far, we have talked only about firms in general without worrying about the different sorts of markets in which they operate. To understand the different types of competition a firm can face, it is necessary, first, to explain clearly what we mean by the word *market*. Economists do not reserve this term for only an organized exchange, such as the London stock exchange, operating in a specific location. In its more general and abstract usage, *market* refers to a set of sellers and buyers whose activities affect the price at which a *particular commodity* is sold. For example, two separate sales of General Motors stock in different parts of the country can be considered to take place in the same market, whereas sales of bread in one stall of a market square and sales of compact discs in the next stall may, in our sense, occur in totally different markets.

Economists distinguish among different kinds of competition in such markets according to how many firms they include, whether the products of the different firms are identical or different, and how easy it is for new firms to enter the markets. *Perfect competition* is at one extreme (many small firms selling an identical product, with easy entry into the market), and *pure monopoly* (a single firm dominating the market) is at the other extreme. In between are hybrid forms—called *monopolistic competition* (many small firms, each selling slightly different products) and *oligopoly* (a few large rival firms)—that share some of the characteristics of both perfect competition and monopoly.

Perfect competition is far from the typical market form in the U.S. economy. Indeed, it is quite rare. Pure monopoly—literally *one* firm—is also infrequently encountered. Most of the products you buy are no doubt supplied by oligopolies or monopolistic competitors—terms that we will define precisely in Chapter 12.

CHAPTERS

THE FIRM AND THE INDUSTRY UNDER PERFECT COMPETITION

Competition . . . brings about the only . . . arrangement of social production which is possible. . . . [Otherwise] what guarantee [do] we have that the necessary quantity and not more of each product will be produced, that we shall not go hungry in regard to corn and meat while we are choked in beet sugar and drowned in potato spirit, that we shall not lack trousers to cover our nakedness while buttons flood us in millions?

FRIEDRICH ENGELS (THE FRIEND AND COAUTHOR OF KARL MARX)

Industries differ dramatically in the number and typical sizes of their firms. Some, such as commercial fishing, encompass a great many small firms. Others, like automobile manufacturing, are composed of a few industrial giants. This chapter deals with a special type of market structure—called *perfect competition*—in which firms are numerous and small. As already noted, this market structure is rarely even approximated in reality. Yet, for reasons that will be pointed out, until a few decades ago most economic theory regarding firms and markets focused on the case of perfect competition.

We begin this chapter by comparing alternative market forms and defining perfect competition precisely. But first, as usual, we set out our puzzle.

CONTENTS

PUZZLE: POLLUTION REDUCTION INCENTIVES THAT ACTUALLY INCREASE POLLUTION

Many economists and other citizens concerned about the environment believe that society can obtain cleaner air and water cheaply and effectively by requiring polluters to pay for the damages they cause. (See Chapter 17 for more details.) Yet people often view pollution charges as just another *tax,* and that word can translate into political poison. Some politicians—reasoning that you can move a donkey along just as effectively by offering it a carrot as by poking it with a stick—have proposed *paying* firms to cut down on their polluting emissions.

At least some theoretical and statistical evidence indicates that such a system of bribes (or, to use a more palatable word, subsidies) does work, *at least up to a point.* Individual polluting firms will, indeed, respond to government payments for decreased emissions by reducing their pollution. But, over the long haul, it turns out that society may well end up with more pollution than before! Subsidy payments to the firms can actually exacerbate pollution problems. How is it possible that subsidies induce each firm to pollute less but in the long run lead to a rise in total pollution? The analysis in this chapter will supplement your own common sense sufficiently to supply the answer.

PERFECT COMPETITION DEFINED

Perfect competition occurs in an industry when that industry is made up of many small firms producing homogeneous products, when there is no impediment to the entry or exit of firms, and when full information is available.

You can appreciate just how special perfect competition is by considering this comprehensive definition. A market is said to operate under **perfect competition** when the following four conditions are satisfied:

1. *Numerous small firms and customers.* **Competitive markets contain so many buyers and sellers that each one constitutes a negligible portion of the whole—so small, in fact, that each player's decisions have no effect on price. This requirement rules out trade associations or other collusive arrangements in which firms work together to influence price.**

2. *Homogeneity of product.* **The product offered by any seller is identical to that supplied by any other seller. (For example, No. 1 red winter wheat is a homogeneous product; different brands of toothpaste are not.) Because products are homogeneous, consumers do not care from which firm they buy, so competition is more powerful.**

3. *Freedom of entry and exit.* **New firms desiring to enter the market face no impediments that previous entrants can avoid, so new firms can easily come in and compete with older firms. Similarly, if production and sale of the good proves unprofitable, no barriers prevent firms from leaving the market.**

4. *Perfect information.* **Each firm and each customer is well informed about available products and prices. They know whether one supplier is selling at a lower price than another.**

These exacting requirements are rarely, if ever, found in practice. One example that comes close to the perfectly competitive standard is a market for common stocks. On any given day, literally millions of buyers and sellers trade Boeing stock. All of the shares are exactly alike, anyone who wishes to sell their Boeing stock can enter the market easily, and most relevant company and industry information is readily available (and virtually free of charge) in the daily newspapers or on the Internet. Many farming and fishing industries also approximate perfect competition, but it is difficult to find many other examples. Our interest in the perfectly competitive model surely does not lie in its ability to describe reality.

Why, then, do we spend time studying perfect competition? The answer takes us back to the central theme of this book. Under perfect competition the market mechanism in many ways performs best. If we want to learn what markets do well, we can put the market's best foot forward by beginning with perfect competition.

As Adam Smith suggested some two centuries ago, perfectly competitive firms use society's scarce resources with maximum efficiency. Also, as Friedrich Engels suggested in the opening quotation of this chapter, only perfect competition can ensure that the economy turns out just those varieties and relative quantities of goods that match consumer preferences. By studying perfect competition, we can learn some of the things an *ideally functioning* market system can accomplish. This is the topic of this chapter and Chapter 14. In Chapters 11 and 12, we will consider other market forms and see how they deviate from the perfectly competitive ideal. Later chapters (especially Chapter 15 and all of Parts 4 and 5) will examine many important tasks that the market does *not* perform well, even under perfect competition. All these chapters combined should provide a balanced assessment of the virtues and vices of the market mechanism.

THE PERFECTLY COMPETITIVE FIRM

To discover what happens in a perfectly competitive market, we must deal separately with the behavior of *individual firms* and the behavior of the *industry* that is constituted by those firms. One basic difference between the firm and the industry under competition relates to *pricing*:

> **Under perfect competition, the firm has no choice but to accept the price that has been determined in the market. It is therefore called a "price taker" (rather than a "price maker").**

The idea that no firm in a perfectly competitive market can exert any control over product price follows from our stringent definition of perfect competition. The presence of a vast number of competitors, each offering identical products, forces each firm to meet but not exceed the price charged by the others, because at any higher price all of the firm's customers would leave it and move their purchases to its rivals.

With two important exceptions, analysis of the behavior of the firm under perfect competition is exactly as we described in Chapters 7 and 8. The two exceptions relate to the special shape of the perfectly competitive firm's demand curve and the freedom of entry and exit, along with their effects on the firm's profits. We will consider each of these special features of perfect competition in turn, beginning with the demand curve.

The Firm's Demand Curve under Perfect Competition

In Chapter 8, we always assumed that the firm faced a downward-sloping demand curve; that is, if a firm wished to sell more (without increasing its advertising or changing its product specifications), it had to reduce its product price. The perfectly competitive firm is an exception to this general principle.

> **A perfectly competitive firm faces a *horizontal* demand curve. This means that it can sell as much as it wants at the prevailing market price. It can double or triple its sales without reducing the price of its product.**

How is this possible? The answer is that the perfectly competitive firm is so insignificant relative to the market as a whole that it has absolutely no influence over price. The farmer who sells his corn through a commodities exchange in Chicago must accept the current quotation that his broker reports to him. Because there are thousands of farmers, the Chicago price per bushel will not budge because farmer Jasmine decides she doesn't like the price and stores a truckload of corn rather than taking it to the grain elevator. Thus, the demand curve for Jasmine's corn is as shown in Figure 1(a). As we can see, the price she is paid in Chicago will be $3 per bushel whether she sells one truckload (point *A*) or two (point *B*) or three (point *C*). This is because that $3 price is determined

*Under perfect competition, the firm is a **price taker**. It has no choice but to accept the price that has been determined in the market.*

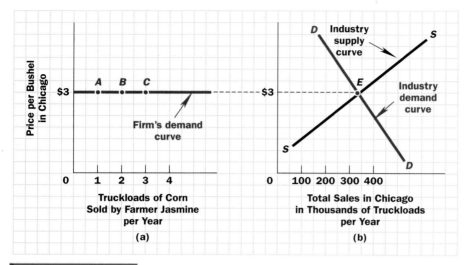

FIGURE 1

Demand Curve for a
Firm under Perfect
Competition

by the intersection of the *indus-try's* supply and demand curves shown in the right-hand portion of the graph, Figure 1(b).

Notice that, in the case of perfect competition, the downward-sloping industry demand curve in Figure 1(b) leads to the horizontal demand curve for the individual firm in Figure 1(a). Also notice that the height of the firm's horizontal demand curve will be the height of the intersection point, *E*, of the industry supply and demand curves. So the firm's demand curve will generally not resemble the demand curve for the industry.

Short-Run Equilibrium for the Perfectly Competitive Firm

We already have sufficient background to study the decisions of a firm operating in a perfectly competitive market. Recall from Chapter 8 that profit maximization requires the firm to pick an output level that makes its *marginal cost equal to its marginal revenue:* MC = MR. The only feature that distinguishes the profit-maximizing equilibrium for the perfectly competitive firm from that of any other type of firm is its horizontal demand curve. We know from Chapter 8 that the firm's demand curve is also its average revenue curve if it sells its product at the same price to each and every customer, because the average revenue a firm gets from selling a commodity is equal to the price of the commodity. That is, if it sells 100 shirts at a price of $18 each, then obviously, the average revenue it obtains from the sale of each shirt will be the average of $18, 18, 18, etc. = $18. So, because the demand curve tells us the price at which the supplier can sell a given quantity, this means it also tells us the average revenue it gets per unit sold when it sells that given quantity. Thus the firm's demand curve and its average revenue curve are identical, by definition. The same curve does two jobs, but it also does a third job. Because this demand curve is horizontal, the competitive firm's *marginal* revenue curve is a horizontal straight line that also coincides with its demand curve; hence, MR = Price (*P*). It is easy to see why this is so.

If the price does not depend on how much the firm sells (which is exactly what a horizontal demand curve means), then each *additional* unit sold brings in an amount of additional revenue (the *marginal* revenue) exactly equal to the market price. So marginal revenue always equals price under perfect competition because the firm is a price taker.[1]

Under perfect competition the firm's demand curve, average revenue curve, and marginal revenue curve are all the same.

As in Chapter 8, once we know the shape and position of a firm's marginal revenue curve, we can use this information and the marginal cost curve to determine its optimal output and profit, as shown in Figure 2. As usual, the profit-maximizing output is that at which MC = MR (point

FIGURE 2

Short-Run Equilibrium
of the Perfectly
Competitive Firm

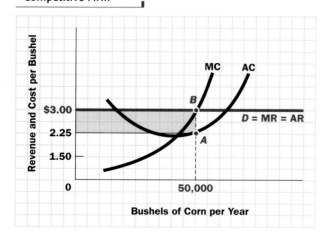

---

[1] There is another way to prove this. We saw in the appendix to Chapter 8 that if the average revenue curve is horizontal and its height is equal to price, we cannot have either MR < AR or MR > AR, because a marginal revenue lower than average revenue must put the average down, and MR > AR must pull the average up. So with the demand curve horizontal we must have P = MR = MR.

B). This occurs at the point where the MC curve cuts the demand curve (under perfect competition, *D* = MR = AR), because, as we have just seen, the firm's output is too small to affect market price. This particular competitive firm produces 50,000 bushels of corn per year—the output level at which MC and MR both equal the market price, $3. Thus:

> Because it is a price taker, the *equilibrium* of a profit-maximizing firm in a perfectly competitive market must occur at an output level at which marginal cost equals price = AR = MR. This is because a horizontal demand curve makes price and MR equal and, therefore, both must equal marginal cost according to the profit-maximizing principle. In symbols:

$$MC = MR = P$$

This idea is illustrated in Table 1, which gives the firm's total and marginal revenue, total and marginal cost, and total profit for different output quantities. We see from column (6) that total profit is maximized at an output of about 50,000 bushels where total profit is $37,500. An increase in output from 40,000 to 50,000 bushels incurs a marginal cost ($26,500) that most nearly equals the corresponding marginal revenue ($30,000), confirming that 50,000 bushels is the profit-maximizing output.[2]

TABLE 1

Revenues, Costs, and Profits of a Perfectly Competitive Firm

(1) Total Quantity	(2) Total Revenue	(3) Marginal Revenue	(4) Total Cost	(5) Marginal Cost	(6) Total Profit
0	$ 0				
		>$30			
10	30		$ 32		$ −2
		>30		>$ 24	
20	60		56		4
		>30		>11.5	
30	90		67.5		22.5
		>30		>18.5	
40	120		86		34
		>30		>26.5	
50	150		112.5		37.5
		>30		>56.5	
60	180		169		11
		>30		>93	
70	210		262		−52

NOTE: Quantity is in thousands of bushels; dollars are in thousands.

Short-Run Profit: Graphic Representation

Our analysis so far tells us how a firm can pick the output that maximizes its profit. It may even be able to earn a substantial profit, but sometimes, even if it succeeds in maximizing profit, the firm may conceivably find itself in trouble because market conditions may make the highest possible profit a *negative* number. If the demand for its product is weak or its costs are high, even the firm's most profitable option may lead to a loss. In the short run, the demand curve can either be high or low relative to costs. To determine whether the firm is making a profit or incurring a loss, we must compare *total* revenue (TR = *P* × *Q*) with *total* cost (TC = AC × *Q*). Because the output (*Q*) is common to both of these amounts, this equation tells us that the process is equivalent to comparing price (*P*) with average cost (AC). If *P* > AC, the firm will earn a profit, and if *P* < AC, it will suffer a loss.

We can, therefore, show the firm's profit in Figure 2, which includes the firm's *average cost* curve. By definition, profit per unit of output is revenue per unit *(P)* minus cost per unit (AC). We see in Figure 2 that average cost at 50,000 bushels per year is only $2.25 per bushel (point *A*), whereas *average revenue* (AR) is $3 per bushel (point *B*). The firm makes a profit of AR − AC = $0.75 per bushel, which appears in the graph as the vertical distance between points *A* and *B*.

Notice that, in addition to showing the *profit per unit*, Figure 2 can be used to show the firm's *total profit*. Total profit is the profit per unit ($0.75 in this example) times the number of units (50,000 per year). Therefore, total profit is represented by the *area* of the shaded rectangle whose height is the profit per unit ($0.75) and whose width is the number of units sold (50,000).[3] In this case, profits are $37,500 per year. In general, total profit at any output is the area of the rectangle whose base equals the level of output and whose height equals AR − AC.

---

[2] Marginal cost is not precisely equal to marginal revenue, because to calculate marginal costs and marginal revenues with perfect accuracy, we would have to increase output one bushel at a time instead of proceeding in leaps of 10,000 bushels. Of course, that would require too much space! In any event, our failure to make a more careful calculation in terms of individual bushels explains why we are unable to find the output at which MR and MC are *exactly* equal.

[3] Recall that the formula for the area of a rectangle is Area = Height × Width.

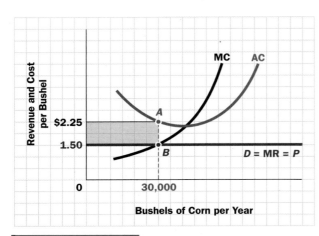

The MC = *P* condition gives us the output that maximizes the perfectly competitive firm's profit. It does not, however, tell us whether the firm is making a profit or incurring a loss. To make this determination, we must compare price (average revenue) with average cost.

The Case of Short-Term Losses

The market is obviously treating the farmer in Figure 2 rather nicely. But what if the corn market were not so generous in its rewards? What if, for example, the market price were only $1.50 per bushel instead of $3? Figure 3 shows the equilibrium of the firm under these circumstances. The cost curves are the same in this diagram as they were in Figure 2, but the demand curve has shifted down to correspond to the market price of $1.50 per bushel. The firm still maximizes profits by producing the level of output at which marginal cost (MC) is equal to price (*P*) — (MC = *P* = MR)—point *B* in the diagram. But this time "maximizing profits" really means minimizing losses, as shown by the shaded rectangle.

At the optimal level of output (30,000 bushels per year), average cost is $2.25 per bushel (point *A*), which exceeds the $1.50 per bushel price (point *B*). The firm therefore incurs a loss of $0.75 per bushel times 30,000 bushels, or $22,500 per year. This loss, which is represented by the area of the gold rectangle in Figure 3, is the best the firm can do. If it selected any other output level, its loss would be even greater.

Shutdown and Break-Even Analysis

Of course, any firm will accept only a limited amount of loss before it stops production. If losses get too big, the firm can simply go out of business. But sometimes it will benefit the firm to continue to operate for a while because of costs that it will still have to pay even if its production ceases. To understand the logic of the choice between shutting down and remaining in operation, at least temporarily to help cover losses, we must return to the distinction between **costs** that are **variable** in the short run and those that are not. Recall from Chapter 7 that costs are not variable if the firm cannot escape them in the short run, either because of a contract (say, with a landlord or a union) or because it has already bought the item whose cost cannot now be escaped (for example, a machine bought on credit, with a contract requiring annual payments for X years).

If the firm stops producing, then its revenue and its short-run variable costs will fall to zero. But its costs that are not variable will remain. If the firm is losing money, in certain cases it will be better off continuing to operate until its obligations to pay the nonvariable (inescapable) costs expire; but in other cases it will do better by shutting down immediately and producing nothing. That decision obviously depends on whether or not by shutting down immediately, the costs the firm can avoid *immediately* are greater that the revenue it gives up by having nothing to sell any longer. More explicitly, two rules govern the decision:

> **Rule 1.** The firm will make a loss if total revenue (TR) is less than total cost (TC). In that case, it should plan to shut down, either in the short run or in the long run.

> **Rule 2.** The firm should continue to operate in the short run if TR exceeds total short-run variable cost (TVC).

The first rule is self-evident. If the firm's revenues do not cover its total costs, then it surely will lose money and, sooner or later, it will have to close. The second rule is a bit more subtle. Suppose that TR is less than TC. If our unfortunate firm continues in operation, it will lose the difference between total cost and total revenue:

Loss if the firm stays in business = TC − TR

A **variable cost** is a cost whose total amount changes when the quantity of output of the supplier changes.

However, if the firm stops producing, both its revenues and short-run variable costs become zero, but its *nonvariable* costs must still be paid:

Loss if the firm shuts down = Nonvariable costs = TC − TVC

Hence, it is best to keep operating as long as the firm's loss if it stays in business is less than its loss if it shuts down:

$$TC - TR < TC - TVC$$

or

TVC < TR, that is, (AVC)Q < PQ, or AVC < P

That is, Rule 2. Its logic is simpler than it appears to be: A firm that is losing money should nevertheless stay in business (temporarily) if its revenue more than covers the variable costs that it can escape immediately, because the surplus of TR over TVC provides earnings that help to cover part of the remaining costs—the cost that the firm cannot escape in the short run. Surely, it is better to earn enough to pay off part of those inescapable costs than for the owners of the firm to bear the entire burden themselves and pay the inescapable costs in their entirety.

Of course, the firm will not stay in business unless there is some output level at which $P - AVC$, the amount available to help cover inescapable costs, is positive. That is, with the price, P, fixed by industry supply and demand, it will not stay in business unless at the output at which AVC is as small as possible, $P > AVC$.

We can illustrate Rule 2 with the two cases shown in Table 2. Case A deals with a firm that loses money but is better off staying in business in the short run. If it shuts down, it will lose its entire $60,000 worth of short-run nonvariable cost. If it continues to operate, its total revenue of $100,000 will exceed its total variable cost (TVC = $80,000) by $20,000. That means continuing operation contributes $20,000 toward meeting nonvariable costs and reduces losses to $40,000. In Case B, in contrast, it pays the firm to shut down because continued operation merely adds to its losses. If the firm operates, it will lose $90,000 (the last entry in Table 2); if it shuts down, it will lose only the $60,000 in inescapable costs, which it must pay whether it operates or not.

We also can analyze the shutdown decision graphically. In Figure 4, the firm will run a loss whether the price is P_1, P_2, or P_3, because none of these prices is high enough to reach the minimum level of average cost (AC). We can show the *lowest* price that keeps the firm from shutting down immediately by introducing one more short-run cost curve: the average variable cost (AVC) curve that shows how AVC varies, depending on the size of the firm's output. Why is this curve relevant? Because, as we have just seen, it pays the firm to remain in operation only if the price exceeds the lowest attainable AVC. An immediate conclusion is

The firm will produce nothing unless price lies above the minimum point on the AVC curve.

In Figure 4, price P_1 is below the minimum average variable cost. With this price, the firm cannot even cover its variable costs and is better off shutting down (producing zero output).

TABLE 2

The Shutdown Decision

	Case A	Case B
Total revenue (TR)	$100	$100
Total variable cost (TVC)	80	130
Short-run nonvariable cost	60	60
Total cost (TC)	140	190
Loss if firm shuts down (= Short-run nonvariable cost)	60	60
Loss if firm does not shut down	40	90

NOTE: Figures are in thousands of dollars.

FIGURE 4

Shutdown Analysis

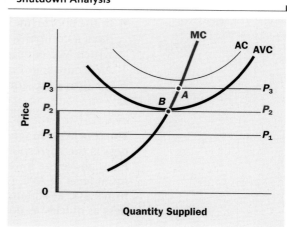

Farming Economics: Ethanol-Driven Price Increases Rock the Food Chain

Because farmers are *price takers,* they simply have to live with the price that is determined by the market's supply and demand. Here is an example:

"Beef prices are up. So are the costs of milk, cereal, eggs, chicken and pork.

And corn is getting the blame. President Bush's call for the nation to cure its addiction to oil stoked a growing demand for ethanol, which is mostly made from corn. Greater demand for corn has inflated prices from a historically stable $2 per bushel to about $4.

That means cattle ranchers have to pay more for animal feed that contains corn. Those costs are reflected in cattle prices, which have gone from about $82.50 per 100 pounds a year ago to $91.15 today.

The corn price increases flow like gravy down the food chain, to grocery stores and menus. The cost of rounded cubed steak at

SOURCE: IndexStock/SuperStock

local Harris Teeters is up from $4.59 last year to $5.29 this year, according to TheGroceryGame.com, which tracks prices. The Palm restaurant chain recently raised prices as much as $2 for a New York strip. And so on. . . .

The heightened demand for corn has decreased the supply of other grains, including soybeans, because farmers are shifting fields to make room for corn. Soybeans are a key ingredient in trans-fat-free cooking oils now in high demand as cities and counties ban fatty oils in restaurants and bakeries. . . . Now Sysco, a Houston food company that is a major supplier of trans-fat-free oils, says it is seeing pricing pressure on the product."

SOURCE: Excerpted from Michael S. Rosenwald, "The Rising Tide of Corn: Ethanol-Driven Demand Felt Across the Market," *The Washington Post,* June 15, 2007, p. D01.

Price P_3 is higher. Although the firm still runs a loss if it sets MC = P at point A (because AC exceeds P_3), it allows the firm to at least cover its short-run variable costs, so it pays to keep operating in the short run. Price P_2 is the borderline case. If the price is P_2, the firm is indifferent between shutting down and staying in business and producing at a level where MC = P (point B). P_2 is thus the *lowest* price at which the firm will produce anything. As we see from the graph, P_2 corresponds to the minimum point on the AVC curve.

The Perfectly Competitive Firm's Short-Run Supply Curve

The **supply curve of a firm** shows the different quantities of output that the firm would be willing to supply at different possible prices during some given period of time.

Without realizing it, we have now derived the **supply curve of the perfectly competitive firm** in the short run. Why? Recall that a supply curve summarizes in a graph the answers to questions such as, "If the price is so and so, how much output will the firm offer for sale?" We can now see that

- In the short run, if the price is high enough for the firm to cover its AVC, then it pays a competitive firm to stay in business and produce the level of output at which MC equals P. Thus, for any price above point B, the lowest point on the AVC curve, in Figure 4, we can read the corresponding quantity supplied from the firm's MC curve.

We can now conclude that

The short-run supply curve of the perfectly competitive firm that is not going out of business is the corresponding portion of its marginal cost curve where P = AR = MR = MC. P lies above the lowest point on the average variable cost curve—that is, above the minimum level of AVC. (But it should be remembered that if the market price is below the firm's AVC at all output levels, as we have just seen, it will pay the firm to go out of business as quickly as possible, dropping its quantity supplied to zero.)

THE PERFECTLY COMPETITIVE INDUSTRY

Now that we have completed the analysis of the perfectly competitive *firm's* supply decision, we turn our attention next to the perfectly competitive *industry*.

The Perfectly Competitive Industry's Short-Run Supply Curve

Once again, we need to distinguish between the short run and the long run, but the distinction is different here. The short run for the *industry* is defined as a period of time too brief for new firms to enter the industry or for old firms to leave, so the number of firms is fixed. By contrast, the long run for the industry is a period of time long enough for any firm to enter or leave as it desires. In addition, in the long run each firm in the industry can adjust its output to its own long-run costs.[4] We begin our analysis of industry equilibrium in the short run.

With the number of firms fixed, it is a simple matter to derive the **supply curve of the perfectly competitive industry** from those of the individual firms. At any given price, we simply *add up* the quantities supplied by each of the firms to arrive at the industry-wide quantity supplied. For example, if each of 1,000 identical firms in the corn industry supplies 45,000 bushels when the price is $2.25 per bushel, then the quantity supplied by the industry at a $2.25 price will be 45,000 bushels per firm × 1,000 firms = 45 million bushels.

This process of deriving the *market* supply curve from the *individual* supply curves of firms is analogous to the way we derived the *market* demand curve from the *individual* consumers' demand curves in Chapter 6. Graphically, what we are doing is *summing the individual supply curves horizontally,* as illustrated in Figure 5. At a price of $2.25, each of the 1,000 identical firms in the industry supplies 45,000 bushels—point *c* in Figure 5(a)—so the industry supplies 45 million bushels—point *C* in Figure 5(b). At a price of $3, each firm supplies 50,000 bushels—point *e* in Figure 5(a)—and so the industry supplies 50 million bushels—point *E* in Figure 5(b). We can carry out similar calculations for any other price. By adding up the quantities supplied by each firm at each possible price, we arrive at the industry supply curve *SS* in Figure 5(b).

> The supply curve of the competitive industry in the short run is derived by *summing* the short-run supply curves of all the firms in the industry *horizontally.*

This adding-up process indicates, incidentally, that the supply curve of the industry will shift to the right whenever a new firm enters the industry.

The **supply curve of an industry** shows the different quantities of output that the industry would supply at different possible prices during some given period of time.

FIGURE 5

Derivation of the Industry Supply Curve from the Supply Curves of the Individual Firms

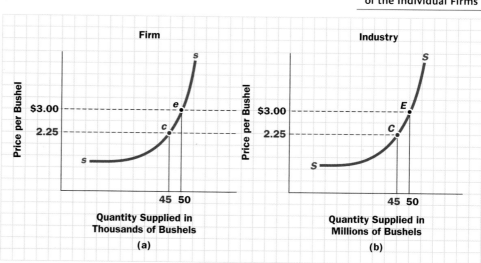

(a) Firm — Quantity Supplied in Thousands of Bushels

(b) Industry — Quantity Supplied in Millions of Bushels

Industry Equilibrium in the Short Run

Now that we have derived the industry supply curve, we need only add a market demand curve to determine the price and quantity that will emerge in equilibrium. We do this for our illustrative corn industry in Figure 6, where the blue industry supply

---

[4] The relationship between short-run and long-run cost curves for the firm was discussed in Chapter 7, pages 141–143.

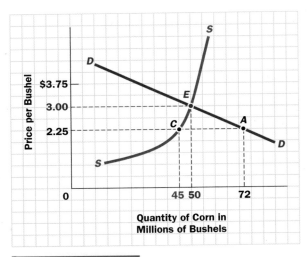

FIGURE 6

Supply-Demand
Equilibrium of a
Perfectly Competitive
Industry

curve, carried over from Figure 5(b), is *SS* and the demand curve is *DD*. The only equilibrium combination of price and quantity is a price of $3 and a quantity of 50 million bushels, at which the supply curve, *SS*, and the demand curve, *DD*, intersect (point *E*). At any lower price, such as $2.25, quantity demanded (72 million bushels, as shown by point *A* on the demand curve) will be higher than the 45-million-bushel quantity supplied (point *C*). Thus, the price will be bid up toward the $3 equilibrium. The opposite will happen at a price such as $3.75, which is above equilibrium.

Note that for the perfectly competitive industry, unlike the perfectly competitive firm, the demand curve normally slopes downward. Why? Each firm by itself is so small that if it alone were to double its output, the effect would hardly be noticeable. But if *every* firm in the industry were to expand its output, that would make a substantial difference. Customers can be induced to buy the additional quantities arriving at the market only if the price of the good falls.

Point *E* is the equilibrium point for the perfectly competitive industry, because only at a price of $3 are sellers willing to offer exactly the amount that consumers want to purchase (in this case, 50 million bushels).

Should we expect price actually to reach, or at least to *approximate,* this equilibrium level? The answer is yes. To see why, we must consider what happens when price is not at its equilibrium level. Suppose that the price is lower—say, $2.25. This low price will stimulate customers to buy more; it will also lead firms to produce less than they would at a price of $3. Our diagram confirms that at a price of $2.25, quantity supplied (45 million bushels) is lower than quantity demanded (72 million bushels). Thus, the availability of unsatisfied buyers will probably lead sellers to raise their prices, which will force the price *upward* in the direction of its equilibrium value, $3.

Similarly, if we begin with a price higher than the equilibrium price, we may readily verify that quantity supplied will exceed quantity demanded. Under these circumstances, frustrated sellers are likely to reduce their prices, so price will be forced downward. In the circumstances depicted in Figure 6, in effect a magnet at the equilibrium price of $3 will pull the actual price in its direction, if for some reason the actual price starts out at some other level.

In practice, prices do move toward equilibrium levels over a sufficiently long period of time in most perfectly competitive markets. Matters eventually appear to work out, as depicted in Figure 6. Of course, numerous transitory influences can jolt any real-world market away from its equilibrium point—a workers' strike that cuts production, a sudden change in consumer tastes, and so on.

Yet, as we have just seen, powerful forces push prices back toward equilibrium—toward the level at which the supply and demand curves intersect. These forces are fundamentally important for economic analysis. If no such forces existed, prices in the real world would bear little resemblance to equilibrium prices, and there would be little reason to study supply-demand analysis. Fortunately, the required equilibrating forces do step in, as appropriate, to bring markets back toward equilibrium.

Industry and Firm Equilibrium in the Long Run

The equilibrium of a perfectly competitive industry in the long run may differ from the short-run equilibrium that we have just studied, for two reasons. First, the number of firms in the industry (1,000 in our example) is not fixed in the long run. Second, as we saw in Chapter 7 (page 129), in the long run firms can vary their plant size and change other commitments that could not be altered in the short run. Hence, the firm's (and the industry's) long-run cost curves are not the same as the short-run cost curves. These differences can be very important, as we will see.

What will lure new firms into the industry or encourage old ones to leave? The answer is *profits*—economic profits; that is, any part of the firm's earnings that exceeds the average earnings of other firms in the economy and thus exceeds the firm's costs, including its opportunity costs. Remember that when a firm selects its optimal level of output by setting MC = P, it may wind up with either a profit, as in Figure 2, or a loss, as in Figure 3. Such profits or losses must be *temporary* for perfectly competitive firms because new firms are free to enter the industry if profits that are greater than the average obtained elsewhere are available in our industry. For the same reason, old firms will leave if they cannot cover their costs in the long run. Suppose that firms in the industry earn very high profits, in excess of the normal rates of return currently available. Then new companies will find it attractive to enter the business, and expanded production will force the market price to fall from its initial level. Why? Recall that the industry supply curve is the horizontal sum of the supply curves of individual firms. Under perfect competition, new firms can enter the industry *on the same terms as existing firms.* Thus, new entrants will have the *same* individual supply curves as the old firms. If the market price did not fall, the entry of new firms would lead to an increased number of firms, with no change in output *per firm.* Consequently, the total quantity supplied to the market would be higher, and it would exceed quantity demanded—which, of course, would also drive prices down. Thus, the entry of new firms *must* push the price down.

Figure 7 shows how the entry process works. In this diagram, the demand curve *DD* and the original (short-run) supply curve S_0S_0 are carried over from Figure 6. The entry of new firms seeking high profits *shifts the industry's short-run supply curve outward to the right,* to S_1S_1. The new market equilibrium at point *A* (rather than at point *E*) indicates that price is $2.25 per bushel and that 72 million bushels are produced and consumed. The entry of new firms reduces price and raises total output.

If the price had not fallen, the quantity supplied after the new firms' entry would have been 80 million bushels—point *F.* Why must the price fall in this case? Because the demand curve for the industry slopes downward, consumers will purchase the increased output only at a reduced price.

To see the point at which entry stops being attracted by high profits, we must consider how entry by new firms affects existing firms' behavior. At first glance, this notion may seem to contradict the idea of perfect competition; perfectly competitive firms are not supposed to be affected by what competitors do, because no individual firm can influence the industry. Indeed, these corn farmers don't care about the entry of new firms. But they *do* care very much about the market price of corn and, as we have just seen, the entry of new firms into the corn-farming industry lowers the price of corn.

In Figure 8, we juxtapose the diagram of perfectly competitive firm equilibrium (Figure 2) with the perfectly competitive industry equilibrium diagram (Figure 7). Before the new firms' entry, the market price was $3, point *E* in Figure 8(b), and each of the 1,000 firms produced 50,000 bushels—the point where marginal cost and price were equal, point *e* in Figure 8(a). Each firm faced the horizontal demand curve D_0 in Figure 8(a). Firms within the industry enjoyed profits because average costs (AC) at 50,000 bushels per firm were less than price.

Now suppose that 600 new firms are attracted by these high profits and enter the industry. Each faces the cost structure indicated by the AC and MC curves in Figure 8(a).

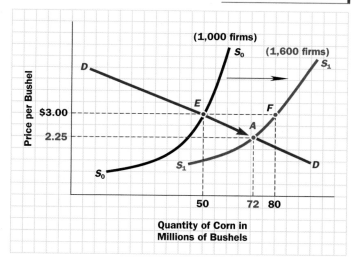

FIGURE 7

A Shift in the Industry Supply Curve Caused by the Entry of New Firms

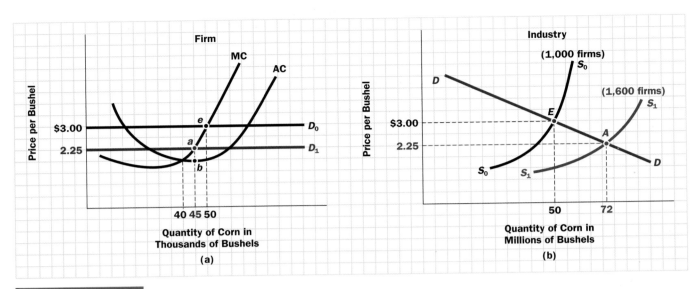

FIGURE 8

The Perfectly
Competitive Firm
and the Perfectly
Competitive Industry

As a result of the new entrants' production, the industry supply curve in Figure 8(b) shifts to the right, and price falls to $2.25 per bushel. Because the height of the firm's horizontal demand curve is, as we have seen, equal to the industry price, the firm's demand curve must now move down to the brick-colored line D_1 *corresponding to the reduced market price.* Firms in the industry react to this demand shift and its associated lower price. As we see in Figure 8(a), each firm reduces its output to 45,000 bushels (point *a*). But now there are 1,600 firms, so total industry output is 45,000 bushels × 1,600 firms = 72 million bushels, point *A* in Figure 8(b).

At point *a* in Figure 8(a), some profits remain available because the $2.25 price still exceeds average cost (point *b* is below point *a*). Thus, the entry process is not yet complete. New firms will stop appearing only when all profits have been competed away. Figures 9(a) and 9(b) show the perfectly competitive firm and the perfectly competitive industry in long-run equilibrium. Only when entry shifts the industry supply curve so far to the right—$S_2 S_2$ in Figure 9(b)—that each individual firm faces a demand curve that has fallen

FIGURE 9

Long-Run Equilibrium
of the Perfectly
Competitive Firm
and Industry

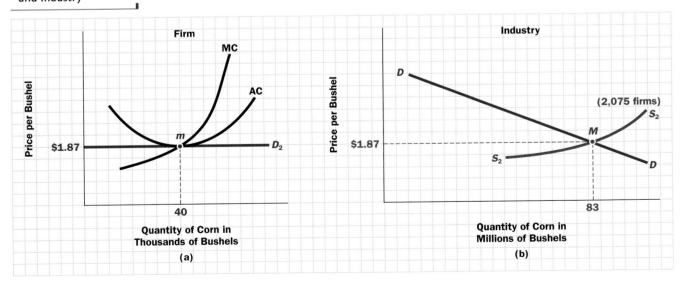

to the level of minimum average cost—point *m* in Figure 9(a)—will all profits be eradicated and entry cease.[5]

At the equilibrium point, *m*, in Figure 9(a), each firm picks its own output level to maximize its profit. As a result, for each firm *P* = MC. But free entry also forces AC to equal *P* in the long run—point *M* in Figure 9(b)—because if *P* were not equal to AC, firms would either earn profits or suffer losses. That would mean, in turn, that firms would find it profitable to enter or leave the industry, which is not compatible with industry equilibrium. Thus:

> **When a perfectly competitive industry is in long-run equilibrium, firms maximize profits so that *P* = MC, and entry forces the price down until it is tangent to the firm's long-run average cost curve (*P* = AC). As a result, in long-run perfectly competitive equilibrium it is always true that for each firm**

$$P = MC = AC$$

Thus, even though every firm earns zero profit, profits are at the maximum that is sustainable.[6]

Zero Economic Profit: The Opportunity Cost of Capital

Why would there be any firms in the industry at all if, in the long run, they do not make a profit? The answer is that the zero profit concept used in economics does not mean the same thing that it does in ordinary, everyday usage. We have already encountered this and discussed its relevance in Chapter 8 (pages 159–160). Here we will explain this important point in a slightly different way.

We have noted that when economists measure average cost, they include the cost of *all* of the firm's inputs, *including the opportunity cost of the capital (the funds) or any other inputs, such as labor, provided by the firm's owners.* Because the firm may not make explicit payments to some of the people who provide it with capital, this element of cost may not be picked up by the firm's accountants. So what economists call zero **economic profit** will correspond to a *positive* amount of profit as measured by conventional accounting techniques. For example, if investors can earn 15 percent by lending their funds elsewhere, then the firm must earn a 15 percent rate of return to cover its opportunity cost of capital. The chance for investors to earn 15 percent on their money by putting it into the firm is what attracts them to do so. True, the 15 percent return is no more than the investors can earn by putting their money elsewhere, but that does not make their 15 percent receipt unattractive.

> **Economic profit** equals net earnings, in the accountant's sense, minus the opportunity costs of capital and of any other inputs supplied by the firm's owners.

> **HOW MUCH DOES IT REALLY COST?** *Opportunity Cost:* **Because economists consider the 15 percent opportunity cost in this example to be the *cost of the firm's capital*, they include it in the AC curve. If the firm cannot earn at least 15 percent on its capital, funds will not be made available to it, because investors can earn greater returns elsewhere. To break even—to earn zero *economic profit*—a firm must earn enough to cover not only the cost of labor, fuel, and raw materials but also the cost of its funds, including the opportunity cost of any funds supplied by the owners of the firm.**

IDEAS FOR
BEYOND THE
FINAL EXAM

An example will illustrate how economic profit and conventional accounting profit differ. Suppose that U.S. government bonds pay 8 percent interest, and the owner of a small shop earns 6 percent on her business investment. This shopkeeper might see this as a

---

[5] If the original short-run equilibrium had involved losses instead of profits, firms would have exited from the industry, shifting the industry supply curve inward, until all losses were eradicated, and we would end up in a position exactly like Figure 9. EXERCISE: To test your understanding, draw the version of Figure 8 that corresponds to this case.

[6] EXERCISE: Show what happens to the equilibrium of the firm and of the industry in Figure 9 if a rise in consumer income leads to an outward shift in the industry demand curve.

6 percent profit, but an economist would see a 2 percent loss on every dollar she has invested in her business. By keeping her money tied up in her firm, the shop owner gives up the chance to buy government bonds and receive an 8 percent return. She is earning *minus 2 percent in economic profit*. With this explanation of economic profit, we can understand the logic behind the zero-profit condition for the long-run industry equilibrium.

> Zero profit in the economic sense simply means that firms are earning a return, but that return is just the same as the normal, economy-wide rate of profit in the accounting sense. This result is guaranteed, in the long run, under perfect competition, by freedom of entry and exit.

The Long-Run Industry Supply Curve

We have now seen basically what lies behind the supply-demand analysis that we first introduced in Chapter 4. Only one thing remains to be explained. Figures 5 through 8 depicted short-run industry supply curves and short-run equilibrium. However, because Figure 9 describes long-run perfectly competitive equilibrium, its industry supply curve must also pertain to the long run.

How does the long-run *industry* supply curve relate to the short-run supply curve? The answer is implicit in what we have just discussed. The long-run industry supply curve evolves from the short-run supply curve via two simultaneous processes. First, new firms enter or some existing ones exit, which shifts the short-run industry supply curve toward its long-run position. Second, and concurrently, as in the long run each firm in the industry is freed from its fixed commitments, the cost curves pertinent to its decisions become its long-run cost curves rather than its short-run cost curves. For example, consider a company that was stuck in the short run with a plant designed to serve 20,000 customers, even though it is now fortunate enough to have 25,000 customers. When it is time to replace the old plant, management will want to build a new plant that can serve the larger number of customers more conveniently, efficiently, and *more cheaply*. The reduced cost that results from the larger plant is the pertinent cost to both the firm and the industry in the long run.

Finally, let us note that the long-run supply curve of the perfectly competitive industry (S_2S_2 in Figure 9) must be identical to the industry's long-run *average* cost curve. This is because in the long run, as we have seen, economic profit must be zero. The price the industry charges cannot exceed the long-run average cost (LRAC) of supplying that quantity because any excess of price over LRAC would constitute a profit opportunity for others that would have attracted new firms and driven price down to average cost. Similarly, price cannot be below LRAC because firms would then have refused to continue to supply that output at this price and output would have fallen, driving price up until it equaled average cost. Therefore, for each possible long-run quantity supplied, the price must equal the industry's long-run average cost. Thus, this long-run industry supply curve is also the industry's average cost curve, and that is the cost curve relevant for determination of long-run equilibrium price and quantity in a standard supply-demand diagram.

These ideas are illustrated in Figure 10, in which the short-run industry supply curve, *SS*, lies above and to the left of the long-run average cost curve, LRAC. Consider any industry output—say, 70 million bushels of corn per year. At that output, the long-run average cost is $1.50 per bushel (point *A*). But if the price charged by farmers were given by the short-run supply curve for that output—that is, $2.62 per bushel (point *B*)—then the firms would earn $1.12 in economic profit on each and every bushel they sold.

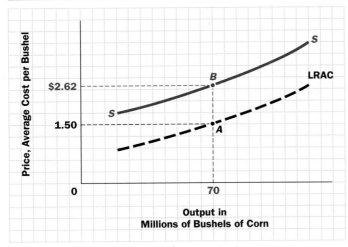

FIGURE 10

Short-Run Industry Supply and Long-Run Industry Average Cost

Such economic profits would induce other firms to enter the industry, which would force prices downward as the industry supply curve shifted outward. So long as this shift did not take *SS* all the way down to LRAC, some economic profits would remain, and so entry would continue. Thus, *SS* must continue to fall until it reaches the position of the long-run average cost curve. Then and only then will entry of new firms cease and long-run equilibrium be attained.

The long-run supply curve of the perfectly competitive industry is also the industry's long-run average cost curve. The industry is driven to that supply curve by the entry or exit of firms and by the adjustment of firms already in the industry.

We will see presently that the identity of the industry's long-run supply curve and its LRAC curve provide us with some important insights.

PERFECT COMPETITION AND ECONOMIC EFFICIENCY

Economists have long admired perfect competition as a thing of beauty, like one of King Tutankhamen's funerary masks. (And it's just as rare!) Adam Smith's invisible hand produces results that are considered *efficient* in a variety of senses that we will examine carefully in Chapter 14. But one aspect of the great efficiency of perfect competition follows immediately from the analysis we have just completed.

We saw earlier that when the firm is in long-run equilibrium, it must have $P = MC = AC$, as indicated by Figure 9(a), but we know that MC does not equal AC at any point on the AC curve that is moving either downhill or uphill (see the appendix to Chapter 8 if you need to be reminded why this is so). This implies that the long-run competitive equilibrium of the firm will occur at the lowest point (the horizontal point) on its long-run AC curve, which is also where that curve is tangent to the firm's horizontal demand curve.

In long-run perfectly competitive equilibrium, every firm produces at the minimum point on its average cost curve. Thus, the outputs of perfectly competitive industries are produced at the lowest possible cost to society.

An example will show why it is most efficient if each firm in a perfectly competitive industry produces at the point where AC is as small as possible. Suppose the industry is producing 12 million bushels of corn. This amount can be produced by 120 farms each producing 100,000 bushels, or by 100 farms each producing 120,000 bushels, or by 200 farms each producing 60,000 bushels. Of course, the job can also be done instead by other numbers of farms, but for simplicity let us consider only these three possibilities.

Suppose that the AC figures for the firm are as shown in Table 3. Suppose, moreover, that an output of 100,000 bushels corresponds to the lowest point on the firm's AC curve, equal to 70 cents per bushel. Which is the cheapest way for the industry to produce its 12-million-bushel output? In other words, what is the cost-minimizing number of firms for the job? Looking at column (5) of Table 3, we see that the industry's total cost of producing the 12-million-bushel output is as low as possible if 120 firms each produce the cost-minimizing output of 100,000 bushels.

TABLE 3
Average Cost for the Firm and Total Cost for the Industry

(1)	(2)	(3)	(4)	(5)
Firm's Output	Firm's Average Cost	Number of Firms	Industry Output	Total Industry Cost
60,000	$0.90	200	12,000,000	$10,800,000
100,000	0.70	120	12,000,000	8,400,000
120,000	0.80	100	12,000,000	9,600,000

NOTE: Output is in bushels.

Why is this so? The answer is not difficult to see. For any *given* industry output Q, because Q is constant in the calculation, *total* industry cost (= AC × Q) will be as small as possible if and only if AC (for *each* firm) is as small as possible—that is, if the number of firms doing the job is such that each is producing the output at which AC is as low as possible.

That this kind of cost efficiency characterizes perfect competition in the long run can be seen in Figures 8 and 9. Before full long-run equilibrium is reached (Figure 8), firms may not be producing in the least costly way. For example, the 50 million bushels being produced by 1,000 firms at points *e* and *E* in Figures 8(a) and 8(b) could be produced more cheaply by more firms, each producing a smaller volume, because the point of minimum average cost lies to the left of point *e* in Figure 8(a). This problem is rectified in the long run by the entry of new firms seeking profit. We see in Figure 9 that after the entry process is complete, every firm is producing at its most efficient (lowest AC) level—40,000 bushels.

As Adam Smith might have put it, even though each farmer cares only about his or her own profits, the corn-farming industry as a whole is *guided by an invisible hand* to produce the amount of corn that society wants at the lowest possible cost.

PUZZLE RESOLVED: WHICH MORE EFFECTIVELY CUTS POLLUTION—
THE CARROT OR THE STICK?

We end by returning to the puzzle with which the chapter began, because we now have all the tools needed to solve it, particularly the observation that the perfectly competitive industry's long-run supply curve is also its LRAC curve. Remember that we asked: Should polluters be *taxed* on their emissions, or should they, instead, be offered *subsidies* to cut emissions? A subsidy—that is, a government payment to the firms that comply—would indeed induce firms to cut their emissions. Nevertheless, the paradoxical result is likely to be an *increase* in total pollution. Let us see now why this is so.

In Figure 11, we have drawn the industry long-run average cost curve (LRAC), XX. We now know that this must also be the industry's long-run supply curve, because if

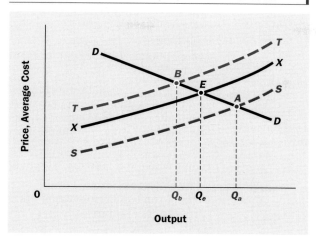

FIGURE 11

Taxes versus Subsidies as Incentives to Cut Pollution

the supply curve lies above (to the left of) LRAC, then economic profits will be earned and entry will drive the supply curve to the right. The opposite would occur if the supply were below and to the right of LRAC.

Now, a tax on business firms clearly raises the long-run average costs of the industry. Suppose that it shifts the industry's LRAC, and thus the long-run supply curve, upward from *XX* to *TT* in the graph. This change will move the equilibrium point from *E* to *B* and reduce the industry's polluting output from Q_e to Q_b. Similarly, a subsidy reduces average cost, so it shifts the LRAC and the long-run supply curve downward and to the right (from *XX* to *SS*). This change moves the equilibrium point from *E* to *A* and *raises the industry's polluting output to Q_a*.

Our paradoxical result follows from the presumption that the more *output* a polluting industry produces, the more *pollution* it will

"So that's where it goes! Well, I'd like to thank you fellows for bringing this to my attention."

emit. Under the tax on emissions, equilibrium moves from *E* to *B*, so the polluting output falls from Q_e to Q_b. Thus, emissions will fall—just as common sense leads us to expect. But, with the subsidy, industry output will *rise* from Q_e to Q_a. Thus, contrary to intuition and despite the fact that each firm emits less, the industry must pollute more!

What explains this strange result? The answer is the *entry* of new firms or the *exit* of old firms. A subsidy will initially bring economic profits to the polluters, which will in turn attract even more polluters into the industry. In essence, a subsidy encourages more polluters to open up for business. But our graph takes us one step beyond this simple observation. It is true that we end up with more polluting firms, but each will be polluting less than before. Thus, we have one influence leading to more pollution and another influence leading to less pollution. Which of these forces will win out? The graph tells us that if a rise in the polluting good's output always increases pollution, then, in a perfectly competitive industry, subsidies *must* lead to increased pollution on balance. The corresponding explanation, entailing the exit of firms that are forced to pay a tax penalty for their emissions, applies to the use of taxes to discourage pollution.

| SUMMARY |

1. **Markets** are classified into several types depending on the number of firms in the industry, the degree of similarity of their products, and the possibility of impediments to entry.

2. The four main market structures discussed by economists are *monopoly* (single-firm production), *oligopoly* (production by a few firms), *monopolistic competition* (production by many firms with somewhat different products), and *perfect competition* (production by many firms with identical products, free entry and exit, and full information).

3. Few, if any, industries satisfy the conditions of **perfect competition** exactly, although some come close. Perfect competition is studied because it is easy to analyze and because it represents a case in which the market mechanism works well, so that it is useful as a yardstick to measure the performance of other market forms.

4. The demand curve of the perfectly competitive firm is horizontal because its output is such a small share of the industry's production that it cannot affect price. With a horizontal demand curve, price, average revenue, and marginal revenue are all equal.

5. The short-run equilibrium of the perfectly competitive firm is at the level of output that maximizes profits—that is, where MR = MC = price. This equilibrium may involve either a profit or a loss.

6. The short-run **supply curve** of the perfectly competitive firm is given by the firm's marginal cost curve.

7. The industry's short-run supply curve under perfect competition is the horizontal sum of the supply curves of all of its firms.

8. In the long-run equilibrium of the perfectly competitive industry, freedom of entry forces each firm to earn zero **economic profit,** or no more than the firm's capital could earn elsewhere (the opportunity cost of the capital).

9. Industry equilibrium under perfect competition is at the point where the industry supply and demand curves intersect.

10. In long-run equilibrium under perfect competition, the firm chooses output such that average cost, marginal cost, and price are all equal. Output is at the point of minimum average cost. The firm's demand curve is tangent to its average cost curve at its minimum point.

11. The competitive industry's long-run supply curve coincides with its long-run average cost curve.

12. Both a tax on the emission of pollutants and a subsidy payment for reductions in those emissions induce firms to cut emissions. However, under perfect competition, a subsidy leads to the entry of more polluting firms and the likelihood of a net increase in total emissions by the industry.

| KEY TERMS |

economic profit   209

perfect competition   198

price taker   199

supply curve of a firm   204

supply curve of an industry · 205

variable cost   202

| TEST YOURSELF |

1. Under what circumstances might you expect the demand curve of the firm to be
   a. Vertical?
   b. Horizontal?
   c. Negatively sloping?
   d. Positively sloping?

2. Explain why $P = MC$ in the short-run equilibrium of the perfectly competitive firm, whereas in long-run equilibrium $P = MC = AC$.

3. Explain why it is not sensible to close a business firm if it earns zero economic profits.

4. If the firm's lowest average cost is $52 and the corresponding average variable cost is $26, what does it pay a perfectly competitive firm to do if
   a. The market price is $51?
   b. The price is $36?
   c. The price is $12?

5. If the market price in a competitive industry were above its equilibrium level, what would you expect to happen?

| DISCUSSION QUESTIONS |

1. Explain why a perfectly competitive firm does not expand its sales without limit if its horizontal demand curve indicates that it can sell as much as it desires at the current market price.

2. Explain why a demand curve is also a curve of average revenue. Recalling that when an average revenue curve is neither rising nor falling, marginal revenue must equal average revenue, explain why it is always true that $P = MR = AR$ for the perfectly competitive firm.

3. Regarding the four attributes of perfect competition (many small firms, freedom of entry, standardized product, and perfect information):

   a. Which is primarily responsible for the fact that the demand curve of a perfectly competitive firm is horizontal?

   b. Which is primarily responsible for the firm's zero economic profits in long-run equilibrium?

4. We indicated in this chapter that the MC curve cuts the AVC (average variable cost) curve at the *minimum* point of the latter. Explain why this must be so. (*Hint:* Because marginal costs are, by definition, entirely composed of variable costs, the MC curve can be considered the curve of *marginal variable costs*. Apply the general relationships between marginals and averages explained in the appendix to Chapter 8.)

5. **(More difficult)** In this chapter we stated that the firm's MC curve goes through the lowest point of its AC curve and also through the lowest point of its AVC curve. Because the AVC curve lies below the AC curve, how can both of these statements be true? Why are they true? (*Hint:* See Figure 4.)

MONOPOLY

The price of monopoly is upon every occasion the highest which can be got.

ADAM SMITH[1]

I n Chapter 10, we described an idealized market system in which all industries are perfectly competitive, and in Chapters 14 and 16 we will describe the virtues of that system. In this chapter, we turn to one of the blemishes—the possibility that some industries may be monopolized—and to the consequences of such a flaw in the market system.

We will indeed find that monopolized markets do not match the ideal performance of perfectly competitive markets. Under monopoly, the market mechanism no longer allocates society's resources efficiently. This suggests that government actions to constrain monopoly may sometimes be able to improve the workings of the market—a possibility that we will study in detail in Chapter 13.

But, first, as usual, we start with a real-life puzzle.

CONTENTS

---

[1] But Adam Smith's statement is incorrect! See Discussion Question 4 at the end of the chapter.

PUZZLE: **WHAT HAPPENED TO AT&T'S "NATURAL MONOPOLY" IN TELEPHONE SERVICE?**

We are all keenly aware of the strong competition in the market for telephone service. How can we miss it? A plethora of firms (old and new) offering telephone service of one kind or another besiege us with television commercials, pop-up ads on the Internet, and mountains of junk mail. The days of "Ma Bell," the affectionate nickname for AT&T's ubiquitous Bell Telephone System—which used to be virtually the only provider of telephone service—are long gone and now seem as quaint and old-fashioned as the horse and buggy. What was it that allowed competition in this industry, which had always been considered by some as a classic example of a "natural monopoly" against which no competitor could be expected to survive (see a fuller definition below)? In this chapter you will learn about the causes and consequences of monopoly and, in the process, obtain insights about the answers to this question.

MONOPOLY *DEFINED*

A **pure monopoly** is an industry in which there is only one supplier of a product for which there are no close substitutes and in which it is very difficult or impossible for another firm to coexist.

The definition of **pure monopoly** has rather stringent requirements. First, only one firm can be present in the industry—the monopolist must be "the only game in town." Second, no close substitutes for the monopolist's product may exist. Thus, even a city's sole provider of natural gas is not considered a pure monopoly because other firms offer close substitutes such as heating oil and electricity. Third, there must be a reason why entry and survival of potential competitors is extremely unlikely. Otherwise, monopolistic behavior and its excessive economic profits could not persist.

These rigid requirements make pure monopoly a rarity in the real world. The telephone company and the post office used to be examples of one-firm industries that faced little or no effective competition, at least in some of their activities, but most firms face at least a degree of competition from substitute products. If only one railroad serves a particular town, it still must compete with bus lines, trucking companies, and airlines. Similarly, the producer of a particular brand of beer may be the only supplier of that specific product, but the firm is not a pure monopolist by our definition. Because many other beers are close substitutes for its product, the firm will lose much of its business if it tries to raise its price far above the prices of other brands.

There is another reason why the unrestrained pure monopoly of economic theory is rarely found in practice. We will learn in this chapter that pure monopoly can have a number of undesirable features. The government has often intervened in markets where a pure monopoly might otherwise prevail, in order to prevent monopolization or to limit the discretion of a monopolist to set its price (for more on types of government intervention to constrain the power of monopolies, see Chapter 13).

If we do not study pure monopoly for its descriptive realism, why *do* we study it? Because, like perfect competition, pure monopoly is a market form that is easier to analyze than the more common market structures that we will consider in the next chapter. Thus, pure monopoly is a stepping-stone toward more realistic models. More important, we will understand the possible evils of monopoly (and some of its possible benefits) most clearly if we examine monopoly in its purest form.

Sources of Monopoly: Barriers to Entry and Cost Advantages

The key requirement for preservation of a monopoly is exclusion of potential rivals from the market. One way to achieve this result is by means of some specific impediment that prevents the establishment of a new firm in the industry. Economists call such impediments **barriers to entry.** Here are some examples.

Barriers to entry are attributes of a market that make it more difficult or expensive for a new firm to open for business than it was for the firms already present in that market.

1. Legal Restrictions The U.S. Postal Service has a monopoly position for some of its services because Congress has given it one. Private companies that may want to compete with the postal service directly in those services are prohibited from doing so by law. Local monopolies of various kinds are sometimes established either because government grants some special privilege to a single firm (for example, the right to operate a food concession in a municipal stadium) or prevents other firms from entering the industry (for instance, by licensing only a single cable television supplier).

2. Patents Some firms benefit from a special, but important, class of legal impediments to entry called **patents.** To encourage inventiveness, the government gives exclusive production rights for a period of time to the inventors of certain products. As long as a patent is in effect, the firm has a protected position and holds a monopoly. For example, Xerox Corporation for many years had (but no longer has) a monopoly in plain-paper copying. Most pharmaceutical companies also obtain monopolies on the medicines they discover. The drugmaker Pfizer, for instance, had a patent on Zoloft, which is a best-selling antidepressant medication. This patent expired at the end of 2005, which opened the door to competition from generic makers of the drug that has intensified, contributing to a decrease in the company's earnings.[2]

A **patent** is a privilege granted to an inventor, whether an individual or a firm, that for a specified period of time prohibits anyone else from producing or using that invention without the permission of the holder of the patent.

3. Control of a Scarce Resource or Input If a certain commodity can be produced only by using a rare input, a company that gains control of the source of that input can establish a monopoly position for itself. Real examples are not easy to find, but the South African diamond syndicate used to come close.

4. Deliberately Erected Entry Barriers A firm may deliberately attempt to make entry into the industry difficult for others. One way is to start costly lawsuits against new rivals, sometimes on trumped-up charges. Another is to spend exorbitant amounts on advertising, thus forcing any potential entrant to match that expenditure.

5. Large Sunk Costs Entry into an industry will, obviously, be very risky if it requires a large investment, especially if that investment is *sunk*—meaning that it cannot be recouped for a considerable period of time. For example, production in an industry may require the firm to construct a large, expensive building of a very special type, and that expenditure will only be covered fully out of returns from company sales far in the future. Thus, the need for a large sunk investment discourages entry into an industry. Many analysts therefore consider sunk costs to be the most important type of "naturally imposed" barrier to entry. For example, the high sunk costs involved in jet airplane production helped Boeing Corporation enjoy a monopoly at the top end of the long-range, wide-body

---

[2] Tim Annett, "The Afternoon Report: Patents & Profits," *The Wall Street Journal* (Eastern edition), Online edition, April 20, 2007.

jet airliner market for many years after the launch of the 747 jumbo jet. The rival aircraft manufacturer Airbus, which with European governments' sponsorship has been able to afford the high investments, has since encroached on Boeing's territory.

Such barriers can keep rivals out and ensure that an industry is monopolized. However, monopoly can also occur in the absence of barriers to entry if a single firm has substantial cost advantages over potential rivals. Two examples of attributes of production that create such advantages are technical superiority and economies of scale.

6. Technical Superiority

A firm whose technological expertise vastly exceeds that of any potential competitor can, for a period of time, maintain a monopoly position. For example, IBM Corporation for many years had little competition in the computer business mainly because of its technological virtuosity. Of course, competitors eventually caught up. More recently, Microsoft Corporation has established a commanding position in the software business, especially for operating systems, through a combination of inventiveness and marketing wizardry.

7. Economies of Scale

If *mere size* gives a large firm a cost advantage over a smaller rival, it is likely to be impossible for anyone to compete with the largest firm in the industry.

Natural Monopoly

This last type of cost advantage is important enough to merit special attention. In some industries, economies of large-scale production or economies of scope (cost reductions from simultaneous production of a large number of related items, such as car motors and bodies, truck parts, and so on) are so extreme that the industry's output can be produced at far lower cost by a single large firm than by a number of smaller firms. In such cases, we say there is a **natural monopoly.** Once a firm becomes large enough relative to the size of the market for its product, its natural cost advantage may well drive the competition out of business whether or not anyone in the relatively large firm has evil intentions.

A monopoly need not be a large firm if the market is small enough. *What matters is the size of a single firm relative to the total market demand for the product.* Thus, a small bank in a rural town or a gasoline station at a less traveled intersection may both be natural monopolies, even though they are very small firms.

Figure 1 shows the sort of average cost (AC) curve that leads to natural monopoly. It has a negative slope throughout, meaning that the more a firm in this industry produces, the lower its average cost will be. Suppose that any firm producing video games has this AC curve and that, initially, there are two firms in the industry. Suppose also that the larger firm is producing 2 million games at an average cost of $2.50 (point *A*), and the smaller firm is producing 1 million games that are no better than its rival's at an average cost of $3.00 (point *B*). Clearly, the larger firm can drive the smaller firm out of business if it offers its output for sale at a price below $3.00 (so the smaller firm can match the price only by running a loss) but above $2.50 (so it can still make a profit). Hence, a monopoly may arise "naturally," even in the absence of barriers to entry.

Once the monopoly is established (producing, say, 2.5 million video games–point *C*), its output is apt to grow even larger, so that its AC will fall even further. The economies of scale act as a very effective deterrent to entry because no new entrant can hope to match the low average cost ($2.00) of the existing monopoly firm. Of course, the public interest may be well served if the natural monopolist uses its low cost to keep its prices low. The danger, however, is that the firm may raise its price once rivals have left the industry.

Many public utilities operate as *regulated* monopoly suppliers for exactly this reason. It is believed that the technology of producing or distributing their output enables them

> A **natural monopoly** is an industry in which advantages of large-scale production make it possible for a single firm to produce the entire output of the market at lower average cost than a number of firms each producing a smaller quantity.

FIGURE 1

Natural Monopoly

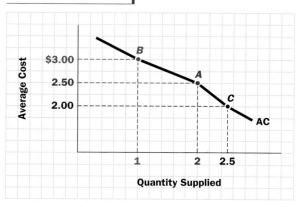

NOTE: Average cost is in dollars per unit; quantity is in millions.

to achieve substantial cost reductions by producing large quantities. It is therefore often considered preferable to permit these firms to achieve lower costs by having the entire market to themselves and then to subject them and their prices to regulatory supervision, rather than to break them up into a number of competing firms. We will examine the issues connected with regulation of natural monopolies in detail in Chapter 13. To summarize this discussion:

> **There are two basic reasons why a monopoly may exist: barriers to entry, such as legal restrictions and patents, and cost advantages of superior technology or large-scale operation that lead to natural monopoly. It is generally considered undesirable to break up a large firm whose costs are low because of scale economies. But barriers to entry are usually considered to be against the public interest except where they are believed to offer offsetting advantages, as in the case of patents, which are designed to encourage invention.**

The rest of this chapter analyzes how a monopoly can be expected to behave if its freedom of action is not limited by the government.

THE MONOPOLIST'S SUPPLY DECISION

A monopoly firm does not have a "supply curve," as we usually define the term. Unlike a firm operating under perfect competition, a monopoly is not at the mercy of the market; the firm does not have to accept the market's price as beyond its control and adjust its output level to that externally fixed price, as the supply curve assumes. Instead, it has the power to set the price, or rather to select the price-quantity combination on the demand curve that suits its interests best.

Put differently, a monopolist is not a *price taker* that must simply adapt to whatever price the forces of supply and demand decree. Rather, a monopolist is a *price maker* that can, if so inclined, raise the product price. Thus, the standard supply-demand analysis described in Chapter 4 does not apply to the determination of price or output in a monopolized industry. But it remains true that, for whatever price the monopolist selects, the demand curve for the product indicates how much consumers will buy.

The demand curve of a monopoly, unlike that of a perfectly competitive firm, is normally downward-sloping, not horizontal. This means that a price rise will not cause the monopoly to lose *all* of its customers, but any increase will cost it *some* business. The higher the price, the less the monopolist can expect to sell.

> **The market cannot impose a price on a monopolist as it imposes a price on the price-taking perfectly competitive firm. But the monopolist cannot select both price and the quantity it sells. In accord with the demand curve, the higher the price it sets, the less it can sell.**

In deciding what price best serves the firm's interests, the monopolist must consider whether profits can be increased by raising or lowering the product's price. Because of the downward-sloping demand curve, the sky is not the limit in pricing by a monopolist. Some price increases are not profitable because they lead to disproportionately large reductions in sales of the products.

In our analysis, we will assume that the monopolist wants to maximize profits. That does not mean that a monopoly is guaranteed a positive profit. If the demand for its product is low, or if the firm is inefficient, even a monopoly may lose money and eventually be forced out of business. However, if a monopoly firm does earn a positive profit, it may be able to continue doing so in the long run because there will be no entry that competes the profits away.

We can use the methods of Chapter 8 to determine which price the profit-maximizing monopolist will prefer. To maximize profits, the monopolist must compare marginal revenue (the addition to total revenue resulting from a one-unit rise in output) with marginal

Is the Software Industry a Natural Monopoly?

Some leading economists believe the software industry is prone to monopoly. Three influences may incline the industry in this direction, as an article in *InfoWorld* describes:

> One factor is diminishing costs: while the first copy of a software program costs millions to produce, the cost to produce subsequent copies is negligible. The second factor is the network effect in which the value of software increases by the number of people using it and developers creating applications for it. The third factor is the lock-in effect, in which the cost of switching to another system (installation, training, application compatibility) persuades users to stick with current systems. . . . These forces create natural barriers to entry for newcomers, and Microsoft's operating-system dominance is a prime example.

SOURCE: AP Photo/Aynsley Floyd

SOURCE: Lynda Radosevich, "Top of the News: How the Software Industry Creates Monopolies," *Infoworld* 20 (May 25, 1998).

cost (the addition to total cost resulting from that additional unit). Figure 2 shows a marginal cost (MC) curve and a marginal revenue (MR) curve for a typical monopolist. Recall that the firm's demand curve (*DD*) is also its average revenue (AR) curve. That is because if a firm sells *Q* units of output, selling every unit of output at the price *P*, then the *average* revenue brought in by a unit of output must be the price, *P*, because the average of a bunch of equal numbers must be that same number. Since the demand curve gives the price at which any particular quantity can be sold, it also automatically indicates the AR (= price) yielded by that quantity.

Notice that the marginal revenue curve is always below the demand curve, meaning that MR is always less than price (*P*). We have already seen that this must be true in the appendix to Chapter 8, where it was demonstrated that if the AR curve slopes downward, the MR curve must lie below the AR curve, because it is this MR < AR that pulls the average down. This important fact is also easy to explain here in common-sense terms. The monopoly firm charges the same price to all of its customers. If the firm wants to increase sales by one unit, it must decrease the price somewhat to all of its customers.

FIGURE 2

Profit-Maximizing Equilibrium for a Monopolist

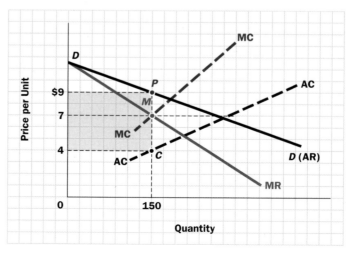

NOTE: Price is in dollars per unit.

When it cuts the price to attract new sales, all previous customers also benefit. Thus, the additional revenue that the monopolist takes in when sales increase by one unit (*marginal revenue*) is the price that the firm collects from the new customers *minus the revenue that it loses by cutting the price paid by all of its old customers.* This means that MR is necessarily less than P = AR; graphically, it implies that the MR curve is below the demand curve, as in Figure 2.

Determining the Profit-Maximizing Output

Like any other firm, the monopoly maximizes its profits by setting marginal revenue (MR) equal to marginal cost (MC). It selects point M in Figure 2, where output is 150 units. But point M does not tell us the monopoly price because, as we have just seen, price exceeds MR for a monopolist. To learn what price the monopolist charges, we must use the demand curve to find the price at which consumers are willing to purchase the profit-maximizing output of 150 units. The answer, as we know, is given by the height of the demand curve at that output—it is given by point P directly above M. The monopoly price is $9 per unit. Not surprisingly, it exceeds both MR and MC (which are equal at $7).

The monopolist depicted in Figure 2 is earning a tidy profit. This profit is shown in the graph by the shaded rectangle whose height is the difference between price (point P) and average cost (point C) and whose width is the quantity produced (150 units). In the example, profits are $5 per unit, or $750.

To study the decisions of a profit-maximizing monopolist:

1. **Find the output at which MR equals MC to select the profit-maximizing output level.**
2. **Find the height of the demand curve *at that level of output* to determine the corresponding price.**
3. **Compare the height of the demand curve with the height of the AC curve at that output to see whether the net result is an economic profit or a loss.**

We also can show a monopolist's profit-maximization calculation numerically. In Table 1, the first two columns show the quantity and price figures that constitute this monopolist's demand curve. Column (3) shows total revenue (TR) for each output, which is the product of price times quantity. Thus, for 3 units of output, we have TR = $92 × 3 = $276. Column (4) shows marginal revenue (MR). For example, when output rises from 3 to 4 units, TR increases from $276 to $320, so MR is $320 − $276 = $44. Column (5) gives the monopolist's total cost for each level of output. Column (6) derives marginal cost (MC) from total cost (TC) in the usual way. Finally, by subtracting TC from TR for each level of output, we obtain total profit in column (7).

The table brings out a number of important points. We note first in columns (2) and (3) that a cut in price may increase or decrease total revenue. When output rises from 1 to 2 units, P falls from $140 to $107 and TR rises from $140 to $214. However, when (between 5 and 6 units of output) P falls from $66 to $50, TR falls from $330 to $300. Next we observe, by comparing columns (2) and (4), that after the first unit, price always exceeds marginal revenue (because the marginal revenue curve *must* lie below the downward-sloping demand [AR] curve). Finally, from columns (4) and (6) we see that MC = MR = $44 when Q is between 3 and 4 units, indicating that this is the level of output that maximizes the monopolist's total profit. This is confirmed in column (7) of the table, which shows that at this output profit reaches its highest level, $110, for any of the output quantities considered in the table.

TABLE 1

A Profit-Maximizing Monopolist's Price-Output Decision

		Revenue		Cost		Total Profit
(1)	(2)	(3)	(4)	(5)	(6)	(7)
Q	P	TR = $P \times Q$	MR	TC	MC	TR − TC
0	—	$ 0		$ 10		$−10
			$140		$60	
1	$140	140		70		70
			74		50	
2	107	214		120		94
			62		46	
3	92	276		166		110
			44		44	
4	80	320		210		110
			10		43	
5	66	330		253		77
			−30		45	
6	50	300		298		2

Comparing Monopoly and Perfect Competition

This completes our analysis of the monopolist's price—output decision. At this point, it is natural to wonder whether there is anything distinctive about the monopoly equilibrium. To find out, we need a standard of comparison. Perfect competition provides this standard because, as we will learn in Chapter 14, it is a theoretical benchmark of ideal performance against which other market structures can be judged. By comparing the results of monopoly with those of perfect competition, we will see why economists since Adam Smith have condemned monopoly as inefficient.

1. A Monopolist's Profit Persists

Monopoly profits are any excess of the profits earned persistently by a monopoly firm over and above those that would be earned if the industry were perfectly competitive.

The first difference between competition and monopoly is a direct consequence of barriers to entry in monopoly. Profits such as those shown in Figure 2 would be competed away by free entry in a perfectly competitive market, because a positive profit would attract new competitors into the business. A competitive firm must earn *zero economic profit* in the long run; that is, it can earn only enough to cover its costs, including the opportunity cost of the owner's capital and labor. But higher **profit** *can* persist under **monopoly**—if the monopoly is protected from the arrival of new competitors by barriers to entry. This can, then, allow monopolists to grow wealthy at the expense of their consumers. But because people find such accumulations of wealth objectionable, monopoly is widely condemned. As a result, monopolies are generally regulated by government, which often limits the profits they can earn.

2. Monopoly Restricts Output to Raise Short-Run Price

Excess monopoly profit can be a problem, but economists believe that the second difference between competition and monopoly is even more worrisome:

> **Compared with the perfectly competitive ideal, the monopolist restricts output and charges a higher price.**

To see that this is so, let us conduct the following thought experiment. Imagine that a court order breaks up the monopoly firm depicted in Figure 2 (and reproduced as Figure 3) into a large number of perfectly competitive firms. Suppose further that the industry demand curve is unchanged by this event and that the MC curve in Figure 3 is also the (horizontal) sum of the MC curves of all the newly created competitive firms. These may be unrealistic assumptions, as we will soon explain; however, they make it easy to compare the output-price combinations that would emerge in the short run under monopoly and perfect competition.

Before making our comparison, we must note that under monopoly, the firm and the industry are exactly the same entity, but under perfect competition, any one firm is just

FIGURE 3

Comparison of a Monopoly and a Perfectly Competitive Industry

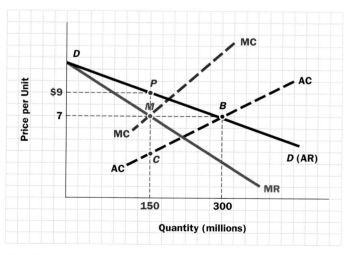

NOTE: Price is in dollars per unit.

a small portion of the industry. So when we measure the performance of monopoly against that of perfect competition, we should compare the monopoly with the entire competitive industry, not with an individual competitive firm. In Figure 3, the monopolist's output is point M at which MC = MR. The long-run competitive output (point B) is greater than the monopoly's because it must be sufficiently large to yield zero economic profit (P = AR = AC).

It is self-evident and not very interesting to observe that the output of the monopolist is virtually certain to be larger than that of a tiny competitive *firm*. The interesting issue is how much of the *entire industry's* product gets into the hands of consumers under the two market forms—that is, how much output is produced by a monopoly as compared with the quantity provided by a similar competitive *industry*.

3. Monopoly Restricts Output to Raise Long-Run Price   As we have seen, monopoly output is determined by the profit-maximization requirement that MC = MR (point M). Moreover, in Chapter 10, we learned that long-run perfectly competitive equilibrium occurs at point B in Figure 3, where price (=AR) and average cost are equal and economic profit is zero.

By comparing point B with the monopolist's equilibrium (point M), we see that the monopolist produces fewer units of output than would a competitive industry with the same demand and cost conditions. Because the demand curve slopes downward, producing less output means that the industry gets away with a higher price. The monopolist's price, indicated by point P on the demand curve and directly above M, exceeds the price that would result from perfect competition at point B. This is the essence of the truth behind the popular view that unregulated monopolists "gouge the public." The monopolist deliberately cuts back the amount of output produced in order to make the product scarcer and thereby force its price upward.

We should note that matters will *always* turn out that way if the average cost curve has a positive slope between the monopoly output level and the competitive output level. That is because we know, in this case, that the MC curve must lie above the AC curve (to review why, see pages 173–174 of Chapter 8). We also have just seen that the MR curve must lie below the demand (AR) curve. It is clear, then, that the point where the MR curve meets the MC curve (the monopoly output) must always lie to the left of the output at which AC and AR meet (the competitive industry output). Consequently, monopoly output will always be the smaller of the two when the curves of the competitive and monopoly industries are identical. With monopoly output lower, its price will always be higher.

4. Monopoly Leads to Inefficient Resource Allocation   We conclude, then, that a monopoly will charge a higher price and produce a smaller output than will a competitive industry with the same demand and cost conditions. Why do economists find this situation so objectionable? Because, as we will learn in Chapter 14, a competitive industry devotes "just the right amount" of society's scarce resources to the production of its particular commodity. Therefore, if a monopolist produces less than a competitive industry, it must be producing too little.

To summarize this discussion of the consequences of monopoly:

Because it is protected from entry, a monopoly firm may earn positive economic profits; that is, profits in excess of the opportunity cost of capital. At the same time, monopoly breeds inefficiency in resource allocation by producing too little output and charging too high a price. For these reasons, some of the virtues of the free market evaporate if an industry becomes monopolized.

Monopoly Is Likely to Shift Demand

This analysis need not always apply. For one thing, it has assumed that the market demand curve is the same whether the industry is competitive or monopolized. But is

this usually so? The demand curve will be the same if the monopoly firm does nothing to expand its market, but that is hardly plausible.

Under perfect competition, purchasers consider the products of all suppliers in an industry to be identical, so no single supplier has any reason to advertise. Advertising expenditure by firm X will bring most of its benefits to the other firms in the industry, because the ads, if they work, will induce customers to buy more of the identical product from among any of its many sellers. But if a monopoly takes over from a perfectly competitive industry, it may very well pay to advertise. If management believes that the creative touch of the advertising agency can make consumers rush to the market to purchase the product whose virtues have been extolled on television, then the firm will allocate a substantial sum of money to accomplish this feat. Take the Eastman Kodak Company, for example. Kodak enjoyed a near monopoly on U.S. film sales from the turn of the century until the 1980s, but that did not stop the company from spending a good deal on advertising. This type of expenditure should shift the demand curve outward. The monopoly's demand curve and that of the competitive industry will then no longer be the same.

The higher demand curve for the monopoly's product may induce it to expand production and therefore reduce the difference between the competitive and the monopolistic output levels indicated in Figure 3. But it may also make it possible for the monopoly to charge even higher prices, so the increased output may not constitute a net gain for consumers.

Monopoly Is Likely to Shift Cost Curves

The advent of a monopoly also may shift the average and marginal cost curves. One reason for higher costs is the advertising we have just been discussing. Another reason is the sheer size of the monopolist's organization, which may lead to bureaucratic inefficiencies, coordination problems, and the like.

At the same time, a monopolist may be able to eliminate certain types of duplication that are unavoidable for a number of small, independent firms: One purchasing agent may do the input-buying job where many buyers were needed before; a few large machines may replace many small items of equipment in the hands of the competitive firms. In addition, the large scale of the monopoly firm's input purchases may permit it to take advantage of quantity discounts by its input suppliers that are not available to small competitive firms.

If the consolidation achieved by a monopoly does shift the marginal cost curve downward, monopoly output will tend to move up closer to the competitive level. The monopoly price will then tend to move down closer to the competitive price.

CAN ANYTHING GOOD BE SAID ABOUT MONOPOLY?

We conclude that our graphic comparison of monopoly and perfect competition is very artificial. It assumes that all other things will remain the same, even though that is unlikely to happen in reality. For that reason and others, there are certain cases in which monopoly may not be as damaging to the public interest as the previous discussion suggests. Let us consider some specific ways in which monopoly can offset some of its undesirable consequences.

Monopoly May Aid Innovation

Some economists have emphasized that it is misleading to compare the cost curves of a monopoly and a competitive industry *at a single point in time*. Because it is protected from rivals and therefore sure to capture the benefits from any cost-saving methods and new products it can invent, a monopoly has particularly strong motivation to invest in research, these economists argue. If this research bears fruit, the monopolist's costs will be lower than those of a competitive industry in the long run, even if they are higher in the short run. Monopoly, according to this view, may be the handmaiden of innovation. Although the argument is an old one, it remains controversial. The statistical evidence is decidedly mixed.

Natural Monopoly: Where Single-Firm Production Is Cheapest

Second, we must remember that the monopoly depicted in Figure 2 is not a natural monopoly, because its average costs increase rather than decrease when its output expands. However, some of the monopolies you find in the real world are "natural" ones. Where a monopoly is natural, costs of production would, by definition, be higher—possibly much higher—if the single large firm were broken up into many smaller firms. (Refer back to Figure 1.) In such cases, it may serve society's interests to allow the monopoly to continue because consumers benefit from the economies of large-scale production. But then it may be appropriate to regulate the monopoly by placing legal limitations on its ability to set its prices.

PRICE DISCRIMINATION UNDER MONOPOLY

So far we have assumed that a monopoly charges the same price to all of its customers, but that is not always true. In reality, monopoly firms can sell the same product to different customers at different prices, even if that price difference is unrelated to any special costs that affect some customers but not others. Such a practice is called **price discrimination.** Pricing is also said to be discriminatory if it costs more to supply a good to Customer A than to Customer B, but A and B are nonetheless charged the same price.

We are all familiar with cases of price discrimination. For example, suppose that Erik and Emily both mail letters from Lewisburg, Pennsylvania, but his goes to New York while hers goes to Hawaii. Both pay the same 44¢ postage even though Hawaii is much farther away from Lewisburg than New York. Bargain airline fares are another example. Passenger C, who obtained a student discount, may find herself seated next to Passenger D, who has paid 25 percent more for the same flight and the same taste-free food.

The airline example shows that price discrimination occurs in industries that are not monopolies. Still, it is easier for a monopolist to charge discriminatory prices than it is for a firm that is affected by competition, because price discrimination means that sales to some customers are more profitable than sales to others. Such discrepancies in profitability tempt rivals, including new entrants into the industry, to charge the more profitable consumers somewhat lower prices in order to lure them away from the firm that is "overcharging" them. Price discriminators sneeringly call this type of targeted entry *cream skimming,* meaning that entrants go after the best-paying customers, leaving the low payers (the "skimmed milk") to the discriminator. Whether desirable or not, such entry certainly makes it more difficult to charge higher prices to the more profitable customers.

Why do firms sometimes engage in price discrimination? You may already suspect the answer: to increase their profits. To see why, let us consider a simple example. Imagine a town with 100 rich families and 1,000 poor ones. The poor families are each willing to buy

Price discrimination is the sale of a given product at different prices to different customers of the firm when there are no differences in the costs of supplying these customers. Prices are also discriminatory if it costs more to supply one customer than another but they are charged the same price.

one video game but cannot afford to pay more than $25. The rich, however, are prepared to buy one per family as long as the price is no higher than $75.

If it cannot price-discriminate, the best the firm can do is to set the price at $25 for everyone, yielding a total revenue of $25 × 1,100 = $27,500. If it charged more, say, $75, it would sell only to the rich and earn just $7,500. If the added cost of producing the 1,000 games for the poorer families is less than the $20,000 in added revenues from the larger sales to the additional poor customers who are led to purchase the games by the lower price ($27,500 − $7,500 = $20,000), then the $25 price must be more profitable than the $75 price.

But what if the game maker can charge different prices to the rich and to the poor—and can prevent the poor from reselling their low-priced merchandise to the rich at a markup? Then the revenue obtainable by the firm from the same 1,100 video game output becomes $25 × 1,000 = $25,000 from selling to the poor plus $75 × 100 = $7,500 from selling to the rich, for a total of $32,500. This is clearly a better deal for the firm than the $27,500 revenue obtainable without price discrimination. Profits are $5,000 higher. In general:

> **When a firm charges discriminatory prices, profits are normally higher than when the firm charges nondiscriminatory (uniform) prices because the firm then divides customers into separate groups and charges each group the price that maximizes its profits from those customers.**

We have constructed our simple example to make the two profit-maximizing prices obvious. In practice, that is not so; the monopolist knows that if it sets a price too high, quantity demanded and hence profits will be too low. The discriminating monopolist's problem is determining the different profit-maximizing prices to charge to different customer groups. The solution to this problem is given by another rule of marginal analysis. For simplicity, suppose that the seller proposes charging two different prices to two customer groups, A and B. Profit maximization requires that the price to Group A and the price to Group B are such that they yield the same *marginal* revenue, so that the MR from *each* customer group is equal to the MC of the product; that is,

> **The marginal revenue from a sale to a Group A customer must be the same as that from a sale to a Group B customer:**

$$MR_a = MR_b$$

The reasoning is straightforward. Basically it amounts to this: Suppose you have been selling widgets to two customers and have two widgets left over. When would you be willing to sell one of this remainder to each customer, rather than selling both to only one of the customers? The obvious answer is that you will sell one to each if neither offers you a higher payment (MR) than the other. Thus, suppose that the sale of an additional video game to a Group A customer who lives in Richtown brings in MR_a = $28 in revenue, whereas the corresponding sale to a Group B customer in Poorborough adds only MR_b = $12. Such an arrangement cannot possibly be a profit-maximizing solution. By switching one unit of its shipments from Poorborough, with its B customers, and sending that unit instead to Richtown's A customers, the firm gives up $12 in revenue to gain $28—a net gain of $16 from the same total quantity of sales. Because a similar argument holds for any other pair of marginal revenues that are unequal, profit maximizing clearly requires that the marginal revenue from each group of customers be equal.

The equal-marginal-revenue rule enables us to determine the profit-maximizing prices and sales volumes for two such groups of customers diagrammatically. The two panels of Figure 4 show the demand curves and corresponding marginal revenue curves for customer groups A and B. Suppose that the firm is selling the quantity Q_a to Group A customers at price P_a. How much must the firm then sell to Group B customers, and at what price, to maximize profits? Our rule gives the answer. The marginal revenue from selling to Group A is equal to H—as we see from point J directly above Q_a on the MR curve

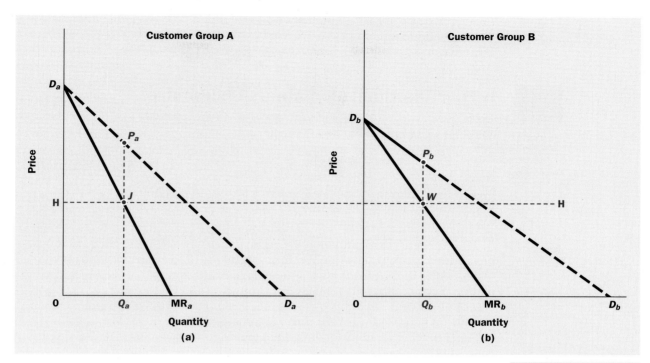

FIGURE 4

Prices and Quantities under Price Discrimination

in Panel (a). The rule tells us that the firm must charge a price to Group B customers that induces them to buy the quantity that yields the same marginal revenue, *H*. We find this quantity by drawing a horizontal line *HH* through point *J* from Figure 4(a) to Figure 4(b). The marginal revenues of the two customer groups will clearly be equal where *HH* cuts the Group B marginal revenue curve—at point *W*. The profit-maximizing sales volume to Group B will be Q_b, directly below point *W*. And at sales volume Q_b, the market B price is clearly given by the corresponding point on the market B demand curve, price P_b directly above Q_b.

> **Given price and output in one of two markets (Figure 4a), to determine the profit-maximizing output and price in the other market (Figure 4b) under price discrimination, do the following:**
>
> 1. **Draw the demand and marginal revenue curves for the different customer groups (Group A and Group B) side by side.**
>
> 2. **For the first market (Group A, Figure 4a), draw a horizontal line through point *J* corresponding to the marginal revenue—quantity combination, which will set the price and quantity for Customer Group A at (P_a, Q_a).**
>
> 3. **Knowing the marginal revenue *H* and output (Q_a), point *J*, for the first market, find the profit-maximizing sales quantity for the second market where the horizontal line cuts the MR curve for the second group of customers, so that the MR levels are the same for both customer groups.**
>
> 4. **Knowing the marginal revenue *H* and point-maximizing sales quantity Q_b for the second market, determine the second customer group's profit-maximizing price P_b, point *W*, by locating the point on the demand curve corresponding to the profit-maximizing quantity.**

That is not quite the end of the story: We have not yet said anything about costs, and we know that profit maximization must take account of costs as well as revenues. We can deal with the cost issue quite easily, at least if the marginal cost of a video game is the same whether supplied to an A customer or a B customer. Even under price discrimination, we still have the fundamental MR = MC rule for profit maximization in each market segment (see page 165 in Chapter 8). The extended profit-maximization rule under price discrimination then must be:

$$MR_a = MR_b = MC$$

Is Price Discrimination Always Undesirable?

Although the word *discrimination* is generally used to refer to reprehensible practices, *price discrimination* may not always be bad. Most people feel strongly that it is appropriate for the post office to charge the same price for all first-class letters going between two points in the United States, regardless of the differences in delivery costs. Similarly, most people approve of discounts on theater tickets sold to students or to senior citizens, even though those prices are obviously discriminatory. The same is widely agreed about lower doctor's fees for needy patients.

Other reasons, in addition to some standard of fairness or justice, may provide a defense for price discrimination in certain cases. One such case arises when it is impossible without price discrimination for a private firm to supply a product that customers want. For an illustration, go back to our numerical example of video-game price discrimination. Suppose that the total cost of producing 100 video games is $8,000, and the total cost of producing 1,100 video games is $30,000. Then our firm cannot cover its costs with a uniform, nondiscriminatory price. If it charged $75 to the 100 rich customers willing to pay that much, its $7,500 total revenue would fall short of its $8,000 total cost. Similarly, charging the uniform price of $25 to all 1,100 customers would yield total revenue of only $27,500, which is less than the $30,000 total cost. Thus, *any* uniform price would drive the firm out of business, depriving customers of the consumers' surplus from purchasing the product. With discriminatory prices, we saw that the firm would earn $32,500, enabling the firm to cover the $30,000 cost of supplying the requirements of both sets of customers.

It is even possible that price discrimination can make a product cheaper than it would otherwise be for *all* customers—even those who pay the higher discriminatory prices. As you may imagine, this can be true only if the production of the commodity involves significant economies of scale. For example, suppose that price discrimination permits the firm to offer lower prices to certain customers, thereby attracting some business that it would not otherwise have. The firm's output will therefore increase. Scale economies can then reduce the firm's marginal costs. If marginal cost falls enough, even the high-priced customer group may end up paying less than it would in the absence of price discrimination.

The conclusion from this discussion is not that price discrimination is always a good thing, but rather that it is *sometimes* desirable. In particular, we must recognize that a firm may be unable to cover its costs without price discrimination—a situation that some observers consider to be relatively common.

PUZZLE RESOLVED: COMPETITION IN TELEPHONE SERVICE

We conclude our discussion of monopoly by returning to the puzzle that began this chapter: Why are phone services around the country threatened by competition in an industry that was once considered the very definition of a natural monopoly? The answer has many parts, notably changes in the government's rules and new rulings by the courts, but the main development that made competition in the industry possible is the huge change in telephone service technology.

Until recently, the market for *local* telephone service was considered a natural monopoly. The primary reason was the need for very expensive transmission facilities, primarily the wires that had to enter every subscriber's home. Local and state governments even disallowed competition in these markets because they believed that it would lead to wasteful duplication of such costly equipment and that this expensive duplication would lead to higher prices. Instead, local utility commissions regulated these monopolies to ensure adequate service and reasonable prices. Because long-distance calls also had to reach the home and office via those costly wires, the firm that owned them would have been in a position to control the industry and perhaps even to turn it into a monopoly once again, if government rules had not prevented it.

SOURCE: © AP Images/PRNewsFoto/Verizon Wireless

Recent changes in communications technology have since made this market riper for competition. Computers and satellite technology have reduced the investment costs of providing phone service. Wherever you live, competition has become a reality, with cell phones that need no wires to connect to households. In addition, voice message transmission via the Internet often is far less costly and easily supplied by rival providers. Local landline phone companies still have some near-monopoly power in their own geographic territories, but that power seems likely to erode before long.

| SUMMARY |

1. A **pure monopoly** is a one-firm industry producing a product for which there are no close substitutes.

2. Monopoly can persist only if there are important cost advantages to single-firm operation or **barriers to free entry**. These barriers may consist of legal impediments (**patents**, licensing), the special risks faced by a potential entrant resulting from the need to incur large sunk investments, or the result of "dirty tricks" designed to make things tough for an entrant.

3. One important case of cost advantages is **natural monopoly**—instances in which only one firm can survive because of significant economies of large-scale production.

4. A monopoly has no supply curve. It maximizes its profit by producing an output at which its marginal revenue equals its marginal cost. Its price is given by the point on its demand curve corresponding to that output.

5. In a monopolistic industry, if demand and cost curves are the same as those of a competitive industry, and if the demand curve has a negative slope and the competitive supply curve has a positive slope, then monopoly output will be lower and price will be higher than they will be in the competitive industry.

6. Economists consider the fact that monopoly output tends to be below the competitive level to constitute an (undesirable) inefficiency.

7. Advertising may enable a monopoly to shift its demand curve above that of a comparable competitive industry. Through economies such as large-scale input purchases, a monopoly may be able to shift its cost curves below those of a competitive industry.

8. A monopoly may be able to increase its profits by engaging in **price discrimination**—charging higher prices for the same goods to customers who are less resistant to price increases, or failing to charge higher prices to customers whom it costs more to serve.

9. The profit-maximizing discriminatory prices, and corresponding sales volumes, for a firm with several different customer groups can be determined with the

help of an extended rule for profit maximization: that the *marginal revenues* from sales to *each* customer group must be equal to one another and to the firm's marginal cost.

10. Price discrimination can sometimes be damaging to the public interest, but at other times it can be beneficial.

Some firms cannot survive without it, and price discrimination may even reduce prices to *all* customers if there are substantial economies of scale.

| KEY TERMS |

barriers to entry   219

monopoly profits   224

natural monopoly   220

patents   219

price discrimination   227

pure monopoly   218

| TEST YOURSELF |

1. Which of the following industries are pure monopolies?

   a. The only supplier of heating fuel in an isolated town

   b. The only supplier of IBM notebook computers in town

   c. The only supplier of digital cameras

   Explain your answers.

2. The following are the demand and total cost schedules for Company Town Water, a local monopoly:

Output in Gallons	Price per Gallon	Total Cost
50,000	$0.28	$ 6,000
100,000	0.26	15,000
150,000	0.22	22,000
200,000	0.20	32,000
250,000	0.16	46,000
300,000	0.12	64,000

How much output will Company Town Water produce, and what price will it charge? Will it earn a profit? How much? (*Hint:* First compute the firm's MR and MC schedules.)

3. Show from the table in Test Yourself Question 2 that for the water company, marginal revenue (per 50,000-gallon unit) is always less than price.

4. A monopoly sells Frisbees to two customer groups. Group A has a downward-sloping straight-line demand curve, whereas the demand curve for Group B is infinitely elastic. Draw the graph determining the profit-maximizing discriminatory prices and sales to the two groups. What will be the price of Frisbees to Group B? Why? How is the price to Group A determined?

| DISCUSSION QUESTIONS |

1. Suppose that a monopoly industry produces less output than a similar competitive industry. Discuss why this may be considered socially undesirable. Is this because it is *always* socially beneficial to produce more of some product?

2. If competitive firms earn zero economic profits, explain why anyone would invest money in them. (*Hint:* What is the role of the opportunity cost of capital in economic profit?)

3. Suppose that a tax of $28 is levied on each item sold by a monopolist, and as a result, it decides to raise its price by exactly $28. Why might this decision be against its own best interests?

4. Use Figure 2 to show that Adam Smith was wrong when he claimed that a monopoly would always charge "the highest price which can be got."

5. General Motors declared bankruptcy in 2009. If it goes out of business altogether, why might that *not* reduce the competition facing rival automaker Ford? (*Hint:* At what price would the assets of the bankrupt companies be offered for sale?)

6. What does your answer to the previous question tell you about the ease or difficulty of entry into the automobile industry?

7. A firm cannot break even by charging uniform (nondiscriminatory) prices, but with price discrimination it can earn a small profit. Explain why in this case consumers *must* be better off if the firm is permitted to charge discriminatory prices.

8. It can be proved that, other things being equal, under price discrimination the price charged to some customer group will be higher the less elastic the demand curve of that group is. Why is that result plausible?

BETWEEN COMPETITION AND MONOPOLY

. . . neither fish nor fowl.

JOHN HEYWOOD (C. 1565)

Most productive activity in the United States, as in any advanced industrial society, falls somewhere between the two extreme market forms we have considered so far. So if we want to understand the workings of the market mechanism in a real, modern economy, we must look at hybrid market structures that fall somewhere between perfect competition and pure monopoly. There are two such market forms—*monopolistic competition* and *oligopoly*—that are analyzed extensively by economists and are extremely important in practice.

Monopolistic competition is a market structure characterized by many small firms selling somewhat different products. Here, each firm's output is so small relative to the total output of closely related and, hence, rival products that the firm does not expect its competitors to respond to or even to *notice* any changes in its own behavior.

Monopolistic competition, or something close to it, is widespread in retailing: shoe stores, restaurants, and gasoline stations are good examples. Most firms in our economy can be classified as monopolistic competitors, because even though they are small, such enterprises are abundant. We begin the chapter by using the theory of the firm described in Chapter 8 to analyze a monopolistically competitive firm's price–output decisions, then we consider the role of entry and exit, as we did in Chapter 10.

Finally we turn to oligopoly, a market structure in which a few large firms dominate the market. The steel, automobile, and airplane manufacturing industries are good examples of oligopolies, despite the increasing number of strong foreign competitors. Probably the largest share of U.S. economic output comes from oligopolists. Although they are fewer in number than monopolistic competitors, many oligopoly firms are extremely large, with annual sales exceeding the total outputs of most countries in the world and even of some of the smaller industrial European countries.

CONTENTS

One critical feature distinguishing an oligopolist from either a monopolist or a perfect competitor is that oligopolists care very much about what other individual firms in the industry do. The resulting *interdependence* of decisions, as we will see, makes oligopoly very difficult to analyze and results in a wide range of behavior patterns. Consequently, economic theory uses not just one but many models of oligopoly (some of which we will review in this chapter), and it is often hard to know which model to apply in any particular situation.

PUZZLE: THREE PUZZLING OBSERVATIONS

We need to study the hybrid market structures considered in this chapter because many economic phenomena cannot be explained in terms of perfect competition or pure monopoly. Here are three examples:

PUZZLE 1: WHY ARE THERE SO MANY RETAILERS? You have undoubtedly seen road intersections with gasoline stations on every corner. Often, two or three of them have no customers at the pumps. There seems to be more gas stations than the number of cars warrants, with a corresponding waste of labor, time, equipment, and other resources. Why—and how—do they all stay in business?

PUZZLE 2: WHY DO OLIGOPOLISTS ADVERTISE MORE THAN "MORE COMPETITIVE" FIRMS? Many big companies use advertising as a principal weapon in their battle for customers, and advertising budgets can constitute very large shares of their expenditures. Such firms spend literally billons of dollars per year on advertising, seeking to leap ahead of their rivals. For instance, Procter & Gamble, the largest U.S. advertiser, reportedly spent $2.8 billion on advertising (about 23 percent of its 2008 net earnings).[1] Yet critics often accuse oligopolistic industries containing only a few giant firms of being "uncompetitive." Farming, in contrast, is considered as close to perfect competition as any industry in our economy, but few, if any, individual farmers spend anything at all on advertising.[2] Why do these allegedly "uncompetitive" oligopolists make such heavy use of combative advertising, whereas very competitive farmers do not?

PUZZLE 3: WHY DO OLIGOPOLISTS SEEM TO CHANGE THEIR PRICES SO INFREQUENTLY? Many prices in the economy change from minute to minute. The very latest prices of commodities such as soybeans, pork bellies, and copper are available online 24 hours a day, seven days a week. If you want to buy one of these commodities at 11:45 A.M. today, you cannot use yesterday's price—or even the price from 11:44 A.M. today—because it has probably changed already. Yet prices of products such as cars and refrigerators generally change only a few times a year at most, even during fairly rapid inflation. Firms that sell cars and refrigerators know that product and input market conditions change all the time. Why don't they adjust their prices more often? This chapter will offer answers to each of these questions.

MONOPOLISTIC COMPETITION

For years, economic theory told us little about market forms in between the two extreme cases of pure monopoly and perfect competition. Then, during the 1930s, Edward Chamberlin of Harvard University and Joan Robinson of Cambridge University (working

---

[1] Source: The Nielsen Company, "U.S. Ad Spending Fell 2.6% in 2008, Nielsen Reports," press release, March 13, 2009, accessed online: http://en-us.nielsen.com/main/news/news_releases; and The Procter & Gamble Company, *2008 Annual Report*, accessed online: http://www.pg.com/annualreport2008.

[2] Farmers' associations, such as Sunkist and various dairy groups, do spend money on advertising.

separately) partially filled this gap and helped to make economic theory more realistic. The market structure they analyzed is called **monopolistic competition.**

Characteristics of Monopolistic Competition

A market is said to operate under conditions of monopolistic competition if it satisfies four requirements, three of which are the same as those for perfect competition:

- *Numerous participants*—that is, many buyers and sellers, all of whom are small
- *Freedom of exit and entry*
- *Perfect information*
- *Heterogeneous products*—as far as the buyer is concerned, each seller's product differs at least somewhat from every other seller's product

Notice that monopolistic competition differs from perfect competition in only the last respect. Perfect competition assumes that the products of different firms in an industry are identical, but under monopolistic competition products differ from seller to seller—in terms of quality, packaging, supplementary services offered (such as windshield washing at a gas station), or merely consumers' perceptions. The attributes that differentiate products need not be "real" in any objective or directly measurable sense. For example, differences in packaging or in associated services can and do distinguish otherwise identical products. However, although two products may perform quite differently in quality tests, if consumers know nothing about this difference, it is irrelevant.

In contrast to a perfect competitor, a monopolistic competitor's demand curve is negatively sloped. Because each seller's product is different, each caters to a set of customers who vary in their loyalty to the particular product. If the firm raises its price somewhat, it will drive *some* of its customers to competitors' offerings, but customers who strongly favor the firm's product will not switch. If one monopolistic competitor lowers its price, it may expect to attract some trade from rivals. However, because different products are imperfect substitutes, it will not lure away *all* of the rivals' business.

For example, if Harriet's Hot Dog House reduces its price slightly, it will attract those customers of Sam's Sausage Shop who were nearly indifferent between the two. If Harriet were to cut her prices further, she would gain some customers who have a slightly greater preference for Sam's product. But even a big cut in Harriet's price will not bring her the hard-core sausage lovers who hate hot dogs. Therefore, monopolistic competitors face a demand curve that is negatively sloped, like that of a monopolist, rather than horizontal, like that of a perfect competitor who will lose all of his business if he insists on a higher price than that charged by a rival.

Because consumers see each product as distinct from all others, a monopolistically competitive firm appears to have something akin to a small monopoly. Can we therefore expect it to earn more than zero economic profit? Like perfect competitors, perhaps monopolistic competitors will obtain economic profits in the short run. In the long run, however, high economic profits will attract new entrants into a monopolistically competitive market—not with products *identical* to an existing firm's, but with products sufficiently similar to absorb the excess economic profits.

If McDonald's is thriving at a particular location, it can confidently expect Burger King or some other fast-food outlet to open a franchise nearby shortly. When one seller adopts a new, attractive package, rivals will soon follow suit with slightly different designs and colors of their own. In this way, freedom of entry ensures that the monopolistically competitive firm earns no higher return on its capital in the long run than that capital could earn elsewhere. In other words, the firm earns no excess economic profits. Just as under perfect competition, competition will drive price down to equal average cost, including the opportunity cost of capital. In this sense, although its product differs somewhat from everyone else's, the firm under monopolistic competition has no more monopoly *power* than does one operating under perfect competition.

Monopolistic competition refers to a market in which products are heterogeneous but which is otherwise the same as a market that is perfectly competitive.

FIGURE 1

Short-Run Equilibrium of the Firm under Monopolistic Competition

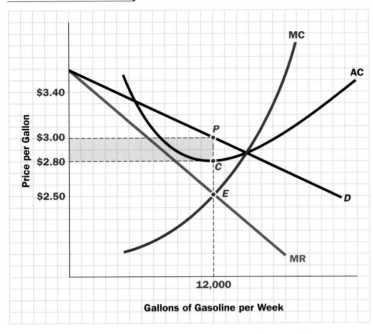

Gallons of Gasoline per Week

Let us now examine the process that ensures that competition will drive economic profits down to zero in the long run, even under monopolistic competition, and see what prices and outputs that process fosters.

Price and Output Determination under Monopolistic Competition

The *short-run* equilibrium of the firm under monopolistic competition differs little from the equilibrium seen under monopoly. Because the firm faces a downward-sloping demand curve (labeled D in Figure 1), its marginal revenue (MR) curve will lie below its demand curve. Like any firm, a monopolistic competitor maximizes profits by producing the output at which marginal revenue equals marginal cost (MC). In Figure 1, the profit-maximizing output for a hypothetical gas station is 12,000 gallons per week, and it sells this output at a price of $3.00 per gallon (point P on the demand curve). The firm makes 20 cents per gallon in profits, as depicted by the vertical distance from C to P.

This analysis, you will note, looks much like Figure 2 in Chapter 11 for a monopoly. The main difference is that monopolistic competitors are likely to face a much flatter demand curve than pure monopolists do, because many products serve as close substitutes for the monopolistic competitor's product. If our gas station raises its price to $3.40 per gallon, most of its customers will go across the street. If it lowers its price to $2.50 per gallon, it will have long lines at its pumps.

The gas station depicted in Figure 1 is enjoying economic profits. Because average cost at 12,000 gallons per week is only $2.80 per gallon (point C), the station makes a profit of 20 cents per gallon on gasoline sales, or $1,200 per week in total, shown by the shaded rectangle. Under monopoly, such profits can persist. Under monopolistic competition, they cannot—because economic profits will entice new firms to enter the market. Although the new gas stations will not offer the identical product, they will offer products that are close enough to take away some business from our firm. (For example, they may sell Conoco or Shell gasoline instead of Exxon gasoline.)

When more firms enter the market, each firm's demand curve will shift downward (to the left). But how far will it shift? The answer is basically the same as it was under perfect competition: Market entry will cease only when the most that the firm can earn is zero economic profit—exactly the same return the firm can earn elsewhere.

Figure 2 depicts the same monopolistically competitive firm as in Figure 1 *after* the adjustment to the long-run equilibrium is complete. The demand curve—and also the MR curve—has been pushed down so far by the entry of new rivals that when the firm equates

FIGURE 2

Long-Run Equilibrium of the Firm under Monopolistic Competition

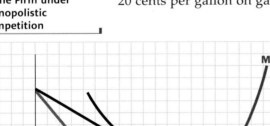

Gallons of Gasoline per Week

MC and MR in an attempt to maximize profits (point *E*), it simultaneously equates price *(P)* and average cost (AC) so that economic profits are zero (point *P*). As compared to the short-run equilibrium depicted in Figure 1, price in long-run equilibrium is *lower* ($2.85 cents per gallon versus $3.00), *more firms* participate in the industry, and each firm produces a *smaller* output (10,000 gallons versus 12,000 gallons) at a *higher* average cost per gallon ($2.85 versus $2.80).[3] In general:

> **Long-run equilibrium under monopolistic competition requires that the firm's output be at a level where its demand curve and its average cost curve meet, and there the two curves must be *tangent*, not crossing.**

Why? Because if the demand curve were above the average cost curve or the two curves intersected, firms could produce output quantities at which price would exceed average cost, which means that participants would be earning economic profits, and that would draw an influx of new close-substitute products that would push down the demand curve. Similarly, if the average cost curve were above the demand curve at every point, the firm would incur an economic loss—it would be unable to obtain returns equal to those that its capital can get elsewhere, and firms would leave the industry.

This analysis of entry is quite similar to the perfectly competitive case. Moreover, the notion that firms under monopolistic competition earn exactly zero economic profits seems to correspond fairly well to what we see in the real world. Gas station operators, whose markets fit the characteristics of monopolistic competition, do not earn notably higher profits than do small farmers, who operate under conditions closer to perfect competition.

The Excess Capacity Theorem and Resource Allocation

One economically significant difference arises between perfect and monopolistic competition. Look at Figure 2 again. The tangency point between the average cost and demand curves, point *P*, occurs along the *negatively sloping portion* of the average cost curve, because *P* is the only point where the AC curve has the same (negative) slope as the demand curve. If the AC curve is U-shaped, the tangency point must therefore lie above and to the left of the *minimum point* on the average cost curve, point *M*. In other words, under monopolistic competition, the demand curve hits the average cost curve in a region where average costs are still declining. Average costs have yet to reach their lowest point. By contrast, the perfectly competitive firm's demand curve is horizontal, so tangency must take place at the minimum point on the average cost curve. You can easily confirm this by referring back to Figure 9(a) in Chapter 10. This difference leads to the following important conclusion:

> **Under monopolistic competition in the long run, the firm will tend to produce an output lower than that which minimizes its unit costs, and hence unit costs of the monopolistic competitor will be higher than necessary. Because the level of output that corresponds to minimum average cost is naturally considered to be the firm's optimal capacity, this result has been called the *excess capacity theorem of monopolistic competition*. Thus, monopolistic competition tends to lead firms to have unused or wasted capacity.**

It follows that if every firm under monopolistic competition were to expand its output, cost per unit of output would be reduced. However, we must be careful about jumping to policy conclusions from that observation. It does *not* follow that *every* monopolistically competitive firm *should* produce more. After all, such an overall increase in industry output means that a smaller portion of the economy's resources will be available for other uses;

---

[3] EXERCISE: Show that if the demand curve fell still further, the firm would incur a loss. What would then happen in the long run?

from the information at hand, we have no way of knowing whether that choice leaves us better or worse off in terms of social benefits.

Even so, the situation depicted in Figure 2 probably represents a substantial *inefficiency*. Although it is not clear that society would gain if *every* firm were to achieve lower costs by expanding its production, society *can* save resources if firms combine into *a smaller number of larger companies* that produce the *same total output*. For example, suppose that in the situation shown in Figure 2, 15 monopolistically competitive firms each sell 10,000 gallons of gasoline per week. The total cost of this output, according to the figures given in the diagram, would be:

$$\text{Number of firms} \times \text{Output per firm} \times \text{Cost per unit} =$$
$$15 \times 10,000 \times \$2.85 = \$427,500$$

If, instead, the number of stations were cut to 10 and each sold 15,000 gallons, total production would be unchanged. But total costs would fall to $10 \times 15,000 \times \$2.70 = \$405,000$, a net saving of \$22,500 *without any cut in total output.*

This result does not depend on the particular numbers that we used in our illustration. It follows directly from the observation that lowering the cost per unit must always reduce the total cost of producing *any* given industry output. That is, producing a *given* output, Q, always must have a lower total cost when average cost is lower: Specifically, if $AC_1 < AC_2$, it must obviously *always* be true that $TC_1 = Q \times AC_1 < Q \times AC_2 = TC_2$. Society must gain in the sense of getting the same total output, Q, as before but at a lower total cost. After all, which do you prefer—a dozen cans of soda for \$0.70 each or the same dozen cans for \$0.55 each?

1ST PUZZLE RESOLVED: EXPLAINING THE ABUNDANCE OF RETAILERS

The excess capacity theorem explains one of the puzzles mentioned at the beginning of this chapter. The highway intersection with four gas stations, where two could serve the available customers with little increase in customer delays and at lower costs, is a real-world example of excess capacity.

The excess capacity theorem seems to imply that too many sellers participate in monopolistically competitive markets and that society would benefit from a reduction in their numbers. However, such a conclusion may be a bit hasty. Even if a smaller number of larger firms can reduce costs, society may not benefit from the change because it will leave consumers with a smaller range of choice. Because all products differ at least slightly under monopolistic competition, a reduction in the number of *firms* means that the number of different *products* falls as well. We achieve greater efficiency at the cost of greater standardization.

In some cases, consumers may agree that this trade-off represents a net gain, particularly if the variety of products available was initially so great that it only confused them. But for some products, most consumers would probably agree that the diversity of choice is worth the extra cost involved. After all, we would probably save money on clothing if every student were required to wear a uniform. But because the uniform is likely to be too hot for some students, too cool for other students, and aesthetically displeasing to almost everyone else, would the cost saving really be a net benefit?

"Why have we come? Because only Earth offers the rock-bottom prices and wide selection of men's, women's, and children's clothing in the styles and sizes we're looking for."

OLIGOPOLY

An **oligopoly** is a market dominated by a few sellers, at least several of which are large enough relative to the total market that they may be able to influence the market price.

In highly developed economies, it is not monopoly, but *oligopoly*, that is virtually synonymous with "big business." Any oligopolistic industry includes a group of giant firms, each of which keeps a watchful eye on the actions of the others. Under oligopoly, rivalry among firms takes its most direct and active form. Here one encounters such actions and reactions as frequent new-product introductions, free samples, and aggressive—if not downright nasty—advertising campaigns. A firm's price decision may elicit cries of pain from its rivals, and firms are often engaged in a continuing battle in which they plan strategies day by day and each major decision induces direct responses by rival firms.

Notice that the definition of oligopoly does not mention the degree of product differentiation. Some oligopolies sell products that are essentially identical (such as steel plate from different steel manufacturers), whereas others sell products that are quite different in consumers' eyes (for example, Chevrolets, Fords, and Hondas). Some oligopolistic industries also contain a considerable number of smaller firms (example: soft drink manufacturers), but they are nevertheless considered oligopolies because a few large firms carry out the bulk of the industry's business and smaller participants must follow their larger rivals' lead to survive at the margins of the industry. Oligopolistic firms often seek to create unique products—unique, at least, in consumers' perceptions. To the extent that an oligopolistic firm can create a unique product in terms of features, location, or appeal, it protects itself from the pressures of competition that will force down its prices and eat into its sales.

Managers of large, oligopolistic firms who have occasion to study economics are somewhat taken aback by the notion of perfect competition, because it is devoid of all harsh competitive activity as they know it. Recall that under perfect competition firm managers make no price decisions—they simply accept the price dictated by market forces and adjust their output accordingly. As we observed at the beginning of the chapter, a perfectly competitive firm does not advertise; it adopts no sales gimmicks; it does not even know most of its competitors. But because oligopolists have some degree of influence on market forces, they do not enjoy the luxury of such anonymity. They worry about prices, spend fortunes on advertising (see "The Mad Scramble to Differentiate the Product" on the next page), and try to understand or even predict their rivals' behavior patterns.

> An **oligopoly** is a market dominated by a few sellers, at least several of which are large enough relative to the total market to be able to influence the market price.

2ND PUZZLE RESOLVED: WHY OLIGOPOLISTS ADVERTISE BUT PERFECTLY COMPETITIVE FIRMS GENERALLY DO NOT

The two reasons for such divergent behavior should be clear, and they explain the puzzling fact that oligopolists advertise far more than the supposedly far more competitive firms in perfectly competitive markets. First, a perfectly competitive firm can sell all it wants at the current market price, so why should it waste money on advertising? By contrast, Ford Motor Company and Toyota cannot sell all the cars they want at the current price. Because they face negatively sloped (and thus less than perfectly elastic) demand curves, if they want to sell more, they must either reduce prices (to move along the demand curve toward greater quantities) or advertise more (to shift their demand curves outward).

Second, because the public believes that the products supplied by firms in a perfectly competitive industry are identical, if Firm A advertises its product, the advertisement is just as likely to bring customers to Firm B as to itself. Under oligopoly, however, consumer products are often *not* identical. Volkswagen advertises to convince consumers that its automobiles are better than Ford's or Toyota's. If the advertising campaign succeeds, Ford and Toyota will be hurt and probably will respond with more advertising of their own. Thus, the firms in an oligopoly with differentiated products *must* compete via advertising, whereas perfectly competitive firms gain little or nothing by doing so.

The Mad Scramble to Differentiate the Product

Competition is fierce in the world of business, and companies will go very far indeed to outdo their rivals. In the summer of 2000, Pizza Hut's advertising campaign was literally out of this world: The firm helped to bankroll Russia's space agency by putting a 10-meter-high, $1.25-million ad on a Proton booster rocket.

More recent advertising stunts include Snapple's 2005 attempt to erect a 25-foot-tall popsicle in Times Square (it melted in the June heat), a glass elevator decorated to look like a giant Oreo cookie dunking into a glass of milk, and deodorant-maker Right Guard's 2008 "pitvertising" campaign: London subway riders with miniature TV screens playing Right Guard commercials sewn into the armpits of their shirts.

SOURCES: "Marketing: Guerrillas in Our Midst," *The Economist*, October 14, 2000, p. 80; Gina Gayle, "Giant Popsicle Melts, Floods New York Park," *Associated Press*, June 22, 2005; and Stephanie Clifford, "Summer Silliness Brings a Pizza Field and a Giant Oreo," *The New York Times*, August 1, 2008.

SOURCE: Courtesy of Pizza Hut

Why Oligopolistic Behavior Is So Difficult to Analyze

Firms in an oligopolistic industry—in particular, the largest of those firms—have some latitude in choosing their product prices and outputs. Furthermore, to survive and thrive in an oligopolistic environment, firms must take direct account of their rivals' responses. Both of these features complicate the analysis of the oligopolistic firm's behavior and prevent us from drawing unambiguous conclusions about resource allocation under oligopoly. Oligopoly is much more difficult to analyze than other forms of economic organization, because oligopolistic decisions are, by their very nature, *interdependent*. Oligopolists *recognize* that the outcomes of their decisions depend on their rivals' responses. For example, Volkswagen managers know that their actions will probably lead to reactions by Ford, which in turn may require a readjustment of Volkswagen's plans, thereby modifying Ford's response, and so on. Where such a sequence of moves and countermoves may lead is difficult enough to ascertain, but the fact that Volkswagen executives recognize this possibility in advance, and may try to second-guess or predict Ford's reactions as they initially decide on a marketing tactic, makes even that first step difficult to analyze and almost impossible to predict.

Truly, almost anything can and sometimes does happen under oligopoly. The early railroad kings went so far as to employ gangs of hoodlums who fought pitched battles to try to squelch rival lines' operations. At the other extreme, oligopolistic firms have employed overt or covert forms of collusion to avoid rivalry altogether—to transform an oligopolistic industry, at least temporarily, into a monopolistic one. In other instances, oligopolistic firms seem to have arranged to live and let live, via price leadership (discussed later) or geographic allocations, dividing up customers by agreement among the firms.

A Shopping List

Because oligopolies in the real world are so diverse, oligopoly models in the theoretical world should also come in various shapes and sizes. An introductory course cannot hope to explain all of the many oligopoly models. This section offers a quick review of some oligopolistic behavior models. In the remainder of the chapter, we turn our attention to a particularly interesting set of models that use methods such as game theory to analyze oligopolistic firm behavior.

1. Ignoring Interdependence   One simple approach to the problem of oligopolistic interdependence is to assume that the oligopolists themselves ignore it—that they behave as if their actions will not elicit reactions from their rivals. Perhaps an oligopolist, finding the "If they think that we think that they think . . . " chain of reasoning too complex, will decide to ignore rivals' behavior. The firm may then just seek to maximize profits, assuming that its decisions will not affect its rivals' strategies. In this case, economists can analyze oligopoly in the same way they look at monopoly, which we described in Chapter 11. Probably no oligopolist totally ignores all of its major rivals' decisions, but many of them seem to do so as they make their more routine decisions, which are nevertheless often quite important.

2. Strategic Interaction   Although *some* oligopolists may ignore interdependence *some* of the time, models based on such behavior probably do not offer a general explanation for *most* oligopoly behavior *most* of the time. The reason is simple: Because they operate in the same market, the price and output decisions of soapsuds makers Brand X and Brand Y *really are* interdependent.

Suppose, for example, that Brand X, Inc., managers decide to cut their soapsuds' price from $1.12 to $1.05, on the assumption that rival Brand Y, Inc., will ignore this move and continue to charge $1.12 per box. Brand X decides to manufacture 5 million boxes per year and to spend $1 million per year on advertising. It may find itself surprised when Brand Y cuts its price to $1.00 per box, raises production to 8 million boxes per year, and sponsors the Super Bowl! In such a case, Brand X's profits will suffer, and the company will wish it had not cut its price in the first place. Most important for our purposes, Brand X managers will learn not to ignore interdependence in the future.

For many oligopolies, then, competition may resemble military operations involving tactics, strategies, moves, and countermoves. Thus, we must consider models that deal explicitly with oligopolistic interdependence.

3. Cartels   The opposite of ignoring interdependence occurs when all firms in an oligopoly try to do something about their interdependence and agree to set price and output, acting as a monopolist would. In a **cartel,** firms collude directly to coordinate their actions to transform the industry into a giant monopoly.

A **cartel** is a group of sellers of a product who have joined together to control its production, sales, and price in the hope of obtaining the advantages of monopoly.

A notable cartel is the Organization of Petroleum Exporting Countries (OPEC), which first began making joint decisions on oil production in the 1970s. For a while, OPEC was one of the most spectacularly successful cartels in history. By restricting output, its member nations managed to quadruple the price of oil between 1973 and 1974. Unlike most cartels, which come apart because of internal bickering or other reasons, OPEC held together through two worldwide recessions and a variety of unsettling political events. It struck again with huge price increases between 1979 and 1980. In the mid-1980s, its members began to act in ways that did not promote the interest of the entire industry and oil prices tumbled, but prices have since risen spectacularly and OPEC continues to dominate the world oil market. (See "OPEC Says Market Woes Cloud Output View" on the next page for more recent news of OPEC and oil prices.)

OPEC's early success is hardly the norm. Cartels are difficult to organize and even more difficult to enforce. Firms struggle to agree on such things as the amount by which each will reduce its output in order to help push up the price. For a cartel to survive, each member must agree to produce no more output than that assigned to it by the group. Yet once the cartel drives up the price and increases profitability, each member faces the temptation to offer secret discounts that lure some of the now very profitable business away from other members. When this happens, or even when members begin to suspect one another of doing so, the collusive agreement often begins to come apart. Each member begins suspecting the others and is tempted to cut its price first, before the others beat it to the punch.

For this reason, cartels usually adopt elaborate policing arrangements. In effect, they spy on each member firm to ensure that it does not sell more than it is supposed to or shave the price below that chosen by the cartel. This means that cartels are unlikely to succeed or to last very long if the firms sell many, varied products whose prices are difficult to compare and whose outputs are difficult to monitor. In addition, if firms frequently negotiate prices on a customer-by-customer basis and often offer special discounts to favored buyers, a cartel may be almost impossible to arrange.

Many economists consider cartels to be the worst form of market organization, in terms of efficiency and consumer welfare. A successful cartel may end up charging the monopoly price and obtaining monopoly profits. But because the firms do not actually combine operations, cartels offer the public no offsetting benefits in the form of economies of large-scale production. For these and other reasons, open collusion on prices and outputs among firms is illegal in the United States, as we will see in Chapter 13. Outright cartel arrangements rarely occur within the United States, although they are common in some other countries. Only one major exception occurs in the United States: Government regulations have sometimes forced industries such as railroads and gas pipeline transportation to behave as cartels. Regulations prohibited these firms from undercutting the prices set by the regulatory agencies—an exception that we will discuss in Chapter 13.

4. Price Leadership and Tacit Collusion   Overt collusion—in which firms actually meet or communicate directly in some other way to decide on prices and outputs—is quite rare, presumably because it is illegal and can result in large fines or other penalties. But some observers think that *tacit collusion*—where firms, without meeting together, try to do unto their competitors as they hope their competitors will do unto them—occurs quite commonly among oligopolists in our economy. Oligopolists who do not want to rock a very profitable boat may seek to find some indirect way of communicating with

OPEC Says Market Woes Cloud Output View

DUBAI, United Arab Emirates—Damping expectations that it will pump more crude to ease high prices, the Organization of Petroleum Exporting Countries said uncertainties over world economic growth were clouding the outlook for oil demand. The 12-member group, which pumps about 40% of the world's oil, said in its monthly market report that a "more bearish economic trend," partly triggered by the U.S. problems with subprime lending, may hurt demand growth in the second half. At this time, though, OPEC expects demand for its crude to rise to 31.14 million barrels a day in the third quarter, and to 31.32 million barrels a day in the fourth quarter, from 30.30 million barrels a day in the second quarter. OPEC expects daily demand for its crude to average under 30.8 million barrels next year, 239,000 barrels a day lower than the 31 million barrels a day forecast for this year. OPEC also said crude inventories are comfortable in the U.S. and for industrialized nations. . . . The International Energy Agency, which monitors oil markets on behalf of industrialized nations, has warned of rising prices if economic growth and oil demand continue to rise and if OPEC doesn't raise crude production.

SOURCE: © Bettmann/CORBIS

SOURCE: Excerpted from Oliver Klaus and Ayesha Daya, "OPEC Says Market Woes Cloud Output View," *The Wall Street Journal*, August 15, 2007, p. A4. Reprinted by permission of *The Wall Street Journal*. Copyright © 2007 Dow Jones & Company, Inc. All Rights Reserved Worldwide.

POLICY DEBATE

ACTING ON RECOGNIZED INTERDEPENDENCE VERSUS "TACIT COLLUSION"

Antitrust laws unequivocally prohibit price fixing—collusion among competitors in which they agree on their pricing policies (see Chapter 13). Suppose that the firms in an industry, recognizing their interdependence, simply decide to go along with each other's decisions? Is this collusion by long distance? Should it be declared illegal? Should the government require such a firm to "make believe" that it does not know how competitors will respond to its price moves? Must firms act as if they were not interdependent? If such requirements make no sense, what should the government require of oligopolistic firms?

The airline industry constantly illustrates this issue and its complexities. In 1992, American Airlines decided that the vast number of different airline fares and discounts hurt all airlines and that the industry needed a simplified fare structure. American offered a new, simplified pricing plan called "value pricing," in the hope that other airlines would copy that structure widely. A few weeks later, Northwest Airlines introduced a special vacation travel deal that undercut American's pricing. This led to a price war, and American had to withdraw its plan, losing considerable money in the process. In this case, American's rivals did not go along with a price leader's decision.

In a more recent set of events, matters worked out differently. The airlines, which have lost money for years, have been seeking ways to cut costs by reducing wages, firing employees, and so on. As oil prices rose in early 2008, these cost-cutting efforts proved insufficient, and airlines began imposing new surcharges and fees on their customers. In May of 2008, American Airlines was the first major carrier to announce that it would charge passengers for the first checked bag. This

SOURCE: © Peter Christopher/Masterfile

move was risky—if other airlines did not adopt similar surcharges, American could lose much of its business to competitors. But even before American's surcharge became effective, two other major airlines followed suit by announcing that they would adopt the same $15 fee for the first checked bag. By the end of 2008, seven major airlines in the United States had enacted similar fees. As of this writing, two of these airlines, Delta and AirTran, have been sued for this parallel conduct. That complaint alleges that Delta and AirTran colluded by explicitly coordinating the introduction of their new luggage fees. Presumably there is no evidence that the other airlines consulted one another before adopting identical surcharges.

---

one another, signaling their intentions and managing the market accordingly. Each tacitly colluding firm hopes that if it does not make things too difficult for its competitors, its rivals will return the favor. For example, three major makers of infant formula—Abbott Laboratories, Bristol-Myers Squibb, and American Home Products—were accused of conspiring against competitors by keeping their wholesale prices only a few cents apart. The formula makers denied any wrongdoing. (See "Acting on Recognized Interdependence versus 'Tacit Collusion'" above for another example.)

One common form of tacit collusion is **price leadership,** an arrangement in which one firm in the industry, in effect, makes pricing decisions for the entire group. Other firms are expected to adopt the prices set by the price leader, even though no explicit agreement exists—only tacit consent. Often, the price leader will be the largest firm in the industry. But in some price-leadership arrangements, the leadership role may rotate from one firm to another. For example, analysts suggested that for many years the steel industry conformed to the price-leadership model, with U.S. Steel and Bethlehem Steel assuming the leadership role at different times.

Price leadership *does* overcome some problems for the firms that result from oligopolistic interdependence, although it does not provide the only possible way of doing so. If Brand X, Inc. acts as price leader for the soapsuds industry, it can predict how Brand Y, Inc. will react to any price increases that it announces: Brand Y will match the increases. Similarly, Brand Z, Inc. executives will be able to predict Brand Y's behavior as long as the price-leadership arrangement holds up.

One problem besetting price leadership is that, although the oligopolists as an industry may benefit by avoiding a damaging **price war,** the *firms* may not benefit equally. The

Under **price leadership,** one firm sets the price for the industry and the others follow.

In a **price war,** each competing firm is determined to sell at a price that is lower than the prices of its rivals, often regardless of whether that price covers the pertinent cost. Typically, in such a price war, Firm A cuts its price below Firm B's price; B retaliates by undercutting A; and so on and on until some of the competitor firms surrender and let themselves be undersold.

price-leading firm may be able to enhance its own profits more easily than any of the other firms in the group can. But if the price leader does not consider its rivals' welfare as it makes price decisions, it may find itself dethroned! Like cartels, such arrangements can easily break down.

Sales Maximization: An Oligopoly Model with Interdependence Ignored

A firm's objective is said to be **sales maximization** if it seeks to adopt prices and output quantities that make its total revenue (the money value of its sales), rather than its profits, as large as possible.

Early in our analysis of the firm we discussed the profit-maximization hypothesis, and we noted that firms have other possible objectives. Among these alternative goals, one has attracted much attention: **sales maximization.**

Modern industrial firms are managed by people who are not the owners of the companies. Paid executives manage the firms, working for the company on a full-time basis. These managers may begin to believe that whatever is good for them as individuals must be good for the company. The owners may be a large and diverse group of stockholders, most of whom own only a tiny fraction of the outstanding stock. They may take little interest in the company's day-to-day operations and may feel no real sense of ownership. In such a situation, managers' goals may influence company decisions more strongly than the owners' goal of profit maximization.

Some statistical evidence, for example, suggests that management's compensation often relates more directly to company *size,* as measured by sales volume, than to *profit.* The president of a large firm generally fetches a much higher salary—and bigger incentive rewards—than the president of a tiny company. Therefore, firm managers may select price—output combinations that maximize *sales* rather than profits. But does sales maximization lead to different outcomes than profit maximization? We shall see shortly that the answer is yes.

The graph in Figure 3 should be familiar by now. It shows the marginal cost (MC) and average cost (AC) curves for a soapsuds firm—in this case Brand X, Inc.—along with its demand and marginal revenue (MR) curves. We have used such diagrams before and thus know that if the company wants to maximize profits, it will select point A, where MC = MR. Brand X will produce 2.5 million boxes of soapsuds per year and sell them at $1 each (point E on the demand curve above A). Because average cost at this level of output is only 80 cents per box, X earns 20 cents economic profit per unit. Total profits are therefore $0.20 \times 2,500,000 = $500,000$ per year. This is the highest attainable profit level for Brand X.

What if Brand X chooses to maximize total sales revenue instead? In this case, it will want to keep producing until MR falls to *zero;* that is, it will select point B. Why? By definition, MR is the *additional* revenue obtained by raising output by one unit. If the firm wishes to maximize total revenue, then whenever MR is positive, it will want to increase output further, and anytime that MR becomes negative, X's management will want to decrease output. Only when MR = 0 can management possibly have maximized total sales revenue.[4]

Thus, if Brand X is a sales maximizer, it will produce 3.75 million boxes of soapsuds per year (point B), and charge 75 cents per box (point F). Because average costs at this level of production are only 69 cents per box, profit per unit is 6 cents and, with 3.75 million units sold, total profit is $225,000. Naturally, this profit is substantially less than the $500,000 profit the firm can achieve if it reduces output to the profit-maximizing level. But that is not the goal of Brand X's management. The firm's sales revenue at point B is 75 cents per unit times 3.75 million units, or $2,812,500, whereas at point A it was only $2,500,000 (2.5 million units at $1.00 each). We conclude that

> **If a firm is maximizing sales revenue, it will produce more output and charge a lower price than it would if it were maximizing profits.**

---

[4] The logic here is exactly the same as the logic that led to the conclusion that a firm maximized profits by setting *marginal profit* equal to zero. If you need to review, consult Chapter 8, especially pages 163–165.

FIGURE 3

**Sales-Maximization
Equilibrium**

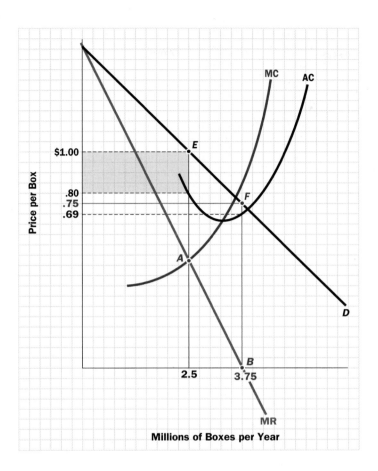

Figure 3 clearly shows that this result holds for Brand X, but does it always hold? The answer is yes. Look again at Figure 3, but ignore the numbers on the axes. At point *A*, where MR = MC, marginal revenue must be positive because it equals marginal cost (which, we may assume, is *always* positive—output can normally not be increased at zero additional cost). At point *B*, MR is equal to zero. Because the marginal revenue curve slopes negatively, the point where it reaches zero (point *B*) must necessarily correspond to a higher output level than does the point where it cuts the marginal cost curve (point *A*). Thus, sales-maximizing firms *always* produce more than profit-maximizing firms and, to sell this greater volume of output, they must charge lower prices.[5]

3RD PUZZLE RESOLVED: THE KINKED DEMAND CURVE MODEL[6]

Another oligopoly analysis model was designed to explain the alleged "stickiness" in oligopolistic pricing, meaning that prices in oligopolistic markets change far less frequently than do competitive market prices—one of the puzzling phenomena with which we began this chapter. The prices of corn, soybeans, pork bellies, and silver—all commodities that trade in markets with large numbers of buyers and sellers—change second by second. But

---

[5] EXERCISE: In the graph, how much below maximum profit is total profit under sales maximization?

[6] Variants of this model were constructed by Hall and Hitch in England and by Sweezy in the United States. See R. L. Hall and C. J. Hitch, "Price Theory and Business Behavior," *Oxford Economic Papers* 2 (May 1939), pp. 12–45; and P. M. Sweezy, "Demand under Conditions of Oligopoly," *Journal of Political Economy* 47 (August 1939), pp. 568–573.

products supplied by oligopolists, such as cars, televisions, and refrigerators, usually change prices only every few months or even more rarely. These products seem to resist frequent price changes, even in inflationary periods.

One reason for such "sticky" prices may be that when an oligopolist cuts its product's price, it can never predict how rival companies will react. One extreme possibility is that Firm Y will ignore Firm X's price cut; that is, Firm Y's price will not change. Alternatively, Firm Y may reduce its price, precisely matching that of Firm X. Accordingly, the model of oligopolistic behavior we discuss next uses two different demand curves. One curve represents the quantities a given oligopolistic firm can sell at different prices *if competitors match its price moves,* and the other demand curve represents what will happen if competitors stubbornly *stick to their initial price levels.*

Point *A* in Figure 4 represents our firm's initial price and output: 1,000 units at $8 each. Two demand curves, *DD* and *dd,* pass through point *A. DD* represents our company's demand if competitors keep their prices fixed, and *dd* indicates what happens when competitors match our firm's price changes.

Of the two, the *DD* curve is the more elastic (flatter with demand, more responsive to price changes), and a moment's thought indicates why this should be so. If our firm cuts its price from its initial level of $8 to, say, $7, and if competitors do not match this cut, we would expect our firm to get a large number of new customers—perhaps its quantity demanded will jump to 1,400 units. However, if its competitors respond by also reducing their prices, its quantity demanded will rise by less—perhaps only to 1,100 units (more inelastic demand curve *dd*). Similarly, when it raises its price, our firm may expect a larger customer flight to its rivals if those rivals fail to match its price increase, and this is indicated by the relative flatness (elasticity) of the curve *DD* in Figure 4, as compared to *dd,* the firm's demand curve when rivals do match our firm's price changes.

How does this relate to sticky oligopolistic prices? The economists who designed this model hypothesized that a typical oligopolistic firm has good reason to fear the worst. If Firm X lowers its prices its rivals will be forced to do the same, because otherwise X's price cut will steal away many of its competitors' customers. The inelastic demand curve, *dd* (that applies when competitors copy X's price cut), will therefore be the relevant curve if Firm X decides on a price *reduction* (points below and to the right of point *A*).

If, on the contrary, Firm X chooses to *increase* its price, management fears that its rivals will respond quite differently than they would to a price cut. The price-raising

The Kinked Demand Curve

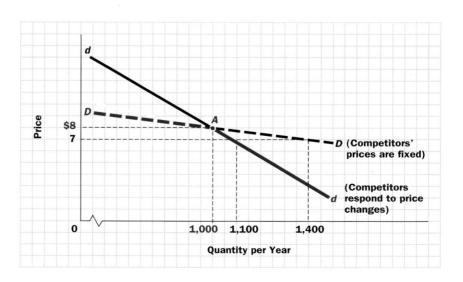

Firm X will fear that its rivals will continue to sit at their old price levels, calmly collecting customers as they flee from X's higher prices. Thus, this time, for price increases, the relevant demand curve (above *A*) will be *DD, not dd.*

In sum, our firm will figure that it will face a segment of the elastic demand curve *DD* if it raises its price and a segment of the inelastic demand curve *dd* if it decreases its price. Its true demand curve will then be given by the heavy brick-colored line, *DAd.* For obvious reasons, it is called a **kinked demand curve.**

The kinked demand curve represents a "heads you lose, tails you lose" proposition in terms of any potential price changes. If a firm raises its price, it will lose many customers (because in that case rivals will [may] not follow, so X's demand is elastic); if it lowers its price, the sales increase will be comparatively small (because then rivals can be expected to have to match the cut, so X's demand is inelastic). In these circumstances, neither a price cut nor a price rise seems beneficial, and management will vary its price only under extreme provocation—that is, only if its costs change enormously.

Figure 5 illustrates this conclusion graphically. The two demand curves, *DD* and *dd,* are carried over precisely from Figure 4. The dashed line labeled MR is the marginal revenue curve associated with *DD,* whereas the solid line labeled mr is the marginal revenue curve associated with *dd.* The marginal revenue curve relevant to the firm's decision making is MR for any output level below 1,000 units, but mr for any output level above 1,000 units. Therefore, the composite marginal revenue curve facing the firm is shown by the gold-highlighted line *DBC*mr with two slopes.

The marginal cost curve drawn in the diagram cuts this composite marginal revenue curve at point *E,* which indicates the profit-maximizing combination of output and price for this oligopolist. Specifically, the quantity supplied at point *E* is 1,000 units, and the price is $8, which we read from the brick-colored demand curve *DAd.*

The unique aspect of this diagram is that the kinked demand curve leads to a marginal revenue curve that takes a sharp plunge between points *B* and *C.* Consequently, even if the MC curve shifts moderately upward or downward, it will still intersect the marginal revenue curve somewhere between *B* and *C* and thus will *not* lead the firm to change its output decision. Therefore, *the firm's price will remain unchanged.* (Try this for yourself in Figure 5.) Oligopoly prices are **"sticky,"** then, in the sense that they do not respond to minor cost changes. Only cost changes large enough to push the MC curve out of the *BC* range will lead to price changes.

A **kinked demand curve** is a demand curve that changes its slope abruptly at some level of output.

A price is called **sticky** if it does not change often, even when there is a moderate change in cost.

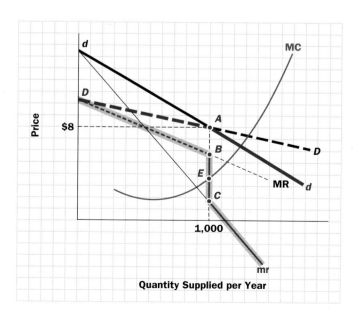

FIGURE 5

The Kinked Demand Curve and Sticky Prices

If this is, in fact, the way oligopolists view their competitors' behavior, we can easily see why they may be reluctant to make frequent price changes. We can also understand why price leadership may arise. The price-leader firm can raise prices at will, confident that the firm will not be left out on a limb (a kink?) by other firms' unwillingness to follow.

The Game Theory Approach

In 1944, the mathematician John von Neumann (1903–1957) and the economist Oskar Morgenstern (1902–1977) contributed a new approach to oligopoly analysis called *game theory*. Game theory is now economists' most widely used analysis of oligopoly behavior. The theory deals with the issue of interdependence directly, taking for granted that the managers of business firms make decisions on the assumption that rival managers are also strategic decision makers. In this model, each oligopolist acts as a competing player in a strategic game.

> A **payoff matrix** shows how much each of two competitors (players) can expect to earn, depending on the strategic choices each of them makes.

Game theory uses two fundamental concepts: *strategy* and the **payoff matrix.** A strategy represents a participant's operational plan. In its simplest form, it may refer to just one possible decision, such as "Add to my product line a new car model that features a DVD player for backseat passengers," or "Cut the price of my car to $19,500." The payoff matrix will be explained presently. For simplicity's sake, we will follow the frequent practice in discussions of game theory and focus on an oligopoly with just two firms—a *duopoly.*

An example will help to explain the analysis. Imagine that the market for telecommunications on a low-income Caribbean island is about to be entered by two cell phone service providers. Say that patent restrictions and other impediments mean that the two companies each have a choice between only one of two cell phones: (1) an expensive, high-tech phone that would have to be sold at a price that gives the seller a low profit margin or (2) a cheaper, low-tech phone with a high profit margin. Furthermore, under this island government's rules, each firm is required to offer the same phone and price for two years. Table 1 illustrates the resulting payoff matrix for one of the two players in this game, Firm A.

This matrix shows how the profits that Firm A can expect to earn depend on the strategy that its sole rival, Firm B, adopts. The choice open to each firm is to select one of the two available strategies—either the "low-tech, high-markup" cell phone or the "high-tech, low-markup" cell phone—without knowing the strategy that the other will choose. The matrix is read like a mileage chart. It shows, for example, that if Firm A chooses the high-tech option (second row of the matrix) and Firm B selects the low-tech option (left-hand column), then A will earn $12 million (lower left-hand square). It also shows the profit payoff to Firm A when it or its rival makes different choices between the two strategies that each firm has available.

TABLE 1

Firm A's Payoff Matrix in a Game with a Dominant Strategy

		Firm B Strategy	
		Low-tech	High-tech
Firm A Strategy	Low-tech	$10m	$–2m
	High-tech	$12m	$3m

Games with Dominant Strategies

> A **dominant strategy** for one of the competitors in a game is a strategy that will yield a higher payoff than any of the other strategies that are possible, no matter what choice of strategy is made by competitors.

How does game theory analyze Firm A's optimal strategic choice? There are a number of related methods. The most direct way is to search for what is called a **dominant strategy,** though, as we will see, it is possible that no such strategy may be available to one or both of the firms. A dominant strategy is defined as one that gives the bigger payoff to the firm that selects it, *no matter which of the two strategies the competitor happens to choose.* As we just said, not all games have such a dominant strategy, but the one illustrated in Table 1 does. Let us see how we know this.

Consider Firm A's decision. Either company can select either the high-tech or the low-tech strategy. Whichever choice B makes, there are two possible profit outcomes for A depending on which strategy it selects. For example, if B selects low-tech, A will either earn $10 million or $12 million, depending on its strategy choice (see the left-hand column of Table 1). So the high-tech strategy, with its $12 million payoff, is clearly A's better decision if B selects low-tech. But what if B turns out to pick high-tech, instead? In that case, we see from the right-hand column of the matrix that if A offers the low-tech product, it will lose $2 million, whereas with that same choice by firm B, A could earn $3 million in profit by choosing high-tech (the lower right-hand entry). So high-tech is again the better choice for A. Clearly, the high-tech option is a *dominant strategy* for firm A, because it will give A a higher profit than the low-tech choice *no matter which option firm B selects.*

Now let us expand the payoff matrix to show simultaneously the earnings of both firms—not, as before, only those of Firm A. In Table 2, this combined payoff matrix reports the profits that each firm can expect to earn, given its own pricing choice and that of its rival. For example, the upper-left square indicates that if both firms decide to offer the low-tech, high-markup model, both A and B will earn $10 million. We also see that if one firm brings in the high-tech model, whereas the other does not, the high-tech supplier will actually raise its profit to $12 million (presumably by capturing more sales) and drive its rival to a $2 million loss. However, if both firms offer the high-tech model, each will be left with a modest $3 million profit.

EXERCISE: Use the same reasoning as above to show that high-tech is also the dominant strategy for Firm B.

Because both firms have a dominant strategy in this example, and it is the same for both, they can both be expected to select it. Each will therefore end up offering the high-tech cell phone, and each will earn $3 million per year.

This example has important implications for policy, because it shows just how competition can force business firms to behave in the way that most benefits consumers, even though it is not the most profitable for the firms. In this example, both firms would have profited most by offering the lower-quality, higher-markup equipment. If they had both chosen the low-tech strategy, they would each have earned $10 million, but at the consumers' expense. However, the presence of a competitor, with its unknown choice, forces each firm to protect itself by choosing the dominant strategy, offering the better (high-tech) product, even though they end up each earning only $3 million. Of course, if the market had been served by a profit-maximizing monopolist, the lone firm would have selected the more profitable low-tech option, and the public would have been denied the better-quality product.

The Moral of the Story: A market that is a *duopoly*, that is, a two-firm oligopoly, may serve the public interest better than a monopoly because of the competition between the two duopolists.

Notice that each firm's fear of what its rival will do virtually forces it to offer the high-tech product and to forgo the higher ($10 million) profit that it could earn if it could trust the other to stick to a lower-quality product. This example illustrates why many observers conclude that, particularly where the number of firms is small, companies should not be permitted to confer or exchange information on prices or product quality. If the two rivals were allowed to collude and act like a monopolist, consumers would be damaged in two ways: They would have to pay more in order to provide the resulting additional profits and, besides, as usually is expected to happen under a monopoly, consumers would get smaller quantities of the products, which may be of lower quality.

Games whose payoff matrices have dominant strategies like that in Table 2 have many other interesting applications. They illustrate how people can get trapped into making both themselves and their rivals worse off. For example, a matrix with the same pattern of payoffs applies to people driving polluting cars in the absence of laws requiring emission

TABLE 2

The Two-Firm Payoff Matrix in a Game with Dominant Strategies

		Firm B Strategy	
		Low-tech	High-tech
Firm A Strategy	Low-tech	A gets $10m B gets $10m	A gets $–2m B gets $12m
	High-tech	A gets $12m B gets $–2m	A gets $3m B gets $3m

controls. Each driver runs a polluting auto because she does not trust other drivers to install emission controls voluntarily. So if she alone goes to the expense of equipping her car with pollution controls, most of the pollution—that from all other cars—will remain in the air. She will have paid for the equipment but have gotten little or no cleaner air benefit. So they all end up with a low payoff (breathing polluted air), even though by getting together and all agreeing to do what is needed to cut emissions, they could all end up with a higher payoff in terms of better health, etc.[7]

Still another interpretation explains why the game in Table 2 is known as the prisoners' dilemma. Instead of a two-firm industry, the prisoners' dilemma involves two burglary suspects who are captured by the police and interrogated in separate rooms. Each suspect has two strategy options: to deny the charge or to confess. If both deny it, both go free, because the police have no other evidence. But if one confesses and the other does not, the silent prisoner can expect the key to his cell to be thrown away while the talker gets off with a light sentence. The dominant solution for each prisoner, then, is to confess and receive the light sentence that results from this choice.

The prisoners' dilemma story confirms the important economic point we made earlier. The reason the two prisoners are both driven to confess, and to bring themselves to justice, is that they are not allowed to communicate and so they do not trust one another. Otherwise, they would collude and promise each other not to confess. The same thing applies to a duopoly. The public interest requires that the duopolists be banned from colluding. If they were permitted to get together and agree on a high price and low-cost, low-quality products, they would earn monopoly profits and the public would suffer the consequences.

The Moral of the Story: It is damaging to the public interest to permit rival firms to collude and to make joint decisions on what prices to charge for their similar products and what quality of product to supply.

Games without Dominant Strategies

We have already observed that games need not offer dominant strategies. An example is easy to provide. For simplicity, Table 3 again shows only the payoffs for Firm A, but this time the hypothetical payoff numbers are different from those in Table 1.

With these new numbers, neither a low-tech nor a high-tech choice is a dominant strategy for A. Suppose A chooses to go with the low-tech product. Then, if B also happens to select low-tech, A will find itself better off (at a $10 million payoff) than if it had chosen a high-tech product (profit = $3 million). But if B goes the other way and offers the high-tech product, A's payoff will be worse ($7 million) with a low-tech product than with one that is high-tech ($8 million payoff). Which of the two options is better for A depends on B's unforeseeable strategy choice. Neither choice by A offers it foolproof protection, so neither of A's possible strategies is dominant.

The decision for A in Table 3 is now much harder than it was before. How can it go about selecting a strategy? One solution proposed in game theory is called the **maximin criterion.** In this strategy, we may envision the management of Firm A reasoning as follows: "If I choose a low-tech strategy, the worst that can happen to me is that my competitor will select the high-tech counterstrategy, which will make my return $7 million (the brick-colored number in the first row of the payoff matrix). Similarly, if I select a high-tech strategy, the worst possible outcome for me is a $3 million profit" (the brick-colored minimum payoff in the second row of the matrix). How can the

The **maximin criterion** requires a player to select the strategy that yields the maximum payoff on the assumption that the opponent will do as much damage as it can.

TABLE 3

Firm A's Payoff Matrix in a Game without a Dominant Strategy

		Firm B Strategy	
		Low-tech	High-tech
Firm A Strategy	Low-tech	$10m	$7m
	High-tech	$3m	$8m

---

[7] EXERCISE: Make up a payoff matrix that tells this story.

managers of Firm A best protect their company from trouble in these circumstances? Game theory suggests that it may be rational to select a strategy based on comparison of the two *minimum* payoffs offered by the two different strategies. If the firm's managers want to cut down the risk, they should pick what can be interpreted as an insurance-policy approach. They should select the strategy that will guarantee them the *highest* of these undesirable minimum payoffs. In other words, expecting the worst outcome for any strategy choice it makes, Firm A should pick the strategy that promises the best of those bad outcomes. In this case, the maximin strategy for Firm A is to offer the low-tech product, whose worst possible outcome is $7 million, whereas the worst outcome if it selects the high-tech product is a profit of only $3 million.

Other Strategies: The Nash Equilibrium

We can interpret the maximin strategy as a pessimist's way to deal with uncertainty. A player who adopts this strategy assumes that the worst will always happen: No matter what move she makes, her opponent will adopt the countermove that does her the most damage. The maximin strategy neglects the possibility that opponents will not have enough information to find out the most damaging countermove. It also ignores the possibility of finding common ground, as when two competitors collude to extract monopoly profit from consumers.

Other strategies are less pessimistic, yet still rational. One of the most analytically useful strategies leads to what is called a **Nash equilibrium.** The mathematician John Nash devised this strategy, for which he won the Nobel Prize in economics in 1994 (after a long period of schizophrenia).[8] The basic idea is simple. In a two-player game, suppose that each firm is trying to decide whether to adopt a blue or a red package for its product. Assume that each firm earns a higher profit if it selects a package color that differs from the other's. Then, if Firm X happens to select a red package, it will obviously be most profitable for Y to select a blue package. Moreover, it will pay each firm to stick with that choice, because blue is Y's most profitable response to X's choice of red, and vice versa.

In general, a Nash equilibrium describes a situation in which both players adopt moves such that each player's move is the most profitable response to the other player's move. Often, no such mutually accommodating solution is possible, but where it is possible, if both players realize this fact and act accordingly, they may both be able to benefit. For example, note how much worse off both firms would be in the preceding example if Firm Y were determined to damage Firm X, at whatever the cost to itself, and adopted a red package, just like X's.

Zero-Sum Games

There is a special but significant situation involving a simple form of payoff matrix that has even been taken up in popular parlance. It is called a **zero-sum game.** The idea is a simple one and is a useful way to think about many issues. A zero-sum game is one in which whatever one player gains, the other must lose. Thus, when one adds up all the gains and losses, the sum is always zero. If I pick your pocket and find $80 in cash, you are $80 poorer and I am $80 richer, so that the sum of the positive gains and negative losses is clearly zero. But if the money was in a wallet with your driver's license and credit cards, and I take the money out and then throw the wallet into a river, it is evidently not zero-sum. You have lost not only the money but also the time and cost of replacing the license and credit cards, whereas I have gained only the money. The payoff matrix of a zero-sum game has a very simple structure. Table 4 provides an example:

A **Nash equilibrium** results when each player adopts the strategy that gives the highest possible payoff if the rival sticks to the strategy it has chosen.

A **zero-sum game** is one in which exactly the amount one competitor gains must be lost by other competitors.

TABLE 4

Zero-Sum Payoff Matrix

		Firm B Strategy	
		Strategy 1	**Strategy 2**
Firm A Strategy	**Strategy 1**	A gets $10m B gets 0	A gets $–2m B gets $12m
	Strategy 2	A gets $4m B gets $6m	A gets $7m B gets $3m

---

[8] As described in the 2001 movie *A Beautiful Mind,* which was based on the book by Sylvia Nasar.

The special feature of this matrix is that the payoffs of the two firms add up to $10 million in each and every payoff square. For example, in the lower left-hand square of Table 4, Firm A's payoff is $4 million and Firm B's payoff is $6 million, for a total of $10 million. You can verify that the sum of the two payoffs is $10 million in each of the other three cells, as well. So if A gains by a strategy change, this must occur, to the penny, at B's expense. If A gains $734, B must lose exactly $734.

The following example will bring out the importance of understanding the zero-sum case as a way to avoid fallacious analysis. It was once thought that international trade was a zero-sum game, because it was believed that each trading nation's objective was to get as much gold as possible from other countries in payment for their purchases. If Brazil ships coffee to France, and the French shippers pay 10,000 ounces of gold for the shipment, then on this view of the matter, Brazil has gained and France has lost exactly the same amount—making it a zero-sum transaction. But a little thought tells us that this view is naïve, because it leaves the coffee shipment itself out of the calculation. Trade is not just about money but also about the goods and services that are traded. If France is too cold to grow good coffee, and Brazil is too hot to produce good wine, and the populations of both countries prefer coffee in the morning and wine in the evening, then it is clear that both will be better off as the result of an exchange of wine for coffee. The game of international trade is far from zero-sum. This is something that must be kept in mind when we consider contentious trade-related issues such as globalization and outsourcing, which will be discussed in Chapter 34.

Repeated Games

The scenarios described so far involve one-time transactions, as when a tourist passes through a city and makes a purchase at a store that he will never visit again. Most business transactions are different. A firm usually sells its products day after day, often to repeat buyers. It must continuously review its pricing decisions, knowing that its rivals are likely to gain information from any repeated behavioral patterns and adapt their response. The important concept of repeated games also offers significant additional insights about the competitive process under oligopoly.

A **repeated game** is one that is played a number of times.

Repeated games give all of the players the opportunity to learn something about each other's behavior patterns and, perhaps, to arrive at mutually beneficial arrangements. By adopting a fairly clear pricing behavior pattern, each firm can attain a reputation that elicits desired responses from competitors.

We return to the example of the product introduction war between Firm A and Firm B to show how this approach works. When we studied the payoff matrix for that game, we assumed that in a single play in which neither player knew anything about the other's behavior pattern, each player was likely to feel forced to adopt its dominant strategy. In other words, each firm offered the low-profit, high-tech product for fear that if it adopted the potentially more profitable low-tech product, its rival would adopt a high-tech product and take customers away. In that way, both firms would end up with low profits.

When games are repeated, the players may be able to escape such a trap. For example, Firm A can cultivate a reputation for selecting a strategy called "*tit for tat.*" Each time Firm B chooses a high-tech product, Firm A responds by also introducing a high-tech product next time, with its limited profit. Firm A also follows a similar repeating strategy if B's product choice is low-tech. After a few repetitions, B will learn that A always matches its decisions. B will then see that it is better off sticking to a more profitable low-tech product. Firm A, too, benefits from its tit-for-tat approach, which will lead both, eventually, to stick permanently to the more profitable low-tech products.

In practice, this amounts to tacit collusion. The two competing firms never actually get together to reach a joint decision on product price and quality, behavior that is illegal. But they watch one another's behavior in their repeated game, and each eventually learns to adapt itself and go along with the other's behavior—which may be anticompetitive and damaging to consumer interests but offers monopoly profits to the tacit colluders. The courts do not have a clear response to this behavior, because it is difficult to argue that firms should not consider all publicly and legitimately available information about its rivals, or that firms should not take this observed rival behavior into consideration when they make their own decisions.

Threats and Credibility   A player can also use *threats* to induce rivals to change their behavior. The trouble is that, if carried out, the threat may well damage both parties. For example, a retailer can threaten to double its output and drive prices down near zero if a rival imitates its product. However, the rival is unlikely to believe the threat, because such a low price harms the threatener as much as the threatened. Such a threat is simply not *credible*, with one exception.

The possibility can become a **credible threat** if the threatener takes steps that commit it to carry out the action. For example, if Firm A signed an irrevocable contract committing it to double its output if Firm B copied A's product, then the threat would become credible, and B would be forced to believe it. But A can make other commitments that make its threat credible. For example, it can build a large plant with plenty of excess capacity. The factory may be very expensive to build, but once built, that cost is irrevocable. If there is only a small *additional* cost of raw material and labor needed to turn out the product, once the cost of the plant has already been paid, then it may not harm A to expand its output of the product, even at a competitor's very low price (if that price exceeds the marginal [variable] cost of the item). So, having built the large factory, the threat to expand output in response to entry becomes credible.

This last possibility leads directly to an important application of game theory: how firms inside an industry ("the old firms") can decide strategically on ways to prevent *new* firms from entering into the industry. To create a credible threat to potential entrants, we see that the old firm may well consider building a bigger factory than it would otherwise want.

Some hypothetical numbers and a typical game theory graph will make the story clear. The old firm faces two options: to build a small factory or a big one. Potential entrant firms also face two options: open for business (that is, enter the industry) or do not enter. Figure 6 shows the four resulting possible decision combinations and the corresponding profits or losses that the two firms may expect in each case.

> A **credible threat** is a threat that does not harm the threatener if it is carried out.

FIGURE 6
Entry and Entry-Blocking Strategy

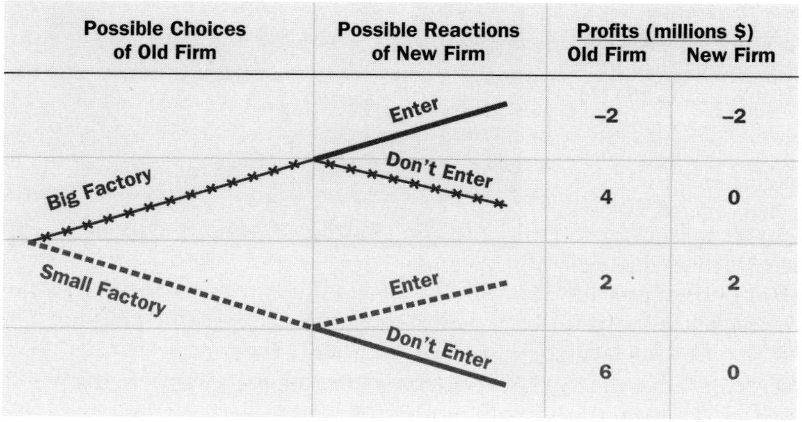

Possible Choices of Old Firm	Possible Reactions of New Firm	Profits (millions $) Old Firm	New Firm
Big Factory	Enter	−2	−2
	Don't Enter	4	0
Small Factory	Enter	2	2
	Don't Enter	6	0

The graph shows that the best outcome for the old firm occurs when it builds a small factory and the new firm decides not to enter. In that case, the old firm will earn $6 million, whereas the new firm will earn nothing, because it never starts up.

However, if the old firm *does* decide to build a small factory, it can be fairly sure that the new firm *will* open up for business, because the new firm can then earn $2 million (rather than zero), as shown by the dashed lines. In the process, the old firm's profit will be reduced, also to $2 million.

If the old firm builds a big factory, its increased output will depress prices and profits. The old firm will now earn only $4 million if the new firm stays out, as shown by the asterisk line, whereas *each* firm will *lose* $2 million if the new firm enters. Obviously, if the old firm builds a big factory, the new firm will be better off staying out of the business rather than subjecting itself to a $2 million loss.

What size factory, then, should the old firm build? When we consider the firms' interactions, to protect itself the old firm must clearly build the large factory with its excess capacity—because this decision will keep the new firm out of the industry, leaving the old firm with a $4 million profit. The moral of the story: "Wasting" money on excess capacity may not be wasteful to the oligopolist firm if it protects the firm's long-term interest.

Of course, game theory is a much richer topic than we have explained here. For example, game theory also provides tools for economists and business managers to analyze coalitions that include groups of firms. It indicates, for cases involving more than two firms, which firms would do well to align themselves together against others. People other than economists also have used game theory to analyze a variety of complicated problems outside the realm of oligopoly theory. Management training programs employ its principles, as do a number of government agencies (see "Application: Game Theory and FCC Auctions" below). Political scientists and military strategists use game theory to formulate and analyze strategy.

Application: Game Theory and FCC Auctions

Since 1994, the Federal Communications Commission (FCC) has conducted competitive bidding auctions of licenses to parts of the electromagnetic spectrum used for such communications services as cell phones and pagers. The FCC used game theory when it designed the online auctions of these so-called *rights to the airways,* and the bidding companies must figure out for themselves how much to offer for the right to service a particular region.

The FCC might simply have decided to price the licenses for the various available regions itself. By conducting auctions, it places the decision-making onus on the bidding companies and their hired game-theorist consultants. The FCC prohibits collusion by the bidders, so each one must decide which sectors it can serve most efficiently, and each must anticipate its competitors' most likely moves and countermoves. The FCC runs these national online auctions continuously. For example, one recent auction offered licenses in the Automated Maritime Telecommunications System (AMTS) spectrum. AMTS is a specialized system of coast stations that provide integrated and interconnected marine voice and data communications, somewhat like a cellular phone system, for tugs, barges, and other vessels on the waterways. The auction raised a total of $1,057,365 from four winning bidders for 10 licenses.

SOURCE: © Paul A. Souders/CORBIS

SOURCE: U.S. Federal Communications Commission, http://www.fcc.gov.

MONOPOLISTIC COMPETITION, OLIGOPOLY, AND PUBLIC WELFARE

How well or poorly do monopolistically competitive or oligopolistic firms perform, from the viewpoint of the general welfare?

We have seen that their performance *can* leave much to be desired. For example, the excess capacity theorem showed us that monopolistic competition can lead to inefficiently high production costs. Similarly, because market forces may not sufficiently restrain their behavior, oligopolists' prices and outputs may differ substantially from socially optimal levels. In particular, when oligopolists organize themselves into a successful cartel, prices will be higher and outputs lower than those associated with their perfectly competitive counterparts. Moreover, some people believe that misleading advertising by corporate giants often distorts consumers' judgments, leading them to buy things they do not need and would otherwise not want. Many social critics feel that such corporate giants wield political power, economic power, and power over the minds of consumers—power that undermines the benefits of Adam Smith's invisible hand.

Because oligopoly behavior varies so widely, the social welfare implications differ from case to case. Some recent economic analysis, however, provides one theoretical case in which oligopolistic behavior and performance quality can be predicted and judged unambiguously.[9] The analysis also can serve as a model for government agencies that are charged with the task of preventing harmful anticompetitive behavior by oligopolistic firms. In this theoretical case, called a **perfectly contestable** market, entry into or exit from the market is costless and unimpeded. Here, the constant threat of the possible entry by new firms forces even the largest existing firm to behave well—to produce efficiently and never overcharge. Otherwise, the firm will be threatened with replacement by an entrant that offers to serve customers more cheaply and efficiently.

> A market is **perfectly contestable** if entry and exit are costless and unimpeded.

We define a market as perfectly contestable if firms can enter it and, if they choose, exit it without losing the money they invested. The crucial issue here is not the amount of capital required to enter the industry, but whether an entrant can withdraw the investment if it wishes. For example, if market entry requires investing in highly *mobile* capital (such as airplanes, trucks, or river barges, which can be moved around easily), the entrant may be able to exit quickly and cheaply.[10] For instance, if a barge operation decides to serve the lower Mississippi River but finds business disappointing, it can easily transfer its boats to, say, the Ohio River.

A profitable market that is also contestable therefore attracts *potential* entrants. Because no barriers to entry or exit exist, firms incur little risk by going into such a market. If their entry turns out to have been a mistake, they can move to another market without loss.

Because perfect competition requires a large number of firms, all of them small relative to the size of the industry, no industry with economies of large-scale production can be perfectly competitive. However, markets that contain a few relatively large firms may be highly contestable, although they are certainly not perfectly competitive. But no real-world industry is *perfectly* contestable, just as no industry is perfectly competitive.

The constant threat of entry forces oligopolists to perform well. Even monopolists must perform well if they do business in a highly contestable market. In particular, perfectly contestable markets have at least two socially desirable characteristics. First, the freedom of entry eliminates any excess economic profits, so in this respect contestable markets

---

[9] See William J. Baumol, John C. Panzar, and Robert D. Willig, *Contestable Markets and the Theory of Industry Structure*, rev. ed. (San Diego: Harcourt Brace Jovanovich, 1988).

[10] Earlier it was thought that air transportation could be classified as a highly contestable industry, but recent evidence suggests that although this judgment may be correct, the story is more complicated than it may initially seem.

resemble perfectly competitive markets. For example, if the current opportunity cost of capital is 12 percent, whereas the firms in a contestable market are earning a return of 18 percent, then new firms will enter the market, expand the industry's outputs, and drive down the prices of its products to the point at which no firm earns any excess profit. To avoid this outcome, established firms must expand output to a level that precludes excess profit. Second, inefficient enterprises cannot survive in a perfectly contestable industry because cost inefficiencies invite replacement of the existing firms by entrants that can provide the same outputs at lower cost and lower prices. Only firms operating at the lowest possible cost can survive. In sum, firms in a perfectly contestable market will be forced to operate as efficiently as possible and to charge prices as low as long-run financial survival permits.

The theory of contestable markets has been widely used by courts and government agencies concerned with the performance of business firms and provides workable guidelines for improved or acceptable behavior in industries in which economies of scale mean that only a small number of firms can or should operate.

A GLANCE BACKWARD: COMPARING THE FOUR MARKET FORMS

We have now completed the set of chapters that has taken us through the four main market forms: perfect competition, monopoly, monopolistic competition, and oligopoly. We hope you have absorbed a lot of information about the workings of these market forms as you read through Chapters 10 through 12, but the large quantity of detail is likely to be confusing. Table 5 presents an overview of the main attributes of each of the market forms to facilitate comparison. It shows that

- Perfect competition and pure monopoly are concepts useful primarily for *analytical* purposes—we find neither very often in reality. There are many monopolistically competitive firms, and oligopolistic firms account for the largest share of the economy's output.
- Profits are zero in long-run equilibrium under perfect competition and monopolistic competition because entry is so easy that high profits attract new rivals into the market.

TABLE 5

Attributes of the Four Market Forms

Market Form	Number of Firms in the Market	Frequency in Reality	Entry Barriers	Public Interest Results	Long-Run Profit	Equilibrium Conditions
Perfect competition	Very many	Rare (if any)	None	Good	Zero	MC = MR = AC = AR = P
Pure monopoly	One	Rare	Likely to be high	Outputs not optimal	May be high	MR = MC
Monopolistic competition	Many	Widespread	Minor	Inefficient	Zero	MR = MC AR = AC
Oligopoly	Few	Produces large share of GDP	Varies	Varies	Varies	Varies

- Consequently, AC = AR in long-run equilibrium under these two market forms. In equilibrium, MC = MR for the profit-maximizing firm under any market form. However, under oligopoly, firms may adopt the strategies described by game theory or they may pursue goals other than profits; for example, they may seek to maximize sales. Therefore, in the equilibrium of the oligopoly firm, MC may be unequal to MR.

- As we will confirm in Chapter 14, the behavior of the perfectly competitive firm and industry theoretically leads to an efficient allocation of resources that maximizes the benefits to consumers, given the resources available to the economy. Monopoly, however, can misallocate resources by restricting output in an attempt to raise prices and profits. Under monopolistic competition, excess capacity and inefficiency are apt to result. And under oligopoly, almost anything can happen, so it is impossible to generalize about its vices or virtues. As will be discussed in Chapter 16, some analysts believe oligopolists have made a significant contribution to the economic growth of the past two centuries that has brought a spectacular increase in average incomes in the world's wealthier countries.

| SUMMARY |

1. Under **monopolistic competition**, there are numerous small buyers and sellers; each firm's product is at least somewhat different from every other firm's product—that is, each firm has a partial "monopoly" over some product characteristics, and thus a downward-sloping demand curve; there is freedom of entry and exit; and all relevant information is known to the sellers and buyers.

2. In long-run equilibrium under monopolistic competition, free entry eliminates economic profits by forcing the firm's downward-sloping demand curve into a position of tangency with its average cost curve. Therefore, output will be below the point at which average cost is lowest. As a result, monopolistic competitors are said to have **excess capacity**.

3. An oligopolistic industry is composed of a few large firms selling similar products in the same market.

4. Under **oligopoly**, each firm carefully watches the major decisions of its rivals and often plans counterstrategies. As a result, rivalry is often vigorous and direct, and the outcome is difficult to predict.

5. One model of oligopoly behavior assumes that oligopolists ignore interdependence and simply maximize profits or sales. Another model assumes that they join together to form a **cartel** and thus act like a monopoly. A third possibility is **price leadership,** where one firm sets prices and the others follow suit.

6. A firm that maximizes sales will continue producing up to the point where marginal revenue is driven down to zero. Consequently, a **sales maximizer** will produce more than a profit maximizer and will charge a lower price.

7. If a firm thinks that its rivals will match any price cut but fail to match any price increase, its demand curve becomes "kinked" and its price will be sticky—in other words, price will be adjusted less frequently than would be true under either perfect competition or pure monopoly.

8. **Game theory** provides new tools for the analysis of business strategies under conditions of oligopoly.

9. A **payoff matrix** shows how much each of two competitors (players) can expect to earn, depending on the strategic choices each of them makes. It is used to analyze the reasoning that applies and the possible outcomes when the payoff to any oligopolist depends on what the other oligopolists in the market will do, so that they are all interdependent.

10. A **dominant strategy** for one of the competitors in a game is a strategy that will yield a higher payoff than any of the other strategies that are possible, no matter what choice of strategy is made by competitors. So selection of a dominant strategy, where it is possible, is a good way for a competitor to avoid risk.

11. In a **maximin** strategy, the player takes the strongest possible precautions against the worst possible outcome of any move it selects.

12. In a **Nash equilibrium**, each player adopts the move that yields the highest possible payoff to itself, given the move selected by the other player.

13. A **zero-sum** game is one in which exactly the amount one competitor gains must be lost by other competitors. The zero-sum game is a useful analytic concept, although rare in the real world.

14. In **repeated games,** a firm can seek to acquire a reputation that induces the other player to make decisions that do not damage its interests. It may also promote its goals by means of **credible threats.**

15. Monopolistic competition and oligopoly can be harmful to the general welfare, but because behavior varies widely, the implications for social welfare also vary from case to case.

| KEY TERMS |

cartel   243

credible threat   255

dominant strategy   250

kinked demand curve   249

maximin criterion   252

monopolistic competition   237

Nash equilibrium   253

oligopoly   241

payoff matrix   250

perfectly contestable market   257

price leadership   245

price war   245

repeated game   254

sales maximization   246

sticky price   249

zero-sum game   253

| TEST YOURSELF |

1. Using game theory, set up a payoff matrix similar to one that Volkswagen's management might employ in analyzing the problem presented in Discussion Question 5.

2. Test Yourself Question 4 at the end of Chapter 11 presented cost and demand data for a monopolist and asked you to find the profit-maximizing solution. Use these same data to find the sales-maximizing solution. In terms of the firm's MR, explain why the answers are different.

3. In the payoff matrix in Table 2, which is Firm B's dominant strategy? Show the calculation that leads to that conclusion.

4. You are given a payoff matrix for a *zero-sum* game. You see that for one pair of strategy choices by the two firms, A's payoff is 9 and B's payoff is 6. For a second set of strategy choices, A's payoff is 7. What is B's payoff?

| DISCUSSION QUESTIONS |

1. How many real industries can you name that are oligopolies? How many operate under monopolistic competition? Perfect competition? Which of these is most difficult to find in reality? Why do you think this is so?

2. Consider some of the products that are widely advertised on television. By what kind of firm is each produced—a perfectly competitive firm, an oligopolistic firm, or another type of firm? How many major products can you think of that are *not* advertised on TV?

3. In what ways may the small retail sellers of the following products differentiate their goods from those of their rivals to make themselves monopolistic competitors: hamburgers, radios, cosmetics?

4. Pricing of securities on the stock market is said to be carried out under conditions in many respects similar to perfect competition. The auto industry is an oligopoly. How often do you think the price of a share of Ford Motor Company's common stock changes? How about the price of a Ford Explorer? How would you explain the difference?

5. Suppose that Volkswagen hires a popular singer to advertise its compact automobiles. The campaign is very successful, and the company increases its share of the compact-car market substantially. What is Ford likely to do?

6. A new entrant, Bargain Airways, cuts air fares between Eastwich and Westwich by 20 percent. Biggie Airlines, which has been operating on this route, responds by cutting fares by 35 percent. What does Biggie hope to achieve?

7. If air transportation were perfectly contestable, why would Biggie Airlines (see Discussion Question 6) fail to achieve the ultimate goal of its price cut?

8. Which of the following industries are most likely to be contestable?

   a. Aluminum production

   b. Barge transportation

   c. Automobile manufacturing

   Explain your answers.

9. Since the deregulation of air transportation, a community served by a single airline is no longer protected by a regulatory agency from monopoly pricing. What market forces, if any, restrict the ability of the airline to raise prices as a pure monopolist would? How effective do you think those market forces are in keeping airfares down?

10. Explain, for a repeated game:

   a. Why it may be advantageous to have the reputation of being a tough guy who always takes revenge against anyone who harms your interests

   b. Why it may be advantageous to have a reputation of irrationality

LIMITING MARKET POWER: REGULATION AND ANTITRUST

. . . the one law you can't repeal is supply and demand.

WILLIAM SAFIRE, *THE NEW YORK TIMES*, JULY 13, 1998

To protect the interests of the public when industries are, or threaten to become, monopolistic or oligopolistic, government in the United States uses two basic tools. Antitrust policy seeks to prevent acquisition of monopoly power and to ban certain monopolistic practices. All business firms are subject to the antitrust laws. In addition, some industries are regulated by rules that constrain firms' pricing and other decisions. Generally, only firms suspected of having the power to act like monopolists are regulated in this way.

CONTENTS

THE PUBLIC INTEREST ISSUE: MONOPOLY POWER VERSUS MERE SIZE

Economies of scale are savings that are obtained through increases in quantities produced. Scale economies occur when an X percent increase in input use raises output by more than X percent, so that the more the firm produces, the lower its per unit costs become.

Monopoly power (or market power) is the ability of a business firm to earn high profits by raising the prices of its products above competitive levels and to keep those prices high for a substantial amount of time.

In Chapters 11 and 12, we learned that when an industry is a monopoly or an oligopoly, the result may not be as desirable in terms of the public interest as it would be if the industry were perfectly competitive. Yet for many industries anything like perfect competition is an impossible goal, and perhaps even an undesirable one. This is true, notably, when the industry's technology provides **economies of scale,** meaning, as you will remember, that the more of its product a firm supplies, the lower the cost of supplying a unit of that product. Scale economies therefore mean that in competition between a large firm and a small one, the big one can usually win. As a result, industries with scale economies usually end up having a small number of firms, each of which has a large share of the industry's sales. In other words, such an industry is usually fated to be a monopoly or an oligopoly.

But what is so bad about that? Sometimes it is not bad at all, because economies of scale, by definition, allow the larger firms to supply the public at lower cost, though of course they do not always do so. In other cases, the public interest will be threatened, because some or all of the firms in the industry will possess **monopoly power.** Monopoly power (or market power) is usually defined as the ability of a firm to earn high profits by raising and keeping the prices of its products substantially above the levels at which those products would be priced in competitive markets. That is, a firm with monopoly power can charge high prices and get away with it—the market will not punish it for doing so. In a competitive industry, in contrast, the market *will* punish a high-price firm by the loss of its customers to rivals with lower prices. Thus, monopoly power is undesirable for several reasons, some of them obvious:

- *High prices reduce the wealth of consumers.* The use of monopoly power is obviously undesirable to consumers because no one likes to pay high prices for purchased commodities. Such high prices may make the firm with monopoly power rich and make the consumers of its products poor. These effects on the distribution of wealth are generally, for obvious reasons, considered undesirable.

- *High prices lead to resource misallocation.* Economists give greater emphasis to a second undesirable effect of prices that exceed the competitive level. Such prices tend to reduce the quantities of the products that consumers demand. In this case, smaller quantities of labor, raw materials, and other inputs will be devoted to production of these high-priced products relative to the quantities that would *best* serve consumer interests. More of those inputs will therefore be transferred to the products of competitive industries. The result will be *underproduction* of the products priced at monopoly levels and *overproduction* of the products of competitive industries. So, as a result of the exercise of monopoly power, the economy does not produce the mix of outputs that best serves the public interest.

- *Monopoly power creates an obstacle to efficiency and innovation.* A firm with monopoly power is a firm that does not face much effective competition—and consequently it does not have as much reason to fear loss of business to others. Where this is so, there is little incentive for management to make the effort to produce efficiently with a minimum of waste or to undertake the expense and risks of innovation. The result is that products may be of poorer quality than they would if the company possessed no monopoly power, and there will be waste in the production process. But, as we will see presently, some economists have suggested another side to this story.

The efficiency problems inherent in monopoly power are among the main reasons for governmental intervention controlling business firms' behavior and other attributes. The critical problem is control of monopoly power and prevention of acts by firms that are designed either to harm or destroy rivals, or to curb the use of that power to exploit the public.

There is a widespread misconception that all big firms have monopoly power, so that the primary purpose of antitrust or regulatory activity should be to break up as many large firms as possible and to constrain the pricing of all large firms that cannot be broken into smaller ones. But this is not a valid conclusion. It is true that firms that have a very small share of their industry's sales cannot wield market power. For reasons studied in Chapter 10, such small firms are price takers, not price makers. They must simply accept the price determined by supply and demand in a competitive market, or the prices determined by larger firms in their industry if those large firms do have market power. But although firms with small market shares never have market power, the converse is not true: Large firms do not always have market power—though some of them surely do.

Why may such power elude the big firm? In an oligopoly characterized by fierce rivalry, each firm may be prevented by the actions of its competitors from raising its price above competitive levels. For example, Coca-Cola and Pepsi each have a very large share of the soft-drink market. It is well known that there is no love between the two companies, so neither dares to raise its prices substantially for fear of driving customers into the arms of its unloved competitor.

Even a monopoly may have little or no monopoly power if entry into its industry is cheap and easy. Such a firm knows that it can retain its monopoly *only if its behavior is not monopolistic.* If it tries to raise its price to monopoly levels for any substantial period of time, then its rivals will have an opportunity to come in and take some or all of its business away. So in industries where entry is very easy, a large firm will have no monopoly power because the perpetual threat of potential entry will keep it from misbehaving. For this reason, government agencies concerned with monopoly issues often explicitly avoid interfering with the actions of firms in industries where entry is clearly cheap and easy.

The primary threat of monopoly and oligopoly to the public interest is monopoly power. This power can lead to excessive prices that exploit consumers, misallocation of resources, and inefficient and noninnovative firms. But firms that are big do not necessarily have market power.

In Part 1 of this chapter, we will discuss how the antitrust laws are used to deal with these issues. In Part 2, we turn to regulation—a second way of dealing with the problems.

PART 1: ANTITRUST LAWS AND POLICIES

In Part 2 of this chapter, we will describe the process of regulation, which governments use to oversee monopoly or oligopoly firms that are deemed to have dangerous power to control their markets. In Part 1, we will now analyze the first of government's instruments for protecting competition: **antitrust policy.** Antitrust policy refers to programs that preclude the deliberate creation of monopoly and prevent powerful firms from engaging in related "anticompetitive practices." Firms accused of violating the U.S. antitrust laws are likely to be sued by the federal government or other private firms. Antitrust suits seek to prevent such undesirable behavior from recurring, provide compensation to the victims, and punish offenders via fines or even imprisonment. For a very brief description of the most notable U.S. antitrust laws see Table 1, "Basic Antitrust Laws," on page 266.

The antitrust agencies generally are not allowed to decide that a firm has violated the antitrust laws. They can only sue a company they suspect of violating those laws in the courts and provide evidence supporting their allegations against the firm, seeking to get the court to punish the claimed misbehavior and prevent its continuation. Still, even the threat of such a lawsuit is a serious matter to the firm, because of the possible punishment if it loses the case and because fighting such a lawsuit can cost the firm hundreds of millions of dollars. What justifies investment of so much power in such government agencies as the Department of Justice and the Federal Trade Commission? What are the purposes of the antitrust laws? How well has antitrust policy succeeded? These are the issues that we will discuss in this part of the chapter.

Antitrust policy refers to programs and laws that preclude the deliberate creation of monopoly and prevent powerful firms from engaging in related "anticompetitive practices."

TABLE 1

Basic Antitrust Laws

Name	Date	Major Provisions
Sherman Act	1890	Prohibits "all contracts, combinations and conspiracies in restraint of trade" (Section 1) and monopolization in interstate and foreign trade (Section 2).
Clayton Act	1914	Prohibits price discrimination, "exclusive contracts" under which sellers prevent buyers from purchasing goods from the sellers' competitors, and "tying contracts" under which a customer who wants to buy some product from a given seller is required as part of the price to agree to buy another product or products from that same seller. Prohibits acquisition by one corporation of another's shares if these acts are likely to reduce competition or tend to create monopoly. Prohibits directors of one company from sitting on the board of a competitor's company.
Federal Trade Commission Act	1914	Established the FTC as an independent agency with authority to prosecute unfair competition and to prevent false and misleading advertising.
Robinson-Patman Act	1936	Prohibits special discounts and other discriminatory concessions to large purchasers unless based on differences in cost or "offered in good faith to meet an equally low price of a competitor."
Celler-Kefauver Antimerger Act	1950	Prohibits any corporation from acquiring the assets of another where the effect is to reduce competition substantially or to tend to create a monopoly.

You Are There: An Antitrust Trial

The charming courtroom is old but recently refurbished, and the air-conditioning is inadequate. It is often difficult to hear what is happening. The defendant firm has been accused of predatory pricing—that is, of charging very low prices in order to drive a competitor out of the market—and is defending itself against a judgment that can run into the billions of dollars.

For the past two months, both sides have called many witnesses—company executives, accountants, statisticians. The female lawyers are dressed in conservative outfits; the men in somewhat seedy two-piece suits. It would not do to appear too wealthy, for this is a jury trial, and the men and women jurors wear casual attire including sneakers, jeans, and sports clothes. Although determined to see justice done, they are having a hard time staying awake under a hurricane of technical arguments and contradictory figures.

The judge follows the proceedings closely, often interrupting with questions of her own. Sometimes she jokes with the witnesses.

The lawyers call in an expert witness who is a specialist in the field—in this case, an economist who has written on predatory pricing. He explains to the court and the jury the current thinking of the economics profession on the definition of predatory pricing and the standards by which one judges whether or not it has occurred. He is persuasive.

But the judge and jury have already heard from another economist, equally distinguished, representing the other side. Their analyses, which were quite technical, reached opposite conclusions though they agree on analytic procedures. Which one are the jurors to believe, and on what basis?

The Size and Scope of an Antitrust Case

Alleged violations of the antitrust laws are usually dealt with by bringing the accused firm to court or by threatening to sue it in the hope that the accused firm will surrender and accept a compromise. Antitrust suits are frequently well-publicized affairs because the accused firms are often the giants of industry—such famous names as Standard Oil, U.S. Steel, the Aluminum Company of America (Alcoa), General Electric, International Business Machines (IBM), American Telephone and Telegraph (AT&T), and Microsoft all have appeared in such proceedings. Even some of the nation's most prestigious colleges and universities have been accused of engaging in a pricing conspiracy.

The magnitude of an antitrust suit is difficult to imagine. After the charges have been filed, it is not unusual for more than five years to elapse before the case even comes to trial. The parties spend this period laboriously preparing their cases. Dozens of lawyers, scores of witnesses, and hundreds of researchers are likely to participate in this process. The trial itself also can run for years. A major case produces literally thousands of volumes of material, and it can easily cost the defendant several hundred million dollars, even if it wins. In addition, if it loses, the defendant may have to pay billions of dollars in fines.

As you may imagine, the power of the government or another firm to haul a company into court on antitrust charges is an awesome one. Win, lose, or draw, such a case imposes a very heavy burden on the accused firm, draining its funds, consuming the time and attention of its management, and delaying business decisions until the outcome of the legal proceedings is determined.

MEASURING MARKET POWER: CONCENTRATION

Concentration: Definition and Measurement— The Herfindahl-Hirschman Index

It is generally agreed that a firm is not strong enough to violate the antitrust laws if it possesses no monopoly power—that is, no power to prevent entry of competitors and to raise prices substantially above competitive levels. So in antitrust lawsuits one issue that is almost invariably argued about is whether the accused company does or does not have monopoly power. In enforcing the antitrust laws, one piece of evidence that the U.S. Department of Justice and the Federal Trade Commission use to test whether a firm under investigation for antitrust violations is likely to possess monopoly power is the **concentration** of the markets in which the firm carries out its activities. A market or an industry is said to be *highly concentrated* if it contains only a few firms, most or all of which sell a large share of the industry's products. In contrast, an industry with many small firms is said to be *unconcentrated*. Thus, concentration is a useful index of the relative bigness of the firms in the industry. Earlier, we noted that big firms do not always have market power, whereas relatively small firms never (or almost never) do. Still, concentration is one useful piece of evidence in deciding whether market power exists in any case under investigation. In particular, if the accused firm can convince the court that it has no such power, the case is likely to be dismissed by the court.

Concentration is measured in a number of ways. The most straightforward method is to calculate what share of the industry's output is sold by some selected number of the industry's firms. Most often a *four-firm* **concentration ratio** is used for this purpose. Thus, if the four largest firms in an industry account for, say, 58 percent of the industry's sales, we say that the four-firm concentration ratio is 0.58.

Another formula now widely used to measure concentration is the **Herfindahl-Hirschman Index (HHI).** This measure is used by the U.S. Department of Justice and the Federal Trade Commission, for example, to decide whether the proposed merger of two firms will lead to excessive concentration in a particular industry. The index is calculated by determining the market share of each of the firms in the industry, squaring each of these numbers, and adding them together. To quote one of the government documents, "For example, a market consisting of four firms with market shares of 30 percent, 30 percent, 20 percent, and 20 percent has an

Concentration of an industry measures the share of the total sales or assets of the industry in the hands of its largest firms.

A **concentration ratio** is the percentage of an industry's output produced by its four largest firms. It is intended to measure the degree to which the industry is dominated by large firms.

The **Herfindahl-Hirschman Index (HHI)** is an alternative and widely used measure of the degree of concentration of an industry. It is calculated, in essence, by adding together the squares of the market shares of the firms in the industry, although the smallest firms may be left out of the calculation because their small market share numbers have a negligible effect on the result.

Protection of Competition, Not Protection of Competitors

The courts have repeatedly emphasized that the antitrust laws are not intended to make life easier for individual firms that encounter difficulties coping with competitive market pressures. The following quotation from a recent decision of the U.S. Supreme Court makes this clear:

> The purpose of the Sherman Act is not to protect businesses from the workings of the market, it is to protect the public from the failure of the market.

SOURCE: *Spectrum Sports Inc. v. McQuillan*, US 122 L.Ed 2d 247 [1993], p. 506.

HHI of 2,600 (or, $30^2 + 30^2 + 20^2 + 20^2 = 2,600$). The HHI ranges from 10,000 (in the case of a pure monopoly) to a number approaching zero (in the case of [near perfect competition])."[1]

The government considers a market to be unconcentrated if its HHI number is less than 1,000, and highly concentrated if that number exceeds 1,800. The HHI offers at least two advantages over the four-firm concentration ratio. Unlike the latter ratio, HHI takes into account data on a much larger percentage of the firms in the market than just the top four. However, the calculation automatically magnifies the weight assigned to the market shares of the larger firms, because the square of a larger number is disproportionately larger than the square of a smaller number. This effect is considered desirable, because these larger firms are the reason the government worries about monopoly power in the market under consideration. It also explains why the HHI works as a measure of concentration. The HHI number rises when concentration grows because the larger the shares of the market's total sales held by the big firms, the disproportionately larger the squared values of those shares will be.

Ultimately, we care about concentration ratios if they are a good measure of market power. The question, then, is this: If an industry becomes more concentrated, will the firms necessarily increase their ability to price their products above competitive levels? Many economists have, in fact, concluded that although increased concentration *often* facilitates or increases market power, it does not *always* do so. Specifically, the following three conclusions are now widely accepted:

- If, after an increase in concentration, an industry still has a very low concentration ratio, then its firms are very unlikely to have any market power either before or after the rise in concentration.
- If circumstances in the industry are in other respects favorable for successful price collusion—that is, an agreement among the firms not to undercut one another's prices or not to compete "too much" in other ways—a rise in concentration will facilitate market power. It will do so by reducing the number of firms that need to be consulted in arriving at an agreement and by decreasing the number of firms that have to be watched to make sure they do not betray the collusive agreement.
- Where entry into and exit from the industry are easy and quite inexpensive, then even when concentration increases, market power will not be enhanced because an excessive price will attract new entrants that will soon force the price down.

---

[1] Department of Justice and Federal Trade Commission, *Horizontal Merger Guidelines*, Washington, D.C., 1993, page 8, footnote.

The Evidence of Concentration in Reality

Concentration data may be the best evidence that we have on the effectiveness of antitrust programs. Table 2 shows concentration ratios and Herfindahl-Hirschman Indexes in a number of industries in the United States. We see that concentration varies greatly from industry to industry: Automobiles, breakfast cereals, and aircraft are produced by highly concentrated industries, but the cement, jewelry, and women's and girls' clothing industries show very little concentration.

During the last century, concentration ratios in the United States, on the average, have remained remarkably constant. It has been estimated that, at the beginning of the twentieth century, 32.9 percent of manufactured goods were produced by industries in which the concentration ratios were 50 percent or more (meaning that at least 50 percent of industry output was produced by the four largest firms). By 1997, the figure had risen only to 33.5 percent. These figures and those for other years are shown in Table 3. As we see, over the course of the twentieth century, concentration in individual U.S. industries has shown little tendency to increase.

Such information may suggest that the antitrust laws have to some degree been effective in inhibiting whatever trend toward bigness may actually exist. Even this very cautious conclusion has been questioned by some observers, who argue that the size of firms has been held down by market forces and technical developments (such as declining computer costs that make it easier for small firms to increase their efficiency, or the takeover of much of freight traffic from large railroads by small trucking firms). These observers argue that antitrust laws have made virtually no difference in the size and the behavior of American business.

TABLE 2		
Concentration Ratios and Herfindahl-Hirschman Indexes for Selected Manufacturing Industries, 2002		
Industry	Four-firm ratio	Herfindahl-Hirschman Index for 50 Largest Companies in the Industry
Precision-turned products	4.1	13.1
Cement and concrete products	11.9	70.5
Womens' and girls' dresses	21.6	185.5
Fine jewelry	21.5	195.3
Bolts, nuts, screws, rivets, and washers	23.7	205.9
Computers and electronic products	18.0	135.0
Fluid milk	42.6	1060.4
Sporting and athletic goods	22.5	182.2
Brooms, brushes, and mops	29.2	346.3
Musical instruments	42.7	606.0
Dolls and stuffed toys	50.8	798.2
Pharmaceutical preparations	34.9	504.6
Ship and boat building	50.8	883.9
Mens' and boys' suits and coats	48.8	1049.0
Fasteners, buttons, needles, and pins	53.1	1461.8
Tortillas	56.1	2031.4
Cookies and crackers	66.6	1629.0
Tires	76.1	1773.8
Aircraft	80.2	2947.6
Breakfast cereal	78.4	2521.3
Automobiles	75.5	1910.9
Electric lamp bulbs and parts	89.6	2848.0
Guided missiles and space vehicles	95.3	Not disclosed
Cigarettes	95.3	Not disclosed

SOURCE: U.S. Census Bureau, "Concentration Ratios in Manufacturing, 2002," 2002 Economic Census, U.S. Department of Commerce, Economics and Statistics Administration, issued May 2006. http://www.census.gov/prod/ec02/ec0231sr1.pdf.

A CRUCIAL PROBLEM FOR ANTITRUST: THE RESEMBLANCE OF MONOPOLIZATION AND VIGOROUS COMPETITION

One problem that haunts most antitrust litigation is that vigorous competition may look very similar to acts that undermine competition and support monopoly power. The resulting danger is that the courts will prohibit, or the antitrust authorities will prosecute, acts that appear to be anticompetitive but are really the opposite.

The difficulty occurs because effective competition by a firm is always tough on its rivals. It forces rivals to charge lower prices, to improve product quality, and to spend money on innovations that will cut their costs and improve their products. Competition will legitimately force competitors out of business if they are inefficient and therefore cannot keep their prices low or provide products of acceptable quality. When competition destroys a rival in this way, however, it is difficult to tell whether the firm was, so to speak, murdered or died of natural causes. In both cases, the surviving competitor bears some responsibility for its rival's failure. On the one hand, if the cause of the rival's demise is legitimate

TABLE 3	
The Historical Trend in Concentration in Manufacturing Industries, 1901–1997	
	Percentage of Value-Added in Industries with Four-Firm Concentration Ratios over 50 Percent
Circa 1901	32.9
1947	24.4
1954	29.9
1958	30.2
1963	33.1
1966	28.6
1970	26.3
1972	29.0
1982	25.2
1987	27.9
1992	26.4
1997	33.5

SOURCES: P. W. McCracken and T. G. Moore, "Competitive and Market Concentration in the American Economy," Subcommittee on Antitrust and Monopoly, U.S. Senate, March 29, 1973; F. M. Scherer, *Industrial Market Structure and Economic Performance* (Boston: Houghton Mifflin, 1980), p. 68; F. M. Scherer and David Ross, *Industrial Market Structure and Economic Performance,* 3rd ed. (Boston: Houghton Mifflin, 1990), p. 84; personal communication with Professor Frederick M. Scherer, March 10, 1993; and personal communication with Andrew W. Hait, Special Reports Branch, U.S. Bureau of the Census, December 2001.

competition, consumers will benefit; on the other hand, if the end of the rival was part of a process of monopoly creation, then the public will end up paying. This very real issue constantly recurs in today's antitrust litigation.

ANTICOMPETITIVE PRACTICES AND ANTITRUST

A central purpose of the antitrust laws is to prevent "anticompetitive practices," which are actions by a powerful firm that threaten to destroy competitors, or force competitors to compete less vigorously, or prevent the entry of new rivals.

Predatory Pricing

Predatory pricing is pricing that threatens to keep a competitor out of the market. It is a price that is so low that it will be profitable for the firm that adopts it only if a rival is driven from the market.

Typical of accusations of anticompetitive behavior is the claim, made frequently in antitrust cases, that the defendant has adopted unjustifiably low prices in order to force other firms to lose money, thereby driving competitors out of business. This practice is called **predatory pricing.** Deciding whether pricing is "predatory" is difficult, both for economists and for courts of law, because low prices generally benefit consumers. Therefore, the courts do not want to discourage firms from cutting prices by being too eager to declare that lower prices are intended to destroy a rival.

One principle widely followed by the courts holds that prices are predatory only if they are below either marginal or average variable costs. The logic of this criterion as a test for whether prices are "too low" is that even under perfect competition, prices will not, in the long run, fall below that level, but will equal marginal costs. Even in cases where prices are below marginal or average variable costs, they may be held to be predatory only under two conditions:

- If evidence shows that the low price would have been profitable only if it succeeded in destroying a rival or in keeping it out of the market.
- When there is a real probability that the allegedly predatory firm could raise prices to monopoly levels after the rival was driven out, thereby profiting from its venture in crime.

Many major firms—including AT&T, American Airlines, and Microsoft—have been accused of predatory pricing. The defendants typically argue that their low prices cover both marginal and average variable costs, that their prices are low because of superior efficiency, and that the lawsuit was brought to prevent the defendants from competing effectively. The courts have generally accepted these arguments. There have been many predatory pricing cases, but few convictions.

The Microsoft Case: Bottlenecks, Bundling, and Network Externalities

The recent litigation involving Microsoft Corporation illustrates two other practices that can conceivably be anticompetitive. Microsoft is the enormously successful supplier of computer operating systems that enable you to communicate with and control your personal computer; it also supplies other very popular computer programs. Microsoft's software sales are huge, and the company is clearly a tough and energetic competitor. The difficulty of distinguishing vigorously competitive behavior from anticompetitive acts is illustrated by the Microsoft antitrust case, in which the U.S. Department of Justice accused the firm of various anticompetitive practices.

The Microsoft case raises many issues, two of which are discussed here as illustrations.

Abuse via Bottlenecks   Microsoft's Windows Vista, an operating system that runs on about 90 percent of all personal computers, is a prime example of a problem referred to as a "bottleneck"—a facility or product in the hands of a single firm, without which competitors find it difficult or even impossible to operate. To reach any substantial proportion of personal computer customers, the producer of any word processor, spreadsheet, or graphics program must use Windows, and there seems little likelihood that any alternative to Windows Vista that is not produced by Microsoft will soon capture the major share of customers.

The bottleneck exists in part because Windows Vista is widely considered a good program, but even more because user compatibility is desirable—computer users need to communicate with one another, and that task is easier if all of them employ the same operating system. That is, there exists a network of users of computer products who want to be able to communicate easily with one another and who therefore desire mutually compatible software. This preference gives Microsoft a big advantage, because it already has so many users that a new purchaser who values such compatibility will be reluctant to buy a competing product that will make it more difficult to communicate with those many users of the Microsoft products. The bottleneck problem arises because Microsoft itself supplies not only Windows Vista but also many applications (such as Word, a word-processing program; Excel, a spreadsheet program; and Internet Explorer, an Internet browser). There is nothing illegal about simply being the owner of a bottleneck. If company X is a railroad with the only train-bearing bridge over a river because no other rail line had the resources or the initiative to build its own bridge, that is surely not anticompetitive. The worry is that a bottleneck owner, like Microsoft, will use its bottleneck product, Windows Vista, in a way that favors its own programs and handicaps programs supplied by its competitors.

Bundling: Legitimate and Illegitimate   Microsoft has promoted its own products by providing them more cheaply to computer manufacturers if these makers buy a *bundle* of Microsoft programs, rather than just Windows Vista alone. This practice means that rival producers of word processors, spreadsheets, and Internet browsers are handicapped in selling their products to PC owners. The question is whether Microsoft's low bundle price is legitimate or if it constitutes a case of predatory pricing whose only purpose is to destroy competitors. Economists often take the position that a **bundling** discount is legitimate if it is less expensive for the firm to supply several products at once than to supply them one at a time and if the price cut corresponds to the cost saving. However, they question the legitimacy of the bundle discount if the cost saving is considerably less than the difference between the bundled price and the sum of the prices of the included products (when bought individually). However, even here, it is argued that if the price of the bundle exceeds its marginal cost or its average variable cost, it is not predatory.

> **Bundling** refers to a pricing arrangement under which the supplier offers substantial discounts to customers if they buy several of the firm's products, so that the price of the bundle of products is less than the sum of the prices of the products if they were bought separately.

USE OF ANTITRUST LAWS TO PREVENT COMPETITION

Finally, let us turn to an issue that some observers consider very serious: the misuse of the antitrust laws to prevent competition. Many firms that have been unable to compete effectively on their own merits have turned to the courts to seek protection from their successful competitors—and some have succeeded.

Firms that try to protect themselves in this way always claim that their rivals have not achieved success through superior ability but rather by means that they call "monopolization." Sometimes the evidence is clear-cut, and the courts can readily discern whether an accused firm has violated the antitrust laws or whether it has simply been too efficient and innovative for the complaining competitor's tastes. In other cases, the issues are complicated, and only a long and painstaking legal proceeding offers any prospect of resolving them.

Various steps have been suggested to deal with the misuse of U.S. antitrust laws. In one proposal, if the courts decide that a firm has been falsely accused by another of violating the antitrust laws, then (as is done in other countries) the accuser will pay the legal costs of the innocent defendant. Another proposal is to subject such suits to prescreening by a government agency, as is done in Japan. But these issues are hardly open-and-shut, for there is no such thing as a perfect legal system. Anything that restricts anticompetitive, private antitrust suits will almost certainly inhibit legitimate attempts by individual firms to defend themselves from genuine acts of monopolization by rival enterprises (for more on this issue, see "Can Antitrust Laws Be Used to *Prevent* Competition?" on page 272).

Doonesbury

BY GARRY TRUDEAU

Can Antitrust Laws Be Used to *Prevent* Competition?

Many observers are concerned that the antitrust laws are often used by inefficient firms to protect themselves from the competition of more efficient rivals. When they are unable to win out in the marketplace, the argument goes, firms simply file lawsuits against their competitors claiming that those rivals have achieved success by means that violate the antitrust laws.

Not only do firms seek protection from the courts against what they describe as "unfair competition" or "predatory practices" but they often sue for compensation that, under the law, can sometimes be three times as large as the damages that they claim to have suffered. Moreover, even if the defendant is found innocent, it must normally pay the very high costs of the litigation itself. Aside from the enormous waste that such lawsuits entail, observers worry that they represent a perversion of the antitrust laws, which were, after all, designed to promote competition, not to prevent it.

Two recent examples illustrate the nature of such litigation. These cases also demonstrate that the courts are often wise enough to throw out such attempts to use the antitrust laws to prevent competition.

Intimate Bookshop versus Barnes & Noble

The Intimate Bookshop, Inc. (Intimate) was an independent bookseller with retail locations throughout the Mid-Atlantic United States. Shortly before it went out of business in 1999, Intimate sued several of its larger rivals, including Barnes & Noble, Inc. (B&N), claiming that Intimate's business losses had been caused by the anticompetitive practices of the larger booksellers and publishers. Specifically, Intimate alleged that B&N was purchasing books from publishers at substantially lower (discriminatory) prices than those paid by Intimate and other independent retail bookstores. The court ruled against Intimate, finding that there was no evidence to show that its losses were caused by anticompetitive conduct (Southern District of New York, 2003).

West Penn versus UPMC and Highmark

West Penn Allegheny Health Systems, Inc. (West Penn), a Pittsburgh area hospital, sued its larger competitor, University of Pittsburgh Medical Center (UPMC), and Highmark, Inc. (Highmark), a local insurance company with a 60 percent market share. At the time that the lawsuit was filed, West Penn was suffering financially, whereas UPMC's revenue was rising dramatically. In its complaint, West Penn claimed that UPMC and Highmark had conspired to protect one another from competition via a campaign of anticompetitive and predatory conduct undertaken in an effort to "destroy" West Penn.

Although the complaint alleged numerous instances of anticompetitive conduct, the court found that all of the allegations were unsupported by any factual specificity and "amount[ed] to nothing more than statements of suspicion." The court also found fault with the relief West Penn sought, which included an order instating nondiscriminatory reimbursement rates that the court noted actually would hurt consumers by raising the costs of both heath care and health insurance (Western District of Pennsylvania, 2009).

PART 2: REGULATION

We turn, next, to regulation, the other of the two traditional instruments used by government to protect consumers from exploitation by firms that are too powerful.

WHAT IS REGULATION?

"**Regulation** of industry" refers to the activities of a number of government agencies that enforce rules about business conduct enacted by Congress or rules that the agencies themselves have adopted. When an industry is suspected of possessing monopoly power and, because of scale economies or for other reasons, it is not considered feasible or desirable to bring effective competition into its markets, the regulatory agency imposes rules upon the firms designed to curb their use of the monopoly power. For example, the agency may place ceilings on the prices the regulated firms can charge, or it may require the firm to submit any change it desires in any of its prices to the agency. Such changes, then, are not permitted until they have been approved by the agency, sometimes after extensive (and expensive) hearings (that is, trials) before the agency, in which the opponents and supporters of the proposed changes, as well as their lawyers and their witnesses, have the opportunity to present their opinions.

Regulation of industry is a process established by law that restricts or controls some specified decisions made by the affected firms; it is designed to protect the public from exploitation by firms with monopoly power. Regulation is usually carried out by a special government agency assigned the task of administering and interpreting the law. That agency also acts as a court in enforcing the regulatory laws.

Regulations designed to limit market power, and economic behavior more generally, affect industries that together provide perhaps 10 percent of the gross domestic product (GDP) of the United States. The list includes telecommunications, railroads, electric utilities, oil pipelines, banks, and the stock markets. Both the federal government and the states have regulatory agencies devoted to such tasks.

Despite its good intentions, regulation has been criticized as a cause of inefficiency and excessive costs to the consuming public. The basic fact about regulation and other forms of government intervention that are designed to affect the operations of markets is that *neither* markets *nor* governmental agencies always work perfectly. In an uncontrolled market, for example, monopoly power can damage the public interest, but excessive or poorly conceived regulations or antitrust decisions also can prove very harmful.

"Won't all these new rules impact adversely on the viability of small businesses with fewer than fifty employees?"

PUZZLE:	WHY DO REGULATORS OFTEN RAISE PRICES?

Regulation sometimes forces consumers to pay *higher* prices than they would pay in its absence. For instance, before the airline industry was deregulated, the flight between New York City and Washington, D.C.—an interstate trip that was controlled by the federal government—was *more* expensive than the flight between San Francisco and Los Angeles—a trip that was not controlled by the federal government, because it took place entirely within the state of California. The California trip was nearly twice as long as the East Coast trip, and it did not have a substantially lower cost per passenger mile for the airline. So why did regulators, whose job it is to protect the public interest, deliberately price the New York–Washington hop about 25 percent higher? Later in the chapter, you will be able to answer this question.

SOME OBJECTIVES OF REGULATION

The regulatory agencies, lawyers, and economists recognize a number of reasons that may justify the regulation of an industry. A primary purpose of regulation is, of course, prevention of abuse of monopoly power. We have seen that such power can easily be acquired in industries characterized by economies of scale and scope and that this power can be used by firms to impose prices that exploit the consumer. We have already discussed these as problems that antitrust activity is designed to control. But this is also a fundamental goal of economic regulation. In contrast, there are other issues that are relevant only to regulation. The following is an example.

Control of Market Power Resulting from Economies of Scale and Scope

As we noted at the beginning of this chapter, a major reason for regulation of industry is to prevent the use of or acquisition of market power by regulated firms. In some industries, it is far cheaper to have production carried out by one firm than by many, and the relatively large firms that result may gain market power. One cause is economies of large-scale production. Railroad tracks are a particularly good example of such economies of scale. The total cost of building and maintaining the tracks when 100 trains traverse them every day is not much higher than when only one train uses them. So, substantial savings in average cost result when rail traffic increases. As we saw in Chapter 7, scale economies lead to an average cost (AC) curve that goes downhill as output increases (see Figure 1). This means that a firm with a large output can cover its costs at a price lower than a firm whose output is smaller. In the figure, point *A* represents the larger firm whose AC is $5, whereas point *B* is the smaller firm with an AC of $7.

Economies of scope are savings that are obtained through simultaneous production of many different products. They occur if a firm that produces many commodities can supply each good more cheaply than a firm that produces fewer commodities.

A single, large firm also may have a cost advantage over a group of small firms when it is cheaper to produce a number of different commodities together rather than making each separately in a different firm. Savings made possible by simultaneous production of many different products by one firm are called **economies of scope**. One clear example of economies of scope is the manufacture of both cars and trucks by the same producer. The techniques employed in producing both commodities are similar, which provides a cost advantage to firms that produce both types of vehicles.

In industries characterized by great economies of scale and scope, costs will be much higher if government intervenes to preserve a large number of small, and therefore costly, firms. Moreover, where economies of scale and scope are strong, society will not be able to preserve free competition, even if it wants to. The large, multiproduct firm will have so great a cost advantage over its rivals that the small firms simply will be unable to survive.

> Where monopoly production is cheapest, so that free competition is not sustainable, the industry is a natural monopoly. When monopoly is cheaper, society may not want to have competition; if free competition is not sustainable, it will not even have a choice in the matter.

Even if society reconciles itself to monopoly in such cases, it will generally not want to let the monopoly firm wield its market power without limits. Therefore, it will consider regulating the company's decisions on matters such as pricing. The first and most universal problem facing the regulator is how to prevent the regulated firm from pricing and taking other actions that exploit the public and undermine the efficiency of the market, but to do so in ways that do not destroy the regulated firm or prevent it from serving the public effectively.

FIGURE 1
Economies of Scale

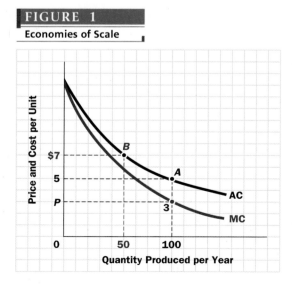

Universal Service and Rate Averaging

A second type of problem in the analysis of regulation stems from another objective of regulation of the prices and other choices of firms in a regulated industry—the desire for "universal service." By this regulators mean the availability of service to everyone at "reasonable prices," particularly to impoverished consumers and small communities where the limited scale of operations may make costs extremely high. In such cases, regulators may encourage or require a public utility (such as an electric power supplier) to serve some of its consumers at a financial loss. This loss on some sales is financially feasible only when the regulated firm is permitted to make up for it by obtaining higher profits on its other sales. Charging higher prices to one set of customers to finance lower prices to another customer group is called **cross-subsidization.**

This sort of cross-subsidization is possible only if the regulated firm is protected from price competition and free entry of new competitors in its other, more profitable markets (in which it charges the higher prices that subsidize the financing of the mandated low prices). If no such protection is provided, potential competitors will sniff out these profit opportunities in the markets where service is supplied at prices well above cost. Many new firms will enter the business and drive prices down in those markets—a practice referred to as *cream skimming*. The entrants choose to enter only the profitable markets and skim away the "cream" of the profits for themselves, leaving the unprofitable markets (the skimmed milk?) to the supplier that had attempted to provide universal service. This phenomenon is one reason why regulatory rules, until recently, made it very difficult or impossible for new firms to enter when and where they saw fit.

Airlines and telecommunications are two industries in which these issues have arisen frequently. In both cases, it was feared that without regulation of entry and rates, or special subsidies, less populous communities would effectively become isolated, losing their airline services and obtaining telephone service only at cripplingly high rates. Many economists question the validity of this argument for regulation, which, they say, calls for hidden subsidies of rural consumers by everyone else. The airline deregulation act provided for government subsidies to help small communities attract airline service. In fact, this market has since been taken over to a considerable extent by specialized "commuter" airlines flying much smaller aircraft than the major airlines, which have withdrawn from many such routes.

A similar issue affects the U.S. Postal Service, which charges the same price to deliver a letter anywhere within the United States, regardless of the distance or the special difficulties and costs of a particular route. To maintain this pricing scheme, the law must protect the Postal Service from direct competition in many of its activities—otherwise, its extreme form of uniform pricing would soon deprive it of its most profitable routes. Thus, the goal of providing universal service leads to the regulation of entry into and exit from the affected industry, and not just price control.

> **Cross-subsidization** means selling one product of the firm at a loss, which is balanced by higher profits on another of the firm's products.

TWO KEY ISSUES THAT FACE REGULATORS

Regulators around the world face (at least) two critical issues that are of fundamental importance for economic policy. They are at the heart of recent legal battles before regulatory agencies almost everywhere.

Setting Prices to Protect Consumers' Interests and Allow Regulated Firms to Cover Their Costs

When governments regulate prices, they usually want to prevent those prices from being so high that they bring monopoly profits to the firm. At the same time, governments want to set prices at levels that are "compensatory"; that is, the prices must be sufficiently high to enable the firms to cover their costs and, consequently, to survive financially.

Regulators also are asked to select prices that best serve the public interest. These goals, as we will see next, can often be at odds.

- *Prices intended to promote the public interest may cause financial problems for firms.* The discussion in Chapter 10 implied that the consumer's welfare is most effectively promoted by setting the price of a product equal to that product's marginal cost, and this will be further confirmed in Chapter 14. But as we will show presently, such a rule would condemn many regulated firms to bankruptcy. What should the regulator do in such a case?
- *Preventing firms with monopoly power from earning excessive profits without eliminating all incentives for efficiency and innovation may prove difficult.* The firm's incentive and reward for the effort and expenditure needed to improve efficiency and to innovate is the higher profit that it expects to obtain if it succeeds. But a frequent objective of regulation is to put a ceiling on profit to prevent monopoly earnings. How can monopoly profits be prevented without destroying incentives?

Let's now analyze these issues, which arise frequently in today's crucial regulatory policy debates.

Marginal versus Average Cost Pricing

Regulatory agencies often have the task of controlling the prices of regulated firms. Acrimonious debate over the proper levels for those prices has filled hundreds of thousands of pages of regulatory-hearing records and has involved literally hundreds of millions of dollars of expenditures in fees for lawyers, expert witnesses, and research. The central question has been: What constitutes the proper formula to set these prices?

Where it is feasible, most economists favor setting price equal to marginal cost because, as we will show in Chapter 14, this pricing policy provides the incentive for firms to produce output quantities that serve consumers' wants most efficiently. However, a serious practical problem often prevents use of marginal cost pricing: In many regulated industries, the firms would go bankrupt if all prices were set equal to marginal costs!

This seems a startling conclusion, but it follows inescapably from three simple facts:

Fact 1. Many regulated industries are characterized by significant economies of large-scale production. As we pointed out earlier, economies of scale are one of the main reasons why certain industries were regulated in the first place.

Fact 2. In an industry with economies of scale, the long-run average cost curve is downward sloping. This means that the long-run average cost falls as the quantity produced rises, as was illustrated by the AC curve in Figure 1. Fact 2 is something we learned back in Chapter 7. The reason, to review briefly, is that where there are economies of scale, if all input quantities are doubled, output will more than double. But total costs will double only if input quantities double. Thus, total costs will rise more slowly than output and so average cost must fall. That is, average cost (AC) is simply total cost (TC) divided by quantity (Q), so with economies of scale, AC = TC/Q must decline when Q increases because the denominator, Q, rises more rapidly than the numerator, TC.

Fact 3. If average cost is declining, then marginal cost must be below average cost. This fact follows directly from one of the general rules relating marginal and average data that were explained in the appendix to Chapter 8. Once again, the logic is simple enough to review briefly. If, for example, your average quiz score is 90 percent but the next quiz pulls your average down to 87 percent, then the grade on the most recent test (the marginal grade) must be below both the old and the new average quiz scores; that is, it takes a marginal grade (or cost) that is below the average to pull the average down.

Putting these three facts together, we conclude that in many regulated industries, marginal cost (MC) will be below average cost, as depicted in Figure 1. Now suppose that regulators set the price (or average revenue, AR) at the level of marginal cost. Because

P then equals MC, *P* (= AR) must be below AC and the firm must lose money, so "*P* equals MC" is simply not an acceptable option. What, then, should be done? One possibility is to set price equal to marginal cost and to use public funds to make up for the deficit. However, government subsidies to large regulated firms are not very popular politically and may also not be sensible.

A second option, which is quite popular among regulators, is to (try to) set price equal to average cost. This method of pricing is, however, neither desirable nor possible to carry out except on the basis of arbitrary decisions. The problem is that almost no firm produces only a single commodity. Almost every company produces a number of different varieties and qualities of some product, and many produce thousands of different products, each with its own price. General Electric, for example, is perhaps best known for the home appliances it produces, but the company also runs the movie studio and cable television channels that comprise NBC Universal, a finance division that provides loans and other business services, and manufacturing divisions that produce everything from airplane engines to surgical accessories. In a multiproduct firm, we cannot even define AC = TC/Q, because to calculate Q (total output), we would have to add up all of the apples and oranges (and all of the other different items) that the firm produces. Of course, we know that we cannot add up apples and oranges. Because we cannot calculate AC for a multiproduct firm, it is hardly possible for the regulator to require *P* to equal AC for each of the firm's products (although regulators sometimes think they can do so).

One way of dealing with the issue is the price-cap approach that was invented by economists but is now widely employed in practice. The procedure and its logic will be described a little later in this chapter.

Preventing Monopoly Profit but Keeping Incentives for Efficiency and Innovation

Opponents of regulation claim that it seriously impairs the efficiency of American industry and reduces the benefits of free markets. One obvious source of inefficiency is the endless paperwork and complex legal proceedings that prevent the firm from responding quickly to changing market conditions.

In addition, economists believe that regulatory interference in pricing causes economic inefficiency. By forcing prices to differ from those that would prevail in a free, competitive market, regulations lead consumers to demand a quantity of the regulated product that does not maximize consumer benefits from the quantity of resources available to the economy. (This resource misallocation issue will be discussed in Chapter 15.)

A third source of inefficiency may be even more important. It occurs because regulators often are required to prevent the regulated firm from earning excessive profits, while offering it financial incentives for maximum efficiency of operation and allowing it enough profit to attract the capital it needs when growing markets justify expansion. It would seem to be ideal if the regulator would permit the firm to earn just the amount of revenue that covers its costs, including the cost of its capital. Thus, if the current rate of profits in competitive markets is 10 percent, the regulated firm should recover its costs plus 10 percent on its investment and not a penny more or less. The trouble with such a rule is that it removes all profit incentive for efficiency, responsiveness to consumer demand, and innovation. In effect, it guarantees just one standard rate of profit to the firm, no more and no less—regardless of whether its management is totally incompetent or extremely talented and hard-working.

Competitive markets do not work this way. Although under perfect competition the average firm will earn just the illustrative 10 percent, a firm with an especially ingenious and efficient management will do better, and a firm with an incompetent management is likely to go broke. It is the possibility of great rewards and harsh punishments that gives the market mechanism its power to cause firms to strive for high efficiency and productivity growth.

When firms are guaranteed fixed returns no matter how well or how poorly they perform, gross inefficiencies often result. For example, many contracts for purchases of military equipment have prices calculated on a so-called cost-plus basis, meaning that the supplier is guaranteed that its costs will be covered and that, in addition, it will receive some prespecified profit, removing a key incentive for management to work hard to improve the firm's performance. Studies of such cost-plus arrangements have confirmed that they lead to enormous supplier inefficiencies. A regulatory arrangement that in effect guarantees a regulated firm its cost plus a "fair rate of return" on its investment obviously has much in common with a cost-plus contract. Fortunately, there are also substantial differences between the two, and so regulatory profit ceilings need not always have serious effects on the firm's incentives for efficiency.

How can one prevent regulated firms from earning excessive profits, but also permit them to earn enough to cover their legitimate costs, attract the capital they need, and, above all, still allow rewards for superior performance and penalties for poor performance?

Price Caps as Incentives for Efficiency   A regulatory innovation designed to prevent monopoly profits while offering incentives for the firm to improve its efficiency is now in use in many countries—for electricity, telephones, and airport services in the United Kingdom, for example, and for telephone rates in the United States and elsewhere.

A **price cap** is a ceiling above which regulators do not permit prices to rise. The cap is designed to provide an efficiency incentive to the firm by allowing it to keep part of any savings in costs it can achieve.

Under this program, regulators assign ceilings (called **price caps**) for the *prices* (not the profits) of the regulated firms. However, the price caps (which are measured in real, inflation-adjusted terms—in other words, they are adjusted for changes in the purchasing power of money) are reduced each year at a rate based on the rate of cost reduction (productivity growth) previously achieved by the regulated firm. Thus, if the regulated firm subsequently achieves cost savings (by innovation or other means) greater than those it obtained in the past, the firm's real costs will fall more rapidly than its real prices do, and it will be permitted to keep the resulting profits as its reward. Of course, there is a catch. If the regulated firm reduces its costs by only 2 percent per year, whereas in the past its costs fell 3 percent per year, the price cap will also fall at a 3 percent rate. The firm will therefore lose profits, although consumers will continue to benefit from falling real prices. So under this arrangement the firm is automatically punished if its cost-reduction performance does not keep up with what it was able to achieve in the past.

Thus, under price-cap regulation, management is constantly forced to look for ever more economical ways of doing things. This approach clearly gives up any attempt to limit the profit of the regulated firm—leaving the possibility of higher profits as an incentive for efficiency. At the same time, it protects the consumer by controlling the firm's prices. Indeed, it makes those prices lower and lower, in real terms.

THE PROS AND CONS OF "BIGNESS"

We have described several goals for antitrust activity including control of monopoly power. Is it desirable, in addition to these regulatory goals, to try to make big firms become smaller? In other words, are the effects of "bigness" always undesirable? We have already seen that only relatively large firms have any likelihood of possessing monopoly power. We also have seen that monopoly power can cause a number of problems, including undesirable effects on income distribution, misallocation of resources, and inhibition of efficiency and innovation.

But we also have seen that big firms, at least sometimes, do not possess monopoly power. More generally, there is another side of the picture. Bigness in industry can also, at least sometimes, benefit the general public. Again, this is true for a number of reasons.

Economies of Large Size

Probably the most important advantage of bigness is found in industries in which technology makes small-scale operation inefficient. One can hardly imagine the costs if automobiles were produced in little workshops rather than giant factories. The notion of a small firm operating a long-distance railroad does not even make sense, and a multiplicity of firms replicating the same railroad service would clearly be incredibly wasteful.

On these grounds, most policy makers have never even considered any attempt to eliminate bigness. Of course, it does not follow that every industry in which firms happen to be big is one in which big firms are best. Some observers argue that many firms, in fact, exceed the sizes required for cost minimization.

Required Scale for Innovation

Some economists have argued that only large firms have the resources and the motivation for really significant innovation. Many important inventions are still contributed by individuals. But, because it is often an expensive, complex, and large-scale undertaking to put a new invention into commercial production, often only large firms can afford the funds and bear the risks that such an effort demands.

Many studies have examined the relationships among firm size, industry competitiveness, and the level of expenditure on research and development (R&D). Although the evidence is far from conclusive, it does indicate that highly competitive industries composed of very small firms tend not to spend a great deal on research. Up to a point, R&D outlays and innovation seem to increase with size of the firm and the concentration of the industry. One reason for this is that many oligopolistic firms use innovation—new products and new processes—as their primary competitive "weapon," forcing them, as time passes, to maintain and even increase their spending on R&D and other innovative activities.

However, some of the most significant innovations introduced in the twentieth century have been contributed by firms that started very small. Examples include the airplane, alternating current (AC) electricity, the photocopier, and the electronic calculator. Yet, the important successive improvements in those products have characteristically come out of the research facilities of large, oligopolistic enterprises.

The bottom line is that bigness in business firms receives a mixed score. In some cases it can produce undesirable results, but in other cases it is necessary for efficiency and low costs and offers other benefits to the public. A rule requiring regulators to combat bigness per se, wherever it occurs, is likely to have undesirable results and would, in any event, be unworkable.

DEREGULATION

Because regulators have sometimes adopted rules and made decisions that were ill-advised and were demonstrably harmful to the public interest, and because the bureaucracy that is needed to enforce regulation is costly and raises business expenses, there have long been demands for reduced regulation. Beginning in the mid-1970s, Congress responded to such arguments by deregulating several industries, such as airlines and trucking, and eliminating most of the powers of the relevant regulatory agencies. In other industries, such as railroads and telecommunications, rule changes now give regulated firms considerably more freedom in decision making. This deregulation process is still under way.

The Effects of Deregulation

One way to deal with the regulation difficulties just discussed is to shut regulation down—that is, simply to leave everything to the free market and get rid of the regulators. Many observers think that would be a good idea in a number of cases, but sometimes it would be unacceptable, as in markets that are virtually pure monopolies. Thus, the move toward deregulation has proceeded slowly, by eliminating regulation in some fields and reducing it in others. Deregulation's effects in the United States are still being debated, but several conclusions seem clear.

1. Effects on Prices
There seems little doubt that deregulation has generally led to lower prices. Airline fares, railroad freight rates, and telephone rates have all declined on the average (again, in real, inflation-adjusted terms) after total or partial deregulation.

At least in the case of the airlines, however, the rate of decline slowed abruptly toward the end of the 1980s. Still, observers conclude that most of these prices are well below the levels that would have prevailed under regulation.

2. Effects on Local Services   At first it was widely feared, even by supporters of deregulation, that smaller and more isolated communities would be deprived of services because small numbers of customers would make those services unprofitable. Some predicted that airlines, railroads, and telephone companies would withdraw from such communities once there was no longer any regulation to force them to stay. The outcome was not as serious as had been anticipated. For example, although larger airlines have left smaller communities, they have usually been replaced by smaller commuter airlines that have often provided more frequent service. In addition, the larger airlines inaugurated a new scheduling pattern called the "hub-and-spoke system" (see the discussion below), which enabled them to continue to serve less traveled destinations profitably.

3. Effects on Entry   As a result of deregulation, older airlines invaded one another's routes, several dozen new airlines sprang up, and about 10,000 new truck operators entered the market. Many of the trucking entrants have since dropped out of the industry, as profits and wages were driven down by competition. Almost all of the new airlines also ran into trouble and were sold to the older airlines. Since 1990, however, many small airlines have been launched and several are now the most profitable firms in the industry. A battle is now shaping up over whether the small airlines need special protection from tough competition by the larger airlines. Here it is also pertinent to note that although many of the small entrant airlines have perished, so have a number of very large carriers, including Eastern Airlines, Braniff, Pan Am, and TWA, all of which had once been major enterprises.

4. Effects on Unions   Deregulation has badly hurt unions such as the Teamsters (of the trucking industry) and the Airline Pilots Association. In the new, competitive climate, firms have been forced to make sharp cuts in their workforces and to resist wage increases and other costly changes in working conditions. Indeed, there has been strong pressure for retrenchment on all of these fronts. It should not be surprising, then, that unions often oppose deregulation.

5. Effects on Product Quality   The public has been unpleasantly surprised by another effect of deregulation. At least in the case of aviation, increased price competition has been accompanied by sharp reductions in "frills." To cut costs, most airlines have eliminated free meals and limited the number of flights to avoid empty seats—which has increased crowding. To fill planes with more passengers, many airlines turned to "hub-and-spoke" systems (see Figure 2). Instead of running a flight directly from a low-demand airport, A, to another low-demand airport, B, the airline flies all passengers from Airport A to its "hub" at Airport H, where all passengers, from many points of origin, who are bound for the same destination, Airport B, are brought together and asked to reboard an airplane flying to B. This system clearly saves money and gives passengers more options as the number of flights between hubs and spokes increases. At the same time, it is surely less convenient for passengers than a direct flight from origin to destination. Critics of deregulation have placed a good deal of emphasis on the reductions in passenger comfort. Economists, however, argue that competition would not bring such results unless passengers as a group prefer the reduction in fares to the greater standards of luxury that preceded them.

6. Effects on Safety   Also in the case of airline deregulation (though the issue can well arise elsewhere), some observers have been concerned that cost cutting after deregulation would lead to skimping on safety measures. As Figure 3

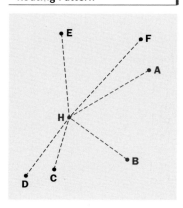

FIGURE 2

A "Hub-and-Spoke" Airline Routing Pattern

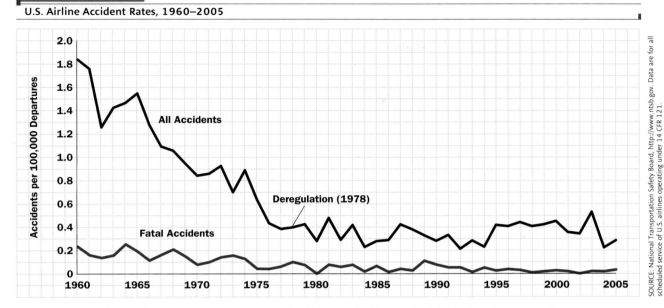

FIGURE 3

U.S. Airline Accident Rates, 1960–2005

NOTE: Accidents resulting from illegal acts, such as suicide or sabotage, are excluded from the National Transportation Safety Board's accident rate computations.

SOURCE: National Transportation Safety Board, http://www.ntsb.gov. Data are for all scheduled service of U.S. airlines operating under 14 CFR 121.

shows, deregulation seems not to have increased the rate of airline accidents. Even so, deregulation may require special vigilance to guard against neglect of safety as a cost-cutting measure. In late 2001, this concern led Congress to legislate a government role in protecting the public from terrorist attacks. Some observers suggest that the reduced profits that competition caused in truck transportation has led truckers to cut corners in terms of safety.

7. Effects on Profits and Wages

As the previous discussion suggested, deregulation has generally strengthened competition, and the increased power of competition has, in turn, tended to depress profits and wages. There is evidence that few airlines, including the largest carriers, have been able to earn profits as high as those in other competitive industries, on average, since the deregulation of the airlines more than two decades ago. Recent events such as the threat of terrorism and rising fuel prices have brought several large airlines to the brink of bankruptcy. This, of course, is just the other side of reduced prices to consumers. In some cases, the profit and wage cuts were very substantial and had significant consequences. The recent financial problems for airlines and trucking firms have already been noted, and the pressures for decreases in the very high earnings of airline pilots have prompted frequent confrontations between these workers and the airlines.

The general conclusion is that deregulation has usually worked out well, but hardly perfectly in promoting the welfare of consumers. Indeed, partial deregulation has sometimes proved to be disastrous, as illustrated by what happened in the electricity industry in California in 2001. There, *wholesale* prices were deregulated, but tight ceilings were imposed on *retail* prices. Firms that bought at wholesale and sold at retail incurred great losses when wholesale prices increased, with a brief period of significant power shortages being the predictable result.

The battle for deregulation is far from over. Even if those who wish for a return to the good old days of regulation (and there are some) do not succeed, many areas exist in which regulation of the old-time variety still retains its grip or has been reintroduced in disguised form.

PUZZLE REVISITED: WHY REGULATORS OFTEN PUSH PRICES UPWARD

We can now return to the puzzle we posed earlier: Why would regulators, who are supposed to protect the interests of the public, raise prices? The answer is that regulators sometimes push for higher prices when they want to prevent the demise of any existing firms in an industry. Earlier, we saw that strong economies of scale and economies of scope may make it impossible for a number of firms to survive. The largest firm in an industry may have such a big cost advantage over its competitors that it can drive them out of the market while still operating at a profit.

Firms that are hurt by such competitive pressures often complain to regulatory commissions that the prices charged by a rival are "unfairly low." These commissions, afraid that unrestrained pricing will reduce the number of firms in the industry, then attempt to "equalize" matters by imposing price floors (below which prices cannot be set). Such price floors are designed to permit all the firms in the industry to operate profitably, including those that operate inefficiently and incur costs far higher than their competitors' costs. That is presumably why, under regulation, the New York–Washington, D.C., air fares were so high.

Many economists maintain that this approach to pricing is a perversion of the idea of competition. The virtue of competition is that, where it occurs, firms force one another to supply consumers with products of high quality at low prices. Any firm that cannot achieve this goal is driven out of business by market forces. A regulatory arrangement may allow efficient and inefficient firms to coexist only by preventing them from competing with one another, but this arrangement merely preserves the appearance of competition while destroying its substance, and it forces consumers to pay the higher prices necessary to keep the inefficient firms alive.

CONCLUDING OBSERVATIONS

As we noted at the beginning of this chapter, monopoly and monopoly power are rightly judged to cause market failure—they prevent the market from serving consumer interests most effectively by providing the products the public desires at the lowest possible prices. The alternative is government intervention, and governments, too, sometimes make imperfect decisions. Thus, before deciding whether to regulate more or deregulate, whether to toughen antitrust laws or loosen them, informed citizens should carefully weigh the prospects for market failure against the possibility of government failure in terms of the contemplated change.

Certainly, monopolists have sometimes succeeded in preventing the introduction of useful new products. They have raised prices to consumers and held down product quality. In contrast, large firms have sometimes been innovative and their service to customers has been considered of high quality.

Government has suffered its own missteps. It has initiated costly lawsuits, sometimes on questionable grounds. It has forced regulated firms to adopt pricing rules that were clearly not beneficial to consumers, and it has handicapped the operations of industries—for example, arguably for a time almost destroying the nation's railroads. Yet government, too, has done useful things in influencing industry behavior, preventing various monopolistic practices, protecting consumers from impure foods and medications, and so on. Most economists believe that by the 1970s government intervention had clearly gone too far in some respects and that deregulation was, consequently, in the public interest. However, the general issue is hardly settled.

| SUMMARY |

1. Antitrust policy includes those policies and programs designed to control the growth of monopoly and to prevent big business from engaging in "anticompetitive" practices.

2. **Predatory pricing** is pricing that is low relative to the marginal or average variable costs of the firm and so threatens to drive a competitor out of the market. For pricing to be considered predatory, there must also be a likelihood that if the prices do destroy a competitor, the firm will acquire market power enabling it to charge prices well above competitive levels.

3. **Bundling** refers to a price reduction given to customers who purchase several of the firm's products simultaneously. It is considered unobjectionable if it is cheaper for the firm to bundle its products so that the price cut merely passes the savings on to customers. However, bundling can be used to destroy competitors that sell only some of the bundled products.

4. The evidence indicates that no significant increase in the **concentration** of individual U.S. industries into fewer, relatively larger firms occurred during the twentieth century. Evidence as to whether antitrust laws have been effective in preventing monopoly is inconclusive, and observers disagree on the subject.

5. Unregulated monopoly is apt to distribute income unfairly, produce undesirably small quantities of output, and provide inadequate motivation for innovation.

6. Sometimes, however, only large firms may have funds sufficient for effective research, development, and innovation. Where economies of scale are available, large firms may also serve customers more cheaply than can small ones.

7. Economic **regulation** is adopted to put brakes on the decisions of industries with monopoly power.

8. In the United States, regulation of prices and other economic decisions is generally applied only to large firms, including railroads, telecommunications, and gas and electricity suppliers.

9. In recent years, we have seen a major push toward reduction of regulation. Among the industries that have been deregulated in whole or in part are air, truck, and rail transportation.

10. Among the major reasons given for regulation are (a) **economies of scale** and **economies of scope,** which make industries into natural monopolies, and (b) the universal service goal, which refers to the provision of service to poor people and isolated areas where supply is unprofitable.

11. Regulators often reject proposals by regulated firms to cut their prices, and sometimes the regulators even force firms to raise their prices. The purposes of such actions are to prevent "unfair competition" and to protect customers of some of the firm's products from being forced to **cross-subsidize** customers of other products. Many economists disagree with most such actions, arguing that the result is usually to stifle competition and make all customers pay more than they otherwise would.

12. Economists generally agree that a firm should be permitted to cut its price as long as it covers its marginal cost. However, in many regulated industries, firms would go bankrupt if all prices were set equal to marginal costs.

13. By putting ceilings on profits to prevent monopoly earnings, regulation can eliminate the firm's incentive for efficiency and innovation. Price caps, which put (inflation-adjusted) ceilings on prices, rather than profits, are used widely to deal with this problem.

| KEY TERMS |

antitrust policy 265	cross-subsidization 275	monopoly power 264
bundling 271	economies of scale 264	predatory pricing 270
concentration of an industry 267	economies of scope 274	price cap 278
concentration ratios 267	Herfindahl-Hirschman Index (HHI) 267	regulation 273

| DISCUSSION QUESTIONS |

1. Why is an electric company in a city often considered to be a natural monopoly? What would happen if two competing electric companies were established? How about telephone companies? How can changes in technology affect your answer?

2. Suppose that a 20 percent cut in the price of coast-to-coast telephone calls brings in so much new business that it permits a long-distance telephone company to cut its charges for service from Chicago to St. Louis, but only by 2 percent. In your opinion, is this practice equitable? Is it a good idea or a bad one?

3. In some regulated industries, regulatory agencies prevented prices from falling, and as a result many firms opened for business in those industries. In your opinion, is this kind of regulation competitive or anticompetitive? Is it a good idea or a bad one?

4. Regulators are highly concerned about the prevention of "predatory pricing." The U.S. Court of Appeals has, however, noted that "the term probably does not have a well-defined meaning, but it certainly bears a sinister connotation." How might one distinguish "predatory" from "nonpredatory" pricing? What would you do about it?

5. Do you think that it is fair or unfair for rural users of telephone service to be cross-subsidized by other telephone users?

6. To provide incentives for increased efficiency, several regulatory agencies have eliminated ceilings on the profits of regulated firms but instead put caps on their prices. Suppose that a regulated firm manages to cut its prices in half, but in the process it doubles its profits. Should rational consumers consider this to be a good or a bad development? Why?

7. A shopkeeper sells his store and signs a contract that restrains him from opening another store in competition with the new owner. The courts have decided that this contract is a reasonable restraint of trade. Can you think of any other types of restraint of trade that seem reasonable? Can you think of any that seem unreasonable?

8. Which of the following industries do you expect to have high concentration ratios: automobile production, aircraft manufacture, hardware production, pharmaceuticals, production of expensive jewelry? Compare your answers with the data in Table 2.

9. Why do you think the specific industries you selected in Discussion Question 8 are highly concentrated?

10. Do you think it is in the public interest to launch an antitrust suit that costs $1 billion? What leads you to your conclusion?

11. In Japan and a number of European countries, the antitrust laws were once much less severe than those in the United States. Do you think that this difference helped or harmed American industry in its efforts to compete with foreign producers? Why?

12. Can you think of some legal rules that may discourage the use of antitrust laws to prevent competition while at the same time not interfering with legitimate antitrust actions?

13. During the oil crisis in the 1970s, long lines at gas stations disappeared soon after price controls were removed and gas prices were permitted to rise. Should this event be interpreted as evidence that the oil companies have monopoly power? Why or why not?

14. Some economists believe that firms rarely attempt predatory pricing because it would be a very risky act even if it were legal. Why may this be so?

15. Firm X cuts its prices, and competing Firm Y soon goes out of business. How would you judge whether this price cut was an act of legitimate and vigorous competition or an anticompetitive act?

Part 4

The Virtues and Limitations of Markets

This book is not a piece of propaganda. And so we recognize that, like most institutions, the market has both shortcomings and benefits, and one of our goals is to describe them both as dispassionately as we can. Chapter 14 describes and analyzes a snapshot picture of the market at its best, showing how remarkably well it can coordinate the vast number of activities and decisions that drive our economy. The next chapter, in contrast, investigates some of the important ways in which the market mechanism, if left entirely to itself, fails to serve the public interest well. In Chapter 15 as well as in Chapter 17, we examine what can be done to remedy these deficiencies—or at least to reduce their undesirable consequences. In Chapter 16, the growth chapter, we depict the economy in motion. There we will see the most incredible of all the accomplishments of the market economy in its ability to bring remarkable increases in standards of living and innovative products that could hardly have been imagined by our ancestors. In short, as Chapter 16 will demonstrate and begin to explain, the growth performance of the market has totally outstripped that of any economy in previous history. Finally, Chapter 18 introduces you to the tax system and the effects of the government on resource allocation in the market economy.

CHAPTERS

THE CASE FOR FREE MARKETS I: THE PRICE SYSTEM

If there existed the universal mind that . . . would register simultaneously all the processes of nature and of society, that could forecast the results of their inter-reactions, such a mind . . . could . . . draw up a faultless and an exhaustive economic plan. . . . In truth, the bureaucracy often conceives that just such a mind is at its disposal; that is why it so easily frees itself from the control of the market.

LEON TROTSKY, A LEADER OF THE RUSSIAN REVOLUTION

Our study of microeconomics focuses on two crucial questions: What does the market do well, and what does it do poorly? By applying what we learned about demand in Chapters 5 and 6, supply in Chapters 7 and 8, and the functioning of perfectly competitive markets in Chapter 10, we can provide a fairly comprehensive answer to the first part of this question. This chapter describes major tasks that the market carries out well—some, indeed, with spectacular effectiveness.

We begin by recalling two important themes from Chapters 3 and 4. First, because all resources are scarce, a society benefits by using them efficiently. Second, to do so, an economy must somehow coordinate the actions of many individual consumers and producers. Specifically, society must somehow choose

- How much of each good to produce
- What input quantities to use in the production process of each commodity
- How to distribute the resulting outputs among consumers

CONTENTS

As suggested by the opening quotation (from someone who was certainly in a position to know), these tasks are exceedingly difficult for a centrally planned economy. That overwhelming difficulty surely contributed to the fall of communism in the late 1980s, and the same difficulty shows up in the few remaining centrally planned economies, such as North Korea and Cuba. But, for the most part, those same tasks appear to be rather simple for a market system. This is why observers with philosophies as diverse as those of Adam Smith and the Russian Revolution's Leon Trotsky have admired the market, and why even countries that maintain very strong central governments have now moved toward market economies.

Do not misinterpret this chapter as a piece of salesmanship. Here, we study the market mechanism at its theoretical very best—when every good is produced under the exacting conditions of perfect competition. Some industries in our economy are reasonable approximations of perfect competition, but many others are as different from this idealized world as the physical world is from a frictionless vacuum tube. Just as the physicist uses the vacuum tube to study the laws of gravity, the economist uses the theoretical concept of a perfectly competitive economy to analyze the virtues of the market. We will spend plenty of time in later chapters studying its vices.

PUZZLE: CROSSING THE SAN FRANCISCO–OAKLAND BAY BRIDGE: IS THE PRICE RIGHT?

In California, the San Francisco–Oakland Bay Bridge is very heavily traveled. The large volume of toll-paying traffic has probably long since paid for the cost of building this bridge, although that is less likely for the nearby San Mateo–Hayward and Dumbarton bridges, which are less crowded. Yet economists argue that the price charged to use the San Francisco–Oakland Bay Bridge should be higher than the prices charged for use of the other two bridges. Why does that make sense? Before you have finished reading this chapter, you may even agree with this seemingly unfair proposition.

SOURCE: © Roger Allyn Lee/SuperStock

EFFICIENT RESOURCE ALLOCATION AND PRICING

The fundamental fact that inputs are scarce means that there are limits to the volume of goods and services that any economic system can produce. In Chapter 3 we illustrated the concept of scarcity with a graphic device called a *production possibilities frontier*, which we repeat here for convenience as Figure 1. The frontier, curve *BC*, depicts all combinations of motorboats and milk that a hypothetical society can produce given the limited resources at its disposal. For example, if it decides to produce 300 motorboats, it will have enough resources left over to produce no more than 500 billion quarts of milk (point *D*). Of course, it is possible, then, to produce fewer than 500 billion quarts of milk—at a point, such as *G*, below the production possibilities frontier. But if a society makes this choice, it is wasting some of its potential output; that is, it is not operating efficiently, as will be explained presently.

In Chapter 3 we defined efficiency rather loosely as the absence of waste. Because this chapter discusses primarily how a competitive market economy allocates resources efficiently, we now need a more precise definition. It is easiest to define an **efficient allocation of resources** by saying what it is not. For example, suppose that we could rearrange our resource allocation so that one group of people would get more of the things it wanted while no one else would have to give up anything. Then, the failure to change the allocation of resources to take advantage of this so far as yet unused opportunity would surely be wasteful—that is, inefficient. When society has taken advantage of every such opportunity for improvement, so that no such possibilities remain for making some people better off without making others worse off, we say that the allocation of resources is efficient.

An **efficient allocation of resources** is one that takes advantage of every opportunity to make some individuals better off in their own estimation while not worsening the lot of anyone else.

To see what this implies for our analysis, let us see what an inefficient set of output quantities looks like in our graph. Because point *G* in Figure 1 is below the frontier, there must be points like *E* on the frontier that lie above and to the right of *G*. At point *E*, we get more of both outputs without any increase in the available input supply, so it is possible to make some people better off without harming anyone. Thus, no point below the frontier can represent an efficient allocation of resources. By contrast, every point on the frontier is efficient because, no matter where on the frontier we start, we cannot get more of one good (by putting more of the available inputs into production of that item) without taking away those input quantities for, and so thereby giving up some of, the other.

This discussion also shows that, normally, many particular allocations of resources will be efficient; in the example, every combination of outputs that is represented by a point on frontier *BC* can be efficient. As a rule, the concept of efficiency cannot tell us which of these efficient allocations is best for society. Yet, as we shall see in this chapter, we can use the concept of efficiency to formulate surprisingly detailed rules to steer us away from situations in which resources would be wasted.

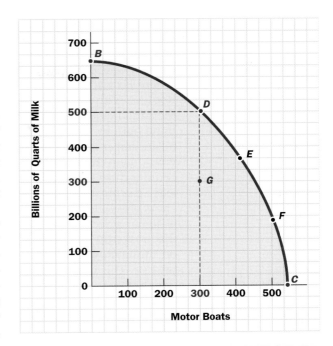

FIGURE 1

Production Possibilities Frontier and Efficiency

FIGURE 2

Toll Bridges of the San Francisco Bay Area

Pricing to Promote Efficiency: An Example

We can use the real example in our opening puzzle about the San Francisco–Oakland Bay Bridge to illustrate the connection between efficiency and the way prices can guide efficient choices. Prices can make all the difference between efficiency and inefficiency by guiding the actions of both suppliers and their customers. We will see now that the prices (tolls) California transportation authorities charge drivers to use San Francisco Bay area bridges can save some of the time that the drivers spend commuting—that is, they can make the commuting process more efficient. We also will see that people may well reject the efficient solution with perhaps reasonable grounds for doing so.

Figure 2 shows a map of the San Francisco Bay area, featuring the five bridges that serve most of the traffic in and around the bay. A traveler going from a location north of Berkeley (point *A*) to Palo Alto (point *B*) can choose among at least three routes:

Route 1: Over the Richmond–San Rafael Bridge, across the Golden Gate Bridge, through San Francisco, and on southward via Highway 101

Route 2: Across the bay on the San Francisco–Oakland Bay Bridge and on southward via Highway 101, as before

Route 3: Down the eastern shore of the bay, across the San Mateo–Hayward Bridge or the Dumbarton Bridge, and then on to Palo Alto (shown in blue in Figure 2)

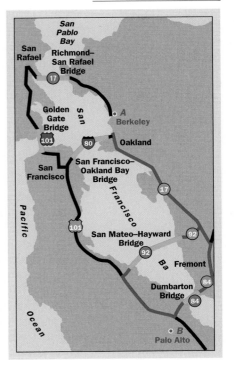

Let's consider which of these three choices uses society's resources—commuter time, gasoline, and so on—most efficiently. The San Francisco–Oakland Bay Bridge is by far the most crowded of the five bridges, carrying approximately 254,000 vehicles per day, followed by the Golden Gate Bridge, which carries about 107,000 per day. The San Mateo–Hayward, Dumbarton, and Richmond–San Rafael bridges carry approximately 92,000, 64,000, and 71,000 vehicles per day, respectively.[1]

[1] Traffic volume for the Golden Gate Bridge is a daily average for the period between July 2007 and June 2008 (accessed online at: http://goldengatebridge.org/research/crossings_revenues.php). Traffic volumes for the four other Bay area bridges are estimates based on one-way vehicle counts for October 21, 2009 (provided by the Bay Area Toll Authority's Public Information Office).

To achieve efficiency, any driver who is indifferent about the two routes should take the one using the least crowded bridges. This would help reduce the amount of travel time wasted by the population as a whole. Specifically, in our illustration, Route 1, using the Golden Gate Bridge, is not a socially desirable way for our driver to get to Palo Alto because it adds too many miles to the trip and because it requires two bridge crossings. Route 2, with its use of the San Francisco–Oakland Bay Bridge, is even worse because of the added delays it causes for everyone else. Route 3, for drivers who are indifferent about these options, is the best choice from the viewpoint of the public interest. This does not mean that it is socially efficient to equalize the traffic among the routes, but it certainly would help travelers get where they are going more quickly if transportation authorities could induce some drivers (those who care least about which of the routes they take) to leave the most crowded routes and switch over to some less crowded ones.

Appropriate prices can promote this sort of efficiency in bridge utilization. Specifically, if higher prices (very likely substantially higher prices) were charged for drivers to cross the most crowded bridges (on which space is a scarce resource), balanced by lower prices on the uncrowded bridges, then more drivers could be induced to use the uncrowded bridges. This is the same reasoning that leads economists to advocate low prices for abundant natural resources and high prices for scarce ones.

Can Price Increases Ever Serve the Public Interest?

This discussion raises a point that people untrained in economics always find extremely difficult to accept: Low prices may not always serve the public interest! The reason is pretty clear. If a price, such as the toll charged for crossing a crowded bridge or the price of gasoline, is set "too low," then consumers will receive the "wrong" market signals. Low prices will encourage them to crowd the bridge even more or to consume more gasoline, thereby squandering society's scarce resources and contributing to the global warming threat.

A striking historical illustration brings out the importance of this role of prices. In 1834, University of Dublin economics professor, Mountifort Longfield, lectured about the price system. He offered the following example:

> Suppose the crop of potatoes in Ireland was to fall short in some year [by] one-sixth of the usual consumption. If [there were no] increase of price, the whole . . . supply of the year would be exhausted in ten months, and for the remaining two months a scene of misery and famine beyond description would ensue. . . . But when prices [increase] the sufferers [often believe] that it is not caused by scarcity. . . . They suppose that there are provisions enough, but that the distress is caused by the insatiable rapacity of the possessors . . . [and] they have generally succeeded in obtaining laws against [the price increases] . . . which alone can prevent the provisions from being entirely consumed long before a new supply can be obtained.[2]

You may be intrigued to know that this talk was given some 10 years before the great potato famine, which caused unspeakable misery and death by starvation and brought many people from Ireland to the United States. The story of the actual potato famine in Ireland is much more complex than Longfield's discussion indicates. Still, the implications of his lecture about the way the price system works are entirely valid.

We can perhaps rephrase Longfield's reasoning more usefully. If the crop fails, potatoes become scarcer. If society is to use its scarce resources efficiently, stretching out the potato supply to last until the next crop arrives, it must cut back on the consumption of potatoes during earlier months—which is just what rising prices will do automatically if free-market mechanisms are allowed to work. However, if the price is held artificially low, consumers will use society's resources inefficiently. In this case, the inefficiency shows up in the form of famine and suffering when people deplete this year's crop months before the next one is harvested.

---

[2] Mountifort Longfield, *Lectures on Political Economy Delivered in Trinity and Michaelmas Terms* (Dublin: W. Curry, Jr., and Company; 1834), pp. 53–56.

Using Economic Principles to Reduce Highway Congestion in Orange County, California

"91 Express Lanes" is a four-lane, 10-mile toll road built in the median of California's crowded Riverside Freeway (State Road 91). Opened in 1995, it was the first variable-priced and fully automated highway in the United States. By varying the price that drivers must pay to use these lanes, the traffic authorities control the congestion on the road and keep the traffic moving. For example, tolls in October 2009 ranged from $1.30 at the most uncongested times (like 3 o'clock in the morning) all the way up to $9.90 during the worst of the rush hour. Faced with high tolls during commuting hours, some drivers choose not to use the lanes at that time. Since 1995, the lanes have saved more than 32 million hours of commuting time. The Orange County Transportation Authority estimates that these time savings are worth $480 million in added economic productivity and quality-of-life benefits.

SOURCE: Orange County Transportation Authority, http://www.91expresslanes.com/learnabout/snapshot.asp.

91 Express Lanes — Toll Schedule — Eastbound
Effective July 1, 2009 — SR-55 to Riverside Co. Line

	Sun	M	Tu	W	Th	F	Sat
Midnight	$1.30	$1.30	$1.30	$1.30	$1.30	$1.30	$1.30
1:00 am	$1.30	$1.30	$1.30	$1.30	$1.30	$1.30	$1.30
2:00 am	$1.30	$1.30	$1.30	$1.30	$1.30	$1.30	$1.30
3:00 am	$1.30	$1.30	$1.30	$1.30	$1.30	$1.30	$1.30
4:00 am	$1.30	$1.30	$1.30	$1.30	$1.30	$1.30	$1.30
5:00 am	$1.30	$1.30	$1.30	$1.30	$1.30	$1.30	$1.30
6:00 am	$1.30	$2.05	$2.05	$2.05	$2.05	$2.05	$1.30
7:00 am	$1.30	$2.05	$2.05	$2.05	$2.05	$2.05	$1.30
8:00 am	$1.65	$2.05	$2.05	$2.05	$2.05	$2.05	$2.05
9:00 am	$1.65	$2.05	$2.05	$2.05	$2.05	$2.05	$2.05
10:00 am	$2.50	$2.05	$2.05	$2.05	$2.05	$2.05	$2.50
11:00 am	$2.50	$2.05	$2.05	$2.05	$2.05	$2.05	$2.50
Noon	$3.00	$2.05	$2.05	$2.05	$2.05	$3.10	$3.00
1:00 pm	$3.00	$2.85	$2.85	$2.85	$3.10	$4.85	$3.00
2:00 pm	$3.00	$4.05	$4.05	$4.05	$4.15	$4.10	$3.00
3:00 pm	$2.50	$4.35	$3.70	$5.45	$5.90	$9.50	$3.00
4:00 pm	$2.50	$6.05	$7.75	$8.25	$9.90	$9.30	$3.00
5:00 pm	$2.50	$5.85	$7.75	$8.25	$9.05	$7.75	$3.00
6:00 pm	$2.50	$4.35	$4.60	$4.10	$4.90	$5.25	$2.50
7:00 pm	$2.50	$3.10	$3.10	$3.10	$4.45	$4.90	$2.05
8:00 pm	$2.50	$2.05	$2.05	$2.05	$2.85	$4.45	$2.05
9:00 pm	$2.05	$2.05	$2.05	$2.05	$2.05	$2.85	$2.05
10:00 pm	$1.30	$1.30	$1.30	$1.30	$1.30	$2.05	$1.30
11:00 pm	$1.30	$1.30	$1.30	$1.30	$1.30	$1.30	$1.30

SOURCE: © Courtesy of the Orange County Transportation Authority

It is not easy to accept the notion that higher prices can serve the public interest better than lower ones. Politicians who voice this view are in the position of the proverbial parent who, before spanking a child, announces, "This is going to hurt me much more than it hurts you!" Because advocacy of higher prices courts political disaster, the political system often rejects the market's increased price solution when resources suddenly become scarcer.

The way that airport officials price landing privileges at crowded airports offers a good example. Airports become particularly congested at "peak hours," just before 9 A.M. and just after 5 P.M. These times are when passengers most often suffer long delays. But many airports continue to charge bargain landing fees throughout the day, even at those crowded hours. That makes it attractive for small corporate jets or other planes carrying only a few passengers to arrive and take off at those hours, worsening the delays. Higher fees for peak-hour landings can discourage such overuse, but they are politically unpopular, and many airports are run by local governments. So we continue to experience late arrivals as a normal feature of air travel. (See "Using Economic Principles to Reduce Highway Congestion in Orange County, California" above for a successful example of pricing to reduce congestion.)

ATTEMPTS TO REPEAL THE LAWS OF SUPPLY AND DEMAND: THE MARKET STRIKES BACK

IDEAS FOR BEYOND THE FINAL EXAM

As we saw in our list of **Ideas for Beyond the Final Exam**, keeping prices low when an increase is appropriate can have serious consequences. We have just observed that it can worsen the effects of shortages of food and other vital goods. We know that inappropriately low prices caused nationwide chaos in gasoline distribution after the sudden decline in Iranian oil exports in 1979. In times of war, constraints on prices have even contributed to the surrender of cities under military siege, deterring those who would otherwise have risked smuggling food supplies through enemy lines. Low prices also have discouraged housing construction in cities where government-imposed upper limits on rents made building construction a losing proposition. Of course, in some cases it is appropriate to resist price increases—when unrestrained monopoly would otherwise succeed in gouging the public, when taxes are imposed on products capriciously and inappropriately, and when rising prices fall so heavily on poor people that rationing becomes the more acceptable option. Before tampering with the market mechanism we must carefully evaluate the potentially serious and even tragic consequences that artificial restrictions on prices can produce.

SCARCITY AND THE NEED TO COORDINATE ECONOMIC DECISIONS

Efficiency becomes a particularly critical issue when we concern ourselves with the workings of the economy as a whole, rather than with narrower topics such as choosing among bridge routes or deciding on the output of a single firm. We can think of an economy as a complex machine with literally millions of component parts. If this machine is to function efficiently, we must find some way to make the parts work in harmony.

A consumer in Madison, Wisconsin, may decide to purchase two dozen eggs, and on the same day thousands of shoppers throughout the country may make similar decisions. None of these purchasers knows or cares about the decisions of the others. Yet scarcity requires that these demands must somehow be coordinated with the production process so that the total quantity of eggs demanded does not exceed the total quantity supplied. Consumers, supermarkets, wholesalers, shippers, and chicken farmers must somehow arrive at mutually consistent decisions, in this case with an increase in egg supplies or a decrease in demand for them; otherwise, the economic process will deteriorate into chaos, as will millions of other such decisions. A machine cannot run with a few missing parts.

In a planned or centrally directed economy, we can easily imagine how such coordination takes place—though implementation is far more difficult than conception. Central planners set production targets for firms and sometimes tell firms how to meet these targets. In extreme cases, consumers may even be told, rather than asked, what they are allowed to consume.

In contrast, a market system uses prices to coordinate economic activity. High prices discourage consumption of the scarcest resources and, where possible, induce expansion of their supplies, whereas low prices discourage consumption of comparatively abundant resources. In this way, Adam Smith's invisible hand uses prices to organize the economy's production.

"Corporate leaders gather in a field outside Darien, Connecticut, where one of them claims to have seen the invisible hand of the marketplace."

The invisible hand has an astonishing capacity to handle enormously complex coordination problems—even those that remain beyond computer capabilities. Like any mechanism, this one has its imperfections, some of them rather serious. But we should not lose sight of the tremendously demanding task that the market constantly does accomplish—unnoticed, undirected, and, in some respects, amazingly well. Let's look at just how the market goes about coordinating economic activity.

Three Coordination Tasks in the Economy

We recalled at the beginning of this chapter that any economic system, planned or unplanned, must find answers to three basic questions of resource allocation:

- *Output selection.* How much of each commodity should be produced, given limited supplies of the needed input resources?
- *Production planning.* What quantity of each of the available inputs should be used to produce each good?
- *Distribution.* How should the resulting products be divided among consumers?

These coordination tasks may at first appear to be tailor-made for a regime of government planning like the one that the former Soviet Union once employed. Yet most economists (even, nowadays, those in the formerly centrally planned economies) believe that it is in exactly these tasks that central direction performs most poorly and, paradoxically, the undisciplined free market performs best, even though no one directs its overall activities.

To understand how the unplanned and unguided market manages the miracle of creating order out of what might otherwise be chaos, let's look at how each of these questions is answered by a system of free and unfettered markets—the method of economic organization that eighteenth-century French economists named **laissez-faire**. Under laissez-faire, the government acts to prevent crime, enforce contracts, and build roads and other types of public works; it does not set prices, however, and interferes as little as possible with the operation of free markets. How does such an economy, *though unmanaged and unguided by anyone,* solve the three coordination problems?

Laissez-faire refers to a situation in which there is minimal government interference with the workings of the market system. The term implies that people should be left alone in carrying out their economic affairs.

Output Selection   A free-market system decides what should be produced via what we have called the "law" of supply and demand. Where there is a shortage (that is, where quantity demanded exceeds quantity supplied), the market mechanism pushes the price upward, thereby encouraging more production and less consumption of the commodity in short supply. Where a surplus arises (that is, where quantity supplied exceeds quantity demanded), the same mechanism works in reverse: the price falls, discouraging production and stimulating consumption.

As an example, suppose that millions of people wake up one morning with a change in taste and thereafter want more omelets. As a result, for the moment, the quantity of eggs demanded exceeds the quantity supplied, but within a few days, the market mechanism swings into action to meet this sudden change in demand. The price of eggs rises, which stimulates egg production. At first, farmers will simply bring more eggs to market by taking them out of storage. Over a somewhat longer time period, chickens that otherwise would have been sold for meat will be kept in the chicken coops laying eggs. Finally, if the high price of eggs persists, farmers will begin to increase their flocks, build more coops, and so on. Thus, a shift in consumer demand leads to a shift in society's resources; more eggs are wanted, so the market mechanism sees to it that more of society's resources are devoted to egg production and marketing.

Similar reactions follow if a technological breakthrough reduces the input quantities needed to produce an item. Electronic calculators are a marvelous example. Calculators used to be so expensive that they could be found only in business firms and scientific laboratories. Then advances in science and engineering reduced their cost dramatically, and the market went to work. With costs sharply reduced, prices fell and the quantity demanded skyrocketed. Electronics firms flocked into the industry to meet this demand, which is to say that more of society's resources were devoted to producing the calculators that were suddenly in such great demand. These examples lead us to conclude that:

> Under laissez-faire, the allocation of society's resources among different products depends on consumer preferences (demands) and the production costs of the goods demanded. Prices (and the resulting profitability of the different products) vary so as to bring the quantity of each commodity produced into line with the quantity demanded.

Notice that no bureaucrat or central planner arranges resource allocation. Instead, an unseen force guides allocation—the lure of profits, which is the invisible hand that guides chicken farmers to increase their flocks when eggs are in greater demand and guides electronics firms to build new factories when the cost of electronic products falls.

Production Planning   Once the market has decided on output composition, the next coordination task is to determine just how those goods will be produced. The production-planning problem includes, among other things, the division of society's scarce inputs among enterprises. Which farm or factory will get how much of which materials? How much of the nation's labor force? Of the produced inputs such as plant and machinery? Such decisions can be crucial. If a factory runs short of an essential input, the entire production process may grind to a halt.

In reality, no economic system can select inputs and outputs separately. The input distribution between the production of cars and the manufacture of washing machines determines the quantities of cars and washing machines that society can obtain. However, it is simpler to think of input and output decisions as if they occur one at a time.

Poland's Transition to a Free-Market Economy

Nearly 20 years have passed since communism collapsed all over Eastern Europe and the former Soviet Union, ending economic central planning and heralding the emergence of a free market in these countries. Nowhere were these changes as dramatic as in Poland, where radical economic reforms constituted no less than "shock therapy."

Poland's transformation into a market economy, though far from complete, has been nearly as drastic as the first post-communist government hoped. Poland had been saddled with a legendarily incompetent, old-fashioned, and badly managed economy, which in its depths managed to run out of things like matches and salt, its paltry living standards bequeathed by a centrally controlled economy. It reached out to the West for help in creating monetary, budget, trade, and legal regimes and is now one of the most robust economies in central Europe and, most recently, one of the newest members of the European Union.

Poland's economy has been growing at an impressive rate. Its average annual GDP grew by more than 4 percent between 1995 and 2005. But despite strong growth and lower unemployment (14 percent in 2006, down from rates as high as 50 percent following the collapse of communism), Poland's GDP per capita remains much lower than that of other European Union member countries. Poland's GDP per capita also varies significantly from region to region, and the gap between the country's large urban centers and rural areas has increased steadily since the mid-1990s. As of 2005, GDP per capita in Warsaw was more than 2.5 times greater than the national average.

Meanwhile, privatization continues slowly. Competition has increased in Poland's telecommunications industry, but major sell-offs of formerly state-controlled power suppliers have been delayed, and the country's two major banking and insurance entities remain state-owned. Despite all of the good news, Poland still has much work to do.

SOURCES: Rudolf Herman, "Rural Poland: Ready for the Chop," *Central European Review*, 1, no. 10 (August 1999); Stanislaw Gomulka, "Macroeconomic Policies and Achievements in Transition Economies, 1989–1999," United Nations' Economic Commission for Europe Annual Seminar, Geneva (May 2, 2000); Michael P. Keane and Eswar S. Prasad, "Poland: Inequality, Transfers, and Growth in Transition," *Finance & Development*, 38, no. 1 (March 2001); Organization for Economic Cooperation and Development (OECD), *OECD Territorial Reviews: Poland* (Paris, OECD, 2008, accessed online at: http://www.oecd.org); and OECD, *Policy Brief: Regional Development* (Paris: OECD, November 2008, accessed online at: http://www.oecd.org).

SOURCE: © GROCHOWIAK EWA/CORBIS SYGMA

SOURCE: © Raymond Gehman/CORBIS

Once again, under laissez-faire it is the price system that apportions labor, fuel, and other inputs among different industries in accord with those industries' requirements. The firm that needs a piece of equipment most urgently will be the last to drop out of the market for that product when prices rise. If millers demand more wheat than is currently available, the price will rise and bring quantity demanded back into line with quantity supplied, always giving priority to those users who are willing to pay the most for grain because it is most valuable to them. Thus:

In a free market, inputs are assigned to the firms that can make the most productive (most profitable) use of them. Firms that cannot make a sufficiently productive use of some input will be priced out of the market for that item.

This task, which sounds so simple, is actually almost unimaginably complex. It is so complex that it has helped to bring down many centrally planned systems because they could not handle the difficulties. We will return to this shortly, as an illustration of how difficult it is to replace the market by a central planning bureau, but first let us consider the third of our three coordination problems.

Distribution of Products among Consumers
The third task of any economy is to decide what consumer gets which of the goods that has been produced. The objective is to

distribute the available supplies to match differing consumer preferences as well as possible. The price mechanism solves this problem by assigning the highest prices to the goods in greatest demand and then letting individual consumers pursue their own self-interests. Consider our example of rising egg prices. As eggs become more expensive, people whose craving for omelets is not terribly strong will begin to buy fewer eggs. In effect, the price acts as a rationing device that apportions the available eggs among consumers who are willing to pay the most for them.

Thus, the price mechanism has an important advantage over other rationing devices: It can respond to individual consumer preferences. If a centrally planned economy rations eggs by distributing the same amount to everyone (say, two eggs per week to each person), then everyone ends up with two eggs whether he likes eggs or detests them. The price system, on the other hand, permits each consumer to set his own priorities. Thus:

IDEAS FOR BEYOND THE FINAL EXAM

THE TRADE-OFF BETWEEN EFFICIENCY AND EQUALITY The price system carries out the distribution process by rationing goods on the basis of preferences and relative incomes. Notice the last three words of the previous sentence. The price system does favor the rich, and this is a problem to which market economies must face up.

However, we may still want to think twice before declaring ourselves opposed to the price system. If equality is our goal, might not a more reasonable solution be to use the tax system to equalize incomes and then let the market mechanism distribute goods in accord with preferences? We take this idea up in Chapter 18, in which we discuss tax policy.

We have just seen, in broad outline, how a laissez-faire economy addresses the three basic issues of resource allocation: what to produce, how to produce it, and how to distribute the resulting products. Because it performs these tasks without central direction and with no apparent concern for the public interest, many radical critics have predicted that such an unplanned system must degenerate into chaos. Yet unplanned, free-market economies are far from chaotic. Quite ironically, it is the centrally planned economies that have often ended up in economic disarray, whereas the invisible hand seems to go about its business seamlessly. Perhaps the best way to appreciate the free market's accomplishments is to consider how a centrally planned system must cope with the coordination problems we have just outlined. Let us examine just one of them: production planning.

Input-Output Analysis: The Near Impossibility of Perfect Central Planning

Of the three coordination tasks of any economy, the assignment of input to specific industries and firms has claimed the most attention of central planners. Why? Because the production processes of the various industries are interdependent. Industry X cannot operate without Industry Y's output, but Industry Y, in turn, needs Industry X's product. The metal supplying industry needs railroads, but the railroads cannot operate without metal for rails and other equipment. The output decisions of the two industries cannot escape this (nonvicious) circle. The entire economy can grind to a halt if planners do not solve such production-planning problems satisfactorily. Failure to adapt to this kind of interdependence has had dire consequences in North Korea, one of the last remaining centrally planned economies. Breakdowns of key economic activities such as the electric supply grid, transportation systems, and other basic industries have each exacerbated the others' failures and created a terrible cycle of economic disaster that contributed to a severe famine in the late 1990s, which killed as many as 2 million people. Hunger continues to be a problem, with an estimated 37 percent of North Koreans still receiving food assistance.[3]

A simple example will further illustrate the point. Unless economic planners allocate enough gasoline to the trucking industry, products will not get to market. And unless planners allocate enough trucks to haul gasoline to gas stations, drivers will have no fuel. Thus, trucking activity depends on gasoline supply, but gasoline supply also depends on

---

[3] "Life Expectancy Plummets, North Korea Says," *The New York Times*, May 16, 2001, http://www.nytimes.com; and "At the Heart of North Korea's Troubles an Intractable Hunger Crisis," *The Washington Post*, March 6, 2009, http://www.washingtonpost.com.

Input-Output Equations: An Example

Imagine an economy with only three outputs: electricity, steel, and coal. Let E, S, and C represent the respective dollar values of these outputs. Suppose that to produce every dollar's worth of steel, $0.20 worth of electricity is used, so that the total electricity demand of steel manufacturers is $0.2S$. Similarly, assume that coal manufacturers use $0.30 of electricity in producing $1 worth of coal, or a total of $0.3C$ units of electricity. Because E dollars of electricity are produced in total, the amount left over for consumers, after subtracting industrial demands for fuel, will be E (available electricity) minus $0.2S$ (used in steel production) minus $0.3C$ (used in coal production). Suppose further that the central planners have decided to supply $15 million worth of electricity to consumers. We end up with the electricity output equation:

$$E - 0.2S - 0.3C = 15$$

The planner will also need such an equation for each of the two other industries, specifying for each of them the net amount intended to be left for consumers after the industrial uses of the product. The full set of equations will then be similar to the following:

$$E - 0.2S - 0.3C = 15$$
$$S - 0.1E - 0.06C = 7$$
$$C - 0.15E - 0.4S = 10$$

These are typical equations in an input-output analysis. In practice, however, such an analysis has dozens and sometimes hundreds of equations with similar numbers of unknowns. This, then, is the logic of input-output analysis.

SOURCE: © Steve Allen/Brand X Picture/Jupiterimages

---

trucking activity. We see again that the decision maker is caught in a circle. Planners must decide both truck and gasoline outputs together, not separately.

Because the output required from any one industry depends on outputs from many other industries, planners can be sure that the production of the various outputs will be sufficient to meet both consumer and industrial demands only by taking explicit account of this interdependence among industries. If they change the output target for one industry, they must also adjust the targets for many other industries. But those changes in turn are likely to require readjustment of the first target change that started it all, leading to still more target change requirements, and so on, indefinitely.

For example, if planners decide to provide consumers with more electricity, then more steel must be produced in order to build more electric generators. Of course, an increase in steel output requires that more iron ore be mined. More mining, in turn, means that still more electricity is needed to light the mines, run the elevators, perhaps operate some of the trains that carry the iron ore, and so on. Any single change in production triggers a chain of adjustments throughout the economy that require still more adjustments that lead to still more adjustments.

There is a solution to this seemingly intractable problem, at least in theory. To decide how much of each output an economy must produce, the planner must use statistics to form a set of equations, one equation representing the input requirements for each product, and then solve those equations simultaneously. The simultaneous solution process deals effectively with the interdependence in the analysis—electricity output depends on steel production, but steel output depends on electricity production—and prevents it from becoming a vicious circle. The technique used to solve these complicated equations—**input-output analysis**—was invented by the late economist Wassily Leontief, who won the 1973 Nobel Prize for his work.

The equations of input-output analysis illustrated in the box, "Input-Output Equations: An Example," above take explicit account of the interdependence among industries by describing precisely how each industry's target output depends on every other

Input-output analysis is a mathematical procedure that takes account of the interdependence among the economy's industries and determines the amount of output each industry must provide as inputs to the other industries in the economy.

industry's target. To keep the discussion from growing too complicated, the example deals with a vastly oversimplified and imaginary economy that has only three industries. Only by solving these equations simultaneously for the required outputs of electricity, steel, coal, and so on can planners ensure a consistent solution that produces the required amounts of each product—including the amount of each product needed to produce every other product.

The illustrative input-output analysis that appears in the box is not provided to make you a master at using the technique yourself. Its true purpose is to help you imagine how very complicated the problems facing central planners can become in the real world. Their task, although analogous to the one described in the box, is enormously more complex. In any real economy, the number of commodities is far greater than the three outputs in the example! In the United States, some large manufacturing companies deal in hundreds of thousands of items, and the armed forces keep several million different items in inventory.

Planners must ultimately make calculations for each single item. It is not enough to plan the right number of bolts in total; they must make sure that the required number of each size is produced. (Try putting 5 million large bolts into 5 million small nuts.) To be sure that their plans will really work, they need a separate equation for every size of bolt and one for every size and type of nut. But then, to replicate the analysis described in the box, they would have to solve several million equations simultaneously! This task would strain even the most powerful computer's capability, but that is not even the main difficulty.

Worse still is the data problem. Each of our three equations requires three pieces of statistical information, making 3×3, or 9 numbers in total. The equation for electricity must indicate how much electricity is needed in steel production, how much in coal production, and how much is demanded by consumers, all on the basis of statistical information that is itself subject to error. Therefore, in a five-industry analysis, 5×5, or 25, pieces of data are needed; a 100-industry analysis requires 100×100, or 10,000, numbers, and a million-item input-output study might need 1 trillion pieces of information. Solving the data-gathering problems is no easy task, to put it mildly. Still other complications arise, but we have seen enough to conclude that:

> **A full, rigorous central-planning solution to the production problem is a tremendous task, requiring an overwhelming quantity of information and some incredibly difficult calculations. Yet this very complex job is carried out automatically and unobtrusively by the price mechanism in an unplanned free-market economy.**

Which Buyers and Which Sellers Get Priority?

Because the supplies of all commodities are limited, some potential customers of a product will end up with none of it. And because demand is not infinite, some potential suppliers of a commodity will find no market available for them. So, which consumers get the scarce commodity and which firms get to supply the goods? Once again, the price mechanism comes to the rescue.

> **Other things being equal, the price mechanism ensures that those consumers who want a scarce commodity most will receive it and that those sellers who can supply it most efficiently will get to supply the commodity.**

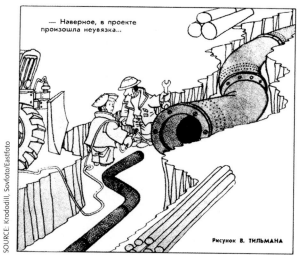

In this cartoon from a Soviet humor magazine, one construction worker comments to another, "A slight mistake in the plans, perhaps." It is interesting that there were many cartoons making fun of the inefficiencies of the Soviet economy in the humor magazines of the USSR before the collapse of communism.

To illustrate, let's look at Figure 3, an ordinary supply-demand graph. For simplicity, suppose we are dealing here with a commodity such as a best-selling novel. We assume also that no one buys more than one copy of the book. The demand curve, *DD*, represents the widely differing preferences of 6,000 potential customers. The first

FIGURE 3

FIGURE 3

Supply-Demand Graph Showing That Price Excludes Only Buyers and Sellers Who Care the Least

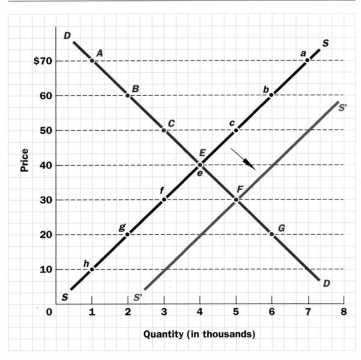

Quantity (in thousands)

1,000 of them are willing to pay as much as $70 for the book, as shown by point *A* on the demand curve (though they would, of course, prefer to pay less). Point *B* shows a second group of 1,000 buyers who will purchase the book at a price of $60 but refuse to spend $70 on it (because they care less about the book than the point *A* consumers). Similarly, point *C* represents the demand of a third group of consumers, to whom the book is even less important, so that they are willing to spend only $50 for a copy. And points *E, F,* and *G* represent sets of consumers with successively lower desires for the book, until at point *G,* consumers are willing to pay only $20 for the book.

With *SS* as the supply curve, the equilibrium point is *E,* where *SS* and *DD* intersect. Under perfect competition, the market price of the book will be $40. Buyers at point *A,* to whom the book is worth $70, will be delighted to buy it for only $40. Similarly, buyers at points *B, C,* and *E* will also buy the book. But the consumers at points *F* and *G,* to whom the book is worth less than $40, will not buy the book. We can see in this example that the book will go to the consumers who value it most (in terms of money), and only those who value it least will be deprived of it.

The price mechanism always ranks potential consumers of a good in the order of the intensity of their preference for the good, as indicated by the amount they are willing to spend for it.

The price system's priority to those consumers who assign most importance to a good goes one step further. Suppose that supply increases, with the supply curve shifting to the right, from *SS* to *S'S'* in the figure. Which consumers will get the increased quantity supplied? Answer: Of those consumers in the group of people who were previously denied the commodity, those who want it most intensely will acquire the product. In the graph, the shift in supply moves the equilibrium point from *E* to *F,* so point *F* consumers will now be included in the group of buyers of the book (along with point *A, B, C,* and *E* consumers), but the point *G* consumers still will not purchase the book. The book is worth more to point *F* consumers ($30) than it is to point *G* consumers, who value it at only $20.

The price system seems to set the right priorities in deciding which prospective consumers of some specific good do receive some of it and which do not. Only one major imperfection arises in this argument, to which we will return in a moment.

First, however, let's look at Figure 3 again, this time from the supplying firm's point of view. Assume that *SS* is the long-run industry supply curve. Point *g* on this curve represents the amount that the industry will supply if the price is $20—that is, the amount that will be supplied by firms whose average cost is no higher than $20, so that the price will cover their cost. Similarly, point *f* represents the output of all firms whose average cost is no higher than $30, so that the group of suppliers now includes some firms that are less efficient (they have higher average cost) than those at point *g.* At point *e,* some of the suppliers will have average costs of $40, but none of the suppliers who are able to make any sales will have an average cost higher than that level. Using the same reasoning, as we move farther along *SS* to points *c, b,* and *a,* increasingly inefficient firms will be included among the suppliers.

Now we examine the supply-demand equilibrium point *e,* at which price is $40. Which suppliers will be able to market their products at this point? Answer: Those at points *g, f,* and *e,* but not firms at points *c, b,* and *a,* because no firm in the last three groups can cover its costs at the equilibrium price. Once again, the price mechanism does its job. It ranks firms in order of their efficiency, as measured by long-run average costs, and brings business to the more efficient firms, leaving out the least efficient potential suppliers.

This example illustrates yet another of the many desirable features of the price mechanism. But there is one fly in the ointment—at least on the demand side of the story. We saw that consumers in group *G* were likely to be denied the scarce commodity we are discussing, because they wanted it less than the other consumers. Group *G* consumers were willing to spend only $20 for the book, whereas the other consumers were willing to spend more for it. But what if some consumers in group *G* want the book very badly but are also very poor? This is an important question—one we will encounter again and again. The price mechanism is like a democracy, but one in which the rule is not "one person, one vote," but rather, "one dollar, one vote." In other words, under the price mechanism rich consumers' preferences get much more attention than poor consumers' desires.

HOW PERFECT COMPETITION ACHIEVES EFFICIENCY: A GRAPHIC ANALYSIS

We have indicated how the market mechanism solves the three basic coordination problems of any economy—what to produce, how to produce it, and how to distribute the goods to consumers. Also, we have suggested that these same tasks pose almost insurmountable difficulties for central planners. One critical question remains: Is the allocation of resources that the market mechanism selects efficient, according to the precise definition of efficiency presented at the start of this chapter? The answer, under the idealized circumstances of perfect competition, is yes. A simple supply-and-demand diagram can be used to give us an intuitive view of why that is so.

Focusing on the market for a single commodity, let us ask whether either an increase or a decrease in the amount of output produced by the market mechanism can yield a greater total net benefit to consumers and producers. Suppose the current output level of swimming lessons in a swimming pool (number of people being taught) is 20 and the total net benefit to all involved in the activity can somehow be evaluated in money terms at $500 per week. Then, if any other number of students yields a total net benefit less than $500, clearly we have reason to conclude that 20 students is the optimum. We will show that, in equilibrium under perfect competition, the market unerringly and automatically will drive toward an equilibrium exactly at that optimal output level, without any central direction, explicit guidance, or planning by anyone. That is one of the remarkable accomplishments of the market mechanism.

To show this, let's begin by defining consumer and producer benefits sufficiently precisely so we can measure them. In Chapter 5 (page 93), we already have encountered the concept we need for the consumer benefits: consumer's surplus. And we will introduce a perfectly analogous concept, called *producer's surplus*, for the other side of the market. Suppose Anne would be willing to purchase a full week of swimming lessons at any price up to $140, but when she arrives at the gym she sees that the lessons are available for sale at a price of $90. Because swimming lessons are worth $140 to her, and she only has to spend $90 to obtain them, the purchase provides her with a net benefit of $140 − $90 = $50. If the lessons had been priced at $140, the result of the purchase would have been a wash—she would have given up $140 and received in exchange a service worth exactly $140 to her. But because the market price happens to be $90, she obtains a net gain worth $50 to her—a surplus—from the transaction. So, as we did in Chapter 5, we define:

The **consumer's surplus** from a purchase is equal to the difference between the maximum amount the consumer would be willing, if necessary, to pay for the item bought and the price that the market actually charges. In a purchase by a rational consumer, the surplus will never be a negative number, because if the price is higher than the maximum amount the potential purchaser is willing to pay, he will simply refuse to buy it.

Producer's surplus is defined exactly analogously. If Ben, a swimming instructor, is willing to provide a week of lessons at any price from $30 up, but the market price happens to be $90, he receives a $60 surplus from the transaction—and is delighted to make such a sale. So we have the definition:

The **producer's surplus** from a sale is the difference between the market price of the item sold and the lowest price at which the supplier would be willing to provide the item.

The **consumer's surplus** from a purchase is equal to the difference between the maximum amount the consumer would be willing, if necessary, to pay for the item bought and the price that the market actually charges.

The **producer's surplus** from a sale is the difference between the market price of the item sold and the lowest price at which the supplier would be willing to provide the item.

Now that we know how the two surpluses are defined and how to measure them, our objective is to see how the total surplus to all buyers and sellers in a market is affected by the quantity produced and sold in the market. We will demonstrate a striking result: that at the perfectly competitive market output level—the output level at which the market supply and demand curves intercept—the total surplus for all participants is as large as possible. To do this, we must turn to our familiar supply-demand analysis and use it to show explicitly the roles played by Anne, Ben, and the others involved in the market.

We begin with a table that assumes for simplicity that there are five potential buyers (Anne, Charles, Elaine, etc.) and five potential competing sellers (Ben, Debbie, etc.) in the market for swimming lessons. We see in Table 1 that at the weekly fee of $90 (third column in the table), Anne, to whom a week's lessons are worth $140 (first column), obtains a consumer's surplus of $50 = $140 − $90.

Similarly, at that price, Charles obtains a surplus of just $30. The consumer's surplus for these two customers is shown by the two light brown areas below the brown demand curve DD in Figure 4(a), corresponding to their purchases (two sets of lessons). For example, the left-most brown bar has its bottom at the price of $90 and its top at the $140 that the lessons are worth to Anne, so that the area of Anne's brown bar area is equal to her surplus, $140 − $90 = $50.

Similarly, Table 1 shows the producer's surpluses that can be earned by the different potential instructors. For example, it shows that the $90 fee gives Ben a surplus of $60 = $90 − $30, because he would be willing to give the lessons even if the fee were as low as $30. In the same way, we see that Debbie obtains a surplus of $40. These two producers' surpluses are shown in Figure 4(a) by the areas of the first two light blue bars areas between the blue supply curve SS and the $90 price line for those two sales. We also note that if both Anne and Charles received lessons, and both Ben and Debbie gave lessons, so that two sets of lessons were provided, the total surplus created by the market would be the sum of their four individual surpluses, $50 + 30 + 60 + 40 = $180—which is the second entry in the fourth column in the table. This is also shown by the area DRTUVS in Figure 4(a) that lies between the brown demand curve and the blue supply curve when only two sets of lessons are provided.

But comparison of Figures 4(a) and 4(b) shows us clearly that two lessons are not enough to make the total surplus generated by the market as large as possible. Specifically, if Elaine also takes lessons, and Frank provides them, this third transaction generates an additional consumer's surplus of $20 and an additional producer's surplus of $20, raising the total to $220. This larger total is shown by summing all the light brown and light blue areas between the demand and supply curves in Figure 4(b). One more set of lessons, the number at which the supply and demand curves intersect at PP, contributes no net gain in surplus, because George and Harriet value the lessons at exactly the prevailing price of $90. In buying and selling the service, these two people exchange money and services that are worth exactly the same to them. Increasing output further, by raising it to a fifth set of lessons, will actually reduce total surplus, because Irene, the potential student, values the lessons at less than their $90 price, whereas Jack, the potential instructor, considers his work worth $120. If Jack were to provide lessons to Irene, they both would obtain negative

TABLE 1

Consumer's and Producer's Surplus in the Swimming Lesson Market (dollars)

Students	(1) Student's Acceptable Maximum Price	(2) Individual Consumer's Surplus	(3) Actual Price	(4) Cumulative Total Surplus	(5) Individual Producer's Surplus	(6) Instructor's Acceptable Minimum Price	Instructors
Anne	$140	$50	$90	$110 = 50 + 60	$60	$ 30	Ben
Charles	120	30	90	180 = 110 + 30 + 40	40	50	Debbie
Elaine	110	20	90	220	20	70	Frank
George	90	0	90	220	0	90	Harriet
Irene	80	−10	90	180	−30	120	Jack

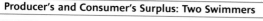

FIGURE 4(a)
Producer's and Consumer's Surplus: Two Swimmers

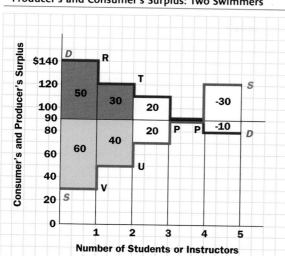

FIGURE 4(b)
Producer's and Consumer's Surplus and Optimal Output

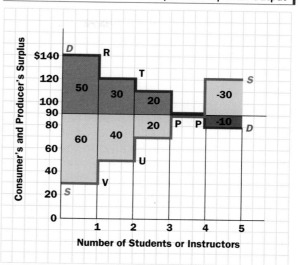

surpluses, represented by the dark blue and dark brown bars toward the right of the graph. These negative surpluses bring the total surplus down from $220 to $180 (the last two entries in column 4 of the table), clearly a net loss to the economy.

Now we come to the payoff from all this reasoning. Looking at Figure 4(a), we see that if total output stops short of the intersection of the supply and demand curve (interval PP), the light blue and brown areas will not be as large as possible. Similarly, if more than that quantity of swimming lessons is supplied, total surplus is decreased (Figure 4(b)). Only when the output quantity corresponds to the intersection of the supply and demand curves is the net surplus earned by both buyers and sellers as large as possible. Three conclusions follow:

1. Because under perfect competition the equilibrium output will be at the intersection of the supply and demand curves, a regime of perfect competition will select output levels that are optimal in terms of the public interest. They yield as large a sum of consumers' and producers' surpluses as possible.

2. If some influence such as monopoly forces output to be smaller (because price is higher) than that under perfect competition, the public interest will be damaged because the quantity of resources allocated to this market will be less than optimal.

3. If something like a government tax reduction induces suppliers to produce an output larger than the competitive level, that will also be a misallocation of resources damaging to the public welfare.

HOW PERFECT COMPETITION ACHIEVES OPTIMAL OUTPUT: MARGINAL ANALYSIS

There is a second way to look at the optimality of outputs under perfect competition's idealized circumstances, this time relating the discussion directly to the definition of efficiency given at the beginning of this chapter. Because a detailed proof of this assertion for all three coordination tasks is long and time-consuming, we will present the proof only for the task we have just been considering—output selection. We will show that, at least in theory, perfect competition does guarantee efficiency in determining the relative quantities of the different commodities that the economy produces.

The proof comes in two steps. First, we derive a criterion for efficient output selection— that is, a test that tells us whether production is being carried out efficiently. Second, we show that the prices that emerge from the market mechanism under perfect competition automatically pass this test.

Step 1: Rule for Efficient Output Selection   We begin by stating the rule for efficient output selection:

IDEAS FOR BEYOND THE FINAL EXAM

THE IMPORTANCE OF THINKING AT THE MARGIN   *Marginal Analysis*: Efficiency in the choice of output quantities requires that, for each of the economy's outputs, the marginal cost (MC) of the last unit produced be equal to the marginal utility (MU) of the last unit consumed.[4] In symbols:

$$MC = MU$$

This rule is yet another example of the basic principle of marginal analysis that we learned in Chapter 8.

The efficient decision about output quantities is the one that maximizes the total benefit (total utility) to society, minus the cost to society of producing the output quantities that are chosen. In other words, the goal is to maximize the surplus that society gains—total utility minus total cost. But, as we saw in Chapter 8, to maximize the difference between total utility and total cost, we must find the outputs that equalize the corresponding marginal figures (marginal utility and marginal cost), as the preceding efficiency rule tells us.

An example will help us to see explicitly why resource allocation must satisfy this rule to be deemed efficient. Suppose that the marginal utility of an additional pound of beef to consumers is $8 but its marginal cost is only $5. Then the value of the resources that would have to be used up to produce one more pound of beef (its MC) would be $3 less than the money value that consumers would willingly pay for that additional pound (its MU). By expanding the output of beef by one pound, society could get more (in MU) out of the economic production process than it was putting in (in MC). We know that the output at which MU exceeds MC cannot be optimal, because society would be better off with an increase in that output level. The opposite is true if the MC of beef exceeds the MU of beef.

Thus, we have shown that, if any product's MU is not equal to MC—whether MU exceeds MC or MC exceeds MU—the economy must be wasting an opportunity to achieve a net improvement in consumers' welfare. This is exactly what we mean by saying society is using resources inefficiently. Just as was true at point *G* in Figure 1, if MC does not equal MU for some commodity, it is possible to rearrange production to make some people better off while harming no one else. It follows, then, that efficient output choice occurs only when MC equals MU for every good.[5]

Step 2: The Price System's Critical Role   Next, we must show that under perfect competition, the price system automatically leads buyers and sellers to behave in a way that equalizes MU and MC.

To see this, recall from Chapter 10 that under perfect competition it is most profitable for each beef-producing firm to produce the quantity at which the marginal cost equals the price (*P*) of beef:

$$MC = P$$

This must be so because, if the marginal cost of beef were less than the price, farmers could add to profits by increasing the size of the herd (or the amount of grain fed to the animals). The reverse would be true if the marginal cost of beef were greater than its price. Thus, under perfect competition, the lure of profits leads each producer of beef (and of every other product) to supply the quantity that makes MC = *P*.

We also learned in Chapter 5 that each consumer will purchase the quantity of beef at which the marginal utility of beef in money terms equals the price of beef:

$$MU = P$$

---

[4] Recall from Chapter 5 that we measure marginal utility in money terms—that is, the amount of money that a consumer is willing to give up for an additional unit of the commodity. Economists usually call this the marginal rate of substitution between the commodity and money.

[5] *Warning:* As described in Chapter 15, markets sometimes perform imperfectly because the decision maker faces a different marginal cost than the marginal cost to society. This situation occurs when the individual who creates the cost can make someone else bear the burden. Consider an example: Firm X's production causes pollution emissions that increase nearby households' laundry bills. In such a case, Firm X will ignore this cost and produce inefficiently large outputs and emissions. We study such problems, called *externalities*, in Chapters 15 and 17.

If consumers did not do so, either an increase or a decrease in their beef purchases would leave them better off.

Putting these last two equations together, we see that the invisible hand enforces the following string of equalities:

$$MC = P = MU$$

If the MC of beef and the MU of beef both equal the same price, P, then they must equal each other. That is, it must be true that the quantity of beef produced and consumed in a perfectly competitive market satisfies the equation:

$$MC = MU$$

This is precisely our rule for efficient output selection. Because the same must be true of every other product supplied by a competitive industry,

> **Under perfect competition, producers and consumers will make uncoordinated decisions that we can expect automatically (and amazingly) to produce exactly the quantity of each good that satisfies the MC = MU rule for efficiency. That is, under the idealized conditions of perfect competition, the market mechanism, without any government intervention and without anyone else directing it or planning for it, is capable of allocating society's scarce resources efficiently.**

The Invisible Hand at Work

This is truly an extraordinary result. How can the price mechanism automatically satisfy all of the exacting requirements for efficiency (that marginal utility equals marginal cost for each and every commodity)—requirements that no central planner can hope to handle because of the masses of statistics and the enormous calculations they entail? This seems analogous to a magician suddenly pulling a rabbit out of a hat!

But, as always, rabbits come out of hats only if they were hidden there in the first place. What really is the mechanism by which our act of magic works? The secret is that the price system lets consumers and producers pursue their own best interests—something they are probably very good at doing. Prices are the dollar costs of commodities to consumers, so in pursuing their own best interests, consumers will buy the commodities that give them the most satisfaction per dollar. Under perfect competition, the price the consumer pays is also equal to MC, because the market's incentives lead each supplier to supply that amount at which this is true.

Because $P = MC$ measures the resource cost (in every firm) of producing one more unit of the good, this means that when consumers buy the commodities that give them the most satisfaction for their money, they will automatically have chosen the set of purchases that yields the most satisfaction obtainable from the resources used up in producing those purchases. In other words, the market mechanism leads consumers to squeeze the greatest possible benefit out of the social resources used up in making the goods and services they buy. So, if resources are priced appropriately ($P = MC$), when consumers make the best use of their money, they must also be making the best use of society's resources. That is the way the market mechanism ensures economic efficiency.

> **When all prices are set equal to marginal costs, the price system gives correct cost signals to consumers. It has set prices at levels that induce consumers to use society's resources with the same care they devote to watching their own money, because the money cost of a good to consumers has been set equal to the opportunity cost of the good to society. A perfectly analogous explanation applies to the decisions of producers.**

This is the magic of the invisible hand. Unlike central planners, consumers need not know how difficult it is to manufacture a certain product or the scarcity of the inputs required by the production process. Everything consumers need to know about supply in making their decisions is embodied in the market price, which, under perfect competition, accurately reflects marginal costs. Similarly, producers do not need to know anything about the psychology and tastes of their individual customers—price movements tell them all they need to know when consumer preferences change.

Other Roles of Prices: Income Distribution and Fairness

So far we have stressed the role of prices that economists emphasize most: Prices guide resource allocation. Prices also command the spotlight in another role: Prices influence the distribution of income between buyers and sellers. For example, high rents often make tenants poorer and landlords richer.

This rather obvious role of prices draws the most attention from the public, politicians, and regulators, and we should not lose sight of it.[6] Markets serve only those demands that are backed up by consumers' desire and ability to pay. The market system may do well in serving poor families, because it gives them more food and clothing than a less efficient economy would provide. But the market system offers far more to wealthy families. Many people think that such an arrangement represents a great injustice, however efficient it may be.

Often, people oppose economists' recommendations for improving the economy's efficiency on the grounds that these proposals are unfair. For example, economists frequently advocate higher prices for transportation facilities at the times of day when the facilities are most crowded. Economists propose a pricing arrangement called "peak, off-peak pricing" under which prices for public transportation are higher during rush hours than during other hours.

The rationale for this proposal should be clear from our discussion of efficiency. A seat on a train is a much scarcer resource during rush hours than it is during other times of the day when the trains run fairly empty. Thus, according to the principles of efficiency outlined in this chapter, seats should be more expensive during rush hours to discourage those consumers with no set schedule from riding the trains during peak periods. The same notion applies to other services. Charges for long-distance telephone calls made at night are generally lower than those in the daytime. And in some places, electricity is cheaper at night, when demand does not strain the supplier's generating capacity.

Yet the proposal that transportation authorities should charge higher fares for public transportation during peak hours—say, from 8:00 A.M. to 9:30 A.M. and from 4:30 P.M. to 6:00 P.M.—often runs into stiff opposition. Opponents say that most of the burden of such higher fares will fall on lower-income working people who have no choice regarding the timing of their trips. For example, a survey of economists and members of Parliament in Great Britain found that, while high peak-period fares were favored by 88 percent of the economists, only 35 percent of the Conservative Party members of Parliament and just 19 percent of the Labour Party members of Parliament approved of this arrangement (see Table 2). We may

TABLE 2

Replies to a Questionnaire

Question: To make the most efficient use of a city's resources, how should subway and bus fares vary during the day?	Economists	Conservative Party Members of Parliament	Labour Party Members of Parliament
a. They should be relatively low during rush hour to transport as many people as possible at lower costs.	1%	0%	40%
b. They should be the same at all times to avoid making travelers alter their schedules because of price differences.	4	60	39
c. They should be relatively high during rush hour to minimize the amount of equipment needed to transport the daily travelers.	88	35	19
d. Impossible to answer on the data and alternatives given.	7	5	2

SOURCE: Excerpt from Samuel Brittan, *Is There an Economic Consensus?* p. 93. Copyright © 1973. Reproduced by permission of Samuel Brittan.

[6] Income distribution is the subject of Part 5.

POLICY DEBATE

USER CHARGES FOR PUBLIC FACILITIES

At a time when budget cutting is the way to popularity for a politician, the notion of charging users for the services that government once gave away for free is under debate. Economists have often advocated such charges for the use of roads, bridges, museums, educational facilities, and the like. Of course, it's true that if the services are provided for "free," the public has to pay for them anyway—just more indirectly through taxes. But if people are asked to pay directly for such services, it can make a big difference.

As an example, let's say a road is financed out of general taxes. In this circumstance, it does not matter how many times Sabrina, the owner of an independent trucking firm, uses the road. She pays the same amount whether she uses it twice a year or every day. But if Sabrina has to pay a toll every time she uses the road, she will have a strong incentive to avoid unnecessary use. That is why advocates of pricing to promote economic efficiency propose more substantial user charges, not only for roads and bridges but also for admission to national parks, for the use of publicly owned grazing lands, and for the use of the television and radio spectrums by broadcasters.

Opponents of user charges contend that these fees are unfair to poor people. Besides, it is argued, the use of public facilities such as libraries, museums, and schools should be encouraged rather than

impeded by user charges. For instance, in New York there is no charge to cross four of the five bridges that connect Brooklyn and Queens with Manhattan. But each time new tolls are proposed, they are met with the cry, "Should I have to pay an admission fee into my own city?!"

SOURCE: © Ron Chapple/Thinkstock Images/Jupiterimages

surmise that these members of the British Parliament reflected the views of the public more accurately than did the economists. In this case, people simply found the efficient solution unfair, and so they refused to adopt it.

Yet Another Free-Market Achievement: Growth versus Efficiency

This chapter has followed the economist's standard approach in evaluating the market mechanism. Economists usually stress efficiency in resource allocation and the role of the market in ensuring such efficiency—the division of resources among alternative uses in a way that misses no opportunity to increase consumer net benefits.

Some other admirers of the market do not place their main emphasis on the free market's efficiency accomplishments. A very diverse group, including businesspeople, politicians, economic historians, leaders such as Dmitry Medvedev and Hu Jintao in formerly communist economies that have become more market-oriented, and even Marxists, appreciate the market primarily for a very different reason—the extraordinary growth in output that market economies have achieved and the historically unprecedented abundance that has resulted.

Historians have estimated that before the arrival of the capitalistic market mechanism, output per person grew with glacial slowness. Today an average American can afford nearly seven times the quantity of goods and services that an individual's income bought 100 years ago. Undoubtedly, the failure to achieve substantial growth and prosperity (and not just inefficiencies in allocating goods) helped to bring about the fall of communism in eastern Europe. Even Karl Marx stressed this role of the market mechanism, waxing lyrical in his description of its accomplishments. Chapter 16 will return to this subject, indicating what a free-market economy can accomplish in terms of economic growth.

PUZZLE RESOLVED: — SAN FRANCISCO BRIDGE PRICING REVISITED

 Our earlier example of the San Francisco Bay area bridges also raises fairness issues. Recall that we concluded from our analysis that efficient bridge use requires higher tolls on the more crowded bridges. Because this principle seems so clear and rational, it is surprising to find out what the actual bridge tolls are: $5 on the Golden Gate Bridge and $4 on all other bridges, even though their average daily traffic varies, with the San Francisco–Oakland Bay Bridge by far the most crowded.[7]

From an efficiency point of view, this uniform toll seems irrational, with the relatively uncrowded bridges assigned the same toll as the most crowded bridge. The explanation lies in some widely held notions of fairness.

Many people feel that it is fair for those who travel on a particular bridge to pay for its costs. In this view, it would be unjust for those who use the crowded San Francisco–Oakland Bay Bridge to pay more in order to subsidize the least crowded Dumbarton Bridge. Naturally, a heavily traveled bridge earns more toll payments and so recoups its building, maintenance, and operating costs more quickly. On the other hand, it is felt that the relatively few users of a less crowded bridge should make a fair contribution toward its costs.

An economically irrational pattern of tolls does nothing to ease congestion on overcrowded bridges and thereby contributes to inefficiency. But one cannot legitimately conclude that advocates of such prices are "stupid." Whether this pattern of tolls is or is not desirable must be decided, at least partly, on the basis of the public's sense of what constitutes fairness and justice in pricing. It also depends on the amount that people are willing to pay in terms of delays, inconvenience, and other inefficiencies to avoid apparent injustices.

Economics alone cannot decide the appropriate trade-off between fairness and efficiency. It cannot even pretend to judge which pricing arrangements are fair and which are unfair. But it can and should indicate whether a particular pricing decision, proposed because it is considered fair, will impose heavy inefficiency costs on the community. Economic analysis also can and should indicate how to appraise these costs, so that the issues can be evaluated on a rational, factual basis.

TOWARD ASSESSMENT OF THE PRICE MECHANISM

We do not mean to imply in our discussion of the case for free markets that the free-enterprise system is an ideal of perfection, without flaw or room for improvement. In fact, it has a number of serious shortcomings that we will explore in subsequent chapters. But recognition of these imperfections should not conceal the price mechanism's enormous accomplishments.

We have shown that, under the proper circumstances, prices are capable of meeting the most exacting requirements of allocative efficiency—requirements that go well beyond any central planning bureau's capacities. Even centrally planned economies use the price mechanism to carry out considerable portions of the task of allocation, most notably in the distribution of consumer goods. No one has invented an instrument for directing the economy that can replace the price mechanism, which no one ever designed or planned for, but which simply grew by itself, a child of the processes of history.

---

[7] Toll schedules for the San Francisco Bay area bridges are from the Bay Area Toll Authority, http://bata.mtc.ca.gov/tolls/schedule.htm, and the Golden Gate Bridge, Highway and Transportation District, http://www.goldengate.org. Note that nowadays these bridge authorities do encourage efficiency by providing faster carpool lanes for buses and cars with three or more passengers; these categories of vehicle cross the five bridges free of charge during weekday rush hours. And the introduction of an electronic toll collection system (FasTrak) that can process almost three times as many vehicles per hour as the manual collection has significantly improved efficiency and reduced congestion. Drivers who do not utilize FasTrak on the Golden Gate Bridge are charged an extra dollar to cross that bridge.

| SUMMARY |

1. Economists consider an allocation of resources to be inefficient if it wastes opportunities to change the use of the economy's resources in any way that makes at least some consumers better off without harming anyone. Resource allocation is considered efficient if there are no such wasted opportunities.

2. Under perfect competition, the free-market mechanism adjusts prices so that the resulting resource allocation is efficient. It induces firms to buy and use inputs in ways that yield the most valuable outputs per unit of input. It distributes products among consumers in ways that match individual preferences. Finally, it produces commodities whose value to consumers exceeds the cost of producing them and assigns the task of production to the potential suppliers who can produce most efficiently.

3. Resource allocation involves three basic coordination tasks:

   a. How much of each good to produce

   b. What quantities of available inputs to use in producing the different goods

   c. How to distribute the goods among different consumers

4. An optimal allocation of society's resources among the commodities the economy produces and consumes is one that maximizes the sum of the consumers' and producers' surpluses derived by everyone in the community. Perfectly competitive equilibrium achieves this goal, at least in theory.

5. Efficient decisions about what goods to produce require that the marginal cost (MC) of producing each good be equal to its marginal utility (MU) to consumers. If the MC of any good differs from its MU, then society can improve resource allocation by changing the amounts produced.

6. Because the market system induces firms to set MC equal to price, and it induces consumers to set MU equal to price, it automatically guarantees satisfaction of the condition that MC should equal MU.

7. Improvements in efficiency occasionally require some prices to increase so as to stimulate supply or to prevent waste in consumption. This is why price increases can sometimes be beneficial to consumers.

8. In addition to resource allocation, prices influence income distribution between buyers and sellers.

9. The price mechanism can be criticized on the ground that it is unfair because it accords wealthy consumers preferential treatment.

| KEY TERMS |

consumer's surplus   299

efficient allocation of resources   288

input-output analysis   296

laissez-faire   293

producer's surplus   299

| TEST YOURSELF |

1. What possible social advantages of price increases arise in the following cases?

   a. Charging higher prices for electrical power on very hot days when many people use air conditioners

   b. Raising water prices in drought-stricken areas

2. In the discussion of Figure 3, there is a set of numbers indicating how much different buyers would be willing to pay for a book. Construct a table for these buyers like the first three columns in Table 1, indicating their consumer's surpluses.

3. As in the previous question, use the numbers in Figure 3 to determine the producer's surpluses and complete your table to correspond to the remaining columns of Table 1.

| DISCUSSION QUESTIONS |

1. Discuss the fairness of the two proposals included in Test Yourself Question 1.

2. Using the concepts of marginal cost (MC) and marginal utility (MU), discuss the nature of the inefficiency in each of the following cases:

   a. An arrangement that offers relatively little coffee and much tea to people who prefer coffee and does the reverse for tea lovers

   b. An arrangement in which skilled mechanics are assigned to ditch digging and unskilled laborers to repairing cars

   c. An arrangement that produces a large quantity of trucks and few cars, assuming that both cost about the same amount to produce and to run but that most people in the community prefer cars to trucks

3. In reality, which of the following circumstances might give rise to each of the situations described in Discussion Question 2 above?

   a. Regulation of output quantities by a government

   b. Rationing of commodities

   c. Assignment of soldiers to different jobs in an army

4. We have said that the economy's three coordination tasks are output selection, production planning, and product distribution. Which of these is done badly in the cases described in Discussion Questions 2a, 2b, and 2c?

5. In a free market, how will the price mechanism deal with each of the inefficiencies described in Discussion Question 2?

6. In the early months after the end of communism in Eastern Europe, there seems to have been an almost superstitious belief that the free market could solve all problems. What sorts of problems do you think the leaders and the citizens of those countries had in mind? Which of those problems is there good reason to believe the market mechanism actually can deal with effectively? What disappointments and sources of disillusionment should have been expected? Which disappointments have resulted?

15

THE SHORTCOMINGS OF FREE MARKETS

When she was good
She was very, very good,
But when she was bad
She was horrid.

HENRY WADSWORTH LONGFELLOW

What does the market do well, and what does it do poorly? These questions are the focus of our microeconomic analysis, and we are well on our way toward finding their answers. In Chapters 4, 10, and 14, we explained the workings of Adam Smith's invisible hand, the instrument by which a perfectly competitive economy allocates resources efficiently without any guidance from government. Of course, that perfectly competitive model is just a theoretical ideal, but our observations of the real world confirm the extraordinary accomplishments of the market mechanism. Free-market economies have achieved levels of output, productive efficiency, variety in available consumer goods, and general prosperity that are unprecedented in history—and are now the envy of the formerly planned economies. We will discuss that phenomenal record of production and growth in detail in Chapter 16.

Yet the market mechanism has its weaknesses. In Chapters 11 and 12, we examined one of these defects—the free market's vulnerability to exploitation by large and powerful business firms, which can lead to both an inappropriate concentration of wealth and resource misallocation. Now we take a more comprehensive view of market failures and study some of the steps that can be taken to remedy them. Clearly, the market does not do everything we want it to do. Amid the vast outpouring of products in our economy, we also find appalling poverty, cities choked by traffic and pollution, and hospitals, educational institutions, and artistic organizations in serious financial trouble. Although our economy produces an overwhelming abundance of material wealth, it seems far less capable of reducing social ills and environmental damage. We will examine the reasons for these failings and indicate why the price system *by itself* may sometimes not be able to deal with them, and sometimes addresses them only after some governmentally imposed changes in the market's pricing practices.

CONTENTS

Our recognition of the market's limitations emphatically does not imply that the public interest calls for abandoning the market. As we will see, many of the imperfections of this economic system are treatable within the market environment, sometimes even by making use of the market mechanism to cure its own deficiencies.

PUZZLE: WHY ARE HEALTH-CARE COSTS IN CANADA RISING?

Long before the U.S. government made its ultimately successful attempt in 2010 to grapple with the problems of health care, Canada adopted a universal health-care program intended to solve the same problem in that country. For this purpose, the Canadian government imposed strong controls over prices and fees. Each province has one insurance plan that reimburses doctors according to a uniform fee schedule; hospitals are put on predetermined overall budgets; and patients pay very low direct, out-of-pocket costs.

SOURCE: © Ron Chapple/Thinkstock Images/Jupiterimages

Many observers believe that Canada has created an efficient, user-friendly system, although some critics disagree. But Canadians clearly have *not* succeeded in containing costs. Despite the price controls, Canadian health-care costs have been rising persistently faster than the general inflation rate, just as they had in the United States, where there once were no such national rules to rein in rising health-care prices. Moreover, some observers contend that Canadian health services are getting worse, with longer waits for diagnostic tests and elective surgery and tighter restrictions on treatments available to patients. Does this trend mean that Canadian health services are especially inefficient or corrupt? There is no evidence for such suspicions. Then why have the Canadians been unable to brake the growth of their health-care costs? This chapter will help you to understand the answer to this question, with its important implications for U.S. policy.

WHAT DOES THE MARKET DO POORLY?

Although we cannot list all of the market's imperfections, we can list some major areas in which it has been accused of failing:

1. Market economies suffer from severe business fluctuations, unemployment, and inflation. (See Chapters 22–33.)
2. The market distributes income unequally. (See Chapter 21.)
3. Where monopoly markets are present, they allocate resources inefficiently. (See Chapter 11.)
4. The market deals poorly with the side effects of many economic activities such as pollution.
5. The market cannot readily provide "public goods," such as national defense and street cleaning.
6. The market may do a poor job of allocating resources between the present and the future.
7. The market mechanism makes public and personal services increasingly expensive, which often induces socially damaging countermeasures by government.

We discuss the first three items in the list elsewhere in this book, as indicated. This chapter deals with the remaining four. To help us analyze these cases, we will first briefly review the concept of efficient resource allocation, discussed in detail in Chapter 14.

EFFICIENT RESOURCE ALLOCATION: A REVIEW

The basic problem of resource allocation is deciding how much of each commodity the economy should produce. At first glance, the solution may seem simple: the more, the better! But this is not necessarily so, as one of our *Ideas for Beyond the Final Exam* indicates.

HOW MUCH DOES IT REALLY COST? *Opportunity Costs:* **Outputs are not created out of thin air. We produce them from scarce supplies of fuel, raw materials, machinery, and labor. If we use these resources to produce, say, more jeans, then we must take resources away from some other products, such as backpacks. To decide whether increasing the production of jeans is a good idea, we must compare the utility of that increase with the loss of utility in producing fewer backpacks. This, as you recall, means we must consider the opportunity cost of increased output. It is *efficient* to increase the output of jeans only if society considers the additional jeans more valuable than the forgone backpacks.**

IDEAS FOR BEYOND THE FINAL EXAM

To illustrate this idea, we repeat a graph you have seen several times in earlier chapters—a *production possibilities frontier*—but we put it to a somewhat different use here. Curve *ABC* in Figure 1 is a **production possibilities frontier** showing the alternative combinations of jeans and backpacks that the economy can produce by reallocating its resources between production of the two goods. Suppose that point *B*, representing the production of 8 million backpacks and 60 million pairs of jeans, constitutes the *optimal* resource allocation. We assume this combination of outputs is the only one that best satisfies society's wants among all the possibilities that are *attainable* (given the technology and resources as represented by the production frontier). That is, we assume that the combination of outputs at point *B* on the frontier yields the highest total consumers' plus producers' surplus for the entire economy. Two questions are pertinent to our discussion of the price system:

1. What prices will get the economy to select point *B*; that is, what prices will yield an *efficient* allocation of resources?
2. How can the wrong set of prices lead to a misallocation of resources?

We discussed the first question in detail in Chapter 14, where we saw that

> An efficient allocation of resources requires the prices that will be reached at equilibrium if there is perfect competition be equal to marginal cost; that is,

$$P = MC$$

This chapter is devoted mainly to the second question: How can the "wrong" prices cause a **misallocation of resources?** The answer to this question is not too difficult, and we can use the case of monopoly as an illustration.

The "law" of demand tells us that a rise in a commodity's price normally will reduce the quantity demanded. Suppose, now, that the backpack industry is a monopoly, so the price of backpacks exceeds their marginal cost—the price they would have in a perfectly competitive market.[1] This will decrease the quantity of backpacks demanded below the 8 million that we have assumed to be socially optimal (point *B* in Figure 1). The economy will move from point *B* to a point such as *K*, where too few backpacks and too many pairs

The **production possibilities frontier** is a curve that shows the maximum quantities of outputs it is possible to produce with the available resource quantities and the current state of technological knowledge.

Resources are misallocated if it is possible to change the way they are used or the combination of goods and services they produce and thereby make consumers and producers better off.

FIGURE 1

The Economy's Production Possibilities Frontier for the Production of Two Goods

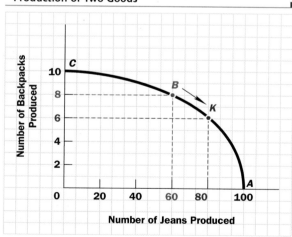

NOTE: Numbers are in millions per year.

---

[1] To review why price under monopoly may be expected to exceed marginal cost, you may want to reread Chapter 11, pages 223–225.

of jeans are being produced for maximal consumer satisfaction. By setting the "wrong" prices, then, the market induces individual consumers to buy quantities that are inconsistent with maximal welfare of all individuals as a group, and thereby prevents the most efficient use of the economy's resources.

If a commodity's price is higher than its marginal cost, the economy will tend to produce less of that item than would maximize consumer benefits. The opposite will occur if an item's price is lower than its marginal cost.

In the rest of this chapter, we will encounter several other significant instances in which the market mechanism may set the "wrong" prices, leading to sale of more of some goods and less of other goods than would yield the highest attainable benefits for the community as a whole.

EXTERNALITIES: GETTING THE PRICES WRONG

We start our discussion of what the market does imperfectly with the fourth item on our list of market failures (since we have studied the first three in previous chapters): The market deals poorly with the incidental side effects of economic activities. This flaw is one of the least obvious yet most consequential of the price system's imperfections.

Many economic activities provide incidental *benefits* to others for whom they are not specifically intended. For example, homeowners who plant beautiful gardens in front of their homes incidentally and unintentionally provide pleasure to neighbors and passersby, even though they receive no payment in return. Economists say that their activity generates a **beneficial externality.** That is, the activity creates benefits that are *external to,* or outside, the intentions and interests of those that are directly involved in the activity. Similarly, some activities incidentally and unintentionally impose *costs* on others. For example, the owners of a motorcycle repair shop create a lot of noise for which they pay no compensation to their deafened neighbors. Economists say these owners produce a **detrimental externality.** Pollution is the classic illustration of a detrimental externality.

> An activity is said to generate a **beneficial** or **detrimental externality** if that activity causes incidental benefits or damages to others not directly involved in the activity and no corresponding compensation is provided to or paid by those who generate the externality.

To see why externalities cause the price system to misallocate resources, you need only recall that the price system achieves efficiency by rewarding producers who serve consumers well—that is, at the lowest possible cost. This argument breaks down, however, as soon as some of the costs and benefits of economic activities are left out of the profit calculation.

When a firm pollutes a river, it uses up some of society's resources (for example, it depletes the valuable oxygen in the water) just as surely as when the firm burns coal. However, if the firm pays for coal but not for the use of clean water, we can expect the firm's management to be economical in its use of coal and wasteful in its use of the water's oxygen. By the same token, a firm that provides unpaid benefits to others is unlikely to be generous in allocating resources to the activity, no matter how socially desirable it may be.

In an important sense, the source of the market mechanism's difficulty here lies in society's rules about property rights. Coal mines are *private property;* their owners will not let anyone take coal without paying for it. Thus, coal is costly and so is not used wastefully. But waterways usually are not private property. Because they belong to everyone in general, they belong to no one in particular. Therefore, anyone can use those waterways as free dumping grounds for wastes that spew poisons into the water and use up the water's oxygen that is vital for underwater life. Because no one pays for the use of the socially valuable dissolved oxygen in a public waterway, people will use that oxygen wastefully. The fact that waterways are exempted from the market's normal control procedures is therefore the source of a detrimental externality.

Externalities and Inefficiency

Using these concepts, we can see precisely why an externality has undesirable effects on the allocation of resources. In discussing externalities, it is crucial to distinguish between *social* and *private* marginal cost. We define **marginal social cost (MSC)** as the sum of two components: (1) **marginal private cost (MPC),** which is the share of an activity's marginal cost that is paid for by the persons who carry out the activity, plus (2) *incidental cost,* which is the share paid by others.

If an increase in a firm's output also increases the smoke its factory spews into the air, then, in addition to direct private costs (as recorded in the company accounts), the expansion of production imposes incidental costs on others. These costs take the form of increased laundry bills, medical expenditures, outlays for air-conditioning and electricity, and the unpleasantness of living in a cloud of noxious fumes. These are all part of the activity's marginal *social* cost.

Where the firm's activities generate detrimental externalities, its marginal social cost will be greater than its marginal private cost, while the business firm will base its pricing only on its private cost because it does not pay the remainder of the social costs of its operation (and generally does not even know how large that remaining cost is). In symbols, MSC > MPC, where MSC is the cost to the entire community, whereas the price charged by the firm is based on MPC. Therefore, the firm's output must be too big because price will be below the truly relevant marginal cost, thereby increasing sales of the commodity that damages the public. In such a case, society would necessarily benefit if output of that product were *reduced*. It would lose some of the product but escape the high marginal social cost. We conclude that

> Where a firm's activity causes detrimental externalities, the marginal benefits of the output will be less than marginal social costs in a free market. Smaller outputs will be socially desirable.

This relationship holds because private enterprise has no motivation to take into account any costs to others for which it does not have to pay. In fact, competition *forces* firms to produce at as low a private cost as possible, because if they don't, rivals will be able to take their customers away. Thus, competition *compels* firms to make extensive use of resources for which they are not required to pay or pay fully. As a result, goods that cause detrimental externalities will be produced in undesirably large amounts, because they have social costs that are not paid by the supplier firms.

The opposite, of course, holds for the case of external benefits. This situation is one where the **marginal social benefit (MSB)** is greater than the **marginal private benefit (MPB).** A clear example is an invention produced by Firm A that gives an idea for another new product or process to an engineer from a different firm, B. Firm B clearly benefits from Firm A's research and development (R&D) spending, and B does not pay anything to A for this gain. In that case, the social benefit—the sum of the benefits to the two firms together—will be greater than the private benefit to the inventor Firm A alone. Thus, the marginal private benefit to investment in R&D will be less than the marginal social benefit, and less R&D will be carried out under private enterprise than social optimality requires.

These principles can be illustrated with the aid of Figure 2. This diagram repeats the two basic curves needed for analysis of the firm's equilibrium: a marginal revenue curve and a marginal cost curve (see Chapter 8). These curves represent the *private* costs and revenues of a particular firm (in this

The **marginal social cost (MSC)** of an activity is the sum of its marginal private cost (MPC) plus its incidental costs (positive or negative) that are borne by others who receive no compensation for the resulting damage to their well-being.

The **marginal private cost (MPC)** is the share of an activity's marginal cost that is paid for by the persons who carry out the activity.

The **marginal social benefit (MSB)** of an activity is the sum of its marginal private benefit (MPB) plus its incidental benefits (positive or negative) that are received by others, and for which those others do not pay.

The **marginal private benefit (MPB)** is the share of an activity's marginal benefit that is received by the persons who carry out the activity.

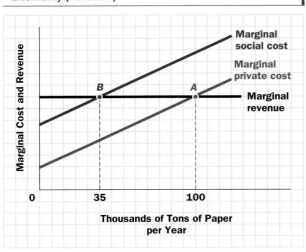

FIGURE 2

Equilibrium of a Firm Whose Output Produces a Detrimental Externality (Pollution)

case, a paper mill). The mill maximizes profits by providing 100,000 tons of output, corresponding to the intersection between the marginal private cost and marginal revenue curves (point *A*).

Now suppose that the factory's wastewater pollutes a nearby estuary, so that its production creates a detrimental externality for which the owners do not pay. Then marginal social cost must be higher than marginal private cost, as shown in the diagram. The output of paper, which is governed by private costs, will be 100,000 tons (point *A*)—an excessive amount from the viewpoint of the public interest, given its environmental consequences.

If, instead of being able to impose the external costs on others, the paper mill's owners were forced to pay them, then their private marginal cost curve would correspond to the higher of the two cost curves. Paper output would then fall to 35,000 tons, corresponding to point *B*, the intersection between the marginal revenue curve and the marginal social cost curve.

The same sort of diagram shows that the opposite relationship will hold when the firm's activity produces beneficial externalities. The firm will produce less of its beneficial output than it would if it were rewarded fully for its activities' benefits. Thus,

> **Where the firm's activity generates beneficial externalities, free markets will produce too little output. Society would be better off with larger output levels.**

We can also see these results with the help of a production possibilities frontier diagram similar to that in Figure 1. In Figure 3, we see the frontier for two industries: electricity generation, which causes air pollution (a detrimental externality), and tulip growing, which makes an area more attractive (a beneficial externality). We have just seen that detrimental externalities make marginal social cost greater than marginal private cost.

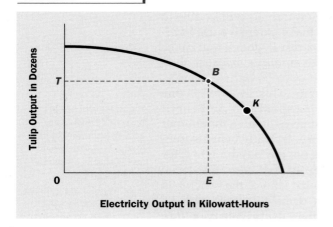

Externalities, Market Equilibrium, and Efficient Resource Allocation

Hence, if the electric company charges a price equal to its own marginal (private) cost, that price will be less than the true marginal social cost. Similarly, in tulip growing, a price equal to marginal private cost will be above the true marginal cost to society.

Earlier in the chapter, we saw that an industry that charges a price above marginal social cost will reduce quantity demanded through this high price, and so it will produce an output too small for an efficient allocation of resources. The opposite will be true for an industry whose price is below marginal social cost. In terms of Figure 3, suppose that point *B* again represents the efficient allocation of resources, involving the production of *E* kilowatt-hours of electricity and *T* dozen tulips.

Because the polluting electricity-generation company charges a price below marginal social cost, it will sell more than *E* kilowatt-hours of electricity. Similarly, because tulip growers generate external benefits and so charge a price above marginal social cost, they will produce less than *T* dozen tulips. The economy will end up with the resource allocation represented by point *K* rather than that at point *B*. There will be too much smoky electricity production and too little attractive tulip growing. More generally:

> **An industry that generates detrimental externalities will have a marginal social cost higher than its marginal private cost. If the price is equal to a firm's own marginal private cost, it will therefore be below the true marginal cost to society. In this way, the market mechanism tends to encourage inefficiently large outputs of products that cause detrimental externalities. The opposite is true of products that cause beneficial externalities; private industry will provide inefficiently small quantities of these products.**

Externalities Are Everywhere

Externalities occur throughout the economy. Many are beneficial. A factory that hires unskilled or semiskilled laborers, for example, gives them on-the-job training and provides the external benefit of better workers to future employers. Benefits to others are also generated when firms invent useful but unpatentable products, or even patentable products that can be imitated by others to some degree.

Detrimental externalities are also widespread. Pollution by factories, cars, and trucks causes some of our most pressing environmental problems. The abandonment of buildings causes the quality of neighborhoods to deteriorate and is the source of serious externalities for cities. And these are only two of many significant examples.

We have yet to mention the most threatening damaging externality of them all—global warming. The authors of this book cannot claim to be experts on the subject, which still gives rise to debate, though the skeptics who deny the dangers or the role of human actions in generating the emissions that are believed to be heating the climate seem to be retreating in their opposition. But it is clear that if the full threat materializes, the cost to humanity will be enormous, with flooding of cities, the turning of formerly flourishing areas into deserts, and possibly even worse. And the likely source of the problem is emissions, not only factories but you and we, the authors of this book, as we drive our cars and grill our steaks. This brings out an important point: Damaging externalities are caused not only by business firms. They are created by the military when they drive their tanks and fly their airplanes, by farmers when they spray their fields, and by consumers such as ourselves. *We all do it.*

Although the market mechanism, acting on its own, does nothing to cure externality problems, there is more to the story. Market economies often have dirty air and rivers and suffer from the effects of improperly disposed toxic wastes, but that does not mean that nonmarket economies do any better. The communist countries of Eastern Europe and the Soviet Union long were known to have a dismal environmental record. When communism fell apart in those countries, the revealed horrors of environmental degradation were hard to believe. It became abundantly clear that central planning is not a guaranteed cure for environmental difficulties.

Moreover, the market mechanism does offer an effective way of dealing with such difficulties. Although markets hardly can be claimed to protect the environment automatically, they offer us a powerful tool for doing so, as we will see shortly.

Government Policy and Externalities

Because of the market's inability to cope with externalities, governments support activities that are believed to generate external benefits. Governments subsidize education, not only because they know it helps promote equal opportunity for all citizens but also because they believe it generates beneficial externalities. For example, educated people normally commit fewer crimes than uneducated people do, so the more we educate people, presumably the less we need to spend on crime prevention. Also, academic research that is a by-product of the educational system has often benefited the entire population and has, indeed, been a major contributor to the nation's economic growth. Biotechnology and advanced computing are just two major scientific breakthroughs that have stemmed from university research. It is believed that if education were offered only by profit-making institutions, the outputs of these beneficial services would be provided at less than optimal levels.

Similarly, governments have begun to increase fines on companies that contribute heavily to air and water pollution. In the years just before George W. Bush's administration, the U.S. Environmental Protection Agency levied more criminal fines and civil penalties against violators than ever before. This is done, of course, as a disincentive for the creation of socially damaging externalities. In other words, it brings the amounts that business firms pay closer to covering all of the costs that their activities generate.

EXTERNALITIES: A SHORTCOMING OF THE MARKET CURED BY MARKET METHODS Externalities are really just failures to price resources so that markets will allocate them efficiently. One effective way to deal with externalities may be to use taxes and subsidies, making polluters pay for the costs they impose on society and paying the generators of beneficial externalities for the incidental benefits of their activities (which can be considered as an offset or deduction from the social cost of the activity).

IDEAS FOR BEYOND THE FINAL EXAM

Externalities Cured by Negotiation: The Coase Theorem

We have just seen how the damage to the public interest that results from externalities can be prevented by government intervention—for example, by taxing damaging externalities. But there are cases in which the market mechanism can take care of the problem *and even obtain an optimal outcome* by negotiation between the individuals who produce the externalities and the individuals who are affected by them. This possibility was first recognized by Ronald Coase, who received the Nobel Prize in 1991.

A simple example will bring out the logic of these cases. Imagine a very profitable factory that creates a lot of noise which prevents the owner of a nearby home from sleeping. Suppose it is possible for the factory owner to muffle the sound of his indispensable machinery at a cost of $10,000, but that the homeowner can protect himself by putting up a noise-muffling wall at a cost of $15,000. The obviously efficient outcome is for the homeowner to pay the factory owner $10,000, and perhaps a bit more, as an inducement to install the muffler, because that will cost the noise victim less than the $15,000 wall. This solution is clearly the socially optimal choice because it protects the victim at the lowest possible cost.

But suppose that, instead of leaving the homeowner to fend for himself, the local municipality passes a law saying that the owner of the factory is responsible for the damage that the noise causes to the homeowner. Then the factory owner will again select the $10,000 muffler in the factory, rather than the wall in the home, because it is the least expensive way to comply with the law.

This example illustrates the second and more surprising feature of the Coase theorem. For it shows that *no matter which of the two parties has the upper hand, the outcome of the negotiation will be the same: the noise will be muffled in the way that has the lowest cost.* Even if the factory owner is not forced to fix the problem, it will pay the homeowner to bribe the factory owner to reduce the noise via the low-cost remedy. And if, instead, the law requires remedial action by the factory owner, he will do exactly the same thing. So, in such cases, there is no need for the government to intervene.

But this ingenious idea has its limitations; there are a number of circumstances in which things do not work out so nicely. First, the story assumes that both parties are coolly rational—they just want to solve the problem at the lowest cost. But suppose the homeowner hates the factory owner and vows never to give the latter even a single dollar, no matter what the alternative costs. Then he will be stuck with either unceasing noise or a $15,000 bill to build a wall in his house.

That isn't the only problem with Coase's proposed solution. Suppose a costly lawsuit is required to get the owners to negotiate. Or suppose there are hundreds of houses nearby, with the noise preventing all the residents from sleeping. Then what is required for the Coase solution to work is a successful negotiation involving hundreds of homeowners and the factory owner. Everyone knows that negotiation involving such a mob will be time consuming, costly, and often yield irrational results. To take this objection even farther, imagine trying to use the Coase solution to solve the pollution problems caused by the hundreds of thousands of automobiles that travel through a major city every day. Surely, only chaos would result. And the externalities on which global warming is blamed are even more complex and involve literally billions of parties. So there are clearly times and places where government intervention in the public interest is indispensable.

For example, the analysis implies that firms that generate beneficial externalities should be given subsidies per unit of their output equal to the difference between their marginal social costs and their marginal private costs. Similarly, detrimental externalities should be taxed so that the firm will have to pay the entire marginal social cost. In terms of Figure 2, after paying the tax, the firm's marginal private cost curve will shift up until it coincides with its marginal social cost curve, so the market price will be set in a manner consistent with efficient resource allocation.

Although this approach works well in principle, it is often difficult to carry out in reality. Social costs are rarely easy to estimate, partly because they are so widely diffused throughout the community (everyone is affected by pollution) and partly because it is difficult to assess many of the costs and benefits (effects on health, unpleasantness of living in smog) in monetary terms. In Chapter 17, which focuses on environmental problems, we will continue our discussion of the pros and cons of the economist's approach to externalities and will outline alternative policies for their control.

PROVISION OF PUBLIC GOODS

A second area in which market failure occurs is the provision of what economists call **public goods.** Public goods are socially valuable commodities whose provision, for reasons we will explain, cannot be financed by private enterprise, or at least not at socially desirable prices. Thus, government must pay for public goods if they are to be provided at all. Standard examples of public goods include everything from national defense to coastal lighthouses.

It is easiest to explain the nature of public goods by contrasting them with **private goods,** which are at the opposite end of the spectrum. *Private goods are characterized by two important attributes.* One can be called **depletability.** If you eat an apple or use a gallon of gasoline, there is that much less fruit or fuel in the world available for others to use. Your consumption depletes the supply available for other people, either temporarily or permanently.

But a pure public good is like the legendary widow's jar of oil, which always remained full, no matter how much oil was poured out. For example, once snow has been removed from a street, improved driving conditions are available to every driver who uses that street, whether 10 or 1,000 cars pass that way. One passing car does not make the road less snow-free for the next driver. The same is true of spraying swamps near a town to kill malarial mosquitoes. The cost of spraying is the same whether the town contains 10,000 or 20,000 people. A resident of the town who benefits from this service does not deplete its advantages to others.

The other property that characterizes private goods but not all public goods is **excludability,** meaning that anyone who does not pay for the good can be excluded from enjoying its benefits. If you do not buy a ticket, you are excluded from the basketball game. If you do not pay for an electric guitar, the storekeeper will not hand it over to you.

But some goods or services, once provided to anyone, automatically become available to many others whom it is difficult, if not impossible, to exclude from the benefits. When the street is cleared of snow, everyone who uses the street benefits, regardless of who paid for the snowplow. If a country provides a strong military, every citizen receives its protection, even persons who do not want it.

A public good is defined as a good that lacks depletability. Very often, it also lacks excludability. Notice two important implications.

First, because nonpaying users usually cannot be excluded from enjoying a public good, suppliers of such goods will find it *difficult or impossible to collect fees* for the benefits they provide. This is the so-called *free-rider* problem. How many people, for example, would *voluntarily* spend close to $6,000 a year to support our national defense establishment? Yet this is roughly what it costs per American family. Services such as national defense and public health, which are not depletable and where excludability is impossible, *cannot* be provided by private enterprise because people will not pay for what they can get free. Because private firms are not in the business of giving services away, the supply of public goods must be left to government and nonprofit institutions.

The second implication we notice is that, because the supply of a public good is not depleted by an additional user, *the marginal (opportunity) cost of serving an additional user is zero.* With marginal cost equal to zero, the basic principle of optimal resource allocation (price equal to marginal cost) calls for provision of public goods and services to anyone who wants them *at no charge.* In other words, not only is it often impossible to charge a market price for a public good, it is often *undesirable* as well. Any nonzero price would discourage some users from enjoying the public good; but this would be inefficient, because one more person's enjoyment of the good costs society nothing. To summarize:

It is usually *not possible* to charge a price for a pure public good because people cannot be excluded from enjoying its benefits. It may also be *undesirable* to charge a price for it because that would discourage some people from benefiting, even though using a public good does not deplete its supply. For both of these reasons, government supplies many public goods. Without government intervention, public goods simply would not be provided.

Referring back to our example in Figure 1, if backpacks were a public good and their production were left to private enterprise, the economy would end up at point *A,* with zero production of backpacks and a far greater output of jeans than is called for by efficient allocation (point *B*). Usually, communities have not let that happen; today they devote a substantial proportion of government expenditure—indeed, the bulk of municipal budgets—to financing of public goods or services believed to generate substantial

A **public good** is a commodity or service whose benefits are not depleted by an additional user and from which it is generally difficult or impossible to exclude people, even if the people are unwilling to pay for the benefits.

A **private good** is a commodity characterized by both depletability and excludability.

A commodity is **depletable** if it is used up when someone consumes it.

A commodity is **excludable** if someone who does not pay for it can be kept from enjoying it.

external benefits. National defense, public health, police and fire protection, and research are among the services governments provide because they offer beneficial externalities or are public goods.

ALLOCATION OF RESOURCES BETWEEN PRESENT AND FUTURE

A third area in which market failure occurs is the division of benefits between today and tomorrow. When a firm invests in a new plant and equipment, more resources are devoted to expanding its capacity to produce consumer goods in the future. But if we devote inputs to building new factories and equipment that will add to production tomorrow, those resources then become unavailable for consumption now. Fuel used to make steel for a new factory building cannot be used to heat homes or drive cars. Thus, the allocation of inputs between current consumption and investment—their allocation between present and future—influences how fast the economy grows. Investment in education has a similar role, because people who are educated today are likely to be more effective producers tomorrow, and if education enables them to contribute inventions, that may increase tomorrow's production even more. That is why economists refer to education as "investment in human capital," thereby thinking of more educated people as analogous to machinery in the factory whose efficiency is increased by modernization.

In principle, the market mechanism should be as efficient in allocating resources between present and future uses as it is in allocating resources among different outputs at any one time. If future demands for a particular commodity, such as personal computers, are expected to be higher than they are today, it pays manufacturers to plan now to build the necessary plant and equipment so they will be ready to turn out the computers when the market expands. More resources are thereby allocated to future consumption.

We can analyze the allocation of resources between present and future with the aid of a production possibilities frontier diagram, such as the one in Figure 1. The question now is how much labor and capital to devote to producing consumers' goods and how much to devote to construction of durable facilities to produce output in the future. Then, instead of jeans and backpacks, the graph will show consumers' goods and number of facilities on its axes, but otherwise it will be exactly the same as Figure 1.

The profit motive directs the flow of resources between one time period and another, just as it handles resource allocation among different industries in a given period. The lure of profits directs resources to those products *and those time periods* in which high prices promise to make output most profitable. But at least one feature of the process of resource allocation among different time periods distinguishes it from the process of allocation among industries—the special role that the *interest rate* plays in allocation among time periods.

The Role of the Interest Rate

If receipt of a given amount of money is delayed until some future time, the recipient incurs an *opportunity cost*—the interest that the money could have earned if it had been received earlier and invested. For example, if the prevailing interest rate is 9 percent and you can persuade someone who owes you $100 to make that payment one year earlier than originally planned, you come out $9 ahead (because you can take the $100 and invest it at 9 percent). Put another way, if the interest rate is 9 percent and the payment of $100 is postponed for one year, you lose the opportunity to earn $9. Thus, the interest rate determines the opportunity cost to a recipient who gets money at some future date instead of now—the lower the interest rate, the lower the opportunity cost. For this reason, as we will see in greater detail in Chapter 19:

> **Low interest rates will persuade people to invest more now in factories and equipment, because that will reduce the opportunity cost of these investments, which yield a large portion of their money returns in the future. Thus, more resources will be devoted to the future by investment in durable production facilities now if interest rates are low. Similarly, high interest rates make durable investment less attractive, because it yields**

much of its benefit only in the future, when it is too late to obtain much of the interest payment that earlier receipt of the earnings would have made possible. Therefore, high interest rates tend to increase the public's use of resources for output today at the expense of reduced future output tomorrow.

On the surface, it seems that the price system can allocate resources among different time periods in the way consumers prefer, because the supply of and demand for loans, which determine the interest rate—the price of a loan—reflects the public's preferences between present and future. Suppose, for example, that the public suddenly became more interested in future consumption (say, people wanted to put more money away for their retirement years). People would save more money, the supply of funds available for lending would increase relative to demand, and interest rates, the price of a loan of money, would tend to fall. This would stimulate investment and add to the future output of goods at the expense of current consumption.

But economists have raised several questions about how effectively the market mechanism allocates resources among different time periods in practice.

How Does It Work in Practice?

One thing that makes economists uneasy is that the interest rate (which is the price that controls resource allocation over time) is also used for a variety of *other* purposes. For instance, sometimes the interest rate is used to deal with business fluctuations. For instance, the government will take steps to push interest rates down in order to induce people to borrow and increase their spending and thereby stimulate business. For this and other similar reasons, governments frequently manipulate interest rates. For example, during the economic crisis of 2007–2008, the Federal Reserve Board—the organization that oversees the activities of banks in the United States—reduced interest rates repeatedly in order to make it cheaper for consumers and firms to borrow and buy consumers' goods or to invest in new plant and equipment. In doing so, policy makers seem to give little thought to the effects on resource allocation between present and future, so we may well worry whether the resulting interest rates were the most appropriate from that point of view.

Second, some economists have suggested that even when the government does not manipulate the interest rate, the market may devote too large a proportion of the economy's resources to immediate consumption. One British economist, A. C. Pigou, argued that people suffer from a "defective telescopic faculty"—that they are too shortsighted to give adequate weight to the future. A "bird in the hand" point of view leads people to spend too much on today's consumption and commit too little to tomorrow's investments.

Third, our economy shortchanges the future when it despoils irreplaceable natural resources, exterminates whole species of plants and animals, floods canyons, "develops" attractive areas into acres of potential slums, and so on. Worst of all, industry, the military, and individuals bequeath a ticking time bomb to the future when they leave behind lethal and slow-acting toxic residues. For example, nuclear wastes may remain dangerous for hundreds or even thousands of years, but their disposal containers are likely to fall apart long before the contents lose their lethal qualities. Such actions are essentially *irreversible*. If a factory is not built this year, the deficiency in facilities provided for the future can be remedied by building it next year. But a natural canyon, once destroyed, can never be replaced. For this reason,

> Many economists believe that *irreversible decisions* have a special significance and must not be left entirely to the decisions of private firms and individuals—that is, to the market.

Some writers, however, have questioned the general conclusion that the free market will not invest enough for the future. They point out that our economy's prosperity has increased fairly steadily from one decade to the next, and that there is reason to expect future generations to have far higher real average incomes and an abundance of consumer goods than we have today, just as we are economically better off than our grandparents. Pressures to increase future investment then may be like taking from the poor to give to the rich—a sort of backward Robin Hood redistribution of income.

SOME OTHER SOURCES OF MARKET FAILURE

We have now surveyed some of the most important imperfections of the market mechanism, but our list is not complete, and it can never be. In this imperfect world, nothing ever works out ideally. Indeed, by examining anything with a sufficiently powerful microscope, one can always detect more blemishes. However, some significant items were omitted from our list. We will conclude with a brief description of three of them and discuss a fourth of special current interest in somewhat greater detail.

Imperfect Information: "Caveat Emptor"

In our analysis of the virtues of the market mechanism in Chapter 14, we assumed that consumers and producers have all the information they need to make good decisions. In reality, this is rarely true. When buying a house or secondhand car or when selecting a doctor, consumers are vividly reminded of how little they know about what they are purchasing. The old cliché, "caveat emptor" (let the buyer beware), applies. Obviously, if participants in the market are ill-informed, they will not always make the optimal decisions described in our theoretical models. (For more on this issue, see "Asymmetric Information, 'Lemons,' and Agents," on the next page.)

Yet not all economists agree that imperfect information is really a failure of the market mechanism. They point out that information, too, is a commodity that costs money to produce. Neither firms nor consumers have complete information because it would be irrational for them to spend the enormous amounts needed to get it. As always, compromise is necessary. One should, ideally, stop buying information at the point where the marginal utility of further information is no greater than its marginal cost. With this amount of information, the business executive or the consumer would be able to make what we call "optimally imperfect" decisions.

Rent Seeking

An army of lawyers, expert witnesses, and business executives crowd our courtrooms and cause enormous costs to pile up through litigation. Business firms seem to sue each other at the slightest provocation, wasting vast resources and delaying business decisions. Why? Because it is possible to make money by such seemingly unproductive activities—through legal battles over profit-making opportunities.

For example, suppose that a municipality awards a contract to produce electricity to Firm A, offering $20 million in profit. It may be worthwhile for Firm B to spend $5 million in a lawsuit against the municipality and Firm A, hoping that the courts will award it the contract (and thus the $20 million profit) instead.

Rent seeking refers to unproductive activity in the pursuit of economic profit—in other words, undeserved profit in excess of competitive earnings.

In general, any source of unusual profit, such as a monopoly, tempts firms to waste economic resources in an effort to obtain control of that source of profit. This process, called **rent seeking** (meaning that the firms hope to obtain earnings without contributing to production), is judged by some observers to be a major source of inefficiency in our economy. (For more on rent seeking, see pages 408–409 in Chapter 19.)

Moral Hazard

Moral hazard refers to the tendency of insurance to discourage policyholders from protecting themselves from risk.

Another widely discussed problem for the market mechanism is associated with insurance. Economists view insurance—which is the provision of protection against risk—as a useful commodity, like shoes or information. But insurance also encourages the very risks against which it provides protection. For example, if an individual has a valuable stamp collection that is fully insured against theft, she has little motivation to protect it against burglars, because if it is stolen she will get her money back from the insurance company. She may, for example, fail to lock it up in a safe-deposit box. This problem—the tendency of insurance to encourage the source of risk—is called **moral hazard,** and it makes a free market in insurance difficult to operate.

Asymmetric Information, "Lemons," and Agents

Have you ever wondered why a six-month-old car sells for so much less than a brand-new one? Economists offer one explanation, having to do with *imperfect information*. The problem is that some small percentage of new automobiles are "lemons" that are plagued by mechanical troubles. The new-car dealer probably knows no more than the buyer about whether a particular car is a lemon. The information known to the two parties, therefore, is said to be *symmetric*, and there is a low probability that a car purchased from a new-car dealer will turn out to be a lemon.

In the used-car market, however, information is *asymmetric*. The person selling the used car knows very well whether the car is a lemon, but the buyer does not. Moreover, a seller who wants to get rid of a relatively new car is likely to be doing so only because it is a lemon. Potential buyers realize that. Hence, if a person is forced to sell a *good* new car because of an unexpected need for cash, he will be stuck with a low price because he cannot *prove* that his car really works well. The moral is that asymmetric information also tends to harm the honest seller.

In addition, asymmetric information leads to the *principal-agent problems*, which are discussed in the text and whose analysis is a major concern of recent economic research. Principal-agent and asymmetric information problems are said to have played a major part in the much-publicized Enron debacle. When that huge energy trading firm collapsed, stockholders—the "principals" (including Enron employees whose retirement money was invested in the firm)—lost their savings. Stockholders are called principals because they are, according to the law, the owners of the firm. But Enron's management, the stockholders' employees (their hired agents), had already deserted the sinking ship with large bonus payments, having sold *their* company stocks while the price was still high. Asymmetric information is crucial here. Principals usually know only *imperfectly* whether their agents are serving their interests faithfully and efficiently or are instead neglecting or even acting against the principals' interests to pursue selfish interests of their own. Misuse of the principals' property, embezzlement, and political corruption are extreme examples of such dereliction of duty by agents and, unfortunately, they seem to occur often.

One way that has been used to address the asymmetric information problem that has often failed spectacularly is based on the following logic. If the earnings of corporate management can be linked quite tightly to company profits or based on the market value of company shares, then by promoting the welfare of stockholders, managers will make themselves better off. Shareholders, even though they know only imperfectly what management is doing, can have greater confidence that management will try to serve their interests well. We will presently discuss what has gone wrong with this approach.

SOURCE: © Photopia

Principals, Agents, and Recent Stock Option Scandals

Yet another important area of concern about the performance of the unconstrained market is called the "principal-agent problem," which has just been mentioned. The economy contains many activities so large and complex that it is out of the question for them to be organized and operated by those most directly concerned. The most striking example is provided by our representative democracy that is, in theory, run by "We the people." But it is obvious that it would be quite impractical to assemble all of the citizens of the country to discuss and decide on the details of proposed legislation on complex matters such as trade policy or rules for protection of the environment. So, instead, the U.S. Constitution requires us to hire politicians via the election process to run the country on our behalf. In economic terminology, we would say that the citizens are the **principals** in the activity of running the country, and the president and members of Congress are the **agents** who are hired by us, the principals, to operate the country on our behalf.

A second example, the one on which we will focus here, is the running of a corporation. A giant corporation such as Intel (the largest producer of microprocessors for computers) has thousands of stockholder-owners. And, like citizens of a country, they are also too numerous to run the firm day by day, making the thousands of required decisions. So these principals, too, hire agents—the corporate management—to do the job. The assigned task of the agents is to run the corporation in a way that best promotes the interests of the stockholders.

The main problem that besets this arrangement, like all principal-agent arrangements, is that the agents cannot always be trusted. All too often they put their own interests ahead of those of their principals, in clear dereliction of duty. Indeed, in just this decade so far, there has been what seems like a flood of corporate scandals, with managements

Agents are people hired to run a complex enterprise on behalf of the **principals,** those whose benefit the enterprise is supposed to serve.

having indiscriminately betrayed stockholders and employees while obtaining for them-selves hundreds of millions of dollars as their supposedly merited rewards. (For examples, see the feature box in Chapter 9 on "Corporate Scandals.")

Economic analysis suggests a solution to the problem: Arrange for the amount that the agents are paid to depend on the degree to which their actions succeed in benefiting the principals. Pay the agents a lot if they achieve much for the principals, and pay them little if they don't. If such an incentive scheme is established, the agents can do well for themselves only by doing well for the stockholders.

The only trouble with this solution is that it is easier to describe on paper than to carry out in practice. First, it is not easy to measure what the agents have actually accomplished. If the company's sales increased, was that because of something management did, or was it largely an accident? The second problem is that unscrupulous managers can often find ways to get around such rules via legal maneuvers or by appointing friends and allies to the company's board of directors, rather than even-handed appointees who can assure the honesty and competence of management.

One seemingly clever device was thought up to do the job of rewarding management for what they achieve: the employee stock option. But corruption within firms and irrational tax laws that undermine their effectiveness, among other impediments, have prevented stock options from doing the job they were intended to do. Let us see what stock options are and why they have often been ineffective.

A **stock option** is, in effect, a contract that allows the person who owns the option to buy a specified quantity of the company's stock at some date in the future that can be chosen, within specified limits, by the owner. But when the option owner pays for the stock, he pays not the price on the day the stock is bought but, rather, the price of the stock on the day the option was obtained. For example, suppose the price of the stock was $40 on February 12, the day the option was acquired. On March 23, the owner considers using the option to buy the stock. If the price has fallen to $30, the option owner will decide not to buy any stock because, if he did, the option contract would require him to spend $40 for a stock worth only $30, clearly a losing proposition. But suppose the stock had gone in the other direction and, on the proposed purchase date, the share's price had risen to $60. Since this means that the option owner could acquire a stock worth $60 for only $40, it would give him an immediate $20 profit—a very good deal.

> A **stock option** is a contract that permits its owner to buy a specified quantity of stocks of a corporation at a future date, but at the price specified in the contract rather than the stock's market price at the date of purchase.

When the price of the company's stock goes down, stock options are not used. Thus, the owner of the option loses only what was paid for the option, if anything. But if the price of the stock rises, the owner can make a profit by "exercising the option"; that is, by using it to buy the stock and pocketing the difference between the price specified in the option and the value of the stock at the time it is bought.

If stock options are granted to a corporation's management under appropriate rules, they may well be a powerful way to deal with the principal-agent problem in corporations. For if managers who own stock options work harder to make the company successful, their actions can raise the market price of the corporation's stock, thereby benefiting the stockholders as well as themselves. In other words, a gift or sale of stock options to management can help align the interests of stockholders and management: They both want the stock price to rise. Few other instruments can ensure such compatibility between the interest of stockholders and managers.

However, the conditions under which stock options are now granted are far from this ideal. They can, for instance, lead management to focus on short-term gains in stock prices, rather than on the long-run performance of the firm. They reward management even when the firm's performance is worse than that of the industry and that of the stock market as a whole. And subservient boards of directors often provide staggering and probably undeserved managerial compensation in the form of huge gifts of stock options.

Unscrupulous managers have learned ways to manipulate stock options and undermine their benefits to stockholders. For instance, there have been cases in which management sent out misleading information indicating, falsely, that the company was about to make large profits. This raised the price of its stock temporarily, giving the holders of stock options an opportunity to use them quickly to buy the stocks at the low prices specified in the options and quickly sell the shares while their market price was still high, thus making a large profit for themselves. Such problems are best attacked directly by requiring the issue of stock options to management to satisfy provisions such as the following:

1. That exercise of those stock options should not be permitted for some substantial period of time, say five years, after they are initially offered;
2. That the stock options be performance-based, meaning that they are contingent on performance by the firm that exceeds that of comparable firms or of the firm's own past record, with the number of stock options granted to management proportioned to the magnitude of the superiority of the firm's performance;
3. That any such grant of options to management be subject to approval by vote of the firm's stockholders; and
4. That the sale of such shares by top management be made public promptly.

Stock options granted on these terms may well lead to a dramatic change in the incentives facing management—and in the desired direction. If the improved incentives created by options succeed in their purpose of fostering higher earnings, the gift of options to management may involve no cost to stockholders. On the contrary, earnings per share will probably be higher than they would otherwise have been, and both managers and shareholders will benefit.

But unfortunately, the existing rules do not contain such provisions to protect the interests of the shareholders (the principals). There are even rules that discourage some of those provisions. For example, under current tax rules, a company obtains some tax advantages if it uses stock options as part of management's compensation. But the law offers those advantages only if the grant of options is not made to depend on how well management performs for the company. Only if the options are given outright, with no difference in reward between cases where management performs its job well and where it does badly, do the current rules offer a tax benefit to the company.

MARKET FAILURE AND GOVERNMENT FAILURE

We have pointed out some of the invisible hand's most noteworthy failures. We seem forced to the conclusion that a market economy, if left entirely to itself, is likely to produce results that are, at least in some respects, far from ideal. We have noted in our discussion, either directly or by implication, some of the things that government can do to correct these deficiencies. But the fact that government often *can* intervene in the economy's operation in a constructive way does not always mean that it actually *will* succeed in doing so. Governments cannot be relied on to behave ideally, any more than business firms can be expected to do so.

It is difficult to make this point in a suitably balanced way. Commentators too often stake out one extreme position or the other. Some people think the market mechanism is inherently unfair and biased by the greed of those who run its enterprises and they look to the government to cure all economic ills. Others deplore government intervention and consider the public sector to be the home of every sort of inefficiency, graft, and bureaucratic stultification. The truth, as usual, lies somewhere in between.

Governments, like humans, are inherently imperfect. The political process leads to compromises that sometimes bear little resemblance to rational decisions. For example, legislators' versions of the policies suggested by economic analysis are sometimes mere caricatures of the economists' ideas. (For a satirical editorial illustrating this point, see "The Politics of Economic Policy.")

Yet often the problems engendered by an unfettered economy are too serious to be left to the free market. The problems of inflation, environmental decay, and the provision of public goods are cases in point. In such instances, government intervention is likely to yield substantial benefits to the general public. However, even when *some* government action is clearly warranted, it may be difficult or impossible to calculate the *optimal* degree

The Politics of Economic Policy

In 1978, Alfred Kahn, a noted economist who served in the administration of President Jimmy Carter, advocated reducing pollution by raising the tax on leaded gasoline and lowering the tax on unleaded gasoline. The *Washington Post*, in an editorial excerpted here, agreed that Kahn's idea was a sound one but worried about what might emerge from Congress:

SOURCE: The Museum of Modern Art, New York, NY Digital Image © The Museum of Modern Art/Licensed by SCALA/Art Resource, NY

If the administration adopts the Kahn plan, recent history offers a pretty clear view of the rest of the story. Mr. Kahn will draft a one-page bill to raise the tax on the one kind of gas and lower it on the other. But the White House political staff will immediately point out that his draft fails to address profound questions of social equity. What about the poor, who buy leaded gas because it's cheaper? What about young people driving old cars? What about the inhabitants of lower Louisiana, who need their outboard motors to get around the swamps and bayous? There will have to be a rebate formula. It will take into account each family's income, the number and ages of its various automobiles and the distance from its front doorstep to the bus stop. The legislative draftsmen at the Energy Department have had a lot of experience with that kind of formula and eventually the 53-page bill will be sent to Congress. . . .

The real fun will start when it arrives at the Senate Finance Committee. First the committee will add tuition tax credits for families with children in private schools. Then, warming to its work, it will vote import quotas on straw hats from Hong Kong, beef from Argentina and automobiles from Japan. . . . [I]t will then add several obscure but pregnant provisions that seem to refer to the tax treatment of certain oil wells in the Gulf states. When the 268-page bill comes to the Senate floor, the administration will narrowly manage to defeat an amendment to improve business confidence by repealing the capital-gains tax and returning to the gold standard.

When the bill gets back to the House, liberal Democrats will denounce it as an outrage and declare all-out war. They will succeed in getting all references to gasoline taxes and the environment stricken—but not, unfortunately, the import quotas or the obscure tax changes for the oil wells. By the time the staff of the Joint Committee on Taxation has straightened out a few technical difficulties, the bill will run to 417 pages and Ralph Nader will be calling on President Carter to veto it. But the feeling at the White House will be that Congress has worked so long and hard on the bill that he has no choice but to sign it. By the time the bill is finally enacted, Mr. Kahn might well wish he had chosen some other instrument of policy.

SOURCE: Alfred E. Kahn, "The Politics of Economic Policy" from the *Washington Post*, December 26, 1978. Reprinted by permission of Alfred E. Kahn, Robert Julius Thorne Professor of Political Economy, Emeritus, Cornell University.

of governmental intervention. There is, then, the danger of intervention so excessive that the society might have been better off without it.

In other areas, the market mechanism is likely to work reasonably well, and small imperfections do not constitute adequate justification for government intervention. In any event, *even where government action is appropriate, we must consider market-like instruments as one possible way to correct market mechanism deficiencies*. The tax incentives described earlier in our discussion of externalities are an outstanding example of what we have in mind.

THE COST DISEASE OF SOME VITAL SERVICES: INVITATION TO GOVERNMENT FAILURE

As our final example, we consider next a problem that is not strictly a *failure* of the market mechanism. Rather, it is a case where the market's behavior creates that illusion and often leads to ill-advised *government* action that threatens the general welfare. This problem concerns dramatically rising prices, as typified by health-care and college tuitions. (For more on health-care costs and the 2010 U.S. health-care reforms, see "The Economics of America's 2010 Health-Care Reform" on page 328.) As a reader of this book, you are well aware that your attendance at an American college is likely to cost as much as $50,000 per year. When the older of the two authors of this book attended graduate school in the mid-1900s, the fee was a little over $100 per year. That is a dramatic rise in cost, and it has hit not only college tuitions. In this section, we will examine the reasons for these rising prices and other disturbing developments in the affected segments of the economy.

Deteriorating Personal Services

Over the years, general standards of living have increased and our material possessions have multiplied. But at the same time, our communities have experienced a decline in the quality of a variety of public and private services. Not just in the United States, but throughout the world, streets and subways, for example, have grown increasingly dirty. Bus, train, and postal services have all been cut back. Amazingly enough, in the 1800s in suburban London, there were twelve mail deliveries per day on weekdays, including Saturdays, and one on Sundays! Today, mail service in the United Kingdom is hardly a subject of admiration anymore.

SOURCE: By Rose for Byrd Newspapers, Harrisburg, VA

BY ROSE FOR BYRD NEWSPAPERS, FREDERICKSBURG, VA.

Parallel cutbacks have occurred in the quality of private services. Milk once used to be delivered to individual homes every day, and it was not necessary to push five buttons successively on the telephone to get to speak to a human being at the bank. Doctors almost never visit patients at home anymore. In many areas a house call, which 50 years ago was a commonplace event, now occurs only rarely. Another example, although undoubtedly a matter for less general concern, is the quality of food served in restaurants. Even some of the most elegant and expensive restaurants serve frozen and reheated meals—charging high prices for what amounts to little more than TV dinners.

Personal Services Are Getting More Expensive

Perhaps most distressing of all, and closely connected with the problems just described, is the persistent and dramatic rise in the *cost* of what we call *personal services*—services that require face-to-face, in-person interaction between the supplier and the consumer, such as health care and education. As a college student, you know how fast college tuitions have been increasing. But you may not realize that the cost of a hospital stay has been going up even more rapidly. Worse still, the cost of health care has denied adequate health services to a substantial portion of our population—the poor and even some members of the middle class. These cost increases have prompted most industrialized countries—most recently, the U.S.—to adopt health-care regulations aimed at controlling costs and keeping care affordable for their citizens.

Consider these facts: Between 1948 and 2008, the Consumer Price Index (CPI) (an official measure of *overall* price rises in the economy) increased at an average rate of about 3.7 percent per year, whereas the price of physicians' services rose about 5.2 percent per year. This difference seems tiny, but compounded over those 60 years it had the effect of increasing the price of a doctor visit, measured in dollars of constant purchasing power, by 229 percent. In the last three decades, the price of hospital care also skyrocketed: The average price of inpatient hospital services increased at an annual rate of about 7.86 percent, compounded continuously. This amounts to a nearly 300 percent increase since 1948, measured in constant dollars from which the effects of inflation have been eliminated.[2]

Virtually every major industrial nation has tried to prevent health-care costs from rising faster than its economy's overall rate of inflation, but none has succeeded, as Figure 4 shows. In this graph, the bar for each country shows its average yearly rate of increase in

---

[2] These figures were derived from data provided by the U.S. Department of Labor, Bureau of Labor Statistics, available at http://www.bls.gov.

FIGURE 4

Average Annual Growth Rates in Real Health-Care Expenditure per Capita between 1960 and 2006

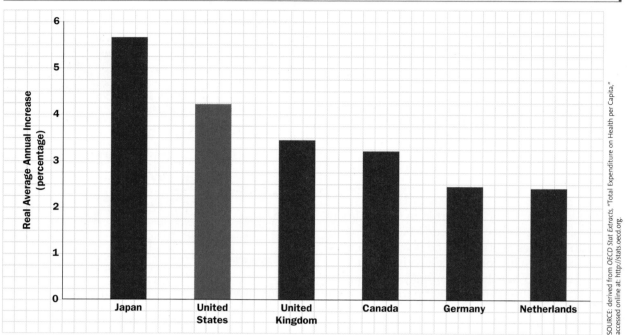

SOURCE: derived from *OECD Stat Extracts,* "Total Expenditure on Health per Capita," accessed online at: http://stats.oecd.org.

real (inflation-adjusted) health-care spending per person between 1960 and 2006. It is clear that the United States did not exhibit the highest rate of increase in real health-care costs.

The cost of education has a similar record—costs in the United States have increased at an average annual rate of 4.5 percent per year in the last decade. Between 1995 and 2004, U.S. increases in education costs were the highest among a group of seven top industrial countries, as shown in Figure 5.

These are remarkable statistics, particularly because doctors' earnings have barely kept up with the economy's overall inflation rate in the post–World War II time period, and teachers' salaries actually fell behind. Persistent cost increases have also plagued other services such as postal delivery and libraries. The soaring costs of education, health care, and police and fire protection place a terrible financial burden on municipal budgets.

FIGURE 5

Average Annual Growth Rates in Real Education Expenditure between 1995 and 2004

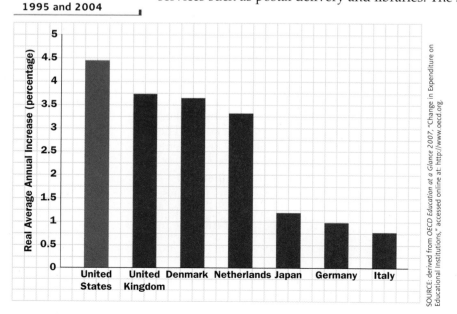

SOURCE: derived from *OECD Education at a Glance 2007,* "Change in Expenditure on Educational Institutions," accessed online at: http://www.oecd.org.

NOTE: Data for 1996–1999 were not available.

Why Are These "In-Person" Services Costing So Much More?

What accounts for the ever-increasing costs? Are they attributable to inefficiencies in government management or to political corruption? Perhaps to some degree to both. But there is also another and a more significant reason—one that cannot be avoided by any municipal administration no matter how pure its conduct and efficient its bureaucrats and one that affects personal services provided by the private sector of the economy just as severely as it does the public sector. The common influence underlying all of these problems of rising cost and deterioration in service quality, which is *economic* in character and expected to grow even more serious with time, has been called the **cost disease of the personal services.**

This "cost disease" stems from the basic nature of personal services: They usually require face-to-face interaction between those who provide the service and those who consume it. Doctors, nurses, teachers, and librarians all engage in activities that require direct, in-person interaction. Moreover, the quality of the service deteriorates if less personal time is provided by doctors, teachers, and librarians to each user of their services.

> The **cost disease of the personal services** is the tendency of the costs and prices of these services to rise persistently faster than those of the average output in the economy.

Uneven Labor Productivity Growth in the Economy

In other parts of the economy, such as manufacturing, no direct personal contact between the consumer and the producer is required. For instance, the buyer of an automobile usually has no idea who worked on its assembly and could not care less how much labor time went into its production. A labor-saving innovation in auto production need not imply a reduction in product quality. As a result, over the years it has proved far easier for technological change to save labor in manufacturing than to save labor in providing many services. In the post–World War II period, for instance, productivity in the United States' (non-farm) business sector grew by an average of 2.2 percent per year.[3] Meanwhile, labor productivity in elementary and secondary education actually *declined*, with the average number of pupils per teacher in public schools falling from about 25 pupils per teacher in 1960–61 to about 15 pupils per teacher in 2006–07.[4] However, this decline may be due, in part, to smaller class sizes.

These disparate productivity performances have grave consequences for prices. When manufacturing wages rise by roughly 2 percent, the cost of manufactured products need not rise because increased output per worker can make up for the rise in wages. But the nature of many personal services makes it very difficult to introduce labor-saving devices in those parts of the service sector. A 2 percent wage increase for teachers or police officers is not usually offset by higher output per worker and must lead to an equivalent rise in municipal budgets. Similarly, a 2 percent wage increase for hairdressers must lead beauty salons to raise their prices.

In the long run, wages for all workers throughout the economy tend to go up and down together, for otherwise an activity whose wage rate falls seriously behind will tend to lose its labor force. So autoworkers and police officers will see their wages rise at roughly the same rate in the long run. But if output per worker—labor productivity—on the assembly line advances, while productivity in the police patrol car does not, then police protection grows ever more expensive, relative to manufacturing, as time goes on. Because labor productivity improvements are very difficult to achieve for most personal services, their costs can be expected to rise more rapidly, year in and year out, than the costs of manufactured products do. Over a period of several decades, this difference in the growth rate of costs of the two sectors adds up, making services enormously more expensive compared with manufactured goods. This imbalance explains why personal services have grown steadily more expensive compared to goods, and they are likely to continue to do so.

A Future of More Goods but Fewer Services: Is It Inevitable?

If some services continue to get ever more expensive in comparison to goods, the implications for life in the future are profound indeed. The cost disease portends a world in which the typical home contains an abundance of goods—luxuries and furnishings that we can hardly imagine. But it is a home that may be surrounded by garbage and perhaps by violence. The cost disease also portends a future in which the services of doctors,

---

[3] Bureau of Labor Statistics, "Productivity Change in the Nonfarm Business Sector, 1947–2008" (chart), 2009, accessed online: ftp://ftp.bls.gov/pub/special.requests/opt/lpr/mfgbardata.txt.

[4] Thomas D. Snyder, Sally A. Dillow, and Charlene M. Hoffman, *Digest of Education Statistics 2008*, Chapter 2, Figure 6, p. 57, Washington, D.C.: National Center for Education Statistics, 2009.

teachers, and police officers are increasingly mass-produced and impersonal, and in which arts and crafts are increasingly supplied only by amateurs because the cost of professional work in these fields is too high.

But this future is by no means inevitable. To see why, we must first recognize that the problem's source, paradoxically, is the growth in our economy's productivity, the amount of output each worker creates in an hour—or rather, the *unevenness* of that growth. Trash removal costs go up not because garbage collectors become less efficient, but because labor in automobile manufacturing becomes *more* efficient, thus enhancing the sanitation worker's potential value on the automotive assembly line. The sanitation worker's wages must go up to keep him at his garbage removal job.

But increasing productivity in goods manufacturing does *not* make a nation poorer. It does *not* make us unable to afford things that we could afford in the past. Indeed, increasing productivity (that is, more output from each work-hour) means that we can afford more of *all* things—televisions, electric toothbrushes, cell phones, medical care, education, and other services.

The role of services in the nation's future depends on how we order our priorities. If we value services sufficiently, we can have more and better services—at some sacrifice in the growth rate of manufactured goods. Whether that is a good choice for society is not for economists to say. But society *does* have a choice, and if we fail to exercise it, matters may proceed relentlessly toward a world in which material goods are abundant and many things that most people now consider primary requisites for a high quality of life are scarce.

The Economics of America's 2010 Health-Care Reform

For more than 50 years, a succession of U.S. presidents attempted unsuccessfully to pass legislation allowing most or all American citizens access to affordable health insurance. Until 2010, the U.S. was the only prosperous country in the world that did not offer such protection. But now, after a bitter battle between Republicans and Democrats, reforms that will provide financial protection to some 32 million previously uninsured people have been signed into law.

The new law prohibits private insurers from rejecting child applicants who have preexisting medical conditions or from charging more to policy holders with medical problems. Insurers also will be forbidden to set a ceiling on a person's lifetime medical expenditures, and children can now be included in their parents' insurance until age 26.

Government subsidies will help some families and small businesses purchase their insurance. New taxes levied on wealthy families' investment income and on high-end insurance plans will help to pay for these reforms.

Perhaps the most controversial aspect of the plan is the requirement that almost everyone (except the very poor) buy health insurance, with fines for those who refuse. Without this provision, however, the program would not work, for the logic of insurance is based on *risk sharing*. Consider an analogy based on fire insurance for homeowners. Suppose that, on average, 99 out of every 100 insured homes are *not* destroyed by fire in a given year. In order to achieve adequate protection for all, the average homeowner who purchases fire insurance must pay only one percent of the cost of rebuilding a destroyed home because most homeowners will never need to use any of the protection they have purchased. Health insurance works similarly. So, if all of the healthy people were to decline to purchase insurance, only the sick would pay in (and, in turn, require payouts to cover the cost of their medical treatments). Such an insurance scheme would likely go bankrupt.

The proponents of the 2010 health-care reform supported it primarily because of the protection it offers to poor and middle-class Americans and to small business firms, for whom rising health-care costs have been a growing burden. But whatever its virtues and vices, there is little reason to expect the new law to end the rapidly rising costs of health care that are explained in this chapter. The fact is that countries throughout the world have tried many different forms of regulation in order to prevent these costs from rising. But few, if any, have succeeded.

SOURCE: JASON REED/Reuters/Landov

Government May Make the Problem Worse

How does the cost disease relate to the central topic of this chapter—the market's performance and its implications for the government's economic role? Here the problem is that the market *does* give the appropriate price signals, but politicians in government are likely to misunderstand these signals and be misled to make decisions that do not promote the public interest most effectively.

Health care is a good example. The cost disease itself is capable of causing health-care costs (say, the price of a hospital stay) to rise more rapidly than the economy's inflation rate because medical care cannot be standardized enough to share in the productivity gains offered by automation and assembly lines. As a result, if we want to maintain standards of care in public hospitals, it is not enough to keep health-care budgets growing at the economy's prevailing inflation rate. Those budgets must actually grow quickly and consistently in order to prevent a decline in quality. For example, when the inflation rate is 4 percent per year, hospitals' budgets may need to increase by 6 percent annually.

In these circumstances, something may seem amiss to a state legislature that increases its hospitals' budgets by only 5 percent per year. Responsible lawmakers will doubtless be disturbed by the fact that the budget is growing steadily, outpacing the inflation rate, and yet standards of quality at public hospitals continue to slip. If the legislators do not realize that the cost disease is causing the problem, they will look for villains—greedy doctors, corrupt or inefficient hospital administrators, and so on. The net result, all too often, is a set of wasteful rules that hamper the freedom of action of hospitals and doctors inappropriately or that tighten hospital budgets below the levels that demands and costs would require if they were determined by the market mechanism rather than by government.

In many cases, *price controls* are proposed for sectors of the economy affected by the cost disease—for medical services, insurance services, and the like. As we know, such price controls can, at best, merely eliminate the symptoms of the disease, and they often create problems that are sometimes more serious than the disease itself.[5]

PUZZLE RESOLVED: EXPLAINING THE RISING COSTS OF CANADIAN HEALTH CARE

This brings us back to the puzzle with which we began the chapter: Why have price controls failed to brake the rise in Canadian health-care costs? The answer is that the medical care system in Canada, like the health-care system in every other industrial country, is struggling with the effects of the cost disease of the personal services. As we have just seen, legislative fiat cannot abolish the productivity-growth patterns that force health-care costs to rise persistently and universally faster than the overall inflation rate. The government-imposed price controls on doctors' fees and hospital budgets have, in fact, led to long waiting lists for Canadians who need high-tech medical procedures and have reduced patients' access to high-priced specialists. The Canadian government has been forced to ease up somewhat on price controls, allowing health-care prices to adapt more closely to costs so as to prevent more serious erosion of medical-care services. The provincial governments are also trying to hold down costs by squeezing the list of services covered by public health insurance, dropping such things as vision tests and physical therapy and forcing Canadians to pay for these things out of their own pockets. The overall quality of service apparently remains high, but the costs have risen persistently more rapidly than the overall inflation rate, just as in the United States.

Figure 4 showed that the U.S. record of increasing health-care costs is by no means the best, but also not the worst, in this sample of six countries for the period 1960 to 2006. The conclusion is that,

SOURCE: From *The Wall Street Journal*—Permission, Cartoon Features Syndicatee

"What really makes this heaven is our great healthcare plan."

---

[5] See Chapter 4, pages 56–57 and 70–71.

although the U.S. health-care reforms may or may not be desirable for other reasons, it is hardly a promising cure for the cost disease. Congress can declare both heart disease and the cost disease of the services to be illegal, but that will do little to cure either disease, and such a law may well impede more effective approaches to the problem.

In sum, the cost disease is not a case where the market performs badly. Rather, it is a case in which the market *appears* to misbehave by singling out certain sectors through particularly large cost increases. Because the market seems to be working badly here, government reactions that can be highly damaging to the public interest are likely; that is, "government failure" may occur.

THE MARKET SYSTEM ON BALANCE

This chapter, like Chapter 14, has deliberately offered a rather unbalanced assessment of the market mechanism. In Chapter 14, we extolled the market's virtues; in this chapter, we catalogued its vices. We come out, as in the nursery rhyme, concluding that the market is either very, very good or it is horrid.

There seems to be nothing moderate about the quality of performance of a market system. As a means of achieving efficiency in the production of ordinary consumer goods and responding to changes in consumer preferences, it is unparalleled. In the next chapter we will see that the market system's performance in terms of innovation and income growth among members of the population is unmatched in human history. It is, in fact, difficult to overstate the accomplishments of the price system in these areas. By contrast, the market has proved itself incapable of coping with business fluctuations, income inequality, or the consequences of monopoly. It has proved to be a very poor allocator of resources among outputs that generate external costs and external benefits, and it has shown itself to be incapable of arranging for the provision of public goods. Some of the most urgent problems that plague our society—the deterioration of services in the cities, the despoliation of our atmosphere, the social unrest attributable to poverty—can be ascribed in part to one or another of these market system shortcomings.

Most economists conclude from these observations that although the market mechanism is virtually irreplaceable, the public interest nevertheless requires considerable modifications in the way it works. Proposals designed to deal directly with the problems of poverty, monopoly, and resource allocation over time abound in economic literature. All of them call for the government to intervene in the economy, either by supplying directly those goods and services that, it is believed, private enterprise does not supply in adequate amounts or by seeking to influence the workings of the economy more indirectly through regulation. We discussed many of these programs in earlier chapters; we will explain others in future chapters.

EPILOGUE: THE UNFORGIVING MARKET, ITS GIFT OF ABUNDANCE, AND ITS DANGEROUS FRIENDS

As we said at the end of Chapter 14, economists' analysis of the free market's accomplishments, although valid enough, may fail to emphasize its central contribution. The same can be said of their analysis of the market's shortcomings.

The market's major contribution to the general welfare may well be its stimulation of *productivity*, which has yielded an abundance of consumer goods, contributed to increases in human longevity, created new products, expanded education, and raised standards of living to levels undreamed of in earlier societies. This is an accomplishment that is yet to be discussed (see Chapter 16). The main shortcoming of the market, according to many observers, lies in the arena of justice and injustice, a subject that economists are no more competent to address than anyone else. The perception that markets are cruel and unjust springs from the very heart of the mechanism. The market mechanism has sometimes been described appropriately as the profit system, because it works by richly rewarding those who succeed in introducing attractive new products or in increasing efficiency sufficiently to permit sharp price reductions of other items. At the same time, it is unforgiving to those who fail, subjecting them to bankruptcy and perhaps to poverty.

Both the wealth awarded to those who succeed and the drastic treatment accorded to those who fail are main sources of the markets' productive power, but they also generate disenchantment and opposition. Consider what has happened in the newly "marketized" countries of Eastern Europe and Asia. Predictably, as enterprise in these countries was freed from government control, a number of wildly successful entrepreneurs have earned high incomes, leading to widespread resentment among the populace and calls for restrictions on entrepreneurial earnings. These critics do not seem to realize that a market without substantial rewards to successful entrepreneurs is a market whose engine has been weakened, if not altogether removed.

Indeed, efficient and effectively competitive markets often elicit support from groups that, at the same time, do their best to undermine that competition. For example, regulators who seek to prevent "excessive competition," and politicians in other countries who arrange for the sale of government enterprises to private owners only to constrain decision making by the new owners at every turn, are, in fact, doing their best to keep markets from working. When the general public demands price controls on interest rates, rents, and health-care services, it is expressing its unwillingness to accept the free market's decisions. Businesspeople who tirelessly proclaim their support for the market system, but who seek to acquire the monopoly power that can distort its activities, are doing the same thing. In short, the market has many professed supporters who genuinely believe in its virtues but whose behavior poses a constant threat to its effectiveness.

We cannot take for granted the success of the newly introduced market mechanism in Eastern Europe. The Russian economy, in its transition from communist government control, has come very slowly out of turmoil, as have other economies in Eastern Europe. Most remarkable has been the performance of China, which has moved rapidly to a market economy, despite its continued dedication to socialist political principles. Even in the older free-enterprise economies, we cannot simply assume that the market will emerge unscathed from the dangerous embrace of its most vocal supporters.

| SUMMARY |

1. At least seven major imperfections are associated with the market mechanism:

   a. Inequality of income distribution

   b. Fluctuations in economic activity (inflation and unemployment)

   c. Monopolistic output restrictions

   d. Beneficial and detrimental externalities

   e. Inadequate provision of public goods

   f. Misallocation of resources between present and future

   g. Deteriorating quality and rising costs of personal services

2. Efficient resource allocation is a matter of balancing the benefits of producing more of one good against the benefits of devoting the required inputs to some other good's production.

3. A detrimental **externality** occurs when an economic activity incidentally does harm to others who are not directly involved in the activity. A beneficial externality occurs when an economic activity incidentally creates benefits for others.

4. When an activity causes a detrimental externality, the activity's **marginal social cost** (including the harm it does to others) must be greater than the **marginal private cost** to those who carry on the activity. The opposite will be true when a beneficial externality occurs.

5. If a product's manufacture causes detrimental externalities, its price will generally not include all of the marginal social cost it causes, because part of the cost will be borne by others. The opposite is true for beneficial externalities.

6. The market will therefore tend to overallocate resources to the production of goods that cause detrimental externalities and underallocate resources to the production of goods that create beneficial externalities. This imbalance is one of the *Ideas for Beyond the Final Exam*.

7. A **public good** is a commodity (such as the guiding beam of a coastal lighthouse) that is not depleted by additional users. It is often difficult to exclude anyone from

the benefits of a public good, even those who refuse to pay for it. A **private good,** in contrast, is characterized by both **excludability** and **depletability.**

8. Free-enterprise firms generally will not produce a public good, even if it is extremely useful to the community, because they cannot charge money for the use of the good.

9. Many observers believe that the market often short-changes the future, particularly when it makes irreversible decisions that destroy natural resources.

10. Complex and large-scale enterprises such as huge corporations cannot be run day-to-day or effectively controlled directly by their owners, the **principals**. So they hire **agents** to run the enterprises on their behalf. The danger is that the agents will operate the enterprises so as to favor their own interests rather than those of the principals.

11. Because personal services—such as education, medical care, and police protection—are activities whose inherent value depends on face-to-face, in-person interaction, they are not amenable to labor-saving innovations and suffer from a **cost disease.** That is, their costs tend to rise persistently and considerably more rapidly than costs in the economy as a whole, where faster productivity increases offset rising input costs. The result can be a distortion in the supply of services by government or the imposition of unwise price controls when the rising cost is misattributed to greed and mismanagement.

| KEY TERMS |

agents   321

beneficial externality   312

cost disease of the personal services   327

depletability   317

detrimental externality   312

excludability   317

marginal private benefit (MPB)   313

marginal private cost (MPC)   313

marginal social benefit (MSB)   313

marginal social cost (MSC)   313

moral hazard   320

principals   321

private good   317

production possibilities frontier   311

public good   317

rent seeking   320

resource misallocation   311

stock options   322

| TEST YOURSELF |

1. What is the opportunity cost to society of a 100-mile truck trip? Why may the price of the gasoline used by the truck not adequately represent that opportunity cost?

2. Suppose that because of a new disease that attacks coffee plants, far more labor and other inputs are required to harvest a pound of coffee than before. How may that change affect the efficient allocation of resources between tea and coffee? How would the prices of coffee and tea react in a free market?

3. Give some examples of goods whose production causes detrimental externalities and some examples of goods whose production creates beneficial externalities.

4. Compare cleaning a dormitory room with cleaning the atmosphere of a city. Which is a public good and which is a private good? Why?

5. **(More difficult)** A firm holds a patent that is estimated to be worth $20 million. The patent is repeatedly challenged in the courts by a large number of (money-seeking) firms, each hoping to grab away the patent. If anyone is free to challenge the patent so that there is free entry into the litigation process, how much will end up being spent in the legal battles? (*Hint:* Under perfect competition, should firms expect to earn any economic profit?)

| DISCUSSION QUESTIONS |

1. Give some other examples of public goods. In each case, explain why additional users do not deplete the good and why it is difficult to exclude people from using it.

2. Think about the goods and services that your local government provides. Which are "public goods" as economists use the term?

3. Explain why the services of a lighthouse are sometimes used as an example of a public good.

4. Explain why education is not a very satisfactory example of a public good.

5. In recent decades, college tuition costs have risen more rapidly than the general price level, even though the wages of college professors have failed to keep pace with the price level. Can you explain why?

16

THE MARKET'S PRIME ACHIEVEMENT: INNOVATION AND GROWTH

Procter & Gamble has a world-class global research and development organization, with more than 7,500 scientists working in 22 research centers in 12 countries around the world. This includes 1,250 Ph.D. scientists. For perspective, this is larger than the combined science faculties at Harvard, Stanford, and MIT.

PROCTER & GAMBLE, R&D'S FORMULA FOR SUCCESS, P&G INNOVATION
HTTP://WWW.PG.COM

Many textbooks, including previous editions of this one, tend to give scant attention to the microeconomics of innovation and growth. This omission is astonishing, given the incredible contribution of the market in this arena to society's economic welfare. It is an achievement whose magnitude was undreamed of by our ancestors, and its benefits far exceed those expected from any other possible modifications in the workings of the market that we know. In this chapter we will begin our discussion of the mechanism that underlies this economic revolution. First, we will try to give you some feeling for the magnitude of this accomplishment—something that is often overlooked because we have come to take innovation and growth for granted. We must note that there are (at least) five contributors to this achievement: government, universities, inventors, entrepreneurs, and competing oligopolists in the high-tech industries. Since here we are interested primarily in the contribution of the market, we will say little about the role of governments and universities, despite their importance. In this chapter we will focus on the part played by the oligopolists, leaving the critical role of the inventors and the entrepreneurs to Chapter 20 in the section of the book on the economy's "factors of production," that is, its main categories of productive inputs.

CONTENTS

This chapter focuses on one extraordinary and important development, the unprecedented expansion in the amount that the market economies produce, on average, for each of their inhabitants and the flood of new products and other inventions that they provide to them. Never before in human history has economic performance ever come close to this achievement. There have, of course, been economies with a striking record of invention, and others have produced valuable contributions to knowledge about astronomy and materials related to other sciences. But none has come close to the enhancement of living standards in our economy and a number of others. What accounts for this near miraculous performance? What is the role of the market in this achievement? No one is absolutely certain of the answers to these questions, but economists have provided some of the relevant insights, insights that can be helpful in ensuring that our economic progress continues and can offer some useful guidance to the impoverished nations, most of whose residents continue to live in poverty.

THE MARKET ECONOMY'S INCREDIBLE GROWTH RECORD

An activity is said to generate a beneficial or detrimental **externality** if that activity causes incidental benefits or damages to others not directly involved in the activity and no corresponding compensation is provided to or paid by those who generate the externality.

The past several chapters have tried to provide a balanced evaluation of the market, describing both its shortcomings and its accomplishments. Among its defects we have listed are attributes such as vulnerability to monopoly power, **externalities** such as damage to the environment, and a propensity to underproduce public goods. On the virtuous side, we showed how the market can allocate resources more efficiently and more in accord with consumer desires than planning and central direction.

But we have saved the best for last—the free market's incredible performance in terms of *innovation* and growth, in which it has far exceeded any other type of economy in ancient or recent history. Whatever else one may think of our economic system, its accomplishment in terms of enhanced income of the population is an astonishing achievement, not remotely paralleled anywhere in the previous history of the world.

Although growth is often viewed as a macroeconomic topic, inventions are provided by individuals or individual laboratories and are brought to market by individual firms. So understanding innovation and its contribution to growth requires microeconomic analysis of the behavior of individual innovators and firms. This chapter will indicate the magnitude of the market's growth accomplishment. Here, and in Chapter 20, we will use our microeconomic tools to analyze how the market has produced that achievement.

Incidentally, part of the discussion may be considered both as a review of some of the analytic tools we have used before and as an additional illustration of the wide variety of subjects they can be used to investigate.

Per-capita income in an economy is the average income of all people in that economy.

The **productivity** of an economy is the value of all goods and services produced there, divided by the total labor time devoted to the economy's productive activities.

In the free-market economies, the growth in **per-capita income** (average income per person) and **productivity** (output per hour of work) has been so enormous that we can hardly comprehend its magnitude.

Still, a few numbers may begin to suggest what growth has accomplished. Today the income of an average American is about $43,368. In contrast, at the beginning of the twentieth century the average individual's was less than $6,000, in terms of today's purchasing power.[1] And if income per person grows as rapidly in the twenty-first century as it did in the twentieth, in the year 2100 our descendants will be earning, on average, an amount equivalent approximately to the purchasing power of more than $300,000 today. Just think what you and your family could purchase if all of your savings and earnings were suddenly

---

[1] Actually, the growth in per-capita income in the United States was even greater than this, very likely substantially so. We have used the most conservative estimate we could find, that of Angus Maddison, to avoid exaggeration of an already astonishing number.

multiplied by seven![2] Looked at another way, an average American family living around 1900 could afford only about *one-seventh* the food, clothing, housing, and other amenities that constitute the standard of living today. That figure is really incredible. Just try to imagine how your family's life would be changed if you suddenly lost more than six out of seven dollars from all of your savings and earnings and you were forced to reduce the family's consumption expenditure correspondingly.

Such economic growth has never been experienced before. In contrast to this explosive expansion of income in recent centuries, average growth rates of per-capita incomes probably approximated *zero* for about the entire 1,500 years before the **Industrial Revolution** (around the time of George Washington). In 1776, even the wealthiest consumers in England, then the world's richest country, could purchase perhaps only a half-dozen consumer goods that had not been available more than a thousand years earlier in ancient Rome. These new products included (highly inaccurate) hunting guns, (fairly inaccurate) watches, paper with printed material on it, window glass, and very little else. No sounds had ever been recorded, so we can never hear Washington's voice. No one had traveled on land faster than on horseback. Messages delivered from the Old World to the New World required weeks and even months, so that the battle of New Orleans (1815) was fought *after* the peace treaty had been signed. And Roman citizens enjoyed a number of amenities, such as hot baths and paved roads, which had practically disappeared long before the American Revolution.

The low income numbers and the resulting economic conditions of the lower economic classes before the Industrial Revolution and for quite a period beyond it are difficult for us to grasp. Regular famines—at least once per decade on average, with starvation widespread and corpses littering the streets—only began to disappear in the eighteenth century. Still, famines continued occasionally well into the nineteenth, and not only in Ireland. For example, in relatively wealthy Belgium, "During the great crisis of 1846, the newspapers would tell daily of cases of death from starvation. . . . [In one town] cases became so frequent that the local policeman was given the job of calling at all houses each day to see if the inhabitants were still alive."[3] But even the living standards of the upper classes were far from enviable (see "Discomforts of the Rich a Few Centuries Ago" on page 336).

By comparison, in the past two centuries, per-capita incomes in the typical **capitalist** economy have risen by amounts ranging from several hundred to several thousand percent. Recent decades have yielded an unmatched outpouring of new products and services: the Internet, color television, the computer, jet aircraft, the VCR and DVD player, the microwave oven, the handheld calculator, the cellular telephone, and so on. And the flood of new products continues.[4] Surely, part of the reason for the collapse of most of the world's communist regimes was their citizens' desire to participate in the growth miracle of the capitalist economies.

There are, of course, many Americans who still live in poverty, but phenomena like mass starvation have disappeared. It is mainly in the nonmarket economies that one finds the 25 percent of the world population that still lives on the equivalent of about $1.25 per person per day.[5]

We can look at this enormous economic progress in the market economies from another angle: by examining how much work it takes to acquire the things we purchase. For

> The **Industrial Revolution** is the stream of new technology and the resulting growth of output that began in England toward the end of the eighteenth century.

> **Capitalism** is an economic system in which most of the production process is controlled by private firms operating in markets with minimal government control. The investors in these firms (called "capitalists") own the firms.

---

[2] Angus Maddison, *The Nature and Functioning of European Capitalism: A Historical and Comparative Perspective* (Groningen, Netherlands: University of Groningen, 1997), p. 34. Real income is not measured in actual dollars, but in dollars whose purchasing power is kept unchanged.

[3] Adrien De Meeüs, *History of the Belgians* (New York: Frederick A. Praeger, 1962), p. 305.

[4] "Could the Emperor Tiberius have eaten grapes in January? Could the Emperor Napoleon have crossed the Atlantic in a night? . . . Could Thomas Aquinas have . . . dispatched [a letter] to 1,000 recipients with the touch of a key, and begun to receive replies within the hour?" (J. Bradford DeLong, *The Economic History of the Twentieth Century: Slouching Toward Utopia?*, Chapter 2, p. 3, draft copy, http://www.j-bradford-delong.net.)

[5] Shaohua Chen and Martin Ravallion, "The Developing World Is Poorer than We Thought, but No Less Successful," Washington, D.C.: World Bank, 2008.

Discomforts of the Rich a Few Centuries Ago

Earlier eras were characterized by miserable living conditions even for the wealthy and powerful. Their wealth did give them ostentatious clothing, exotic foods, and armies of servants. But the problem for them was that little of the technology of human comfort had yet been invented.

The standards of discomfort for the rich and powerful before the Industrial Revolution are illustrated by the oft-cited report by the Princess Palatine (German sister-in-law of the mighty French king Louis XIV) that in the winter of 1695, the wine froze in the glasses at the king's table in the Palace of Versailles! Even throughout the nineteenth century, in much of the United States it was expected that every winter the ink would freeze in the inkwells.

A description of the 1732 journey of the pregnant Wilhelmina, favorite sister of Frederick the Great, between Berlin and Bayreuth is also revealing:

Ten strenuous, abnormally frigid days were spent upon roads, bad enough in summer, now deep with snow. On the second day the carriage in which Wilhelmina was riding turned over.

SOURCE: © Comstock Images/Jupiterimages

She was buried under an avalanche of luggage. . . . Everyone expected a miscarriage and wanted Wilhelmina to rest in bed for several days. . . . Mountains appeared after Leibzig had been passed. . . . Wilhelmina was frightened by the steepness of the roads and preferred to get out and walk to being whacked about as the carriage jolted from boulder to boulder.

Statistics and other pieces of evidence tell a story consistent with such anecdotes. Using genealogical records, it has been estimated that between 1550 and 1700 the average longevity for the general male and female population slightly exceeded that for members of the nobility for a substantial part of this period.

SOURCES: Fernand Braudel, *Civilization and Capitalism, 15th to 18th Century*, vol. 1 (New York: Harper & Row, 1979), p. 299; Constance Wright, *A Royal Affinity* (London: Frederick Muller, 1965), p. 142; and Robert W. Fogel, "Nutrition and the Decline of Mortality since 1700: Some Preliminary Findings," in S. L. Engerman and R. E. Gallman, eds., *Long-Term Factors in American Economic Growth* (Chicago: University of Chicago Press, 1986).

example, in 1919, the average U.S. worker had to labor nearly an hour to buy a pound of chicken. At today's wages and poultry prices, less than 5 minutes of labor is required for the purpose! Figure 1 (Minutes of Work) shows how much cheaper a variety of snack foods have become over the past century.

Food is not the only item that has become much less costly in terms of the labor time needed to pay for it. Figure 2 (Hours of Work) shows the great cost reductions of various

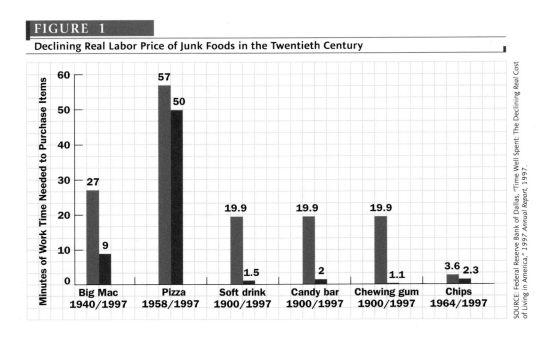

FIGURE 1

Declining Real Labor Price of Junk Foods in the Twentieth Century

SOURCE: Federal Reserve Bank of Dallas, "Time Well Spent: The Declining *Real* Cost of Living in America," *1997 Annual Report*, 1997.

FIGURE 2

Declining Real Labor Price of Electronic Products in the Twentieth Century

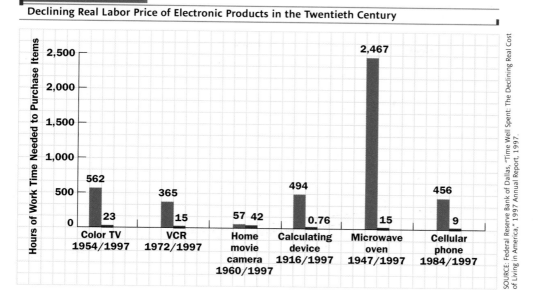

SOURCE: Federal Reserve Bank of Dallas, "Time Well Spent: The Declining Real Cost of Living in America," 1997 Annual Report, 1997.

types of electronic equipment—a cut of 98 percent in the cost of a color TV between 1954 and 1997, 96 percent in the cost of a VCR between 1972 and 1997, and 99 percent in the cost of a microwave oven between 1947 and 1997. Of course, the most sensational decrease of all has been in the cost of computers. Computer capability is standardized in terms of the number of MIPS (millions of instructions per second) that the computer is capable of handling. These days, it costs about 27 minutes of labor per 1 MIPS capacity. In 1984, it cost the wages of 52 *hours* of labor; in 1970, the cost was 1.24 *lifetimes* of labor; and in 1944, the price was a barely believable 733,000 *lifetimes* of labor.[6,7] In this chapter, we will investigate the free market's extraordinary record of growth and economic progress.

GDP (gross domestic product) is a measure of the total amount the economy produces domestically in a year.

The history of the growth in income per person can be summed up with a graph depicting estimates of the United Kingdom's **GDP** per capita for five centuries (Figure 4). It is clear that the pattern of the graph is characterized by a rising slope that grows dramatically ever steeper.

The bottom line is that in the long run, the economic welfare of a nation's entire population is heavily dependent on its performance in terms of innovation and the speed of growth in its production per person, and no economy has been able to approximate anything near these accomplishments of the modern market economies.

---

[6] But the magic of productivity growth has not yet succeeded in invading every sector of the U.S. economy. In particular, the process of college teaching seems to have been able to escape the cost-reducing ability of productivity growth. Figure 3 (Work Time Needed to Buy a College Education) shows the consequences. Between 1965 and 1995, the cost of a college education rose 33 percent at public universities, whereas at private universities it went up by more than 150 percent, from 500 to 1,300 labor hours. All of these figures on changing labor-value prices are taken from Federal Reserve Bank of Dallas, *Time Well Spent: The Declining Real Cost of Living in America, 1997 Annual Report* (Dallas, Tex., 1997).

[7] The data cited here are evidently more than a decade old. Unfortunately, we have not been able to find any studies of the subject that are more recent.

FIGURE 3

Work Time Needed to Buy a College Education, 1965 versus 1995

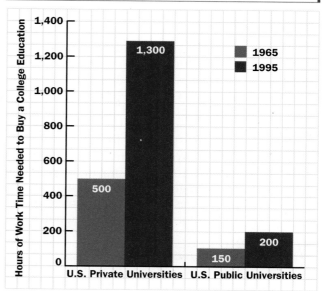

SOURCE: Federal Reserve Bank of Dallas, "Time Well Spent: The Declining Real Cost of Living in America," 1997 Annual Report, 1997.

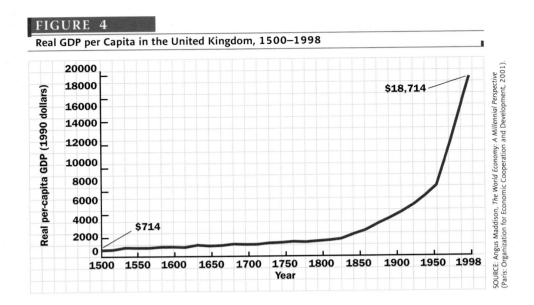

FIGURE 4

Real GDP per Capita in the United Kingdom, 1500–1998

$18,714

$714

Real per-capita GDP (1990 dollars)

Year

SOURCE: Angus Maddison, *The World Economy: A Millennial Perspective* (Paris: Organization for Economic Cooperation and Development, 2001).

INNOVATION, NOT INVENTION, IS THE UNIQUE FREE-MARKET ACCOMPLISHMENT

Invention is the creation of new products or processes or the ideas that underlie them.

Innovation is the process that begins with invention and includes improvement to prepare the invention for practical use and marketing of the invention or its products.

The search for explanations of the capitalist growth miracle must focus on its unprecedented outpouring of innovation, and to that we will soon turn. But first it is important to distinguish the key term *innovation* from the related word *invention*. **Invention** is used by economists to mean what its usual definition asserts: the creation of new products or processes, or at least the ideas that underlie them. But the term **innovation** means more than that; it refers to the entire extended process of which invention is only the initial step. Innovation includes development of the invention's design to the point at which it is ready for practical use, its introduction to the market, and its subsequent utilization by the economy. The distinction is critical here because it underlies much of the difference between the accomplishments of the capitalist economy and those of any and all of its predecessors, including those earlier economies with remarkable records of invention.

Invention is nothing new. Ancient China, for example, invented printing, paper, playing cards, the spinning wheel, the wheelbarrow, an elaborate water clock, the umbrella, and, of course, gunpowder, to name but a few. But despite China's talent for the creation of novel technology, its performance in adoption and utilization of these inventions was hardly outstanding. More than once inventions were diverted to amusement rather than productive use or, like the wondrous water clock, soon forgotten.[8] Even in the former Soviet Union, with its cadre of very capable scientists and engineers, there is evidence of a respectable record of invention but a remarkably poor record of utilization of these inventions—except in military activity. The reason is that the economic institutions in both ancient China and the former Soviet Union not only failed to offer incentives for innovative activity but actually provided strong motivation for its determined avoidance.

In China, inventions often were confiscated by the government, with no reward for the inventors. In the former Soviet Union, factory managers resisted the installation of improved equipment or the adoption of improved products because the necessary retooling period could cut down the factory's production, on which the manager's reward was based. In short, although the free market's record of invention is noteworthy, it is its performance in innovation that is unique.

---

[8] This persisted into a much more recent era. Westerners bringing mechanical clocks as gifts to the Chinese emperors found that timekeeping accuracy elicited little appreciation, but marching or dancing figures run by the clockworks were highly valued.

SOURCES OF FREE-MARKET INNOVATION: THE ROLE OF THE ENTREPRENEUR

As already mentioned, there are many obvious sources of innovation. Some innovations are contributed by universities and government research agencies, which are not inherently market-driven. Then there are the well-known products of individual inventors, such as Thomas Edison and Alexander Graham Bell. In addition, innovative entrepreneurs, those who keep their eyes open for promising inventions and take action to see that they are employed effectively by business firms and others, play an important part in directing the inventions to their most effective uses. Finally, there are the outputs of industrial laboratories in giant corporations. These last two sources—the private entrepreneur and the giant corporations—clearly are directly embedded in the workings of the market economy. In this chapter we will focus on the role of the big firms in the economy's innovation, leaving the entrepreneurs, the creators of new business firms, and their crucial place in the innovation process until later when we discuss the contribution and activities of this important factor of production in Chapter 20. Here we will only note that, throughout history, the presence or absence of innovating entrepreneurs appears to have been crucial for the growth and innovative accomplishments of their economies.

Stimulating Demand via Sensational New Products

The iPhone was perhaps the most talked about technological gadget of 2007, beginning with Steve Jobs's announcement during his keynote talk at the 2007 MacWorld Expo and ending with *Time* naming it Invention of the Year. The following excerpt describes the anticipation surrounding the iPhone's official launch on June 29:

> It's hard to determine the wackiest aspect of iPhone craziness leading up to the launch of Apple's eagerly (to say the least) awaited venture into the cell-phone world on June 29. Was it the relentless media attention, which blended nuts-and-bolts business coverage with the obsessive overkill of a Paris Hilton stalkfest? Or was it the lunacy of the people dying to get those phones at the earliest possible moment? Standing outside New York's Fifth Avenue Apple store on launch day, with dozens of reporters interviewing the masses who braved days of heat and rain to snare their palm-size prize, there was a sense of being in the middle of a Zeitgeist hurricane.
>
> The iPhone itself is off to a ring-a-ding start, selling an estimated 500,000 to 700,000 units the first weekend. And the reviews are uniformly positive. (My own take, after three weeks of iPhoning, still holds: though there's still work to be done, the beautiful screen, the clever multitouch navigation and the well-designed and -integrated applications make this gizmo a genuine breakthrough.)
>
> But sales figures and reviews don't speak to the unprecedented hoopla. What was it that made a five-ounce slab of silicon, aluminum and glass so important to us? In part, you can chalk it up to the iPod factor. Before 2001, Apple was a company that made cool computers that only a small fraction of the public cared to buy. But over the next few years, 100 million customers discovered Apple's tiny music player, and bonded with it as they had with no previous gadget. The same crowd welcomed the news that Apple was going mobile. "Everyone we talk to hates their phones," Steve Jobs told me the week before the launch, in an attempt to explain the iPhone anticipation.
>
> We've heard a lot recently about of the 40th anniversary of the Beatles' landmark "Sgt. Pepper" album. Back in 1967, new releases by universally loved bands like the Beatles, the Rolling Stones and the Beach Boys were anticipated breathlessly, and greeted by monster sales, heated analysis and sonic ubiquity. In 1967, it was "All You Need Is Love." In 2007, it's "All You Need Is AT&T Activation." Welcome to the summer of technolust.

Breakthrough Invention and the Entrepreneurial Firm

Individual inventors and entrepreneurs continued to be the primary source of innovation in the market economies until the end of the nineteenth century, when large corporations began to play a critical role in the process. But the part played by large corporations is very different from that of the more freewheeling and flexible small enterprises. Research activity in large business organizations is inherently cautious and focuses on small, relatively limited improvements in current technology. The big established firms tend to avoid the great risks that revolutionary breakthroughs involve. The true breakthrough inventions, rather, are often still the domain of small or newly founded enterprises, guided by enterprising owners, although success of an invention can rapidly transform a start-up firm into a business giant.

There is no clear boundary between inventions that can be considered revolutionary breakthroughs and those that are "merely" cumulative incremental improvements, but some inventions clearly fall into the former category. For example, the electric light, alternating electric current, the internal combustion engine, and the electronic computer must surely be deemed revolutionary. In contrast, successive models of washing machines and refrigerators—with each new model a bit longer-lasting, a bit less susceptible to breakdown, and a bit easier to use—clearly constitute a sequence of incremental improvements.

There is a striking degree of asymmetry between small and large firms in their introduction of breakthrough versus incremental invention. The U.S. Small Business Administration has prepared a list of breakthrough innovations of the twentieth century for which small firms are responsible, and its menu of inventions literally spans the range from A to Z, from air-conditioning to the zipper. Included in the list are the cotton picker, the electronic spreadsheet, FM radio, the helicopter, the integrated circuit, the instant camera, quick-frozen food, the vacuum tube, and the photocopier, among a host of others, many of enormous significance for our economy (Table 1 reproduces part of the list).

TABLE 1
Some Important Innovations by U.S. Small Firms in the Twentieth Century

Air-Conditioning	Heart Valve	Photo Typesetting
Airplane	Helicopter	Polaroid Camera
Assembly Line	High Resolution CAT Scanner	Portable Computer
Audio Tape Recorder	Human Growth Hormone	Prefabricated Housing
Biosynthetic Insulin	Hydraulic Brake	Quick-Frozen Food
Catalytic Petroleum Cracking	Integrated Circuit	Safety Razor
Cotton Picker	Microprocessor	Soft Contact Lens
Defibrillator	Nuclear Magnetic Resonance Scanner	Solid-Fuel Rocket Engine
DNA Fingerprinting	Optical Scanner	Vacuum Tube
Electronic Spreadsheet	Oral Contraceptives	Xerography
FM Radio	Overnight National Delivery	X-Ray Telescope
Geodesic Dome	Pacemaker	Zipper
Gyrocompass	Personal Computer	

SOURCE: U.S. Small Business Administration, *The State of Small Business: A Report of the President, 1994* (Washington, D.C: U.S. Government Printing Office, 1995), p. 114.

Research and development (R&D) is the activity of firms, universities, and government agencies that seeks to invent new products and processes and to improve those inventions so that they are ready for the market or other users.

A high proportion of the revolutionary new ideas of the past two centuries have been, and are likely to continue to be, provided by independent innovators who operate small business enterprises. The small entrepreneurial firms have played a leading role in the portion of business **research and development (R&D)** activity that is engaged in the search for the revolutionary breakthroughs that are such a critical part of the growth machine that is provided by the market economy.

MICROECONOMIC ANALYSIS OF THE INNOVATIVE OLIGOPOLY FIRM

The Large Enterprises and Their Innovation "Assembly Lines"

As we see in Figure 5, private investment in R&D has risen sharply in the last three decades (with only a few slowdowns in funding during those years). Increasingly, at least

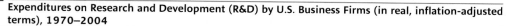

FIGURE 5

Expenditures on Research and Development (R&D) by U.S. Business Firms (in real, inflation-adjusted terms), 1970–2004

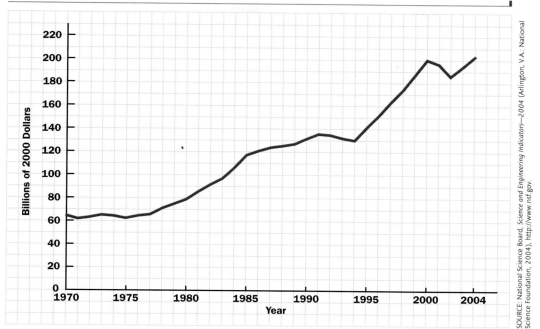

SOURCE: National Science Board, *Science and Engineering Indicators—2004* (Arlington, V.A.: National Science Foundation, 2004). http://www.nsf.gov.

in the United States, the financing for innovation has been supplied by large oligopolistic enterprises, rather than by independent inventors or small, newly founded entrepreneurial firms. In 2007, 90 percent of R&D expenditure in the United States was paid for by private companies; most of this outlay was provided by the larger firms.[9] Even seemingly "low-tech" companies like the consumer products giant Procter & Gamble (noted for outputs like cleaning and personal care products) employ small armies of R&D personnel (as evidenced in the quotation at the beginning of the chapter). These large firms are driven to do this by powerful market pressures of competitive innovation.

Innovation has, in fact, become a prime weapon of choice for competitive battles in substantial sectors of the economy. Of course, prices are still important, but it is improved products and methods of production that really capture the attention of the firm's managers. Product lines as diverse as computers and computer software, automobiles, cameras, and machinery all feature constant improvements, which are instantly and widely advertised.

The result is a kind of innovation arms race in which no firm in a high-tech industry can afford to fall behind its rivals. Indeed, only by staying abreast of the others can the firm hope to preserve its place in the market. In its innovation, it is forced to run as fast as it can just to stand still—because its rivals are doing the same. Any firm that can come up with a better model than its rivals will gain a critical advantage.

Firms in many high-tech industries—such as computers, medical equipment, aeronautics, and even automobiles—struggle for market position in this way. The managers of firms cannot afford to neglect R&D activities. For if a firm fails to adopt the latest technology—even if the technology is created by others—then rival firms can easily take the lead and make disastrous inroads into the slower firm's sales. Often, for the firm, innovation is literally a matter of life and death.

A **high-tech (high-technology)** firm or industry is one whose products, equipment, and production methods utilize highly advanced technology that is constantly modified and improved. Examples are the aerospace, scientific instruments, computer, communications, and pharmaceutical industries.

---

[9] For instance, the U.S. National Science Foundation reports that, in 2007, the largest manufacturing firms (each employing 10,000 or more workers) accounted for 58 percent of R&D in the manufacturing sector of the economy (National Science Foundation, Division of Science Resources Statistics, "U.S. Business R&D Expenditures Increase in 2007: Small Companies Performed 19% of Nation's Business R&D," Arlington, V.A., July 2009, accessed online at: http://www.nsf.gov.).

Thus, especially in high-tech sectors, firms dare not leave innovation to chance, or to the haphazard contributions of independent inventors tinkering in their basements and garages. Rather, competitive markets force firms to take over the innovation process themselves and (in the immortal words of the great comedian W. C. Fields) "to remove all elements of chance" from the undertaking.[10] Many business firms today routinely budget for R&D, hire scientists and engineers to do the job, and systematically decide how to promote and price their innovations.

> This "arms-race" feature of an industry's innovation process probably plays a critical role in the continuing outpouring of innovations that characterize the market economy. The capitalist economy itself has become a giant *innovation machine* the predictable output of which is a stream of improved technology. Never in any other type of economy has there existed such an innovation machine—an assembly line that *forces* the economy to bring one invention after another from the drawing board all the way to the market, as though it were a meat plant producing frankfurters, rather than a high-tech enterprise generating product improvements.

In their effort to contain the risks inherent in the innovation process, large business firms have tended to slant their efforts toward small *incremental improvements* rather than revolutionary breakthroughs. User-friendliness, increased reliability, marginal additions to application, expansions of capacity, flexibility in design—these and many other types of improvement have come out of the industrial R&D facilities, with impressive consistency, year after year, and often preannounced and preadvertised. They produce longer-lasting light bulbs, more reliable air bags to protect automobile passengers, and clearer TV screens. But they usually do not invent anything of the magnitude of the airplane, computer, or antibiotics.

Thus, the products of these innovative activities are often modest, each making a very small improvement in a product or its production process. Nevertheless, taken in the aggregate, these small improvements have accomplished a great deal. An example is the airplane. The comfort, speed, and reliability of the modern passenger aircraft and the complexity and power of today's military flying machines clearly have turned the Wright brothers' original revolutionary device into a historical curiosity. Most of the sophistication, speed, and reliability of today's aviation equipment is attributable to the combined incremental additions made by routine research activities in corporate facilities.

There are even more startling examples of the innovative contributions of the large companies, whose incremental advances can compound to results of enormous magnitude. It is reported, for example, that between 1971 and 2007, the "clock speed" of Intel's microprocessor chips—that is, the number of instructions each chip can carry out per second—increased by some *three million percent*, reaching about three billion computations per second. During the same time period, the number of transistors embedded in a single chip expanded by more than *35 million percent*—from 2,300 in 1971 to 820 million in 2007.[11] Added up, these advances surely contributed enormously more computing capacity than was provided by the original revolutionary breakthrough of the invention of the electronic computer. Of course, that initial invention was an indispensable necessity for all of the later improvements. But it is only the combined work of the two together that made possible the powerful and inexpensive apparatus that serves us so effectively today. Other careful observers have extended such examples and have concluded that incremental innovation activities of the large firms have been responsible for a very respectable share of the contribution of innovation to economic growth in the twentieth century.

In the growth process, the individual entrepreneurs (whom we will discuss in Chapter 20) and the giant firms have played roles that are different but essential for one another. The

---

[10] This phrase is uttered when Fields, playing a card shark, seeks to lure an unsuspecting novice into a card game, whereupon his intended victim questions the morality of "games of chance." Fields hastens to reassure him: "Young man, when you play with me, all elements of chance have been removed!"

[11] Intel Corporation, "The Evolution of a Revolution," accessed online at: http://download.intel.com/pressroom/kits/IntelProcessorHistory.pdf.

Predicting the Future: A Feebleness of Imagination?

There is one area where futurists have suffered not from inflated hopes but from a feebleness of imagination: the information revolution. In an article titled "Brains That Click" in the March 1949 issue of *Popular Mechanics,* the author enthused over a state-of-the-art supercomputer called the ENIAC (for Electronic Numerical Integrator and Computer). But he knew it was just the beginning. "Where a calculator like the ENIAC today is equipped with 18,000 vacuum tubes and weighs 30 tons," he predicted, "computers in the future may have only 1,000 tubes and perhaps weigh only 1½ tons." Today's amused denizens of the Internet have used their laptops and desktop PCs—each vastly more powerful than the pitiful ENIAC—to lampoon the quotation on scores of pages across the World Wide Web. Also spreading like a virus through cyberspace are words attributed to I.B.M.'s former chairman Thomas J. Watson in 1943: that there is a world market for perhaps five computers. Back then it seemed sensible that only nations or the largest corporations would be able to afford such mammoth contraptions. Again and again, prognosticators made the mistake of assuming that computers would be like rocket ships or other ordinary machines. The mightier you wanted to make them, the bigger, more expensive and more energy-hungry they would have to be. It defied common sense to envision what exists today, a technology where making something smaller causes it to be more powerful, with denser skeins of circuitry squeezed into increasingly tinier spaces.

And that's just the beginning of the magic. As the parts become closer together they can exchange information more rapidly. Designers can take a circuit diagram and photograph it onto a silicon chip. As the focus of the projector grows sharper, the circuits become finer and more tightly packed. With a design in place, chips can be stamped out like pages on a printing press.

These devices—the most complex things produced by the human mind—can be made indefinitely small because of a crucial distinction. While ordinary machines work by manipulating stuff, computers manipulate information, symbols which are essentially weightless. A bit of information, a 1 or a 0, can be indicated by a pencil mark in a checkbox, by a microscopic spot on a magnetic disk or by the briefest pulse of electricity or scintilla of light.

According to Moore's famous law, the number of components that can be packed onto a single chip doubles every year or two. The latest Pentium chip contains 42 million transistors, each doing the job of one of ENIAC's glowing tubes but far more rapidly and efficiently.

The end is not in sight. By some estimates, the shrinking will continue over coming decades until each component is the size of a single atom, registering a bit of information by the position of an orbiting electron.

SOURCE: © Bettmann/CORBIS

breakthrough ideas have been contributed disproportionately by the entrepreneurs in their pursuit of the temporary monopoly profits that successful innovations promise. The giant firms have specialized in a constant stream of incremental improvements that protect them from destruction by competitors who constantly seek to beat them at the innovation game. Together, the contributions of the two groups have played a critical role in the growth of the market economies as far back as ancient Mesopotamia, well before the rise of ancient Greece and Rome. But the internal R&D units of the giant firms had their inception only in the latter half of the nineteenth century.

> **The innovation arm's race in which no innovating firm dares to fall behind in its innovative efforts is an incredibly powerful mechanism underlying the tremendous economic growth accomplishments of the market economies.**

Next, we turn from our description of the facts related to the market's accomplishments in innovation and economic growth to see what the tools of microeconomic analysis can help us to understand about these achievements.

The Profits of Innovation: Schumpeter's Model

The modern microtheory of innovation and its rewards had its origins in the work of the late Professor Joseph Schumpeter. His model (1911) argues that the successful innovative entrepreneur's reward is a monopoly profit, which accrues because the entrepreneur is the first to bring a new product into the market. Having no rivals, that profit temporarily exceeds what can be earned under perfect competition. This high profit attracts imitating rivals into the market who seek to share those profits. By "reverse engineering" the new product, that is, by in effect taking it apart and seeing how it works, these imitators are able to enter the market with their rival product and thereby erode the initial entrepreneur's "monopolistic"earnings. Eventually, those economic profits will be reduced to zero, because entry by imitators will continue as long as earnings are higher than that.

The Schumpeterian analysis shows how the entrepreneur in this model is driven to work, without letup, for economic growth. To prevent termination of the monopoly rewards, the entrepreneur can never desist from further innovation and cannot rest on his laurels. Thus, the analysis clearly describes the tight association between innovative entrepreneurship and growth.

But reality does not follow Schumpeter's story in detail. As will be shown in Chapter 20, in reality the financial returns of many innovators are very low, and failure of their efforts and investments are not uncommon. Yet, many discussions of innovation start with the assumption that innovators can expect to earn very high profits. Indeed, huge rewards do often accrue to those who introduce unusually successful innovations. We have all heard of innovators like Thomas Edison, Alexander Graham Bell, and, more recently, Bill Gates, Steven Jobs, and others in the computer industry who have acquired great riches from their ability to invent or to bring innovations to market. Of course, for every successful innovator, many others have plowed their family savings into new gadgets and lost all they have spent. The evidence indicates that inventors on average earn zero economic profits, or even lose money.

This possibility also appears likely when we consider big-business investment in R&D. As we saw in Chapter 10, if an industry is perfectly competitive, entry will occur until economic profits are forced down to zero. Put another way, perfect competition permits firms to earn just what they need to pay investors for the funds they provide—no more and no less. This must be so because if a typical firm in one industry earns more than firms in other industries, investors will put more money into the more profitable industry. Any excess economic profit will lead to an expansion of industry output, which will drive prices down and squeeze profits.

Because there are some barriers to entry into innovation, we cannot be certain that economic profits from invention will tend *exactly* toward zero, but we can expect them to be very low on average. In other words, although inventive activity sometimes pays off handsomely, large R&D investments also can fail spectacularly, so that the average economic profits come out close to zero. In particular, a large firm with a big R&D division may work simultaneously on many possible innovations. The "law of averages" suggests that some of these efforts will fail and some will succeed. So we should not be surprised to find near-zero economic profit even in industries with a great deal of innovative activity.

Although we have no systematic study of all inventive activities, high-tech industries provide a useful illustration—especially the computer industry, where many founders have made fortunes and received much publicity. According to corporate management guru Peter F. Drucker, "The computer industry hasn't made a dime. . . . Intel and Microsoft make money, but look at all the people who were losing money all the world over. It is doubtful the industry has yet broken even."[12] But is this true everywhere? One study looked at companies that went public from 1975 to 1992, most of which were high-tech firms, and found their rate of return to be about average (that is, zero economic profit), once the researchers adjusted for risk and company size.[13] In Chapter 20 we will see that the typical earnings of innovating entrepreneurs are apparently even lower.

---

[12] As cited in Jane Katz, "To Market, to Market: Strategy in High-Tech Business," *Federal Reserve Bank of Boston Regional Review* (Fall 1996), www.bos.frb.org.

[13] Alon Brav and Paul A. Gompers, "Myth or Reality? The Long-Run Underperformance of Initial Public Offerings: Evidence from Venture and Nonventure Capital-Backed Companies," *Journal of Finance,* 52, no. 5 (December 1997): 1791–1821.

Financing the Innovation "Arms Race": High R&D Costs and "Monopoly Profits"

In our discussion of the Schumpeterian model in the preceding section we hinted at our skepticism over what he describes as the monopoly profits of the entrepreneur. Large-scale innovative activity is expensive. Firms must spend substantial amounts of money, year after year. In some firms, the costs of R&D can account for as much as 40 percent of the company's total costs. If an innovative firm is to stay in business, the products it supplies must be priced so as to enable the firm to recover those expenditures.

This effort requires an approach to pricing that is very different from the one we studied in earlier chapters. Previously we concluded that in a competitive market, prices tend to be set approximately equal to marginal costs, assuming this price would bring in enough revenue to keep the firm in business. To see the reason for the difference between this case and that of the innovative firm, consider the case of Jim—an organic wheat farmer—who decides to grow 1,000 more bushels of wheat than he did last year. That level of production will require him to rent x more acres of land, to buy y more bags of fertilizer and z more bags of seed, to hire h more hours of labor, and to borrow b more dollars from the bank. The prices of these inputs tell Jim how much he must spend to get the added output. If this added cost is divided by the 1,000 added bushels, we have an (approximate) calculation of the marginal cost of a bushel, including the marginal return to capital—Jim's loan payment to the bank. If the price of organic wheat is set by the market so that it covers this amount, evidently price is equal to marginal cost and is also enough to keep the farm in business. It is enough to keep Jim's farm going because *all* of his costs, including the cost of renting more land, are costs of *adding* to his output—in essence, all of his costs take the form of marginal or added costs.

Contrast this case with a software firm that has just spent $20 million to create a valuable new computer program. If the firm supplies one more unit of the program (or even 1,000 more units of the program), what is its added cost? The answer is nearly zero—just the cost of making a new CD, packaging it, and shipping it. One of the firm's main costs is that of R&D, but no *added* R&D cost is incurred when another purchaser acquires the already-designed program. So the firm's heavy R&D expenditure contributes nothing to *marginal* cost. A price that covers only the marginal cost of one more copy of the program can hardly amount to more than, say, $5. That price cannot begin to cover the $20 million in R&D cost—a cost the firm will probably have to replicate in the next year to keep the program up-to-date and up to competitive standards. So, pricing software—or any other products of a firm with high and continuing R&D costs—at marginal cost is a recipe for financial suicide. Prices of the products of innovating firms simply cannot follow the familiar formula: $P = MC$. Rather, entry will force the expectable lifetime earnings of an invention just high enough to yield zero economic profit, covering marginal costs, opportunity costs, and the fixed cost of the invention's R&D. True, the earnings will be higher initially, before imitators enter and depress market earnings. But those early high earnings will just be a substantial contribution to recovery of the fixed R&D outlays, not anything resembling monopoly profits. Of course, there are some cases in which innovators do earn monopoly profits, as is equally true in industries that contribute little innovation. But freedom of entry into the innovation process means that this will not be the ordinary state of affairs, as the courts of the United States have recognized in dealing with antitrust cases entailing innovation.

> **Firms that are forced by competition to spend a great deal on research and development year after year, but that use the results of the R&D to improve a product whose marginal costs are low, cannot expect to recover their R&D costs if they set their prices equal or close to marginal costs, as occurs under perfect competition.**

This pricing situation is troubling because it can mislead the government agencies charged with preventing firms from acting as monopolists. Many of the people who work in these agencies have been trained using textbooks such as this one, and they have come away from their studies with the valid (but possibly irrelevant) conclusion that under perfect competition price must equal marginal cost. So, when they encounter prices in innovative firms that are nowhere near marginal costs, their suspicions are sometimes aroused. Is this firm exploiting the public by charging prices higher than marginal costs? Should something be done to make the company price its products as wheat farmer Jim does? We can see now that doing so may well bring innovative activity to a virtual standstill. Of course, most of the government authorities who are concerned with monopolistic behavior know better than that, but their suspicions are nevertheless aroused by finding cases of $P > MC$. In addition, some of them really do misunderstand the issue, and thereby constitute a threat to innovative activity by business.

How Much Will a Profit-Maximizing Firm Spend on Innovation?

The legendary "Eureka! I have found it!" scenario, in which the lone inventor working in a basement or garage happens to come up with a brilliant invention, may not be amenable to conventional economic analysis. But innovation in a modern corporation is easier to analyze by using the standard tools of the theory of the firm because R&D budgeting looks a lot like other business decisions, such as those about how much to produce or how much to spend on advertising. We can study all of these standard business decisions using the same tools of marginal analysis that we studied in Chapters 5, 7, and 8. The key questions are: How much can we expect firms to spend on R&D? How much can they expect to earn by doing so? And how will competition affect their innovative activity?

We have already just considered how much they can expect to earn and have asked and answered similar questions before, when we studied how basic marginal analysis addresses business decision making. If the firm seeks to maximize its profits, it will expand its spending on R&D up to the point at which the marginal cost of additional R&D equals the marginal revenue.

By now, the logic should be familiar. A level of R&D spending (call it X dollars) at which marginal revenue (MR) is, for example, *greater* than marginal cost (MC) cannot possibly represent the profit-maximizing amount for the company to spend on R&D. For, if MR exceeds MC, the company can increase its profits by spending more than X dollars on R&D. The opposite will be true if MR < MC. In that case, the firm can increase its profits by *decreasing* R&D spending. So X dollars cannot be the optimal level of spending if, at that level of expenditure, either MR > MC or MR < MC. It follows that the profit-maximizing level of spending on R&D can only be an amount—say, Y dollars—at which MR = MC. You will recognize this argument, for we have repeated it many times in earlier chapters when we discussed other business decisions, such as those related to price and quantity of output.

This analysis simultaneously tells us everything, and nothing, about the R&D decision. It tells us everything because its conclusion is correct. If the firm is a profit maximizer, and if we know its MR and its MC curves for R&D investment, then the MR = MC rule does, in theory, tell us exactly how much the profit-seeking firm should invest in R&D. But the discussion so far tells us nothing about the shape of "typical" marginal revenue and marginal cost curves for R&D, nor does it tell us how the competitive pressures that play such an important role in R&D decisions affect those curves. We turn next to these crucial matters.

A Kinked Revenue Curve Model of Spending on Innovation

Our discussion thus far has left a basic question unanswered. If innovation is so expensive and so risky, and if the economic profits expected from innovation approach zero, why do firms do it? Why doesn't every firm refuse to participate in this unattractive game? The answer, at least in part, is that competitive markets leave them no choice. If firms do not keep up with their competitors in terms of product attractiveness and improved process efficiency that lowers costs, they will lose out to their rivals and end up losing money. Clearly, firms prefer zero economic profits—profits that yield only normal competitive returns to investors—to negative profits and investor flight.

This observation also enables us to investigate how much the firm will spend on R&D, using a microeconomic model very similar to one we encountered in Chapter 12—the kinked demand curve model that we used to explain why prices tend to be "sticky" in oligopoly markets. The underlying mechanism there was an asymmetry in the firm's expectations about its competitors. The firm hesitates to lower its price for fear that its rivals will match the price cut, causing the firm to end up with only a few new customers but dramatically reduced revenues; that is, if the firm lowers its price it will be dealing with an inelastic demand curve. But the firm can be expected to fear that if it *increases* its price, the others will *not* follow suit, so that it will be left all by itself with an overpriced product. It will lose many customers—the relevant portion of its demand curve for price increases will be highly elastic. And we have seen that with an inelastic demand curve a price cut will reduce total revenue and the same is true of a price rise when demand is elastic. So, a firm with such beliefs will want to set its price at the industry level—no more and no less—and leave it there unless the competitive situation changes drastically.

The innovation story is similar. Imagine an industry with, say, five firms of roughly equal size. Company X sees that each of the other firms in the industry spends approximately $20 million per year on R&D. Then our firm will generally find it unattractive to spend either less or more than this amount. It will not dare to spend much less than $20 million on its own R&D because if it does so, it risks falling behind its rivals in the unceasing race to introduce product improvements, for its rivals may well continue to spend the customary $20 million, leaving our firm's next product model behind, without new features as attractive as those of rival products. But Company X will see little point in raising the ante to, say, $30 million because it knows that its competitors will be driven to follow suit, all of them simply expanding their innovative efforts simultaneously, with none gaining any new lead over its rivals. So neither a cut in R&D spending nor a rise in such spending will promise to add to profits, because rivals are likely to match any increased spending and nullify its prospective advantages, whereas the competitors can be expected *not* to replicate any R&D spending cut by our firm, hoping in this way to lure customers away from our enterprise. As a result, we can expect that the firms will hesitate to make *any* significant changes in the amount they spend on innovative activity, neither raising their expenditure nor reducing it.

But that's not the end of the story. All the firms in the industry will continue to invest the same amount as they have in the past, even if the cost of R&D shifts down moderately or some other minor change occurs, until one of them enjoys a research breakthrough leading to a wonderful new product. That fortunate firm will then expand its investment in the breakthrough product, because doing so will pay off *even if the other firms in the industry match the increase.* Thus the MR curve for the breakthrough firm will move to the right, and so will its profit-maximizing R&D budget level—to an amount larger than $20 million. Other companies in the industry will then be forced to follow. So now the industry norm will no longer be a $20 million annual investment but some larger amount, say, $25 million per firm. No firm will be the first to drop back to the old $20 million level, fearing that its rivals would not follow such a retrenchment move. So the MR = MC equilibrium point will now be $25 million of R&D spending. Again, the common story of armaments races among countries parallels the story of innovation battles among firms.

The process we have just described assumes that competition forces firms in the industry to keep up with one another in their R&D investments. But once they have

"You will never catch up with the new technology."

caught up, the investment level remains fairly constant until one firm breaks ranks and increases its spending. Then, all other firms follow suit, but none dares to drop back. Such an arrangement is described as a **ratchet,** in analogy to the mechanical device that prevents a wound-up spring from suddenly unwinding. This arrangement normally holds technological spending steady, sometimes permits it to move forward, but generally does not allow it to retreat. Thus, we can expect R&D spending to expand from time to time. Once the new level is reached, the ratchet—enforced by the competitive market—prevents firms from retreating to the previous lower level.[14]

A **ratchet** is an arrangement that permits some economic variable, such as investment or advertising, to increase but prevents that variable from subsequently decreasing.

Ratcheting acts as a critical part of the mechanism that produces the extraordinary growth records of free-enterprise economies and differentiates them from all other known economic systems. Competitive pressures force firms to run as fast as they can in the innovation race just to keep up with the others.

Innovation as a Public Good

An innovation, once created, usually does not only contribute to the output of the firm that discovered the breakthrough. At little or no additional cost, the new technology can also add to the outputs produced by other enterprises, often in other industries. This public good property[15] of technical knowledge enables those who adopt the innovation (with or without the inventor's permission) to adopt it more cheaply.

In Chapter 15, we used the term *public good* to describe any input or output that is not depleted when used once but rather can be used over and over by more users with little or no additional cost. Such goods can be made available to the entire public without additional cost over that of supplying it to a single individual. Analogously, R&D expenses need not be duplicated when firms use knowledge repeatedly to produce output. For instance, Thomas Edison and his colleagues worked for many months and used up much material before they finally found a way to create a viable light bulb. But they did not have to repeat that outlay on experiments to produce their second light bulb. Similarly, if Edison had permitted another firm to use the technology, that firm would not have needed to repeat the expensive research that yielded the first light bulb. Innovation is like the oil lamp in the ancient Hanukkah legend: a lamp that miraculously replenished its fuel and could provide light day after day without any additional oil.

That is one distinguishing feature of any knowledge. Both coal and technical knowledge contribute to output. But when a ton of coal is used as fuel, it cannot be used again. A second ton of coal must be mined and burned to run the engine longer. Once technical knowledge is created, however, it can be used over and over again without ever being depleted.

Effects of Process Research on Outputs and Prices

A **product innovation** is the introduction of a good or service that is entirely new or involves major modifications of earlier products.

As a last example of how standard analytic tools of microeconomic analysis can help us to deal with innovation, we turn to the effects of innovation on outputs and prices. We will consider a single monopoly firm that makes decisions independently of other enterprises' activities and decisions.

Innovation is often divided into two types: **product innovations,** which consist of the introduction of a new item (such as a photocopying machine or a video camera), and

---

[14] This statement somewhat exaggerates the effectiveness of ratchets in preventing the economy from *ever* sliding backward in its R&D expenditures. After all, even in machinery, ratchets sometimes slip. Firms may, for example, be forced to cut back their R&D expenditure if business is extremely bad. They may also make mistakes in planning how much to spend on investment or become discouraged by repeated failures of their research division to come up with saleable products. The economy's ratchets are indeed imperfect, but they nevertheless exist. They cannot completely prevent backsliding in R&D expenditure, but they can be a powerful influence that is effective in resisting such retreats.

[15] For review of the concept of *public goods,* see Chapter 15, pages 316–318.

process innovations, which entail an improvement in the way in which commodities are produced, making them cheaper to buy. At this point, we will discuss only process innovations, because they are easier to analyze.

A successful process innovation can be expected to expand the output of the product that uses the process and to reduce the product's price, for a very simple reason: A process innovation normally leads to a downward shift in the firm's marginal and average cost curves but, because it involves no change in the product, it should not cause any change in the demand and marginal revenue curves.

A standard graph familiar from earlier chapters can demonstrate these results. Figure 6 shows MR and *DD* (demand), the firm's marginal revenue and demand (average revenue) curves, respectively, for the production of widgets. The graph also shows MC_1, the marginal cost curve of widgets *before* the process innovation, and MC_2, the marginal cost curve *after* the innovation is adopted. MC_2 is naturally lower than MC_1 because the innovation has reduced the cost of making widgets. Before the innovation, the quantity produced by our profit-maximizing firm is Q_1, the quantity at which MR = MC_1 (at point E_1). The corresponding price is P_1, the point on the demand curve (*DD*) above quantity Q_1. After the process innovation, the marginal cost curve shifts downward to MC_2. That new marginal cost curve meets the downward-sloping MR curve at point E_2, which lies to the right of E_1. This means that the profit-maximizing output quantity must increase from Q_1 to Q_2, and, because of the downward slope of the demand curve, price must fall from P_1 to P_2. Thus, we have shown, as suggested earlier, that

> **A cost-cutting process innovation increases the output and decreases the price of the product that a profit-making firm supplies with the help of the innovation.**

A **process innovation** is an innovation that changes the way in which a commodity is produced.

FIGURE 6

Effect of Process Innovations on Prices and Outputs

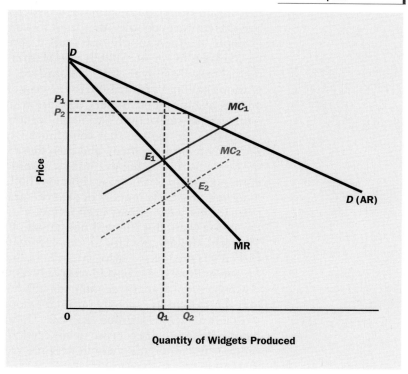

DO FREE MARKETS SPEND ENOUGH ON R&D ACTIVITIES?

We have seen that today's market economies turn out innovations at a pace and complexity never seen before in human history. Business firms, the U.S. government, universities, and others spend a good deal on research and innovation. As we noted before, in 2007, more than $269 billion (about 1.9 percent of the United States' total GDP) was spent on these activities, with business firms funding close to 90 percent of that amount.[16] Yet we may well ask, is this amount too small or too large a share of GDP? That is, would the general public benefit or lose if more resources were devoted to innovation? Some economic analysis suggests that there is a fundamental reason for believing that, despite our impressive successes in this arena, we still do not spend enough.

As usual, there is a trade-off to spending more than we currently do. If we devote more resources to innovation this year, less will be left over to produce clothing, food, or new

---

[16] National Science Foundation, Division of Science Resources Statistics, "U.S. Business R&D Expenditures Increase in 2007," Arlington, V.A., July 2009, accessed online at: http://www.nsf.org.

TV programs—goods and services that contribute primarily to today's consumption rather than tomorrow's. With smaller supplies of these items, their prices will rise. On the other hand, if we devote more resources to innovation, we will probably get better and cheaper products in the future. So, as with any investment, R&D expenditures entail a trade-off between the present and the future. More R&D spending means that consumers get less to consume this year, but they get more and better products in the future. The question is, how much is enough?

Innovation as a Beneficial Externality

Many economists believe that private enterprise does not devote enough resources to innovation, because the acquisition of new technical knowledge generates large externalities. Recall from Chapter 15 that an externality is an effect of a business transaction that benefits or hurts people other than those who directly take part in the transaction.[17] For example, if a food supply firm finds it necessary to clean the snow off its street on a winter morning to get supplies to its restaurant customers on time, well before the slow municipal snow-removal effort is launched, then all the neighbors of the firm will benefit without having to contribute to the cost of rapid street clearing. Here, the business firm and its restaurant customers who are waiting for timely delivery are the direct participants in the transaction, and neighborhood homes receive the gains from the beneficial externality. So we see that sometimes externalities benefit unconnected third parties, rather than harming them, and then those who carry out the transaction reap only part of the benefits. As another example, suppose your roommate, an advanced engineering student, comes up with a more efficient battery that turns out to benefit laptop computer manufacturers, the makers of electric cars, and many others. Your roommate may get a prize for her work or may even receive a royalty payment from the companies that license her innovation. But she will not get all of the benefits. This is true of most innovations: They benefit the innovator to some degree, but large parts of the benefits—some estimates exceed 90 percent(!)[18]—also go to others. Such beneficial externalities mean that a firm that invests in R&D can expect to reap only a fraction of the profits from the innovation.

Consequently, many economists believe that the free market induces private firms to invest less than the socially optimal amount in activities that generate external benefits, with innovation as a prime example. They believe that many innovations whose benefits would exceed their costs are never carried out because any firm that spent the money to produce the innovation would get only part of the benefit, and that part would be insufficient to cover the firm's costs. Instead, governments finance a good deal of innovation and research activity, which is carried out in government laboratories and in research institutions such as universities.

The externality problem is probably most severe for what is called **basic research**—that is, research that deals with science and general principles rather than improvement of a specific product. (Research

"Oh, if only it were so simple."

Basic research refers to research that seeks to provide scientific knowledge and general principles rather than coming up with any specific marketable inventions.

---

[17] For review, see Chapter 15, pages 312–316.

[18] See William D. Nordhaus, "Schumpeterian Profits in the American Economy: Theory and Measurement," Working Paper 10433 (Cambridge, M.A: National Bureau of Economic Research, 2004).

of the latter sort, which is directly related to commercial or other uses, is called **applied research**.) For example, some further research on the nature of electricity and magnetism may yield enormous economic benefits in the near or distant future, but for the moment it satisfies only physicists' curiosity. Few business firms will finance such research. Of course, the economy would be much less productive in the long run if no one did it. That is why the governments of the United States and a number of other industrialized countries finance basic research, and why economists generally favor such funding.

Applied research is research whose goal is to invent or improve particular products or processes, often for profit. Note, however, that the military and government health-related agencies provide examples of not-for-profit applied research.

Why the Shortfall in Innovation Spending May Not Be So Big After All

The notion that we are spending far too small a share of GDP on innovation is not really plausible. Looking about us, we see a flood of new products and processes, but certainly nothing that suggests a dearth of new technology. A number of economists are now offering reasons that suggest why there may be no shortfall, or why any shortfall that occurs may be relatively limited.

Here only one of the reasons will be suggested: the existence of profitable markets in *licensing* of innovation to others. As we will see later in this chapter, many firms permit others, even their closest competitors, to use their private technology—for a fee. That fee becomes the market price for a license to use the technology. To take this idea to its extreme, imagine that all innovating firms are successful in profitably licensing their technology to every firm and individual that can benefit from it. Then the externality problem would disappear. The reason is straightforward: A beneficial externality, after all, is simply a good deed for which the doer of the deed is not paid, or not paid adequately, for the benefit he or she creates. For this reason, the outputs that yield beneficial externalities can generally be expected to be too low from the general welfare point of view. But if the supplier can somehow arrange to be paid sufficiently, the incentive to supply an adequate amount of the beneficial product will plainly be restored. So a profitable market for technology licenses is said to help in "internalizing the externality," by getting the supplier paid for supplying the valuable innovation and by restoring the incentive for further innovation.

A related but lesser-known phenomenon occurs when many firms try to reduce their risks by **technology trading**—getting paid for another firm's use of its technology by receiving in exchange the right to use the other firm's technology. This type of deal can be thought of as bartering, rather than selling, technology licenses. Either way, the innovator firm receives some compensation for the use of its technology by others.

The implication is that even if innovating firms do not receive full compensation for the benefits that their technology provides to others, those firms seem to have become quite adept at getting some substantial portion of the appropriate payment. The result is that the innovation externalities may not be nearly as serious a handicap to innovation as the theory may have led some observers to suspect.

Technology trading is an arrangement in which a firm voluntarily makes its privately owned technology available to other firms either in exchange for access to the technology of the second company or for an agreed-upon fee.

THE MARKET ECONOMY AND THE SPEEDY DISSEMINATION OF NEW TECHNOLOGY

Another attribute of the market economy that is vital for its growth is the fact that new technology now spreads with impressive speed, meaning that obsolete products and processes do not long survive or hold back economic growth. The evidence indicates that dissemination is not only surprisingly rapid but has also been growing more so with remarkable consistency for more than a century (see "The Speed-Up of Technology Dissemination" on page 352).

The Speed-Up of Technology Dissemination

A recent study of 46 major product innovations found that, in less than a century, the average time between the commercial introduction of a new product and the time of entry of competitors supplying the same or similar products fell precipitously from almost 33 years at the inception of the twentieth century to just 3.4 years in the period 1967–1986.* Moreover, as shown in Figure 7 below, the decline was remarkably steady and persistent.

* Rajshree Agarwal and Michael Gort, "First Mover Advantage and the Speed of Competitive Entry, 1887–1986," *Journal of Law and Economics,* XLIV (April 2001), pp. 161–177. The authors report that other studies support their results.

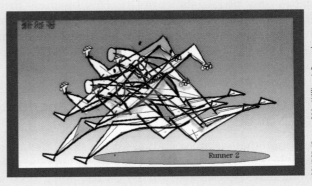

SOURCE: "Runner 2" by William J. Baumol

FIGURE 7

Increased Speed with Which Competition of Similar Products Faces the Seller of an Innovative Product

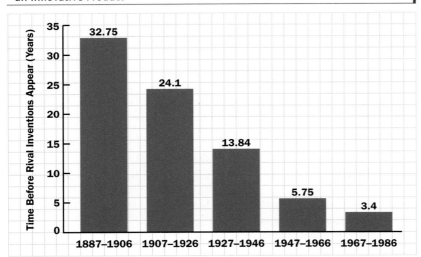

SOURCE: Rajshree Agarwal and Michael Gort "First Mover Advantage and the Speed of Competitive Entry, 1887–1986," *Journal of Law and Economics,* XLIV (April 2001), pp. 161–177.

What underlies this increase in the rapid spread of inventions? It may seem that when a business firm obtains a promising new invention, it will naturally do all it can to bar its competitors' access to the new technology so as to retain a competitive advantage over its rivals. In reality, this is often not so. If a firm can get a sufficiently high price by licensing its technology to others, it may be just as profitable to do that as to reserve the innovations for its own exclusive use. This is not just a theoretical possibility. Newspaper reports indicate, for example, that more than 20 percent of IBM's profits in 2000 were obtained from its technology licenses.

There is another incentive for firms to trade innovations with others, including their competitors. Fearing that their own laboratories may conceivably fail in all R&D undertakings in a particular time period, while competitors may have better luck, firms often enter into agreements with a competitor to *share* all successful future innovations for a specified time period—say, the next five years. Such agreements reduce risk for *both* firms. In photography, for example, one camera manufacturer may introduce an improved automatic-focus device, a second firm may develop an automatic light adjustment, and a third may invent a way to make the camera more compact. Each of these three firms can keep its invention to itself, but if they get together and agree to produce cameras combining all their new features, they will be able to market a product clearly superior to anything produced individually. They will also be in a far better position to meet competition from another camera manufacturer.

Cross licensing of patents occurs when each of two firms agrees to let the other use some specified set of its patents, either at a price specified in their agreement or in return for access to the other firm's patents.

Many firms and industries engage in this practice of **cross licensing.** For example, IBM cross-licenses patents with *each* of its major competitors. One study of technology exchange among American steel minimills, which are now world leaders in steel productivity, found that *all but one* of the 11 firms regularly and routinely exchanged information with the others. Firms would sometimes train the employees of competing

Collaboration, Rather Than Competition, in Innovation

Even some of the largest companies in the world find that collaboration, rather than competition, can sometimes give them an advantage in the global economy. For instance, Sony and Sharp, two leading manufacturers of consumer electronics, have launched a joint venture to produce and sell high-definition Liquid Crystal Display (LCD) televisions. The two companies will jointly own Sharp's newest LCD plant in Sakai City, Japan, which will produce LCD panels for both companies' television lines.

Part of the multinational conglomerate, Sony Group, Sony Corporation is a leading manufacturer of consumer electronics, with more than 170,000 employees in Japan. Sharp Corporation employs just 22,600 people in Japan, but specializes in manufacturing LCD televisions, DVD players, and Blu-ray Disc players.

The Sony-Sharp joint venture allows Sharp to share the cost of its new LCD factory—the first in the world to use tenth-generation glass substrates—with Sony, which, in turn, will be able to incorporate Sharp's leading-edge LCD panels into its new televisions.

SOURCE: ULTRA.F/Jupiter Images

SOURCE: "Sharp and Sony Enter into Definitive Agreement regarding Joint Venture to Produce and Sell Large-Sized LCD Panels and Modules," press release, July 30, 2009, accessed online at: http://www.sony.net/SonyInfo/News/Press/200907/09-0730E/index.html.

firms or send their own personnel to competing facilities to help set up unfamiliar equipment.[19]

Indeed, business firms provide their technology to others for a profit so commonly that MIT has run a seminar teaching firms how to earn more from their technology-rental business. There is even an international association of technology licensing firms, with thousands of members.

Inventions are becoming available more quickly to other firms, including competitors of the firms that own them. Moreover, competitive pressures ensure that these innovations are rapidly put to use.

CONCLUSION: THE MARKET ECONOMY AND ITS INNOVATION ASSEMBLY LINE

Although we devoted a lot of attention to the virtues and vices of the market system in earlier chapters, those chapters barely mentioned what may be its greatest strength. Free-market capitalism has proved to be the most powerful engine of economic growth and innovation ever known. The increased creation, faster dissemination, and accelerated utilization of inventions is surely no accident. There is something about the way the modern economy works that makes it outstrip all of its predecessors in terms of the creation and utilization of new technology—and to do so with little letup for more than two centuries. Never before in history have the economic returns to the average person in the economically advanced economies risen so far and so quickly, and this, arguably, is by far the most spectacular economic accomplishment of the market mechanism.

| SUMMARY |

1. The growth records and **per-capita incomes** achieved by market economies far exceed those attained by any other form of economic organization. **Innovation** is one of the main sources of that economic growth.

2. Small firms created by **entrepreneurs** account for a substantial proportion of the economy's breakthrough

inventions, whereas larger companies specialize in incremental improvements that over time often add up to very major advances.

3. Innovation in free-market economies is stimulated by competition among business firms, which try to outdo one another in terms of the attractiveness of their new

[19] Eric Von Hippel, *The Sources of Innovation* (New York: Oxford University Press, 1988), p. 79.

and improved products and in the efficiency of their productive processes.

4. Innovative entrepreneurial firms are driven to provide a stream of innovations because otherwise rivals are likely to introduce substitute products that will erode the profits from any one innovation. Among large competing firms frequent innovation is a matter of life and death because a firm with obsolete products or processes will lose its customers to rivals.

5. The large amounts that competition forces many firms to spend on R&D and the low marginal costs of the consumer goods sometimes produced with the resulting innovations often mean that if the firms set $P = MC$, as is done under perfect competition, the innovating firms will not be able to recover their costs.

6. As with any other decision, a profit-maximizing firm will invest in R&D up to the point at which the expected MR equals the MC of that expenditure.

7. Competition can force firms to set their R&D spending at levels corresponding to those of their rivals.

8. The typical level of R&D spending in an industry will sometimes increase, but it will rarely decline because no firm dares to be the first to cut back on such spending.

9. **Process innovations** can be shown by MR = MC analysis to increase outputs and decrease prices, even in monopoly firms.

10. Many economists believe that private investment in innovation will fall short of the socially optimal level, because the externalities from innovation mean that inventors do not obtain all of the benefits of their innovations.

11. Firms often seek to reduce the risks of their R&D activities by entering into agreements with other firms to share one another's technology. They may also sell access to their technology to others.

| KEY TERMS |

applied research 351

basic research 350

capitalism 335

cross licensing 352

externality 334

GDP 337

high-tech 341

Industrial Revolution 335

innovation 338

Invention 338

per-capita income 334

process innovation 349

product innovation 348

productivity 334

ratchet 348

research and development (R&D) 340

technology trading 351

| DISCUSSION QUESTIONS |

1. To understand how much the free-enterprise economy has increased living standards, try to envision the daily life of a middle-class family in a major American city just after the Civil War, when the average purchasing power is estimated to have been less than one-ninth of today's. What do you think they ate? How much clothing did they own? What were their living quarters like? What share of their budget was available for vacations and entertainment?

2. Name five common products introduced since you were born.

3. Name some companies that advertise that their products are "new" or "improved."

4. Explain why firms in an industry that spends a large amount of money on advertising may feel locked into their current advertising budgets, with no one firm daring to cut its expenditure. Describe the analogy with competition in innovation.

5. Alexander Graham Bell beat Elisha Grey to the patent office by several hours, so that Bell obtained the patent on the telephone. Imagine how much that patent turned out to be worth. How much do you think Grey got for his effort and expenditure on development of the invention? How does that help explain the possibility that *average* economic profits from innovation are close to zero?

6. If average economic profits from investment in innovation are close to zero, why would many people be anxious to invest in innovation?

7. Explain how firms that share their technology with competitors benefit by improving their ability to compete against new entrants.

8. What are the possible advantages to the general welfare when firms make their technology automatically available to others (while, of course, charging a price for use of the technology)?

9. Why may it be unprofitable for a firm to spend much more on R&D than its competitors do?

10. Define the following terms:

   a. Externality

   b. Public good

   c. Ratchet

   Explain the applicability of these concepts to the innovative economy.

11. From the point of view of the general welfare, do you think spending on R&D in the United States is too low? Too high? Just about right? Why?

EXTERNALITIES, THE ENVIRONMENT, AND NATURAL RESOURCES

Environmental taxes are perhaps the most powerful tool societies have for forging economies that protect human and environmental health.

DAVID MALIN ROODMAN, WORLDWATCH INSTITUTE

conomics is useful in pointing out both the accomplishments of the market and its shortcomings. But that is only half the battle. Economic analysis would be quite arid if it could not offer us any remedial suggestions for dealing with the market's shortcomings. In Chapter 13, we investigated one of the market's important imperfections: monopoly, or limited competition. In this chapter, we will look at another significant market imperfection studied by microeconomists: *externalities*. In Chapter 15, we learned that externalities—the incidental benefits or damages imposed on people not directly involved in an economic activity—can cause the market mechanism to malfunction. In Part 1 of this chapter, we study a particularly important application of this idea: externalities as a way to explain environmental problems. We will consider the extent to which the price mechanism bears responsibility for these problems and see how that same mechanism can be harnessed to help remedy them. In Part 2 of this chapter, we address a closely related subject: the depletion of natural resources. We will discuss fears that the world is quickly using up many of its vital natural resources and see how the price mechanism can help with this problem as well.

CONTENTS

| PUZZLE: | THOSE RESILIENT NATURAL RESOURCE SUPPLIES |

It is a plain fact that the earth is endowed with only finite quantities of such vital resources as oil, copper, tin, and coal. This reality underlies many worried forecasts about the inevitable, and imminent, exhaustion of one resource or another. For instance, on page 370, "The Permanent Fuel Crisis" lists a number of bleak prophecies about oil production in the United States, all of which proved far off the mark.

In reality, far from running out, available supplies of many key minerals and fuels are *growing*. Known supplies of most minerals have grown at least as fast as production and in many cases have far outstripped it. For example, in 1950 world reserves of tin were estimated at 6 million metric tons (mmt). Between 1950 and 2000, 11 mmt of tin were mined from the earth. Nonetheless, at the end of 2000 world reserves of tin had *increased* to 10 mmt. By the end of 2007, world reserves had declined to 6.1 mmt but were still considered to be in slight oversupply. Similarly, for iron ore (which is used to make steel), known U.S. stocks in 1950 were 46 mmt, but at the end of 2007, U.S. stocks had fallen to 2.9 mmt. A similar odd story is true for U.S. stocks of zinc, copper, and many more minerals.[1] How is this possible? Aren't the quantities of these resources finite? Economic principles, as we will see later in this chapter, help to clear up these mysteries.

PART 1: THE ECONOMICS OF ENVIRONMENTAL PROTECTION

Environmental problems are not new. For example, in the Middle Ages, English kings repeatedly denounced the massive pollution of the river Thames, which, they reported, had grown so bad that it was impeding navigation of the tiny medieval ships! What *is* new and different is the attention we now give to environmental problems. Much of the increased interest stems from rising incomes, which have reduced our concerns about our most basic needs of food, clothing, and shelter and have allowed us the luxury of concentrating on the *quality* of life.

Economic thought on the subject of environmental degradation preceded the outburst of public concern by nearly half a century. In 1911, the British economist Arthur C. Pigou wrote a remarkable book called *The Economics of Welfare,* which for the first time explained environmental problems in terms of externalities. Pigou also outlined an approach to environmental policy that is still favored by most economists today and is gradually winning over lawmakers, bureaucrats, and even cautious environmentalists (as the opening quotation suggests). His analysis indicated a system of monetary *pollution charges* that polluters are forced to pay can be an effective means to control pollution. In this way, the price mechanism can remedy one of its own shortcomings!

REVIEW—EXTERNALITIES: A CRITICAL SHORTCOMING OF THE MARKET MECHANISM

An activity is said to generate a beneficial or detrimental **externality** if that activity causes incidental benefits or damages to others not directly involved in the activity, and no corresponding compensation is provided to or paid by those who generate the externality.

In our discussion in Chapter 15, we emphasized that externalities are found throughout the economy. For example, pollution of the air and waterways is to a considerable degree contributed by factories and motor vehicles as an incidental by-product of their activities that damages other members of society. Similarly, another car's entry onto an overcrowded highway adds to delays that other travelers must endure, thereby causing those drivers and passengers to suffer a *detrimental* **externality.** But externalities can also be *beneficial* to third parties. In Chapter 16, when discussing the microeconomics of innovation

[1] U.S. Geological Survey, *Historical Statistics for Mineral and Material Commodities in the United States,* 2008, http://minerals.usgs.gov/ds/2005/140/#data; and U.S. Geological Survey, *Minerals Yearbook: Tin,* various years, http://minerals.usgs.gov/minerals.

and growth, we emphasized that the vital innovative activities, to which society devotes huge quantities of resources, usually provide beneficial externalities to persons who neither invest in innovation nor work in any research and development establishments.

EXTERNALITIES: A SHORTCOMING OF THE MARKET THAT CAN BE CURED BY MARKET METHODS Because those who create harmful externalities do not pay for the damage done to others, they have little incentive to desist. In this way, the market tends to create an undesired abundance of damaging externalities. Similarly, because those who create beneficial externalities are not compensated for doing so, they have little incentive to supply as large a quantity as will best serve the interests of society. Therefore, the market tends to supply an undesirably small amount of such beneficial externalities. In sum, economists conclude that unless something is done about it, the market will provide an overabundance of harmful externalities and an undersupply of desirable ones. Either case is far from ideal.

IDEAS FOR BEYOND THE FINAL EXAM

Externalities are one of our *Ideas for Beyond the Final Exam* because they have such important consequences for the welfare of society and the efficient functioning of the economy. They affect the health of the population and threaten our natural resource heritage and perhaps even the survival of the human race. This chapter discusses the character and magnitude of the problem and the methods that can be used to contain its harmful consequences.

In this chapter, we focus on one of the most highly publicized externalities—pollution. Toxic fumes from a chemical plant affect not only the plant's employees and customers but also other people not directly associated with the plant. Because the firm does not pay for this *incidental* damage, the firm's owners have no financial incentive to limit their emissions of pollution, especially because pollution controls cost money. Instead, the polluting firm will find it profitable to continue its toxic emissions as though the fumes caused no external damage to the community.

The Facts: Is the World Really Getting Steadily More Polluted?

First, let's look at the facts. The popular press often gives the impression that environmental problems have been growing steadily worse and that *all* pollution is attributable to modern industrialization and the profit system. The problems are, indeed, serious and some of them are extremely urgent, but it is nevertheless possible to exaggerate them.

For one thing, pollution is nothing new. Medieval cities were pestholes; streets and rivers were littered with garbage and the air stank of rotting wastes—a level of filth that was accepted as normal. Early in the twentieth century, the automobile was actually hailed for its major *improvement* in the cleanliness of city streets, which until then had fought a losing battle against the proliferation of horse dung (see "Four-Legged Polluters" on page 359 for more on this issue).

Since World War II, there has been marked progress in solving a number of pollution problems. Air quality has improved in U.S. cities during the past three decades, and concentrations of most air pollutants continue to decline. Most dramatic has been the nearly 100 percent decrease in ambient concentrations of lead since the 1970s. Figure 1 portrays the encouraging trends in national air pollution levels. With the exception of ozone, average concentrations are well below the national ambient air quality standards (NAAQS) established by the U.S. Environmental Protection Agency (EPA). Rapid declines in automobile pollution have played a large role in this improvement, along with decreases in emissions from power plants. There have also been some spectacular gains in water quality. In the Great Lakes region, where the Cuyahoga River once caught fire because of its toxic load and where Lake Erie was pronounced dead, tough pollution controls have gradually brought a recovery.

The Europeans have made progress as well. For example, the infamous killing fogs of London, once the staple backdrop of British mystery fiction, are a thing of the past because of the air quality improvement since 1950. The Thames River has been cleaned up enough to allow large-scale fishing of giant conger eels to resume after a 150-year hiatus.

FIGURE 1

Air Quality Trends in the United States, 1975–2001

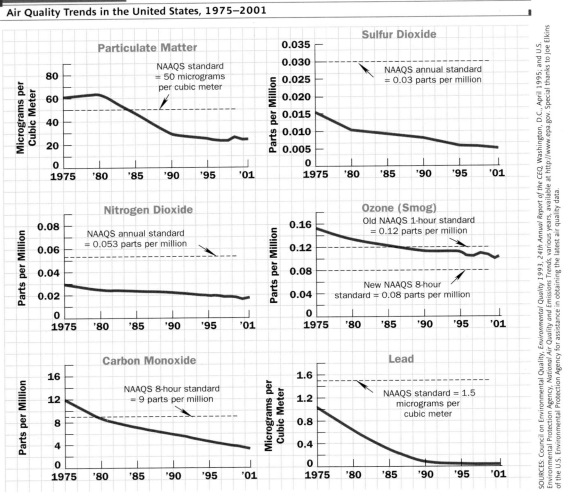

NOTE: Measures are average ambient concentrations of the six pollutants for which the U.S. Environmental Protection Agency has established National Ambient Air Quality Standards (NAAQS). After 1987, particulate matter is measured by PM10 only, an indicator of those particles smaller than 10 micrometers.

The point is that pollution problems are not a uniquely modern phenomenon, nor is every part of the environment deteriorating relentlessly.

Free-market economies certainly have no monopoly on pollution. Although it may seem that a centrally planned economy should be able to cope much better with the environmental problems caused by externalities, such economies have in reality been the *biggest* environmental disasters. China, the last large communist society, has some of the world's worst air pollution, mainly from the burning of low-quality, high-sulfur coal and a dearth of pollution controls. Urban ozone levels in China are far greater than those in Los Angeles, a place where, Americans tend to think, smog was invented.

Grave environmental problems also continue to plague Eastern Europe and the countries of the former Soviet Union. Poland, despite considerable improvement since 1989, continues to battle very serious air pollution problems. Particularly in the cities, high pollution levels contribute to health problems. The collapse of communism in the former Soviet Union revealed a staggering array of environmental horrors, including massive poisoning of air, ground, and water in the vicinity of industrial plants and the devastation of the Aral Sea, once the world's fourth-largest inland sea, but now reduced to less than half its previous size. Many Russians live in environmentally hazardous conditions, and especially severe problems are found in Chechnya, where millions of barrels of oil have seeped into the ground from the region's black-market oil industry. Radioactive pollutants from

Four-Legged Polluters

When Pigs Roamed Broadway

Broadway's affinity with ham has an enduring quality. In the 1860s, however, two species competed for attention in the heart of the city—one panting on stage, the other squealing and grunting in the streets. The pig in the city was a paradox—an element of rural culture transposed to urban life. Pigs roamed the streets rooting for food, the stink from their wastes poisoning the air. Because they ate garbage, the pigs were tolerated to a degree in the absence of adequate sanitation facilities. But this dubious contribution to municipal services was tiny in comparison with the nuisance they caused. From the nation's capital to Midwestern "porkopolis," we are told, squares and parks amounted to public hogpens. . . . in Kansas City the confusion and stench of patrolling hogs were so penetrating that Oscar Wilde observed, "They made granite eyes weep."

Equine Smells

In city streets clogged with automobiles, the vision of a horse and buggy produces strong nostalgia. A century ago it produced a different feeling—distress, owing to the horse for what he dropped and to the buggy for spreading it. Of the three million horses in American cities at the beginning of the twentieth century, New York had some 150,000, the healthier ones each producing between twenty and twenty-five pounds of manure a day. These dumplings were numerous on every street, attracting swarms of flies and radiating a powerful stench. The ambiance was further debased by the presence on almost every block of stables filled with urine-saturated hay. During dry spells the pounding traffic refined the manure to dust, which blew "from the pavement as a sharp, piercing powder, to cover our clothes, ruin our furniture and flow up into our nostrils." . . . The steadily increasing production [of manure] caused the more pessimistic observers to fear that American cities would disappear like Pompeii—but not under ashes.

SOURCE: © Bettmann/CORBIS

SOURCE: Excerpted from Otto L. Bettman, *The Good Old Days—They Were Terrible!* (New York: Random House; 1974), pp. 2–3.

50 years of plutonium production, processing, and storage at the Mayak industrial complex have turned nearby Lake Karachay into one of the most polluted places on earth. The result has been widespread illness and countless premature deaths in these areas.[2]

Yet our own environment here in the United States is hardly free from problems. Despite improvements, many U.S. urban areas still suffer many days of unhealthful air quality, particularly during the summer months. According to the EPA, approximately 105.6 million Americans (just over one-third of the population) were living in areas where pollution levels in 2006 still exceeded at least one of the national air quality standards adopted by the federal government.[3] Ozone (the presence of which high above the earth protects humans from the fiercest part of the sun's ultraviolet radiation) is the most important component of serious ground-level urban air pollution—smog—and remains a pervasive problem in the United States. Even formerly pristine wilderness areas are threatened by air pollution (see "Visibility Impairment from Air Pollution at Canyonlands National Park" on the next page).

Our world is frequently subjected to new pollutants, some far more dangerous than those we have reduced, although less visible and less malodorous. Improperly dumped toxic substances—such as PCBs (polychlorinated biphenyls), chlorinated hydrocarbons, dioxins, heavy metals, and radioactive materials—can cause cancer and threaten life and health in other ways. The danger presented by some of these substances can persist for thousands of years, causing all but irreversible damage.

---

[2] Central Intelligence Agency, *The World Factbook*, https://www.cia.gov; "Poland: Areas of Concern," Resource Renewal Institute, http://www.rri.org; and "Russia: Environmental Issues," U.S. Department of Energy, Energy Information Administration, http://www.eia.doe.gov.

[3] U.S. Environmental Protection Agency, Office of Air Quality Planning and Standards, "Latest Findings on National Air Quality: Status and Trends Through 2006," January 2008, Research Triangle Park, N.C.: U.S. EPA.

This photo shows the significant glacial retreat in the Swiss Alps caused by global warming.

All these problems pale when compared to a global environmental threat—the long-term warming of the earth's atmosphere. Scientists have demonstrated that the documented global warming of the past century, and especially in the past decade, is at least partly a consequence of human activities that have increased "greenhouse gases" in the atmosphere. Most climatologists agree that the carbon dioxide buildup from the burning of fossil fuels such as oil, natural gas, and coal is a prime contributor to this problem. Forecasts of future warming range from 1.8° to 6.3° Fahrenheit by the year 2100, a dramatic change that may shift world rain patterns, disrupt agriculture, threaten coastal cities with inundation, and expand deserts (for more on this topic, see "Big Arctic Perils Seen in Warming, Survey Finds" on the next page).

Although environmental problems are neither new nor confined to capitalist, industrialized economies, we continue to inflict damage on ourselves and our surroundings.

The Role of Individuals and Governments in Environmental Damage

Many people think of industry as the primary villain in environmental damage. But this is not necessarily true.

Although business firms do their share in harming the environment, private individuals and government are also major contributors.

For example, individual car owners are responsible for much of the air pollution in cities. Wood-burning stoves and fireplaces are a source of particulate pollution (smoke). Wastes from flush toilets and residential washing machines also cause significant harm.

Governments, too, add to the problem. Municipal treatment plant wastes are a major source of water pollution. Military aircraft expel exhaust fumes and cause noise pollution. Obsolete atomic materials and by-products associated with chemical and nuclear weapons are among the most dangerous of all wastes, and their disposal remains an unsolved problem. Governments have also constructed giant dams and reservoirs that flooded farmlands and destroyed canyons. Swamp drainage has altered local ecology, and canal building has diverted the flow of rivers. The U.S. Army Corps of Engineers has been accused of acting on the basis of a so-called *edifice complex*.

Visibility Impairment from Air Pollution at Canyonlands National Park

Even in such pristine and remote areas as Utah's Canyonlands National Park, air pollution degrades visibility, as these two photos show.

. . . a clear day

. . . a hazy day

SOURCE: U.S. Environmental Protection Agency, Office of Air & Radiation, *Visibility Impairment,* http://www.epa.gov/air/visibility/parks/canyonld.html.

Pollution and the Law of Conservation of Matter and Energy

The physical law of conservation of matter and energy tells us that objects cannot disappear—at most they can be changed into something else. Petroleum, for instance, can be transformed into heat (and smoke) or into plastic—but it will never vanish. This means that after a raw material has been used, either it must be used again (recycled) or it becomes a waste product that requires disposal.

If it is not recycled, any input used in production must ultimately become a waste product. It may end up in some municipal dump; it may literally go up in smoke, contributing to atmospheric pollution; or it may be transformed into heat, warming up adjacent

Big Arctic Perils Seen in Warming, Survey Finds

A comprehensive four-year study of warming in the Arctic shows that heat-trapping gases from tailpipes and smokestacks around the world are contributing to profound environmental changes, including sharp retreats of glaciers and sea ice, thawing of permafrost and shifts in the weather, the oceans and the atmosphere.

The study, commissioned by eight nations with Arctic territory, including the United States, [and conducted by 300 scientists] says the changes are likely to harm native communities, wildlife and economic activity but also to offer some benefits, like longer growing seasons. . . .

The report says that "while some historical changes in climate have resulted from natural causes and variations, the strength of the trends and the patterns of change that have emerged in recent decades indicate that human influences, resulting primarily from increased emissions of carbon dioxide and other greenhouse gases, have now become the dominant factor."

The Arctic "is now experiencing some of the most rapid and severe climate change on Earth," the report says, adding, "Over the next years, climate change is expected to accelerate, contributing to major physical, ecological, social and economic changes, many of which have already begun. . . ."

Prompt efforts to curb greenhouse-gas emissions could slow the pace of change, allowing communities and wildlife to adapt, the report says. But it also stresses that further warming and melting are unavoidable, given the century-long buildup of the gases, mainly carbon dioxide. . . .

The potential benefits of the changes include projected growth in marine fish stocks and improved prospects for agriculture and timber harvests in some regions, as well as expanded access to Arctic waters.

But the list of potential harms is far longer.

The retreat of sea ice, the report says, "is very likely to have devastating consequences for polar bears, ice-living seals and local people for whom these animals are a primary food source."

Oil and gas deposits on land are likely to be harder to extract as tundra thaws, limiting the frozen season when drilling convoys can traverse the otherwise spongy ground, the report says. Alaska has already seen the "tundra travel" season on the North Slope shrink to 100 days from about 200 days a year in 1970.

The report concludes that the consequences of the fast-paced Arctic warming will be global. In particular, the accelerated melting of Greenland's two-mile-high sheets of ice will cause sea levels to rise around the world.

SOURCE: From Andrew C. Revkin, "Big Arctic Perils Seen in Warming, Survey Finds", in *The New York Times*, October 30, 2004. Used by permission of the author.

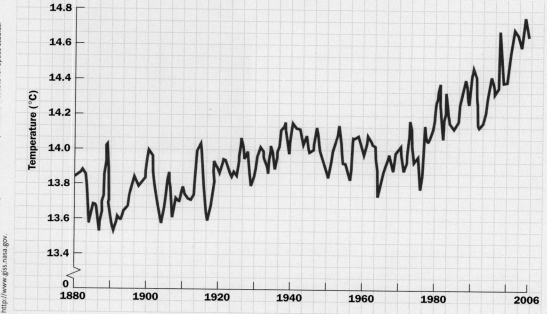

Annual Mean Global Surface Air Temperature, 1880–2006

SOURCE: National Aeronautics and Space Administration, Goddard Institute for Space Studies. http://www.giss.nasa.gov.

waterways and killing aquatic life. But the laws of physics tell us nothing can be done to make used inputs disappear altogether.

We create an extraordinary amount of solid waste—each American discards close to 4.6 pounds of trash every *day*, despite our efforts to reduce this waste. Fortunately, in the face of this rising tide of garbage, recycling rates for many commonly used materials (such as aluminum, paper, and glass) are rising in the United States and many other industrial countries. In the United States, recycling has increased substantially. According to the EPA, Americans recycled 33 percent of municipal solid waste in 2007, a rate that has more than tripled since 1980.[4] As of 2005, 30 percent of the municipal waste generated by the 30 OECD member countries was recycled or composted—up from just 18 percent during the mid-1990s.[5]

Our very existence makes some environmental damage inevitable. To eat and protect ourselves from the elements, people must inevitably use up the earth's resources and generate wastes.

Environmental damage cannot be reduced to zero. As long as the human race survives, eliminating such damage completely is impossible.

Why do economists believe that, although environmental damage cannot be reduced to zero, the *public interest* requires it to be reduced below its free-market level? The reason is clear from our previous analysis: Why do economists conclude that the market mechanism, which is so good at providing approximately the right number of hockey sticks and hair dryers, generates too much pollution? Pollution is an externality, which means that it

Garbage! Economic Incentives to Create Less of It and Recycle More of It

The U.S. Environmental Protection Agency estimates that 7,100 American communities (covering about 25 percent of the U.S. population) operate "pay-as-you-throw" programs (also known as unit pricing or variable-rate pricing), in which residents are charged for the collection of household garbage based on the amount they throw away. This creates a direct economic incentive to generate less garbage and to recycle more of what is generated. Rather than paying a flat fee for waste disposal (or simply receiving waste disposal services without any sense of what the cost is—as is true when a municipality provides trash collection services and pays for them out of general revenues), these programs require residents to pay for municipal waste disposal based on the number of bags or cans of trash placed at the curb or dropped off at a trash disposal facility. It is no surprise that it works! It has been shown that variable-rate PAYT programs have substantially reduced the tonnage of waste shipped to disposal facilities. One recent study estimated that these programs have reduced residential disposal by about 17 percent, with 6 percent attributable to source reduction (less garbage generated), 5–6 percent attributable to increases in recycling, and 4–5 percent attributable to decreases in the amount of yard waste that residents put into their garbage cans.

SOURCE: © Brand X Pictures/Jupiterimages

SOURCE: Lisa Skumatz and David Freeman, "Pay as You Throw in the U.S.: 2006 Update and Analyses," prepared for U.S. EPA by Skumatz Economic Research Associates, Superior, CO, December 2006.

---

[4] U.S. Environmental Protection Agency, *Municipal Solid Waste Generation, Recycling, and Disposal in the United States: Facts and Figures 2007*, available at http://www.epa.gov. We should point out that recycling is not always as benign as it seems. The very process of preparing materials for reuse often can produce dangerous emissions. The recycling of waste oil is a clear example, because used petroleum products are often combined with toxic chemicals that can be released in the recycling process.

[5] *OECD Environmental Outlook to 2030*, Paris: Organisation for Economic Co-operation and Development, 2008, p. 246, accessed online at: http://titania.sourceoecd.org/vl=1517583/cl=44/nw=1/rpsv/cgi-bin/fulltextew.pl?prpsv=/ij/oecdthemes/99980061/v2008n1/s14/p459.idx.

results from a price mechanism malfunction that prevents the market from doing its usual effective job of carrying out consumers' wishes.

Here, *failure of the pricing system* is caused by a pollution-generating firm's ability to use up some of the community's clean air or water without paying for the privilege. Just as the firm would undoubtedly use oil and electricity wastefully if they were available at no charge, so it will use "free" air wastefully, despoiling it with chemical fumes far beyond the level justified by the public interest. The problem is that *price* has not been permitted to play its usual role here. Instead of having to pay for the pure air that it uses up, a polluting firm gets that valuable resource free of charge.

Externalities play a crucial role affecting the quality of life. They show why the market mechanism, which is so efficient in supplying consumers' goods, has a much poorer record in terms of environmental effects. The problem of pollution illustrates the importance of externalities for public policy.

The magnitude of our pollution problems is largely attributable to the fact that the market lets individuals, firms, and government agencies deplete such resources as clean water and pure air without charging them any money for using up those resources.

It follows that one way of dealing with pollution problems is to charge those who emit pollution, and those who despoil the environment in other ways, a price commensurate with the costs they impose on society.

BASIC APPROACHES TO ENVIRONMENTAL POLICY

In broad terms, there are three ways to control activities that damage the environment:

- *Voluntary efforts,* such as nonmandatory investment in pollution-control equipment by firms motivated by social responsibility or voluntary recycling of solid wastes by consumers.
- *Direct controls,* which either (1) impose legal ceilings on the amount any polluter is permitted to emit or (2) specify how particular activities must be carried out. For example, direct controls may prohibit backyard garbage incinerators or high-sulfur coal burning or require smokestack "scrubbers" to capture the emissions of power plants.
- *Taxes on pollution, tradeable emissions permits,* or the use of other monetary incentives or penalties to make it unattractive financially for pollution emitters to continue to pollute as usual.

As we will see next, all of these methods have useful roles.

1. Voluntarism   Voluntarism, though admirable, often has proved weak and unreliable. Some well-intentioned business firms, for example, have voluntarily made sincere attempts to adopt environmentally beneficial practices. Yet competition has usually prevented them from spending more than token amounts for this purpose. No business, whatever its virtues, can long afford to spend so much on "good works" that rivals can easily underprice it. As a result, voluntary business programs sometimes have been more helpful to the companies' public relations activities than to the environment.

Yet voluntary measures do have their place. They are appropriate where surveillance and, consequently, enforcement is impractical, as in the prevention of littering by campers in isolated areas, where appeals to people's consciences are the only alternative. And in brief but serious emergencies, which do not allow for time to plan and enact a systematic program, voluntary compliance may be the only workable approach.

Several major cities have, for example, experienced episodes of temporary but dangerous concentrations of pollutants, forcing the authorities to appeal to the public for drastic emissions cuts. Public response to appeals requiring cooperation for short periods often has been enthusiastic and gratifying, particularly when civic pride was a factor. During the 1984 Summer Olympic Games, for example, Los Angeles city officials asked motorists to carpool, businesses to stagger work hours, and truckers to restrict themselves to essential deliveries and to avoid rush hours. The result was an extraordinary decrease in traffic and smog, such that the 6,000-foot San Gabriel Mountains suddenly became visible behind the city.

Direct controls are government rules that tell organizations or individuals what processes or raw materials they may use or what products they are permitted to supply or purchase.

2. Direct Controls   **Direct controls** have traditionally been the chief instrument of environmental policy in the United States (the so-called *command-and-control approach*). The federal government, through the Environmental Protection Agency, formulates standards for air and water quality and requires state and local governments to adopt rules that will ensure achievement of those goals. For example, the standards for automobile emissions require new automobiles to pass tests showing that their emissions do not exceed specified amounts. As another example, localities sometimes prohibit industry's use of particularly "dirty" fuels or require firms to adopt processes to "clean" those fuels.

Pollution charges (taxes on emissions) are taxes that polluters are required to pay. The amount they pay depends on what they emit and in what quantities.

3. Taxes on Pollution Emissions   Most economists agree that relying exclusively on direct controls is a mistake and that, in most cases, *financial penalties*, or **pollution charges**, on polluters can do the same job more dependably, effectively, and economically.

The most common suggestion is that governments permit firms to pollute all they want but be forced to pay a tax for the privilege, in order to make them want to pollute less. Under such a plan, the quantity of the polluter's emissions is metered just like the use of electricity. At the end of the month the government sends the polluter a bill charging a stipulated amount for each gallon (or other unit) of emissions. (The amount can also vary with the emissions' quality, with a higher tax rate being imposed on emissions that are more dangerous or unpleasant.) Thus, in such a scheme, the more environmental damage done, the more the polluter pays. Emissions taxes are deliberately designed to *encourage* polluters to take advantage of the tax loophole—by polluting less, the polluter can reduce the amount of tax owed.

Businesses *do* respond to such taxes. One well-known example is the Ruhr River basin in Germany, where emissions taxes have been used for many years. Although the Ruhr is a heavily concentrated industrial center, the rivers that are protected by taxes are clean enough for fishing and other recreational purposes. Firms have also found it profitable to avoid taxes by extracting pollutants from their liquid discharges and recycling them. (See "Making the Polluter Pay" for another example of the response to taxes.)

Emissions Taxes versus Direct Controls

It is important to see why taxes on emissions may prove more effective and reliable than direct controls. Direct controls rely on the criminal justice system for enforcement. But a polluter who violates the rules must first be caught. Then the regulatory agency must decide whether it has enough evidence to prosecute. Next, the agency must win its case in court. Finally, the court must impose a penalty strong enough to matter. If any one of these steps does not occur, the polluter gets away with the environmentally damaging activities.

Enforcement Issues   Enforcement of direct controls requires vigilance and enthusiasm by the regulatory agency, which must assign the resources and persons needed to carry out enforcement. However, in many cases the resources devoted to enforcement are pitifully small. The effectiveness of direct controls also depends on the speed and rigor of the court system. Yet the courts are often slow and lenient. In the notorious case of the Reserve Mining Company, more than a decade of litigation was required to stop this company from pouring its wastes (which contain asbestos-like fibers believed to cause cancer) into Lake Superior, the drinking water source for a number of communities.

Finally, direct controls work only if the legal system imposes substantial penalties on violators. In the late 1990s, there were some significant penalties imposed in several cases (for instance, in 1998 Louisiana Pacific Corporation was fined $37 million

Making the Polluter Pay

In the Netherlands, a set of charges originally intended only to cover the costs of wastewater treatment has produced a classic demonstration of the pollution-preventing power of charges themselves. Since 1970, gradually rising fees for emissions of organic material and heavy metals into canals, rivers, and lakes have spurred companies to cut emissions, but without dictating how. Between 1976 and 1994, emissions of cadmium, copper, lead, mercury, and zinc plummeted 86–97 percent, primarily because of the charges, according to statistical analyses. . . . And demand for pollution control equipment has spurred Dutch manufacturers to develop better models, lowering costs and turning the country into a global leader in the market. The taxes have in effect sought the path of least economic resistance—of least cost—in cleaning up the country's waters.

Industrial Discharges of Selected Heavy Metals into Surface Waters of the Netherlands, 1976–1994

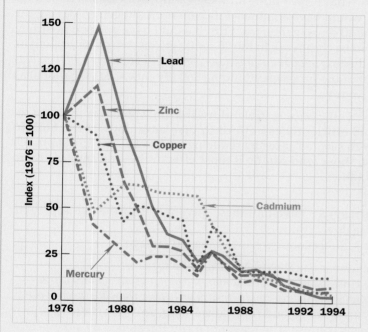

SOURCE: © Hill Creek Picutres/Index Stock Imagery, Inc.

SOURCE: David Malin Roodman, "Getting the Signals Right: Tax Reform to Protect the Environment and the Economy" from Worldwatch Institute, *Worldwatch Paper 134*, 1997, http://www.worldwatch.org. Reprinted by permission.

for violations of the Clean Air Act; and in 1999 Royal Caribbean Cruises Ltd., one of the world's largest cruise lines, agreed to pay $18 million for dumping oil and hazardous chemicals in U.S. waters). In 2007, American Electric Power (AEP) agreed to pay a $15 million civil penalty and a $4.6 billion settlement—the largest of its kind in the history of the Clean Air Act—for failing to install required pollution controls at some of its coal-fired electric power plants. Some polluters have served prison terms for their misdeeds. Much more often, however, large firms have been convicted of polluting and fined amounts beneath the notice of even a relatively small corporation. Spread out over 10 years, AEP's $4.6 billion settlement looks pretty small next to the company's $14.4 billion in revenues in 2008.[6] Under the second Bush administration, environmental fines and the prosecution of polluters fell off significantly.

In contrast, pollution taxes are automatic and certain. No one need be caught, prosecuted, convicted, and punished. The tax bills are sent out automatically by the untiring tax collector. The only sure way for the polluter to avoid paying pollution charges is to pollute less.

[6] "Record-Breaking $4.6 Billion Clean Air Act Settlement Announced," National Resources Defense Council press release, October 9, 2007, accessed online: http://www.nrdc.org/media/2007/071009.asp.

Efficiency in Cleanup   A second important advantage of emissions taxes is that they tend to cost less than direct controls. Statistical estimates for several pollution-control programs suggest that the cost of doing the job through direct controls can easily be twice as high as under the tax alternative. Why should there be such a difference? Under direct controls, emissions cutbacks are usually *not* apportioned among the various firms on the basis of ability to reduce pollution cheaply and efficiently.

Suppose it costs Firm A only 3 cents per gallon to reduce emissions, whereas Firm B must spend 20 cents per gallon to do the same job. If each firm spews out 2,000 gallons of pollution per day, authorities can achieve a 50 percent reduction in pollution by ordering both firms to limit emissions to 1,000 gallons per day. This may or may not be fair, but it is certainly not efficient. The social cost will be 1,000 $\times$ 3 cents (or $30) to Firm A, and 1,000 $\times$ 20 cents (or $200) to Firm B, a total of $230. If the government had instead imposed a tax of 10 cents per gallon, Firm A would have done all the cleanup work by itself, at a far lower total cost. Why? Firm A would have eliminated its emissions altogether, paying the 3 cents/gallon cost to avoid the 10 cents/gallon tax. Firm B would have gone on polluting as before, because the tax would be cheaper than the 20 cents/gallon cost of controlling its pollution. In this way, under the tax, *total daily emissions would still be cut by 2,000 gallons per day*, but the total daily cost of the program would be $60 (3 cents $\times$ 2,000 gallons) as opposed to $230 under direct controls.

The secret of a pollution tax's efficiency is straightforward. Only polluters that can reduce emissions cheaply and efficiently can afford to take advantage of the built-in loophole—the opportunity to save on taxes by reducing emissions. The tax approach therefore assigns the job to those who can do it most effectively—and rewards them by letting them escape the tax.

Advantages and Disadvantages   Given all these advantages of the tax approach, why would anyone want to use direct controls?

In three important situations, direct controls have a clear advantage:

- *Where an emission is so dangerous that it must be prohibited altogether.*
- *Where a sudden change in circumstances—for example, a dangerous air-quality crisis—calls for prompt and substantial changes in conduct, such as temporary reductions in use of cars.* Tax rule changes are difficult and time-consuming, so direct controls will usually do a better job in such a case. The mayor of a city threatened by a dangerous air-quality crisis can, for example, forbid use of private passenger cars until the crisis passes.
- *Where effective and dependable pollution-metering devices have not been invented or are prohibitively costly to install and operate.* In such cases, authorities cannot operate an effective tax program because they cannot determine the emissions levels of an individual polluter and so cannot calculate the tax bill. The only effective option may be to require firms to use "clean" fuel or install emissions-purification equipment.

Another Financial Device to Protect the Environment: Emissions Permits

Emissions permits are licenses issued by government specifying the maximum amount the license holder is allowed to emit. The licenses are restricted to permit a limited amount of emissions in total. Often, they must be purchased from the government or on a special market.

The basic idea underlying the emissions-tax approach to environmental protection is that financial incentives induce polluters to reduce their environmental damage. At least one other form of financial inducement can accomplish the same thing: requiring polluters to buy **emissions permits** that authorize the emission of a specified quantity of pollutant. Such permits can be offered for sale in limited quantities fixed by the government authorities at prices set by demand and supply.

Under this arrangement, the environmental agency decides what quantity of emissions per unit of time (say, per year) is tolerable and then issues a batch of permits authorizing (altogether) just that amount of pollution. The permits are sold to the highest bidders, with the price determined by demand and supply. The price will be high if the number of permits offered for sale is small and many firms need permits to carry out their industrial activities. Similarly, the price of a permit will be low if authorities issue many permits but the quantity of pollution that firms demand is small.

Emissions permits basically work like a tax—they make it too expensive for firms to continue polluting as much as before. However, the permit approach has some advantages over taxes. For example, it reduces *uncertainty* about the *quantity* of pollution that will be emitted. Under a tax, we cannot be sure about this quantity in advance, because it depends on polluters' future response to a given tax rate. In the case of permits, environmental authorities decide on an emissions ceiling in advance, then issue permits authorizing just that amount of emissions. When the U.S. EPA first introduced tradeable emissions permits in 1995, many people were outraged by the notion of such "licenses to pollute." Nowadays, one hears few complaints, because tradeable permit programs have turned out to be such a huge success. One of the best examples is the "acid rain" market for sulfur dioxide permits (in which the main players are the large electricity-generating utility companies). This "cap and trade" program (in which the EPA sets limitations on total SO_2 emissions and issues the number of tradeable permits, called *allowances*, that will keep emissions within those limits) has lowered pollution levels while saving billions of dollars in polluter costs. In 2008, more than 13.9 million SO_2 allowances were traded, the vast majority in private over-the-counter transactions, with the EPA providing online systems of allowance tracking, emissions tracking, and continuous emissions monitoring. The Chicago Board of Trade runs EPA's annual auction of a small percentage of allowances, which generates valuable information about the going price of allowances. These markets are open to anyone, so environmental activists can buy these permits and "retire" them, thereby improving the quality of the air (for example, during the 2004 auction, the Acid Rain Retirement Fund, a Portland, Maine–based nonprofit organization, bought 7 allowances at a price of $2,100; at the same time, Ohio-based American Electric Power bought 75,000 allowances for $20,813,800).[7] (See "EPA's Clean Air Markets" on page 368 for more on the sulfur dioxide market and other programs involving tradeable emissions permits.)

Despite the good news about economic incentives in cap and trade for sulfur dioxide and other pollutants, it must be noted that politics can sometimes interfere with environmental programs. For example, in 2007 the U.S. Supreme Court overturned a Bush administration attempt to relax Clean Air Act rules for aging electric power plants. And, in another decision on the same day (April 2, 2007), the court held that the Clean Air Act gives the U.S. Environmental Protection Agency the power to regulate carbon dioxide and other global-warming pollutants, contrary to arguments by the Bush administration.

TWO CHEERS FOR THE MARKET

In Part 1 of this chapter, we have learned that environmental protection cannot be left to the free market. Because of the large externalities involved, the market will systematically allocate insufficient resources to the job. However, this market failure does not imply that we should disregard the price mechanism. On the contrary, we have seen that a legislated market solution based on pollution charges may often be the best way to protect the environment. At least *in this case, the market mechanism's power can be harnessed to correct its own failings.*

We turn now, in the second part of this chapter, to the issue of natural resources, where the market mechanism also plays a crucial role.

---

[7] Source: http://epa.gov/airmarkets.

EPA's Clean Air Markets

The Environmental Protection Agency's Clean Air Markets let participants in the sulfur dioxide (SO_2) and nitrogen oxide (NO_x) pollution permits markets record trades directly on the internet. A trading unit is called an allowance and is equivalent to one ton of air emissions. EPA's tracking systems record official SO_2 and NO_x allowance transfers under existing emission "cap and trade" programs. Anyone anywhere in the world can participate in the market, and hundreds of companies, brokers, and individuals are already engaged in trading.

Emissions "cap and trade" programs ensure that environmental goals are met (by setting a cap on emissions and allowing polluters to trade allowances among themselves), while providing companies with an alternative to the installation of costly pollution control technologies in complying with the law. This approach was first used nationally by EPA in its acid rain program to reduce SO_2 and then utilized by the northeastern states to reduce NO_x. It has also been used in Southern California to reduce SO_2 and NO_x and in Chicago to reduce volatile organic compounds, the prime ingredient in the formation of ground-level ozone (smog). The cap and trade programs effectively reduce air pollution by setting a permanent cap on emissions, then allowing trading within that cap. As a prerequisite to trading, EPA requires rigorous monitoring and reporting standards, and mandates that companies pay automatic fees to the government for any emissions above the legal limit. Rigorous monitoring is essential to ensuring certainty and consistency in the program and to confirming that each allowance traded represents one ton of emissions, regardless of where it is generated. It is this certainty and consistency that enable creation of a robust market for allowances, free from the need for government review and approval of transactions. EPA emphasizes, however, that no matter how many allowances a utility holds, it will not be permitted to emit amounts of pollutant that would violate the national or state atmospheric (ambient) health-protection standards. Additional cap and trade programs have been proposed by Congress to reduce electricity industry emissions in the United States, and dozens of countries around the world are considering such programs.

SOURCE: © 2002 PhotoDisc

SOURCE: U.S. Environmental Protection Agency, "$20 Billion Emission Trading Market Goes Online," EPA Newsroom, www.epa.gov, December 4, 2001. The Clean Air Markets web site is at http://www.epa.gov/airmarkets.

▪ PART 2: THE ECONOMICS OF NATURAL RESOURCES

Since Fuel is become so expensive, and will of course grow scarcer and dearer; any new Proposal for saving the [fuel] . . . may at least be thought worth Consideration.

BENJAMIN FRANKLIN, 1744

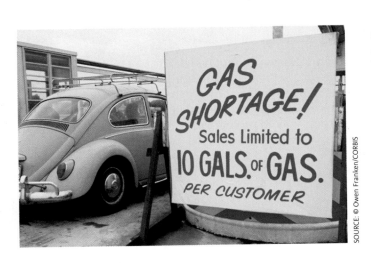

SOURCE: © Owen Franken/CORBIS

One of the most significant forms of environmental damage occurs when we waste natural resources. Earlier in this chapter, we saw that externalities can lead to just this sort of waste—as when governments, individuals, or business firms use up clean air and clean water without cost or penalty. There is a close analytic connection between the economics of environmental protection that we have just investigated and the economics of natural resources, to which we now turn.

More than 30 years ago, the world was rocked by a sudden "energy crisis." Oil prices shot up and consumers found themselves waiting in long lines to buy gasoline. This event had profound effects throughout the world and ended the widespread assumption that the stock of natural resources was unlimited and simply ours for the taking. Indeed, back in the late 1970s and early 1980s, there was near panic about the threatened exhaustion of many natural resources. The front page of a leading magazine even asked, "Are we running out of *everything*?"

Natural resources have always been scarce, and they have often been used wastefully. Nevertheless, we are not about to run out of the most vital resources. In many cases, substitutes are available, and many of the shortages of the 1970s can largely be ascribed to the folly of government programs rather than the imminent exhaustion of natural resources.

ECONOMIC ANALYSIS: THE FREE MARKET AND PRICING OF DEPLETABLE RESOURCES

If statistics on known mineral reserves keep rising as surprisingly as those reported in the puzzle with which this chapter began, we may begin to regard them skeptically and question whether the statistics are wrong or whether we are really not running out of a number of valuable resources, despite their finite supply and their continued use. Is there another indicator of resource depletion that is more reliable? Most economists say there is one—*the price of the resource.*

Scarcity and Rising Prices

According to economic analysis, a better indicator of the degree of depletion of a resource is its price. As a resource becomes scarcer, we expect its price to rise for several reasons. One reason is that we do not deplete a resource simply by gradually using up a homogeneous product, every unit of which is equally available. Rather, we generally use up the most accessible and highest-quality deposits first; only then do we turn to less accessible supplies that are more costly to retrieve or deposits of lower purity or quality. Oil is a clear example. First, Americans relied primarily on the most easily found domestic oil. Then they turned to imports from the Middle East with their higher transport costs. At that point it was not yet profitable to embark on the dangerous and extremely costly process of bringing up oil from the floor of the North Sea. We know that the United States still possesses a tremendous amount of petroleum embedded in shale (rock), but so far this oil has been too difficult and, therefore, too costly to extract.

> **Increasing scarcity of a resource such as oil is not usually a matter of imminent and total disappearance. Rather, it involves exhaustion of the most accessible and cheapest sources so that new supplies become more costly.**

Supply-Demand Analysis and Consumption

Growing scarcity also raises resource prices for the usual supply-demand reason. As we know, goods in short supply tend to become more expensive. To see just how this process works for natural resources, imagine a mythical mineral, "economite," consistent in quality, which has negligible extraction and transportation costs. How quickly will the reserves of this mineral be used up, and what will happen to its price as time passes?

> **The basic law of pricing of a depletable resource tells us that as its stocks are used up, its price in a perfectly competitive market will rise every year by greater and greater dollar amounts.**

Although we can predict the price of economite without knowing anything about its supply or consumer demand for it, we do need to know something about supply and demand to determine what will happen to economite's consumption—the rate at which it will be used up.

The Permanent Fuel Crisis

Humanity has a long history of panicking about the imminent exhaustion of natural resources. In the thirteenth century, a large part of Europe's forests was cut down, primarily for use in metalworking (much of it for armor). Wood prices rose, and there was a good deal of talk about depletion of fuel stocks. People have been doing it ever since, as the accompanying table illustrates.

	Past Petroleum Prophecies (and Realities)		
Date	U.S. Production Rate	Prophecy	Reality
1866	0.005	Synthetics are available if oil production should end. *U.S. Revenue Commission*	In the next 82 years, the U.S. produces 37 billion barrels with no need for synthetics.
1891	0.05	Little or no chance for oil in Kansas or Texas. *U.S. Geological Survey*	Production exceeds 14 billion barrels in these two states since 1891.
1914	0.27	Total future production only 5.7 billion barrels. *Official of U.S. Bureau of Mines*	More than 34 billion barrels produced since 1914, or six times the prediction.
1920	0.45	U.S. needs foreign oil and synthetics; peak domestic production almost reached. *Director, U.S. Geological Survey*	1948 U.S. production exceeds consumption and is more than four times 1920 output.
1939	1.3	U.S. oil supplies will last only 13 years. *Radio Broadcasts by Interior Department*	New oil found since 1939 exceeds the 13 years' supply known at that time.
1947	1.9	Sufficient oil cannot be found in the United States. *Chief of Petroleum Division, State Department*	4.3 billion barrels found in 1948, the largest volume in history and twice U.S. consumption.
1949	2.0	End of U.S. oil supply almost in sight. *Secretary of the Interior*	Recent industry data show ability to increase U.S. production by more than 1 million barrels daily in the next five years.

NOTE: U.S. oil production rate in billions of barrels per year.

SOURCE: William M. Brown, "The Outlook for Future Petroleum Supplies," in Julian L. Simon and Herman Kahn, eds., *The Resourceful Earth: A Response to Global 2000* (Oxford, U.K.: Basil Blackwell; 1984), p. 362, who cite Presidential Energy Program, Hearings before the Subcommittee on Energy and Power of the Committee on Interstate and Foreign Commerce, House of Representatives, 1st session on the implication of the President's proposals in the Energy Independence Act of 1975, Serial No. 94-20, p. 643. February 17, 18, 20, and 21, 1975.

Figure 2(a) is a demand curve for economite, *DD*, which shows the amount people want to use up *per year* at various price levels. On the vertical axis, we show how the price must rise from year to year from $100 per ton in the initial year to $110 per ton in the next year, and so on. Because of the demand curve's negative slope, it follows that consumption of this mineral will fall each year. That is, *if there is no shift in the demand curve, as in Panel (a),* consumption will fall from 100,000 tons initially to 95,000 tons the next year, and so on.

In reality, such demand curves rarely stay still. As the economy grows and population and incomes increase, demand curves shift outward—a pattern that has probably been true for most scarce resources. Such shifts in the demand curve will offset at least part of the reduction in quantity demanded that results from rising prices. Nevertheless, rising prices do cut consumption growth relative to what it would have been if price had remained unchanged. Figure 2(b) depicts an outward shift in demand from curve D_1D_1 in the initial period to curve D_2D_2 a year later. If price had remained constant at the initial value, $100 per ton, quantity consumed per year would have risen from 100,000 tons to 120,000 tons. But because with a given supply curve price must rise, say to $110 per ton, quantity demanded will increase only to 110,000 tons. Thus, whether or not the demand curve shifts, we conclude:

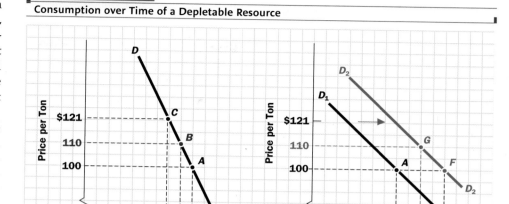

FIGURE 2

Consumption over Time of a Depletable Resource

(a)

(b)

NOTE: Quantity is in thousands of tons per year.

The ever-rising prices accompanying increasing scarcity of a depletable resource discourage consumption (encourage conservation). Even if quantity demanded grows, it will not grow as much as it would if prices were not rising.

ACTUAL RESOURCE PRICES IN THE TWENTIETH CENTURY

How do the facts match up with this theoretical analysis? Not too well, as we will see now. Figure 3 shows the behavior of the prices of three critical metals—lead, zinc, and copper—since the beginning of the twentieth century. This graph shows the prices of these three resources relative to other prices in the economy (in other words, the *real* prices, after adjustment for any inflation or deflation that affected the purchasing power of the dollar).

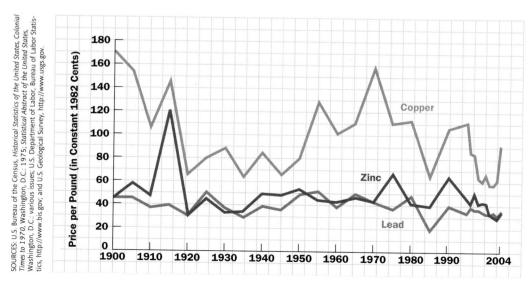

SOURCES: U.S. Bureau of the Census, *Historical Statistics of the United States, Colonial Times to 1970*, Washington, D.C.; 1975; *Statistical Abstract of the United States*, Washington, D.C.: various issues; U.S. Department of Labor, Bureau of Labor Statistics, http://www.bis.gov; and U.S. Geological Survey, http://www.usgs.gov.

FIGURE 3

Prices of Lead, Zinc, and Copper, 1900–2004, in Real (Inflation-Adjusted) Terms

NOTE: Prices are in constant 1982 cents, as deflated by the producer price index for all commodities.

What we find is that instead of rising steadily, as the theory leads us to expect, zinc prices remained amazingly constant, as has the price of lead, even though both minerals are gradually being used up. The price of copper has been all over the map but also has shown no upward trend.

Figure 4 shows the real price of crude oil in the United States since 1948 (again, adjusted for inflation). It gives price at the wellhead—that is, at the point of production—with no transportation cost included. Notice how constant these prices were until the first "energy crisis" in 1973, when oil prices rose precipitously. A second and even more dramatic increase occurred in the late 1970s and early 1980s. After that, real oil prices remained well below their "energy crisis" levels, until 2003, when oil prices increased significantly again. In the summer of 2008, oil prices climbed well above $100 a barrel.[8]

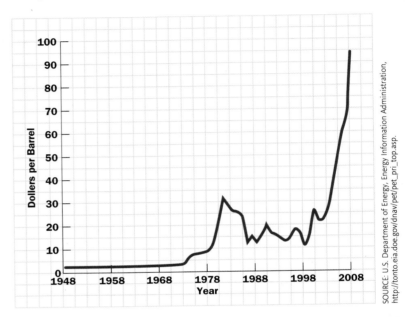

FIGURE 4

Average Price of Domestic Oil at the Wellhead, 1948–2008

SOURCE: U.S. Department of Energy, Energy Information Administration, http://tonto.eia.doe.gov/dnav/pet/pet_pri_top.asp.

Interferences with Price Patterns

How does one explain this strange behavior in the prices of finite resources, which surely are being used up, even if only gradually? Although many things can interfere with price patterns, we will mention only three:

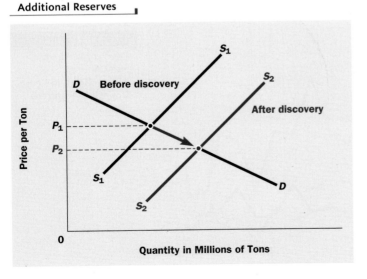

FIGURE 5

Price Effects of a Discovery of Additional Reserves

1. *Discoveries of reserves whose existence was previously not suspected.* If we were to stumble upon a huge and easily accessible reserve of economite, which came as a complete surprise to the market, the price of this mineral would obviously fall. The discovery of the new reserves leads people to recognize that the supply of economite is much larger than previously thought. A rightward shift of the supply curve (from curve S_1S_1 to curve S_2S_2) results, because the suppliers' cost of any given quantity is reduced by the discovery, so it will pay them to supply a larger quantity at any given price. Like any outward shift in a supply curve, this change can be expected to cause a price decrease (from P_1 to P_2).

A clear historical example was the Spaniards' sixteenth-century discovery of gold and silver in Mexico and South America, which led to substantial

---

[8] Jad Mouawad, "Oil Prices Take a Nerve-Rattling Jump Past $138," *The New York Times*, June 7, 2008, accessed online at: http://www.nytimes.com.

drops in European prices of these precious metals. The same effect can result from innovations that use resources more efficiently. *If a new invention doubles the number of miles one can travel on a gallon of gasoline, that is tantamount to doubling the supply of petroleum that still remains in the ground.*

2. *The invention of new methods of mining or refining that may significantly reduce extraction costs.* This development can also lead to a rightward shift in the supply curve, as suppliers become able to deliver a larger quantity at any given price. The situation is therefore again represented by a diagram like Figure 5—only now a reduction in cost, not a new discovery of reserves, shifts the supply curve to the right. (See "Necessity Is the Mother of Invention: Innovation Can Increase Resources" below for a real-world example.)

3. *Price controls that hold prices down or decrease them.* A legislature can pass a law prohibiting the sale of the resource at a price higher than P^* (see Figure 6). Often this strategy doesn't work; in many cases an illegal black market emerges, where suppliers charge very high prices more or less secretly. But when price controls do work, shortages usually follow. Because the objective is to make the legal ceiling price, P^*, lower than the market equilibrium price, P, then at price P^* quantity demanded (5 million tons in the figure) will be higher than the free-market level (4 million tons). Similarly, we may expect quantity supplied (2 million tons in the figure) to be less than its free-market level (again, 4 million tons). Thus, as always happens in these cases, quantity supplied is less than quantity demanded, and a shortage results (measured in Figure 6 by the length of AB, or 3 million tons).

FIGURE 6
Controls on the Price of a Resource

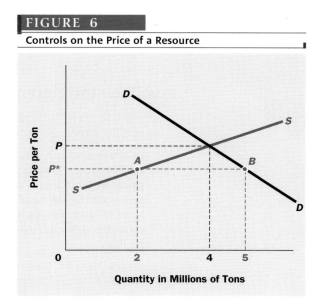

Necessity Is the Mother of Invention: Innovation Can Increase Resources

One study of technological innovation in natural resource industries describes how economic necessity compels firms to search hard for ways to extract resources more efficiently, thereby increasing the available supply:

> The U.S. petroleum industry faced a squeeze between competition from low-cost foreign producers and the upward pressure exerted on costs by the depletion of easily accessible domestic reserves. Under these conditions, it was imperative to develop techniques that would allow exploitation of known reserves at competitive costs. Initial extraction had removed as little as 30 percent of the oil in some abandoned reservoirs. This was largely because traditional vertical drilling methods limited the amount of oil that could be economically removed from reserves with complex structures. With the development of horizontal drilling, it became possible to approach a reservoir from any angle and thus to drain it more thoroughly.

SOURCE: © AP Images

SOURCE: R. David Simpson, ed., *Productivity in Natural Resource Industries: Improvement Through Innovation*, Washington, D.C.: Resources for the Future, 1999, pp. 17–18.

Many economists believe that this is exactly what happened after 1971 when President Nixon decided to experiment with price controls. It was then that the economy experienced a plague of shortages, and we seemed to be "running out of nearly everything." After price controls ended in 1974, most of the shortages disappeared.

We can explain each of our examples of minerals whose price did not rise by one or more of these influences. For example, copper and zinc have benefited from technological changes that lowered their extraction costs. In addition, the development of direct electroplating techniques has made copper production much more efficient. In the case of lead, new mines in Missouri held abundant quantities of ore that were much easier to extract and much cheaper to refine than what had been available before. Obviously, real events are more complex than a naïve reading of theoretical models might lead us to believe.

Is Price Interference Justified?

Despite these influences, if a resource does become scarce and costly to obtain, its price must ultimately rise unless government interferes. Moreover:

> **In a free market, quantity demanded can never exceed quantity supplied, even if a finite resource is undergoing rapid depletion. The reason is simple: In any free market, price will automatically adjust to eliminate any difference between quantity supplied and quantity demanded.**
>
> **In theory, any shortage—any excess of quantity demanded over quantity supplied—must be artificial, ascribable to a decision to prevent the price mechanism from doing its job.**

To say that the cause is artificial, of course, does not settle the basic issue—whether freedom of price adjustments is desirable when resources are scarce, or whether interference with the pricing process is justified.

Many economists believe that this is a case in which the disease—shortages and their resulting economic problems—is far worse than the cure—deregulation of prices. They hold that the general public is misguided in regarding these price rises as the problem, when in fact they are part of the (admittedly rather painful) cure.

It is, of course, easy to understand why no consumer loves a price rise. It is also easy to understand why many consumers attribute any such price increase to a conspiracy by greedy suppliers who somehow deliberately arrange for shortages to force prices upward. Sometimes, this view is even correct. For example, the members of the Organization of Petroleum Exporting Countries (OPEC) have openly and frankly tried to influence the flow of oil in order to increase its price—and have often succeeded. But it is important to recognize from the principles of supply and demand that when a resource grows scarce, its price will tend to rise automatically, even without any conspiracies or plots.

On the Virtues of Rising Prices

Rising prices help to control resource depletion in three basic ways:

- They discourage consumption and waste and provide an inducement for conservation.
- They stimulate more efficient resource use by industry, providing incentives for employment of processes that are more sparing in their use of the resource or that use substitute resources.
- They encourage innovation—the discovery of other, more abundant resources that can serve the same role and of new techniques that permit these other resources to be used economically.

PUZZLE REVISITED: GROWING RESERVES OF EXHAUSTIBLE NATURAL RESOURCES

Earlier we saw, strangely enough, that reserves of many mineral resources have actually been increasing, despite growing world production that uses these resources. This paradox has a straightforward economic explanation: Rising mineral reserves are a tribute to the success of pricing and exploration activity. Minerals are not discovered by accident. Rather, exploration and discovery entail costly work requiring geologists, engineers, and expensive machinery. Industry does not consider this money worth spending when reserves are high and mineral prices are low.

In the twentieth century, every time some mineral's known reserves fell and its price tended to rise, exploration increased until the decline was offset. The law of supply and demand worked. In the 1970s, for example, the rising price of oil led to very substantial increases in oil exploration, which helped to build up reserves. Although, to protect ourselves from OPEC, it may not be wise for us to *consume* more oil from American sources, it certainly does seem prudent for us to increase our reserves through exploration. Increased profitability of exploration is perhaps the most effective way to achieve that goal.

| SUMMARY |

1. Pollution is as old as human history. Contrary to popular notions, some forms of pollution were actually decreasing even before government programs were initiated to protect the environment.

2. Both planned and market economies suffer from substantial environmental problems.

3. The production of commodities *must* cause waste disposal problems unless everything is recycled, but even recycling processes cause pollution (and use up energy).

4. Industrial activity causes environmental damage, but so does the activity of private individuals (as when people drive cars that emit pollutants). Government agencies also damage the environment (as when military airplanes emit noise and exhaust fumes or a hydroelectric project floods large areas).

5. Pollution is an **externality**—when a factory emits smoke, it dirties the air in nearby neighborhoods and may damage the health of persons who neither work for the factory nor buy its products. Hence, the public interest in pollution control is not best served by the free market. This conclusion is another of our *Ideas for Beyond the Final Exam.*

6. Pollution can be controlled by voluntary programs, **direct controls, pollution charges** (taxes on emissions), or other monetary incentives for emissions reduction.

7. Most economists believe that the monetary incentives approach is the most efficient and effective way to control damaging externalities.

8. The quantity demanded of a scarce resource can exceed the quantity supplied only if something prevents the market mechanism from operating freely.

9. As a resource grows scarce on a free market, its price will rise, inducing increased conservation by consumers, increased exploration for new reserves, and increased substitution of other items that can serve the same purpose.

10. In the twentieth century, the relative prices of many resources remained roughly constant, largely because of the discovery of new reserves and cost-saving innovations.

11. In the 1970s, OPEC succeeded in raising petroleum's relative price, but the price increase led to a substantial decline in world demand as well as to an increase in production in countries outside OPEC.

12. *Known reserves* of depletable scarce resources have not tended to fall with time, because as the price of the resource rises with increasing scarcity, increased exploration for new reserves becomes profitable.

| KEY TERMS |

direct controls   364

emissions permits   366

externality   356

pollution charges (taxes on emissions)   364

| TEST YOURSELF |

1. Production of Commodity X creates 10 pounds of emissions for every unit of X produced. The demand and supply curves for X are described by the following table:

Price	Quantity Demanded	Quantity Supplied
$10	80	100
9	85	95
8	90	90
7	95	85
6	100	80
5	105	75

What is the equilibrium price and quantity, and how much pollution will be emitted?

2. Using the data in Test Yourself Question 1, if the price of X to consumers is $9, and the government imposes a tax of $2 per unit, show that because suppliers get only $7, they will produce only 85 units of output, not the 95 units of output they would produce if they received the full $9 per unit.

3. With the tax described in Test Yourself Question 2, how much pollution will be emitted?

4. Compare your answers to Test Yourself Questions 1 and 3 and show how large a reduction in pollution emissions occurs because of the $2 tax on the polluting output.

| DISCUSSION QUESTIONS |

1. What sorts of pollution problems would you expect in a small African village? In a city in India? In the People's Republic of China? In New York City?

2. Suppose you are assigned the task of drafting a law to impose a tax on smoke emissions. What provisions would you put into the law?

   a. How would you decide the size of the tax?

   b. What would you do about smoke emitted by a municipal electricity plant?

   c. Would you use the same tax rate in densely and sparsely settled areas?

   What information will you need to collect before determining what you would do about each of the preceding provisions?

3. Discuss some valid and some invalid objections to letting rising prices eliminate shortages of supplies of scarce resources.

4. Why may an increase in fuel prices lead to more conservation after several years have passed than it does in the months following the price increase? What does your answer imply about the relative sizes of the long-run and short-run elasticity of demand for fuel?

TAXATION AND RESOURCE ALLOCATION

The taxing power of the government must be used to provide revenues for legitimate government purposes. It must not be used to regulate the economy or bring about social change.

RONALD REAGAN

"Nothing is certain but death and taxes," proclaims an old adage. In recent decades, American politics seems to have turned this aphorism on its head. It seems that the surest route to political death is to raise taxes—and the surest route to winning elections is to cut them.

Tax-cutting fever first swept the nation during the presidency of Ronald Reagan, who won two landslide elections. After pledging not to raise taxes, President George Bush (the first) agreed to some small tax increases in 1990—a decision that some think cost him the 1992 election. Next came President Bill Clinton, who made income-tax increases for upper-income taxpayers a major component of his deficit-reduction plan in 1993. The next year, the Democrats were annihilated at the polls by a Republican party pledging to cut taxes. Clinton won reelection in 1996 anyway. But President George Bush (the second) defeated Al Gore in 2000 partly on the basis of his promise to cut taxes, and then won reelection in 2004 partly because John Kerry, like Clinton, proposed to repeal part of the Bush tax cuts. During the 2008 campaign, whether or not to extend the Bush tax cuts was a hot political issue once again. The Democratic candidate, Barack Obama, pledged to roll back some of the tax cuts, but Republican John McCain campaigned not only on extending the Bush tax cuts, but on adding still more. As this book goes to press, it appears that President Obama and the Democratically-controlled congress will let many of the Bush tax cuts expire at the end of 2010, but no one knows for sure.

Antitax sentiment is nothing new in the United States, a country that was born partly out of a tax revolt. But taxes are inevitable in any modern, mixed economy. Although the vast majority of economic activities in the United States are left to the private sector, some—such as provision of national defense and highways—are reserved for the government. And any such government spending requires tax revenues to pay the bills. So do transfer programs such as Social Security and unemployment insurance.

In addition, the government sometimes uses the tax system to promote some social goal. For example, we learned in the previous chapter that policy makers can use taxes to correct misallocations of resources caused by externalities, including those that contribute to global climate change.

CONTENTS

This chapter discusses the types of taxes that are used to raise what President Reagan called "revenues for legitimate government purposes," the effects of taxes on resource allocation and income distribution, and the principles that distinguish "good" taxes from "bad" ones.

ISSUE:	SHOULD THE BUSH TAX CUTS BE (PARTLY) REPEALED?

 President George W. Bush was one of the biggest tax cutters in U.S. history. He proposed, and Congress passed, tax cuts in 2001, 2002, and 2003. These bills reduced personal income-tax rates substantially, phased out the estate tax, and created a preferentially low tax rate on dividends—among other things. However, the legislation made most of the tax cuts temporary (with different "sunset" years), so they will expire in 2010 unless Congress explicitly reenacts them. Probably for that reason, repeal or extension of the Bush tax cuts became an issue in the 2008 presidential campaign and still is.

The Bush tax cuts have been controversial since their inception. Supporters, including most Republicans, credit them with the economy's rapid growth in 2003 and 2004 and argue that they should be made permanent. Critics, including most Democrats, blame the tax cuts for ballooning the federal budget deficit and suggest that the tax cuts for upper-income households should be repealed because the nation cannot afford them.

In this chapter, you will learn the principles by which tax systems are judged. Then we will apply those principles to appraising the Bush tax cuts.

THE LEVEL AND TYPES OF TAXATION

Many Americans believe that taxes have been gobbling up an ever-increasing share of the U.S. economy. Figure 1, however, shows that this supposition is not true. By charting the behavior of both federal and state and local taxes *as a percentage of gross domestic product (GDP)* since 1929, we see that the share of federal taxes in GDP was rather steady from the early 1950s until around 2000. It climbed from less than 4 percent in 1929 to 20 percent during World War II, fell back to 15 percent in the immediate postwar period, and fluctuated mainly in the 18 to 21 percent range until the Bush tax cuts pushed it down below 17 percent. More recently, it has rebounded back into the 18–19 percent range.

The share of GDP taken by state and local taxes climbed substantially from World War II until the early 1970s. But since then it, too, has remained remarkably stable—at about 10 to 11 percent. Whether these shares are too high or too low is a matter of some debate. In any event,

The shares of GDP taken in taxes by the federal, state, and local governments have been approximately constant for about 40 years.

Americans have always felt that taxes are both too many and too high. Sometimes it seems that the tax collector is everywhere. We have income and payroll taxes deducted from our paychecks, sales taxes added to our purchases, and property taxes levied on our homes. We pay gasoline taxes, liquor taxes, cigarette taxes, and telephone taxes. Not surprisingly, tax cuts are more popular politically than are tax increases. Yet, as we noted in Chapter 2, by international standards Americans are among the most lightly taxed people in the world. (See Figure 13 of Chapter 2, on page 35.)

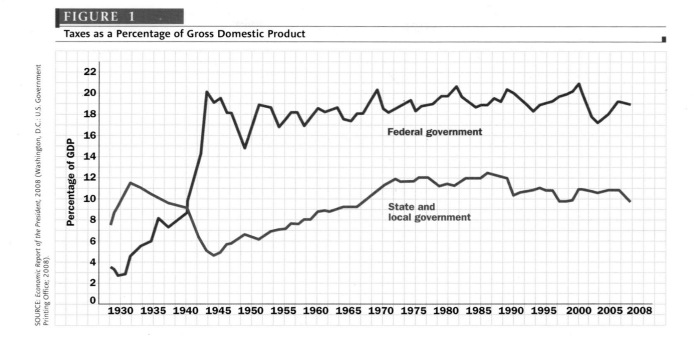

FIGURE 1

Taxes as a Percentage of Gross Domestic Product

SOURCE: *Economic Report of the President, 2008* (Washington, D.C.: U.S. Government Printing Office, 2008).

Progressive, Proportional, and Regressive Taxes

Economists classify taxes as progressive, proportional, or regressive. Under a **progressive tax** like the personal income tax, the fraction of income paid in taxes rises as a person's income increases. Under a **proportional tax** like the payroll tax, this fraction is constant. Under a **regressive tax** like the notorious *head tax,* which charges every person the same amount, the fraction of income paid to the tax collector *declines* as income rises.[1] Because the fraction of income paid in taxes is called the **average tax rate,** we can reformulate these definitions as they appear in the margin.

Often, however, the average tax rate is less interesting than the **marginal tax rate,** which is the fraction of each *additional* dollar that is paid to the tax collector. The reason, as we will see, is that the *marginal* tax rate, not the *average* tax rate, most directly affects economic incentives. Those who advocate tax cuts emphasize the virtues of low *marginal* rates.

Direct versus Indirect Taxes

Another way to classify taxes is to categorize them as either **direct taxes** or **indirect taxes.** Direct taxes are levied directly on *people;* primary examples are *income taxes* and *estate taxes.* In contrast, indirect taxes are levied on particular activities, such as buying cigarettes, gasoline, or using the telephone. But, of course, people ultimately pay them—hence the name, "indirect" taxes.

The federal government raises revenues mainly by direct taxes, whereas states and localities rely more heavily on indirect taxes. *Sales taxes* and *property taxes* are the most important indirect taxes in the United States, although many other countries, including the members of the European Union (EU), rely heavily on the *value-added tax (VAT)*—a tax that has often been discussed, but never adopted, in the United States.

THE FEDERAL TAX SYSTEM

The **personal income tax** is the biggest source of revenue to the federal government. Few people realize that the payroll tax—a tax levied on wages and salaries up to a certain limit

A **progressive tax** is one in which the average tax rate paid by an individual rises as income rises.

A **proportional tax** is one in which the average tax rate is the same at all income levels.

A **regressive tax** is one in which the average tax rate falls as income rises.

The **average tax rate** is the ratio of taxes to income.

The **marginal tax rate** is the fraction of each *additional* dollar of income that is paid in taxes.

Direct taxes are taxes levied directly on people.

Indirect taxes are taxes levied on specific economic activities.

The **personal income tax** is a tax levied on the income of an individual or a family, typically with a progressive rate structure.

---

[1] In 1990, Prime Minister Margaret Thatcher caused riots in the United Kingdom by instituting a head tax.

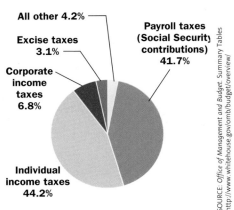

All other 4.2%

Excise taxes
3.1%

Corporate
income
taxes
6.8%

Payroll taxes
(Social Security
contributions)
41.7%

Individual
income taxes
44.2%

SOURCE: Office of Management and Budget, Summary Tables
http://www.whitehouse.gov/omb/budget/overview/

FIGURE 2

Sources of Federal
Revenue

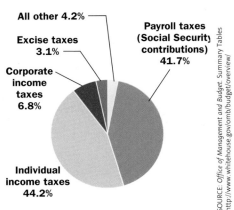

SOURCE: © The New Yorker
Collection 1986, Mick Stevens
From cartoonbank.com. All
Rights Reserved.

TABLE 1

Federal Personal Income Tax Rates in 2008
for a Married Couple Filing Jointly

Taxable Income	Tax	Average Tax Rate	Marginal Tax Rate
$ 10,000	$ 1,000	10.0%	10.0%
25,000	2,919	11.7	15.0
50,000	6,669	13.3	15.0
100,000	17,375	17.4	25.0
150,000	30,264	20.2	28.0
250,000	60,322	24.1	33.0
1,000,000	320,363	32.0	35.0

A **tax loophole** is a special provision in the tax code that reduces taxation below normal rates (perhaps to zero) if certain conditions are met.

A particular source of income is **tax exempt** if income from that source is not taxable.

A **tax deduction** is a sum of money that may be subtracted before the taxpayer computes taxable income.

and paid by employers and employees—is the next biggest source. Furthermore, payroll taxes have been growing more rapidly than income taxes for decades. In 1960, payroll tax collections were just 36 percent as large as personal income-tax collections; in the recessionary economy of 2009, this figure reached almost 95 percent. In fact, most Americans today pay more in payroll taxes than they do in income taxes.

The rest of the federal government's revenues come mostly from the *corporate income tax* and from various excise (sales) taxes. Figure 2 shows the breakdown of federal revenues for the fiscal year 2009 budget. Let us now look at these taxes in more detail.

The Federal Personal Income Tax

The tax on individual incomes traces its origins to the Sixteenth Amendment to the U.S. Constitution in 1913, but it remained inconsequential until the beginning of World War II. Washington then raised the tax substantially to finance the war, and it has been the major source of federal revenue ever since.

Many taxpayers have little or no additional tax to pay when the April 15 day of reckoning comes around, because employers *withhold* income taxes from payrolls and forward those funds to the U.S. Treasury. In fact, many taxpayers are "overwithheld" during the year and receive refund checks from Uncle Sam. Nevertheless, most taxpayers (including the authors of this book!) dread the arrival of their Form 1040 because of its legendary complexity.

The personal income tax is *progressive.* That fact is evident in Table 1, which shows that average tax rates rise as income rises. Ignoring a few complications, the current tax law has six basic marginal rates, each of which applies within a specific tax bracket. As income rises above certain points, the marginal tax rate increases from 10 percent to 15 percent, then to 25 percent, 28 percent, and then finally to 33 percent and 35 percent on very high incomes (more than about $370,000 of taxable income for a married couple).

Actually, the income tax is less progressive than it seems because of a variety of **tax loopholes.** Let us examine a few major ones.

Tax-Exempt Status of Municipal Bond Interest   To help state and local governments and certain public authorities raise funds, Congress has made interest on their bonds **tax exempt** under the federal income tax. Whether or not it was Congress's intent, this provision has turned out to be one of the biggest loopholes for the very rich, who invest much of their wealth in tax-free municipal bonds. Such tax-conscious investing has long been the principal reason why some multimillionaires pay so little income tax.

Tax Benefits for Homeowners   Among the sacred cows of the U.S. income-tax system is the deductibility of payments that homeowners make for mortgage interest and property taxes. These **tax deductions** substantially reduce homeowners' tax bills and give them preferential treatment compared to renters. Clearly, Congress's intent is to encourage home ownership. However, because homeowners are, on the average, richer than renters, this loophole also erodes the progressivity of the income tax.

Why call this a "loophole," when other interest expenses and taxes (such as those paid by shopkeepers, for example) are considered legitimate deductions? The answer is that, unlike shopkeepers, homeowners do not pay taxes on the income they earn by incurring these expenses. The reason is that the "income" from owning a home accrues not in cash, but in the form of living rent-free.

An example will illustrate the point. Jack and Jill are neighbors. Each earns $60,000 per year and lives in a $200,000 house. The difference is that Jack owns his home, whereas Jill rents. Most observers would agree that Jack and Jill *should* pay the same income tax. Will they? Suppose Jack pays $4,000 per year in local property taxes and has a $160,000 mortgage at an 8 percent interest rate, which costs him $12,800 per year in interest. Both property taxes and mortgage interest are tax deductible, so he gets to deduct $16,800 in housing expenses, but Jill, who may pay $16,800 per year in rent, does not. Thus, Jill's tax burden is higher than Jack's.

We could go on listing more tax loopholes, but enough has been said to illustrate the main point:

Every tax loophole encourages particular patterns of behavior and favors particular types of people. Furthermore, because most loopholes mainly benefit the rich, they erode the progressivity of the income tax.

The Payroll Tax

The second most important tax in the United States is the **payroll tax,** the proceeds of which are earmarked to be paid into various "trust funds." These funds, in turn, are used mainly to pay for Social Security, Medicare, and unemployment benefits. The payroll tax is levied at a fixed percentage rate (now about 16 percent), shared about equally between employees and employers. For example, a firm paying an employee a gross monthly wage of $5,000 will deduct $400 (8 percent of $5,000) from that worker's check, add an additional $400 of its own funds, and send the $800 to the government.

On the surface, this tax seems to be *proportional,* but it is actually highly *regressive,* for two reasons. First, only wages and salaries are subject to the tax; interest and dividends are not. Second, because Social Security benefits are subject to upper limits, earnings above a certain level (which changes each year) are exempt from the Social Security tax. In 2009, this level was $106,800 per year. Above this limit, the *marginal payroll tax rate* is zero.[2]

> The **payroll tax** is a tax levied on the earnings from work. In the United States, the tax starts at the first dollar earned and ends at an upper limit that increases each year.

The Corporate Income Tax

The tax on corporate profits is also considered a "direct" tax, because corporations are fictitious "people" in the eyes of the law. All large corporations currently pay a basic marginal tax rate of 35 percent. (Firms with smaller profits pay a lower rate.) Because the tax applies only to *profits*—not to income—all wages, rents, and interest paid by corporations are deducted before the tax is applied. Since World War II, corporate income-tax collections have accounted for a declining share of federal revenue. But the low corporate profits of recent years shrank this share to under 7 percent in 2009.

> The **corporate income tax** is a tax levied on the profits of corporations, after all expenditures on wages, interest, rent, and purchases of other inputs are deducted.

Excise Taxes

An **excise tax** is a sales tax on the purchase of a particular good or service. Although sales taxes are mainly reserved for state and local governments in the United States, the federal government does levy excise taxes on a hodgepodge of miscellaneous goods and services, including cigarettes, alcoholic beverages, gasoline, and tires.

Although these taxes constitute a minor source of federal government revenue, raising revenue is not their only goal. Some taxes seek to discourage consumption of a good by raising its price. For example, there are steep excise taxes on cigarettes and alcoholic beverages, but their main purpose is not to raise revenue. The clear intent is to discourage smoking and drinking.

> An **excise tax** is a tax levied on the purchase of some specific good or service.

The Payroll Tax and the Social Security System

In government statistical documents, payroll taxes are euphemistically called "contributions for social insurance," although these "contributions" are far from voluntary. The term signifies the fact that, unlike other taxes, the proceeds from this particular tax are set aside in "trust funds" to pay benefits to Social Security recipients and others.

> The **Social Security System** raises funds from the payroll tax and pays Social Security benefits to retirees.

---

[2] However, the portion of the payroll tax that pays for Medicare is applied to all earnings, without limit.

POLICY DEBATE

PRIVATIZING SOCIAL SECURITY

According to the government's long-range projections, Social Security benefits that have already been promised exceed expected future payroll tax receipts by a wide margin. Thus, although Social Security faces no immediate financial problem, something must be done eventually to put the system on a sound financial footing.

You don't have to be an actuary to see that some combination of higher payroll taxes (or some other revenue source) and lower Social Security benefits will be needed to do the job. But both alternatives are politically unpalatable. This dilemma led President Bush to suggest another way out: *privatizing* part of the Social Security System.

What does that mean? Simply that some portion of current payroll taxes would be diverted away from the Social Security trust fund and directed into private investment

SOURCE: © AP Images

accounts, owned and controlled by individual workers. The idea is that these private accounts would earn higher returns than the Social Security trust fund, which invests all of its money in U.S. government bonds. If so, the private accounts would grow rapidly, relieving the trust fund of some of the burden of paying future benefits. But critics worry that many individuals would not be wise investors.

After his reelection in 2004, President Bush presented his own specific privatization plan and began to press for it. But Congress would have none of it, even though it was then dominated by Republicans. In the 2008 campaign, most Democrats made a point of opposing privatization, and few Republicans supported it with any vigor. It looks like Social Security privatization is dead for now.

The standard notion of a trust fund does not apply. Some private pension plans *are* trust funds. You pay money into them while you are working, the trustees invest those savings for you, and you withdraw it bit by bit in your retirement years. The Social Security system does *not* function that way. For most of its history, the system has simply taken the payroll tax payments of current workers and handed them over to current retirees. The benefit checks that your grandparents receive each month are not, in any real sense, dividends on the investments they made while they worked. Instead, these checks are paid out of the payroll taxes that your parents (or you) pay each month.

For many years, this "pay-as-you-go" system managed to give every generation of retirees more in benefits than it had contributed in payroll taxes. Social Security "contributions" were, indeed, a good investment. How was this miracle achieved? It relied heavily on growth—both population growth and wage growth. As long as the population grows, there are more and more young people to tax. Similarly, as long as real wages keep rising, the same payroll tax *rates* permit the government to pay benefits to each generation in excess of that generation's contributions. Ten percent of today's average real wage, after all, is a good deal more than 10 percent of the real wages your grandfather earned 50 years ago.

Unfortunately, the growth magic stopped working in the 1970s, for several reasons. First, growth in real wages slowed dramatically, while Social Security benefits continued to grow rapidly. As a result, the burden of financing Social Security grew more onerous.

Second, population growth slowed significantly in the United States. Birthrates in this country were very high from the close of World War II until about 1960 (the postwar baby boom) and fell thereafter. As a result, the fraction of the U.S. population that is older than age 65 has climbed from only 7.5 percent in 1945 to over 12.5 percent today, and it is certain to go much higher in the coming decades as baby boomers retire. Thus, there are fewer working people available to support each retired person.

Third, life expectancy keeps rising while the average retirement age keeps falling. These facts are undoubtedly good news for Americans, but they are bad news for the financial health of the Social Security system. The reason is simple: As people live longer and retire younger, they spend more and more years in retirement. When Congress set the normal Social Security retirement age at 65, many Americans did not live that long. Nowadays most do, and many live 20 years or more beyond retirement.

With the growth magic over and the long-run funding of Social Security clearly at risk in 1983, Congress trimmed Social Security benefits (mainly by raising the normal retirement age to 67 in stages) and increased payroll taxes to shore up the system's finances. Furthermore, Social Security abandoned its tradition of pay-as-you-go financing. Congress decided instead to start accumulating funds *in advance* so that the Social Security Administration would be able to pay the baby boomers' retirement benefits.

Since then, the trust fund has taken in more money than it has paid out. The Social Security surplus is now running at about $180 billion per year. If current projections of population, real wages, and retirement behavior prove reasonably accurate, these annual surpluses will accumulate into a huge trust fund balance in a few more years and then start to be drawn down. Unfortunately, the long-run funding problem has not been solved, for those same projections show the trust fund running out of money by about 2037. It is therefore clear that some combination of lower Social Security benefits and higher payroll taxes looms on the long-run horizon, unless some way is found to inject more money into the system. (See the box "Privatizing Social Security" on the previous page.)

THE STATE AND LOCAL TAX SYSTEM

Indirect taxes are the backbone of state and local government revenues, although most states also levy income taxes. *Sales taxes* are the principal source of revenue to the states, whereas cities and towns rely heavily on *property taxes*. Figure 3 shows the breakdown of state and local government receipts by source.

Sales and Excise Taxes

These days, all but five states, many large cities, and a few counties levy broad-based sales taxes on purchases of goods and services, with certain specific exemptions. For example, food is exempted from sales tax in many states. Overall sales tax rates typically run in the 5 to 8 percent range. In addition, most states impose special excise taxes on such things as tobacco products, liquor, gasoline, and luxury items.

Property Taxes

Municipalities raise revenue by taxing properties, such as houses and office buildings. Educational and religious institutions are normally exempt from these **property tax** levies. The usual procedure is to *assess* each taxable property based on its market value and then to place a tax rate on the community's total assessed value that yields enough revenue to cover expenditures on local services. Property taxes generally run between 1 and 3 percent of true market value.

Considerable political controversy has surrounded the property tax for years. Because local property taxes provide the main source of financing for public schools, wealthy communities with expensive real estate are able to afford higher-quality schools than poor communities. A simple arithmetical example will clarify why. Suppose real estate holdings in Richtown average $300,000 per family, whereas real estate holdings in Poortown average only $100,000 per family. If both towns levy a 2 percent property tax to pay for their schools, Richtown will generate $6,000 per family in tax receipts, but Poortown will generate only $2,000.

Glaring inequalities like this have led courts in many states to declare unconstitutional the financing of public schools by local property taxes, because doing so deprives children in poorer districts of an equal opportunity to receive high-quality education. These legal

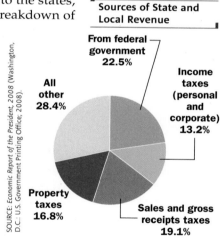

FIGURE 3

Sources of State and Local Revenue

From federal government 22.5%

Income taxes (personal and corporate) 13.2%

All other 28.4%

Property taxes 16.8%

Sales and gross receipts taxes 19.1%

SOURCE: *Economic Report of the President, 2008* (Washington, D.C.: U.S. Government Printing Office, 2008).

The **property tax** is levied on the assessed values of taxable properties, such as houses and office buildings.

decisions, in turn, have created considerable political turmoil as state legislatures scrambled to find ways to fund their schools while complying with court rulings. Many states have been grappling with this problem for years.

Fiscal Federalism

Figure 3 points out an interesting fact: Grants from the federal government are a major source of revenue to state and local governments. In addition, grants from the states are vital to local governments. This system of transfers from one level of government to the next, which has a long history, is referred to as **fiscal federalism.**

Aid from this source has come traditionally in the form of *restricted grants*—that is, money given from one level of government to the next on the condition that it be spent for a specific purpose. For example, the U.S. government may grant funds to a state *if* that state promises to use the money to build highways. Alternatively a state government may give money to a school district to spend on a specific educational program.

The system of grants from the federal government to the states has often been the subject of political controversy. Supporters of large grants see state governments as more flexible and closer to the people. They also view the states as "laboratories of democracy," where creative solutions to make government more efficient can be developed. Critics of grant programs argue that the history of state governments gives little reason to see them as efficient providers of public services. These people worry that minimum national standards in welfare and health care might be sacrificed as states husband their limited financial resources.

> **Fiscal federalism** refers to the system of grants from one level of government to the next.

THE CONCEPT OF EQUITY IN TAXATION

Taxes are judged on two criteria: *equity* (Is the tax fair?) and *efficiency* (Does the tax interfere with the workings of the market economy?). Although economists are mostly concerned with the second criterion, public discussions about tax proposals focus almost exclusively on the first. Let us, therefore, begin our discussion by investigating the concept of equitable taxation.

Horizontal Equity

There are three distinct concepts of tax equity. The first, **horizontal equity,** simply asserts that *equally situated individuals should be taxed equally*. Few would quarrel with this principle. Because it is often difficult to apply in practice, violations of horizontal equity can be found throughout the tax code.

Consider, for example, the personal income tax. Horizontal equity calls for two families with the same income to pay the same tax. But what if one family has eight children and the other has none? Well, you answer, we must define "equally situated" to include equal family sizes, so only families with the same number of children can be compared on grounds of horizontal equity. But what if one family has unusually high medical expenses and the other has none? Are they still "equally situated"? By now, the point should be clear: Determining when two families are equally situated is no simple task. In fact, the U.S. tax code contains literally scores of requirements that must be met before two families are construed as equal.

> **Horizontal equity** is the notion that equally situated individuals should be taxed equally.

Vertical Equity

The second concept of fair taxation seems to flow naturally from the first. If equals are to be treated equally, it appears that *unequals should be treated unequally*. This precept is known as **vertical equity.**

Just saying this does not get us very far, however, because vertical equity is a slippery concept. Often it is translated into the **ability-to-pay principle,** which states that *those*

> **Vertical equity** refers to the notion that differently situated individuals should be taxed differently in a way that society deems to be fair.

> The **ability-to-pay principle** of taxation refers to the idea that people with greater ability to pay taxes should pay higher taxes.

most able to pay should pay the highest taxes. Unfortunately, this principle still leaves a definitional problem similar to the problem of defining "equally situated": How do we measure ability to pay? The nature of each tax often provides a straightforward answer. In income taxation, we measure ability to pay by income; in property taxation, we measure it by property value; and so on.

But an even thornier problem arises when we try to translate this concept into concrete terms. Consider the three alternative income-tax plans listed in Table 2. Families with higher incomes pay higher taxes under all three plans, so each plan can claim to follow the ability-to-pay principle. Yet the three have radically different distributive consequences. Plan 1 is a progressive tax, like the individual income

TABLE 2						
Three Alternative Income-Tax Plans						
	Plan 1		Plan 2		Plan 3	
Income	Tax	Average Tax Rate	Tax	Average Tax Rate	Tax	Average Tax Rate
$10,000	$ 300	3%	$1,000	10%	$1,000	10%
50,000	8,000	16	5,000	10	3,000	6
250,000	70,000	28	25,000	10	7,500	3

tax in the United States: The average tax rate is higher for richer families. Plan 2 is a proportional tax: Every family pays 10 percent of its income. Plan 3 is regressive: Because tax payments rise more slowly than income, the average tax rate for richer families is lower than that for poorer families.

Which plan comes closest to the ideal notion of vertical equity? Many people find that Plan 3, the regressive tax, offends their sense of fairness. People agree much less over the relative merits of progressive versus proportional taxes. Some people take the notion of vertical equity to be synonymous with progressivity. Other things being equal, progressive taxes are seen as "good" taxes in some ethical sense, whereas regressive taxes are seen as "bad." On these grounds, advocates of greater equality support progressive income taxes and oppose regressive sales taxes. But other people disagree and find proportional taxes to be "fair."

The Benefits Principle

Whereas the principles of horizontal and vertical equity, for all their ambiguities and practical problems, at least do not conflict with one another, the final principle of fair taxation often violates commonly accepted notions of vertical equity. According to the **benefits principle of taxation,** those who reap the benefits from government services should pay the taxes.

The benefits principle is often used to justify earmarking the proceeds from certain taxes for specific public services. For example, receipts from gasoline taxes typically go to finance construction and maintenance of roads. Thus, those who use the roads pay the taxes—and roughly in proportion to their usage. Most people seem to find this system fair. But in other contexts—such as public schools and hospitals—the body politic has been loath to apply the benefits principle because it clashes so dramatically with common notions of fairness. (Should sick people pay for public hospitals?) So most public services are financed out of general tax revenues rather than by direct charges for their use.

The **benefits principle of taxation** holds that people who derive benefits from a service should pay the taxes that finance it.

THE CONCEPT OF EFFICIENCY IN TAXATION

Economic efficiency is among the most central concepts of economics. The economy is said to be efficient if it has used every available opportunity to make someone better off without making anyone else worse off. In this sense, taxes almost always introduce *inefficiencies.* That is, if the tax were removed, some people could be made better off without anyone being harmed.

However, that is not a terribly pertinent comparison. The government does, after all, need revenue to pay for the services it provides. So, when economists discuss the notion of "efficient" taxation, they are usually seeking taxes that cause the *least amount of inefficiency for a given amount of tax revenue.* Or, in the more colorful words of Jean-Baptiste Colbert, treasurer to King Louis IV of France, "The art of taxation consists in so plucking the goose to obtain the largest amount of feathers, with the least possible amount of hissing."

To explain the concept of efficient taxation, we need to introduce a new term. Economists define the **burden of a tax** as the amount the taxpayer would have to be given to be just as well off in the presence of the tax as in its absence. An example will clarify this notion and also make clear why:

The **burden of a tax** to an individual is the amount one would have to be given to be just as well off with the tax as without it.

The burden of a tax normally exceeds the revenue raised by the tax.

Suppose the government, in the interest of energy conservation, levies a high tax on the biggest gas-guzzling cars, with progressively lower taxes on smaller cars.[3] For example, a simple tax schedule might be the following:

Car Type	Tax
Hummer	$1,000
Chrysler 300	500
Toyota Prius	0

Harry has a taste for big SUVs and has recently been buying Hummers. Once the new tax takes effect, he has three options: He can still buy a Hummer and pay $1,000 in tax; he can switch to a Chrysler 300 and avoid half the tax; or he can switch to the hybrid Toyota Prius and avoid the entire tax.

If Harry sticks with the Hummer, we have a case in which the burden of the tax is exactly equal to the tax he pays. Why? Because if someone gave Harry $1,000, he would be in exactly the same position as he was before the tax was enacted. In general:

When a tax induces no change in economic behavior, the burden of the tax is measured accurately by the revenue collected.

However, this result is not what we normally expect to happen, and it is certainly not what the government intends by levying a tax on gas-guzzling vehicles. Normally, we expect taxes to induce some people to alter their behavior in ways that reduce or avoid tax payments. So let us look into Harry's other two options.

If Harry decides to purchase a Chrysler, he pays only $500 in tax, but that $500 *understates* his burden. If we give Harry $500, his tax bill will be covered, but he will still be chagrined by the fact that he no longer drives a Hummer. How much money would it take to make Harry just as well off as he was before the tax? Only Harry knows for sure, but we do know that it is more than the $500 tax that he pays. Whatever that (unknown) amount is, the amount by which it exceeds the $500 tax bill is called the **excess burden** of the tax.

The **excess burden** of a tax to an individual is the amount by which the burden of the tax exceeds the tax that is paid.

Harry's final option makes the importance of understanding excess burden even more clear. If he switches to a Prius, Harry will pay no tax. Are we therefore to say he has suffered no burden? Clearly not, for he longs for the Hummer that he no longer drives. The general principle is

Whenever a tax induces people to change their behavior—that is, whenever it "distorts" their choices—the tax has an *excess burden*. In such a case, the revenue collected systematically understates the true burden of the tax.

The excess burdens that arise from tax-induced changes in economic behavior are precisely the *inefficiencies* we noted at the outset of this section. The basic precept of efficient taxation is to try to devise a tax system that *minimizes* these inefficiencies. In particular:

In comparing two taxes that raise the same total revenue, the one that produces less excess burden is the more efficient.

Notice the proviso that the two taxes being compared must yield the *same* revenue. We are really interested in the *total* burden of each tax. Because

Total burden = Tax collections + Excess burden

---

[3] A tax like the one described here has been in effect since 1984.

we can unambiguously state that the tax with less *excess* burden is more efficient only when tax collections are equal.

Excess burdens arise when consumers and firms alter their behavior on account of taxation. This precept of sound tax policy can be restated in a way that is reminiscent of President Reagan's statement at the beginning of this chapter:

> **In designing a tax system to raise revenue, the government should try to raise any given amount of revenue through taxes that induce the smallest changes in behavior.**

Sometimes, however, a tax is levied not primarily as a revenue raiser, but as a way to induce individuals or firms to alter their behavior—in contrast to President Reagan's dictum. For example, proposals for taxes on carbon-based fuels like coal and gasoline are designed to induce people to use fewer of them. The possibility of using taxes to change consumer behavior will be discussed later in this chapter.

Tax Loopholes and Excess Burden

We noted earlier that loopholes make the income tax less progressive than it appears to be on paper. Now that we have learned that tax-induced changes in behavior lead to excess burdens, we can understand the second reason why tax specialists condemn tax loopholes: Loopholes make the income tax less *efficient* than it could be. Why? Because most loopholes involve imposing different tax rates on different types of income. Given a choice between paying, say, a 35 percent marginal tax rate on one type of income and a 15 percent rate on another, most rational taxpayers will favor the latter. Thus:

> **When different income-earning activities are taxed at different marginal rates, economic choices are distorted by tax considerations, which in turn impairs economic efficiency.**

Our example is hardly hypothetical. Upper-bracket taxpayers in the United States now pay a 35 percent tax on income that comes in the form of wages or interest but only 15 percent on income that comes in the form of capital gains or dividends. It is no wonder, then, that such people shun interest and seek capital gains—often in the stock market.

One major objective shared by tax reformers is to enhance both the equity and efficiency of the personal income tax by closing loopholes and lowering tax rates. The Tax Reform Act of 1986—the pride and joy of tax reformers—did exactly that, but by now that law is ancient history. Since 1986, Congress has allowed a number of tax loopholes to reappear and keeps creating new ones. Critics on both sides of the aisle have long bemoaned the tax system's legendary complexity and yearned for a simpler tax code with fewer loopholes. But so far, those pleas have gone unheeded.

SHIFTING THE TAX BURDEN: TAX INCIDENCE

When economists speak of the **incidence of a tax,** they are referring to who actually bears the burden of the tax. In discussing the tax on gas-guzzling autos, we adhered to what has been called the *flypaper theory of tax incidence:* the burden of any tax sticks where the government puts it. In this case, the burden stays on Harry, our SUV fan, but often things do not work out this way.

The **incidence of a tax** is an allocation of the burden of the tax to specific individuals or groups.

Consider, for example, what will happen if the government levies a $1,000 tax on SUVs like Hummers. We learned how to deal with such a tax in a supply-and-demand diagram back in Chapter 4: The supply curve shifts up by the amount of the tax—in this case, $1,000. Figure 4 shows such a shift by the movement from S_0S_0 to S_1S_1. If the demand curve DD does not shift, the market equilibrium moves from point A to point B. The quantity of SUVs declines as Harrys all over America react to the higher price by buying fewer SUVs. Notice that the price rises from $40,000 to $40,600, an increase of $600. People who continue buying these vehicles therefore bear a burden of only $600—less than the tax that they pay!

FIGURE 4

The Incidence of an
Excise Tax

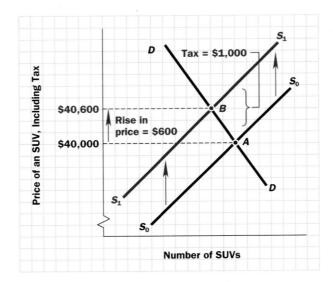

The American Way of Tax

The humorist Russell Baker discussed the problem of excess burden in this classic newspaper column. It seems that every time his mythical Mr. Figg took a step to avoid paying taxes and to satisfy the tax man, he became less and less happy.

New York—The Tax Man was very cross about Figg. Figg's way of life did not conform to the way of life several governments wanted Figg to pursue.

"What's the idea of living in a rental apartment over a delicatessen in the city, Figg?" he inquired.

Figg explained that he liked urban life. In that case, said the Tax Man, he was raising Figg's city sales and income taxes. "If you want them cut, you'll have to move out to the suburbs," he said.

Figg gave up the city and rented a suburban house but the Tax Man was not satisfied. He squeezed Figg until beads of blood popped out along the seams of Figg's wallet.

"Mercy, good Tax Man," Figg gasped. "Tell me how to live so that I may please my government, and I shall obey."

The Tax Man told Figg to quit renting and buy a house. The government wanted everyone to accept large mortgage loans from bankers. If Figg complied, it would cut his taxes.

Figg bought a house, which he did not want, in a suburb where he did not want to live, and he invited his friends and relatives to attend a party celebrating his surrender to a way of life that pleased his governments.

"I have had enough of this, Figg," the Tax Man declared. "Your government doesn't want you entertaining friends and relatives. This will cost you plenty."

Figg immediately threw out all of his friends and relatives, then asked the Tax Man what sort of people his government wished him to entertain. "Business associates," said the Tax Man. "Entertain plenty of business associates, and I shall cut your taxes."

To make the Tax Man and his government happy, Figg began entertaining people he didn't like in the house he didn't want in the suburb where he didn't want to live.

Then was the Tax Man enraged indeed. "Figg!" he thundered, "I will not cut your taxes for entertaining straw bosses, truck drivers and pothole fixers."

"Why not?" said Figg. "These are the people I associate with in my business."

"Which is what?" asked the Tax Man.

"Earning my pay by the sweat of my brow," said Figg.

"Your government is not going to bribe you for performing salaried labor," said the Tax Man. "Don't you know, you imbecile, that tax rates on salaried income are higher than on any other kind?"

And he taxed the sweat of Figg's brow at a ferocious rate.

"Get into business, or minerals, or international oil," warned the Tax Man, "or I shall make your taxes as the taxes of 10."

Figg went into business, which he hated, and entertained people he didn't like in the house he didn't want in the suburb where he did not want to live, and the Tax Man and all the governments and the nation were happy.

Figg began to make a profit. The Tax Man was outraged.

"What's the idea of making a profit, Figg?" he demanded, placing his iron grip on Figg's bank account.

"Spare me," Figg pleaded.

"Only if you sell your business!" roared the Tax Man.

"After forcing me to get into business, the Government now wants me to get out of business?" asked Figg.

"Exactly" said the Tax Man. "Sell, and I'll tax the profit from the sale at a delightfully low capital-gain rate of only 25 percent. Otherwise, I'll take the meat ax to those profits."

Does this mean that the tax imposes a *negative* excess burden? Certainly not. What it means is that consumers who refrain from buying the taxed commodity manage to *shift* part of the tax burden away from consumers as a whole, including those who continue to buy SUVs. Who are the victims of this **tax shifting**? There are two main candidates. First are the automakers or, more precisely, their stockholders. To the extent that the tax reduces auto sales and profits, stockholders bear the burden. The other principal candidates are autoworkers. To the extent that reduced production leads to layoffs or lower wages, these workers bear part of the tax burden.

People who have never studied economics almost always believe in the flypaper theory of incidence, which holds that sales taxes are borne by consumers, property taxes are borne by homeowners, and taxes on corporations are borne by stockholders. Perhaps the most important lesson of this chapter is that

The flypaper theory of incidence is typically wrong.

Failure to grasp this basic point has led to all sorts of misguided tax legislation in which members of Congress or state legislatures, *thinking* they were placing a tax burden on one group of people, inadvertently placed it squarely on another. Of course, in some cases the flypaper theory of incidence is roughly correct. So let us consider some specific examples of tax incidence.

> **Tax shifting** occurs when the economic reactions to a tax cause prices and outputs in the economy to change, thereby shifting part of the burden of the tax onto others.

The Incidence of Excise Taxes

Excise taxes have already been covered by our SUV example, because Figure 4 could represent any commodity that is taxed. Our basic finding is that *part* of the burden will fall on consumers of the taxed commodity (including those who stop buying it because of the tax), and part will be borne by the firms and workers who produce the commodity.

How is the burden shared between buyers and sellers? It all depends on the slopes of the demand and supply curves. Intuitively speaking, if consumers are very loyal to the taxed commodity, they will continue to buy almost the same amount regardless of price. In that case, they will get stuck with most of the tax bill because they have left themselves vulnerable to it. Thus:

The more *inelastic* the demand for the product, the larger the share of the tax that consumers will pay.

Similarly, if suppliers are determined to offer the same amount of the product no matter how low the price, then they will wind up paying most of the tax. That is:

The more *inelastic* the supply curve, the larger the share of the tax that suppliers will pay.

One extreme case arises when no one stops buying SUVs when their prices rise. The demand curve becomes vertical, like the demand curve *DD* in Figure 5. Then no tax shifting can take place. When the supply curve shifts upward by the amount of the tax ($1,000), the price of an SUV (inclusive of tax) rises by the full $1,000—from $40,000 to $41,000. So consumers bear the entire burden.

The other extreme case arises when the supply curve is totally inelastic, as depicted by the vertical line *SS* in Figure 6. Because the number of SUVs supplied is the same at any price, the supply curve will not shift when a tax is imposed. Consequently, automakers must bear the full burden of any tax that is placed on their product. Figure 6 shows that the tax does not change the market price (including tax), which, of course, means that the price received by sellers must fall by the full amount of the tax.

Demand and supply schedules for most goods and services are not as extreme as those depicted in Figures 5

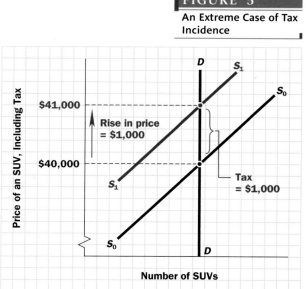

FIGURE 5

An Extreme Case of Tax Incidence

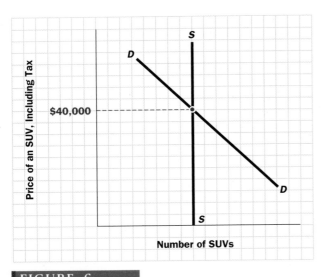

$40,000 - - - - - - - - - - - - - - -

Price of an SUV, Including Tax

S
D

D

S

Number of SUVs

FIGURE 6

Another Extreme Case
of Tax Incidence

and 6, so buyers and sellers normally share the burden. Precisely how it is shared depends on the elasticities of the supply and demand curves.[4]

The Incidence of the Payroll Tax

Economists view the payroll tax as an excise tax on the employment of labor. As mentioned earlier, the U.S. payroll tax comes in two parts: Half is levied on employees (via payroll deductions) and half on employers. A fundamental point, which people who have never studied economics often fail to grasp, is that

The ultimate incidence of a payroll tax is the same whether it is levied on employers or on employees.

A simple numerical example will illustrate why this must be so. Consider an employee earning $100 per day with a 16 percent payroll tax that is shared equally between the employer and the employee, as under present U.S. law. To hire this worker, a firm must pay $100 in wages to the worker plus $8 in taxes to the government—for a total daily cost of $108. But how much does the worker receive? He gets $100 in wages paid by the employer less $8 deducted and sent to the government, or $92 per day. The difference between wages *paid* and wages *received* is $108 − $92 = $16, the amount of the tax.

Now suppose Congress tries to "shift" the burden of the tax entirely onto firms by raising the employer's tax to $16 while lowering the employee's tax to zero. At first, with the daily wage fixed at $100, the firm's total labor costs (including tax) rise to $116 per day, and workers' net income rises to $100 per day. Congress seems to have achieved its goal.

This achievement is fleeting, however, for what we have just described is not an equilibrium situation. With the daily cost of labor at $116 for firms, the quantity of labor *demanded* will be *less* than it was when labor cost only $108 per day. Similarly, with take-home pay up to $100 for workers, the quantity of labor *supplied* will be *more* than it was when the after-tax wage was only $92. Therefore, a *surplus of labor* on the market will develop (an excess of quantity supplied over quantity demanded), and this surplus will place downward pressure on wages.

How far will wages have to fall? We can easily see that an *after-tax* wage of $92 will restore equilibrium. If daily take-home pay is $92, the same as it was before the tax change, quantity supplied will be the same. From the firm's perspective, labor now costs $108 per day ($92 in wages plus $16 in taxes), just as it did before the tax change. Firms will, therefore, demand the same quantity of labor as they did when the payroll tax was shared. Thus, in the end, the market will completely frustrate the intent of Congress.

The payroll tax is an excellent example of a case in which Congress, misled by the flypaper theory of incidence, thinks it is "taxing firms" when it raises the employer's share and "taxing workers" when it raises the employee's share. In truth, who really pays the tax in the long run depends on the incidence of the payroll tax. But no lasting difference results from a change in the employee's and the employer's shares.

So who, in fact, bears the burden? Like any excise tax, the incidence of the payroll tax depends on the elasticities of the supply and demand schedules. In the case of labor, a large body of empirical evidence points to the conclusion that the quantity of labor supplied is not very responsive to price for most population groups. The supply curve is almost vertical, like that shown in Figure 6. The result: Workers as a group can shift little of the burden of the payroll tax to employers.

Employers *can* shift it in most cases. To firms, their share of the payroll tax is an additional cost of using labor. When payroll taxes go up, firms try to substitute cheaper

---

[4] For concrete examples, see Test Yourself Questions 3 and 4 at the end of this chapter.

factors of production (such as capital) for labor wherever they can. This effort reduces the quantity of labor demanded, lowering the wage received by workers. Thus market forces shift part of the tax burden from firms to workers.

To the extent that the supply curve of labor has some positive slope, the quantity of labor supplied will fall when the wage goes down, allowing workers to shift some of the burden back onto firms, but firms, in turn, can shift that burden onto consumers by raising their prices. As we know from Part 3, prices in competitive markets generally rise when costs (such as labor costs) increase. It is doubtful, therefore, that firms bear much of the payroll tax burden. The flypaper theory of incidence could not be farther from the truth. Even though the tax is collected by the firm, it is really borne by workers and consumers.

WHEN TAXATION CAN IMPROVE EFFICIENCY

We have spent much of this chapter discussing the inefficiencies and excess burdens that arise from taxation. Before we finish this discussion, we must point out two things.

First, economic efficiency is not society's only goal. For example, a tax on energy causes "inefficiencies" if it changes people's behavior patterns. These changes may be just what the government intends. The government wants people to conserve energy and is willing to tolerate some economic inefficiency to accomplish this goal. We can, of course, argue whether the conservation achieved is worth the efficiency loss. The general point is that

Some taxes that introduce economic inefficiencies may nonetheless be good social policy if they help to achieve some other goal.

We have already mentioned the excise tax on cigarettes, which aims to change behavior. Another important example is the high tax on alcoholic beverages.

A second, and more fundamental, point is that

Some taxes that change economic behavior may lead to efficiency *gains*, rather than to efficiency *losses*.

As you might suspect, this favorable outcome is possible only when the system has an inefficiency prior to the tax. In such a case, an appropriate tax may help set things right. One important example of this phenomenon was discussed at length in the previous chapter. Because firms and individuals who despoil clean air and water often do so without paying any price, these precious resources are used inefficiently. A corrective tax on pollution can remedy this problem.

EQUITY, EFFICIENCY, AND THE OPTIMAL TAX

In a perfect world, the ideal tax would raise the revenues the government needs, reflect society's views on equity in taxation, and induce no changes in economic behavior—and so have no excess burden. Unfortunately, there is no such tax.

Sometimes, in fact, the taxes with the smallest excess burdens are the most regressive. For instance, a head tax, which charges every person the same number of dollars, is incredibly regressive. It is also perfectly efficient. Because no change in economic behavior will enable anyone to avoid it, no one has any reason to change behavior. As we have noted, the regressive payroll tax also seems to have small excess burdens.

Fortunately, however, there is a tax that, although not ideal, still scores highly on both the equity and efficiency criteria: a comprehensive personal income tax with few loopholes. Although it is true that income taxes can be avoided by earning less income, we have already observed that in reality the supply of labor responds little to tax policy. People also can reduce their tax bills by investing in relatively safe assets (such as government bonds) rather than riskier ones (such as common stocks), because safer assets pay lower rates of return. But it is not clear that the income tax actually induces such behavior. Why?

Because although the government shares in the *profits* when investments turn out well, it also shares in the *losses* when investments turn sour. Finally, because an income tax reduces the return on saving, many economists have worried that it would discourage saving and thus retard economic growth.[5] Empirical evidence, however, does not suggest that such reactions happen to any great extent. On balance, then, although unresolved questions remain and research is continuing,

> **Most of the research to date suggests that a comprehensive personal income tax with no loopholes would induce few of the behavioral reactions that cause inefficiencies and thus would have a rather small excess burden.**

On the equity criterion, we know that personal income taxes can be made as progressive as society deems desirable, though if marginal tax rates on rich people get extremely high, some of the potential efficiency losses might become more serious than they are now. On both grounds, then, many economists—including both liberals and conservatives—view a comprehensive personal income tax as one of the best ways for a government to raise revenue. They differ, however, over how progressive the income tax should be, with some conservatives favoring a proportional tax.

ISSUE REVISITED: THE PROS AND CONS OF REPEALING THE BUSH TAX CUTS

How do the tax cuts enacted in 2001 and 2003 stack up against these criteria? Should these tax cuts be maintained or repealed?

First, the Bush tax cuts concentrated on reducing *marginal* tax rates. They therefore can be expected to improve economic *efficiency*, at least modestly. That effect is a clear plus, which—not surprisingly—is touted by supporters.

Second, however, the tax cuts were skewed toward upper-bracket taxpayers, thereby reducing the *progressivity* of the tax system. Whether that change is a plus or a minus depends on your attitude toward inequality. Some Americans wondered why the very rich should get such large tax breaks. Others pointed out that the people who received the biggest tax cuts in 2001–2003 were the people who paid the highest taxes. Naturally, this aspect of the tax cuts has been a bone of contention between Democrats and Republicans since 2001—and remains so today.

Third, a number of critics of the tax cuts worried about their large *magnitude*. Can we really afford such generosity, they asked, or does the government need the money for what President Reagan called "legitimate government purposes"? In answering this question back in 2001, when large budget *surpluses* were looming, President Bush argued that the government should return some of the money to the people who paid the (unneeded) taxes, but the surpluses evaporated quickly after September 11, 2001, and the federal government began running sizable deficits—which ballooned during the recent recession. Democrats see repeal of the Bush tax cuts as an appealing way to raise revenue, whereas Republicans insist that deficits be attacked only on the spending side.

So where does this partial accounting of the pros and cons of repealing the Bush tax cuts leave us? As usual in a serious public policy debate, with plenty of room for reasonable people to disagree! As we said back in Chapter 1, economics is not supposed to give you all the *answers*. It is supposed to teach you how to ask the right *questions*. Now you know what they are.

---

[5] For this reason, some economists prefer a tax on consumption to a tax on income.

| SUMMARY |

1. Taxes in the United States have been quite constant as a percentage of gross domestic product since the early 1970s. The federal tax share fell sharply after 2001, but it has risen since.

2. The U.S. government raises most of its revenue by **direct taxes,** such as the personal and corporate income taxes and the payroll tax. Of these taxes, the payroll tax is increasing most rapidly.

3. For decades, the Social Security System relied successfully on pay-as-you-go financing. In recent years, however, it has been accumulating a large trust fund to be used to pay benefits to future retirees. But experts do not think that trust fund will be large enough.

4. State and local governments raise most of their tax revenues by **indirect taxes.** States rely mainly on sales taxes, whereas localities depend on property taxes.

5. Controversy has arisen over whether local property taxes are an equitable way to finance public education.

6. In our multilevel system of government, the federal government makes a variety of grants to state and local governments, and states in turn make grants to municipalities and school districts. This system of intergovernmental transfers is called **fiscal federalism.**

7. The three concepts of fair, or "equitable," taxation occasionally conflict. **Horizontal equity** simply calls for equals to be treated equally. **Vertical equity,** which calls for unequals to be treated unequally, has often been translated into the **ability-to-pay principle**—namely, that people who are better able to pay taxes should be taxed more heavily. The **benefits principle** of tax equity ignores ability to pay and seeks to tax people according to the benefits they receive.

8. The **burden of a tax** is the amount of money an individual would have to be given to be as well off with the tax as without it. This burden normally exceeds the taxes that are paid, and the difference between the two amounts is called the **excess burden** of the tax.

9. Excess burden arises whenever a tax induces some people or firms to change their behavior. Because excess burdens signal economic inefficiencies, the basic principle of efficient taxation is to utilize taxes that have small excess burdens.

10. When people change their behavior on account of a tax, they often **shift** the burden of the tax onto someone else. For this reason, the "flypaper theory of **tax incidence**"—the belief that the burden of any tax sticks where Congress puts it—is often incorrect.

11. The burden of a sales or excise tax normally is shared between suppliers and consumers. The manner in which it is shared depends on the elasticities of supply and demand.

12. The payroll tax works like an excise tax on labor services. Because the supply of labor is much less elastic than the demand for labor, workers bear most of the burden of the payroll tax—including both the employer's and the employee's shares.

13. Sometimes "inefficient" taxes—that is, taxes that cause a good deal of excess burden—are nonetheless desirable because the changes in behavior they induce further some other social goal.

14. When there are inefficiencies in the system for reasons other than the tax system (for example, externalities), taxation can conceivably improve efficiency.

| KEY TERMS |

ability-to-pay principle   384
average tax rate   379
benefits principle of taxation   385
burden of a tax   386
corporate income tax   381
direct taxes   379
economic efficiency   385
excess burden   386

excise tax   381
fiscal federalism   384
horizontal equity   384
incidence of a tax   387
indirect taxes   379
marginal tax rate   379
payroll tax   381
personal income tax   379
progressive taxes   379

property tax   383
proportional taxes   379
regressive taxes   379
Social Security System   381
tax deductions   380
tax exempt   380
tax loopholes   380
tax shifting   389
vertical equity   384

| TEST YOURSELF |

1. Using the following hypothetical income-tax table, compute the marginal and average tax rates. Is the tax progressive, proportional, or regressive?

Income	Income Tax
$20,000	$2,000
30,000	2,700
40,000	3,200
50,000	3,500

2. Which concept of tax equity, if any, seems to be served by each of the following?

   a. The progressive income tax

   b. The excise tax on cigarettes

   c. The gasoline tax

3. Suppose the supply-and-demand schedules for cigarettes are as follows:

Price per Carton	Quantity Demanded	Quantity Supplied
$3.00	360	160
3.25	330	180
3.50	300	200
3.75	270	220
4.00	240	240
4.25	210	260
4.50	180	280
4.75	150	300
5.00	120	320

NOTE: Quantity is in millions of cartons per year.

   a. What are the equilibrium price and equilibrium quantity?

   b. Now the government levies a $1.25 per carton excise tax on cigarettes. What are the new equilibrium price paid by consumers, the price received by producers, and the quantity?

   c. Explain why it makes no difference whether Congress levies the $1.25 tax on the consumer or the producer. (Relate your answer to the discussion of the payroll tax in the text.)

   d. Suppose the tax is levied on the producers. How much of the tax are producers able to shift onto consumers? Explain how they manage to do so.

   e. Will there be any excess burden from this tax? Why? Who bears this excess burden?

   f. By how much has cigarette consumption declined on account of the tax? Why might the government be happy about this outcome, despite the excess burden?

4. Now suppose the supply schedule is instead as follows:

Price per Carton	Quantity Supplied
$3.00	60
3.25	105
3.50	150
3.75	195
4.00	240
4.25	285
4.50	330
4.75	375
5.00	420

NOTE: Quantity is in millions of cartons per year.

   a. What are the equilibrium price and equilibrium quantity in the absence of a tax?

   b. What are the equilibrium price and equilibrium quantity in the presence of a $1.25 per carton excise tax?

   c. Explain why your answer to part b differs from your answer to part b of the previous question, and relate this difference to the discussion of the incidence of an excise tax in this chapter.

5. The country of Taxmania produces only two commodities: rice and caviar. The poor spend all their income on rice, whereas the rich purchase both goods. Both demand for and supply of rice are quite inelastic. In the caviar market, both supply and demand are quite elastic. Which good would be heavily taxed if Taxmanians cared mostly about efficiency? What if they cared mostly about vertical equity?

| DISCUSSION QUESTIONS |

1. "Americans are overtaxed. The federal government should continue cutting taxes." Comment.

2. Soon after taking office in 2001, President Bush proposed a series of large tax cuts, including lower bracket rates and repeal of the estate tax. Critics argued that these tax cuts were excessive in magnitude and regressive in their distributional impact. Why did they say that? Do you agree?

3. Use the example of Mr. Figg (see the box, "The American Way of Tax" on page 388) to explain the concepts of efficient taxes and excess burden.

4. Think of some tax that you personally pay. What steps have you taken or could you take to reduce your tax payments? Is there an excess burden on you? Why or why not?

5. Discuss President Reagan's statement on taxes quoted on the first page of this chapter. Do you agree with him?

6. Use the criteria of equity and efficiency in taxation to evaluate the idea of taxing capital gains at a lower rate than other sources of income.

THE DISTRIBUTION OF INCOME

I n Part 5, we examine how a market economy distributes its income, using the price mechanism, with the prices of the inputs to the production process determined by supply and demand; that is, we investigate what determines the share of total output that goes to workers, to landowners, to investors, etc. We will see that the market assigns a central role to the marginal productivity of each of these recipients—how much of a marginal contribution each makes to the economy's total output.

In Chapter 19, we will study the payments made for the use of capital (interest), land (rent), and the reward to entrepreneurs (profits). Because most people earn their incomes primarily from wages and salaries, and because these payments constitute nearly three-quarters of U.S. national income, our analysis of the payments to labor (wages) merits a separate chapter (Chapter 20). In Chapter 21, we turn to some important problems in the distribution of income—poverty, inequality, and discrimination.

CHAPTERS

PRICING THE FACTORS OF PRODUCTION

Rent is that portion of the produce of the earth which is paid to the landlord for use of the original and indestructible powers of the soil.

DAVID RICARDO (1772–1823)

I n Chapter 15, we noted that the market mechanism cannot be counted on to distribute income in accord with ethical notions of fairness, and we listed this as one of the market's shortcomings. But there is much more to say about how income is distributed in a market economy.

The market mechanism distributes income through its payments to the **factors of production.** Everyone owns some potentially usable factors of production—the inputs used in the production process. Many of us have only our own labor; but some of us also have funds that we can lend, land that we can rent, or natural resources that we can sell at prices determined by supply and demand. The distribution of income in a market economy is determined by the prices of the factors of production and by the amounts that are employed. For example, if wages are low and unequal and unemployment is high, obviously many people will be poor.

Factors of production are the broad categories—land, labor, capital, exhaustible natural resources, and entrepreneurship—into which we classify the economy's different productive inputs.

CONTENTS

PUZZLE:	WHY DOES A HIGHER RETURN TO SAVINGS REDUCE THE AMOUNTS SOME PEOPLE SAVE?

The rate of interest is the price one obtains by saving some money and lending it to others—for example, lending the money to a bank (by depositing the money into a bank account) or lending the money to a corporation (by buying its bonds). We normally expect that a rise in the price of a loan (like the price of anything else) will reduce the quantity demanded and increase the quantity supplied. In fact, many people who save their money and lend it to others do the opposite—they *reduce* the amount they lend when the rate of interest goes up. How can that make sense?

The same puzzle affects other factors of production. For example, when wages, the price of labor, rise, workers often decide to work less, perhaps taking longer vacations. Why don't they work more when pay is better? The explanation will be discussed later in the chapter.

It is useful to group the factors of production into five broad categories: land, labor, capital, exhaustible natural resources, and a rather mysterious input called **entrepreneurship.** In this chapter, we will look at two of them—the interest paid to capital and the rent of land.

But first, because there is a great deal of misperception about the distribution of income among workers, suppliers of capital, and landlords, let's see how much these three groups actually earn. Of all the payments made to factors of production in the United States in 2006, interest payments accounted for about 4.5 percent; land rents were minuscule, making up only 0.7 percent; corporate profits accounted for 15 percent; and income of other business proprietors made up 9.4 percent. In total, the payments to all the factors of production that we deal with in this chapter amounted to about 30 percent of national factor income. Where did the rest of it go? The answer is that 70 percent of 2006 national factor income consisted of employee compensation—that is, wages and salaries.[1]

There are many other serious misunderstandings about the nature of income distribution and about what government can do to influence it, and discussions of the subject are often emotional. That's because the distribution of income is the one area in economics in which any one individual's interests almost inevitably conflict with the interests of someone else. By definition, if I get a larger slice of the total income pie, then you end up with a smaller slice. Still, as we will see in the next chapter, it is possible to get more for oneself by increasing the size of the pie, and then everyone can benefit.

Entrepreneurship is the act of starting new firms, introducing new products and technological innovations, and, in general, taking the risks that are necessary to seek out business opportunities.

THE PRINCIPLE OF MARGINAL PRODUCTIVITY

The **marginal physical product (MPP)** of an input is the increase in output that results from a one-unit increase in the use of the input, holding the amounts of all other inputs constant.

The **marginal revenue product (MRP)** of an input is the money value of the additional sales that a firm obtains by selling the marginal physical product of that input.

By now it should not surprise you that supply and demand determine the prices of inputs as well as the prices of goods and services. The supply sides of the markets for the various factors differ enormously, so we must discuss each factor market separately. We can use one basic principle, the *principle of marginal productivity,* to explain how much of any input a profit-maximizing firm will demand, given the price of that input. To review the principle, we must first recall two concepts from Chapter 7: **marginal physical product (MPP)** and **marginal revenue product (MRP).**

Table 1 helps us review these two concepts in terms of Naomi's Natural Farm, which has to decide how much organic corn, priced at $10 per bag, to feed its chickens. The *marginal*

---

[1] *National Income and Product Accounts,* U.S. Department of Commerce, Bureau of Economic Analysis, available at http://www.bea.gov. (Note: This calculation consists of the Bureau of Economic Analysis categories, Compensation of Employees, Proprietors' Income with IVA and CCAdj., Rental Income of Persons with CCAdj., Corporate Profits with IVA and CCAdj., and Net Interest and Miscellaneous Payments, all as a percentage of Net National Factor Income.)

physical product (MPP) column tells us how many additional pounds of chicken each additional bag of corn will yield. For example, according to the table, the fourth bag increases output by 34 pounds. The *marginal revenue product* (MRP) column tells us how many dollars this marginal physical product is worth. In Table 1, we assume Naomi's prized, natural chickens sell at $0.75 per pound, so the MRP of the fourth bag of corn is $0.75 per pound times 34 pounds, or $25.50 (last column of the table).

> **The marginal productivity principle states that in competitive factor markets, the profit-maximizing firm will hire or buy the quantity of any input at which the marginal revenue product equals the price of the input.**

The basic logic behind this principle is simple, as we saw before. We know that the firm's profit from acquiring an additional unit of an input is the input's marginal revenue product minus its marginal cost (which is the price of the additional unit of input). If the input's marginal revenue product is greater than its price, it will pay the profit-seeking firm to acquire more of that input because an additional unit of input brings the firm revenue that exceeds its cost. The firm should purchase that input up to the amount at which diminishing returns reduce the MRP to the level of the input's price, so that further expansion yields zero further addition to profit. By similar reasoning, if MRP is less than price, then the firm is using too much of the input. We see in Table 1 that about seven bags is the optimal amount of corn for Naomi to use each week, because an eighth bag brings in a marginal revenue product of only $6.75, which is less than the $10 cost of buying the bag.

One corollary of the principle of marginal productivity is obvious: The quantity of any input demanded depends on its price. The lower the price of corn, the more it pays the farm to buy. In our example, it pays Naomi to use between seven and eight bags when the price per bag is $10. But if corn were more expensive—say, $20 per bag—that high price would exceed the value of the marginal product of either the sixth or seventh bag. It would, therefore, pay the firm to stop at five bags of corn. Thus, *marginal productivity analysis shows that the quantity demanded of an input normally declines as the input price rises.* The "law" of demand applies to inputs just as it applies to consumer goods.

TABLE 1

Naomi's Natural Farm Schedules for TPP, MPP, APP, and MRP of Corn

(1) Corn Input (Bags)	(2) TPP: Total Physical Product (chicken, lbs)	(3) MPP: Marginal Physical Product per Bag	(4) APP: Average Physical Product per Bag	(5) MRP: Marginal Revenue Product per Bag
0	0.0 lbs	14.0 lbs	0.0 lbs	$10.50
1	14.0	22.0	14.0	16.50
2	36.0	30.0	18.0	22.50
3	66.0	34.0	22.0	25.50
4	100.0	30.0	25.0	22.50
5	130.0	26.0	26.0	19.50
6	156.0	19.0	26.0	14.25
7	175.0	9.0	25.0	6.75
8	184.0	1.4	23.0	1.05
9	185.4	−5.4	20.6	−4.05
10	180.0	−15.0	18.0	−11.25
11	165.0	−21.0	15.0	−15.75
12	144.0		12.0	

INPUTS AND THEIR DERIVED DEMAND CURVES

We can, in fact, be much more specific about how much of each input a profit-maximizing firm will demand. That's because the marginal productivity principle tells us precisely how to derive the demand curve for any input from its marginal revenue product (MRP) curve.

Figure 1 graphs the MRP schedule from Table 1, showing the marginal revenue product for corn (MRP$_c$) rising and then declining as Naomi feeds more and more corn to her chickens. In the figure, we focus on three possible prices for a bag of corn: $20, $15, and $10. As we have just seen, the optimal purchase rule requires Naomi to keep increasing her use of corn until her MRP begins to fall and eventually is reduced to the price of corn. At a price of $20 per bag, we see that the quantity demanded is about 5.6 bags of corn per week (point *A*); at that point, MRP equals price. Similarly, if the price of corn is $15 per bag, quantity demanded is about 6.8 bags per week (point *B*). Finally, at a price of $10 per bag, the quantity demanded would be about 7.7 bags per week (point *C*). Points *A*, *B*, and *C* are therefore three points on the demand curve for corn. By repeating this exercise for any other price, we learn that because the

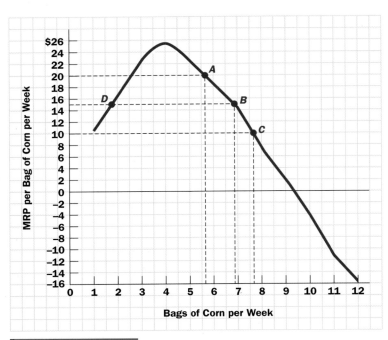

FIGURE 1

Marginal Revenue Product Graph for Naomi's Natural Farm

The **derived demand** for an input is the demand for the input by producers as determined by the demand for the final product that the input is used to produce.

profit-maximizing purchase of an input occurs at the point where the MRP has *fallen* down to the level of the input price,

> **The demand curve for any input is the downward-sloping portion of its marginal revenue product curve.[2]**

The demand for corn or labor (or for any other input) is called a **derived demand** because it is derived from the underlying demand for the final product (poultry in this case). For example, suppose that a surge in demand drives organic chicken prices to $1.50 per pound. Then, at each level of corn usage, the marginal revenue product will be twice as large as when poultry brought $0.75 per pound. This effect appears in Figure 2 as an upward shift of the (derived) demand curve for corn, from D_0D_0 to D_1D_1, even though the marginal physical product curves have not changed. Thus, an outward shift in demand for poultry leads to an outward shift in the demand for corn.[3] We conclude that, in general:

An outward shift in the demand curve for any commodity causes an outward shift of the derived demand curve for all factors utilized in the production of that commodity.

Similarly, an inward shift in the demand curve for a commodity leads to inward shifts in the demand curves for factors used in producing that commodity.

This completes our discussion of the *demand* side of the analysis of input pricing. The most noteworthy feature of the discussion is the fact that the same marginal productivity principle serves as the foundation for the demand schedule for each and every type of input. In particular, as we will see in Chapter 20, the marginal productivity principle serves as the basis for the determination of the demand for *labor*—that crucial input whose financial reward plays so important a role in an economy's standard of living. On the demand side, one analysis fits almost all.

The supply side for each input, however, entails a very different story. Here we must deal with each of the main production factors individually. We must do so because, as we will see, the supply relationships of the different inputs vary considerably. We begin with *interest payments*, or the return on capital. First, we must define a few key terms.

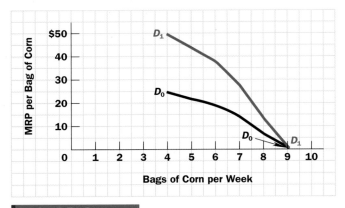

FIGURE 2

A Shift in the Demand Curve for Corn

---

[2] Why is the demand curve restricted to only the downward-sloping portion of the MRP curve? The logic of the marginal productivity principle dictates this constraint. For example, if the price of corn were $15.00 per bag, Figure 1 shows that MRP = P at two input quantities: (approximately) 1.75 bags (point D) and 6.8 bags (point B). Point D cannot be the optimal stopping point, however, because the MRP of a second bag ($16.50) is greater than the cost of the third bag ($15.00); that is, the firm makes more money by expanding its input use beyond 1.5 bags per week. A similar profitable opportunity for expansion occurs anytime P = MRP and the MRP curve slopes upward at the current price. This must be so, because then an increase in the quantity of input used by the firm will raise MRP above the input's price. It follows that a profit-maximizing firm will always demand an input quantity that is in the range where MRP is diminishing.

[3] To make Figure 2 easier to read, the (irrelevant) upward-sloping portion and the negative portion of each curve have been omitted.

INVESTMENT, CAPITAL, AND INTEREST

Although people sometimes use the words *investment* and *capital* as if they were interchangeable, it is important to distinguish between them. Economists define **capital** as the *inventory* (or stock) of plant, equipment, and other productive resources owned by a business firm, an individual, or some other organization. **Investment** is the amount by which capital *grows*. A warehouse owned by a firm is part of its capital. Expansion of the warehouse by adding a new area to the building is an investment. So, when economists use the word *investment,* they do not mean just the transfer of money. The higher the level of investment, the *faster* the amount of capital that the investor possesses grows. The relation between investment and capital is often explained by the analogy of filling a bathtub: The accumulated water in the tub is analogous to the *stock* of capital, whereas the flow of water from the faucet (which adds to the tub's water) is like the *flow* of investment. Just as the faucet must be turned on for more water to accumulate, the capital stock increases only when investment continues. If investment ceases, the capital stock stops growing (but does not disappear). In other words, if investment is zero, the capital stock does not fall to zero but remains constant (just as when you turn off the faucet the tub doesn't suddenly empty, but rather the level of the water stays the same).

> **Capital** refers to an inventory (*stock*) of plant, equipment, and other (generally durable) productive resources held by a business firm, an individual, or some other organization.

> **Investment** is the *flow* of resources into the production of new capital. It is the labor, steel, and other inputs devoted to the *construction* of factories, warehouses, railroads, and other pieces of capital during some period of time.

The process of building up capital by investing and then using this capital in production can be divided into five steps, listed below and summarized in Figure 3:

Step 1. The firm decides to enlarge its stock of capital.

Step 2. The firm raises the funds to finance its expansion, either by tapping outside sources such as banks or by holding onto some of its own earnings rather than paying them out to company owners.

Step 3. The firm uses these funds to hire the inputs needed to build factories, warehouses, and the like. This step is the act of investment.

Step 4. After the investment is completed, the firm ends up with a larger stock of capital.

Step 5. The firm uses the capital (along with other inputs) either to expand production or to reduce costs. At this point, the firm starts earning returns on its investment.

"I can't sleep. I just got this incredible craving for capital."

Notice that investors put *money* into the investment process—either their own or funds borrowed from others. Then, through a series of steps, firms transform the funds into physical inputs suitable for production use. If investors borrow the funds, they must

FIGURE 3

The Investment Production Process

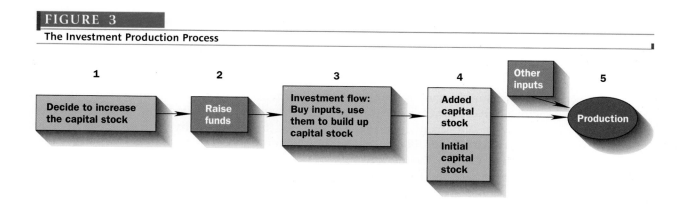

Interest is the payment for the use of funds employed in the production of capital; it is measured as the percent per year of the value of the funds tied up in the capital.

someday return those amounts to the lender with some payment for their use. This payment is called **interest,** and it is calculated as an annual percentage of the amount borrowed. For example, if an investor borrows $1,000 at an interest rate of 12 percent per year, the annual interest payment is $120.

The Demand for Funds

The rate of interest is the *price* at which funds can be rented (borrowed). Just like other factor prices, interest rates are determined by supply and demand.

On the demand side of the market for loans are borrowers—people or institutions that, for one reason or another, wish to spend more than they currently have. Individuals or families borrow to buy homes or automobiles or other expensive products. Sometimes, as we know, they borrow because they want to consume more than they can afford, which can get them into financial trouble. But often, borrowing makes good sense as a way to manage their finances when they experience a temporary drop in income. It also makes sense to borrow money to buy an item such as a home that will be used for many years. This long product life makes it appropriate for people to pay for the item as it is used, rather than all at once when it is purchased.

Businesses use loans primarily to finance investment. To the business executive who borrows funds to finance an investment and pays interest in return, the funds really represent an intermediate step toward the acquisition of the machines, buildings, inventories, and other forms of physical capital that the firm will purchase. The marginal productivity principle governs the quantity of funds demanded, just as it governs the quantity of corn demanded for chicken feed. Specifically:

> **Firms will demand the quantity of borrowed funds that makes the marginal revenue product of the investment financed by the funds just equal to the interest payment charged for borrowing.**

One noteworthy feature of capital distinguishes it from other inputs, such as corn. When Naomi feeds corn to her chickens, the input is used once and then it is gone. But a blast furnace, which is part of a steel company's capital, normally lasts many years. The furnace is a *durable* good; because it is durable, it contributes not only to today's production but also to future production. This fact makes calculation of the marginal revenue product more complex for a capital good than for other inputs.

To determine whether the MRP of a capital good is greater than the cost of financing it (that is, to decide whether an investment is profitable), we need a way to compare money values received at different times. For, other things being equal, a dollar to be received in 2011 is worth less than a dollar in 2010 because the recipient of the 2010 dollar has an additional year in which to use it to earn more money; for example, he can lend it out for an additional year and earn the additional interest. To make such comparisons between money obtained at different dates, economists and businesspeople use a calculation procedure called *discounting*. We will explain discounting in detail in the appendix to this chapter, but it is not necessary to master this technique in an introductory course. There are really only two important attributes of discounting to learn here:

- **A sum of money received at a future date is worth less than the same sum of money received today.**
- **This difference in values between money today and money in the future is greater when the rate of interest is higher.**

We can easily understand why this is so. To illustrate our first point, consider what you could do with a dollar that you received today rather than a year from today. If the annual rate of interest were 10 percent, you could lend it out (for example, by putting it in a savings account) and receive $1.10 in a year's time—your original $1.00 plus $0.10 interest. For this reason, money received today is worth more than the same number of dollars received later.

Now for our second point. Suppose the annual rate of interest is 15 percent rather than the 10 percent in the previous example. In this case, $1.00 invested today would grow to

$1.15 (rather than $1.10) in a year's time, which means that $1.15 received a year from today would be equivalent to $1.00 received today, and so, when the interest rate is 15 percent, $1.10 a year in the future must now be worth less than $1.00 today. In contrast, when the interest rate is only 10 percent per year, $1.10 to be received a year from today is equivalent to $1 of today's money, as we have seen. This illustrates the second of our two points.

The rate of interest is a crucial determinant of the economy's level of investment. It strongly influences the amount of current consumption that consumers will choose to forgo in order to use the resources to build machines and factories that can increase the output of consumers' goods in the future. The interest rate is crucial in determining the allocation of society's resources between present and future—an issue that we discussed in Chapter 15 (pages 318–319). Let us see, then, how the market sets interest rates.

The Downward-Sloping Demand Curve for Funds

A rise in the price of borrowed funds, like a rise in the price of any item, usually decreases quantity demanded. But when the money is used for investment by the firm the situation is a little more complicated than the relation between price and a consumers' good. The two attributes of discounting discussed above help to explain the special reasons why the demand curve for funds has a negative slope.

Recall that the demand for borrowed funds, like the demand for all inputs, is a *derived demand,* derived from the desire to invest in capital goods. But firms will receive part—perhaps all—of a machine or factory's marginal revenue product in the future. Hence, the value of the MRP *in terms of today's money* shrinks as the interest rate rises. Why? Because a given future return on investment in a machine or factory becomes worth less (it must be *discounted* more) when the rate of interest rises, as our illustration of the second point about discounting showed. As a consequence of this shrinkage, a machine that appears to be a good investment when the interest rate is 10 percent may look like a terrible investment if interest rates rise to 15 percent; that is, the higher the interest rate, the fewer machines a firm will demand. That is so because investing in the machines would use up money that could earn more interest in a savings account. Thus, the demand curve for machines and other forms of capital will have a negative slope—the higher the interest rate, the smaller the quantity that firms will demand.

> As the interest rate on borrowing rises, more and more investments that previously looked profitable start to look unprofitable. The demand for borrowing for investment purposes, therefore, is lower at higher rates of interest.

Note that, although this analysis clearly applies to a firm's purchase of capital goods such as plant and equipment, it may also apply to the company's land and labor purchases. Firms often finance both of these expenditures via borrowed funds, and these inputs' marginal revenue products may accrue only months or even years after the inputs have been bought and put to work. (For example, it may take quite some time before newly acquired agricultural land will yield a marketable crop.) Thus, just as in the case of capital investments, a rise in the interest rate will reduce the quantity demanded of investment goods such as land and labor, just as it cuts the derived demand for investment in plant and equipment.

Figure 4 depicts a derived demand schedule for loans, with the interest rate on the vertical axis as the loan's cost to a borrower. Its negative slope illustrates the conclusion we have just stated:

> The higher the interest rate, the less people and firms will want to borrow to finance their investments.

FIGURE 4

The Derived Demand Curve for Loans

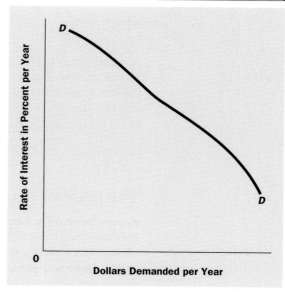

PUZZLE RESOLVED: THE SUPPLY OF FUNDS

Somewhat different relationships arise on the supply side of the market for funds—where the suppliers or *lenders* are consumers, banks, and other business firms. Funds lent out are usually returned to the owner (with interest) only over a period of time. Loans will look better to lenders when they bear higher interest rates, so the supply schedule for loans rather naturally may be expected to slope upward—at higher rates of interest, lenders supply more funds. Such a supply schedule appears as the curve *SS* in Figure 5, where we also reproduce the demand curve, *DD,* from Figure 4. Here, the free-market interest rate is 7.5 percent.

However, not all supply curves for funds slope uphill to the right like curve *SS.* As we stated in the puzzle at the beginning of the chapter, sometimes a rise in the interest rate (the price of loans that is the financial reward for saving) will lead people to save less, rather than more. An example will help to explain the reason for this apparently curious behavior, which, as we will see, can sometimes be sensible behavior. Say Jim is saving to buy a $10,000 used tractor in three years. If he lends money out at interest in the interim, suppose Jim must save $3,100 per year to reach his goal. If interest rates were higher, he could get away with saving less than

$3,100 per year and still reach his $10,000 goal because every year, with the higher interest, he would get larger interest payments on his savings. Thus, Jim's saving (and lending) may decline as a result of the rise in interest rate. This argument applies fully only to savers, like Jim, with a fixed accumulation goal, but similar considerations affect the calculations of other savers. So when the rate of interest rises, some people save more but some save less.

Generally, we expect the quantity of loans supplied to rise at least somewhat when the interest reward rises, so the supply curve will have a positive slope, like *SS* in Figure 5. However, for reasons similar to those indicated in Jim's example, the increase in the economy's saving that results from a rise in the interest rate is usually quite small. That is why we have drawn the supply curve to be so steep. The rise in the amount supplied by some lenders is partially offset by a decline in the amounts lent by savers with fixed goals (like Jim, who is putting money away to buy a tractor, or Jasmine, who is saving for an expensive camera).

FIGURE 5

Equilibrium in the Market for Loans

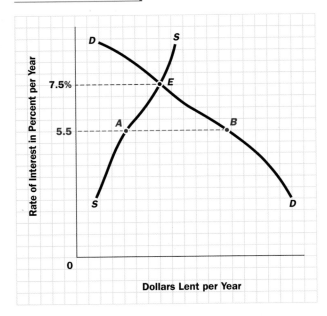

Having examined the relevant demand and supply curves, we are now in a position to discuss the determination of the equilibrium rate of interest. This is summed up in Figure 5, in which the equilibrium is, as always, at point *E,* where quantity supplied equals quantity demanded. We conclude, again, that the equilibrium interest rate on loans is 7.5 percent in the example in the graph.

The Issue of Usury Laws: Are Interest Rates Too High?

People have often been dissatisfied with the market mechanism's determination of interest rates. Fears that interest rates, if left unregulated, would climb to exorbitant levels have made usury laws (which place upper limits on money-lending rates) quite popular in many times and places. Attempts to control interest payments date back to biblical days, and in the Middle Ages the influence of the church even led to total prohibition of interest payments in much of Europe. The same is true today in Moslem countries. In the United

States, the patchwork of state usury laws was mostly dismantled during the 1980s when the banking industry was deregulated.

Unscrupulous lenders often manage to evade usury laws, charging interest rates even higher than the free-market equilibrium rate. Even when usury laws are effective, they interfere with the operation of supply and demand and, as we will demonstrate, they may harm economic efficiency.

Look at Figure 5 again but, this time, assume it depicts the supply of bank loans to consumers. Consider what happens if a usury law prohibits interest rates higher than 5.5 percent per year on consumer loans. At 5.5 percent, the quantity supplied (point A in Figure 5) falls short of the quantity demanded (point B). This means that many applicants for consumer loans are being turned down even though banks consider them to be creditworthy.

Who gains and who loses from this usury law? The gainers are the lucky consumers who get loans at 5.5 percent even though they would have been willing to pay 7.5 percent. The losers are found on both the supply side and the demand side: the consumers who would have been willing and able to get credit at 7.5 percent but who are turned down at 5.5 percent, and the banks that could have made profitable loans at rates of up to 7.5 percent if there were no interest-rate ceiling.

This analysis explains why usury laws can be politically popular. Few people sympathize with bank stockholders, and the consumers who get loans at lower rates are, naturally, pleased with the result of usury laws. Other consumers, who would like to borrow at 5.5 percent but cannot because quantity supplied is less than quantity demanded, are likely to blame the bank for refusing to lend, rather than blaming the government for outlawing mutually beneficial transactions.

Concern over high interest rates can be rational. It may, for example, be appropriate to combat homelessness by making financing of housing cheaper for poor people. Of course, it may be much more rational for the government to subsidize the interest on housing for the poor rather than to declare high interest rates illegal, in effect pretending that those costs can simply be legislated away, as a usury ceiling tries to do.[4]

THE DETERMINATION OF RENT

The factor of production we will discuss next is land. Rent, the payment for the use of land, is another price that, when left to the market, often seems to settle at politically unpopular levels. Rent controls are a frequent solution. We discussed the effects of rent controls in Chapter 4 (pages 72–73), and we will say a bit more about them later in this chapter. Our main focus here is the determination of rents by free markets.

The market for land is characterized by a special feature on the supply side. Land is a factor of production whose total quantity supplied is (roughly) unchanging and virtually unchangeable: The same quantity is available at every possible price. Indeed, classical economists used this notion as the working definition of land, and the definition seems to fit, at least approximately. Although people may drain swamps, clear forests, fertilize fields, build skyscrapers, or convert land from one use (a farm) to another (a housing development), human effort cannot change the total supply of land by very much.

What does this fact tell us about how the market determines land rents? Figure 6 helps to provide an answer. The vertical supply curve *SS* means that no matter what

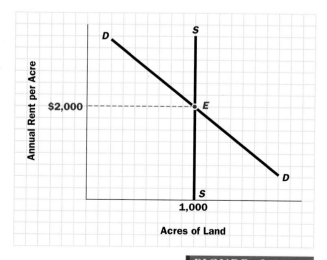

FIGURE 6

Determination of Land Rent in Littleville

---

[4] The law also sometimes concerns itself with discrimination in lending against women or members of ethnic minority groups. Strong evidence suggests the existence of sex and race discrimination in lending. For example, as late as the nineteenth century, married women were often denied loans without the explicit permission of their husbands, even when the women had substantial independent incomes.

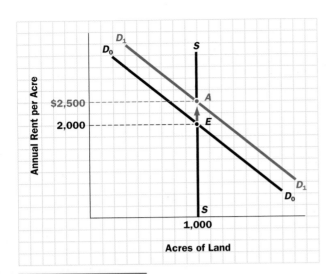

the level of rents, there are only 1,000 acres of land in a small hamlet called Littleville. The demand curve, *DD*, slopes downward and is a typical marginal revenue product curve, predicated on the notion that the use of land, like everything else, is subject to diminishing returns. The free-market price is determined, as usual, by the intersection of the supply and demand curves at point *E*. In this example, each acre of land in Littleville rents for $2,000 per year. The first interesting feature of this diagram is that, because quantity supplied is rigidly fixed at 1,000 acres whatever the price, the market level of rent is entirely determined by the market's demand side. This leads to the second special feature: Any shift in the demand curve that raises (or lowers) it by *X* dollars will raise (or lower) the equilibrium price of land by precisely the same amount—*X* dollars.

If, for example, a major university relocates to Littleville, attracting more people who want to live there, the *DD* curve will shift outward, as depicted in Figure 7. Equilibrium in the market will shift from point *E* to point *A*. The same 1,000 acres of land will be available, but now each acre will command a rent of $2,500 per acre. The landlords will collect more rent, even though society gets no more of the input—land—from the landlords in return for its additional payment.

The same process also works in reverse, however. If the university shuts its doors and the demand for land declines as a result, the landlords will suffer even though they did not contribute to the decline in the demand for land. (To see this, simply reverse the logic of Figure 7. The demand curve begins at D_1D_1 and shifts to D_0D_0.)

This discussion shows the special feature of rent that leads economists to distinguish it from payments to other factors of production. An **economic rent** is an "extra" payment for a factor of production (such as land) that does not change the amount of the factor that is supplied. Society is not compensated for a rise in its rent payments by any increase in the quantity of land it obtains. Economic rent is thus the portion of the factor payment that exceeds the minimum payment necessary to induce that factor to be supplied.

As late as the end of the nineteenth century, the idea of economic rent exerted a powerful influence far beyond technical economic writings. American journalist Henry George was nearly elected mayor of New York in 1886, running on the platform that all government should be financed by a "single tax" levied on landlords, who, he said, are the only ones who earn incomes without contributing to the productive process. George said that landlords reap the fruits of economic growth without contributing to economic progress. He based his logic on the notion that landowners do not increase the supply of their factor of production—the quantity of land—when rents increase.

Economic rent is the portion of the earnings of a factor of production that exceeds the minimum amount necessary to induce that factor to be supplied.

Land Rents: Further Analysis

If all plots of land were identical, our previous discussion would be virtually all there is to the theory of land rent. But plots of land *do* differ—in geographical location, topography, nearness to marketplaces, soil quality, and so on. The early economists, notably David Ricardo, took this disparity into account in their analysis of rent determination—a remarkable nineteenth-century piece of economic logic still considered valid today.

The basic notion is that capital invested in any piece of land must yield the same rate of return per dollar invested as capital invested in any other piece that is actually in use. Why? If it were not so, capitalist renters would bid against one another for the more profitable pieces of land. This competition would go on until the rents they would have to pay for these parcels were driven up to a point that eliminated their advantages over other parcels.

Suppose that a farmer produces a crop on one piece of land for $160,000 per year in labor, fertilizer, fuel, and other nonland costs, whereas a neighbor who is no more efficient produces the same crop for $120,000 on a second piece of land. The rent on the second parcel must be *exactly* $40,000 per year higher than the rent on the first, because otherwise production on one plot would be cheaper than on the other. If, for example, the rent difference were only $30,000 per year, it would be $10,000 cheaper to produce on the second plot of land. No one would want to rent the first plot and every grower would instead bid for the second plot. Rent on the first plot would be forced down by the lack of customers, and rent on the second plot would be driven up by eager bidders. These pressures would come to an end only when the rent difference reached $40,000, so that both plots became equally profitable.

At any given time, some low-quality pieces of land are so inferior that it does not pay to use them at all—remote deserts are a prime example. Any land that is exactly on the borderline between being used and not being used is called **marginal land.** By this definition, marginal land earns no rent because if its owner charged any for it, no one would willingly pay to use it.

We combine these two observations—that the difference between the costs of producing on any two pieces of land must equal the difference between their rents and that zero rent is charged on marginal land—to conclude that

> **Rent on any piece of land will equal the difference between the cost of producing the output on that land and the cost of producing it on marginal land.**

That is, competition for the superior plots of land will permit the landowners to charge prices that capture the full advantages of their superior parcels.

This analysis helps us to understand more completely the effects of an outward shift in the demand curve for land. Suppose population growth raises demand for land. Naturally, rents will rise. But we can be more specific than this statement. In response to an outward shift in the demand curve, two things will happen:

- *It will now pay to employ some land whose use was formerly unprofitable.* The land that was previously on the zero-rent margin will no longer be on the borderline, and some land that is so poor that it was formerly not even worth considering will now just reach the borderline of profitability. The settling of the American West illustrates this process strikingly. Land that once could not be given away is often now very valuable.
- *People will begin to exploit already-used land more intensively.* Farmers will use more labor and fertilizer to squeeze larger amounts of crops out of their acreage, as has happened in recent decades. Urban real estate that previously held two-story houses will now be used for high-rise buildings.

These two events will increase rents in a predictable fashion. Because the land that is considered marginal *after* the change must be inferior to the land that was considered marginal previously, rents must rise by the difference in yields between the old and new marginal lands. Table 2 illustrates this point. In the table, we deal with three pieces of land: A, a very productive piece; B, a piece that was initially considered only marginal; and C, a piece that is inferior to B but nevertheless becomes marginal when the demand curve for land shifts upward and to the right.

The crop costs $80,000 more when produced on B than on A, and $12,000 more when produced on C than on B. Suppose, initially, that demand for the crop is so low that Farmer Jones does not plant crops in field C. Farmer Jones is on the fence about whether to plant crops in field B. Because field B is marginal, it is just on the margin between being used and being left idle—it will command no rent. We know that the rent on field A will be equal to the $80,000 cost advantage of A over B. Now suppose demand for the crop increases enough so that plot C becomes marginal land.

Marginal land is land that is just on the borderline of being used—that is, any land the use of which would be unprofitable if the farmer had to pay even a penny of rent.

TABLE 2

Nonrent Costs and Rent on Three Pieces of Land

Type of Land	Nonland Cost of Producing a Given Crop	Total Rent Before	After
A. A tract that was better than marginal before and after	$120,000	$80,000	$92,000
B. A tract that was marginal before but is attractive now	200,000	0	12,000
C. A tract that was previously not worth using but is now marginal	212,000	0	0

Then field B commands a rent of $12,000, the cost advantage of B over C. Plot A's rent now must rise from $80,000 to $92,000, the size of its cost advantage over C, the newly marginal land.

In addition to the quality differences among pieces of land, a second influence pushes land rents up: increased intensity of use of land that is already under cultivation. As farmers apply more fertilizer and labor to their land, the marginal productivity of the land increases, just as factory workers become more productive when more is invested in their equipment. Once again, the landowner can capture this productivity increase in the form of higher rents. (If you do not understand why, refer back to Figure 7 and recall that the demand curves are marginal revenue product curves—that is, they indicate the amount that capitalists are willing to pay landlords to use their land.) Thus, we can summarize the theory of rent as follows:

As the use of land increases, landlords receive higher payments from two sources:

- **Increased demand leads the community to employ land previously not good enough to use; the advantage of previously used land over the new marginal land increases, and rents go up correspondingly.**
- **Land is used more intensively; the marginal revenue product of land rises, thereby increasing the ability of the producer who uses the land to pay rent.**

Generalization: Economic Rent Seeking

Economists refer to the payments for land as "rents," but land is not the only scarce input with a fixed supply, at least in the short run. Toward the beginning of the twentieth century, some economists realized that the economic analysis of rent can be applied to inputs *other* than land. As we will see, this extension yielded some noteworthy insights.

The concept of rent can be used to analyze such common phenomena as lobbying in the U.S. Congress (attempts to influence the votes of members of Congress) by industrial groups, lawsuits between rival firms, and battles over exclusive licenses (as for a television station). Such interfirm battles can waste very valuable economic resources—for

Land Prices Around the World

Supply and demand do not equalize prices for identical commodities offered by different sellers when the commodity, such as land, cannot be transferred from one geographic market to another. In 2008, for example, retailers on the Avenue des Champs-Elysees in Paris paid an average of $1,134 per square foot, per year. In comparison, shop space on Milan's Via Montenapoleone cost $983 per square foot each year, and retail real estate on New Bond Street in London cost $810 per square foot per year. A fifteen-block stretch of 5th Avenue, between Central Park and 42nd Street in New York City, ranked as the most expensive retail real estate in the world, at $1,850 per square foot in 2008.

SOURCE: © Adina Tovy/Robert Harding/Jupiterimages

SOURCE: Matt Woolsey, "World's Most Valuable Addresses," *Forbes*, December 22, 2008, http://www.forbes.com/2008/12/22/most-valuable-addresses-forbeslife-cx_mw_1222realestate.html.

example, the time that executives, bureaucrats, judges, lawyers, and economists spend preparing and battling court trials. Because this valuable time could have been used in production, such activities entail large *opportunity costs*. Rent analysis offers insights into the reasons for these battles and provides a way to assess what *quantity* of resources people waste as they seek economic rents for scarce resources.

How is economic rent—which is a payment to a factor of production above and beyond the amount necessary to get the factor to make its contribution to production—relevant in such cases? Gordon Tullock, an economist also trained in legal matters, first identified the phenomenon of rent seeking as the search and battle for opportunities to charge or collect those payments above and beyond the amount necessary to create the source of the income.

An obvious source of such rents is a monopoly license. For example, a license to operate the only television station in town will yield enormous advertising profits, far above the amount needed for the station to operate. That's why rent seekers swoop down when such licenses become available. Similarly, the powerful lobby for U.S. sweetener producers, including corn and beet growers as well as cane sugar farmers, pressures Congress to impede cane sugar imports, because free importation would cut prices (and rents) substantially. Such activities need not increase the quantities of product supplied, just as higher rents do not increase the supply of land. That is why any resulting earnings are called "rent" and why the effort to obtain such earnings that contribute nothing to output is called "rent seeking."

How much of society's resources will be wasted in such a process? Rent-seeking theory can give us some idea. Consider a race for a monopoly cable TV license that, once awarded, will keep competing stations from operating. *Nothing prevents anyone from entering the race* to grab the license. Anyone can hire the lobbyists and lawyers or offer the bribes needed in the battle for such a lucrative license. Thus, although the cable business itself may not be competitive, the process of fighting for the license can be very competitive.

Of course, we know from the analysis of long-run equilibrium under perfect competition (Chapter 10, pages 206–209) that in such markets, economic profits approximate zero—in other words, revenues just cover costs. If owners expect a cable license to yield, say, $900 million over its life in rent, then rent seekers (that is, the companies competing to gain the license in the first place) are likely to waste something close to that amount as they fight for the license.

Why? Suppose each of 10 bidders has an equal chance at winning the license. To each bidder, that chance should be worth about $90 million—1 chance in 10 of getting $900 million. If the average bidder spends only $70 million on the battle, each firm will still value the battle for the license at $90 million minus $70 million. This fact will tempt an eleventh bidder to enter and raise the ante to, say, $80 million in lobbying fees, hoping to grab the rent. This process of attraction of additional bidders stops only when all of the excess rent available has been wasted on the rent-seeking process, so there is no further motivation for still more people to bid.

Rent as a Component of an Input's Compensation

We can use the concept of economic rent to divide the payment for any input into two parts. The first part is simply the minimum payment needed to acquire the input—for example, the cost of producing a ball bearing or the compensation people require in exchange for the unpleasantness, hard work, and loss of leisure involved in performing labor. The owners of the input must be offered this first part of the factor payment if they are to supply the input willingly. If workers do not receive at least this first part, they will not supply their labor.

The second part of the payment is a *bonus* that does not go to every input, but only to inputs of particularly high quality, like the payment to the owner of higher-quality land in our earlier example. Payments to workers with exceptional natural skills are a good illustration of the generalized rent concept. Because these bonuses are like the extra payment for a better piece of land, they are called *economic rents*. Indeed, like the rent of land, an increase in the amount of economic rent paid to an input may not increase the *quantity* of that input supplied. This second part of the payment—the economic rent—is pure gravy. The skillful worker is happy to have it as an extra, but it is not a deciding consideration in the choice of whether or not to work.

An Application of Rent Theory: Salaries of Professional Athletes

Professional athletes may seem to have little in common with plots of farmland. Yet to an economist, the same analysis—the theory of economic rent—explains how the market arrives at the amounts paid to each of these "factors of production." To understand why, let's look at a hypothetical basketball team, the Lost Lakers, and its seven-foot star center, Dapper Dan. First, we must note that there is only one Dapper Dan. That is, he is a scarce input whose supply is fixed just like the supply of land. Because he is in fixed supply, the price of his services is determined in a way similar to that of land rents.

A moment's thought shows how the general notion of economic rent applies both to land and to Dapper Dan. The total quantity of land available for use is the same whether rent is high, low, or zero; only limited payments to landlords are necessary to induce them to supply land to the market. By definition, then, a considerable proportion of the payments to landholders for their land is economic rent—payments above and beyond those necessary for landlords to provide land to the economy. Dapper Dan is (almost) similar to land in this respect. His athletic talents are unique and cannot be reproduced. What determines the payment to such a factor? Because the quantity supplied of such a unique, nonreproducible factor is absolutely fixed (there's only one Dapper Dan), and therefore unresponsive to price, the analysis of rent that we summarized in Figure 6 applies, and the position of the demand curve for Dapper Dan's services is determined by the superiority of his services over those of other players.

Suppose the Lost Lakers team also includes a marginal player, Weary Willy, winner of last year's Least Valuable Player award. Willy earns the $50,000 per year necessary to obtain his services. Suppose also that if no other option were available, Dapper Dan would be willing to play basketball for $50,000 per year, rather than working as a hamburger flipper, the only other job for which he is qualified. But Dan knows he can do better than that. He estimates, quite accurately, that his presence on the team brings in $10 million of added revenue over and above what the team would obtain if Dan were replaced by a player of Willy's caliber. In that case, Dan and his agent ought to be able to obtain $10 million *more* per year than is paid to Willy. As a result, Dan obtains a salary of $10,050,000, of which $10 million is economic rent—exactly analogous to the previous rent example involving different pieces of land of unequal quality. Note that the team gets no more of Dapper Dan's working time in return for the rent payment. (See "A-Rod: Earning Lots of Economic Rent" on the facing page for a real-world example.)

Almost all inputs, including employees, earn some economic rent. What sorts of inputs earn no rent? Only those inputs that can be provided by a number of suppliers at equal and constant cost and with identical quality earn no rents. For instance, no ball-bearing supplier will ever receive any rent on a ball bearing, at least in the long run, because any desired number of them, *of equal quality*, can be produced by any of the competing suppliers at (roughly) constant costs and can contribute equal amounts to the profits of those who use them. If one ball-bearing supplier tried to charge a price above their *x*-cent cost, another manufacturer would undercut the first supplier and take its customers away. Hence, the competitive price includes no economic rent.

Rent Controls: The Misplaced Analogy

Why is the analysis of economic rent important? Because only economic rent can be taxed away without reducing the quantity of the input supplied. Here common English gets in the way of sound reasoning. Many people feel, in effect, that the *rent* they pay to their landlord is economic rent. After all, their apartments will still be there if they pay $1,500 per month, or $500, or $100. This view, although true in the short run, is quite shortsighted.

"A-Rod": Earning Lots of Economic Rent

In case you think that our discussion of economic rent is mere academic theorizing, check out these numbers: In 2000, in a deal that sent shock waves through the baseball establishment, shortstop Alex Rodriguez signed a 10-year, $252-million contract with the Texas Rangers. His salary of more than $25 million per year makes him one of the highest-paid professional athletes in sports history. It is safe to assume that most of his salary is economic rent—in other words, he would still be willing to play baseball if no team offered him much more than a far smaller amount.

Less than four years later, the Rangers, finding themselves unable to afford A-Rod's huge salary, traded their superstar shortstop to the New York Yankees—who can afford him. In fact, however, the Rangers will still pay part of Rodriguez's salary through the year 2010. But the saga continued: In October 2007, after the Yankees failed to reach the playoffs, A-Rod opted out of his contract and became a free agent. Six weeks later, he signed a new $275 million 10-year contract with the Yankees organization. That move paid off for the Yankees—in 2009 they defeated the Philadelphia Phillies to win the World Series.

SOURCE: © Jason Szenes/EPA/Landov

Like the ball-bearing producer, the owner of a building cannot expect to earn *economic rent* because too many other potential owners whose costs of construction are roughly the same will also offer apartments if rents are high. If the market price temporarily included some economic rent—that is, if price exceeded production costs plus the opportunity cost of the required capital—other builders would start new construction that would drive the price down. Far from being in perfectly *inelastic* (vertical) supply, like raw land, buildings come rather close to being in perfectly *elastic* (horizontal) supply, like ball bearings. As we have learned from the theory of rent, this means that builders and owners of buildings cannot collect economic rent in the long run.

Because apartment owners collect very little economic rent, payments by tenants in a free market must be just enough to keep those apartments on the market (the very definition of zero economic rent). If rent controls push these prices down, the apartments will start disappearing from the market.[5] Among other unfortunate results, we can therefore expect rent controls to contribute to homelessness—though it is, of course, not the only influence behind this distressing phenomenon.

PAYMENTS TO BUSINESS OWNERS: ARE PROFITS TOO HIGH OR TOO LOW?

We turn next to business profits, the discussion of which often seems to elicit more passion than logic. With the exception of some economists, almost no one thinks that profit rates are at the right level. Critics point accusingly to some giant corporations' billion-dollar profits and argue that they are unconscionably high; they then call for much stiffer taxes on profits. On the other hand, the Chambers of Commerce, National Association of Manufacturers, and other business groups complain that regulations

---

[5] None of this is meant to imply that temporary rent controls in certain locations cannot have desirable effects in the short run. In the short run, the supply of apartments and houses really is fixed, and large shifts in demand can hand windfall gains to landlords—gains that are true, if temporary, economic rents. Controls that eliminate such windfalls should not cause serious problems. But knowing when the "short run" fades into the "long run" can be tricky. "Temporary" rent control laws have a way of becoming rather permanent.

and "ruinous" competition keep profits too low, and they constantly petition Congress for tax relief.

The public has many misconceptions about the nature of the U.S. economy, but probably none is farther from reality than popular perceptions of what American corporations earn in profits. Try the following experiment. Ask five of your friends who have never had an economics course what fraction of the nation's income they imagine is pure profit to companies. Although the correct answer varies from year to year, business profits in 2006 made up 12.4 percent of gross domestic product (GDP) (before taxes).[6] A comparable percentage of the prices you pay represents before-tax profit. Most people think this figure is much, much higher (see "Public Opinion on Profits" on page 31 in Chapter 2).

As you can see, economists are reluctant to brand factor prices as "too low" or "too high" in some moral or ethical sense. Rather, they are likely to ask first: What is the market equilibrium price? Then they will ask whether there are any good reasons to interfere with the market solution. This analysis, however, is not so easily applied to the case of *profits*, because it is difficult to use supply-and-demand analysis when you do not know which factor of production earns profit.

In both a bookkeeping sense and an economic sense, *profits are the residual*. They are what remains from the selling price after all other factors have been paid.

But which production factor earns this reward? Which factor's marginal productivity constitutes the profit rate?

What Accounts for Profits?

Economic profit is the total revenue of a firm minus all of its costs, including the interest payments and opportunity costs of the capital it obtains from its investors.

Economic profit, as we learned in Chapter 10, is the amount a firm earns *over and above the payments for all inputs,* including the interest payments for the capital it uses and the opportunity cost of any capital provided by the owners of the firm. The payment that firm owners receive to compensate them for the opportunity cost of their capital (and that in common parlance is considered profit) is closely related to interest rates but is not part of *economic profit*. In an imaginary (and dull) world in which everything was certain and unchanging, capitalists who invested money in firms would simply earn the market rate of interest on their funds. Profits beyond this level would be competed away. Payment for capital below this level could not persist, because capitalists would withdraw their funds from firms and deposit them in banks. Capitalists in such a world would be mere moneylenders.

But the real world is not at all like this. Some capitalists are much more than moneylenders, and the amounts they earn often exceed current interest rates by a huge margin. This substantial earning can be a rent, of the sort we have just been considering. But now we are discussing other sources of profit, which are obtained in return for some productive service by the recipient (see "Nimble Entrepreneurship: Snatching Victory from the Jaws of Defeat" for an example). However, we can list three primary ways in which profits above "normal" interest rate levels can be earned.

1. Monopoly Power   If a firm can establish a monopoly with some or all of its products, even for a short while, it can use that monopoly power to earn monopoly profits. We analyzed the nature of these monopoly earnings in Chapter 11.

2. Risk Bearing   Firms often engage in financially risky activities, subjecting the capitalist investors in the firm (as well as its employees) to some financial peril. For example, when a firm prospects for oil, it must drill exploratory wells hoping to find petroleum at

---

[6] SOURCE: *National Income and Product Accounts,* U.S. Department of Commerce, Bureau of Economic Analysis, available at http://www.bea.gov.

Nimble Entrepreneurship: Snatching Victory from the Jaws of Defeat

"The path to entrepreneurial success is not always obvious. In fact, in the case of Scale Computing of Indianapolis, failure was the springboard.

Jeff Ready, the chief executive of Scale Computing, and his business partners said they originally thought they would use the artificial-intelligence technology they had developed at a previous start-up company to recast stock prices and make a fortune as hedge fund gurus.

But by the time they had built their 'magic box,' the economy had turned grim and they were unable to raise the $100 million they thought they needed. It was only after potential customers rejected other software technology ideas that they realized their device could be marketed as a more practical product: a data storage system. Two years later, the orders are pouring in.

Andrew Zacharakis, a professor of entrepreneurship at Babson College outside Boston, said Scale Computing's owners followed a classic entrepreneurial path of shifting gears as necessary to seize real, as opposed to perceived, opportunities."

SOURCE: Image copyright Tatuasha, 2009. Used under license from Shutterstock.com

SOURCE: Excerpted from Brent Bowers, "Finding the Path to Success by Changing Directions," *The New York Times*, September 9, 2009, accessed online at http://www.nytimes.com.

the bottom. Of course, many such exploratory wells end up as dry holes, and the costs then bring no return. Lucky investors, on the other hand, do find oil and are rewarded handsomely—more than the competitive return on the firm's capital. The extra income pays the firm for bearing risk.

A few lucky individuals make out well in this process, but many suffer heavy losses. How well can we expect risk takers to do, on the average? If 1 exploratory drilling out of 10 typically pays off, do we expect its return to be exactly 10 times as high as the interest rate, so that the *average* firm will earn exactly the normal rate of interest? The answer is that the payoff will be *more* than 10 times the interest rate if investors dislike gambling—that is, if they prefer to avoid risk. Why? Because investors who are risk averse will not be willing to put their money into a business that faces such long odds—10 to 1—unless the market provides compensation for the financial peril.

In reality, nothing guarantees that things will always work out this way. Some people love to gamble and tend to be overly optimistic. They may plunge into projects to a degree unjustified by the odds. Average payoffs to such gamblers in risky undertakings may end up below the interest rate. The successful investor will still make a good profit, just like the lucky winner in Las Vegas. The average participant, however, will have to pay for the privilege of bearing risk.

3. Returns to Innovation

The third major source of profits is perhaps the most important of all for social welfare. People who introduce new outputs or new production methods or find new markets for the commodities that the firm sells are called *innovative entrepreneurs*. The first entrepreneur able to innovate and market a desirable new product or employ a new cost-saving machine will garner a higher profit than what an uninnovative (but otherwise similar) business manager would earn. Innovation differs from invention. Whereas **invention** generates new ideas, **innovation** takes the next step by putting the new idea into practical use. Businesspeople are rarely inventors, but they are often innovators.

When an entrepreneur innovates, even if the new product or new process is not protected by patents, the entrepreneur will be one step ahead of competitors. If the market

Invention is the act of generating an idea for a new product or a new method for making an old product.

Innovation also includes the next step, the act of putting the new idea into practical use.

likes the innovation, the entrepreneur will be able to capture most of the sales, either by offering customers a better product or by supplying the product more cheaply. In either case, the entrepreneur will temporarily have some monopoly power as the competitors weaken and will receive monopoly profit for the initiative.

And the benefit to the community can be substantial. Innovative entrepreneurs have played a crucial role in recognizing promising inventions and ensuring that they are put to productive use. They have contributed enormously to the rapid growth of per-capita income and the flood of new products that have emerged in the past several centuries. The crucial role of the entrepreneur will be discussed more fully in the following chapter, which will complete the elements of the story of economic growth that was begun in Chapter 16.

Taxing Profits

Thus, we can consider profits in excess of market interest rates to be the return on entrepreneurial talent. But this definition is not really very helpful, because no one can say exactly what entrepreneurial talent is. Certainly we cannot measure it; nor can we teach it in a college course, although business schools may try. We do not know whether the observed profit rate provides more than the minimum reward necessary to attract entrepreneurial talent into the market. This relationship between observed profit rates and minimum necessary rewards is crucial when we start to consider the policy ramifications of taxes on profits—a contentious issue, indeed.

Consider a profits tax levied on oil companies. If oil companies earn profits well above the minimum required to attract entrepreneurial talent, those profits contain a large element of economic rent. In that case, we could tax away these excess profits (rents) without fear of reducing oil production. In contrast, if oil company profits do not include economic rents, then a windfall profits tax can seriously curtail oil exploration and, hence, production.

This example illustrates the general problem of deciding how heavily governments should tax profits. Critics of big business who call for high, if not confiscatory, profits taxes seem to believe that profits are mostly economic rent. If they are wrong—if, in fact, most of the observed profits are necessary to attract people into entrepreneurial roles—then a high profits tax can be dangerous. Such a tax would threaten the very lifeblood of the capitalist system. Business lobbying groups claim, predictably enough, that current tax policy creates precisely this threat. Unfortunately, neither group has offered much evidence to support its conclusion.

CRITICISMS OF MARGINAL PRODUCTIVITY THEORY

The theory of factor pricing described in this chapter once again uses supply-demand analysis. Factor pricing theory also relies heavily on the principle of marginal productivity to derive the shape and position of the demand curve for various inputs. Indeed, some economists refer to the analysis (rather misleadingly) as the *marginal productivity theory of distribution*, when it is, at best, only a theory of the demand side of the pertinent market.

Over the years, factor pricing analysis has been subject to attack on many grounds. One frequent accusation, which is largely (but not entirely) groundless, is the assertion that marginal productivity theory merely attempts to justify the income distribution that the capitalist system yields—in other words, that it is a piece of pro-capitalist propaganda. According to this argument, when marginal productivity theory claims that each factor is paid exactly its marginal revenue product, it is only a sneaky way of saying that each factor is paid exactly what it deserves. These critics claim that the theory legitimizes the gross inequities of the system—the poverty of many and the great wealth of a few.

This argument is straightforward but wrong. First, payments are made not to factors of production, but rather to the people who happen to own them. If an acre of land earns

$2,000 because that is its marginal revenue product, it does not mean, nor is it meant to imply, that the landlord *deserves* any particular payment, because he may even have acquired the land by fraud.

Second, an input's MRP does not depend only on "how hard it works" but also on how much of it happens to be employed—because, according to the "law" of diminishing returns, beyond some level of employment, the more of an input that is employed, the lower its MRP. Thus, a factor's MRP is not and cannot legitimately be interpreted as a measure of the intensity of its "productive effort." In any event, what an input "deserves," in some moral sense, may depend on more than what it does in the factory. For example, workers who are sick or have many children may be considered more deserving, even if they are no more productive than their healthy or childless counterparts.

On these and other grounds, no economist today claims that marginal productivity analysis shows that distribution under capitalism is either just or unjust. It is simply wrong to claim that marginal productivity theory is pro-capitalist propaganda. The marginal productivity principle is just as relevant to organizing production in a socialist society as it is in a capitalist one.

Other critics have attacked marginal productivity theory for using rather complicated reasoning to tell us very little about the really urgent problems of income distribution. In this view, it is all very well to say that everything depends on supply and demand and to express this idea in terms of many complicated equations (many of which appear in more advanced books and articles). But these equations do not tell us what to do about such serious distribution problems as malnutrition among the indigenous populations in Latin America or poverty among minority groups in the United States.

Although it does exaggerate the situation somewhat, there is some truth to this criticism. We have seen in this chapter that the theory provides some insights into real policy matters, though not as many as we would like. Later in the book, we will see that economists do have useful things to say about the problems of poverty and underdevelopment, but very little of what we can say about these issues arises out of marginal productivity analysis.

Perhaps, in the end, what should be said for marginal productivity theory is this: As the best model we have at the moment, marginal productivity theory offers us some valuable insights into the way the economy works, and until we find a more powerful model, we are better off using the tools that we do have.

| SUMMARY |

1. A profit-maximizing firm purchases the quantity of any input at which the price of the input equals its **marginal revenue product** (MRP). Consequently, the firm's demand curve for an input is (the downward-sloping portion of) that input's MRP curve.

2. **Investment** in a firm is the amount that is added to the firm's capital, which is its plant, equipment, inventory, and other productive inputs that tie up the company's money.

3. **Interest** rates are determined by the supply of and demand for funds. The demand for funds is a **derived demand,** because these funds are used to finance business investment whose profitability depends on the demand for the final products turned out with the aid of such investment. In this way, the demand for funds depends on the marginal revenue productivity of capital.

4. A dollar obtainable sooner is worth more than a dollar obtainable later because of the interest that can be earned on that dollar in the interim.

5. Increased demand for a good that needs land to produce it will drive up the price of land either because inferior land will be brought into use or because land will be used more intensively.

6. Rent controls do not significantly affect the supply of land, but they do tend to reduce the supply of buildings.

7. **Economic rent** is any payment to the supplier of a factor of production that is greater than the minimum amount needed to induce the factor to be supplied.

8. **Factors of production** that are unique in quality and difficult or impossible to reproduce will tend to be paid relatively high economic rents because of their scarcity.

9. Factors of production that are easy to produce at a constant cost and that are provided by many suppliers will earn little or no economic rent.

10. **Economic profits** over and above the cost of **capital** are earned (a) by exercise of monopoly power, (b) as payments for bearing risk, and (c) as the earnings of successful **innovation.**

11. The desirability of increased taxation of profits depends on the taxes' effects on the supply of managerial talent. If most profits are economic rents, then higher profits taxes will have few undesirable effects. If most profits are necessary to attract good managers or entrepreneurs into the market, then higher profits taxes can weaken the capitalist economy.

| KEY TERMS |

capital   401

derived demand   400

economic profit   412

economic rent   406

entrepreneurship   398

factors of production   397

innovation   413

interest   402

invention   413

investment   401

marginal land   407

marginal physical product (MPP)   398

marginal revenue product (MRP)   398

| TEST YOURSELF |

1. Which of the following inputs do you think include relatively large economic rents in their earnings?

   a. Nuts and bolts

   b. Petroleum

   c. A champion racehorse

   Use supply-demand analysis to explain your answer.

2. Three machines are employed in an isolated area. They each produce 2,000 units of output per month, the first requiring $20,000 in raw materials, the second $25,000, and the third $28,000. What would you expect to be the monthly charge for the first and second machines if the services of the third machine can be hired at a price of $9,000 per month? Which parts of the charges for the first two machines are economic rent?

3. Economists conclude that a tax on the revenues of firms will be shifted in part to consumers of the products of those firms in the form of higher prices. However, they believe that a tax on the rent of land usually cannot be shifted and must be paid entirely by the landlord. What explains the difference? (*Hint:* draw the supply-demand graphs.)

4. Many economists argue that a tax on apartment buildings is likely to reduce the supply of apartments, but that a tax on all land, including the land on which apartment buildings stand, will not reduce the supply of apartments. Can you explain the difference? How is this answer related to the answer to Test Yourself Question 3?

5. Distinguish between investment and capital.

6. Explain the difference between an invention and an innovation. Give an example of each.

7. What is the difference between interest and profit? Who earns interest, in return for what contribution to production? Who earns economic profit, in return for what contribution to production?

| DISCUSSION QUESTIONS |

1. A profit-maximizing firm expands its purchase of any input up to the point where diminishing returns have reduced the marginal revenue product so that it equals the input price. Why does it not pay the firm to "quit while it is ahead," buying so small a quantity of the input that the input's MRP remains greater than its price?

2. If you have a contract under which you will be paid $10,000 two years from now, why do you become richer if the rate of interest falls?

3. Do you know any entrepreneurs? How do they earn a living? How do they differ from managers?

4. "Marginal productivity does not determine how much a worker will earn—it determines only how many workers will be hired at a given wage. Therefore, marginal productivity analysis is a theory of demand for labor, not a theory of distribution." What, then, do you think determines wages? Does marginal productivity affect their level? If so, how?

5. **(More difficult)** American savings rates are among the lowest of any industrial country. This has caused concern about our ability to finance new plants and equipment for U.S. industry. Some politicians and others have advocated lower taxes on saving as a remedy. Do you expect such a program to be very effective? Why?

6. If rent constitutes only 2 percent of the incomes of Americans, why may the concept nevertheless be significant?

7. Litigation in which one company sues another often involves costs for lawyers and other court costs literally amounting to hundreds of millions of dollars per case. What does rent have to do with the matter?

| APPENDIX | *Discounting and Present Value*

Frequently in business and economic problems it is necessary to compare sums of money received (or paid) at different dates. Consider, for example, the purchase of a machine that costs $11,000 and will yield a marginal revenue product of $14,520 two years from today. If the machine can be financed by a two-year loan bearing 10 percent interest, it will cost the firm $1,100 in interest at the end of each year, plus $11,000 in repayment of the principal (the amount originally borrowed) at the end of the second year. (See the table that follows.) Is the machine a good investment?

Costs and Benefits of Investing in a Machine

	End of Year 1	End of Year 2
Benefits		
Marginal revenue product of the machine	$0	$14,520
Costs		
Interest	1,100	1,100
Repayment of principal on loan	0	11,000
Total Cost	1,100	12,100

The total costs of owning the machine over the two-year period ($1,100 + $12,100 = $13,200) are less than the total benefits ($14,520). But this is clearly an invalid comparison, because the $14,520 in future benefits is not worth $14,520 *in terms of today's money.* Adding up dollars received (or paid) at different dates is a bit like adding apples and oranges.

The process that has been invented for making the magnitudes of payments at different dates comparable to one another is called **discounting**, or **computing the present value.**

To illustrate the concept of present value, let us ask how much $1 received a year from today is worth in terms of today's money. If the rate of interest is 10 percent, the answer is about 91 cents. Why? Because if we invest 91 cents today at 10 percent interest, it will grow to 91 cents plus 9.1 cents in interest = 100.1 cents in a year. That is, at the end of a year a payment of $100 will leave the recipient about as well off as he would have been if he had instead received $91 now. Similar considerations apply to any rate of interest. In general:

If the rate of interest is *i*, the present value of $1 to be received in a year is

$$\frac{\$1.00}{(1 + i)}$$

This is so, because in a year

$$\frac{\$1.00}{(1 + i)}$$

will grow to the original amount plus the interest payment; that is,

$$\frac{\$1.00}{(1 + i)} + \frac{\$1.00}{(1 + i)} \times i = \frac{\$1.00}{(1 + i)} \times (1 + i) = \$1$$

What about money to be received two years from today? Using the same reasoning, and supposing the interest rate is 10 percent so that $1 + i = 1.1$, $1.00 invested today will grow to $1.00 times (1.1) = $1.10 after one year and will grow to $1.00 times (1.1) times (1.1) = $1.00 times $(1.1)^2$ = $1.21 after two years. Consequently, the present value of $1.00 to be received two years from today is

$$\frac{\$1.00}{(1 + i)^2} = \frac{\$1.00}{1.21} = 82.64 \text{ cents}$$

A similar analysis applies to money received three years from today, four years from today, and so on.

The general formula for the present value of $1.00 to be received N years from today when the rate of interest is *i* is

$$\frac{\$1.00}{(1 + i)^N}$$

The present value formula is based on the two variables that determine the present value of any future flow of money: the rate of interest (*i*) and the amount of time you have to wait before you get it (*N*).

Let us now apply this analysis to our example. The present value of the $14,520 revenue is easy to calculate because it all comes two years from today. Because the rate of interest is assumed to be 10 percent ($i = 0.1$), we have:

$$\text{Present value of revenues} = \frac{\$14,520}{(1.1)^2}$$
$$= \frac{\$14,520}{1.21}$$
$$= \$12,000$$

The present value of the costs is a bit trickier in this example because costs occur at two different dates. The present value of the first interest payment is

$$\frac{\$1,100}{(1 + i)} = \frac{\$1,100}{1.1} = \$1,000$$

The present value of the final payment of interest plus principal is

$$\frac{\$12,100}{(1 + i)^2} = \frac{\$12,100}{(1.1)^2} = \$10,000$$

Now that we have expressed each sum in terms of its present value, it is permissible to add them up. So the present value of all costs is

Present value of costs = $1,000 + $10,000

= $11,000

Comparing this figure to the $12,000 present value of the revenues clearly shows that the machine really is a good investment. We can use the same calculation procedure for all investment decisions.

| SUMMARY |

1. To determine whether a loss or a gain will result from a decision whose costs and returns will come at several different periods of time, we must discount all the figures represented by these gains and losses to obtain their present value.

2. For discounting purposes, we use the present value formula for X dollars receivable N years from now with an interest rate i:

$$\text{Present value} = \frac{X}{(1 + i)^N}$$

3. We then combine the present values of all the returns and all the costs. If the sum of the present values of the returns is greater than the sum of the present values of the costs, then the decision to invest will promise a net gain.

| KEY TERM |

**discounting, or computing the
present value   417**

| TEST YOURSELF |

1. Compute the present value of $1,000 to be received in three years if the rate of interest is 11 percent.

2. A government bond pays $100 in interest each year for three years and also returns the principal of $1,000 in the third year. How much is it worth in terms of today's money if the rate of interest is 8 percent? If the rate of interest is 12 percent?

LABOR AND ENTREPRENEURSHIP: THE HUMAN INPUTS

Octavius (a wealthy young Englishman): "I believe most intensely in the dignity of labor."
The chauffeur: "That's because you never done any."

GEORGE BERNARD SHAW, *MAN AND SUPERMAN*, ACT II

"O for a muse of fire that would ascend/ The brightest heaven of invention"

WILLIAM SHAKESPEARE, *HENRY V*, ACT I, SCENE I

Two human factors of production can be credited with major contributions to a nation's production and economic growth—the labor force and the entrepreneurs. The former contribute the physical and mental effort required for production. The latter organize the workers' efforts and ensure that they are provided with the capital and the raw materials their activities require. They also find new ways to carry out these processes, invent new products, and find new markets in which to sell them. We begin this chapter with a discussion of the economics of labor activity, and then we will turn to the entrepreneurs.

CONTENTS

PART 1: THE MARKETS FOR LABOR

Labor costs account for by far the largest share of gross domestic product (GDP). As noted in Chapter 19, the earnings of labor amount to almost three-quarters of national income. Wages also represent the primary source of personal income for the vast majority of Americans. For more than a century, wages were the centerpiece of the American dream. In almost every decade, the purchasing power of a typical worker's earnings grew substantially, and the U.S. working class evolved into a comfortable middle class—the envy of the world and an irresistible lure for millions of immigrants. Then, something changed fundamentally in ways economists do not yet fully understand.

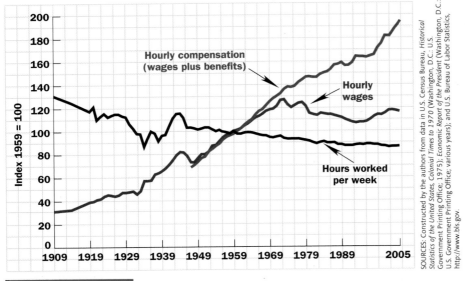

SOURCES: Constructed by the authors from data in U.S. Census Bureau, *Historical Statistics of the United States, Colonial Times to 1970* (Washington, D.C.: U.S. Government Printing Office, 1975); *Economic Report of the President* (Washington, D.C.: U.S. Government Printing Office; various years); and U.S. Bureau of Labor Statistics, http://www.bls.gov.

FIGURE 1

Index of Trends in Wages, Compensation, and Work Hours, 1909–2005 (in Real, Inflation-Adjusted Terms)

Figure 1 shows that average real wages (wages adjusted for changes in the purchasing power of the dollar) stopped their upward march around 1973 and, by some (disputed) calculations, even declined. In contrast, hourly *compensation* (wages plus fringe benefits) did not fall. Fringe benefits include things like health insurance, retirement payments, and education subsidies that employers provide to their employees. But compensation *growth* did slow markedly.[1] The graph also shows that average hours worked per week have declined by almost 35 percent since the early 1900s, even when wages and compensation were increasing. (The big drop in hours worked during the 1930s was a consequence of the Great Depression, and the sharp rise in hours worked during the 1940s was attributable to World War II.) During most of the 1990s, average hours worked per week remained virtually constant, then, after 2000, started to drop slowly once again.

PUZZLE: ENTREPRENEURS EARN LESS THAN MOST PEOPLE THINK—WHY SO LITTLE?

The most obvious incentive for innovative entrepreneurs to devote the time, effort, and investment to innovative activity is the great wealth and enormous prestige that success in their undertaking appears to promise, as in the case of superstar inventors such as Eli Whitney, James Watt, Elias Singer, Thomas Edison, the Wright Brothers, etc. But a healthy dose of reality may be in order. Thomas Astebro* reports on the basis of a sample of 1,091 inventions that, "only between 7–9 percent reach the market. Of the 75 inventions that did, six received returns above 1400 percent, 60 percent obtained negative returns and the median was negative" (p. 226).

SOURCE: © Library of Congress - digital version copyright Science Faction / Getty Images

---

[1] The sharp increases in compensation over the years reflect, at least in part, the rising cost of services such as health care, rather than an increase in the quantity and quality of benefits provided to workers. We explored the reasons for the rising costs of services in Chapter 15.

Perhaps even more striking is the recent work of economist William Nordhaus.** "Using data from the U.S. non-farm business section, I estimate that innovators are able to capture about *2.2 percent* of the total [benefits of] innovation . . . the rate of profit on [their investments] over the 1948–2001 period is estimated to be 0.19 percent per year" (p. 34).

So we see that the innovative entrepreneur's activities are a lottery that offers just a few mega-prizes, like so many of the lotteries that capture the headlines. An innovator's activity is much like a mega-lottery, or like the pursuit of an occupation that offers a limited number of superstar positions. A very well-recognized attribute of lotteries is their built-in unfairness. The average payout is sure to be less than the per-ticket-holder take of the lottery operator—that is why he is in the business. The evidence does indeed support the hypothesis that the inventors and the entrepreneurs are characterized by a degree of optimism well above the norm. Research shows that they are inclined to believe, much more than other people do, that they really are likely to win the grand prize of the lottery.

But that is hardly the end of the story. Each of these activities—innovative entrepreneurship and the purchase of lottery tickets—also provides an important payoff of a second sort. Both activities offer distinct psychological rewards in contemplating the *prospects* of glory, of wealth and fame, yielding the pleasure and excitement of anticipation, even if the winnings never materialize. They are, indeed, the stuff that dreams are made of.

* Astebro, Thomas, "The Return to Independent Invention: Evidence of Unrealistic Optimism, Risk Seeking or Skewness Loving," *The Economic Journal*, January 2003, pp. 226–238.

** Nordhaus, William D., "Schumpeterian Profits in the American Economy: Theory and Measurement," Working Paper 10433, Cambridge, MA: National Bureau of Economic Research, 2004.

Slowing wage growth has been accompanied by an expanding *income gap* between the rich and the poor, as will be discussed in Chapter 21. In 2008, the income share of the poorest fifth of households was about 3.4 percent of the U.S. total, whereas the richest fifth's income share had reached about 50 percent.[2] As of 2005, more than one in five American children lives in poverty, a rate about twice as high as in the big economies of Western Europe.[3]

Along with this, the prospective gap between your income as a future college graduate and the incomes of your contemporaries who have not attended college has widened sharply. For instance, in 1973 male college graduates earned about 38 percent more than their high school–educated counterparts, and female college graduates earned about 50 percent more than their high school–educated counterparts. By 2005, college-educated men and women were earning about 80 percent more and 72 percent more, respectively, than men and women with only high school educations.[4] As of 2007, median annual income for high school graduates in the United States was $27,000. In comparison, college graduates earned $47,000 and those with advanced degrees earned $61,000. These developments have profound and distressing implications for the future of our society as a whole. We will discuss some of the possible causes later in the chapter.

WAGE DETERMINATION IN COMPETITIVE MARKETS

To understand such labor issues, we must first investigate how wages are determined. In a completely free labor market, wages (the price of labor) would be determined by supply and demand, just like any other price. On the demand side, we would find that the demand curve for labor is derived like the demand curve for any other input—by labor's marginal revenue product, in the manner described in Chapter 19. However, the labor market has a number of distinctive features on the supply side.

[2] U.S. Census Bureau, "Income, Poverty, and Health Insurance Coverage in the United States: 2008," September 2009, accessed online at: http://www.census.gov.

[3] United Nations Children's Fund, "Child Poverty in Rich Countries 2005," *Innocenti Report Card*, no. 6 (2005), Florence, Italy: Innocenti Research Center, accessed online at: http://www.unicef.org.

[4] Lawrence Mishel, Jared Bernstein, and Sylvia Allegretto, *The State of Working America, 2006/2007* (Ithaca, N.Y: ILR Press, Cornell University Press, 2007), http://www.epi.org; and U.S. Census Bureau, "Educational Attainment in the United States: 2007," January 2009, accessed online at: http://www.census.gov.

Though the labor market is generally far from perfectly competitive, we start our investigation by describing the theory of competitive labor markets in which the buyers are large numbers of tiny firms and the sellers are individual workers who act independently of one another. In this model, both buyers and sellers are too small to have any choice but to accept the wage rate determined by the impersonal forces of supply and demand.

The Demand for Labor and the Determination of Wages

The **marginal revenue product of labor (MRP$_L$)** is the increase in the employer's total revenue that results when it hires an additional unit of labor.

Much of what we can say about the demand for labor was already said about the demand for inputs in general in earlier chapters. Workers are hired (primarily) by profit-maximizing firms, which hire an input quantity at which the input's price (the market wage) equals its marginal revenue product (MRP). In this chapter, **MRP$_L$** is the abbreviation we will use for the **marginal revenue product of labor.** Recall that MRP$_L$ is the addition to the firm's revenue that it obtains by hiring one additional worker. It is equal to the additional amount that worker produces (the worker's marginal physical product, or MPP) multiplied by the price of that product. In other words, to determine how much additional money that worker brings in, we multiply the amount she produces by the price of the commodity she produces.[5]

If the MRP$_L$ exceeds the price of labor (the wage), by the usual reasoning of marginal analysis the firm can increase its profit by hiring at least one more worker either to produce more output or to substitute for some other input. The reverse is true when the MRP$_L$ is less than its wage. Thus, the derived demand and, consequently, the demand curve for labor are determined by labor's marginal revenue product. Such a demand curve is shown as the blue curve *DD* in Figure 2. The figure also includes a brick-colored supply curve, labeled *SS*. Since in a competitive labor market equilibrium will be at the wage that equates the quantity supplied with the quantity demanded, equilibrium occurs at point *E*, where demand curve *DD* crosses supply curve *SS*. The equilibrium wage is $300 per week and equilibrium employment is 500,000 workers. Here because 500,000 workers will be employed at a wage of $300 per week, the total income of the workers will be $300 × 0.5 million = $150 million.

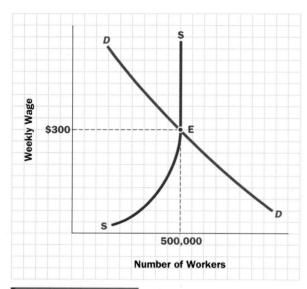

FIGURE 2

Equilibrium in a Competitive Labor Market

Influences on MRP$_L$: Shifts in the Demand for Labor

What determines MRP$_L$? The answer offers some important insights about the labor market.

Some obvious influences can change labor's MRP. For example, increased education can improve the ability of the labor force to master difficult technology, raising MRP. Economists use the phrase **investment in human capital** to refer to spending on education and other means to increase labor's knowledge and skills. Such spending is analogous to investment in the firm's plant and equipment because both are outlays today that increase production both now *and in the future.*

Workers can also improve their skills through experience, called *on-the-job training,* and in a variety of ways that give them added information and increase their mental and physical dexterity.

Because the demand for labor is a *derived demand,* anything that enhances the demand for the goods and services that labor produces can shift the labor demand curve upward. So in a period of economic prosperity when consumers will have more to spend, their demand for products will shift upward, which in turn will raise the price of the worker's

Investment in human capital is any expenditure on an individual that increases that person's future earning power or productivity.

---

[5] To review, see Chapter 7, pages 130–131.

product, thereby shifting upward the MRP curve—the demand for labor. That, of course, is why unemployment is always low during a period of prosperity.

Technical Change, Productivity Growth, and the Demand for Labor

Another critical influence on the MRP_L is the quality and quantity of the *other* inputs used by workers. Especially important is innovation that improves machinery, power sources, and other productive instruments that adds to what can be produced by a given amount of labor, and so crucially affects the levels of wages and employment.

Technical change that increases the worker's productivity has two effects that work in opposite directions. First, increased productivity clearly implies an increase in the worker's marginal physical product—the quantity of widgets that an additional worker can produce will rise. Second, because of the resulting reduction in labor cost and the increased output of widgets, we can expect that when productivity rises, widget prices will fall. Now recall that

Marginal revenue product of labor in widget production = 5 price of widgets multiplied by the worker's marginal widget output:

$$MRP = P \text{ (of widgets)} \times MPP$$

Because an increase in productivity raises MPP but reduces *P*, we cannot be sure of the net effect on MRP—that is, the net effect on the demand curve for labor.[6]

PRODUCTIVITY GROWTH: *Productivity Growth Is (Almost) Everything in the Long Run* In the long run, rising productivity has always improved the standard of living for both workers and the owners of other factors of production. As we indicated in one of our *Ideas for Beyond the Final Exam*, in the long run nothing contributes more to the economic well-being of the nation than rising productivity. Today workers enjoy far longer lives, better health, more education, and more luxury goods than they did a century ago or in any previous period in history. The fact that an hour of labor today can produce a large multiple of what our ancestors could create in an hour can increase everyone's average income. In the short run, labor-saving technological change sometimes cuts employment and holds down wages. Historically, however, in the long run it has not reduced employment. It has raised workers' incomes and increased real wages. In the United States, in the last century, productivity per hour of labor grew about eightfold, and the purchasing power of the wage a worker earns in an hour was multiplied nearly fivefold.

The Service Economy and the Demand for Labor

Although productivity growth has not led to any long-term upward trend in unemployment, it *has* cut jobs drastically in some parts of the economy, sending the labor force to other economic sectors for employment. Agriculture is the prime example. It has been estimated that at the time of the American Revolution, nearly 90 percent of the U.S. labor force had agricultural jobs and eked out what today would be considered a meager standard of living. Yet today, with just 0.32 percent of the nation's labor working on farms, the United States produces such a surplus of products that it sometimes seems unmanageable. At first, after the huge drop in farm jobs was under way, the farm workers shifted to manufacturing, as growing U.S. incomes raised demand for industrial products sharply. Then productivity in manufacturing took off, and workers again had to move elsewhere into the service sector of the economy. Indeed, it has transformed the United States into a "service economy," with more than three-quarters of the labor force employed in services such as telecommunications, software design, health care, teaching, and restaurants.

---

[6] However, experience shows that, in the very short run, an increase in labor productivity (that is, of labor-saving technology) often causes a downward shift in the demand for labor, which holds down wages. If firms can meet the current demand for their products with 10 percent fewer workers than they needed last year, they will be tempted to "downsize," which is a polite way of saying that they will fire some workers. This does sometimes occur, so workers' widespread fear of labor-saving technology is, to some degree, justified.

It has been argued that this has occurred because other countries are stealing away the U.S. manufacturing business base, but this is simply untrue. As Figure 3 reports, the service sector has become dominant in *all* the major industrial economies. No industrial economy has been able to avoid it by stealing manufacturing markets away from the others. More relevant to our concerns here is another worry: that the workers driven from manufacturing into the service sector of the economy have predominantly become low-paid dishwashers and hamburger flippers. That is true in some cases, but the majority of new service jobs created in the past half-century are in the information sector of the economy, including computation, research, and teaching, all occupations requiring both education and specialized skills.

SOURCES: Organization for Economic Cooperation and Development, *Quarterly Labor Force Statistics*, various issues; and *OECD in Figures*, various years, http://www.sourceoecd.org.

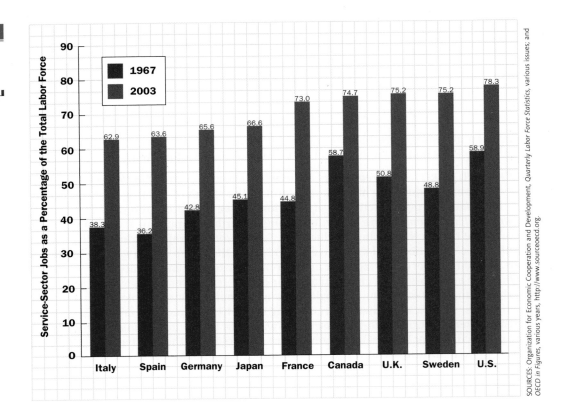

FIGURE 3

The Growing Share of Service-Sector Jobs in Nine Countries, 1967 and 2003

THE SUPPLY OF LABOR

We turn next to labor supply, which has undergone several significant labor supply trends in recent decades.

First, the expansion of the total labor force has continued, much of it ascribable to sheer growth of the nation's population. From this, the number of jobholders has grown—from about 60 million jobholders right after World War II to about 145 million in 2008.

Second, the proportion of the population with jobs has also grown, from about 58 percent after World War II to 65.2 percent in 2009. This is called *a rise in labor force participation*.

Third, there are new groups of workers, notably women, who today hold proportionately more jobs (46 percent of the workforce) than before (except in wartime).

Finally, the labor supply conditions have been affected by a continued and large relative decline in union membership. There has been a significant fall in the share of American workers who belong to unions, whose stated purpose is to protect their interests. Unions seek to bargain for all the workers in a firm or an industry, thus eliminating competition among workers over jobs and wages, and we will consider them later in this chapter. First, we discuss some other supply-side influences.

Rising Labor-Force Participation

One significant development in labor supply in the industrial countries is the increase in the number of family members who hold jobs. In 2008, 66 percent of the 59 million American married-couple families had two wage earners, compared with only 40 percent in 1970.[7] It used to be that the "head of the household" (usually the husband) was ordinarily the only breadwinner. Today, however, married women also hold jobs. This is in part attributable to lagging wages, forcing both heads of the family into gainful employment. Rapidly rising medical costs and costs of education add to these financial pressures.

Participation in the labor force has increased for other reasons as well: liberation of women from their traditional role in the family, and progress in education of minorities that increased their job opportunities. Not so long ago, an African-American executive in a major business firm was unheard of, and an employed wife was considered disgraceful because it implied that her husband could not support her properly. Today this has changed drastically, although discrimination is by no means over. These changes have affected the labor market. For a while the increase in supply may have held back wages. This is, of course, what the usual supply-demand graph for a labor market tells us—when the supply curve of labor shifts to the right, the price of labor (that is, the wage) can be expected to fall. Second, it has been argued that a combination of discrimination and the initial lack of experience of these new entrants into the labor market (which temporarily reduced their MRP_L) had a similar effect. Discrimination against women or African-American or Hispanic workers in the labor market can force them to accept wages lower than those paid to white male employees with comparable ability (as will be discussed more fully in the appendix to the next chapter, Chapter 21). Lack of experience can have a similar effect, but for a reason that is less objectionable: If workers acquire skill through experience on the job (on-the-job training), then, on the average, inexperienced workers can be expected to have lower MRP_L, so the demand curve for the inexperienced workers will also be low, and lower wages will follow.

An Important Labor Supply Conundrum

For most commodities, an increase in their prices leads to an increase in the quantities supplied, whereas a price decline reduces the amounts supplied; that is, supply curves slope upward. But the striking historical trends in labor supply tell a very different story. Supply has tended to fall when wages rose and to rise when wages fell. Throughout the first three-quarters of the twentieth century, real wages rose, as Figure 1 clearly showed. Yet labor asked for and received reductions in the length of the workday and workweek. At the beginning of the century, the standard workweek was 50 to 60 hours (with virtually no vacations). Since then, labor hours have generally declined to an average workweek of about 34 hours.

In the last two decades, as the rise in real wages has ceased or at least slowed markedly, people have increased the quantity of labor they supply.

Where has the common-sense view of this matter gone wrong? Why, as hourly wages rose for 75 years, did workers not sell more of the hours they had available instead of pressing for a shorter and shorter workweek? And why, in recent years, have they sold more of their labor time as real wage rates stopped rising?

A simple observation helps us to answer these questions: Given the fixed amount of time in a week, a person's decision to *supply* more labor to firms is simultaneously a decision to *demand* less leisure time for himself. The leisure time can be interpreted simply as what is left over after the time spent at work. Assuming that, deducting the necessary time for eating and sleeping, a worker has 90 usable hours in a week, then a decision to spend 40 of those hours working is simultaneously a decision to demand 50 of them for other purposes.

---

[7] U.S. Census Bureau, *Current Population Survey,* http://www.census.gov.

This offers us a substantial insight into the relationship between wages and labor supply. Economists say that a rise in wages has two effects on the worker's demand for leisure—the substitution effect and the income effect, that tell us a good deal about the labor market.

> The **substitution effect** of a wage increase is the resulting incentive to work more because of the higher relative reward to labor.

1. Substitution Effect

The **substitution effect** of an increase in the price of any good is the resulting switch of customers to a substitute product whose price has not risen. An increase in the price of fish, for example, can lead consumers to buy more meat. The same is true of wages and the demand for leisure. For instance, if you decide not to work overtime this weekend, the price you pay for that increase in leisure (the opportunity cost) is the amount of wage you have to give up as a result. An increase in wages makes leisure more expensive. So a wage increase can induce workers to buy less leisure time (and more of other things). Thus:

The substitution effect of higher wages leads most workers to want to work more.

2. Income Effect

An increase in the price of any good, other things equal, clearly increases the real incomes of sellers of the good. That rise in income affects the amount of the good (as well as the amounts of other items) that the individual demands. This indirect effect of a price change on demand, called the **income effect** of the price change, is especially important in the case of wages. Higher wages make consumers richer. We expect this increased wealth to raise the demand for most goods, including leisure. So:

> The **income effect** of a rise in wages is the resulting rise of workers' purchasing power that enables them to afford more leisure.

The income effect of higher wages leads most workers to want to work less (that is, demand more leisure), whereas the income effect of lower wages makes them want to work more.

Putting these two effects together, we conclude that some workers may react to an increase in their wage rate by wanting to work more, whereas others may react by wanting to working less. For the market as a whole, therefore, higher wages can lead to either a larger or a smaller quantity of labor supplied. Statistical studies of this issue in the United States have arrived at the following conclusions:

- The response of labor supply to wage changes is not very strong for most workers.
- For low-wage workers, the substitution effect seems clearly dominant, so they work more when wages rise.
- For high-wage workers, the income effect just about offsets the substitution effect, so they do not work more when wages rise.

Figure 4 depicts these approximate "facts." It shows labor supply rising (slightly) as wages rise up to point *A, as substitution effects outweigh income effects.* Thereafter, labor supply is roughly constant as wages rise and income effects become just as important as substitution effects up to point *B.* At still higher wages, above point *B,* income effects may overwhelm substitution effects, so that rising wages can even cut the quantity of labor supplied.

Thus, it is even possible that when wages are raised high enough, further wage increases will lead workers to purchase more leisure and therefore to work less (see "The Income Effect: Is Time More Valuable Than Money?" on the next page). The supply curve of labor is

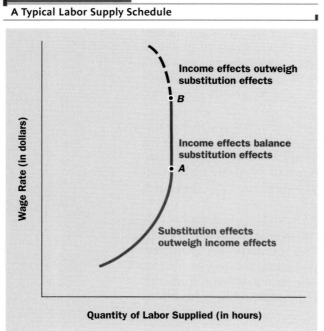

FIGURE 4

A Typical Labor Supply Schedule

Income effects outweigh substitution effects

B

Income effects balance substitution effects

A

Substitution effects outweigh income effects

Wage Rate (in dollars)

Quantity of Labor Supplied (in hours)

The Income Effect: Is Time More Valuable Than Money?

"Time is now more valuable than money wherever you stand on the career ladder, according to a survey of more than 1,000 junior and senior professionals. The survey, by Universum, found that 40 per cent of junior employees—those with one to eight years' work experience—and 50 per cent of senior professionals—with more than eight years' experience—ranked flexible working hours as the most attractive perk that an employer could offer. This compares with 31 per cent of junior staff and 36 per cent of senior staff who put competitive compensation first.

Workers are placing increasing importance on their personal lives and are not afraid to make demands of their employers, the survey shows. Work-life balance is No. 1 on the list of short-term career goals for 43 per cent of junior staff and 60 per cent of more senior staff. . . .

Employers are aware that workers' demands are changing. 'Money is no longer what drives people,' says Sasha Hardman, the HR associate director of Allen & Overy, a law firm. 'They want interesting work, the opportunity to progress, to work with interesting people and a good work-life balance. . . .'"

SOURCE: © 2010 Pixland/Jupiterimages

SOURCE: Excerpted from Clare Dight, "It's No Longer Just About the Money, You Know," *The Times* (of London), January 17, 2008, p. 8.

---

then said to be **backward-bending,** as illustrated by the broken portion of the curve above point *B* in Figure 4.

Does this theory of labor supply apply to college students? A study of the hours worked by students at Princeton University found that it does.[8] Estimated substitution effects of higher wages on the labor supply of Princeton students were positive and income effects were negative, just as the theory predicts. Apparently, substitution effects outweighed income effects by a slim margin, so that higher wages attracted a somewhat greater supply of labor. Specifically, a 10 percent rise in wages increased the hours of work of the Princeton student body by about 3 percent.

> A supply curve of labor is **backward-bending** when a rise in an initially low wage leads to a rise in quantity of labor supplied, but a rise in a wage that was already high reduces the amount supplied.

The Labor Supply Conundrum Resolved

We can now answer our earlier question: Why is it that, historically, rising wages have reduced labor supply and falling wages have increased it?

Rising wages enable the worker to provide for her family with fewer hours of work. As a result, the worker can afford to purchase more leisure without a cut in living standards. Thus, the income effect of increasing wages induces workers to work fewer hours. Similarly, falling wages reduce the worker's income. To preserve the family's living standard, she must seek additional hours of work; and the worker's spouse may have to leave their children in day care and take a job.

Thus, it is the strong income effect of rising wages that apparently accounts for the fact that labor supply has responded in the "wrong" direction, with workers working ever-shorter hours as real wages rose and longer hours as wages fell.

---

[8] Mary P. Hurley, "An Investigation of Employment among Princeton Undergraduates during the Academic Year," senior thesis, Department of Economics, Princeton University, May 1975.

WHY DO WAGES DIFFER?

Earlier in the chapter, we saw how wages are determined in a free-market economy: In a competitive labor market, the equilibrium wage occurs where quantity supplied equals quantity demanded (refer back to Figure 3). In reality, of course, no single wage level applies to all workers. Some workers are paid very well, whereas others are forced to accept meager earnings. We all know that certain groups in our society (the young, the disadvantaged, the uneducated) earn relatively low wages and that some of our most severe social ills (poverty, crime, drug addiction) are related to this fact. But why are some wages so low while others are so high? The explanation is important, because it can help us determine what to do to help poorly paid workers increase their earnings and move up toward the income levels of the more fortunate suppliers of labor.

In the most general terms, the explanation of wage differences is the fact that there is not one labor market but many—each with its own supply and demand curves and its own equilibrium wage. Supply-demand analysis implies that wages are relatively high in markets where demand is high relative to supply, as in Figure 5(a). This, however, doesn't tell us what we need to know about wage differentials. To make the analysis useful, we still must breathe some life into the supply-and-demand curves.

FIGURE 5

Wage Differentials

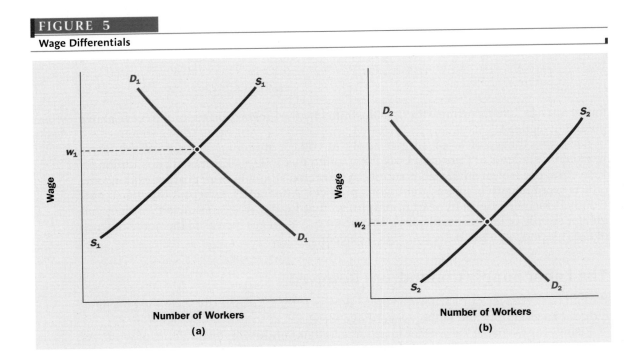

Number of Workers
(a)

Number of Workers
(b)

Labor Demand in General

We start with demand. The demand for labor is greater in some markets than in others because it is guided by workers' *marginal physical product* (MPP), and that depends, of course, on the worker's *abilities* and *degree of effort* on the job. But, there is also the influence of the *other factors of production* that workers use to produce output. Workers in U.S. industry are more productive than workers in many other countries at least partly because they have generous supplies of machinery, natural resources, and technical know-how, and so they earn high wages.

The marginal product of some workers can also be increased relative to that of others by superior education, training, and experience.

Labor Supply in General

Turning next to the supply of labor, it is clear that the *size of the available working population relative to the magnitude of industrial activity* in a given area is important. It helps explain why construction wages soared in New Orleans as a result of the rebuilding efforts after Hurricane Katrina: Demand rose while supply was reduced by the loss of a working population.

The *nonmonetary* attractiveness of any job will also clearly influence the supply of workers to it. Jobs that people find pleasant and satisfying—such as teaching in suburban schools—will attract a large supply of labor and will consequently pay a relatively low wage. In contrast, a premium will have to be paid to attract workers to jobs that are onerous, disagreeable, or dangerous—such as washing the windows of skyscrapers.

Finally, the amount of ability and training needed to enter a particular job or profession is relevant to its supply of labor. Brain surgeons and professional ice skaters earn generous incomes because there are few people as highly skilled as they and because it is time-consuming and expensive to acquire these skills even for those who have the ability.

Investment in Human Capital

The idea that education is an investment is likely to be familiar even to students who have never thought explicitly about it. You made a conscious decision to go to college rather than to enter the labor market, and you are probably acutely aware that this decision is now costing you money—lots of money. Think of a high school friend who chose not to go to college and is now working. You are deliberately giving up a chance at a similar income in order to acquire more education.

In this sense, your education is an *investment* in yourself—a *human investment*. Like a firm that devotes some of its money to build a plant that will yield profits at some future date, you are investing in your own future, hoping that your college education will help you earn more than your high school–educated friend or enable you to find a more pleasant or prestigious job when you graduate. Economists call activities such as going to college investments in human capital because such activities give the person many of the attributes of a capital investment.

One implication of **human capital theory** is that college graduates should earn substantially more than high school graduates to compensate them for their extra investments in schooling. Do they? Your college investment will probably pay off. Indeed, as already noted, college graduates now earn nearly twice as much as their high school-educated peers, and the gap is rising.[9]

> **The large income differentials earned by college graduates provide an excellent "return" on the tuition payments and sacrificed earnings that they "invested" while in school.**

But what is it about more educated people that makes firms willing to pay them higher wages?

Most human capital theorists assume that students in high schools and colleges acquire skills that are productive in the marketplace, thereby raising their marginal revenue products. In this view, educational institutions are factories that take less productive workers as their raw materials, apply doses of training, and create more productive workers as outputs.

Human capital theory focuses on the expenditures that have been made to increase the productive capacity of workers via education or other means. It is analogous to investment in better machines as a way to increase their productivity.

Teenagers: a Disadvantaged Group in the Labor Market

As we have observed, the "labor market" is really composed of many submarkets for labor of different types, each with its own supply-and-demand curves. One particular labor market always seems to have higher unemployment than the labor force as a whole: the job market for teenagers.

Figure 6 shows that teenage unemployment rates have consistently been much higher than the overall unemployment rate, and black teenagers have fared worse than white

[9] U.S. Census Bureau, "Educational Attainment in the United States: 2007," January 2009, accessed online at: http://www.census.gov.

SOURCES: *Economic Report of the President* (Washington, D.C.: U.S. Government Printing Office; various years); and U.S. Bureau of Labor Statistics, http://www.bls.gov.

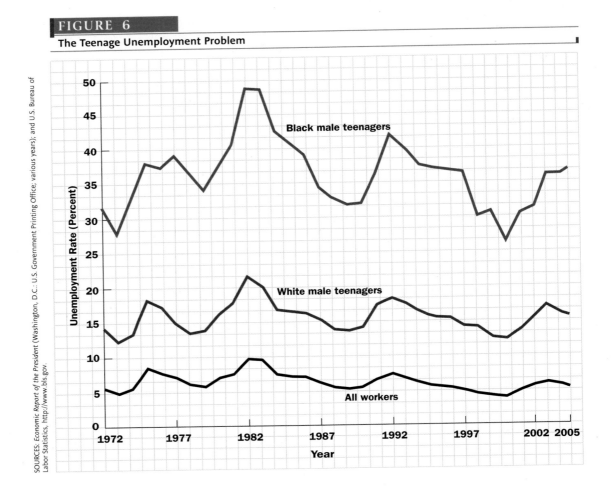

FIGURE 6

The Teenage Unemployment Problem

teenagers. For the most part, however, the three unemployment rates have moved up and down together, as the figure shows. The graph indicates that whenever the unemployment rate for all workers goes up or down, the teenage (defined here as a person aged 16 to 19 years) unemployment rate almost always moves in the same direction, but more dramatically. Thus, when things are generally bad, things are much, much worse for teenage workers, and especially for black teenage workers. Despite social and legislative pressures against race discrimination, efforts to improve the quality of education available to children in the inner cities, and many related programs, there has been no relative improvement in black teenage unemployment in recent years.

One reason is that teenagers generally have not completed their educations and have little job experience, so their marginal revenue products tend to be relatively low. Until recently, many economists argued that this fact, together with minimum wage laws that prevent teenagers from accepting wages commensurate with their low marginal revenue products, is the main cause of high teenage unemployment. The reasoning is that legally imposed high wages make it too expensive to hire teenagers. Recent studies suggest, however, that a rise in minimum wage produces little, if any, cut in demand for teen labor.

UNIONS AND COLLECTIVE BARGAINING

Our analysis of competitive labor markets has so far not dealt with one rather distinctive feature of the markets for labor: The supply of labor is not at all competitive in many labor markets; instead, it is controlled by a labor monopoly, a **labor union.**

Although they are significant, unions in the United States are not nearly as important as is popularly supposed. For example, most people who are unfamiliar with the data are astonished to learn that less than 13 percent of American workers belong to unions. This percentage is about half of what it was in the heyday of unionism in the mid-1950s. Figure 7 shows that in 1930, unions had enrolled slightly less than 7 percent of the U.S. labor force, and by 1933 this figure had slipped to barely more than 5 percent. Since the 1950s, the unionization rate has fallen with few interruptions.

One reason unionization in the United States has been declining is the shift of the U.S. labor force (like that experienced in every other industrial country) into service industries and out of manufacturing, where unions traditionally had their base. In addition, American workers' preferences seem to have shifted away from unions. The increasing share of women in the labor force may have contributed to this trend, because women have traditionally been less prone than men to join unions.

Finally, American unions came under increasing pressure in the 1990s and early 2000s because of stronger competition both at home and abroad. In response, firm after firm has closed plants and eliminated jobs. This "downsizing" trend has made it even more difficult for unions to win concessions that improve the economic positions of their members. That, in turn, has reduced the attractiveness of union membership.

> A **labor union** is an organization made up of a group of workers (usually with the same specialization, such as plumbing or costume design, or in the same industry). The unions represent the workers in negotiations with employers over issues such as wages, vacations, and sick leave.

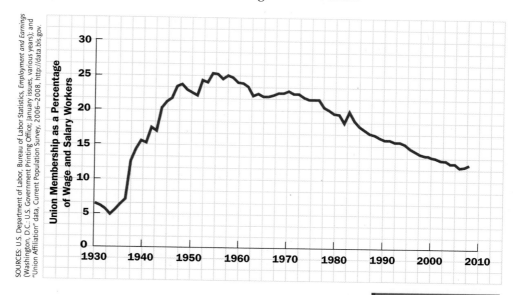

SOURCES: U.S. Department of Labor, Bureau of Labor Statistics, *Employment and Earnings* (Washington, D.C.: U.S. Government Printing Office, January issues, various years); and "Union Affiliation" data, Current Population Survey, 2006–2008, http://data.bls.gov.

In the United States, union membership levels are much lower than in most other industrialized countries. For example, as of 2007, about 25 percent of German workers and 75 percent of Danish workers belonged to unions.[10] The differences are striking and doubtless have something to do with the American tradition of "rugged individualism." But there are also other influences involved. In the United States, growing conservatism has apparently led to growing hostility toward unions.

Unions as Labor Monopolies

Unions require that we alter our economic analysis of the labor market in much the same way that monopolies required us to alter our analysis of the goods market (see Chapter 11). Recall that a monopoly seller of goods selects the point on its demand curve that maximizes its profits. Much the same idea applies to a union, which is, after all, a monopoly seller of labor. It too faces a demand curve—derived this time from the marginal revenue product schedules of firms—and can choose the point on that curve that suits it best.

The problem for the economist trying to analyze union behavior—and perhaps also for the union leader trying to select a course of action—is how to decide which point on the demand curve is "best" for the union and its members. There is no obvious single goal analogous to profit maximization that clearly determines what a union should do. Instead, there are a number of *alternative* goals that sound plausible.

---

[10] Small or declining membership may not necessarily be the same thing as declining influence. For example, union membership in France (8 percent of French workers, as of 2007) is lower than in the United States, but unions are much more powerful because of their formal role the French welfare system (Sources: "Déjà vu?: Special Report, Trade Unions," *The Economist* magazine, June 7, 2003, http://www.economist.com; and OECD, "Union Members and Employees" data, 2007, accessed online at: http://stats.oecd.org.).

The Way It Was

The calamitous Triangle Shirtwaist Factory fire of 1911, in which 146 women and girls lost their lives, was a landmark in American labor history. It galvanized public opinion behind the movement to improve conditions, hours, and wages in the sweatshops. Pauline Newman went to work in the factory, located on what is now New York University's campus, at the age of eight. Many of her friends lost their lives in the fire. She went on to become an organizer and executive of the newly formed International Ladies Garment Workers' Union. In her words:

> We started work at seven-thirty in the morning, and during the busy season we worked until nine in the evening. They didn't pay you any overtime and they didn't give you anything for supper money. . . .
>
> The employers didn't recognize anyone working for them as a human being. You were not allowed to sing. . . . We weren't allowed to talk to each other. . . . If you went to the toilet and you were there longer than the floor lady thought you should be, you would be laid off for half a day and sent home. And, of course, that meant no pay.
>
> You were not allowed to have your lunch on the fire escape in the summertime. The door was locked to keep us in. That's why so many people were trapped when the fire broke out. . . . You were expected to work every day if they needed you and the pay was the same whether you worked extra or not.
>
> Conditions were dreadful in those days. We didn't have anything. . . . There was no welfare, no pension, no unemployment insurance. There was nothing. . . . There was so much feeling against unions then. The judges, when one of our girls came before him, said to her: "You're not striking against your employer, you know, young lady. You're striking against God," and sentenced her to two weeks.
>
> I wasn't at the Triangle Shirtwaist Factory when the fire broke out, but a lot of my friends were. . . . The thing that bothered me was the employers got a lawyer. How anyone could have *defended* them! Because I'm quite sure that the fire was planned for insurance purposes. And no one is going to convince me otherwise. And when they testified that the door to the fire escape was open, it was a lie! It was never open. Locked all the time.

The Triangle Factory, now part of New York University

SOURCE: © AP Images

One hundred and forty-six people sacrificed, and the judge fined Blank and Harris seventy-five dollars!

The Problem Persists

The following newspaper excerpts show that unsafe working conditions continue to produce tragedies, even in this day and age:

***China Daily* (Beijing), February 25, 2006:** "At least 65 people were killed and more than 100 hurt when a fire swept through a locked textile factory crowded with night-shift workers in southern Bangladesh. Up to 500 people, mainly women, were believed to be working in the KTS Composite Textile factory in the southern city of Chittagong when the fire broke out on Thursday night, local fire chief Rashedul Islam said.

Firefighters had found the main entrance to the factory locked, he said, and were forced to rescue trapped workers by breaking open windows and using ropes. . . .

The toll might have been higher, but people working in neighboring factories brought in bamboo ladders and ropes to rescue those trapped on the upper floors, factory security guard Ful Mia said."

***The Daily Record* (Scotland), July 9, 2006:** "Nine people were killed in a chemical factory explosion yesterday—after bosses locked workers inside. . . .

The death toll at the factory in Kenya's capital Nairobi could rise because police have not been able to account for all of the 36 people who were in the building at the time of the explosion.

Most of the victims died because the factory owners locked them inside the building after the blast, claiming that they wanted to prevent people from stealing valuables.

Mutinda Nzuki, who was waiting outside to be hired as a casual worker when the tragedy occurred, said: 'The doors were all locked. It was horrific. The screams from inside were horrendous.'"

SOURCES: Excerpted from Joan Morrison and Charlotte Fox Zabusky (1980), *American Mosaic: The Immigrant Experience in the Words of Those Who Lived It* (New York: E. P. Dutton), reprinted by permission of the publisher, E. P. Dutton, Inc.; from "At Least 65 Die in Textile Factory Fire," *China Daily*, February 25, 2006, accessed online at http://www.chinadaily.com.cn; and from "Nine Dead in Factory Explosion," *The Daily Record* (of Scotland), July 9, 2006, p. 23.

The union leadership may, for example, decide that the size of the union is more or less fixed and try to force employers to pay the highest wage they will pay without firing any of the union members. But this tactic is a high-risk strategy for a union. Firms forced to pay such high wages will be at a competitive disadvantage compared with firms that have nonunion labor, and they may even be forced to shut down. Alternatively, union leaders may assign priority to increasing the size of their union. They may even try to make employment as large as possible by accepting a wage just above the competitive level. One way, but certainly not the only way, to strike a balance between the conflicting goals of maximizing wages and maximizing employment is to maximize the total earnings of all workers taken together.

Monopsony and Bilateral Monopoly

Our analysis thus far oversimplifies matters in several important respects. For one thing, it envisions a market situation in which one powerful union is dealing with many powerless employers: We have assumed that the labor market is monopolized on the selling side but is competitive on the buying side. Some industries more or less fit this model. The giant Teamsters' union negotiates with a trucking industry consisting of thousands of firms, most of them quite small and powerless, and most unions in the construction industry are much larger than the firms.

But many cases simply do not fit the model. The huge auto manufacturing corporations do not stand idly by while the United Automobile Workers (UAW) union picks its favorite point on the demand curve for autoworkers. Nor does the steelworkers' union sit across the bargaining table from representatives of a perfectly competitive industry. In these and other industries, although the union certainly has a good deal of monopoly power over labor supply, the firms also have some *monopsony* power over labor demand. (A **monopsony** is a buyer's monopoly—a case where sellers have only one purchaser for their products.) As a result, the firms may deliberately reduce the quantity of labor they demand as a way to force down the equilibrium level of wages. We can calculate the profit-maximizing restriction of the quantity of labor in the same way that we determined a monopolist's profit-maximizing restriction of output in Chapter 11.

> A **monopsony** is a market situation in which there is only one buyer.

It is difficult to predict the wage and employment decisions that will emerge when both the buying and selling sides of a market are monopolized—a situation called **bilateral monopoly.** The difficulties here are similar to those we encountered in considering the behavior of oligopolistic industries in Chapter 12. Just as one oligopolist is acutely aware that its rivals are likely to react to anything the oligopolistic employer does, so either side in a bilateral monopoly knows that any move it makes will elicit a countermove by the other. This knowledge makes the first decision that much more complicated. In practice, the outcome of bilateral monopoly depends on economic logic, on the relative power of the union and management, on the skill and preparation of the negotiators, and partly on luck.

> A **bilateral monopoly** is a market situation in which there is both a monopoly on the selling side and a monopsony on the buying side.

Still, we can be a bit more concrete about the outcome of the wage determination process under bilateral monopoly. A monopsonist employer unrestrained by a union will use its market power to force wages down below the competitive level, just as a monopoly seller uses its market power to force prices higher. It accomplishes this by reducing its demand for labor below what would otherwise be the profit-maximizing amount, thereby cutting both wages and the number of workers employed.

However, a union may be in a position to prevent this decline from happening. It can deliberately set a floor on wages, pledging its members not to work at all at any wage level below this floor, forcing the monopsony employer to pay higher wages and yet hire more workers than the employer otherwise would.

In reality, large, oligopolistic firms do often engage in similar one-on-one wage bargaining with the unions of their employees, and the resulting bargaining process closely resembles that of the bilateral monopoly model.

Collective Bargaining and Strikes

The process by which unions and management settle on a labor contract is called **collective bargaining.** Unfortunately, nothing as simple as a supply-demand diagram can tell us what wage level will emerge from a collective bargaining session.

> **Collective bargaining** is the process of negotiation of wages and working conditions between a union and the firms in the industry.

Furthermore, actual collective bargaining sessions range over many more issues than just wages. Pensions, health and life insurance, overtime pay, seniority privileges, and work conditions are often crucial issues. Many labor contracts specify in great detail the rights of labor and management to set work conditions—and also provide elaborate procedures for resolving grievances and disputes. The final contract that emerges from collective bargaining may well run to many pages of fine print.

SOURCES: U.S. Department of Labor, Bureau of Labor Statistics, *Monthly Labor Review*, various issues; and http://www.bls.gov.

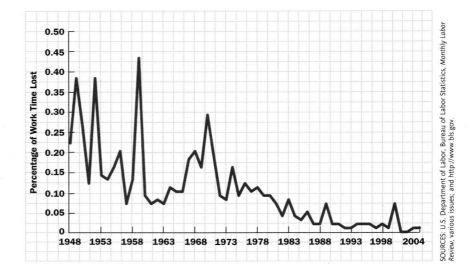

FIGURE 8

Work Time Lost in the
United States Because
of Strikes, 1948–2004

To force management to accept its demands, unions generally threaten strikes or work slowdowns. Firms may even threaten to close the plant to prevent a strike (called a *lockout*).

Fortunately, strikes are not nearly so common as many people believe. Figure 8 reports the percentage of work time lost as a result of strikes in the United States from 1948 to 2004. This fraction has varied greatly from year to year but has never been very large. The fraction of total work time lost has been under one-tenth of 1 percent since 1979 and has dwindled to insignificance at less than five-hundredths of 1 percent since 2001. Despite the headline-grabbing nature of major national strikes, the total amount of work time lost to strikes is truly trivial—far less, for example, than the time lost to coffee breaks! Compared with other nations, the United States suffers more from strikes than, say, Japan, but it has many fewer strikes than Canada (see Figure 9).

FIGURE 9

Incidence of Strikes in
Eight Industrial
Countries, 1996–2000

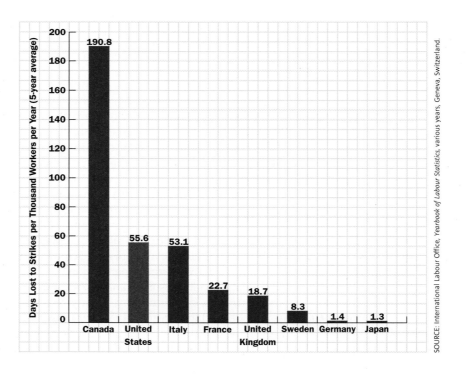

SOURCE: International Labour Office, *Yearbook of Labour Statistics*, various years, Geneva, Switzerland.

PART 2: THE ENTREPRENEUR: THE OTHER HUMAN INPUT

We think of the market mechanism as totally unguided—no one designed it and no one controls its operations. That is somewhat misleading, because there is an important category of individuals, the entrepreneurs, who contribute guidance to some critical market activities. Specifically, it is they who organize and establish new firms. Moreover, not only do they design new enterprises but they often use these new firms to introduce innovations that play such a critical part in the economic growth important to living standards described in Chapter 16. Thus, the entrepreneur may be thought of as the secret behind the market's greatest achievement—unprecedented rates of economic growth.

Anyone who creates a new business firm is usually called an "entrepreneur." Most such new firms are merely repeats of companies that already exist: a new dress manufacturer or a new grocery. But a small proportion of the entrepreneurs are special. They start a business that sells a new product or uses a new production method or opens up in a new market; in short, they *innovate*. The distinction is critical, because it is only the innovating entrepreneur that we can associate unreservedly with growth of the economy. Generally, they are not inventors themselves, but their prime capability is alertness in recognizing the promising inventions of others and in finding how those inventions have to be adjusted to make them attractive to buyers and to ensure that they are put to effective use.

ENTREPRENEURSHIP AND GROWTH

Some historical examples will bring out the importance of innovating entrepreneurs' contributions. The steam engine is a prime illustration. Many people have the mistaken idea that James Watt invented the steam engine, but there were many steam engines in operation in England decades before Watt's improvement, which increased the effectiveness and efficiency of a steam engine substantially. Moreover, a working steam engine had long before been constructed by Heron of Alexandria, probably in the first century A.D. But that engine was never put to practical use. Abraham Lincoln tells us that:

HISTORY OF ENTREPRENEURSHIP

OCTOBER 19 - 21, 2006

> . . . as much as two thousand years ago the power of steam was not only observed, but an ingenious toy was actually made and put in motion by it, at Alexandria. . . .

What appears strange is, that neither the inventor of the toy, nor anyone else, for so long a time afterwards, should perceive that steam would move *useful* machinery as well as a toy. (Abraham Lincoln, "Lecture on Discoveries and Inventions," 1858).

SOURCE: © Birmingham Museums and Art Gallery

Why was this machine not put to productive use in Rome? A plausible answer is that there were no innovative entrepreneurs in Rome such as appeared during the Industrial Revolution. Later we will discuss why. Heron, having no entrepreneur partner available to him, evidently sold this and his many other inventions to Roman priests who used these then-astonishing devices to demonstrate the priest's magical powers to the members of his cult.

Contrast this with the case of James Watt, who did have an entrepreneur partner, Matthew Boulton. Boulton went about England selling Watt's engine to the owners of mines, where they were used to pump out water, their only use at that time. On one sales trip, Boulton discovered, however, that the market for such pumps was saturated—every mine he visited already had a Boulton-Watt pump. Then it came to him that the engine could also do other things, such as running cloth-making machinery and locomotives. He talked Watt into designing the necessary adaptation for these new purposes and, as they say, the rest is history.

This is not the only example where entrepreneurship made the difference between productive and nonproductive use of an invention. It is well known that the Chinese many centuries ago produced a flood of great inventions, not only gunpowder but also the wheelbarrow, printing with movable type, the spinning wheel, playing cards, and elaborate clocks, among others. But these inventions, too, escaped widespread and productive use. And there is every reason to conclude that this failure, too, was caused by the absence of interested entrepreneurs like Matthew Boulton.

The Entrepreneur's Prices and Profits

An **innovative entrepreneur** is someone who introduces into the economy a new product or a new process for producing goods or finds a new market for the sale of commodities or a new way of conducting business.

Just as we did with capital, land, and labor, to understand the economics of **innovative entrepreneurship** we must investigate its financial arrangements. Since entrepreneurs are generally self-employed, there is no such thing as the "price" of entrepreneurship corresponding to the price of land or the wage of labor, because the services of the entrepreneur are not sold directly to anyone. There are, however, two things that are close to such a concept. First, there is the amount the entrepreneurs earn from their activity and, second, there is the price of the products that they supply and that are affected by their innovations.

The following widely cited story explaining the economics of innovative entrepreneurship was originally contributed by the late Harvard economist Joseph Schumpeter. It begins when the alert innovative entrepreneur either creates or recognizes a new and better product, acquires it, and brings it to market, where it makes older substitutes obsolete, in a process described as "creative destruction," as when the automobile drove the buggy manufacturers out of business. As the first provider of the improved product, the entrepreneur initially faces little or no competition, and the resulting monopoly power enables the entrepreneur to sell the new product at a price that is high relative to its costs and yields abundant profit. This generous profit gets the attention of other individuals with entrepreneurial ambitions, who seek to enter the market with competitive and imitative products. Those imitative products, incidentally, may differ somewhat from our entrepreneur's to avoid patent problems but are close enough to the original to attract customers. This competitive entry first reduces and finally brings to an end the temporary excess of price over the competitive level that was initially enjoyed by the entrepreneur. Now, with only zero economic profits available from his first innovation, the entrepreneur is forced to look for other inventive products to bring to market, in hopes of continuing to earn more than zero economic profits.

Thus, there is no rest for the innovators. They can never afford to be satisfied with their past achievements if they want their stream of temporary high profits to continue. Yesterday's invention soon is ancient history, and unless successor inventions are introduced soon enough by the inventor-entrepreneur partners, rivals will indeed succeed in entering and even taking over the market and will dry up the initial entrepreneur's stream of profits. So the entrepreneurs have no choice. They must seek to generate a stream of innovations, and that is one key part of the free-market's success story—the market provides a mechanism designed to change innovation from an occasional happening with a large element of accident into a systematic process that ensures, so far as ingenuity and current knowledge permit, the injection of a stream of inventions into the economy, one after another.[11]

---

[11] This scenario seems to tell us that the entrepreneur's activity offers him a stream of profits above the competitive level. But we will see that the real story is considerably different. It will be shown that, in equilibrium, the high initial earnings that inventors and innovative entrepreneurs obtain (if they are lucky) will often just enable them to recoup the R&D expenses they underwent in creating the product and the amounts they had to spend in bringing the novel product to market.

Fixed Costs and Public Good Attributes in Invention and Entrepreneurship

There are two special features of invention that are essential for full understanding of its economics: first, the *fixed-cost* characteristic of the required R&D expenditures and many of the other costs entailed in bringing an invention to market successfully and, second, the *public good attribute* of invention.

The first of these refers to the fact that once the entrepreneur has spent the R&D funding necessary to create an invention and to improve it sufficiently to make it a market success and the amount needed to bring the novelty to the attention of consumers, these amounts of money will be fixed—this quantity of money will be the same whether the product has 500 purchasers or 5 million. The amount of metal the new product uses will clearly have a positive marginal cost—the greater the number of buyers who purchase it, the more metal the manufacturer of the item will require. But the added sales will not require any additional R&D expenditures. The marginal R&D costs will be zero. The total cost of acquiring the information is the same, whether the idea is used by 100 people or a million.

Second, and related to this, the information that underlies the invention is what economists call "a public good." It will be recalled from the discussion in Chapter 15 (pages 316–318) that this kind of good is one such that none of it is used up (depleted) when an additional person uses it. Unlike the nation's wheat inventory, which goes down every time some bread is eaten, another reading of the specifications of an invention does not reduce the amount of information it contains. In this sense, all information is a public good—its supply is not depleted by an increase in the number of people who use it.

Now, both of these attributes mean that there is a significant portion of the cost of an invention that is totally absent from marginal cost. If more people buy the new product or more people use its specifications, that does not increase the firm's R&D cost or any other similar cost elements, and since marginal cost is by definition that addition to cost that results from an increase of the output of a product, there is no portion of R&D, or the other similar costs, that is included in the firm's MC figure.

This has several implications. First, invention cannot be successful financially if the price is set equal to marginal cost, as must happen in a perfectly competitive market (see Chapter 10, pages 200–201 to review this). Such a price would not cover any of the R&D cost and the related outlays, which, as we have just seen, are entirely absent from the marginal cost of an innovation. So for innovative products, $P = MC$ is a recipe for financial loss and disaster in an innovative firm established by an innovative entrepreneur.

Second, this means that what appear to be initial monopoly profits in Schumpeter's scenario may only be the amount of revenue needed to cover those fixed R&D costs and any similar outlays. Indeed, in a perfectly competitive market in which there is innovation, that is precisely what we must expect. Assuming that just about anyone can start an invention project in her garage or basement, we would expect, for the usual reason, that entry by inventors and entrepreneurs competing for market share will continue so long as there are economic profits to be earned. This entry, as in the usual story, will drive prices down to the point where the expected revenues will just cover all the costs, including the fixed R&D costs *and no more*. That, theoretically, will be the long-run equilibrium of the market, and Schumpeter's initial "monopoly earnings" will just be the form taken by recovery of the R&D costs, and *zero economic profits to inventors as a group is exactly what they can expect to earn on average.* For good reason, this is now the story generally accepted by economic theorists. And, as we will see next, it can lead us to even further insights than have so far been described.

Discriminatory Pricing of an Innovative Product over Its Life Cycle

There are, of course, also reasons other than growing competition by imitators of a successful new product that account for its typically declining cost and falling price. Obviously, experience will teach its suppliers how to produce the novel item more efficiently so that its cost will often be lowered by ever-improved technology. Moreover, if the product turns out to please or even excite consumers (see the story of the iPhone on page 339 in Chapter 16), costs may also be reduced by economies of scale offered by machinery with larger capacity and other cost-saving attributes.

The other accepted scenario, the one that we have just gone over, tells us that the price of an innovative product will initially be high and then will gradually be driven down by competition until there comes a point in its lifetime when it brings in no further profits. But that is only a vague description of these prices. Can we provide an analysis that provides a more specific formula to determine those magnitudes at the times that intervene between these two dates? The answer is that if the market is competitive, standard economic analysis does, indeed, enable us to do so to the extent that we could explain the other price decisions of the firm in earlier chapters.

To understand this we must first recall the concept of discriminatory prices and the way in which such prices are determined by a profit-maximizing firm. It will be recalled that when the firm sells the same product to one group of customers at a lower price than it sells it to another, even though it costs exactly the same to serve the two groups, the prices that are charged are called "discriminatory."

Now firms can and do discriminate in price between groups on the basis of some of their attributes, for example, using senior-citizen discounts. They also sometimes discriminate between locations, charging lower prices in cities where they face more competition. Finally, they can discriminate between customers who buy at different times, as when they charge more for a necklace the day before Christmas than the day after the holiday. A moment's thought shows that this last story involves discrimination between different dates: high prices before competition for a new product arrives in the market and ever-lower prices at later dates as more and more competitors enter. We see that the logic is the same as the discrimination between cities with different numbers of competitors.

Moreover, we saw earlier in the book that there is a formula that gives us the profit-maximizing prices when those prices are discriminatory. That formula was straightforward: If the firm is charging different prices to two groups of customers, it should supply to each group that quantity, Q, at which marginal revenue from these sales is equal to marginal cost. Then, to determine the profit-maximizing price for each of the two customer groups, just examine each group's demand curve for the product and select the price that will just induce the customers in each group to purchase the quantity of the product at which its MC = MR and is therefore profit maximizing.

The logic is exactly the same as we have already used many times before. If for either group its own MR is not equal to MC, it will raise the firm's profit to ship (at least) a little more or a little less to those customers, depending on whether MR or MC is the larger.[12]

---

[12] There is more that we can learn about those prices, which fit right in with the less analytical story that was told in the previous section. Here, we start off by recalling two other conclusions we have encountered before: (1) Other things being equal, the less competition there is in a market, the less elastic the firm's demand curve will be, for reasons that will soon be recalled; and (2) other things being equal, as will be shown again, the less elastic the demand of a group of customers, the higher the profit-maximizing price will be. What these two observations lead us to conclude is fully consistent with the story, but with the difference that we have just obtained a formula to derive those profit-maximizing prices. What these two conclusions show, as Schumpeter argued, is that when an innovation is first brought to market, because competition is sparse or nonexistent at first, the demand for the new product can be expected to be (significantly) less elastic than it becomes later, when more competition appears. Then, from the other of the two preceding conclusions, this tells us that in the early days, just after the new product comes to market the profit-maximizing MC = MR price will be higher than that price will become later.

To complete this analysis, we need only two observations about competition, elasticity and prices that underlie the story. The logic of these observations is simple and easy to explain intuitively. First, when there are few or no competitors the firm can raise its price without driving many customers into the arms of rivals. But this is just another way of saying that when competition is more limited demand will be more inelastic; that is, a given price rise will drive away a relatively small share of the firm's customers. That is exactly how we define an inelastic demand.

Second, when demand is more inelastic, as we have just recalled, a rise in price will be more profitable because it will drive away few customers, thereby raising revenues more, while at the same time cutting the firm's input expenditure, because total sales will have been decreased somewhat by the higher prices.

These paragraphs may be considered as a review of some of our earlier analysis of business decisions, but we also see now how rich that analysis can be, throwing light on the analysis of innovation and the pricing policies that the market leads innovators to adopt.

Negative Financial Rewards for Entrepreneurial Activity?

This takes us through the pricing story except for one thing—the earlier assertion that if there is freedom of entry into the entrepreneurial activities, this will tend to drive the average economic profits of entrepreneurs and inventors to zero. That may seem like an implausible conclusion. After all, we are talking about the activities that raised Bill Gates to the position of richest man in the world. Indeed, we will show next that, in reality, the zero economic profit conclusion is wrong. But the surprising evidence is the opposite of what one might expect—the actual economic profits, on average, are *lower, not higher,* than zero!

SOURCE: © Jeff J Mitchell/Getty Images

Clearly, if this is true, more explanation of what goes on is required. In much of the next few paragraphs it will be convenient to think of entrepreneurs simply as self-employed people who prefer to be their own bosses rather than hiring themselves out to an ongoing enterprise. There are several studies of relevant data that show the self-employed have earnings significantly lower than those of employees with similar education and experience.

All of this implies that when individuals decide to become an entrepreneur or an inventor, they must expect to earn profits so low that they entail some financial sacrifice, rather than the reverse. That is, they must expect to suffer a substantial opportunity cost relative to what they could have earned by working in a business firm owned by others. How can that possibly be true? Why, with such a low payoff to be expected, would they do such work voluntarily?

PUZZLE RESOLVED: **WHY ARE ENTREPRENEURIAL EARNINGS SURPRISINGLY LOW?**

We can now seek to provide the answer to the puzzle presented earlier in this chapter. We are not sure why entrepreneurs on average earn so little—but here are some possibilities. Strange as this may seem, there are grounds to conclude that in a competitive market this is not an abnormality. There are two reasons. The first is the very high rewards generated by the relatively few outstanding successes provide an incentive found in many other activities, such as investment in lotteries with multi-million-dollar payoffs or in occupations such as acting, in both of which actual average earnings are very low indeed.

The willingness of entrepreneurs to invest their lives and fortunes in such risky activity implies that they are either highly overoptimistic or that they enjoy such gambles. There is strong evidence that over optimism is characteristic of entrepreneurs. "The available evidence certainly supports the notion that entrepreneurs are unrealistically optimistic. 68% of respondents to [one] survey of American entrepreneurs thought the odds of their business succeeding were better than for others in the same sector while only 5% thought that they were worse. . . . [Another survey found that] all respondents over-optimistically expect to live longer than the life tables suggest, but that entrepreneurs are substantially more likely to think they will live longer. These authors also establish that optimism is significantly positively associated with the propensity to be an entrepreneur."[*]

Thus, undervaluation of risk and very large rewards to the few blockbuster innovations can indeed lead the average reward of the entrepreneur to be lower than that of others in the economy with comparable ability and performance.

There is a second reason for such low *financial* rewards, for the entrepreneur also receives a second payment in a form that can be considered to be a different currency.

In the case of the entrepreneur, the second currency is the psychological reward of independence, that is, the absence of subservience to a directing superior and the

---

[*] Simon C. Parker (2005), *The Economics of Entrepreneurship: What We Know and What We Don't*, Hanover, Mass.: now Publishers Inc..

excitement of participation in the innovation process (which is readily observed in the biographies of innovative entrepreneurs). In a competitive equilibrium, if entrepreneurship is far more pleasant than working for others, the financial rewards to entrepreneurship must normally be below the earnings of equally capable individuals who take more "boring" jobs in established business firms. For if the wages in the two jobs, one very pleasant and one highly unpleasant, were the same, qualified individuals would be unwilling to accept the far less enjoyable of the two positions. The resulting scarcity of job takers would drive up the wages in the unpleasant position and the abundance of job seekers for the other position would drive those wages down. In the end, the difference in payoffs in the two jobs must make up for the difference in their attractiveness.

Thus, we must conclude that the role of entrepreneur must offer satisfaction considerably greater than that provided by working for others and so, makes entrepreneurs willing to undertake this activity even though it is, on average, so much less rewarding financially.

INSTITUTIONS AND THE SUPPLY OF INNOVATIVE ENTREPRENEURSHIP

What is there about the modern free-market economy that allows this innovation process to flourish and make its fundamental contribution to rates of economic growth that have never previously been experienced in human history? The answer is primarily found in the new institutions that grew up along with the capitalist economy, perhaps partly as a historical accident.

Before the Industrial Revolution there were societies that also had their share of enterprising individuals who profited by doing things in a way that was different from that of their ancestors. The type of invention that was profitable and honorific was likely to be military or could be used to promote religious practices or even entailed outright corruption. We have already noted how Heron of Alexandria used his steam engine and his other inventions to promote the powers of the Roman priesthood and was very likely well compensated by them for his efforts. Use of the fantastically varied and potentially valuable inventions of medieval China was impeded by the fact that the incentives provided to the most enterprising individuals did not encourage them to take steps to introduce those inventions to productive activity. Rather they strove, often for years, to become part of the mandarin officialdom, where they expected to acquire wealth through the resultant power to profit through corruption. And all through history the most honored avenue to wealth and power was the military, through essentially private armies, often using innovative military equipment and tactics to acquire wealth through booty, ransom, land grabbing, enslavement of captives, and other associated means.

By the eighteenth century in England and in the former American colonies, government had become sufficiently powerful to prevent the exercise of military entrepreneurship via the organization of private armies. Other unproductive forms of enterprise had also become more difficult to carry out as a result of laws and customs that prohibited or at least handicapped them. And, at the same time, new institutions were adopted that made innovative entrepreneurship safer, easier, and more profitable. For example, the patent system, unknown in ancient societies, was created directly for the United States in the Constitution.

The basic point is that enterprising individuals are neither more nor less moral than those who are engaged in any other career. The entrepreneur's special talent, as one noted student of the subject has observed, is the ability to spot new and so-far-unused profit-making opportunities. But which activities promise to be profitable depends on current government rules and the nature of the pressures that stem from various influential sources. Today, the entrepreneurs, in their search for profits, are encouraged to innovate by a variety of rules that provide protection for such activity when it contributes to production and to the choices available to consumers. Now we have legal institutions, such as sanctity of property, that prohibits arbitrary expropriation by the king and his nobles, the patent system that helps the inventor and the innovative entrepreneur to reap rewards from their efforts, as well as enforceability of contracts by the courts, bankruptcy protection permitting those who have made unfortunate business decisions to try again, and many more. But this was not always so. These rules were quite new at the time of the Industrial Revolution, and for the first time they assured entrepreneurs and innovators that they could keep the wealth generated by their efforts. This assurance not only provided the incentives that attracted individuals into the struggle for innovation, it also served as an irresistible lure for the entry of competitors. The appearance of the early innovating entrepreneurs and their success brought in more entrepreneurs, but it also gave rise to ever-fiercer competition, using innovation as a weapon. And this provided the driving force for innovation that is present and fully effective only in the market economies.

Today, entrepreneurs continue to be an indispensable ingredient in the unprecedented growth performance of the market. By ensuring that inventions are put to use quickly and effectively, they ensure that our ability to produce and to improve quality will continue to grow. But in order to keep this process going, we must be careful to prevent the adoption of rules that undercut these activities and remove the incentives for entrepreneurs to keep up their productivity-enhancing efforts. That is one of the key morals that emerges from the experience of economic history since the Industrial Revolution.

| SUMMARY |

1. In a free market, the wage rate and the level of employment are determined by the interaction of supply and demand. Workers in great demand or short supply command high wages. Similarly, low wages go to workers who are in abundant supply or who have skills that are not in great demand.

2. The demand curve for labor, like the demand curve for any factor of production, is derived from the **marginal revenue product curve.** It slopes downward because of the "law" of diminishing marginal returns.

3. The demand curve for labor can be shifted upward by an increase in education or on-the-job training that raises the workers' marginal physical products or by an increase in demand for those products that raises product price and therefore also increases labor's MRP.

4. Labor-saving innovations may either raise or lower workers' wages and available jobs in the short run. Because they are tantamount to increased productivity, in the long run they generally raise the incomes of workers along with those of other members of the community.

5. Because of conflicting **income and substitution effects,** the quantity of labor supplied may rise or fall as a result of an increase in wages. Historical data show that hours of work per week have fallen as wages have risen, suggesting that income effects may be dominant in the long run.

6. Most skills can be acquired by means of **investment in human capital,** such as education.

7. **Human capital theory** assumes that people make educational decisions in much the same way as businesses make investment decisions, and it tacitly assumes that people learn things in school that increase their productivity in jobs.

8. Less than 13 percent of all U.S. workers belong to **unions,** which we can think of as monopoly sellers of labor.

Compared with many other industrialized countries, unions in the United States have as members a smaller share of the labor force and are less radical politically.

9. Unions probably succeed in forcing wages to be higher and employment to be lower than they would be in a perfectly competitive labor market.

10. Strikes play an important role in collective bargaining as a way of dividing the fruits of economic activity between big business and big labor. But strikes are not nearly so common as is often supposed.

11. For about two decades Americans have experienced three noteworthy trends: (a) a decline in union membership of more than 30 percent, (b) a steady fall in real wages partly offset by rising fringe benefits, and (c) a rise in the income gap between well-paid and poorly paid workers.

12. Innovative entrepreneurs look for new products or new productive processes or new markets and try to have them put to profitable use.

13. In a widely recognized model of this process, just after entrepreneurs bring new products to market they face no competition and earn monopoly profits, but then competitors enter with imitations of any successful new product and gradually drive the prices down to competitive levels. So, to continue to earn profits the entrepreneur must soon find another innovation to bring to market.

14. The R&D spending on a new product and on breaking into the market is a fixed cost with public good properties, so the amount it adds to marginal cost is zero.

15. Therefore, to cover those fixed costs and earn at least zero economic profit overall, price must exceed marginal cost, unlike a perfectly competitive market where $P = MC$.

16. To cover the fixed cost of R&D, etc., and with the threat of growing competition by imitators, the entrepreneur

will, in effect, charge discriminatory prices, that is, different prices for the same product on sales to early buyers than they will charge to later buyers.

17. The profit-maximizing rule for the discriminatory price variation at different dates will be the same as always applies under price discrimination; that is, if the marginal cost of supplying earlier customers is the same as doing so for later customers, then the quantities supplied at the two dates must be such that the marginal revenues at the two dates are equal.

18. Entrepreneurs will do what it takes to achieve wealth, power, and prestige by innovation. So before there were laws protecting private property, enforcing contracts, and offering patent protection to innovators, they would often organize private armies, take bribes, and find new ways to get special favors from people in power, rather than promoting productive innovation. Since about the time of the Industrial Revolution the laws have changed, and it has become more profitable for entrepreneurs to undertake productive innovations.

| KEY TERMS |

backward-bending   427

bilateral monopoly   433

collective bargaining   433

human capital theory   429

income effect   426

innovative entrepreneurship   436

investment in human capital   422

labor union   431

marginal revenue product of labor (MRP$_L$)   422

monopsony   433

substitution effect   426

| TEST YOURSELF |

1. The following table shows the number of pizzas that can be produced by a large pizza parlor employing various numbers of pizza chefs.

Number of Chefs	Number of Pizzas per Day
1	40
2	64
3	82
4	92
5	100
6	92

a. Find the marginal physical product schedule of the pizza chefs.

b. Assuming a price of $9 per pizza, find the marginal revenue product schedule.

c. If chefs are paid $100 per day, how many chefs will this pizza parlor employ? How would your answer change if chefs' wages rose to $125 per day?

d. Suppose the price of pizza increases from $9 to $12. Show what happens to the derived demand curve for chefs.

2. Discuss the concept of the financial rate of return on a college education. If this return is less than the return on a bank account, does that mean you should quit college? Why might you want to stay in school anyway? Are there circumstances under which it might be rational not to go to college, even when the financial returns to college are very high?

3. In which of the following industries is wage determination most plausibly explained by the model of perfect competition? The model of pure monopoly? The model of bilateral monopoly?

a. Odd-job repairs in private homes

b. Manufacture of low-priced clothing for children

c. Auto manufacturing

4. Can you think of some types of workers whose marginal products probably were raised by computerization? Are there any whose marginal products were probably reduced? Can you characterize the difference between the two types of jobs in general terms?

5. Suppose you are the sole producer of commodity X, which was just invented to clean the snow from sidewalks more efficiently, and you have produced enough to sell for two winters. If the quantity you expect to sell in 2011 would yield MR = $400 and in 2012 it will be $300, what can you do to try to increase your total profit?

6. Explain what a doubling of the number of customers for your snow cleaner will do to the R&D component of your marginal costs.

7. If two jobs are available, one of which is fun and very respectable and the other unpleasant and dangerous, where would you expect wages to be higher? Is that really so in practice?

8. Assume the inventor of the snow cleaner gets only 3 percent of the benefits, the remainder consisting of reduced medical bills for back pain. In the general public, explain why this is an externality. How large is it? Is it a beneficial externality? How will it affect the number of snow cleaners it is most profitable to manufacture, as compared to the number that best contributes to the general welfare?

| DISCUSSION QUESTIONS |

1. Colleges are known to pay rather low wages for student labor. Can this trend be explained by the operation of supply and demand in the local labor markets? Is the concept of monopsony of any use? How might things differ if students formed a union?

2. College professors are highly skilled (or at least highly educated!) laborers, yet their wages are not very high. Is this a refutation of the marginal productivity theory?

3. It seems to be a well-established fact that workers with more years of education typically receive higher wages. What are some possible reasons for this trend?

4. Approximately what fraction of the U.S. labor force belongs to unions? (Try asking this question of a person who has never studied economics.) Why do you think this fraction is so low?

5. What are some reasonable goals for a union? Use the tools of supply and demand to explain how a union might pursue its goals, whatever they are. Consider a union that has been in the news recently. What was it trying to accomplish?

6. "Strikes are simply intolerable and should be outlawed." Comment on this statement.

7. In a bitter strike battle between Eastern Airlines and several of its unions, it was clear from the beginning that the airline was in serious financial trouble. The airline was, indeed, eventually forced to close down, costing many jobs. Discuss what might nevertheless have led the unions to hold out so tenaciously.

8. Since about 1980, GDP per capita (that is, the average real income per person) in the United States has risen fairly substantially. Yet real wages have failed to rise. What do you think may explain this phenomenon?

9. If you were the youngest son of an English nobleman in the Middle Ages, what could you do to make your fortune? What kinds of innovation would be appreciated by people in power?

10. How did Julius Caesar attain his position in Rome and in history? In what sense can his activities be said to have been entrepreneurial?

11. Why do you think China, with all its incredible inventions, fell behind economically?

12. What are some of the U.S. laws and other rules that played a critical role in the attainment of leadership in per-capita income and innovation?

13. What steps should the United States consider undertaking to protect itself from the fate of other countries that once were economic leaders of the world and then fell far behind?

14. Why do you think even though high school education in other countries is widely considered to be better than that in the United States every country sends its best and brightest to the United States to get their Doctorate degrees?

21

POVERTY, INEQUALITY, AND DISCRIMINATION

The white man knows how to make everything, but he does not know how to distribute it.

SITTING BULL

The last two chapters analyzed how factor prices—wages, rents, and interest rates—are determined in a market economy. One reason for concern about this issue is that these payments determine the *incomes* of the people who own the factors. The study of factor pricing, therefore, is an indirect way to learn about how the market *distributes income* among individuals.

In this chapter, we turn directly to the problem of income distribution. Specifically, we seek answers to the following questions: How unequal are incomes in the United States, and why? How can society decide rationally on how much equality it wants? And, once this decision is made, what policies are available to pursue this goal?

CONTENTS

ISSUE: WERE THE BUSH TAX CUTS UNFAIR?

Reducing taxes was the major thrust of President George W. Bush's economic policy. Tax cuts were passed in 2001, 2002, 2003, and 2004, amounting in total to a substantial reduction in the federal tax burden—or, as some critics put it, a large reduction in the tax burdens of the rich. And that is precisely the fairness issue. One of the chief criticisms of the Bush tax cuts was that they were distributively *unfair,* that wealthy Americans were the chief beneficiaries while people of modest means received little. According to one estimate, the lower 60 percent of income earners—a majority of the population—received just 13.7 percent of the tax cuts while the top 1 percent received 24.2 percent.[1] To people concerned with income inequality, that was *prima facie* evidence that the tax cuts were unfair. And, for this reason, every Democratic candidate for the 2008 presidential nomination, including Barack Obama, pledged to roll back some of the tax cuts for the rich—which President Obama subsequently proposed.

President Bush and his supporters responded to these criticisms in a variety of ways. One was to deny the unfairness. It is natural, they said, for upper-bracket taxpayers to get a disproportionate share of the tax cuts for a simple reason: They pay a disproportionate share of the taxes. But a second retort pointed out that lower tax rates improve incentives and enhance economic efficiency—topics that we addressed in Chapter 18. Fairness is in the eye of the beholder, they maintained, but one thing we do know is that lower tax rates improve economic performance. Largely for this reason, Senator John McCain, during the 2008 campaign, pledged to continue the Bush tax cuts.

Which side of this 2008 debate—which lingers on—had it right? Should we worry more about the distributive consequences of the Bush tax cuts or welcome their efficiency effects? It's a good question, but one, as we shall see, without a clear answer.

IDEAS FOR BEYOND THE FINAL EXAM

As we will show in this chapter, the debate over the Bush tax cuts provides a classic example of the trade-off between equality and efficiency that we introduced in Chapter 1. Some conservatives seem so enamored of the efficiency gains from lower tax rates that they ignore, or even deny, the distributive consequences. Some liberals, by contrast, argue that tax cuts that are so "unfair" should be rejected regardless of their potential efficiency benefits.

Economists prefer to avoid such absolutes and to think in terms of trade-offs instead. To reap gains on one front, society often must make sacrifices on another. A policy is not necessarily ill-conceived simply because it has an undesirable effect on income inequality, provided it makes a sufficiently important contribution to efficiency. But policies with very adverse distributive consequences may deserve to be rejected, even if they would raise the nation's total output.

Admitting that there is a *trade-off between equality and efficiency*—namely, that tax cuts that favor the rich may nonetheless enhance economic efficiency—may not be the best way to win votes. But it does face up to reality. And in that way, it helps us to think through the inherently political decisions about what should be done.

If we are to understand these complex issues, a good place to start is, as always, with the facts.

THE FACTS: POVERTY

In 1962, social critic Michael Harrington published a little book called *The Other America,* which turned out to have a profound effect on American society. Harrington's "other Americans" were the poor who lived in the land of plenty. Ill-clothed in the richest country

---

[1] Isaac Shapiro and Joel Friedman, "Tax Returns: A Comprehensive Assessment of the Bush Administration Tax Cuts," Center on Budget and Policy Priorities, April 2004, p. 19.

The Poorest Place in America?

Pine Ridge [South Dakota] lies in the poorest county in America, with 75 percent unemployment and an average family income of $3,700 per year. The life expectancy for men is 48 years, 25 years below the national average. The infant mortality rate is the highest in the country. Bad health, disease, drugs, and alcohol have ravaged the Oglala Sioux. Their culture has been diluted by television and their language is gradually dying out.

. . . [P]eople on the reservation . . . agree that the tribe's funds are chronically mismanaged, that nepotism rules job placement and that a handful of people are getting rich while the rest of the tribe struggles to survive. . . . But . . . hardly anyone outside the reservation knows what's going on at Pine Ridge.

SOURCE: Julie Winokur, "Bury the News at Wounded Knee," at http://www.archive.salon.com/news/feature/2000/03/13/pine_ridge/index.html.

SOURCE: © Bob Rowan; Progressive Image/CORBIS

on earth, inadequately nourished in a nation where obesity was a problem, infirm in a country with some of the world's highest health standards, these people lived an almost unknown existence in their dilapidated hovels, according to Harrington. To make matters worse, this deprivation often condemned the children of the "other Americans" to repeat the lives of their parents. There was, Harrington argued, a "cycle of poverty" that could be broken only by government action.

The work of Harrington and others touched the hearts of many Americans who, it seemed, really had no idea of the abominable living conditions of some other people in the country. Within a few years, the growing outrage over the plight of the poor had crystallized into a "War on Poverty," which President Lyndon Johnson declared in 1964.

Counting the Poor: The Poverty Line

As part of this program, the government adopted an official definition of *poverty:* The poor were those families with incomes less than $3,000 in 1964. This dividing line between the poor and nonpoor was called the **poverty line,** and a goal was established: to get all Americans above the poverty line by the nation's bicentennial in 1976. (The goal was not met.) The poverty line was subsequently modified to account for differences in family size and other considerations, and it is now also adjusted each year to reflect changes in the cost of living. In 2009, the poverty line for a family of four was just over $25,300 and 13.2 percent of all Americans remained in poverty by official definitions.

The **poverty line** is an amount of income below which a family is considered "poor."

Who are the poor? Relative to their proportions in the overall population, they are more likely to be black than white and more likely to be female than male. They are less educated and in poorer health than the population as a whole. About 35 percent of the poor are children.

America made substantial progress toward eliminating poverty in the decade from 1963 to 1973; the percentage of people living below the poverty line dropped from 20 percent to 11 percent (see Figure 1). But thereafter, slower economic growth and cutbacks in social welfare programs reversed the trend. By 1983, the poverty rate was back to what it had been in the 1960s. After that, the poverty rate increased and decreased with no clear trend until the great economic boom of the 1990s restored it almost to its 1970s low. Poverty rose again when the economy slumped early in this decade, but then recovered a bit of the lost ground in 2005 and 2006, before increasing again during the 2008–2009 recession.

High poverty rates worry many people, especially because poverty seems often to be associated with homelessness, illegitimacy, drug dependency, and ill-health. However, some critics argue that the official data badly overstate the number of poor persons. Some

FIGURE 1

Progress in the War on Poverty

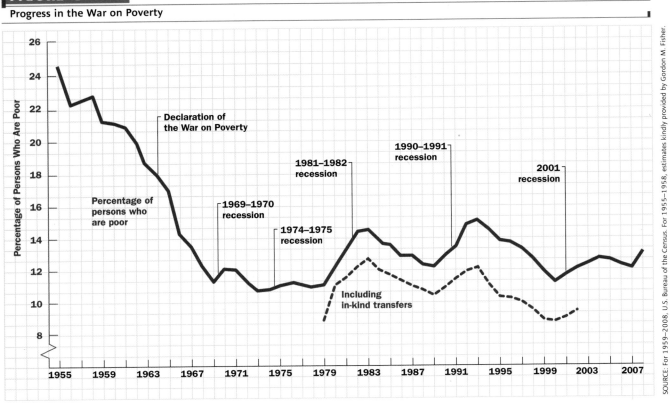

SOURCE: For 1959–2008, U.S. Bureau of the Census. For 1955–1958, estimates kindly provided by Gordon M. Fisher.

even go so far as to claim that poverty would be considered a thing of the past if the official definition (based on cash income) were amended to include the many goods that the poor receive in kind: public education, public housing, health care, food, and the like.

These criticisms prompted the Census Bureau to develop several experimental measures of poverty that account for the value of goods given in kind. If these new measures are accepted as valid, fewer people are classified as poor, but the basic patterns remain the same: Poverty went up and down from the late 1970s until about 1993 with no clear trend and then declined until 2000, when it started heading up again.

Absolute versus Relative Poverty

This debate raises a fundamental question: How do we define "the poor"? Continuing economic growth will eventually pull almost everyone above any arbitrarily established poverty line. Would that mark the end of poverty? Some would say yes, but would insist that the biblical injunction is right: "The poor ye have always with you."

We can define poverty two ways. The more optimistic definition uses an *absolute concept of poverty*: If you fall short of a certain minimum standard of living, you are poor; once you pass this standard, you are no longer poor. The more pessimistic definition relies on a *relative concept of poverty*: The poor are those who fall too far behind the average income.

Each definition has advantages and disadvantages. The basic problem with the absolute poverty concept is that it is arbitrary. Who sets the line? Most of the people of Bangladesh would consider themselves quite prosperous if they lived a bit below the U.S. poverty line. Similarly, the standard of living that we now call "poor" would not have been considered so in America in 1900, and certainly not in Europe during the Middle Ages. Different times and different places apparently call for different poverty lines.

Because the concept of poverty seems to be culturally—not physiologically—determined, it must be a relative concept. For example, the European Union (EU) places the poverty line at half the national average income—which means that the poverty line automatically rises as the EU grows richer.

Once we move from an absolute to a relative concept of poverty, any sharp distinction between the poor and the nonpoor starts to blur. At least in part, the poor are so poor because the rich are so rich. If we follow this line of thought far enough, we are led away from the narrow problem of *poverty* and toward the broader problem of *income inequality*.

THE FACTS: INEQUALITY

Nothing in the market mechanism guarantees equality of incomes. On the contrary, the market system tends to allow or even foster inequality because the basic source of its great efficiency is its system of rewards and penalties. The market is generous to those who succeed in operating efficient enterprises that respond to consumer demands, but it ruthlessly penalizes those who are unable or unwilling to satisfy consumer demands efficiently. Recent developments in the United States have demonstrated these tendencies dramatically, as inequalities have risen notably.

The market's financial punishment of those who try and fail can be severe. At times the market even brings down the great and powerful. Robert Morris, once perhaps the wealthiest resident of the American colonies, ended up in debtors' prison. Some of the greatest American fortunes in the late nineteenth century were made in the railroads, most of which subsequently went bankrupt. When the Internet euphoria ended in 2000, many former multimillionaires (and a few former billionaires) found themselves jobless and nearly destitute. Most recently, the financial crisis of 2007–2009 humbled some of America's greatest financial institutions.

Most people have a good idea that the gulf between the rich and the poor is wide, but few have any concept of where they stand in the income distribution. For example, during a 1995 congressional debate over tax cuts for "the middle class," one member of Congress with an annual income in excess of $150,000 declared himself a member of the "middle class," if not indeed of the "lower-middle class"!

Table 1 offers some statistics on the income distribution among U.S. households in 2008. But before looking at them, try the following experiment. First, write down what you think your household's before-tax income was in 2008. (If you do not know, take a guess.) Next, try to guess what percentage of American households had incomes *lower* than this amount. Finally, if we divide America into three broad income classes—rich, middle class, and poor—to which group do you think your household belongs?

Now that you have written down answers to these three questions, look at the income distribution data for 2008 in Table 1. If you are like most college students, these figures may surprise you. First, if we adopt the tentative definition that the lowest 20 percent are the "poor," the highest 20 percent are the "rich," and the middle 60 percent are the "middle class," many fewer of you belong to the celebrated "middle class" than you thought. In fact, the cutoff point that defined membership in the "rich" class in 2008 was only about $100,000 before taxes, an income level exceeded by the parents of many college students. (Your parents may be shocked to learn that they are rich!)

Next, use Table 1 to estimate the fraction of U.S. households that have incomes lower than yours. (The table caption has instructions to help you make this estimate.) Many students who come from households of moderate

TABLE 1

Distribution of Household Income in the United States in 2008

Income Range	Households in This Range	Households in This and Lower Ranges
Less than $5,000	3.0%	3.0%
$5,000 to $9,999	4.1	7.1
$10,000 to $14,999	5.8	12.9
$15,000 to $24,999	11.8	24.7
$25,000 to $34,999	10.9	35.6
$35,000 to $49,000	14.0	49.6
$50,000 to $74,999	17.9	67.5
$75,000 to $99,999	11.9	79.4
$100,000 or more	20.5	100.0

SOURCE: U.S. Bureau of the Census.

NOTE: If your household income falls close to one of the endpoints of the ranges indicated here, you can approximate the fraction of households with income lower than yours by just looking at the last column. If your household's income falls within one of the ranges, you can interpolate the answer. Example: Your household's income was $80,000. This is 20 percent of the way from $75,000 to $100,000, so your household was richer than roughly 0.20 × 11.9 percent = 2.4 percent of the households in this class. Adding this to the percentage of households in lower classes (67.5 percent in this case) gives the answer—about 70 percent of all households earned less than yours.

TABLE 2

Income Shares in Selected Years

Income Group	2008	1990	1980	1970
Lowest fifth	3.4	3.9	4.3	4.1
Second fifth	8.6	9.6	10.3	10.8
Middle fifth	14.7	15.9	16.9	17.4
Fourth fifth	23.3	24.0	24.9	24.5
Highest fifth	50.0	46.6	43.7	43.3

prosperity feel instinctively that they stand perhaps a bit above the middle of the income distribution. So they estimate that a little more than half of all families have lower incomes. In fact, the median income among American households in 2008 was only $50,300.

This exercise has perhaps brought us down to earth. America is not nearly as rich as Madison Avenue would like us to believe. Let us now look past the average level of income and see how the pie is divided. Table 2 shows the shares of income accruing to each fifth of the population in 2008 and several earlier years. In a perfectly equal society, all the numbers in this table would be "20 percent," because each fifth of the population would receive one-fifth of the income. In fact, as the table shows, reality is far from this perfect equality. In 2008, for example, the poorest fifth of all households had just 3.4 percent of the total income, whereas the richest fifth had 50.0 percent, almost 15 times as much.

These data for 2008 give us a snapshot of the U.S. income distribution. But to interpret them, we must know what the distribution looked like in earlier years or what it looks like in other countries. The historical data in Table 2 shows that

The distribution of income in the United States has grown substantially more unequal since about 1980.

Specifically, the share of the poorest fifth is now the lowest, and the share of the richest fifth is almost the highest since the government began collecting data in 1947. America is not a very class-conscious society, and for years only specialists paid much attention to data like those in Table 2. But income inequality has captured increasing public attention of late as more and more American families sense that they are losing ground to the people at the top. There is particular, and well-justified, concern that the real earnings of wage earners below the middle have fallen further and further behind the wages at the top. These trends toward widening income and wage disparities have been going on for almost three decades now, which is a long time.

Comparing the United States with other countries is much more difficult because no two nations use precisely the same definition of income distribution. The Luxembourg Income Study is the leading international effort to produce comparable data for many countries. In its latest comparison of the income distributions of 20 high-income (mostly European) countries, Sweden and Finland had the most equal income distributions, with Norway, The Netherlands, and Belgium close behind. The United States stood out as having the most inequality. Thus, it appears that

"The poor are getting poorer, but with the rich getting richer it all averages out in the long run."

The United States has more income inequality than most other industrialized countries.

SOME REASONS FOR UNEQUAL INCOMES

Let us now begin to formulate a list of the *causes* of income inequality. Here are some that come to mind.

Differences in Ability   Everyone knows that people have different capabilities. Some can run faster, ski better, do calculations more quickly, type more accurately, and so on. Hence, it should not be surprising that some people are more adept at earning income. Precisely what sort of ability is relevant to earning income has been a matter of intense debate among economists, sociologists, and psychologists for decades. The talents that

How Important Is the Bell Curve?

Over a decade ago, social critic Charles Murray and psychologist Richard Herrnstein created a furor with a book claiming that genetically inherited intelligence is overwhelmingly important to economic success. The book's title, *The Bell Curve,* referred to the shape of the distribution of scores on conventional IQ tests (see chart), which shows most people clustered near the middle, with small minorities on either end.

Critics of government antipoverty efforts were attracted to the book's central message: that the poor are poor in large measure because they are not very smart. Among the most stunning claims made by Herrnstein and Murray was that much of the observed economic gap between blacks and whites could be attributed to the fact that blacks' IQ scores were, on average, lower than those of whites.

Although *The Bell Curve* received a blitz of media attention, social scientists generally gave the analysis low marks. No one doubts that intelligence contributes to economic success, nor that genetics has some bearing on intelligence. But the scientific evidence on the strength of each link is in great dispute. Many experts on IQ, for example, argue that environmental factors may be more important than genetics in determining intelligence and that "true" intelligence may differ from measured IQ. Furthermore, few, if any, economists believe that cognitive ability is the main ingredient in economic success.

The bottom line, according to most scholars, is that the black–white IQ gap does not go very far in explaining racial income inequalities. Nor can we be certain that much of the measured IQ gap is biologically, rather than culturally, determined.

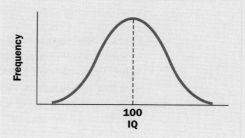

make for success in school have some effect, but hardly an overwhelming one. The same is true of innate intelligence—"IQ" (see the box, "How Important Is the Bell Curve?"). It is clear that some types of inventiveness are richly rewarded by the market, as is that elusive characteristic we have discussed in earlier chapters: entrepreneurial ability. Also, it is obvious that poor health often impairs earning ability.

Differences in Intensity of Work   Some people work longer hours than others or labor more intensely when they are on the job. These disparities lead to income differences that are largely voluntary.

Risk Taking   Most people who acquire large sums of money do so by taking risks—by investing their money in the stock market, in a small start-up company, or in some other uncertain venture. Those who gamble and succeed become wealthy. Perhaps the most spectacular example is Bill Gates, believed to be the richest person in the world, who dropped out of Harvard to start a small company that we now know as Microsoft. Of course, those who try and fail often go broke. Most people prefer not to take such chances and end up somewhere in between. This is another way in which income differences arise voluntarily.

Compensating Wage Differentials   Some jobs are more arduous than others, or more dangerous, or more unpleasant for other reasons. To induce people to take these jobs, some sort of financial incentive normally must be offered. For example, factory workers who work the night shift normally receive higher wages than those who work during the day.

Schooling and Other Types of Training   Chapter 20 analyzed schooling and other types of training as "investments in human capital." As explained there, this phrase refers to the idea that people sacrifice current income to improve their skills so that their future incomes will be higher. When this is done, income differentials naturally rise. Although it is generally agreed that differences in schooling are an important cause of income differentials, this particular cause has both voluntary and involuntary aspects. Young men or women who choose not to go to college have made voluntary decisions that affect their incomes. Many never get the choice: Their parents simply cannot afford to send them. For them, the resulting income differential is not voluntary.

Work Experience   It is well-known to most people and well documented by scholarly research that more experienced workers earn higher wages.

Inherited Wealth   Not all income is derived from work. Some represents the return on invested wealth, and part of this wealth is inherited. Although this cause of inequality applies to few people, many of America's superrich got that way through inheritance. Think of the Rockefellers or, more recently, the Waltons (of Wal-Mart fame). Financial wealth is not the only type of capital that can be inherited—so can human capital. In part, this inheritance happens naturally through genetics: High-ability parents tend to have high-ability children, although the link is an imperfect one. But it also happens partly for economic reasons: Well-to-do parents send their children to the best schools, thereby transforming their own financial wealth into human wealth for their children. This type of inheritance affects many more people than the financial type.

Luck   No observer of our society can fail to notice the role that chance plays in income inequalities. Some of the rich and some of the poor got there largely by good or bad fortune. Two Internet entrepreneurs work equally hard, but only one develops the hot web site that makes him rich. A farmer digs for water, but strikes oil instead. A storekeeper near the World Trade Center disaster is driven out of business for lack of customers. The list could go on and on. Many large income differentials arise purely by chance.

THE FACTS: DISCRIMINATION

Some of the factors we have just listed lead to income differentials that are widely accepted as "just." For example, most people believe it is fair for people who work harder to receive higher incomes. Other factors on our list ignite heated debates. For example, some people view income differentials that arise purely by chance as perfectly acceptable, whereas others find these same differentials intolerable. However, almost no one is willing to condone income inequalities that arise from discrimination.

Economic discrimination occurs when equivalent factors of production receive different payments for equal contributions to output.

The facts about discrimination are not easy to come by. **Economic discrimination** is said to occur when equivalent factors of production receive different payments for equal contributions to output. But this definition is difficult to apply in practice because we cannot always tell when two factors of production are "equivalent."

Few people would call it "discrimination" if a woman with only a high school diploma receives a lower salary than a man with a college degree. Even if a man and a woman have the same education, the man may have 10 more years of work experience than the woman does. If they receive different wages for this reason, is that discriminatory?

In principle, we should compare men and women with equal *productivities*. If women receive lower wages than men who do the same work, we would attribute the difference to discrimination. But discrimination normally takes much more subtle forms than paying unequal wages for equal work. For instance, employers can simply relegate women to inferior jobs, thereby justifying their lower salaries.

One clearly *incorrect* way to measure discrimination is to compare the different groups' typical incomes. Table 3 displays such data for white men, white women, black men, and black women in 2008. Virtually everyone agrees that the amount of discrimination is less than these differentials suggest, but far greater than zero. Precisely how much is a topic of continuing economic research. Several studies suggest that about half of the observed wage differential between black men and white men, and at least half of the differential between white women and white men, arises from discrimination in the

TABLE 3

Median Incomes in 2008

Population Group	Median Income	Percentage of White Male Income
White males	$35,120	100
Black males	25,118	72
White females	20,350	58
Black females	20,203	58

NOTE: For persons 15 years old and older.

SOURCE: U.S. Bureau of the Census.

labor market (although more might be due to discrimination in education, and so on). Other studies have reached somewhat different conclusions.

THE TRADE-OFF BETWEEN EQUALITY AND EFFICIENCY

We have noted that America has more income inequality than other wealthy nations, and we have observed that inequality in the United States has been on the rise for about 30 years. Should society try to reverse this trend? Here economics *alone* cannot provide an answer, although it can inform the discussion. Value judgments are needed to supplement the economic analysis.

Some people say, "That's the way the ball bounces." If the market mechanism happens to produce high and rising inequality, so be it. To these conservatives, government has no business intervening to reduce income inequalities. If it does, they argue, economic efficiency will be impaired. But others beg to differ. Their vision of a "good society" does not countenance high and rising inequality, especially when those at the bottom are so poor. These liberals want the government to promulgate policies that reduce income disparities—programs such as income support for the poor, antidiscrimination statutes, and progressive income and inheritance taxes.

Economic analysis cannot tell us how important it is to promote greater equality. That value-laden judgment falls more into the realm of political theory and philosophy, maybe even psychology. It is a question over which reasonable people can and do differ. But economics can tell us quite a bit about the costs, in terms of reduced efficiency, of alternative policies to promote greater equality. Specifically:

> **THE TRADE-OFF BETWEEN EQUALITY AND EFFICIENCY**   Policies that redistribute income reduce the rewards of high-income earners while raising the rewards of low-income earners. Hence, such policies reduce the incentive to earn high income. Such incentive effects give rise to a trade-off that is one of the most fundamental in all of economics, and one of our *Ideas for Beyond the Final Exam.*
>
> Measures taken to *increase* the amount of economic equality normally *reduce* economic efficiency, that is, reduce society's total output. So, in trying to divide the pie more equally, we may inadvertently reduce its size.

**IDEAS FOR
BEYOND THE
FINAL EXAM**

This annoying trade-off does not mean that all attempts to reduce inequality are misguided. That is where the economic analysis comes in—to temper and inform our value judgments. Basic economic principles teach us two lessons on which we will elaborate in the balance of this chapter:

1. **There are better and worse ways to promote equality. In pursuing further income equality (or fighting poverty), we should seek policies that do the least possible harm to incentives and efficiency.**

2. **Equality is bought at a price. Thus, like any commodity, society must rationally decide how much to "purchase." We will probably want to spend some of our potential income on equality, but certainly not all of it.**

The first lesson is obvious: *We should accomplish any desired redistribution by utilizing the most efficient redistributive policies.* By picking these policies, rather than less efficient ones, we can "buy" whatever degree of equality we want at a lower "price" in terms of lost output. In the rest of this chapter, we will discuss alternative policies and try to indicate which ones damage incentives least.

The second lesson is somewhat less obvious: *Neither complete laissez-faire nor complete equality would normally be society's optimal choice.* To see why, let's take the argument in two steps. At one extreme, it is easy to understand why we should not seek perfect equality. Ask yourself what would happen if we tried to achieve complete equality of incomes by putting a 100 percent income tax on all income and then dividing the tax receipts equally among the population. No one would have any incentive to work, to invest, to take risks, or to do anything else to earn money, because the rewards for all such activities would have disappeared. The nation's total production would fall drastically. Only someone with a fanatic desire for equality would favor such an outcome.

The argument at the other extreme is more subtle. Let's assume (a) that almost everyone would favor greater equality if nothing had to be sacrificed to achieve it, and (b) that complete *laissez-faire* results in more inequality than society wants. There will presumably be some small redistributive policies that have essentially no adverse effects on incentives. Example: Levying a 0.1 percent tax on the incomes of billionaires and giving the proceeds to poor children. In a democracy, policies like that would presumably receive nearly unanimous approval. It follows that society should always carry out *some* redistribution, even if it is minor.

We have therefore established our result: The socially optimal amount of equality is presumably *more* than the unfettered operation of free markets would produce, but *less* than complete equality. The government should therefore presumably undertake *some* redistribution of income, but not too much.

It is astonishing how much confusion is caused by a failure to understand these two lessons. Proponents of greater equality often feel obliged to deny that the programs they advocate will hurt incentives at all. Sometimes these vehement denials are so patently unrealistic that they undermine the very case that the egalitarians are trying to make. Conservatives who oppose such policies also undercut the strength of their case by making outlandish claims about the efficiency losses from redistribution.

IDEAS FOR BEYOND THE FINAL EXAM

Neither side, it seems, is willing to acknowledge the fundamental trade-off between equality and efficiency. As a result, the debate generates more heat than light. Because these debates will likely continue for the rest of your lives, we hope that some understanding of this trade-off stays with you well *Beyond the Final Exam*.

The trade-off idea applies directly to the debate over extending or repealing the Bush tax cuts. The tax cuts did worsen income inequality, but they also improved incentives and therefore contributed to greater economic efficiency. Depending on your value judgments, you might therefore approve or disapprove of the policies.

"There is a perfect example of what is wrong with this country today."

"There is a perfect example of what is wrong with this country today."

This case illustrates the point that merely understanding the trade-off will not tell you what to do. We know that the optimal amount of equality lies between two extremes, but we do not know what it actually is. Nor can we expect people to agree on the optimal degree of inequality, because the answer depends on value judgments: Just how much is more equality worth to you?

Arthur Okun, one-time chairman of the Council of Economic Advisers, described the issue graphically. Imagine that money is liquid and that you have a bucket that can be used to move money from the rich to the poor. Unfortunately, the bucket leaks. As you move the money, some gets lost. (These are the efficiency losses from redistribution.) Will you use the bucket if only 1 cent is lost for each $1 you move? Almost everyone would say yes. However, what if you lose 90 cents, so that each $1 taken from the rich results in only 10 cents for the poor? Only the most extreme egalitarians will still say yes. Now try the more difficult questions. What if 20 to 40 cents is lost for each $1 that you move? If you can answer questions such as these, you can decide how much equality you want, for you will have expressed your value judgments in quantitative terms.

POLICIES TO COMBAT POVERTY

Let us take it for granted that the nation wants to reduce poverty, at least somewhat. Which policies promote this goal? Which of these does the least harm to incentives and hence is most efficient?

Education as a Way Out

Education is often advertised as one of the principal ways to escape from poverty. No doubt many people have used this route successfully, and still do. And the evidence points clearly to the conclusion that more education boosts earnings.

However, delivering quality education to poor children is no simple matter. Many of them, especially in the inner cities, are ill-equipped to learn and attend schools that are ill-equipped to teach. Despite some gratifying progress in recent years, dropout rates remain dismayingly high. An astonishing number of youths leave the public school system without even acquiring basic literacy. All of these problems are familiar; none is easy to solve.

In truth, our educational system must serve many goals, and the alleviation of poverty is not the major one. If it were, we would certainly spend more money on preschool and inner-city children and less on college education than we do today. Furthermore, education is not an effective way to lift *adults* out of poverty. Its effects are delayed for a generation or more.

The Welfare Debate and the Trade-Off

By contrast, a variety of programs collectively known as "welfare" are specifically designed to alleviate poverty, meant to help adults as well as children, and intended to have quick effects. The best known and most heavily criticized of these programs used to be *Aid to Families with Dependent Children (AFDC)*. AFDC provided direct cash grants to families that had children but no breadwinner, generally because the father was absent or unknown and the mother could not or did not work.

When Bill Clinton campaigned in 1992 on a promise to "end welfare as we know it," many Americans shared his dissatisfaction with the system. Why? Because AFDC was a classic example of an inefficient redistributive program. One major reason was that it provided no incentive for welfare mothers to earn income. Once monthly earnings passed a few hundred dollars, AFDC payments were reduced by $1 for each $1 that the family earned as wages. Thus, if a member of the family got a job, the family was subjected to a 100 percent marginal tax rate! Little wonder, then, that many welfare recipients did not look very hard for work. In addition, critics argued that "the welfare mess" was too bureaucratic, too expensive, and might even be hurting the very people it was designed to help—by, for example, encouraging out-of-wedlock births and fostering a culture of dependence on the state.

In 1996, Congress redeemed President Clinton's campaign pledge by replacing AFDC with a new welfare program: **Temporary Assistance to Needy Families (TANF)**. Notice the word *temporary*. TANF limits eligibility for welfare checks to two years at a time and five years over a person's lifetime. Before recipients reach these time limits, they are supposed to have found jobs. The new law also gave states much greater latitude to design their own welfare systems, thereby greatly reducing federal influence over welfare. And, indeed, the generosity of TANF now varies tremendously across the 50 states.

The new welfare law was highly controversial when it was enacted. Critics argued that it would throw many needy families to the wolves when their benefits ran out. Supporters argued that it would give them "a hand up, instead of a handout"—and would save the taxpayers money to boot. This debate offered another illustration of the trade-off between equality and efficiency and how poorly understood it is. Critics of TANF argued that the new law was mean-spirited because it reduced the amount of income support that poor mothers could receive. Supporters argued that TANF provided better work incentives than AFDC.

From 1996 to 2000, the economy boomed, jobs were plentiful, and the welfare rolls shrank dramatically. So the new system was not put to the test until the economy slowed in 2000 and 2001 and jobs became scarcer. When the welfare rolls did *not* soar in the weak job market of 2001–2003, TANF passed its first test with flying colors. This success, supporters claimed, proved that the new system worked well. However, studies of the welfare population found very high poverty rates among those who had exited the TANF program. They also found that roughly half of the people eligible for TANF benefits were not receiving them. Furthermore, because many poor women cycle in and out of welfare, few had yet reached the five-year lifetime limit. For all of these reasons, the debate over welfare reform goes on. Studies of TANF during the 2008–2009 recession have yet to be completed.

Food Stamps   A second prominent welfare program is Food Stamps, which burgeoned in the 1970s and was cut back several times in the 1980s and 1990s. Under this program, poor families receive "stamps"—which nowadays are actually delivered via an electronic benefits card—that they can use to purchase food. The size of each family's Food Stamp benefit depends on its income: The poorer the family, the greater the benefit.

Transfers in Kind   In addition to TANF and Food Stamps, the government provides many poor people with a number of important goods and services, either at no charge or at prices that are well below market levels. Medical care under the Medicaid program and subsidized public housing are two notable examples.[2] These programs significantly enhance the living standards of the poor. However, most of them offer benefits that decline as family income rises. Taken as a whole, all of the antipoverty programs together put some poor families in a position where they are taxed extremely heavily if their earnings rise. When this situation occurs, the incentive to work becomes quite weak.

The Negative Income Tax

How can we do the job better? Can we design a simple structure that gets income into the hands of the poor without destroying their incentives to work? The solution suggested most frequently by economists is called the **negative income tax (NIT)**.

The **negative income tax (NIT)** is a program where people below a certain income range would receive a payment from the government.

Table 4 illustrates how a NIT works. A particular NIT plan is defined by picking two numbers: a minimum income level below which no family is allowed to fall (the "guarantee") and a rate at which benefits are "taxed away" as income rises. The table considers a plan with a $12,000 guaranteed income and a 50 percent tax rate. Thus, a family with no earnings (top row) would receive a $12,000 payment (a "negative tax") from the government. A family earning $4,000 (second row) would have the basic benefit reduced by 50 percent of its earnings, or $2,000. Thus, it would receive $10,000 from the government plus the $4,000 earned income for a total income of $14,000.

TABLE 4		
Illustration of a Negative Income Tax Plan		
Benefits Earnings	Total Paid	Income
$ 0	$12,000	$12,000
4,000	10,000	14,000
8,000	8,000	16,000
12,000	6,000	18,000
16,000	4,000	20,000
20,000	2,000	22,000
24,000	0	24,000

Notice in Table 4 that, with a 50 percent tax rate, the increase in total income as earnings rise is always *half* of the increase in earnings. Thus, recipients always have some incentive to work. Notice also that there is a level of income at which benefits cease—$24,000 in this example. This "break-even" level is not a third number that policy makers can select freely. Rather, it is dictated by the choices of the guarantee and the tax rate. In our example, $12,000 is the maximum possible benefit, and benefits are reduced by 50 cents for each $1 of earnings. Hence, benefits will be reduced to zero when 50 percent of earnings is equal to $12,000—which occurs when earnings are $24,000. The general relation is

Guarantee = Tax rate × Break-even level

The fact that the break-even level is completely determined by the guarantee and the tax rate creates a vexing problem. To make a real dent in the poverty problem, the guarantee must be placed fairly close to the poverty line. But then any moderate tax rate will push the break-even level far *above* the poverty line. As a result, families who are not considered "poor" (although they are certainly not rich) will also receive benefits. For example, a low tax rate of 33⅓ percent means that some benefits are paid to families whose income is as high as three times the guarantee level.

---

[2] *Medicaid* programs pay for the health care of low-income people; *Medicare* is available to all seniors, regardless of income.

The solution seems obvious: raise the tax rate to bring the guarantee and the break-even level closer together. Then the incentive to work shrinks, and with it the principal rationale for the NIT in the first place. So the NIT is no panacea for the ills of the welfare system. Difficult choices must still be made.

The Negative Income Tax and Work Incentives   The NIT should increase work incentives for welfare recipients. However, we have just seen that a number of families who are now too well off to collect welfare inevitably would become eligible for NIT payments. For these people, the NIT imposes work disincentives by subjecting them to the relatively high NIT tax rate. Government-sponsored experiments back in the 1960s found that recipients of NIT benefits did in fact work less than nonrecipients, but only by a slight amount.

Largely because of its superior work incentives, economists believe that a NIT is a more efficient way to redistribute income than the existing multifaceted welfare system. If this view is correct, then replacing the current welfare system with a NIT would lead to both more equality *and* more efficiency. But this does not mean that equalization would become cost-free. There is still a trade-off: By increasing equality, we still diminish the nation's output.

The Negative Income Tax and Reality   The NIT is often mistakenly viewed as an "academic" idea that does not exist in practice. But, in fact, America has two important programs that strongly resemble a NIT. One is the Food Stamps program already mentioned. Food Stamp benefits decline as earnings rise, and Food Stamps are used like cash in many poor neighborhoods. Hence, Food Stamp benefits look very much like the NIT plan illustrated in Table 4.

The second program is an important feature of the income tax code, called the **Earned Income Tax Credit (EITC)**. It works as follows. As earnings rise from zero to some threshold (which was about $12,500 in 2009 for a worker with two children), the federal government supplements the earnings of the working poor by giving them what amounts to a grant that is proportional to their earnings. Once earnings pass a second threshold (about $16,500 in 2009), the government starts taking this grant back, just as a NIT would. The EITC dates back to 1975 but was made substantially more generous in 1993. It is now America's biggest income-support program, reaching over 25 million families.

> The **Earned Income Tax Credit (EITC)** is a program in which the federal government gives out grants to certain families proportional to their earnings.

OTHER POLICIES TO COMBAT INEQUALITY

If we take the broader view that society's objective is not just to eliminate poverty, but to reduce income disparities, then the fact that many nonpoor families would receive benefits under a NIT is perhaps not a serious drawback. After all, unless the plan is outlandishly generous, these families' incomes will still fall well below the average. Even so, the NIT is largely thought of as an antipoverty program, not as a tool for general income equalization.

The Personal Income Tax

By contrast, the federal personal income tax *is* thought of as a way to promote greater equality. Indeed, it is probably given far more credit in this regard than it actually deserves. Because the income tax is *progressive*, it takes a larger share of income from the rich than from the poor.[3] Thus, incomes *after* tax are distributed more equally than incomes *before* tax. The actual amount of redistribution achieved by the personal income tax is quite small—and even that was reduced by the tax cuts of 2001–2003.

Death Duties and Other Taxes

Taxes on inheritances and estates levied by both states and the federal government also equalize incomes. In this case, they seem clearly aimed at limiting the incomes of the rich,

---

[3] For definitions of progressive, proportional, and regressive taxes, see Chapter 18.

or at least at limiting their ability to transfer this largesse from one generation to the next. But the amount of money involved is too small to make much difference to the overall income distribution. Total receipts from estate and gift taxes by all levels of government provide less than 1 percent of total tax revenues.

Nonetheless, the federal estate tax has been a hot political issue since 2001 when Congress voted to eliminate it, but in a rather unusual way. Under current law, the estate tax was phased out in January 2010, but then it will miraculously reappear in 2011 unless Congress acts! So it is a good bet that the estate tax law will be changed again in the coming years. Exactly how is not so clear.

Most experts agree that the many other taxes in the U.S. system—including sales taxes, payroll taxes, and property taxes—are decidedly regressive as a group. On balance, the evidence seems to suggest that

The U.S. tax system as a whole is only slightly progressive.

POLICIES TO COMBAT DISCRIMINATION

The policies we have just considered are all based on taxes and transfer payments—on moving dollars from one set of hands to another. A quite different approach has been used to fight *discrimination*: Governments have made it *illegal* to discriminate.

Perhaps the major milestone in the war against discrimination was the *Civil Rights Act of 1964*, which outlawed many forms of discrimination and established the *Equal Employment Opportunity Commission (EEOC)*. When you read in a want ad that the company is "an equal opportunity employer," the firm is proclaiming its compliance with this and related legislation.

Originally, policy makers sought to attack the problem by outlawing discrimination in rates of pay and in hiring standards—and by devoting resources to enforcing these provisions. Some progress in reducing discrimination by race and sex undoubtedly was made between 1964 and the early 1970s. However, many people felt the pace was too slow. One reason was that discrimination in the labor market proved to be more subtle than was first thought. Only rarely could officials find definitive proof that unequal pay was being given for equal work, because determining when work was "equal" turned out to be a formidable task.

To combat this problem, a new and controversial approach was added to the antidiscrimination arsenal. Firms and other organizations with suspiciously small representations of minorities or women in their workforces were required not just to end discriminatory practices but also to demonstrate that they were taking **affirmative action** to remedy this imbalance. That is, they had to document the fact that they were making efforts to locate members of minority groups and females and then to hire them if they were qualified.

Affirmative action refers to active efforts to locate and hire members of underrepresented groups.

This approach to fighting discrimination remains controversial to this day. Critics, including many Republicans in Congress, claim that affirmative action amounts to numerical quotas and compulsory hiring of unqualified workers simply because they are black or female. If this allegation is true, it exacts a toll on economic efficiency. Proponents of affirmative action, including many Democrats, argue that affirmative action is needed to redress past wrongs and to prevent discriminatory employers from claiming that they are unable to find qualified minority or female employees. (See the box "Should Affirmative Action Be Abolished?" on the next page.)

The difficulty revolves around the impossibility of deciding who is "qualified" and who is not based on *purely objective criteria.* What one person sees as government coercion to hire an unqualified applicant to fill a quota, another sees as a discriminatory employer being forced to mend his or her ways. Nothing in this book, or anywhere else, will teach you which view is correct in any particular instance.

The controversy over affirmative action once again illustrates *the trade-off between equality and efficiency.* Putting more women and members of minority groups into high-paying jobs would certainly make the income distribution more equal. Supporters of affirmative action seek that result. But if affirmative action disrupts industry and requires firms to replace

POLICY DEBATE

SHOULD AFFIRMATIVE ACTION BE ABOLISHED?

Affirmative action was controversial from the start. It became a particularly hot political issue in the 1990s and 2000s, as conservative politicians reacted to what they perceived to be one of the chief grievances of the "angry white male."

A number of critics believe that affirmative action has outlived its usefulness. It is time, they say, to rely on "race-blind" standards that judge each person on his or her individual merits. Any other system of selection is unfair, they insist, especially when affirmative action programs devolve into rigid quotas by race or sex—as they frequently do.

Although no federal laws were changed, an important 1995 Supreme Court ruling in *Adarand* v. *Pena* set new and tougher standards for federal affirmative action programs. This ruling prompted President Clinton to order a comprehensive review of federal programs that favored minorities in such matters as hiring and awarding contracts. Although a few programs were cut back or eliminated, the review generally concluded that the United States was still so far from being a "color-blind" society that affirmative action was still needed, and the president continued to defend affirmative action against Republican efforts to eliminate it.

Some state governments, however, went much farther than the federal government. California and Texas, for example, abolished several affirmative action programs at their

state universities. (In California, this action followed a contentious statewide referendum on the matter.) When they did, minority enrollments plummeted so dramatically that a few opponents of affirmative action had well-publicized second thoughts.

The issue remains open. Few people actually like affirmative action—it offends many people's sense of fairness, and even many supporters view it as a necessary evil. New appointments to the Supreme Court have made the Court less and less sympathetic to affirmative action over the years.

SOURCE: © Paul J. Richards/AFP/Getty Images

"qualified" white males with other, "less qualified" workers, the nation's productivity will suffer. Opponents of affirmative action are disturbed by these potential efficiency losses. How far should these programs be pushed? A good question, but one without a good answer.

A LOOK BACK

We have now completed three chapters on the distribution of income. So this may be an opportune moment to pause and see how this analysis relates to our central theme: *What does the market do well, and what does it do poorly?*

We have learned that a market economy relies on the marginal productivity principle to assign an income to each individual. In so doing, the market attaches high prices to scarce factors and low prices to abundant ones and therefore guides firms to use society's resources *efficiently*. This ability is one of the market's great strengths.

However, by attaching high prices to some factors and low prices to others, the market mechanism may create a distribution of income that is quite unequal. Some people wind up fabulously rich, whereas others wind up miserably poor. For this reason, the market has been widely criticized for centuries for doing a rather poor job of distributing income in accord with commonly held notions of *fairness* and *equity*.

On balance, most observers feel that both the praise and the criticism are well justified: The market mechanism is extraordinarily good at promoting efficiency but not very good at promoting equality. As we said at the outset, the market has both virtues and vices.

| SUMMARY |

1. The United States declared a "War on Poverty" in 1964, and within a decade the fraction of families below the official **poverty line** had dropped substantially. Today, the poverty rate is higher than it was in the 1970s.

2. In the United States today, the richest 20 percent of households receive about 50 percent of the income, whereas the poorest 20 percent of households receive less than 3½ percent. These numbers reflect a considerable increase in inequality since about 1980. The U.S. income distribution also appears to be more unequal than those of most other industrial nations.

3. Individual incomes differ for many reasons. Differences in natural abilities, in the desire to work hard and to take risks, in schooling and experience, and in inherited wealth all account for income disparities. **Economic discrimination** also plays a role. All of these factors, however, explain only part of the inequality that we observe. A portion of the rest is due simply to good or bad luck, and the balance is unexplained.

4. There is a trade-off between the goals of reducing inequality and enhancing economic efficiency. Namely, policies that help on the equality front normally harm efficiency, and vice versa.

5. Because of this trade-off, there is in principle an optimal degree of inequality for any society. Society finds this optimum in the same way that a consumer decides how much to buy of different commodities: The trade-off tells us how costly it is to "purchase" more equality, and preferences then determine how much should be "bought." However, because people have different value judgments about the importance of equality, they disagree over the ideal amount of equality.

6. Whatever goal for equality is selected, society can gain by using more efficient redistributive policies because such policies let us "buy" any given amount of equality at a lower price in terms of lost output. Economists claim, for example, that a **negative income tax** is an efficient redistributive tool.

7. But the negative income tax is no panacea for all inequality-related problems. Its primary virtue is the way it preserves incentives to work. But if this goal is accomplished by keeping the tax rate low, then either the minimum guaranteed level of income will have to be low or many nonpoor families will become eligible to receive benefits.

8. The goal of income equality is also pursued through the tax system, especially through the progressive federal income tax and death duties. But other taxes are typically regressive, so the tax system as a whole is only slightly progressive.

9. Discrimination has been attacked by making it illegal, rather than through the tax and transfer system. But simply declaring discrimination to be illegal is much easier than actually ending discrimination. The **trade-off between equality and efficiency** applies once again: Strict enforcement of **affirmative action** will certainly reduce discrimination and increase income equality, but it may do so at a cost in terms of economic efficiency.

| KEY TERMS |

absolute concept of poverty   **448**

affirmative action   **458**

Earned Income Tax Credit (EITC)   **457**

economic discrimination   **452**

Food Stamps   **456**

negative income tax (NIT)   **456**

poverty line   **447**

relative concept of poverty   **448**

Temporary Assistance to Needy Families (TANF)   **455**

| TEST YOURSELF |

1. Define the poverty rate. Does it rise or fall during recessions?

2. Since the official poverty line was set at $3,000 in 1964, prices have risen by about a factor of 7. If the poverty line was adjusted only for inflation, what would it be now? How does that compare with the actual poverty line?

| DISCUSSION QUESTIONS |

1. Discuss the "leaky bucket" analogy (page 454) with your classmates. What maximum amount of income would you personally allow to leak from the bucket in transferring money from the rich to the poor? Explain why people differ in their answers to this question.

2. Suppose you were to design a negative income tax system for the United States. Pick a guaranteed income level and a tax rate that seem reasonable to you. What break-even level of income is implied by these choices? Construct a version of Table 4 for the plan you have just devised.

3. Suppose the War on Poverty were starting anew and you were part of a presidential commission assigned the task of defining the poor. Would you choose an absolute or a relative concept of poverty? Why? What would be your specific definition of poverty?

4. Discuss the concept of the "optimal amount of inequality." What are some of the practical problems in determining how much inequality really is optimal?

5. A number of conservative politicians and economists advocate replacing the progressive income tax with a "flat tax" that would apply the same, low tax rate to all income above a certain exempt amount. One argument against making this change is that the distribution of income has grown much more unequal since the 1970s. Does the evidence support that view? Is it a decisive argument against a flat tax? How is the trade-off between equality and efficiency involved here?

| APPENDIX | *The Economic Theory of Discrimination*

Although discrimination is often thought of as a noneconomic topic, economic analysis can actually tell us quite a bit about its economic effects. This appendix uses some of the analysis we have provided in previous chapters to shed light on two specific questions:

1. Must *prejudice,* which we define as arising when one group dislikes associating with another group, lead to *economic discrimination* as defined in the chapter (unequal pay for equal work)?

2. Do "natural" economic forces tend either to erode or to exacerbate discrimination over time?

Exactly *who* is prejudiced or discriminatory turns out to be critical to the answers, as we will now see.

DISCRIMINATION BY EMPLOYERS

Most attention seems to focus on discrimination by employers, so let us start there. What happens if, for example, some firms refuse to hire blacks? Figure 2 will help us find the answer. Panel (a) pertains to firms that discriminate; Panel (b) pertains to firms that do not. Supply and demand curves for labor in each market are shown in the figure, based on the analysis of Chapter 20. We suppose that the two demand curves are identical.

However, the supply curve in market (b) must be farther to the right than the supply curve in market (a) because both whites *and* blacks can work in market (b), whereas only whites can work in market (a). The result is that wages will be lower in market (b) than they are in market (a). Because all the blacks are forced into market (b), we conclude that employers discriminate against them in the economic sense of that word.

Now consider the situation from the *employers'* point of view. Firms in market (a) pay more for labor (W_a is greater than W_b), so the nondiscriminatory firms in market (b) have a cost advantage. As we learned in earlier chapters, the forces of competition will shift more and more of the total market to the low-cost (nondiscriminatory) producers, eventually driving the discriminators out of business. Of course, this only happens if there is effective competition. If the discriminating firm in market (a) has a protected monopoly, it will be able to stay in business. But it will still pay for the privilege of discriminating by earning lower monopoly profits than it otherwise would (because it will pay higher wages than necessary).

DISCRIMINATION BY FELLOW WORKERS

So, *if* employers are the source of discrimination, competitive forces tend to reduce discrimination over time. Such optimistic conclusions do not follow, however, if it is fellow workers who are prejudiced. Consider what happens, for example, if men object to having women as their supervisors. If male workers will not give their full cooperation, female supervisors will be less effective than male supervisors and hence will earn lower wages. Here prejudice *does* lead to discrimination. Furthermore, in this case, firms that put women into supervisory positions will be at a competitive *disadvantage* relative to firms that do not. So market forces will not erode discrimination.

FIGURE 2

Wage Discrimination

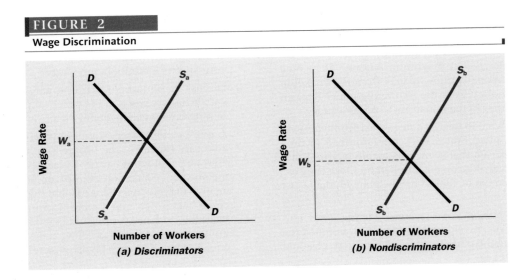

(a) Discriminators · (b) Nondiscriminators

STATISTICAL DISCRIMINATION

A final type of discrimination, called **statistical discrimination,** may be the most stubborn of all. And it can exist even when there is no prejudice.

> **Statistical discrimination** is said to occur when the productivity of a particular worker is estimated to be low just because that worker belongs to a particular group (such as women).

Let us look at an important example. It is, of course, a biological fact that only women give birth. It is also a fact that most working women who have babies leave their jobs for a while to care for their newborns. Employers recognize both facts. What they cannot know, however, is *which* women of child-bearing age will leave the labor force for this reason.

Suppose three candidates apply for a job that requires a long-term commitment. Susan plans to quit after a few years to raise a family. Jane does not plan to have any children. Jack is a man. If he knew all the facts, the employer might not want Susan, but would be equally happy with either Jane or Jack. But the employer cannot differentiate between Susan and Jane. He therefore presumes that either one, being a young woman, is more likely than Jack to quit to raise a family. So he hires Jack, even though Jane is just as good a prospect. Thus Jane is a victim of statistical discrimination.

Lest it be thought that this example actually justifies discrimination against women on economic grounds, it should be noted that most women return to work within six months after childbirth. Furthermore, women typically have less absenteeism and job turnover for nonpregnancy health reasons than men do. The box "Are Women Better Workers?" argues that employers often fail to take these other sex-related differences into account and thus mistakenly favor men.

THE ROLES OF THE MARKET AND THE GOVERNMENT

In terms of the two questions with which we began this appendix, we conclude that different types of discrimination lead to different answers. Prejudice will often, but not always, lead to economic discrimination, and discrimination may occur even in the absence of prejudice. Finally, the forces of competition tend to erode some, but not all, of the inequities produced by discrimination.

However, the victims of discrimination are not the only losers when discrimination occurs. Society also loses whenever discriminatory practices impair economic efficiency. Thus reasonable antidiscrimination policies should be able to enhance both equality and efficiency. For this reason, most observers believe that we should not rely on market forces *alone* to combat discrimination. The government has a clear role to play.

Are Women Better Workers?

In the piece excerpted here, economist Audrey Freedman argues that a female employee can be a better bargain than a male, even though only women request pregnancy leaves and it is mainly women who miss workdays for child-care reasons.

It is undeniable . . . that women, not men, take pregnancy leaves. It is also undeniable that women are the primary nurturers in a family. They are the most likely to be responsible for the care and support of children, as well as their elderly parents. If we stop there . . . women in business are more costly than men.

But the built-in bias of that analysis is the failure to account for far more costly drains on corporate productivity from behavior that is more characteristic of men than of women.

For example, men are more likely to be heavy users of alcohol. This gender-related habit causes businesses to suffer excessive medical costs, serious performance losses, and productivity drains. Yet, the male-dominated corporate hierarchy most often chooses to ignore these "good old boy" habits.

Drug abuse among the fast-movers of Wall Street seems to be understood as a normal response to the pressures of taking risks with other people's money. The consequences in loss of judgment are tolerated. They are not calculated as a male-related cost of business. . . .

In addition, in our culture, lawlessness and violence are found far more often among men than women. The statistics on criminals and prison population are obvious, yet we seem to be unable to recognize these as primarily male behaviors.

A top executive of a major airline once commented to me that his company's greatest problem is machismo in the cockpit—pilots and copilots fighting over the controls. There is an obvious solution: Hire pilots from that half of the population that is less susceptible to the attacks of rage that afflict macho males.

SOURCE: (c)1986 Etta Hulme. Reprinted by permission of Etta Hulme and the *Fort Worth Star Telegram.*

SOURCE: Audrey Freedman, "Those Costly 'Good Old Boys,'" *The New York Times,* July 12, 1989, p. A23. Copyright 1989 by the New York Times Company. Reprinted by permission.

| SUMMARY |

1. Prejudice by employers will result in discrimination in rates of pay and in partial segregation of the workplace. However, the forces of competition should erode this type of discrimination.

2. Prejudice by fellow workers will result in wage discrimination, and perhaps even in segregated workplaces. But competition will not erode this type of discrimination.

3. Discrimination may also arise even when there is no prejudice. This is called **statistical discrimination**.

| KEY TERM |

statistical discrimination   462

THE UNITED STATES IN THE WORLD ECONOMY

"Globalization" became a buzzword in the 1990s—and it remains one today. Some people extol its virtues and view it as something to be encouraged. Others deplore its (real or imagined) costs and seek to stop globalization in its tracks. For example, globalization is often viewed as a threat to the livelihoods of American workers.

We will examine several aspects of the globalization debate in Part 6. Love it or hate it, one thing is clear: The United States is thoroughly integrated into a broader world economy. What happens in the United States influences other countries, and events abroad reverberate back here. Trillions of dollars' worth of goods and services—American software, Chinese toys, Japanese cars—are traded across international borders each year. A vastly larger dollar volume of financial transactions—trade in stocks, bonds, and bank deposits, for example—takes place in the global economy at lightning speed.

We have mentioned these subjects before, but Part 6 brings international factors from the wings to center stage. Chapter 22 studies the factors that underlie *international trade*.

If you want to understand why so many Americans are worried about international trade, why many thoughtful observers think we need to overhaul the international monetary system, or why there was so much economic turmoil in Southeast Asia, Russia, and Latin America during the last 15 years or so, read this chapter with care.

CHAPTERS

22

INTERNATIONAL TRADE AND COMPARATIVE ADVANTAGE

No nation was ever ruined by trade.

BENJAMIN FRANKLIN

conomists emphasize international trade as the source of many of the benefits of *globalization*—a loosely defined term that indicates a closer knitting together of the world's national economies. Of course, countries have always been linked in various ways. The Vikings, after all, landed in North America—not to mention Christopher Columbus. In recent decades, however, dramatic improvements in transportation, telecommunications, and international relations have drawn the nations of the world ever closer together economically. This process of globalization is often portrayed as something new. In fact, it is not, as the box "Is Globalization Something New?" on the next page points out. Still, it is changing the way the people of the world live.

Economic events in other countries affect the United States for both macroeconomic and microeconomic reasons. This chapter studies some of the *microeconomic* linkages among nations: How are patterns and prices of world trade determined? How and why do governments often interfere with foreign trade? The central idea of this chapter is one we have encountered before (in Chapters 1 and 3): the *principle of comparative advantage.*

CONTENTS

Is Globalization Something New?

Few people realize that the industrialized world was, in fact, highly globalized prior to World War I, before the ravages of two world wars and the Great Depression severed many international linkages. Furthermore, as the British magazine *The Economist* pointed out more than a decade ago, globalization has not gone nearly as far as many people imagine.

Despite much loose talk about the "new" global economy, today's international economic integration is not unprecedented. The 50 years before the first world war saw large cross-border flows of goods, capital and people. That period of globalisation, like the present one, was driven by reductions in trade barriers and by sharp falls in transport costs, thanks to the development of railways and steamships. The present surge of globalisation is in a way a resumption of that previous trend. . . .

Two forces have been driving [globalization]. The first is technology. With the costs of communication and computing falling rapidly, the natural barriers of time and space that separate national markets have been falling too. The cost of a three-minute telephone call between New York and London has fallen from $300 (in 1996 dollars) in 1930 to $1 today . . .

The second driving force has been liberalisation. . . . Almost all countries have lowered barriers to trade. . . . [T]he ratio of trade to output . . . has increased sharply in most countries since 1950. But by this measure Britain and France are only slightly more open to trade today than they were in 1913. . . .

Product markets are still nowhere near as integrated across borders as they are within nations. Consider the example of trade between the United States and Canada, one of the least restricted trading borders in the world. On average, trade between a Canadian province and an American state is 20 times smaller than domestic trade between two Canadian provinces, after adjusting for distance and income levels.

The financial markets are not yet truly integrated either. Despite the newfound popularity of international investing, capital markets were by some measures more integrated at the start of this century than they are now. . . . [And] labour is less mobile than it was in the second half of the 19th century, when some 60m people left Europe for the New World.

SOURCE: © AP Images

SOURCE: "Schools Brief: One World?" from *The Economist*, October 18, 1997. Copyright © 1997 The Economist Newspaper Ltd. All rights reserved. Reprinted with permission. Further reproduction prohibited. http://www.economist.com.

| ISSUE: | HOW CAN AMERICANS COMPETE WITH "CHEAP FOREIGN LABOR"? |

Americans (and the citizens of many other nations) often want their government to limit or prevent import competition. Why? One major reason is the common belief that imports take bread out of American workers' mouths. According to this view, "cheap foreign labor" steals jobs from Americans and pressures U.S. businesses to lower wages. For many years, attention focused on the phenomenon of manufacturing jobs moving abroad. Lately, there has been a great deal of concern over the "offshoring" of a wide variety of service jobs—ranging from call center operators to lawyers. Such worries were prominently voiced in the 2008 presidential campaign. For example, during the Democratic primaries, Senators Hillary Clinton and Barack Obama competed over who could be more disparaging toward the North American Free Trade Agreement (NAFTA), arguing that competition from cheap Mexican labor had destroyed many good American jobs.

Oddly enough, the facts appear to be grossly inconsistent with the theory that trade kills jobs. For one thing, wages in most countries that export to the United States have risen dramatically in recent decades—much faster than wages here. Table 1 shows hourly compensation rates in eight countries on three continents, each expressed as a percentage of hourly compensation in the United States, in 1975 and 2005. Only workers in Mexico lost ground to American workers over this 30-year period. Labor in

Europe gained substantially on their U.S. counterparts—rising in Britain, for example, from just above half the U.S. standard to above-U.S. levels. And the wage gains in Asia were nothing short of spectacular. Labor compensation in South Korea, for example, soared from just 5 percent of U.S. levels to more than half.[1] Yet, while all this was going on, American imports of automobiles from Japan, electronics from Taiwan, and textiles from Korea expanded rapidly.

Ironically, then, the United States' dominant position in the international marketplace *deteriorated* just as wage levels in Europe and Asia were rising closer to our own. Clearly, something other than exploiting cheap foreign labor must be driving international trade—in contrast to what the "commonsense" view of the matter suggests. In this chapter, we will see precisely what is wrong with this commonsense view.

TABLE 1		
Labor Costs in Industrialized Countries as a Percentage of U.S. Labor Costs		
	1975	2005
France	73%	104%
United Kingdom	54	109
Spain	41	75
Japan	48	92
South Korea	5	57
Taiwan	6	27
Mexico	24	11
Canada	99	101

SOURCE: U.S. Bureau of Labor Statistics.

NOTE: Data are compensation estimates per hour, converted at exchange rates, and relate to production workers in the manufacturing sector.

WHY TRADE?

The earth's resources are distributed unequally across the planet. Although the United States produces its own coal and wheat, it depends almost *entirely* on the rest of the world for such basic items as rubber and coffee. Similarly, the Persian Gulf states have little land that is suitable for farming but sit atop huge pools of oil—something we are constantly reminded of by geopolitical events. Because of the seemingly whimsical distribution of the earth's resources, every nation must trade with others to acquire what it lacks.

Even if countries had all the resources they needed, other differences in natural endowments such as climate, terrain, and so on would lead them to engage in trade. Americans *could* grow their own bananas and coffee in hothouses, albeit with great difficulty. These crops are grown much more efficiently in Honduras and Brazil, though, where the climates are appropriate.

The skills of a nation's labor force also play a role. If New Zealand has a large group of efficient farmers and few workers with industrial experience, whereas the opposite is true in Japan, it makes sense for New Zealand to specialize in agriculture and let Japan concentrate on manufacturing.

Finally, a small country that tried to produce every product its citizens want to consume would end up with many industries that are simply too small to utilize modern mass-production techniques or to take advantage of other economies of large-scale operations. For example, some countries operate their own international airlines for reasons that can only be described as political, not economic.

To summarize, the main reason why nations trade with one another is to exploit the many advantages of **specialization,** some of which were discussed in Chapter 3. International trade greatly enhances living standards for all parties involved because:

> **Specialization** means that a country devotes its energies and resources to only a small proportion of the world's productive activities.

1. **Every country lacks some vital resources that it can get only by trading with others.**
2. **Each country's climate, labor force, and other endowments make it a relatively efficient producer of some goods and a relatively inefficient producer of others.**
3. **Specialization permits larger outputs via the advantages of large-scale production.**

Mutual Gains from Trade

Many people have long believed that one nation gains from trade only at the expense of another. After all, nothing new is produced by the mere act of trading. So if one country gains from a swap, it has been argued for centuries, the other country must necessarily lose. One consequence of this mistaken belief was and continues to be attitudes that call for each country to try to take advantage of its trading partners on the (fallacious) grounds that one nation's gain must be another's loss.

---

[1] China would be an even more extreme example, but we lack Chinese data dating back to 1975.

Yet, as Adam Smith emphasized, and as we learned in Chapter 3, both parties must expect to gain something from any *voluntary exchange*. Otherwise, why would they agree to trade?

How can mere exchange of goods leave both parties better off? The answer is that although trade does not increase the total output of goods, it does allow each party to acquire items better suited to its tastes. Suppose Levi has four cookies and nothing to drink, whereas Malcolm has two glasses of milk and nothing to eat. A trade of two of Levi's cookies for one of Malcolm's glasses of milk will not increase the total supply of either milk or cookies, but it almost certainly will make both boys better off.

By exactly the same logic, both the United States and Mexico must reap gains when Mexicans voluntarily ship their tomatoes to the United States in return for American chemicals. In general, as we emphasized in Chapter 3:

IDEAS FOR BEYOND THE FINAL EXAM

TRADE IS A WIN-WIN SITUATION Both parties must expect to gain from any *voluntary exchange.* Trade brings about mutual gains by redistributing products so that both parties end up holding more preferred combinations of goods than they held before. This principle, which is one of our *Ideas for Beyond the Final Exam*, applies to nations just as it does to individuals.

INTERNATIONAL VERSUS INTRANATIONAL TRADE

The 50 states of the United States may be the most eloquent testimonial to the large gains that can be realized from specialization and free trade. Florida specializes in growing oranges, Michigan builds cars, California makes software and computers, and New York specializes in finance. All of these states trade freely with one another and, as a result, enjoy great prosperity. Try to imagine how much lower your standard of living would be if you consumed only items produced in your own state.

The essential logic behind international trade is no different from that underlying trade among different states; the basic reasons for trade are equally applicable within a country or among countries. Why, then, do we study international trade as a special subject? There are at least three reasons.

Political Factors in International Trade

First, domestic trade takes place under a single national government, whereas foreign trade always involves at least two governments. But a nation's government is normally much less concerned about the welfare of other countries' citizens than it is about its own. So, for example, the U.S. Constitution prohibits tariffs on trade among states, but it does not prohibit the United States from imposing tariffs on imports from abroad. One major issue in the economic analysis of international trade is the use and misuse of political impediments to international trade.

The Many Currencies Involved in International Trade

Second, all trade within the borders of the United States is carried out in U.S. dollars, whereas trade across national borders almost always involves at least two currencies. Rates of exchange between different currencies can and do change. In 1985, it took about 250 Japanese yen to buy a dollar; now it takes fewer than half that many. Variability in exchange rates brings with it a host of complications and policy problems.

Impediments to Mobility of Labor and Capital

Third, it is much easier for labor and capital to move about within a country than to move from one nation to another. If jobs are plentiful in California but scarce in Ohio, workers can move freely to follow the job opportunities. Of course, personal costs such as the financial burden of moving and the psychological burden of leaving friends and familiar surroundings may discourage mobility. But such relocations are not inhibited by immigration quotas, by laws restricting the employment of foreigners, or by the need to learn a new language.

There are also greater impediments to the transfer of capital across national boundaries than to its movement within a country. For example, many countries have rules limiting foreign ownership. Even the United States limits foreign ownership of broadcast outlets and airlines and, recently, political furors arose when a Chinese company sought to purchase a U.S. oil company and when a Middle Eastern company offered to take over the management of several U.S. ports. Foreign investment is also subject to special political risks, such as the danger of outright expropriation or nationalization after a change in government.

Even if nothing as extreme as expropriation occurs, capital invested abroad faces significant risks from exchange rate variations. An investment valued at 250 million yen is worth $2.5 million to American investors when the dollar is worth 100 yen, but it is worth only $1 million when it takes 250 yen to buy a dollar.

THE LAW OF COMPARATIVE ADVANTAGE

The gains from international specialization and trade are clear and intuitive when one country is better at producing one item and its trading partner is better at producing another. For example, no one finds it surprising that Brazil sells coffee to the United States and the United States exports software to Brazil. We know that coffee can be produced using less labor and other inputs in Brazil than in the United States. Likewise, the United States can produce software at a lower resource cost than can Brazil.

In such a situation, we say that Brazil has an **absolute advantage** in coffee production, and the United States has an absolute advantage in software production. In such cases, it is obvious that both countries can gain by producing the item in which they have an absolute advantage and then trading with one another.

What is much less obvious, but equally true, is that these gains from international trade still exist *even if one country is more efficient than the other in producing everything*. This lesson, the principle of **comparative advantage,** is one we first encountered in Chapter 3.[2] It is, in fact, one of the most important of our *Ideas for Beyond the Final Exam*, so we repeat it here for convenience.

> **THE SURPRISING PRINCIPLE OF COMPARATIVE ADVANTAGE** Even if one country is at an absolute *dis*advantage relative to another country in the production of every good, it still has a *comparative advantage* in making the good at which it is *least inefficient* (compared with the other country).

The great classical economist David Ricardo (1772–1823) discovered about 200 years ago that two countries can still gain from trade even if one is more efficient than the other in *every* industry—that is, even if one has an absolute advantage in producing every commodity.

In determining the most efficient patterns of production, it is *comparative* advantage, not *absolute* advantage, that matters. Thus a country can gain by importing a good even if that good can be produced more efficiently at home. Such imports make sense if they enable the country to specialize in producing goods at which it is *even more* efficient.

The Arithmetic of Comparative Advantage

Let's see precisely how comparative advantage works using a hypothetical example first suggested in Chapter 3. Table 2 gives a rather exaggerated impression of the trading positions of the United States and Japan a few years ago. We imagine that labor is the only

*One country is said to have an **absolute advantage** over another in the production of a particular good if it can produce that good using smaller quantities of resources than can the other country.*

*One country is said to have a **comparative advantage** over another in the production of a particular good relative to other goods if it produces that good less inefficiently as compared with the other country.*

IDEAS FOR BEYOND THE FINAL EXAM

---

[2] To review, see page 49.

TABLE 2

Alternative Outputs from One Year of Labor Input

	In the U.S.	In Japan
Computers	50	10
Televisions	50	40

TABLE 3

Example of the Gains from Trade

	U.S.	Japan	Total
Computers	+25,000	−10,000	**+15,000**
Televisions	−25,000	+40,000	**+15,000**

input used to produce computers and television sets in the two countries and that the United States has an absolute advantage in manufacturing both goods. In this example, one year's worth of labor can produce either 50 computers or 50 TV sets in the United States but only 10 computers or 40 televisions in Japan. So the United States is the more efficient producer of both goods. Nonetheless, as we will now show, it pays for the United States to specialize in producing computers and trade with Japan to get the TV sets it wants.

To demonstrate this point, we begin by noting that the United States has a comparative advantage in *computers,* whereas Japan has a comparative advantage in producing *televisions.* Specifically, the numbers in Table 2 show that the United States can produce 50 televisions with one year's labor, whereas Japan can produce only 40, giving the United States a 25 percent efficient edge over Japan. However, the United States is five times as efficient as Japan in producing computers: it can produce 50 per year of labor rather than 10. Because America's competitive edge is far greater in computers than in televisions, we say that the United States has a *comparative advantage* in computers.

From the Japanese perspective, these same numbers indicate that Japan is only *slightly less* efficient than the United States in TV production but *drastically less* efficient in computer production. So Japan's comparative advantage is in producing televisions. According to Ricardo's law of comparative advantage, then, the two countries can gain if the United States specializes in producing computers, Japan specializes in producing TVs, and the two countries trade.

Let's verify that this conclusion is true. Suppose Japan transfers 1,000 years of labor out of the computer industry and into TV manufacturing. According to the figures in Table 2, its computer output will fall by 10,000 units, whereas its TV output will rise by 40,000 units. This information is recorded in the middle column of Table 3. Suppose, at the same time, the United States transfers 500 years of labor out of television manufacturing (thereby losing 25,000 TVs) and into computer making (thereby gaining 25,000 computers). Table 3 shows us that these transfers of resources between the two countries increase the *world's* production of *both* outputs. Together, the two countries now have 15,000 additional TVs and 15,000 additional computers—a nice outcome.

Was there some sleight of hand here? How did *both* the United States *and* Japan gain *both* computers *and* TVs? The explanation is that the process we have just described involves more than just a swap of a fixed bundle of commodities, as in our earlier cookies-and-milk example. It also involves *a change in the production arrangements.* Some of Japan's inefficient computer production is taken over by more efficient American makers. And some of America's TV production is taken over by Japanese television companies, which are *less inefficient* at making TVs than Japanese computer manufacturers are at making computers. In this way, *world productivity is increased.* The underlying principle is both simple and fundamental:

> When every country does what it can do best, all countries can benefit because more of every commodity can be produced without increasing the amounts of labor and other resources used.

Where does the United States hold and lack comparative advantage? Among our big export powerhouses are the aerospace industry, agriculture, chemicals, high-tech services, financial services, entertainment, and higher education. We are, of course, huge importers of petroleum, television sets, automobiles, computers, clothing, toys, and much else.

The Graphics of Comparative Advantage

The gains from trade also can be illustrated graphically, and doing so helps us understand whether such gains are large or small.

The lines *US* and *JN* in Figure 1 are closely related to the production possibilities frontiers of the two countries, differing only in that they pretend that each country has the

same amount of labor available.[3] In this case, we assume that each has 1 million person-years of labor. For
example, Table 2 tells us that for each 1 million years of
labor, the United States can produce 50 million TVs
and no computers (point *U* in Figure 1), 50 million
computers and no TVs (point *S*), or any combination
between (the line *US*). Similar reasoning leads to line
JN for Japan.

America's *actual* production possibilities frontier
would be even higher, relative to Japan's, than shown in
Figure 1 because the U.S. population is larger. But Figure 1 is more useful because it highlights the differences
in *efficiency* (rather than in mere size), and this is what
determines both absolute and comparative advantage.
Let's see how.

The fact that line *US* lies *above* line *JN* means that the
United States can manufacture more televisions and
more computers than Japan *with the same amount of
labor.* This difference reflects our assumption that the
United States has an *absolute* advantage in both
commodities.

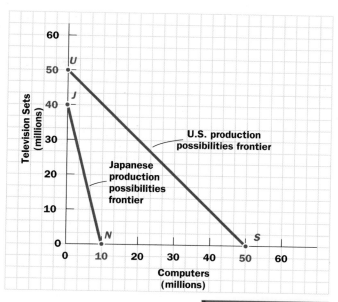

Production Possibilities
Frontiers for Two
Countries (person-years
of labor)

America's *comparative* advantage in computer production and Japan's comparative advantage in TV production are shown in a different way: by the relative *slopes* of the two
lines. Look back to Table 2, which shows that the United States can acquire a computer on
its own by giving up one TV. Thus, the *opportunity cost* of a computer in the United States
is one television set. This opportunity cost is depicted graphically by the slope of the U.S.
production possibilities frontier in Figure 1, which is $OU/OS = 50/50 = 1$.

Table 2 also tells us that the opportunity cost of a computer in Japan is four TVs. This
relationship is depicted in Figure 1 by the slope of Japan's production possibilities frontier, which is $OJ/ON = 40/10 = 4$.

> A country's *absolute* advantage in production over another country is shown by its hav-
> ing a higher per capita production possibilities frontier. The difference in the *compara-
> tive* advantages between the two countries is shown by the difference in the slopes of
> their frontiers.

Because opportunity costs differ in the two countries, gains are possible if the two
countries specialize and trade with one another. Specifically, it is cheaper, in terms of real
resources forgone, for *either* country to acquire its computers in the United States. By a
similar line of reasoning, the opportunity cost of TVs is higher in the United States than in
Japan, so it makes sense for both countries to acquire their televisions in Japan.[4]

Notice that if the slopes of the two production possibilities frontiers, *JN* and *US*, were
equal, then opportunity costs would be the same in each country. In that case, no potential gains would arise from trade. Gains from trade arise from *differences* across countries,
not from similarities. This is an important point about which people are often confused. It
is often argued that two very different countries, such as the United States and Mexico,
cannot gain much by trading with one another. The fact is just the opposite:

> Two very similar countries may gain little from trade. Large gains from trade are most
> likely when countries are very different.

The pattern is apparent in U.S. trade statistics—with one big exception. Canada, a country
very similar to the United States, is our biggest trading partner. But that is mainly because
the two nations share a huge and very porous border. However, our next three biggest

---

[3] To review the concept of the production possibilities frontier, see Chapter 3.
[4] EXERCISE: Provide this line of reasoning.

trading partners, in order, are China, Mexico, and Japan—three countries very different from the United States.

How nations divide the gains from trade depends on the prices that emerge from world trade—a complicated topic taken up in the appendix to this chapter. But we already know enough to see that world trade must, in our example, leave a computer costing more than one TV and less than four. Why? Because if a computer bought less than one TV (its opportunity cost in the United States) on the world market, the United States would produce its own TVs rather than buying them from Japan. And if a computer cost more than four TVs (its opportunity cost in Japan), Japan would prefer to produce its own computers rather than buy them from the United States. So we conclude that, if both countries are to trade, the rate of exchange between TVs and computers must end up somewhere between 4:1 and 1:1. Generalizing:

> **If two countries voluntarily trade two goods with one another, the rate of exchange between the goods must fall in between the price ratios that would prevail in the two countries in the absence of trade.**

To illustrate the gains from trade in our concrete example, suppose the world price ratio settles at 2:1—meaning that one computer costs as much as two televisions. How much, precisely, do the United States and Japan gain from world trade in this case?

Figure 2 helps us visualize the answers. The blue production possibilities frontiers, *US* in Panel (b) and *JN* in Panel (a), are the same as in Figure 1. But the United States can do better than line *US*. Specifically, with a world price ratio of 2:1, the United States can buy two TVs for each computer it gives up, rather than just one (which is the opportunity cost of a computer in the United States). Hence, if the United States produces only computers— point *S* in Figure 2(b)—and buys its TVs from Japan, America's *consumption possibilities* will be as indicated by the brick-colored line that begins at point *S* and has a slope of two—that is, each computer sold brings the United States two television sets. (It ends at point *A* because 40 million TV sets is the most that Japan can produce.) Because trade allows the United States to choose a point on *AS* rather than on *US*, trade opens up consumption possibilities that were simply not available before (shaded gray in the diagram).

FIGURE 2

The Gains from Trade

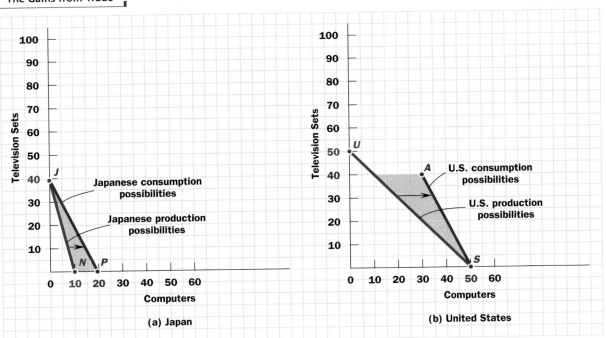

NOTE: Quantities are in millions.

A similar story applies to Japan. If the Japanese produce only television sets—point *J* in Figure 2(a)—they can acquire a computer from the United States for every two TVs they give up as they move along the brick-colored line *JP* (whose slope is two). This result is better than they can achieve on their own, because a sacrifice of two TVs in Japan yields only one-half of a computer. Hence, world trade enlarges Japan's consumption possibilities from *JN* to *JP*.

Figure 2 shows graphically that gains from trade arise to the extent that world prices (2:1 in our example) differ from domestic opportunity costs (4:1 and 1:1 in our example). How the two countries share the gains from trade depends on the exact prices that emerge from world trade. As explained in the appendix, that in turn depends on relative supplies and demands in the two countries.

Must Specialization Be Complete?

In our simple numerical and graphical examples, international specialization is always *complete*—for example, the United States makes all the computers and Japan makes all the TV sets. But if you look at the real world, you will find mostly *incomplete* specialization. For example, the United States is the world's biggest importer of both petroleum and automobiles, but we also manufacture lots of cars and drill for lots of oil. In fact, we even export some cars. This stark discrepancy between theory and fact might worry you. Is something wrong with the theory of comparative advantage?

Actually, there are many reasons why specialization is typically incomplete, despite the validity of the principle of comparative advantage. Two of them are simple enough to merit mentioning right here.

First, some countries are just too small to provide the world's entire output, even when they have a strong comparative advantage in the good in question. In our numerical example, Japan just might not have enough labor and other resources to produce the entire world output of televisions. If so, some TV sets would have to be produced in the United States.

Second, you may have noticed that in this chapter we have drawn all the production possibilities frontiers (PPFs) as *straight lines*, whereas they were always *curved* in previous chapters. The reason is purely pedagogical: We wanted to create simple examples that lend themselves to numerical solutions. It is undoubtedly more realistic to assume that PPFs are curved. That sort of technology leads to incomplete specialization, which is a complication best left to more advanced courses.

ISSUE RESOLVED: COMPARATIVE ADVANTAGE EXPOSES THE

"CHEAP FOREIGN LABOR" FALLACY

The principle of comparative advantage takes us a long way toward understanding the fallacy in the "cheap foreign labor" argument described at the beginning of this chapter. Given the assumed productive efficiency of American labor, and the inefficiency of Japanese labor, we would expect wages to be much higher in the United States.

In these circumstances, one might expect American workers to be apprehensive about an agreement to permit open trade between the two countries: "How can we hope to meet the unfair competition of those underpaid Japanese workers?" Japanese laborers might also be concerned: "How can we hope to meet the competition of those Americans, who are so efficient in producing everything?"

The principle of comparative advantage shows us that both fears are unjustified. As we have just seen, when trade opens up between Japan and the United States, *workers in both countries will be able to earn higher real wages than before* because of the increased productivity that comes through specialization.

As Figure 2 shows, once trade opens up, Japanese workers should be able to acquire more TVs and more computers than they did before. As a consequence, their living standards should rise, even though they have been left vulnerable to competition from the super-efficient Americans. Workers in the United States should also end up with more TVs and more computers. So their living standards should also rise, even though they have been exposed to competition from cheap Japanese labor.

These higher standards of living, of course, reflect the higher real wages earned because workers become more productive in both countries. The lesson to be learned here is elementary:

Nothing helps raise living standards more than a greater abundance of goods.

TARIFFS, QUOTAS, AND OTHER INTERFERENCES WITH TRADE

Despite the large mutual gains from international trade, nations often interfere with the free movement of goods and services across national borders. In fact, until the rise of the free-trade movement about 200 years ago (with Adam Smith and David Ricardo as its vanguard), it was taken for granted that one of the essential tasks of government was to impede trade, presumably in the national interest.

Then, as now, many people argued that the proper aim of government policy was to promote exports and discourage imports, for doing so would increase the amount of money foreigners owed the nation. According to this so-called **mercantilist** view, a nation's wealth consists of the amount of gold or other monies at its command.

Mercantilism is a doctrine that holds that exports are good for a country, whereas imports are harmful.

Obviously, governments can pursue such a policy only within certain limits. A country *must* import vital foodstuffs and critical raw materials that it cannot provide for itself. Moreover, mercantilists ignore a simple piece of arithmetic: It is mathematically impossible for *every* country to sell more than it buys, because one country's exports must be some other country's imports. If everyone competes in this game by cutting imports to the bone, then exports must shrivel up, too. The result is that everyone will be deprived of the mutual gains from trade. Indeed, that is precisely what happens in a trade war.

After the protectionist 1930s, the United States moved away from mercantilist policies designed to impede imports and gradually assumed a leading role in promoting free trade. Over the past 60 years, tariffs and other trade barriers have come down dramatically.

In 1995, the United States led the world to complete the Uruguay Round of tariff reductions and, just before that, the country joined Canada and Mexico in the North American Free Trade Agreement (NAFTA). The latter caused a political firestorm in the United States in 1993 and 1994, with critic (and 1992 presidential candidate) Ross Perot predicting a "giant sucking sound" as American workers lost their jobs to competition from "cheap Mexican labor." (Does that argument sound familiar?) Most of the world's trading nations are now formally engaged in a new multiyear round of trade talks, under guidelines adopted in Doha, Qatar, in 2001. (See the box, "Liberalizing World Trade: The Doha Round.")

Modern governments use three main devices when seeking to control trade: tariffs, quotas, and export subsidies.

A **tariff** is simply a tax on imports. An importer of cars, for example, may be charged $2,000 for each auto brought into the country. Such a tax will, of course, make automobiles more expensive and favor domestic models over imports. It will also raise revenue for the government. In fact, tariffs were a major source of tax revenue for the U.S. government during the eighteenth and nineteenth centuries—and also a major source of political controversy. Nowadays, the United States is a low-tariff country, with only a few notable exceptions. However, many other countries rely on heavy tariffs to protect their industries. Indeed, tariff rates of 100 percent or more are not unknown in some countries.

A **tariff** is a tax on imports.

A **quota** is a legal limit on the amount of a good that may be imported. For example, the government might allow no more than 5 million foreign cars to be imported in a year. In some cases, governments ban the importation of certain goods outright—a quota of zero. The United States now imposes quotas on a smattering of goods, including textiles, meat, and sugar. Most imports, however, are not subject to quotas. By reducing supply,

A **quota** specifies the maximum amount of a good that is permitted into the country from abroad per unit of time.

quotas naturally raise the prices of the goods subject to quotas. For example, sugar is vastly more expensive in the United States than it is elsewhere in the world.

An **export subsidy** is a government payment to an exporter. By reducing the exporter's costs, such subsidies permit exporters to lower their selling prices and compete more effectively in world trade. Overt export subsidies are minor in the United States. But some foreign governments use them extensively to assist their domestic industries—a practice that provokes bitter complaints from American manufacturers about "unfair competition." For example, years of heavy government subsidies helped the European Airbus consortium take a sizable share of the world commercial aircraft market away from U.S. manufacturers like Boeing and McDonnell-Douglas—a trend that has lately reversed.

> An **export subsidy** is a payment by the government to exporters to permit them to reduce the selling prices of their goods so they can compete more effectively in foreign markets.

Tariffs versus Quotas

Although both tariffs and quotas reduce international trade and increase the prices of domestically produced goods, there are some important differences between these two ways to protect domestic industries.

First, under a quota, profits from the higher price in the importing country usually go into the pockets of the foreign and domestic sellers of the products. Limitations on supply (from abroad) mean (a) that customers in the importing country must pay more for the product and (b) that suppliers, whether foreign or domestic, receive more for every unit they sell. For example, the right to sell sugar in the United States under the tight sugar quota has been extremely valuable for decades. Privileged foreign and domestic firms can make a lot of money from quota rights.

By contrast, when trade is restricted by a tariff instead, some of the "profits" go as tax revenues to the government of the importing country. (Domestic producers still benefit, because they are exempt from the tariff.) In this respect, a tariff is certainly a better proposition than a quota for the country that enacts it.

Another important distinction between the two measures arises from their different implications for productive efficiency. Because a tariff handicaps all foreign suppliers

Liberalizing World Trade: The Doha Round

The time and place were not auspicious: an international gathering in the Persian Gulf just two months after the September 11, 2001, terrorists attacks. Nerves were frayed, security was extremely tight, and memories of a failed trade meeting in Seattle in 1999 lingered on. Yet representatives of more than 140 nations, meeting in Doha, Qatar, in November 2001, managed to agree on the outlines of a new round of comprehensive trade negotiations—one that now appears unlikely to be completed.

The so-called Doha Round focuses on bringing down tariffs, subsidies, and other restrictions on world trade in agriculture, services, and a variety of manufactured goods. It also seeks greater protection for intellectual property rights, while making sure that poor countries have access to modern pharmaceuticals at prices they can afford. Reform of the World Trade Organization's own rules and procedures is also on the agenda. Perhaps most surprisingly, the United States has even promised to consider changes in its antidumping laws, which are used to keep many foreign goods out of U.S. markets. (Dumping is explained at the end of this chapter.)

Large-scale trade negotiations such as this one, involving more than 100 countries and many different issues, take years to complete. (The last one, the Uruguay Round, took seven years.) And the Doha Round almost collapsed in 2003 and again in 2006 when negotiating sessions got nowhere. In early 2010, there was not much optimism that the contentious agricultural issues could be resolved, leaving many observers doubting that the Doha Round would ever be completed. But no one knows what the future may bring.

SOURCE: © Patrick Baz/AFP/Getty Images

equally, it awards sales to those firms and nations that can supply the goods most cheaply—presumably because they are more efficient. A quota, by contrast, necessarily awards its import licenses more or less capriciously—perhaps in proportion to past sales or even based on political favoritism. There is no reason to expect the most efficient suppliers will get the import permits. For example, the U.S. sugar quota was for years suspected of being a major source of corruption in the Caribbean.

If a country must inhibit imports, two important reasons support a preference for tariffs over quotas:

1. **Some of the revenues resulting from tariffs go to the government of the importing country rather than to foreign and domestic producers.**

2. **Unlike quotas, tariffs offer special benefits to more efficient exporters.**

WHY INHIBIT TRADE?

To state that tariffs provide a better way to inhibit international trade than quotas leaves open a far more basic question: Why limit trade in the first place? It has been estimated that trade restrictions cost American consumers more than $70 billion per year in the form of higher prices. Why should they be asked to pay these higher prices? A number of answers have been given. Let's examine each in turn.

Gaining a Price Advantage for Domestic Firms

A tariff forces foreign exporters to sell more cheaply by restricting their market access. If the foreign firms do not cut their prices, they will be unable to sell their goods. So, in effect, a tariff amounts to government intervention to rig prices in favor of domestic producers.[5]

Not bad, you say. However, this technique works only as long as foreigners accept the tariff exploitation passively—which they rarely do. More often, they retaliate by imposing tariffs or quotas of their own on imports from the country that began the tariff game. Such tit-for-tat behavior can easily lead to a trade war in which everyone loses through the resulting reductions in trade. Something like this, in fact, happened to the world economy in the 1930s, and it helped prolong the worldwide depression. Preventing such trade wars is one main reason why nations that belong to the World Trade Organization (WTO) pledge not to raise tariffs.

Tariffs or quotas can benefit particular domestic industries in a country that is able to impose them without fear of retaliation. But when every country uses them, every country is likely to lose in the long run.

Protecting Particular Industries

The second, and probably more frequent, reason why countries restrict trade is to protect particular favored industries from foreign competition. If foreigners can produce steel or shoes more cheaply, domestic businesses and unions in these industries are quick to demand protection. And their governments may be quite willing to grant it.

The "cheap foreign labor" argument is most likely to be invoked in this context. Protective tariffs and quotas are explicitly designed to rescue firms that are too inefficient to compete with foreign exporters in an open world market. But it is precisely this harsh competition that gives consumers the chief benefits of international specialization: better products at lower prices. So protection comes at a cost.

---

[5] For more details on this, see the appendix to this chapter.

Thinking back to our numerical example of comparative advantage, we can well imagine the indignant complaints from Japanese computer makers as the opening of trade with the United States leads to increased imports of American-made computers. At the same time, American TV manufacturers would probably express outrage over the flood of imported TVs from Japan. Yet it is Japanese specialization in televisions and U.S. specialization in computers that enables citizens of both countries to enjoy higher standards of living. If governments interfere with this process, consumers in both countries will lose out.

Industries threatened by foreign competition often argue that some form of protection against imports is needed to prevent job losses. For example, the U.S. steel industry has made exactly this argument time and time again since the 1960s—most recently in 2001, when world steel prices plummeted and imports surged. And the U.S. government has usually delivered some protection in response. But basic macroeconomics teaches us that there are better ways to stimulate employment, such as raising aggregate demand.

A program that limits foreign competition will be more effective at preserving employment *in the particular protected industry.* However, such job gains typically come at a high cost to consumers and to the economy. Table 4 estimates some of the costs to American consumers of using tariffs and quotas to save jobs in selected industries. In every case, the costs far exceed the annual wages of the workers in the protected industries—ranging as high as $600,000 per job for the sugar quota.

Nevertheless, complaints over proposals to reduce tariffs or quotas may be justified unless something is done to ease the cost to individual workers of switching to the product lines that trade makes profitable.

TABLE 4	
Estimated Costs of Protectionism to Consumers	
Industry	Cost per Job Saved
Apparel	$139,000
Costume jewelry	97,000
Shipping	415,000
Sugar	600,000
Textiles	202,000
Women's footwear	102,000

SOURCE: Gary C. Hufbauer and Kimberly Ann Elliott, *Measuring the Costs of Protectionism in the United States* (Washington, D.C.: Institute for International Economics; January 1994), Table 1.3, pp. 12–13.

The argument for free trade between countries cannot be considered airtight if governments do not assist the citizens in each country who are harmed whenever patterns of production change drastically—as would happen, for example, if governments suddenly reduced tariff and quota barriers.

Owners of television factories in the United States and of computer factories in Japan may see large investments suddenly rendered unprofitable. Workers in those industries may see their special skills and training devalued in the marketplace. Displaced workers also pay heavy intangible costs—they may need to move to new locations and/or new industries, uprooting their families, losing old friends and neighbors, and so on. Although the *majority* of citizens undoubtedly gain from free trade, that is no consolation to those who are its victims.

To mitigate these problems, the U.S. government follows two basic approaches. First, our trade laws offer temporary protection from sudden surges of imports, on the grounds that unexpected changes in trade patterns do not give businesses and workers enough time to adjust.

Second, the government has set up **trade adjustment assistance** programs to help workers and businesses that lose their jobs or their markets to imports. Firms may be eligible for technical assistance, government loans or loan guarantees, and permission to delay tax payments. Workers may qualify for retraining programs, longer periods of unemployment compensation, and funds to defray moving costs. Each form of assistance is designed to ease the burden on the victims of free trade so that the rest of us can enjoy its considerable benefits.

Trade adjustment assistance provides special unemployment benefits, loans, retraining programs, and other aid to workers and firms that are harmed by foreign competition.

National Defense and Other Noneconomic Considerations

A third rationale for trade protection is the need to maintain national defense. For example, even if the United States were not the most efficient producer of aircraft, it might still be rational to produce our own military aircraft so that no foreign government could ever cut off supplies of this strategic product.

How Popular Is Protectionism?

Since World War II, the world has mainly been moving toward freer trade and away from protection. The people of the world are not convinced that this trend is desirable, though. In what was probably the most comprehensive polling ever conducted on the subject, a Canadian firm asked almost 13,000 people in 22 countries the following question in 1998: "Which of the following two broad approaches do you think would be the best way to improve the economic and employment situation in this country—protecting our local industries by restricting imports, or removing import restrictions to increase our international trade?" The protectionist response narrowly outnumbered the free-trade response by a 47 percent to 42 percent margin. (The rest were undecided.) Protectionist sentiment was much stronger in the United States, however, where the margin was 56 percent to 37 percent. (See the accompanying graph.)

That was in 1998. In the United States (and elsewhere), there is clear evidence that protectionist sentiment is actually gaining in popularity. For example, a *Wall Street Journal*/NBC News poll in 1999 found that 39 percent of Americans believed that trade agreements have helped the United States, whereas 30 percent believed they had hurt. When that same question was asked in 2007, only 28 percent thought trade agreements had helped, whereas 46 percent thought they had hurt.

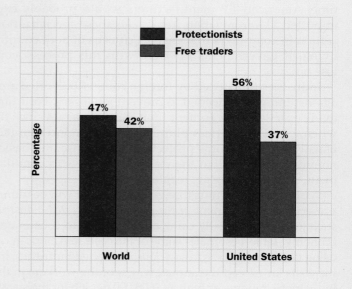

SOURCES: "How Popular Is Protectionism?" *The Economist*, January 2, 1999; and Grant Aldonas, Robert Lawrence, and Matthew Slaughter, *Succeeding in the Global Economy*, Financial Services Forum Policy Research, June 2007, p. 10.

The national defense argument is fine as far as it goes, but it poses a clear danger: Even industries with the most peripheral relationship to defense are likely to invoke this argument on their behalf. For instance, for years the U.S. watchmaking industry argued for protection on the grounds that its skilled craftsmen would be invaluable in wartime!

Similarly, the United States has occasionally banned either exports to or imports from nations such as Cuba, Iran, and Iraq on political grounds. Such actions may have important economic effects, creating either bonanzas or disasters for particular American industries. But they are justified by politics, not by economics. Noneconomic reasons also explain quotas on importation of whaling products and on the furs of other endangered species.

The Infant-Industry Argument

The **infant-industry argument** for trade protection holds that new industries need to be protected from foreign competition until they develop and flourish.

Yet a fourth common rationale for protectionism is the so-called **infant-industry argument**, which has been prominent in the United States at least since Alexander Hamilton wrote his *Report on Manufactures*. Promising new industries often need breathing room to flourish and grow. If we expose these infants to the rigors of international competition too soon, the argument goes, they may never develop to the point where they can survive on their own in the international marketplace.

This argument, although valid in certain instances, is less defensible than it seems at first. Protecting an infant industry is justifiable only if the prospective future gains are sufficient to repay the up-front costs of protectionism. But if the industry is likely to be so profitable in the future, why doesn't private capital rush in to take advantage of the prospective net profits? After all, the annals of business are full of cases in which a new product or a new firm lost money at first but profited handsomely later on. In recent times, Apple, Yahoo!, Google, and eBay all lost money in their early days.

The infant-industry argument for protection stands up to scrutiny only if private funds are unavailable for some reason, despite an industry's glowing profit prospects. Even then it may make more sense to provide a government loan rather than to provide trade protection.

In an advanced economy such as ours, with well-developed capital markets to fund new businesses, it is difficult to think of legitimate examples where the infant-industry argument applies. Even if such a case were found, we would have to be careful that the industry not remain in diapers forever. In too many cases, industries are awarded protection when young and, somehow, never mature to the point where protection can be withdrawn. We must be wary of infants that never grow up.

Strategic Trade Policy

A stronger argument for (temporary) protection has substantially influenced trade policy in the United States and elsewhere. Proponents of this line of thinking agree that free trade for all is the best system. But they point out that we live in an imperfect world in which many nations refuse to play by the rules of the free-trade game. And they fear that a nation that pursues free trade in a protectionist world is likely to lose out. It therefore makes sense, they argue, to threaten to protect your markets unless other nations agree to open theirs.

The United States has followed this strategy in trade negotiations with several countries in recent years. In one prominent case, the U.S. government threatened to impose high tariffs on several European luxury goods unless Europe opened its markets to imported bananas from the Americas. A few years later, the European Union turned the tables, threatening to increase tariffs on a variety of U.S. goods unless we changed a tax provision that amounted to an export subsidy. In each case, a dangerous trade war was narrowly averted when an agreement was struck at the eleventh hour.

The **strategic argument for protection** is a difficult one for economists to counter. Although it recognizes the superiority of free trade, it argues that *threatening* protectionism is the best way to achieve that end. (See the box "Can Protectionism Save Free Trade?" on the next page.) Such a strategy might work, but it clearly involves great risks. If threats that the United States will turn protectionist induce other countries to scrap their existing protectionist policies, then the gamble will have succeeded. But if the gamble fails, protectionism increases.

> The **strategic argument for protection** holds that a nation may sometimes have to threaten protectionism to induce other countries to drop their own protectionist measures.

CAN CHEAP IMPORTS HURT A COUNTRY?

One of the most curious—and illogical—features of the protectionist position is the fear of low import prices. Countries that subsidize their exports are often accused of **dumping**—of getting rid of their goods at unjustifiably low prices. Economists find this argument strange. As a nation of consumers, we should be indignant when foreigners charge us *high* prices, not *low* ones. That commonsense rule guides every consumer's daily life. Only from the topsy-turvy viewpoint of an industry seeking protection are low prices seen as counter to the public interest.

> **Dumping** means selling goods in a foreign market at lower prices than those charged in the home market.

Ultimately, the best interests of any country are served when its imports are as cheap as possible. It would be ideal for the United States if the rest of the world were willing to provide us with goods at no charge. We could then live in luxury at the expense of other countries.

However, benefits to the United States as a whole do not necessarily accrue to every single American. If quotas on, say, sugar imports were dropped, American consumers and industries that purchase sugar would gain from lower prices. At the same time, however, owners of sugar fields and their employees would suffer serious losses in the form of lower profits, lower wages, and lost jobs—losses they would fight fiercely to prevent. For this reason, politics often leads to the adoption of protectionist measures that would likely be rejected on strictly economic criteria.

ISSUE: LAST LOOK AT THE "CHEAP FOREIGN LABOR" ARGUMENT

The preceding discussion reveals the fundamental fallacy in the argument that the United States as a whole should fear cheap foreign labor. The average American worker's living standard must rise, not fall, if other countries willingly supply their products to us more cheaply. As long as the government's monetary and fiscal policies succeed in maintaining high levels of employment, we cannot possibly lose by getting world products at bargain prices. Indeed, this is precisely what happened to the U.S. economy in the late 1990s. Even though imports poured in at low prices, unemployment in the United States fell to its lowest rate in a generation. Even in 2007, with a financial crisis and a massive trade deficit equal to 5.1 percent of GDP, the U.S. unemployment rate averaged only 4.6 percent.

We must add a few important qualifications, however. First, our macroeconomic policy may not always be effective. If workers displaced by foreign competition cannot find new jobs, they will indeed suffer from international trade. But high unemploy-

Can Protectionism Save Free Trade?

In this classic column, William Safire shook off his long-standing attachment to free trade and argued eloquently for retaliation against protectionist nations.

Free trade is economic motherhood. Protectionism is economic evil incarnate. . . . Never should government interfere in the efficiency of international competition.

Since childhood, these have been the tenets of my faith. If it meant that certain businesses in this country went belly-up, so be it. . . . If it meant that Americans would be thrown out of work by overseas companies paying coolie wages, that was tough. . . .

The thing to keep in mind, I was taught, was the Big Picture and the Long Run. America, the great exporter, had far more to gain than to lose from free trade; attempts to protect inefficient industries here would ultimately cost more American jobs.

While playing with my David Ricardo doll and learning nursery rhymes about comparative advantage, I was listening to another laissez-fairy tale: Government's role in the world of business should be limited to keeping business honest and competitive. In God we antitrusted. Let businesses operate in the free marketplace.

Now American businesses are no longer competing with foreign companies. They are competing with foreign governments who help their local businesses. That means the world arena no longer offers a free marketplace; instead, most other governments are pushing a policy that can be called helpfulism.

Helpfulism works like this: A government like Japan decides to get behind its baseball-bat industry. It pumps in capital, knocks off marginal operators, finds subtle ways to discourage imports of Louisville Sluggers, and selects target areas for export blitzes. Pretty soon, the favored Japanese companies are driving foreign competitors batty.

How do we compete with helpfulism? One way is to complain that it is unfair; that draws a horselaugh. Another way is to demand a "Reagan Round" of trade negotiations under GATT, the Gentlemen's Agreement To Talk, which is equally laughable.

Yet another way is to join the helpfuls by subsidizing our exports and permitting our companies to try monopolistic tricks abroad not permitted at home. But all that makes us feel guilty, with good reason.

The other way to deal with helpfulism is through—here comes the dreadful word—protection. Or, if you prefer a euphemism, retaliation. Or if that is still too severe, reciprocity. Whatever its name, it is a way of saying to the cutthroat cartelists we sweetly call our trading partners: "You have bent the rules out of shape. Change your practices to conform to the agreed-upon rules, or we will export a taste of your own medicine."

A little balance, then, from the free trade theorists. The demand for what the Pentagon used to call "protective reaction" is not demagoguery, not shortsighted, not self-defeating. On the contrary, the overseas pirates of protectionism and exemplars of helpfulism need to be taught the basic lesson in trade, which is: tit for tat.

SOURCE: William Safire, "Smoot-Hawley Lives," *The New York Times,* March 17, 1983. Copyright © 1983 by The New York Times Company. All rights reserved. Used by permission and protected by the Copyright Laws of the United States. The printing, copying, redistribution, or retransmission of the material without express written permission is prohibited.

SOURCE: © David Burnett/Contact Press Images

ment reflects a shortcoming of the government's monetary and fiscal policies, not of its international trade policies. That said, it is a huge problem right now, making trade liberalization guide unpopular.

Second, we have noted that an abrupt stiffening of foreign competition can hurt U.S. workers by not allowing them adequate time to adapt to the new conditions. If change occurs fairly gradually, workers can be retrained and move into the industries that now require their services. Indeed, if the change is slow enough, normal attrition may suffice. But competition that inflicts its damage overnight is certain to impose real costs on the affected workers—costs that are no less painful for being temporary. That is why our trade laws make provisions for people and industries damaged by import surges.

In fact, the economic world is constantly changing. The recent emergence of China, India, and other third-world countries, for example, has created stiff new competition for workers in America and other rich nations—competition they never imagined when they signed up for jobs that may now be imperiled by international trade. The same is true of many workers in service jobs (ranging from call center operators to lawyers) who never dreamed that their jobs might be done electronically from thousands of miles away. It is not irrational, and it is certainly not protectionist, for countries like the United States to use trade adjustment assistance and other tools to cushion the blow for these workers.

These are, after all, only qualifications to an overwhelming argument. They call for intelligent monetary and fiscal policies and for transitional assistance to unemployed workers, not for abandonment of free trade. In general, the nation as a whole need not fear competition from cheap foreign labor.

In the long run, labor will be "cheap" only where it is not very productive. Wages will be high in countries with high labor productivity, and this high productivity will enable those countries to compete effectively in international trade despite their high wages. It is thus misleading to say that the United States held its own in the international marketplace until recently *despite* high wages. Rather, it is much more accurate to note that the higher wages of American workers were a result of higher

Unfair Foreign Competition

Satire and ridicule are often more persuasive than logic and statistics. Exasperated by the spread of protectionism under the prevailing mercantilist philosophy, the French economist Frédéric Bastiat decided to take the protectionist argument to its illogical conclusion. The fictitious petition of the French candlemakers to the Chamber of Deputies, written in 1845 and excerpted below, has become a classic in the battle for free trade.

We are subject to the intolerable competition of a foreign rival, who enjoys, it would seem, such superior facilities for the production of light, that he is enabled to inundate our national market at so exceedingly reduced a price, that, the moment he makes his appearance, he draws off all custom for us; and thus an important branch of French industry, with all its innumerable ramifications, is suddenly reduced to a state of complete stagnation. This rival is no other than the sun.

Our petition is, that it would please your honorable body to pass a law whereby shall be directed the shutting up of all windows, dormers, skylights, shutters, curtains, in a word, all openings, holes, chinks, and fissures through which the light of the sun is used to penetrate our dwellings, to the prejudice of the profitable manufactures which we flatter ourselves we have been enabled to bestow upon the country. . . .

We foresee your objections, gentlemen; but there is not one that you can oppose to us . . . which is not equally opposed to your own practice and the principle which guides your policy. . . . Labor and nature concur in different proportions, according to country and climate, in every article of production. . . . If a Lisbon orange can be sold at half the price of a Parisian one, it is because a natural and gratuitous heat does for the one what the other only obtains from an artificial and consequently expensive one. . . .

Does it not argue the greatest inconsistency to check as you do the importation of coal, iron, cheese, and goods of foreign manufacture, merely because and even in proportion as their price approaches zero, while at the same time you freely admit, and without limitation, the light of the sun, whose price is during the whole day at zero?

SOURCE: © Culver Pictures

SOURCE: Frédéric Bastiat, *Economic Sophisms* (New York: G. P. Putnam's Sons, 1922).

worker productivity, which gave the United States a major competitive edge—an edge we still have, by the way.

Remember, where standards of living are concerned, it is *absolute* advantage, not *comparative* advantage, that counts. The country that is most efficient in producing every output can pay its workers more in every industry.

| SUMMARY |

1. Countries trade for many reasons. Two of the most important are that differences in their natural resources and other inputs create discrepancies in the efficiency with which they can produce different goods, and that specialization offers greater economies of large-scale production.

2. Voluntary trade will generally be advantageous to both parties in an exchange. This concept is one of our *Ideas for Beyond the Final Exam.*

3. International trade is more complicated than trade within a nation because of political factors, differing national currencies, and impediments to the movement of labor and capital across national borders.

4. Two countries will gain from trade with each other if each nation exports goods in which it has a **comparative advantage.** Even a country that is inefficient across the board will benefit by exporting the goods in whose production it is *least inefficient.* This concept is another of the *Ideas for Beyond the Final Exam.*

5. When countries specialize and trade, each can enjoy consumption possibilities that exceed its production possibilities.

6. The "cheap foreign labor" argument ignores the principle of comparative advantage, which shows that real wages (which determine living standards) can rise in both importing and exporting countries as a result of **specialization.**

7. **Tariffs** and **quotas** aim to protect a country's industries from foreign competition. Such protection may sometimes be advantageous to that country, but not if foreign countries adopt tariffs and quotas of their own in retaliation.

8. From the point of view of the country that imposes them, tariffs offer at least two advantages over quotas: Some of the gains go to the government rather than to foreign producers, and they provide greater incentive for efficient production.

9. When a nation eliminates protection in favor of free trade, some industries and their workers will lose out. Equity then demands that these people and firms be compensated in some way. The U.S. government offers protection from import surges and various forms of **trade adjustment assistance** to help those workers and industries adapt to the new conditions.

10. Several arguments for protectionism can, under the right circumstances, have validity. They include the national defense argument, the infant-industry argument, and the use of trade restrictions for strategic purposes. But each of these arguments is frequently abused.

11. **Dumping** will hurt certain domestic producers, but it benefits domestic consumers.

| KEY TERMS |

absolute advantage   471

comparative advantage   471

dumping   481

export subsidy   477

infant-industry argument   480

mercantilism   476

quota   476

specialization   469

strategic argument for protection   481

tariff   476

trade adjustment assistance   479

| TEST YOURSELF |

1. The following table describes the number of yards of cloth and barrels of wine that can be produced with a week's worth of labor in England and Portugal. Assume that no other inputs are needed.

	In England	In Portugal
Cloth	8 yards	12 yards
Wine	2 barrels	6 barrels

   a. If there is no trade, what is the price of wine in terms of cloth in England?

   b. If there is no trade, what is the price of wine in terms of cloth in Portugal?

   c. Suppose each country has 1 million weeks of labor available per year. Draw the production possibilities frontier for each country.

   d. Which country has an absolute advantage in the production of which good(s)? Which country has a comparative advantage in the production of which good(s)?

   e. If the countries start trading with each other, which country will specialize and export which good?

   f. What can be said about the price at which trade will take place?

2. Suppose that the United States and Mexico are the only two countries in the world and that labor is the only productive input. In the United States, a worker can produce 12 bushels of wheat *or* 2 barrels of oil in a day. In Mexico, a worker can produce 2 bushels of wheat *or* 4 barrels of oil per day.

   a. What will be the price ratio between the two commodities (that is, the price of oil in terms of wheat) in each country if there is no trade?

   b. If free trade is allowed and there are no transportation costs, which commodity would the United States import? What about Mexico?

   c. In what range would the price ratio have to fall under free trade? Why?

   d. Picking one possible post-trade price ratio, show clearly how it is possible for both countries to benefit from free trade.

| DISCUSSION QUESTIONS |

1. You have a dozen shirts and your roommate has six pairs of shoes worth roughly the same amount of money. You decide to swap six shirts for three pairs of shoes. In financial terms, neither of you gains anything. Explain why you are nevertheless both likely to be better off.

2. In the eighteenth century, some writers argued that one person in a trade could be made better off only by gaining at the expense of the other. Explain the fallacy in this argument.

3. Country A has a cold climate with a short growing season, but a highly skilled labor force (think of Finland). What sorts of products do you think it is likely to produce? What are the characteristics of the countries with which you would expect it to trade?

4. After the removal of a quota on sugar, many U.S. sugar farms go bankrupt. Discuss the pros and cons of removing the quota in the short and long runs.

5. Country A has a mercantilist government that believes it is always best to export more than it imports. As a consequence, it exports more to Country B every year than it imports from Country B. After 100 years of this arrangement, both countries are destroyed in an earthquake. What were the advantages or disadvantages of the surplus to Country A? To Country B?

6. Under current trade law, the president of the United States must report periodically to Congress on countries engaging in unfair trade practices that inhibit U.S. exports. How would you define an "unfair" trade practice? Suppose Country X exports much more to the United States than it imports, year after year. Does that constitute evidence that Country X's trade practices are unfair? What would constitute such evidence?

7. Suppose the United States finds Country X guilty of unfair trade practices and penalizes it with import quotas. So U.S. imports from Country X fall. Suppose, further, that Country X does not alter its trade practices in any way. Is the United States better or worse off? What about Country X?

| APPENDIX | *Supply, Demand, and Pricing in World Trade*

As noted in the text, price determination in a world market with free trade depends on supply and demand conditions in each of the countries participating in the market. This appendix works out some of the details in a two-country example.

When applied to international trade, the usual supply-demand model must deal with (at least) *two demand curves:* that of the exporting country and that of the importing country. In addition, it may also involve *two supply curves,* because the importing country may produce part of its own consumption. (For example, the United States, which is the world's biggest importer of oil, nonetheless produces quite a bit of domestic oil.) Furthermore, equilibrium does *not* take place at the intersection point of *either* pair of supply-demand curves. Why? Because if the two countries trade at all, the exporting nation must supply more than it demands while the importing nation must demand more than it supplies.

All three of these complications are illustrated in Figure 3, which shows the supply and demand curves of a country that *exports* wheat in Panel (a) and of a country that *imports* wheat in Panel (b). For simplicity, we assume that these countries do not deal with anyone else. Where will the two-country wheat market reach equilibrium?

Under free trade, the equilibrium price must satisfy two requirements:

1. **The quantity of wheat *exported* by one country must equal the quantity of wheat *imported* by the other country, for that is how *world* supply and demand balance.**

2. **The price of wheat must be the same in both countries.**[6]

In Figure 3, these two conditions are met at a price of $2.50 per bushel. At that price, the distance *AB* between what the exporting country produces and what it consumes equals the distance *CD* between what the importing country consumes and what it produces. This means that the amount the exporting country wants to sell at $2.50 per bushel exactly equals the amount the importing country wants to buy at that price.

At any higher price, producers in both countries would want to sell more and consumers in both countries would want to buy less. For example, if the price rose to $3.25 per bushel, the exporter's quantity supplied would rise from *B* to *F* and its quantity demanded would fall from *A* to *E,* as shown in Panel (a). As a result, more wheat would be available for export—*EF* rather than *AB*. For exactly the same reason, the price increase would cause higher production and lower sales in the importing country, leading to a reduction in imports from *CD* to *GH* in Panel (b).

But this means that the higher price, $3.25 per bushel, cannot be sustained in a free and competitive international market. With export supply *EF* far greater than import demand *GH*, there would be pressure on price to fall back toward the $2.50 equilibrium price.

FIGURE 3

Supply-Demand Equilibrium in the International Wheat Trade

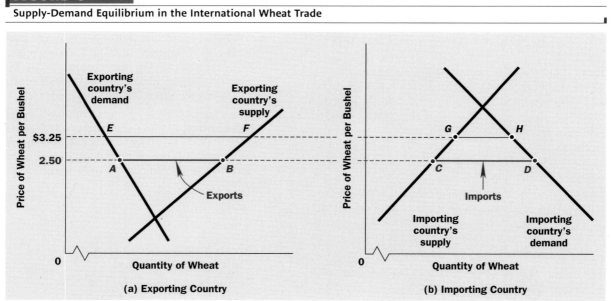

(a) Exporting Country

(b) Importing Country

---

[6] To keep things simple, we ignore such details as the costs of shipping wheat from one country to the other.

Similar reasoning shows that no price below $2.50 can be sustained. Thus:

> In international trade, the equilibrium price is the one that makes the exporting country want to export exactly the amount that the importing country wants to import. Equilibrium will thus occur at a price at which the horizontal distance *AB* in Figure 3(a) (the excess of the exporter's quantity supplied over its quantity demanded) is equal to the horizontal distance *CD* in Figure 3(b) (the excess of the importer's quantity demanded over its quantity supplied). At this price, the *world's* quantity demanded equals the *world's* quantity supplied.

HOW TARIFFS AND QUOTAS WORK

However, as noted in the text, nations do not always let markets operate freely. Sometimes they intervene with quotas that limit imports or with tariffs that make imports more expensive. Although both tariffs and quotas restrict supplies coming from abroad and drive up prices, they operate slightly differently. A tariff works by raising prices, which in turn reduces the quantity of imports demanded. The sequence associated with a quota is just the reverse—a restriction in supply forces prices to rise.

The supply and demand curves in Figure 4 illustrate how tariffs and quotas work. Just as in Figure 3, the equilibrium price of wheat under free trade is $2.50 per bushel (in both countries). At this price, the exporting country produces 125 million bushels—point *B* in Panel (a)—and consumes 80 million

(point *A*). So its exports are 45 million bushels—the distance *AB*. Similarly, the importing country consumes 95 million bushels—point *D* in Panel (b)—and produces only 50 million (point *C*), so its imports are also 45 million bushels—the distance *CD*.

Now suppose the government of the importing nation imposes a *quota* limiting imports to 30 million bushels. The free-trade equilibrium with imports of 45 million bushels is now illegal. Instead, the market must equilibrate at a point where both exports and imports are only 30 million bushels. As Figure 4 indicates, this requirement implies that there must be different prices in the two countries.

Imports in Panel (b) will be 30 million bushels—the distance *QT*—only when the price of wheat in the importing nation is $3.25 per bushel, because only at this price will quantity demanded exceed domestic quantity supplied by 30 million bushels. Similarly, exports in Panel (a) will be 30 million bushels—the distance *RS*—only when the price in the exporting country is $2.00 per bushel. At this price, quantity supplied exceeds quantity demanded in the exporting country by 30 million bushels. Thus, the quota *raises* the price in the importing country to $3.25 and *lowers* the price in the exporting country to $2.00. In general:

> An import quota on a product normally reduces the volume of that product traded, raises the price in the importing country, and reduces the price in the exporting country.

A tariff can accomplish exactly the same restriction of trade. In our example, a quota of 30 million bushels

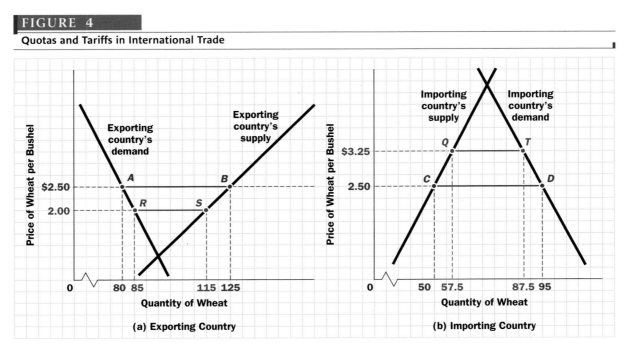

FIGURE 4

Quotas and Tariffs in International Trade

(a) Exporting Country

(b) Importing Country

NOTE: Quantities are in millions of bushels.

leads to a price that is $1.25 higher in the importing country than in the exporting country ($3.25 versus $2.00). Suppose that, instead of a quota, the importing nation were to impose a $1.25 per bushel *tariff*. International trade equilibrium would then have to satisfy the following two requirements:

1. **The quantity of wheat *exported* by one country must equal the quantity of wheat *imported* by the other, just as before.**

2. **The price that consumers in the importing country pay for wheat must *exceed* the price that suppliers in the exporting country receive by the amount of the tariff (which is $1.25 in the example).**

By consulting the graphs in Figure 4, you can see exactly where these two requirements are met. If the exporter produces at S and consumes at R, while the importer produces at Q and consumes at T, then exports and imports are equal (at 30 million bushels), and the two domestic prices differ by exactly $1.25. (They are $3.25 and $2.00.) But this is exactly the same equilibrium we found under the quota. What we have just discovered is a general result of international trade theory:

Any restriction of imports that is accomplished by a quota normally can also be accomplished by a tariff.

In this case, the tariff corresponding to an import quota of 30 million bushels is $1.25 per bushel.

We mentioned in the text that a tariff (or a quota) forces foreign producers to sell more cheaply. Figure 4 shows how this works. Suppose, as in Panel (b), that a $1.25 tariff on wheat raises the price in the importing country from $2.50 to $3.25 per bushel. This higher price drives down imports from an amount represented by the length of the brick-colored line CD to the smaller amount represented by the blue line QT. In the exporting country, this change means an equal reduction in exports, as illustrated by the change from AB to RS in Panel (a).

As a result, the price at which the exporting country can sell its wheat is driven down—from $2.50 to $2.00 in the example. Meanwhile, producers in the importing country, which are exempt from the tariff, can charge $3.25 per bushel. Thus, as noted in the text, a tariff (or a quota) can be thought of as a way to "rig" the domestic market in favor of domestic firms.

| SUMMARY |

1. The prices of goods traded between countries are determined by supply and demand, but one must consider explicitly the demand curve and the supply curve of *each* country involved. Thus, the equilibrium price must make the excess of quantity supplied over quantity demanded in the exporting country equal to the excess of quantity demanded over quantity supplied in the importing country.

2. When trade is restricted, the combinations of prices and quantities in the various countries that are achieved by a quota can also be achieved by a tariff.

3. Tariffs or quotas favor domestic producers over foreign producers.

| TEST YOURSELF |

1. The following table presents the demand and supply curves for microcomputers in Japan and the United States.

Price per Computer	Quantity Demanded in U.S.	Quantity Supplied in U.S.	Quantity Demanded in Japan	Quantity Supplied in Japan
1	90	30	50	50
2	80	35	40	55
3	70	40	30	60
4	60	45	20	65
5	50	50	10	70
6	40	55	0	75

NOTE: Price and quantity are in thousands.

a. Draw the demand and supply curves for the United States on one diagram and those for Japan on another one.

b. If the United States and Japan do not trade, what are the equilibrium price and quantity in the computer market in the United States? In Japan?

c. Now suppose trade is opened up between the two countries. What will be the equilibrium price in the world market for computers? What has happened to the price of computers in the United States? In Japan?

d. Which country will export computers? How many?

e. When trade opens, what happens to the quantity of computers produced, and therefore employment, in the computer industry in the United States? In Japan? Who benefits and who loses *initially* from free trade?

Answers to odd-numbered Discussion Questions are available on the text support site at academic.cengage.com/economics/baumol.

CHAPTER 1:
What Is Economics?

Answers to Appendix Questions

1.

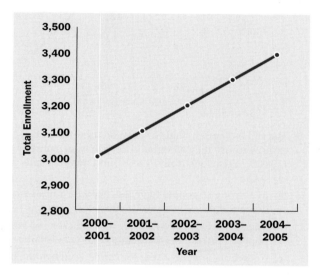

Slope is 100 interpreted as 100 new students each academic year.

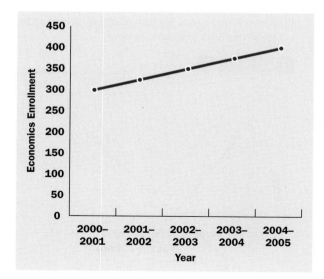

Slope is 25 interpreted as 25 new economics students each academic year.

3.

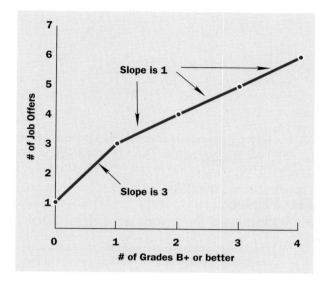

A marginal increase in the number of job offers is relatively larger with the first good grade compared to additional good grades.

5. A = 30 hr labor and 40 yd cloth = 20 units of output.

B = 40 hr labor and 28 yd cloth = 20 units of output.

Common: 20 units of output; Difference: Amount of labor and cloth charge—more labor, less cloth.

CHAPTER 3:
The Fundamental Economic Problem: Scarcity and Choice

1. This question asks the students to apply opportunity cost to a straightforward decision: to rent or buy. After buying the house, the person would no longer have to pay $24,000 annual rent. On the other hand, she would lose the $8,000 she currently earns in interest from her bank account. She would be ahead by $16,000, and the purchase is therefore a good deal. In order to get a service (housing) for which she had been willing to pay $24,000, she only has to give up (that is, the opportunity cost is) goods and services worth $8,000. It is worth pointing out to students that if she did continue to rent the house, it must be because the services she receives from the landlord are worth more than $16,000. Also, it is important to realize that this question is very simplified—it ignores home equity, property taxes, etc.

FIGURE 1

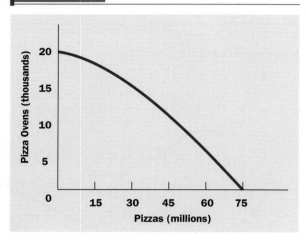

3. In case (b), the production possibilities frontier will be further from the origin in 2009, since Stromboli will have more pizza ovens with which it can produce more pizzas.

CHAPTER 4:
Supply and Demand: An Initial Look

1. (a) The demand curve for a medicine that means life or death for a patient will be vertical, provided the patient has access to any money at all. One would not expect a decline in quantity demanded as the price rises, if that decline meant that the patient would die.

   (b) The demand curve for french fries in a food court with many other stands will be fairly flat, perhaps even horizontal. If the firm raises its price at all, many if not most of its customers will just move to a different stand. Thus a small change in price results in a large change in the amount of fries bought.

3. The answers to all three parts are shown in Figure 2.

   (a) Initially, the equilibrium price is $250, and the equilibrium quantity is 35 million bicycles, as shown by the intersection of D_0 and S_0.

   (b) If demand falls by 8 million bikes per year, the new demand curve is D_1. The price falls to $210, and the quantity falls to 31 million, as shown by the intersection of D_1 and S_0. Although demand falls by 8 million at each price, the quantity exchanged falls by only 4 million because the price fall has induced a movement out along the new demand curve, as well as a movement back along the old supply curve.

   (c) If supply falls by 8 million bikes per year, the new supply curve is S_1. The price rises to $300, and the quantity falls to 31 million, as shown by the intersection of D_0 and S_1. Although supply falls by 8 million at each price, the quantity exchanged falls by only 4 million because the price increase has induced a movement out along the new supply curve, as well as a movement back along the old demand curve.

   (d) If demand and supply each fall by 8 million bikes per year, the equilibrium price is $250, and the

equilibrium quantity is 27 million bicycles, as shown by the intersection of D_1 and S_1.

FIGURE 2

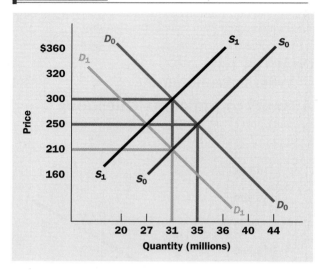

5. The same diagram, Figure 4, can be used for all three cases, because they all entail a decline in demand, from D_0 to D_1. Price falls from P_0 to P_1, and quantity falls from Q_0 to Q_1.

   (a) In a drought, people have less need for umbrellas, so demand falls.

   (b) Popcorn is a complement for movie tickets, so when popcorn prices rise, the demand for tickets falls.

   (c) Coca-Cola is a substitute for coffee, so when the price of the soda falls, the demand for coffee falls.

7. (a) Each price in Table 2 is raised by 50 cents.

   (b) No answer needed.

   (c) Yes, consumption is reduced.

   (d) The price rise is less than the 50 cent tax.

   (e) There is no answer for this question—this may be a good question to discuss in class.

FIGURE 4

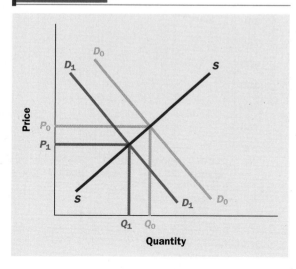

CHAPTER 5:
Consumer Choice: Individual and Market Demand

1. The total utility from 22 gallons is greater, since it is equal to the total utility (or usefulness) of the first 14 gallons, plus the total utility of the next 8.*

3. Normal: (a) and (d). Inferior: (b) and (c).

5.

Baskets	Marginal Utility ($)	Total Utility ($)
0	—	—
1	6	6
2	4	10
3	3	13
4	1	14

At a price of $3 per basket Jim will buy 3 baskets.

7.

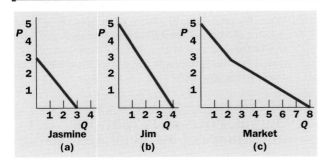

FIGURE 2

Jasmine (a)   Jim (b)   Market (c)

Answers to Appendix Questions

1.

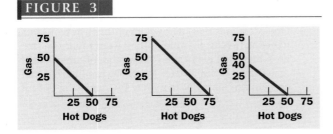

FIGURE 3

Hot Dogs   Hot Dogs   Hot Dogs

3. The slope of an indifference curve is the maximum number of units of the good on the Y-axis (say, cookies) the consumer is willing to give up to get one more unit of the good on the X-axis (say, compact discs). An indifference curve that is U-shaped with respect to the origin has a relatively large slope towards the upper left side and a relatively small slope towards the lower right. This indicates that a consumer who has many cookies but few compact discs is willing to give up a lot of cookies in order to get one more compact disc—but when the tables are turned, the consumer who has many compact discs and only a few cookies is willing to give up only a small number of cookies to get an additional compact disc. This is consistent with the idea of

diminishing marginal utility in the case of one good considered alone.

CHAPTER 6:
Demand and Elasticity

1. The answer depends upon the product, but general variables include tastes, prestige value of the product, income levels, population, prices of substitutes and complements, and new uses to which the product can be put.

3. (a) Goods with low price elasticity of demand (inelastic demand).

 (b) Goods with low price elasticity of demand (inelastic demand).

 (c) Goods with high price elasticity of demand (elastic demand).

 (d) Goods with high price elasticity of demand (elastic demand).

5. Using the formula in the text, (change in quantity/change in price) times (price/quantity), where price and quantity are the average of the beginning and ending values, the elasticity is $(15,000/5) \times (22.5/17,500) = 3.86$.

7. Complements: (b) and (c)

 Substitutes: (a) and (d)

CHAPTER 7:
Production, Inputs, and Cost: Building Blocks for Supply Analysis

1.

Output	TFC (thousands of dollars)	AFC (thousands of dollars)
0	360	—
1	360	360
2	360	180
3	360	120
4	360	90
5	360	72
6	360	60

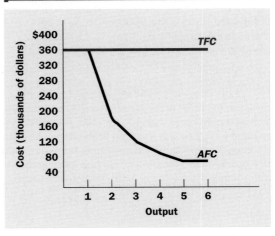

FIGURE 1

3.

Output	TC (thousands of dollars)	AC (thousands of dollars)
0	360	—
1	400	400
2	440	220
3	480	160
4	536	134
5	600	120
6	720	120

FIGURE 3

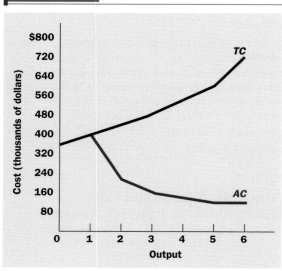

5. It can raise its profits by increasing its use of oil. Adding 1 gallon of oil will raise its revenues by $2.20, and its cost by only $2.07, leaving it with an increase in profits of $0.13.

7.

	150,000 Bushels	325,000 Bushels
Wages	$40,000	$ 80,000
Rent	45,000	90,000
Total Cost	85,000	170,000
Average Cost	0.57	0.52

When returns to scale diminish, average costs fall.

9. For labor, the MPP is 16, the price is $12, and the ratio of the two is a bit more than 1.3; for land, the MPP is 1,400, the price is $1,200, and the ratio of the two is less than 1.2. Since the two ratios are not equal, the farmer is not minimizing costs. She should increase labor and reduce land, thereby reducing the MPP of the former and increasing the MPP of the latter.

Answers to Appendix Questions

1.

FIGURE 4

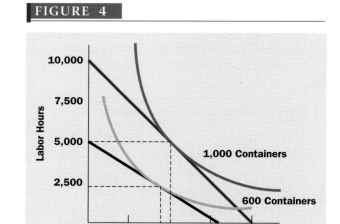

3. When the price ratio of glue to labor falls, the ratio of glue to labor used rises. Therefore, the expansion path, which shows the amounts of glue and labor used as output rises, given unchanging factor prices, becomes flatter, or closer to the glue axis.

CHAPTER 8:
Output, Price, and Profit: The Importance of Marginal Analysis

1. Unfortunately for the firm, exchange is voluntary. Assuming that the demand curve is negatively sloped, when the firm prices its product at $18, it will find buyers for less than 2 million units, and it will discover its inventory rising by more than 1 million units.

3. One presumes that the owners of the firm would like to get as rich as possible. If they were to maximize their marginal profit, they would be forgoing wealth. A marginal profit greater than zero implies that the owners can make more money by increasing output.

5.

Garages	TR	AR	TC	AC	TP
0	$ 0	$ 0	$ 12	$—	−$12
1	30	30	40	40	−10
2	56	28	56	28	0
3	78	26	66	22	12
4	96	24	74	18.5	22
5	110	22	80	16	30
6	120	20	87	14.5	33
7	126	18	96	13.7	30
8	128	16	112	14	16
9	126	14	144	16	−18
10	120	12	190	19	−70

When average cost is equal to average revenue (at two garages in this example), the firm makes no profit. This is because for average revenue to equal average cost, total revenue must equal total cost.

7. At one unit, average and marginal cost are identical. Beyond one unit, since average cost is falling, marginal cost lies below average cost, as shown in Figure 1.

FIGURE 1

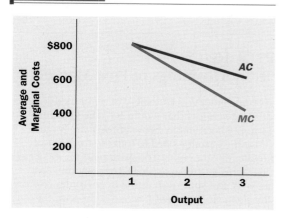

Answers to Appendix Questions

1.

Date	Total Grade	Average Grade	Marginal Grade
9/30	65	65	65
10/28	140	70	75
11/26	230	77	90
12/13	315	79	85
1/24	410	82	95

Note: numbers are rounded for simplicity.

CHAPTER 9:
Investing in Business: Stocks and Bonds

1. The value of the bond times the interest rate (0.06) equals the annual payment ($3.00). So the price of the bond is the annual payment divided by the interest rate: $3.00/0.06 = $50.00.

3. For corporations, bonds are riskier than stocks. For individual investors, stocks are riskier than bonds.

5. Ultimately, the answer to this question depends on whether or not either of these two company stocks have no risk or infinite risk. Barring those possibilities, a portfolio will lower the risk.

CHAPTER 10:
The Firm and the Industry Under Perfect Competition

1. (a) A demand curve might be vertical for a good that is absolutely necessary to the continuance of life, or for a good which is so cheap, and which has so few close substitutes, that a rise in price would barely be noticed by the consumer.

   (b) A demand curve facing a firm in a perfectly competitive industry is horizontal. Because the products of the different firms are identical, and because there are so many firms, no single firm can take a production decision that is large enough to affect industry supply enough to alter the price.

   (c) A firm's demand curve will be negatively sloping if the firm's output is a relatively large portion of the industry's output, or if the firm's output is differentiated from the output of the other firms and is identifiable. Under such circumstances, if the firm seeks to sell a significantly higher output, it will have to lower its selling price in order to attract new business.

   (d) A firm's demand curve might be positively sloping if it could somehow persuade the public that the quality of the good it was selling was signaled by its price.

3. If a firm is earning zero economic profit, the owner's invested capital is earning the same return it could earn in another use, while the owner's labor (if she is working in the firm) is earning the same income it could earn elsewhere, so the owner has no incentive to close the firm.

5. If the market price is above equilibrium, profits will attract new firms into the industry. The increase in supply will reduce the price to its equilibrium, zero-profit level.

CHAPTER 11:
Monopoly

1. (a) Pure monopolist. There is no good substitute for heat (bulky sweaters don't help a great deal), and one firm controls the source.

   (b) Not a pure monopolist. Consumers can buy close substitutes—that is to say, other types of personal computers—from other firms.

   (c) Not a pure monopolist. The one supplier of instant cameras is likely to have more market power than the one supplier of Getty gasoline, but still many other types of cameras are substitutes for instant cameras.

3. The price per 50,000-gallon unit is found by multiplying by 50,000. As the following table shows, for each level of output, marginal revenue is less than price.

Output	Price	MR
50,000	$14,000	$14,000
100,000	13,000	12,000
150,000	11,000	7,000
200,000	10,000	7,000
250,000	8,000	0
300,000	6,000	−4,000

CHAPTER 12:
Between Competition and Monopoly

1. The payoff matrix for GM might be Table 1:

TABLE 1

	Hire a Movie Star	Cut Price	New Product
Hire a new star			
Hire a new ad agency			
Cut price			
New product			

It is, of course, hard to tell what the entries in the payoff matrix will be.

3. In Table 2, we can see that if Firm A chooses the Low-Tech option, Firm B would be better off choosing the High-Tech option since it would get a payoff of $12 million (vs. $10 million if it chooses Low-Tech). If Firm A chooses the High-Tech option, Firm B would be better off choosing the High-Tech option once again because it would get a payoff of $3 million (vs. −$2 million for the Low-Tech option). Therefore, High-Tech is Firm B's dominant strategy since it is the best strategy regardless of Firm A's strategy.

CHAPTER 14:
The Case for Free Markets I: The Price System

1. (a) If there is enough electrical generating capacity to run all the air conditioners on very hot days, much of that capacity will be idle, and therefore wasted, on most days. Charging higher prices on the hot days will restrict usage at those times and therefore reduce the power-generating capacity that must be built. The resources saved can be used for something else.

   (b) In a drought-stricken area, there has to be a way to reduce water usage; otherwise, the society will simply run out and not have water for its most critical, life-saving uses. Raising the price of water can accomplish this, by inducing people to use water only for high-priority purposes.

2. and 3.

Buyers	Buyers' Acceptable Price	Individual Buyer's Marginal Surplus	Actual Price	Cumulative Total Surplus	Individual Firm's Marginal Surplus	Firms' Acceptable Price	Firms
A	$70	$30	$40	$30	$30	$10	h
B	60	20	40	50=30+20	20	20	g
C	50	10	40	60=50+10	10	30	f
E	40	0	40	60=60+0	0	40	e
F	30	−10	40	50=60−10	−10	50	c
G	20	−20	40	30=50−20	−20	60	b
					−30	70	a

CHAPTER 15:
The Shortcomings of Free Markets

1. The opportunity cost to society of a trip by a truck is the goods and services that would have been available had the trip not been made. Some of these are forgone because the gasoline used to fuel the truck is not available for other uses. The price paid for the gasoline likely represents this part of the opportunity cost quite well. But some part of the opportunity cost consists of the clean environment forgone because of the truck's pollutants. This is not included in the price of the gas.

3. Examples of goods causing detrimental externalities: the use of substances in spray cans, which depletes the atmosphere's ozone layer, minerals that are strip-mined, forest products that destroy natural habitats when the trees are cut. Examples of goods creating beneficial externalities: freshly painted houses, workers who are trained in one firm and then work for another.

5. About $20 million will be spent in the legal battles. If any less were spent, it would be advantageous for another litigant to spend more, since the prize is worth $20 million. Perfect competition eliminates economic profits.

CHAPTER 17:
Externalities, the Environment, and Natural Resources

1. At equilibrium, the price is $8, and 90 units of X are sold. Consequently, 900 pounds of pollution are emitted.

3. There are now 850 pounds of emissions.

CHAPTER 18:
Taxation and Resource Allocation

1. The tax is regressive, since the average tax rate falls as income rises:

Income	Tax	Tax Rate Marginal	Tax Rate Average
$20,000	$2,000	0.10	0.10
30,000	2,700	0.07	0.09
40,000	3,200	0.05	0.08
50,000	3,500	0.03	0.07

3. (a) Before the tax is imposed, the equilibrium price is $4.00 and the equilibrium quantity is 240 million cartons.

(b) After the tax is imposed, the supply curve shifts up by the amount of the tax to:

Price (including tax)	Price (excluding tax)	Quantity Demanded	Quantity Supplied
$4.25	$3.00	210	160
4.50	3.25	180	180
4.75	3.50	150	200
5.00	3.75	120	240

So the new equilibrium quantity will be 180 million cartons. The new equilibrium price paid by the consumers (including the tax) will be $4.50, whereas the price received by the producers (excluding the tax) will be $3.25.

(c) Regardless of who pay it, the tax is a wedge of $1.25 between the price paid by the consumer and the price received by the seller. In the situation described in part (b), the seller may list the price at $3.25, and then require the buyer to pay a tax of $1.25 above this. Or the seller may list the price at $4.50, including tax, and give $1.25 of this to the government. In either case, the net price paid by the consumer is $4.50, the net price received by the seller is $3.25, and the equilibrium quantity is 180.

(d) The sellers shift $0.50 of the tax to the buyers, since the market price rises from $4.00 to $4.50. They do this by reducing output, which raises the market price.

(e) There is excess burden borne by both buyers and sellers. The buyers' excess burden arises from the fact that they are purchasing fewer cigarettes than before the tax. The sellers' excess burden arises from the fact that they are producing fewer cigarettes than before.

(f) Cigarette consumption has fallen from 240 million cartons to 180 million cartons. This may actually be the goal that the government sought, in its attempt to improve health.

5. If Taxmanians care mostly about efficiency, they will tax rice most heavily. Since the elasticities of supply and demand are both low, there will be little reduction in the quantity of rice traded as a consequence of the tax, and therefore little excess burden. If they care mostly about vertical equity, they will tax caviar most heavily, since this tax will fall only on the rich, not the poor. A tax on rice would be vertically inequitable, since the poor spend all of their income on rice while the rich spend only part of their income on rice.

CHAPTER 19:
Pricing the Factors of Production

1. (a) Nuts and bolts: no economic rent. Many manufacturers easily produce nuts and bolts, and in the long run their costs are constant, that is to say, the supply curve is close to horizontal. If the price were lower, they would not be produced.

(b) Petroleum: some economic rent. Petroleum has a positively sloped supply curve; some would be produced at a low price and as the price increases, more is produced (from wells that are more expensive to drill and maintain). When demand conditions are such that the price is above the minimum price, therefore, some of the oil is earning economic rent; that is, income greater than would be needed to have it produced.

(c) A champion racehorse: almost all economic rent. The supply curve is vertical at a quantity of one; no matter what the price, the racehorse will still exist. Possibly at very low prices it might not be worth it to the owner and trainer to bring the horse to its full racing potential, but with that exception, all the rest of the horse's earnings are economic rent.

3. Firms can shift part of a tax on their revenue by reducing their output and raising the price to the consumers. But owners of land cannot reduce the amount of land when a land tax is imposed, and therefore they cannot raise the price and shift the tax.

5. Capital includes various means of production that have themselves previously been produced, such as the goods produced by a factory, the equipment in that factory, and any other resources the factory uses to make its final products. Investment is an addition to capital.

7. Interest is the return to the suppliers of capital or the lenders of funds. Profit is the return to entrepreneurship, and it accrues to people who take risks, who innovate, and/or who secure a monopoly position.

Answers to Appendix Questions

1. The present value of $1,000 to be received in 3 years, when the rate of interest is 11 percent, is $1,000 divided by $(1.11)^3$, or $1,000/1.368 = $730.99.

CHAPTER 20:
Labor: The Human Inputs

1.

Number of Chefs	Number of Pizzas per Day	Marginal Physical Product	Marginal Revenue Product when $P = 9	Marginal Revenue Product when $P = 12
1	40	40	$360	$480
2	64	24	216	288
3	82	18	162	216
4	92	10	90	120
5	100	8	72	96
6	92	−8	−72	−96

(a) The MPP schedule is in the third column.

(b) The fourth column contains the MRP schedule, when pizzas sell for $9.

(c) If the wage rate is $100, the pizza parlor hires three chefs. It would not pay to hire the fourth, because the wage would exceed the MRP. If the wage rose to $125, employment would still be three chefs.

(d) The MRP schedule for pizzas priced at $12 is shown in the fifth column. At a wage of $100, the firm hires four chefs, and at a wage of $125, employment would be cut to three chefs.

3. (a) Odd-job repairs in private homes: perfect competition.

(b) Low-priced clothing for women: pure monopoly.

(c) Auto manufacturing: bilateral monopoly.

5. You can reduce the price in year 2010 and raise the price in 2011, thereby selling more in 2010, with its higher MR, and leaving less to sell in 2011, with its lower MR.

7. One would expect the wage of the unpleasant, dangerous job to be higher to induce individuals to take that job, but it doesn't always work out that way in reality.

CHAPTER 21:
Poverty, Inequality, and Discrimination

1. The poverty rate is the percentage of families whose annual income falls below the poverty line. The rate increases during recessions.

CHAPTER 22:
International Trade and Comparative Advantage

1. (a) In the absence of trade, 1 barrel of wine costs 4 yards of cloth in England.

(b) In the absence of trade, 1 barrel of wine costs 2 yards of cloth in Portugal.

(c)

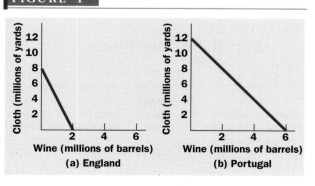

FIGURE 1

(a) England

(b) Portugal

(d) Portugal has the absolute advantage in the production of both goods, and the comparative advantage in wine. England has the comparative advantage in cloth.

(e) When trade opens, England will specialize in cloth and export it to Portugal, which in turn will specialize in wine and export it to England.

(f) In the international market, the price of a barrel of wine will wind up somewhere between 4 yards and 2 yards of cloth, perhaps 3. Stated another way, the price of 1 yard of cloth will be between $1/2$ gallon of wine and $1/4$ gallon of wine.

Answers to Appendix Questions

1. (a)

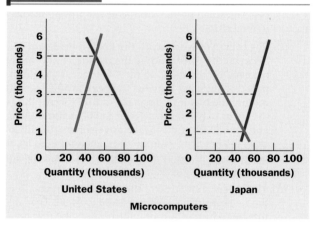

FIGURE 3

United States

Japan

Microcomputers

(b) If there is no trade, in the United States the equilibrium price is $5,000 and the equilibrium quantity is 50,000 units. In Japan, the price is $1,000 and the quantity is 50,000.

(c) The new world price will be $3,000 because, at that price, *world* quantity demanded is 100,000 units (70,000 plus 30,000) and *world* quantity supplied is also 100,000 units (40,000 plus 60,000). The price of computers has fallen in the United States and risen in Japan. (*Note:* To arrive at the answer graphically, construct *world* demand and supply curves. The equilibrium will be found at a world price of $3,000.)

(d) Japan will export 30,000 computers.

(e) In the United States, computer production falls from 50,000 to 40,000, and therefore employment in the computer industry falls. In Japan, computer production rises from 50,000 to 60,000, with a consequent increase in employment. Initially, American consumers and Japanese computer producers (both employers and employees) are helped by free trade, whereas American computer producers and Japanese consumers are hurt.

Glossary

45° line Rays through the origin with a slope of 1 are called 45° lines because they form an angle of 45° with the horizontal axis. A 45° line marks off points where the variables measured on each axis have equal values. (p. 17)

Ability-to-pay principle The ability-to-pay principle of taxation refers to the idea that people with greater ability to pay taxes should pay higher taxes. (p. 384)

Absolute advantage One country is said to have an absolute advantage over another in the production of a particular good if it can produce that good using smaller quantities of resources than can the other country. (p. 471)

Abstraction Abstraction means ignoring many details so as to focus on the most important elements of a problem. (p. 8)

Affirmative action Affirmative action refers to active efforts to locate and hire members of underrepresented groups. (p. 458)

Agents Agents are people hired to run a complex enterprise on behalf of the principals, those whose benefit the enterprise is supposed to serve. (p. 321)

Allocation of resources Allocation of resources refers to the society's decisions on how to divide up its scarce input resources among the different outputs produced in the economy and among the different firms or other organizations that produce those outputs. (p. 47)

Antitrust policy Antitrust policy refers to programs and laws that preclude the deliberate creation of monopoly and prevent powerful firms from engaging in related "anticompetitive practices." (p. 265)

Applied research Applied research is research whose goal is to invent or improve particular products or processes, often for profit. Note, however, that the military and government health-related agencies provide examples of not-for-profit applied research. (p. 351)

Average physical product (APP) The average physical product (APP) is the total physical product (TPP) divided by the quantity of input. Thus, APP = TPP/X where X = the quantity of input. (p. 130)

Average revenue (AR) The average revenue (AR) is total revenue (TR) divided by quantity. (p. 160)

Average tax rate The average tax rate is the ratio of taxes to income. (p. 379)

Backward-bending A supply curve of labor is backward-bending when a rise in an initially low wage leads to a rise in quantity of labor supplied, but a rise in a wage that was already high reduces the amount supplied. (p. 427)

Barriers to entry Barriers to entry are attributes of a market that make it more difficult or expensive for a new firm to open for business than it was for the firms already present in that market. (p. 219)

Basic research Basic research refers to research that seeks to provide scientific knowledge and general principles rather than coming up with any specific marketable inventions. (p. 350)

Beneficial or detrimental externality An activity is said to generate a beneficial or detrimental externality if that activity causes incidental benefits or damages to others not directly involved in the activity and no corresponding compensation is provided to or paid by those who generate the externality. (p. 312)

Benefits principle The benefits principle of taxation holds that people who derive benefits from a service should pay the taxes that finance it. (p. 385)

Bilateral monopoly A bilateral monopoly is a market situation in which there is both a monopoly on the selling side and a monopsony on the buying side. (p. 433)

Bond A bond is simply an IOU sold by a corporation that promises to pay the holder of the bond a fixed sum of money at the specified *maturity* date

and some other fixed amount of money (the *coupon* or *interest payment*) every year up to the date of maturity. (p. 180)

Budget line, household The budget line for a household graphically represents all possible combinations of two commodities that it can purchase, given the prices of the commodities and some fixed amount of money at its disposal. (p. 100)

Budget line, firm A firm's budget line is the locus of all points representing every input combination of inputs that the producer can afford to buy with a given amount of money and given input prices. (p. 150)

Bundling Bundling refers to a pricing arrangement under which the supplier offers substantial discounts to customers if they buy several of the firm's products, so that the price of the bundle of products is less than the sum of the prices of the products if they were bought separately. (p. 271)

Burden of a tax The burden of a tax to an individual is the amount one would have to be given to be just as well off with the tax as without it. (p. 386)

Capital A nation's capital is its available supply of plant, equipment, and software. It is the result of past decisions to make *investments* in these items. (p. 401)

Capitalism Capitalism is an economic system in which most of the production process is controlled by private firms operating in markets with minimal government control. The investors in these firms (called "capitalists") own the firms. (p. 335)

Cartel A cartel is a group of sellers of a product who have joined together to control its production, sale, and price in the hope of obtaining the advantages of monopoly. (p. 243)

Closed economy A closed economy is one that does not trade with other nations in either goods or assets. (p. 24)

497

Collective bargaining Collective bargaining is the process of negotiation of wages and working conditions between a union and the firms in the industry. (p. 433)

Common stock A common stock (also called a share) of a corporation is a piece of paper that gives the holder of the stock a share of the ownership of the company. (p. 180)

Comparative advantage One country is said to have a comparative advantage over another in the production of a particular good *relative to other goods* if it produces that good less inefficiently as compared with the other country. (pp. 49, 471)

Complements Two goods are called complements if an increase in the quantity consumed of one increases the quantity demanded of the other, all other things remaining constant. (p. 117)

Concentration of an industry Concentration of an industry measures the share of the total sales or assets of the industry in the hands of its largest firms. (p. 267)

Concentration ratio A concentration ratio is the percentage of an industry's output produced by its four largest firms. It is intended to measure the degree to which the industry is dominated by large firms. (p. 267)

Consumer's surplus Consumer's surplus is the difference between the value to the consumer of the quantity of Commodity X purchased and the amount that the market requires the consumer to pay for that quantity of X. (pp. 93, 299)

Corporate income tax The corporate income tax is a tax levied on the profits of corporations, after all expenditures on wages, interest, rent, and purchases of other inputs are deducted. (p. 381)

Corporation A corporation is a firm that has the legal status of a fictional individual. This fictional individual is owned by a number of persons, called its *stockholders*, and is run by a set of elected officers and a board of directors, whose chairperson is often also in a powerful position. (p. 179)

Correlated Two variables are said to be correlated if they tend to go up or down together. Correlation need not imply causation. (p. 11)

Cost disease of the personal services The cost disease of the personal services is the tendency of the costs and prices of these services to rise persistently faster than those of the average output in the economy. (p. 327)

Credible threat A credible threat is a threat that does not harm the threatener if it is carried out. (p. 255)

Credit default swap A credit default swap (CDS) is a financial instrument that functions like an insurance policy that protects a lender. The buyer of a CDS pays the seller for insuring against a third-party's default on a debt that is owed to the former. If the third party defaults on the debt, failing to make the required repayment, the seller of the CDS must pay a lump sum to the buyer of the CDS. (p. 188)

Cross elasticity of demand The cross elasticity of demand for product X to a change in the price of another product, Y, is the ratio of the percentage change in quantity demanded of X to the percentage change in the price of Y that brings about the change in quantity demanded. (p. 117)

Cross licensing Cross licensing of patents occurs when each of two firms agrees to let the other use some specified set of its patents, either at a price specified in their agreement or in return for access to the other firm's patents. (p. 352)

Cross-subsidization Cross-subsidization means selling one product of the firm at a loss, which is balanced by higher profits on another of the firm's products. (p. 275)

Demand curve A demand curve is a graphical depiction of a demand schedule. It shows how the quantity demanded of some product will change as the price of that product changes during a specified period of time, holding all other determinants of quantity demanded constant. (p. 58)

Demand schedule A demand schedule is a table showing how the quantity demanded of some product during a

specified period of time changes as the price of that product changes, holding all other determinants of quantity demanded constant. (p. 58)

Depletable A commodity is depletable if it is used up when someone consumes it. (p. 317)

Derivative A derivative is a financial instrument whose value depends on the prices of some other assets. For example, a derivative contract may entitle its owner to buy 100 shares of Company X's stock at a price of $30 in four months, where $30 may be higher or lower than the market price of that stock at the specified date. (p. 188)

Derived demand The derived demand for an input is the demand for the input by producers as determined by the demand for the final product that the input is used to produce. (p. 400)

Direct controls Direct controls are government rules that tell organizations or individuals what processes or raw materials they may use or what products they are permitted to supply or purchase. (p. 364)

Direct taxes Direct taxes are taxes levied directly on people. (p. 379)

Discounting, or computing the present value The process that has been invented for making the magnitudes of payments at different dates comparable to one another is called discounting, or computing the present value. (p. 417)

Division of labor Division of labor means breaking up a task into a number of smaller, more *specialized* tasks so that each worker can become more adept at a particular job. (p. 48)

Dominant strategy A dominant strategy for one of the competitors in a game is a strategy that will yield a higher payoff than any of the other strategies that are possible, no matter what choice of strategy is made by competitors. (p. 250)

Dumping Dumping means selling goods in a foreign market at lower prices than those charged in the home market. (p. 481)

Earned Income Tax Credit (EITC) The Earned Income Tax Credit (EITC) is a federal program like a negative income tax. It supplements earnings up to a point via an income tax credit and, beyond that point, taxes those benefits away. (p. 457)

Economic discrimination Economic discrimination occurs when equivalent factors of production receive different payments for equal contributions to output. (p. 452)

Economic model An economic model is a simplified, small-scale version of some aspect of the economy. Economic models are often expressed in equations, by graphs, or in words. (p. 11)

Economic profit Economic profit equals net earnings, in the accountant's sense, minus the *opportunity costs* of capital and of any other inputs supplied by the firm's owners. (pp. 159, 209, 412)

Economic rent Economic rent is any portion of the payment to labor or any other input that does not lead to an increase in the amount of labor supplied. (p. 406)

Economies of scale Economies of scale are savings that are obtained through increases in quantities produced. Scale economies occur when an *X* percent increase in input use raises output by *more than X* percent, so that the more the firm produces, the lower its per unit costs become. (pp. 142, 264)

Economies of scope Economies of scope are savings that are obtained through simultaneous production of many different products. They occur if a firm that produces many commodities can supply each good more cheaply than a firm that produces fewer commodities. (p. 274)

Efficiency A set of outputs is said to be produced efficiently if, given current technological knowledge, there is no way one can produce larger amounts of any output without using larger input amounts or giving up some quantity of another output. (p. 47)

Efficient allocation of resources An efficient allocation of resources is one that takes advantage of every opportunity to make some individuals better off in their own estimation while not worsening the lot of anyone else. (p. 288)

Elastic demand curve A demand curve is elastic when a given percentage price change leads to a larger percentage change in quantity demanded. (p. 112)

Emissions permits Emissions permits are licenses issued by government specifying the maximum amount the license holder is allowed to emit. The licenses are restricted to permit a limited amount of emissions in total. Often, they must be purchased from the government or on a special market. (p. 366)

Entrepreneurship Entrepreneurship is the act of starting new firms, introducing new products and technological innovations, and, in general, taking the risks that are necessary to seek out business opportunities. (p. 398)

Equilibrium An equilibrium is a situation in which there are no inherent forces that produce change. Changes away from an equilibrium position will occur only as a result of "outside events" that disturb the status quo. (p. 65)

Equities Equities and *common stocks* are essentially the same thing—pieces of paper issued by a company that give the holder a share of the ownership of that company and offers payments to the holder that are called *dividends*. The amount of these payments may be high, low, and sometimes even zero, depending on the company's profit earnings (or losses) during the time period for which the dividends are paid. (p. 184)

Excess burden The excess burden of a tax to an individual is the amount by which the burden of the tax exceeds the tax that is paid. (p. 386)

Excise tax An excise tax is a tax levied on the purchase of some specific good or service. (p. 381)

Excludable A commodity is excludable if someone who does not pay for it can be kept from enjoying it. (p. 317)

Expansion path The expansion path is the locus of the firm's cost-minimizing input combinations for all relevant output levels. (p. 151)

Export subsidy An export subsidy is a payment by the government to exporters to permit them to reduce the selling prices of their goods so they can compete more effectively in foreign markets. (p. 477)

Externality An activity is said to generate a beneficial or detrimental externality if that activity causes incidental benefits or damages to others not directly involved in the activity, and no corresponding compensation is provided to or paid by those who generate the externality. (pp. 312, 334, 356)

Factors of production Inputs or factors of production are the labor, machinery, buildings, and natural resources used to make outputs. (pp. 22, 397)

Fiscal federalism Fiscal federalism refers to the system of grants from one level of government to the next. (p. 384)

Fixed cost A fixed cost is the cost of an input whose quantity does not rise when output goes up, one that the firm requires to produce any output at all. The total cost of such indivisible inputs does not change when the output changes. Any other cost of the firm's operation is called a variable cost. (p. 129)

Gross domestic product (GDP) Gross domestic product (GDP) is the sum of the money values of all final goods and services produced in the domestic economy and sold on organized markets during a specified period of time, usually a year. (pp. 23, 337)

Herfindahl-Hirschman Index (HHI) The Herfindahl-Hirschman Index (HHI) is an alternative and widely used measure of the degree of concentration of an industry. It is calculated, in essence, by adding together the squares of the market shares of the firms in the industry, although the smallest firms may be left out of the calculation because their small market share numbers have a negligible effect on the result. (p. 267)

High-tech (high-technology) A high-tech (high-technology) firm or industry is one whose products, equipment and production methods utilize highly advanced technology that is constantly modified and improved. Examples are the aerospace, scientific instruments, computer, communications, and pharmaceutical industries. (p. 341)

Horizontal equity Horizontal equity is the notion that equally situated individuals should be taxed equally. (p. 384)

Human capital theory Human capital theory focuses on the expenditures that have been made to increase the productive capacity of workers via education or other means. It is analogous to investment in better machines as a way to increase their productivity. (p. 429)

Incidence of a tax The incidence of a tax is an allocation of the burden of the tax to specific individuals or groups. (p. 387)

Income effect The income effect of a rise in wages is the resulting rise of workers' purchasing power that enables them to afford more leisure. (p. 426)

Income elasticity of demand Income elasticity of demand is the ratio of the percentage change in quantity demanded to the percentage change in income. (p. 116)

Increasing returns to scale Production is said to involve economies of scale, also referred to as increasing returns to scale, if, when all input quantities are increased by X percent, the quantity of output rises by more than X percent. (p. 142)

Index fund An index fund is a mutual fund that chooses a particular stock price index and then buys the stocks (or most of the stocks) that are included in the index. The value of an investment in an index fund depends on what happens to the prices of all stocks in that index. (p. 184)

Indifference curve An indifference curve is a line connecting all combinations of the commodities that are equally desirable to the consumer. (p. 102)

Indirect taxes Indirect taxes are taxes levied on specific economic activities. (p. 379)

Industrial Revolution The Industrial Revolution is the stream of new technology and the resulting growth of output that began in England toward the end of the eighteenth century. (p. 335)

Inelastic demand curve A demand curve is inelastic when a given percentage price change leads to a smaller percentage change in quantity demanded. (p. 112)

Infant-industry argument The infant-industry argument for trade protection holds that new industries need to be protected from foreign competition until they develop and flourish. (p. 480)

Inferior good An inferior good is a commodity whose quantity demanded falls when the purchaser's real income rises, all other things remaining equal. (p. 96)

Inflation Inflation refers to a sustained increase in the general price level. Inflation occurs when prices in an economy rise rapidly. The rate of inflation is calculated by averaging the percentage growth rate of the prices of a selected sample of commodities. (p. 181)

Innovation Innovation is the process that begins with invention and includes improvement to prepare the invention for practical use and marketing of the invention or its products. (pp. 338, 413)

Innovative entrepreneur An innovative entrepreneur is someone who introduces into the economy a new product or a new process for producing goods, or finds a new market for the sale of commodities or a new way of conducting business. (p. 436)

Input-output analysis Input-output analysis is a mathematical procedure that takes account of the interdependence among the economy's industries and determines the amount of output each industry must provide as inputs to the other industries in the economy. (p. 296)

Inputs Inputs or factors of production are the labor, machinery, buildings, and natural resources used to make outputs. (pp. 22, 42)

Interest Interest is the payment for the use of funds employed in the production of capital; it is measured as the percent per year of the value of the funds tied up in the capital. (p. 402)

Interest rate The interest rate is the amount that borrowers currently pay to lenders per dollar of the money borrowed—it is the current market price of a loan. (p. 181)

Invention Invention is the act of discovering new products or new ways of making products. (pp. 338, 413)

Investment Investment is the *flow* of resources into the production of new capital. It is the labor, steel, and other inputs devoted to the *construction* of factories, warehouses, railroads, and other pieces of capital during some period of time. (p. 401)

Investment in human capital Investment in human capital is any expenditure on an individual that increases that person's future earning power or productivity. (p. 422)

Invisible hand The invisible hand is a phrase used by Adam Smith to describe how, by pursuing their own self-interests, people in a market system are "led by an invisible hand" to promote the well-being of the community. (p. 56)

Kinked demand curve A kinked demand curve is a demand curve that changes its slope abruptly at some level of output. (p. 249)

Labor union A labor union is an organization made up of a group of workers (usually with the same specialization, such as plumbing or costume design, or in the same industry). The unions represent the workers in negotiations with employers over issues such as wages, vacations, and sick leave. (p. 431)

Laissez-faire Laissez-faire refers to a situation in which there is minimal government interference with the workings of the market system. The term implies that people should be left alone in carrying out their economic affairs. (p. 293)

"Law" of demand The "law" of demand states that a lower price generally increases the amount of a commodity that people in a market are willing to buy. Therefore, for most goods, market demand curves have negative slopes. (p. 97)

"Law" of diminishing marginal utility The "law" of diminishing marginal utility asserts that additional units of a commodity are worth less and less to a consumer in money terms. As the individual's consumption increases, the marginal utility of each additional unit declines. (p. 87)

Law of supply and demand The law of supply and demand states that in a free market the forces of supply and demand generally push the price toward the level at which quantity supplied and quantity demanded are equal. (p. 66)

Limited liability Limited liability is a legal obligation of a firm's owners to pay back company debts only with the money they have already invested in the firm. (p. 180)

Long run The long run is a period of time long enough for all of the firm's current commitments to come to an end. (p. 129)

Marginal analysis Marginal analysis is a method for calculating optimal choices—the choices that best promote the decision maker's objective. It works by testing whether, and by how much, a small change in a decision will move things toward or away from the goal. (p. 88)

Marginal land Marginal land is land that is just on the borderline of being used—that is, any land the use of which would be unprofitable if the farmer had to pay even a penny of rent. (p. 407)

Marginal physical product (MPP) The marginal physical product (MPP) of an input is the increase in total output that results from a one-unit increase in the input quantity, holding the amounts of all other inputs constant. (pp. 131, 398)

Marginal private benefit (MPB) The marginal private benefit (MPB) is the share of an activity's marginal benefit that is received by the persons who carry out the activity. (p. 313)

Marginal private cost (MPC) The marginal private cost (MPC) is the share of an activity's marginal cost that is paid for by the persons who carry out the activity. (p. 313)

Marginal profit Marginal profit is the addition to total profit resulting from one more unit of output. (p. 163)

Marginal revenue (MR) Marginal revenue (MR) is the addition to total revenue resulting from the addition of one unit to total output. Geometrically, marginal revenue is the slope of the total revenue curve at the pertinent output quantity. Its formula is $MR_1 = TR_1 - TR_0$, and so on. (p. 160)

Marginal revenue product (MRP) The marginal revenue product (MRP) of an input is the money value of the additional sales that a firm obtains by selling the marginal physical product of that input. (pp. 133, 398)

Marginal revenue product of labor (MRP_L) The marginal revenue product of labor (MRP_L) is the increase in the employer's total revenue that results when it hires an additional unit of labor. (p. 422)

Marginal social benefit (MSB) The marginal social benefit (MSB) of an activity is the sum of its marginal private benefit (MPB) plus its incidental benefits (positive or negative) that are received by others, and for which those others do not pay. (p. 313)

Marginal social cost (MSC) The marginal social cost (MSC) of an activity is the sum of its marginal private cost (MPC) plus its incidental costs (positive or negative) that are borne by others who receive no compensation for the resulting damage to their well-being. (p. 313)

Marginal tax rate The marginal tax rate is the fraction of each *additional* dollar of income that is paid in taxes. (p. 379)

Marginal utility The marginal utility of a commodity to a consumer (measured in money terms) is the maximum amount of money that she or he is willing to pay for *one more unit* of that commodity. (p. 86)

Market demand curve A market demand curve shows how the total quantity of some product demanded by *all* consumers in the market during a specified period of time changes as the price of that product changes, holding all other things constant. (p. 96)

Market system A market system is a form of economic organization in which resource allocation decisions are left to individual producers and consumers acting in their own best interests without central direction. (p. 50)

Maximin criterion The maximin criterion requires a player to select the strategy that yields the maximum payoff on the assumption that the opponent will do as much damage as it can. (p. 252)

Mediation Mediation takes place during collective bargaining when a neutral individual is assigned the job of persuading the two parties to reach an agreement. (p. 441)

Mercantilism Mercantilism is a doctrine that holds that exports are good for a country, whereas imports are harmful. (p. 476)

Misallocated resources Resources are misallocated if it is possible to change the way they are used or the combination of goods and services they produce and thereby make consumers and producers better off. (p. 311)

Mixed economy A mixed economy is one with some public influence over the workings of free markets. There may also be some public ownership mixed in with private property. (p. 36)

Monopolistic competition Monopolistic competition refers to a market in which products are heterogeneous but which is otherwise the same as a market that is perfectly competitive. (p. 237)

Monopoly power Monopoly power (or market power) is the ability of a business firm to earn high profits by raising the prices of its products above competitive levels and to keep those prices high for a substantial amount of time. (p. 264)

Monopoly profits Monopoly profits are any excess of the profits earned persistently by a monopoly firm over and above those that would be earned if the industry were perfectly competitive. (p. 224)

Monopsony A monopsony is a market situation in which there is only one buyer. (p. 433)

Moral hazard Moral hazard refers to the tendency of insurance to discourage policyholders from protecting themselves from risk. (p. 320)

Mutual fund A mutual fund, in which individual investors can buy shares, is a private investment firm that holds a portfolio of securities. Investors can choose among a large variety of mutual funds, such as stock funds, bond funds, and so forth. (p. 184)

Nash equilibrium A Nash equilibrium results when each player adopts the strategy that gives the highest possible payoff if the rival sticks to the strategy it has chosen. (p. 253)

Natural monopoly A natural monopoly is an industry in which advantages of largescale production make it possible for a single firm to produce the entire output of the market at lower average cost than a number of firms, each producing a smaller quantity. (p. 220)

Negative income tax (NIT) The negative income tax (NIT) is a program where people below a certain income range would receive a payment from the government. (p. 456)

Oligopoly An oligopoly is a market dominated by a few sellers, at least several of which are large enough relative to the total market to be able to influence the market price. (p. 241)

Open economy An open economy is one that trades with other nations in goods and services, and perhaps also trades in financial assets. (p. 24)

Opportunity cost The opportunity cost of a decision is the value of the next best alternative that must be given up because of that decision (for example, working instead of going to school). (pp. 4, 41)

Optimal decision An optimal decision is one that best serves the objectives of the decision maker, whatever those objectives may be. It is selected by explicit or implicit comparison with the possible alternative choices. The term *optimal* connotes neither approval nor disapproval of the objective itself. (pp. 42, 119, 156)

Origin (of a graph) The "0" point in the lower-left corner of a graph where the axes meet is called the origin. Both variables are equal to zero at the origin. (p. 13)

Outputs The outputs of a firm or an economy are the goods and services it produces. (pp. 22, 42)

Patent A patent is a privilege granted to an inventor, whether an individual or a firm, that for a specified period of time prohibits anyone else from producing or using that invention without the permission of the holder of the patent. (p. 219)

Payoff matrix A payoff matrix shows how much each of two competitors (players) can expect to earn, depending on the strategic choices each of them makes. (p. 250)

Payroll tax The payroll tax is a tax levied on the earnings from work. In the United States, the tax starts at the first dollar earned and ends at an upper limit that increases each year. (p. 381)

Per capita income Per capita income in an economy is the average income of all people in that economy. (p. 334)

Perfect competition Perfect competition occurs in an industry when that industry is made up of many small firms producing homogeneous products, when there is no impediment to the entry or exit of firms, and when full information is available. (p. 198)

Perfectly contestable A market is perfectly contestable if entry and exit are costless and unimpeded. (p. 257)

Personal income tax The personal income tax is a tax levied on the income of an individual or a family, typically with a progressive rate structure. (p. 379)

Plowback Plowback (or retained earnings) is the portion of a corporation's profits that management decides to keep and reinvest in the firm's operations rather than paying out as dividends to stockholders. (p. 182)

Pollution charges Pollution charges (taxes on emissions) are taxes that polluters are required to pay. The amount they pay depends on what they emit and in what quantities. (p. 364)

Portfolio diversification Portfolio diversification means inclusion of a number and variety of stocks, bonds, and other such items in an individual's portfolio. If the individual owns airline stocks, for example, diversification requires the purchase of a stock or bond in a very different industry, such as breakfast cereal production. (p. 184)

Poverty line The poverty line is an amount of income below which a family is considered "poor." (p. 447)

Predatory pricing Predatory pricing is pricing that threatens to keep a competitor out of the market. It is a price that is so low that it will be profitable for the firm that adopts it only if a rival is driven from the market. (p. 270)

Price cap A price cap is a ceiling above which regulators do not permit prices to rise. The cap is designed to provide an efficiency incentive to the firm by allowing it to keep part of any savings in costs it can achieve. (p. 278)

Price ceiling A price ceiling is a maximum that the price charged for a commodity cannot legally exceed. (p. 70)

Price discrimination Price discrimination is the sale of a given product at different prices to different customers of the firm, when there are no differences in the costs of supplying these customers. Prices are also discriminatory if it costs more to supply one customer than another, but they are charged the same price. (p. 227)

(Price) elasticity of demand The (price) elasticity of demand is the ratio of the *percentage* change in quantity demanded to the *percentage* change in price that brings about the change in quantity demanded. (p. 109)

Price floor A price floor is a legal minimum below which the price charged for a commodity is not permitted to fall. (p. 73)

Price leadership Under price leadership, one firm sets the price for the industry and the others follow. (p. 245)

Price taker Under perfect competition, the firm is a price taker. It has no choice but to accept the price that has been determined in the market. (p. 199)

Price war In a price war, each competing firm is determined to sell at a price that is lower than the prices of its rivals, often regardless of whether that price covers the pertinent cost. Typically, in such a price war, Firm A cuts its price below Firm B's price; B retaliates by undercutting A; and so on and on until some of the competitor firms surrender and let themselves be undersold. (p. 245)

Principals Agents are people hired to run a complex enterprise on behalf of the principals, those whose benefit the enterprise is supposed to serve. (p. 321)

Principle of increasing costs The principle of increasing costs states that as the production of a good expands, the opportunity cost of producing another unit generally increases. (p. 44)

Private good A private good is a commodity characterized by both depletability and excludability. (p. 317)

Process innovation A process innovation is an innovation that changes the way in which a commodity is produced. (p. 349)

Producer's surplus The producer's surplus from a sale is the difference between the market price of the item sold and the lowest price at which the supplier would be willing to provide the item. (p. 299)

Product innovation A product innovation is the introduction of a good or service that is entirely new or involves major modifications of earlier products. (p. 348)

Production indifference curve A production indifference curve (sometimes called an *isoquant*) is a curve showing all the different quantities of two inputs that are just sufficient to produce a given quantity of output. (p. 149)

Production indifference map A production indifference map is a graph whose axes show the quantities of two inputs that are used to produce some output. A curve in the graph corresponds to some given quantity of that output, and the different points on that curve show the different quantities of the two inputs that are just enough to produce the given output. (p. 18)

Production possibilities frontier The production possibilities frontier is a curve that shows the maximum quantities of outputs it is possible to produce with the available resource quantities and the current state of technological knowledge. (pp. 43, 311)

Productivity Productivity is the amount of output produced by a unit of input. (p. 334)

Progressive tax A progressive tax is one in which the average tax rate paid by an individual rises as income rises. (pp. 35, 379)

Property tax The property tax is levied on the assessed values of taxable properties, such as houses and office buildings. (p. 383)

Proportional tax A proportional tax is one in which the average tax rate is the same at all income levels. (p. 379)

Public good A public good is a commodity or service whose benefits are *not depleted* by an additional user and from which it is generally difficult or *impossible to exclude* people, even if the people are unwilling to pay for the benefits. (p. 317)

Pure monopoly A pure monopoly is an industry in which there is only one supplier of a product for which there are no close substitutes and in which it is very difficult or impossible for another firm to coexist. (p. 218)

Quantity demanded The quantity demanded is the number of units of a good that consumers are willing and can afford to buy over a specified period of time. (p. 57)

Quantity supplied The quantity supplied is the number of units that sellers want to sell over a specified period of time. (p. 61)

Quota A quota specifies the maximum amount of a good that is permitted into the country from abroad per unit of time. (p. 476)

Random walk The time path of a variable such as the price of a stock is said to constitute a random walk if its magnitude in one period (say, May 2, 2005) is equal to its value in the preceding period (May 1, 2005) plus a completely random number. That is: Price on May 2, 2005 = Price on May 1, 2005 + Random number, where the random number (positive or negative) can be obtained by a roll of dice or some such procedure. (p. 190)

Ratchet A ratchet is an arrangement that permits some economic variable, such as investment or advertising, to increase, but prevents that variable from subsequently decreasing. (p. 348)

Ray through the origin (or Ray) Lines whose *Y*-intercept is zero have so many special uses in economics and other disciplines that they have been given a special name: a ray through the origin, or a ray. (p. 16)

Recession A recession is a period of time during which the total output of the economy declines. (p. 24)

Regressive tax A regressive tax is one in which the average tax rate falls as income rises. (p. 379)

Regulation Regulation of industry is a process established by law that restricts or controls some specified decisions made by the affected firms; it is designed to protect the public from exploitation by firms with monopoly power. Regulation is usually carried out by a special government agency assigned the task of administering and interpreting the law. That agency also acts as a court in enforcing the regulatory laws. (p. 273)

Rent seeking Rent seeking refers to unproductive activity in the pursuit of economic profit—in other words, profit in excess of competitive earnings. (p. 320)

Repeated game A repeated game is one that is played over again a number of times. (p. 254)

Required reserves Required reserves are the minimum amount of reserves (in cash or the equivalent) required by law. Normally, required reserves are proportional to the volume of deposits. (p. 635)

Research and development (R&D) Research and development (R&D) is the activity of firms, universities, and government agencies that seeks to invent new products and processes and to improve those inventions so that they are ready for the market or other users. (p. 340)

Resources Resources are the instruments provided by nature or by people that are used to create goods and services. Natural resources include minerals, soil, water, and air. Labor is a scarce resource, partly because of time limitations (the day has only 24 hours) and partly because the number of skilled workers is limited. Factories and machines are resources made by people. These three types of resources are often referred to as *land, labor,* and *capital.* They are also called *inputs* or *factors of production.* (p. 40)

Retained earnings Plowback (or retained earnings) is the portion of a corporation's profits that management decides to keep and reinvest in the firm's operations rather than paying out as dividends to stockholders. (p. 182)

Sales maximization A firm's objective is said to be sales maximization if it seeks to adopt prices and output quantities that make its total revenue (its "sales"), rather than its profits, as large as possible. (p. 246)

Securities Securities are financial instruments *other than* insurance policies and fixed annuities that are offered for sale to investors and which guarantee a set payment each year. Securities can be divided into three main categories: debt securities (e.g., bonds that are loans from the investor to the company), equity securities (e.g., common stocks, whose purchaser obtains a share of the company that creates those stocks), and derivative contracts that are essentially a bundle of other investments. (p. 181)

Shift in a demand curve A shift in a demand curve occurs when any relevant variable other than price changes. If consumers want to buy *more* at any and all given prices than they wanted previously, the demand curve shifts to the right (or outward). If they desire *less* at any given price, the demand curve shifts to the left (or inward). (p. 59)

Short run The short run is a period of time during which some of the firm's cost commitments will not have ended. (p. 129)

Shortage A shortage is an excess of quantity demanded over quantity supplied. When there is a shortage, buyers cannot purchase the quantities they desire at the current price. (p. 65)

Slope of a budget line The slope of a budget line is the amount of one commodity that the market requires an individual to give up to obtain one additional unit of another commodity without any change in the amount of money spent. (p. 103)

Slope of a curved line The slope of a curved line at a particular point is defined as the slope of the straight line that is tangent to the curve at that point. (p. 15)

Slope of an indifference curve The slope of an indifference curve, referred to as the marginal rate of substitution (MRS) between the commodities, represents the maximum amount of one commodity that the consumer is willing to give up in exchange for one more unit of another commodity. (p. 103)

Slope of a straight line The slope of a straight line is the ratio of the vertical change to the corresponding horizontal change as we move to the right along the line between two points on that line, or, as it is often said, the ratio of the "rise" over the "run." (p. 14)

Social Security System The Social Security System raises funds from the payroll tax and pays Social Security benefits to retirees. (p. 381)

Specialization Specialization means that a country devotes its energies and resources to only a small proportion of the world's productive activities. (p. 469)

Speculation Individuals who engage in speculation deliberately invest in risky assets, hoping to obtain profits from future changes in the prices of these assets. (p. 189)

Statistical discrimination Statistical discrimination is said to occur when the productivity of a particular worker is estimated to be low just because that worker belongs to a particular group (such as women). (p. 462)

Sticky price A price is called sticky if it does not change often even when there is a moderate change in cost. (p. 249)

Stock option A stock option is a contract that permits its owner to buy a specified quantity of stocks of a corporation at a future date, but at the price specified in the contract rather than the stock's market price at the date of purchase. (p. 322)

Stock price index A stock price index, such as the S&P 500, is an average of the prices of a large set of stocks. These stocks are selected to represent the price movements of the entire stock market, or some specified segment of the market, and the chosen set is rarely changed. (p. 184)

Strategic argument for protection The strategic argument for protection holds that a nation may sometimes have to threaten protectionism to induce other countries to drop their own protectionist measures. (p. 481)

Substitutes Two goods are called substitutes if an increase in the quantity consumed of one cuts the quantity demanded of the other, all other things remaining constant. (p. 117)

Substitution effect The substitution effect of a wage increase is the resulting incentive to work more because of the higher relative reward to labor. (p. 426)

Supply curve A supply curve is a graphical depiction of a supply schedule. It shows how the quantity supplied of some product will change as the price of that product changes during a specified period of time, holding all other determinants of quantity supplied constant. (p. 62)

Supply curve of a firm The supply curve of a firm shows the different quantities of output that the firm would be willing to supply at different possible prices during some given period of time. (p. 204)

Supply curve of an industry The supply curve of an industry shows the different quantities of output that the industry would supply at different possible prices during some given period of time. (p. 205)

Supply-demand diagram A supply-demand diagram graphs the supply and demand curves together. It also determines the equilibrium price and quantity. (p. 64)

Supply schedule A supply schedule is a table showing how the quantity supplied of some product changes as the price of that product changes during a specified period of time, holding all other determinants of quantity supplied constant. (p. 61)

Surplus A surplus is an excess of quantity supplied over quantity demanded. When there is a surplus, sellers cannot sell the quantities they desire to supply at the current price. (p. 65)

Takeover A takeover is the acquisition by an outside group (the raiders) of a controlling proportion of a company's stock. When the old management opposes the takeover attempt, it is called a *hostile takeover attempt*. (p. 188)

Tangent A tangent to the curve is a *straight* line that *touches*, but does not *cut*, the curve at a particular point. (p. 16)

Tariff A tariff is a tax on imports. (p. 476)

Tax deduction A tax deduction is a sum of money that may be subtracted before the taxpayer computes his or her taxable income. (p. 380)

Tax exempt A particular source of income is tax exempt if income from that source is not taxable. (p. 380)

Tax loophole A tax loophole is a special provision in the tax code that reduces taxation below normal rates (perhaps to zero) if certain conditions are met. (p. 380)

Tax shifting Tax shifting occurs when the economic reactions to a tax cause prices and outputs in the economy to change, thereby shifting part of the burden of the tax onto others. (p. 389)

Technology trading Technology trading is an arrangement in which a firm voluntarily makes its privately owned technology available to other firms either in exchange for access to the technology of the second company or for an agreed-upon fee. (p. 351)

Theory A theory is a deliberate simplification of relationships used to explain how those relationships work. (p. 10)

Total monetary utility The total utility of a quantity of a good to a consumer (measured in money terms) is the maximum amount of money that he or she is willing to give up in exchange for it. (p. 86)

Total physical product (TPP) The firm's total physical product (TPP) is the amount of output it obtains in total from a given quantity of input. (p. 130)

Total profit The total profit of a firm is its net earnings during some period of time. It is equal to the total amount of money the firm gets from sales of its products (the firm's total revenue) minus the total amount that it spends to make and market those products (total cost). (p. 158)

Total revenue The total revenue of a supplier firm is the total amount of money it receives from the purchasers of its products, without any deduction of costs. (p. 159)

Trade adjustment assistance Trade adjustment assistance provides special unemployment benefits, loans, retraining programs, and other aid to workers and firms that are harmed by foreign competition. (p. 479)

Transfer payments Transfer payments are sums of money that the government gives certain individuals as outright grants rather than as payments for services rendered to employers. Some common examples are Social Security and unemployment benefits. (p. 35)

Unit-elastic demand curve A demand curve is unit-elastic when a given percentage price change leads to the same percentage change in quantity demanded. (p. 112)

Variable A variable is something measured by a number; it is used to analyze what happens to other things when the size of that number changes (varies). (p. 13)

Variable cost A variable cost is a cost whose total amount changes when the quantity of output of the supplier changes. (pp. 129, 202)

Vertical equity Vertical equity refers to the notion that differently situated individuals should be taxed differently in a way that society deems to be fair. (p. 384)

Y-intercept The Y-intercept of a line or a curve is the point at which it touches the vertical axis (the Y-axis). The X-intercept is defined similarly. (p. 16)

Zero-sum game A zero-sum game is one in which exactly the amount one competitor gains must be lost by other competitors. (p. 253)

Index

Year	(1) Gross Domestic Product	(2) Personal Consumption Expenditure	(3) Gross Private Domestic Investment	(4) Government Purchases	(5) Net Exports	(6) Gross Domestic Product	(7) Personal Consumption Expenditure	(8) Gross Private Domestic Investment	(9) Government Purchases	(10) Net Exports	(11) Real GDP per capita
	(in billions of dollars)					(in billions of chained 2000 dollars)ª					(In chained 2000 dollars
1929	103.6	77.4	16.5	9.4	0.4	977.0	736.6	101.7	146.5	−9.4	8,016
1933	56.4	45.9	1.7	8.7	0.1	716.4	601.1	18.9	157.2	−10.2	5,700
1939	92.2	67.2	9.3	14.8	0.8	1072.8	811.1	86.2	238.6	−4.7	8,188
1945	223.0	120.0	10.8	93.0	-0.8	2012.4	1001.4	74.7	1402.2	−26.8	14,382
1950	293.7	192.2	54.1	46.7	0.7	2006.0	1283.3	253.2	492.4	−9.0	13,225
1955	414.7	258.8	69.0	86.4	0.5	2500.3	1544.5	285.0	779.3	−14.3	15,128
1960	526.4	331.8	78.9	111.5	4.2	2830.9	1784.4	296.5	871.0	−12.7	15,661
1965	719.1	443.8	118.2	151.4	5.6	3610.1	2241.8	437.3	1048.7	−18.9	18,576
1970	1038.3	648.3	152.4	233.7	4.0	4269.9	2740.2	475.1	1233.7	−52.0	20,820
1971	1126.8	701.6	178.2	246.4	0.6	4413.3	2844.6	529.3	1206.9	−60.6	21,249
1972	1237.9	770.2	207.6	263.4	-3.4	4647.7	3019.5	591.9	1198.1	−73.5	22,140
1973	1382.3	852.0	244.5	281.7	4.1	4917.0	3169.1	661.3	1193.9	−51.9	23,200
1974	1499.5	932.9	249.4	317.9	-0.8	4889.9	3142.8	612.6	1224.0	−29.4	22,861
1975	1637.7	1033.8	230.2	357.7	16.0	4879.5	3214.1	504.1	1251.6	−2.4	22,592
1976	1824.6	1151.3	292.0	383.0	-1.6	5141.3	3393.1	605.9	1257.2	−37.0	23,575
1977	2030.1	1277.8	361.3	414.1	-23.1	5377.7	3535.9	697.4	1271.0	−61.1	24,412
1978	2293.8	1427.6	438.0	453.6	-25.4	5677.6	3691.8	781.5	1308.4	−61.9	25,503
1979	2562.2	1591.2	492.9	500.7	-22.5	5855.0	3779.5	806.4	1332.8	−41.0	26,010
1980	2788.1	1755.8	479.3	566.1	-13.1	5839.0	3766.2	717.9	1358.8	12.6	25,640
1981	3126.8	1939.5	572.4	627.5	-12.5	5987.2	3823.3	782.4	1371.2	8.3	26,030
1982	3253.2	2075.5	517.2	680.4	-20.0	5870.9	3876.7	672.8	1395.3	−12.6	25,282
1983	3534.6	2288.6	564.3	733.4	-51.7	6136.2	4098.3	735.5	1446.3	−60.2	26,186
1984	3930.9	2501.1	735.6	796.9	-102.7	6577.1	4315.6	952.1	1494.9	−122.4	27,823
1985	4217.5	2717.6	736.2	878.9	-115.2	6849.3	4540.4	943.3	1599.0	−141.5	28,717
1986	4460.1	2896.7	746.5	949.3	-132.5	7086.5	4724.5	936.9	1696.2	−156.3	29,443
1987	4736.4	3097.0	785.0	999.4	-145.0	7313.3	4870.3	965.7	1737.1	−148.4	30,115
1988	5100.4	3350.1	821.6	1038.9	-110.1	7613.9	5066.6	988.5	1758.9	−106.8	31,069
1989	5482.1	3594.5	874.9	1100.6	-87.9	7885.9	5209.9	1028.1	1806.8	−79.2	31,877
1990	5800.5	3835.5	861.0	1181.7	-77.6	8033.9	5316.2	993.5	1864.0	−54.7	32,112
1991	5992.1	3980.1	802.9	1236.1	-27.0	8015.1	5324.2	912.7	1884.4	−14.6	31,614
1992	6342.3	4236.9	864.8	1273.5	-32.8	8287.1	5505.7	986.7	1893.2	−15.9	32,255
1993	6667.4	4483.6	953.3	1294.8	-64.4	8523.4	5701.2	1074.8	1878.2	−52.1	32,747
1994	7085.2	4750.8	1097.3	1329.8	-92.7	8870.7	5918.9	1220.9	1878.0	−79.4	33,67
1995	7414.7	4987.3	1144.0	1374.0	-90.7	9093.7	6079.0	1258.9	1888.9	−98.8	34,11
1996	7838.5	5273.6	1240.2	1421.0	-96.3	9433.9	6291.2	1370.3	1907.9	-110.7	34,97
1997	8332.4	5570.6	1388.7	1474.4	-101.4	9854.3	6523.4	1540.8	1943.8	−139.8	36,10
1998	8793.5	5918.5	1510.8	1526.1	-161.8	10283.5	6865.5	1695.1	1985.0	−252.6	37,23
1999	9353.5	6342.8	1641.5	1631.3	-262.1	10779.8	7240.9	1844.3	2056.1	-356.6	38,59
2000	9951.5	6830.4	1772.2	1731.0	-382.1	11226.0	7608.1	1970.3	2097.8	−451.6	39,79
2001	10286.2	7148.8	1661.9	1846.4	-371.0	11347.2	7813.9	1831.9	2178.3	−472.1	39,7'
2002	10642.3	7439.2	1647.0	1983.3	-427.2	11553.0	8021.9	1807.0	2279.6	-548.8	40,1
2003	11142.1	7804.0	1729.7	2112.6	-504.1	11840.7	8247.6	1871.6	2330.5	-603.9	40,7
2004	11867.8	8285.1	1968.6	2232.8	-618.7	12263.8	8532.7	2058.2	2362.0	-688.0	41,8
2005	12638.4	8819.0	2172.2	2369.9	-722.7	12638.4	8819.0	2172.2	2369.9	-722.7	42,6
2006	13398.9	9322.7	2327.2	2518.4	-769.3	12976.2	9073.5	2230.4	2402.1	-729.2	43,4
2007	14077.6	9826.4	2288.5	2676.5	-713.8	13254.1	9313.9	2146.2	2443.1	-647.7	43,9
2008	14441.4	10129.9	2136.1	2883.2	-707.8	13312.2	9290.9	1989.4	2518.1	-494.3	43,7
2009	14256.0	10089.0	1628.8	2930.7	-392.4	12987.4	9235.1	1541.5	2564.6	-355.6	42,2

a Components do not add up to GDP due to chain method of deflation.
b Persons 14 years and older for 1920-1945; thereafter, persons 16 years and older.
c Moody's Aaa rating.
d Trade – weighted average of broad group of U.S. trading partners.
e National income and product accounts basis; calendar years.